LINCOLN'S RISE TO THE PRESIDENCY

Abraham Lincoln. This photograph, probably made by S. M. Fassett in Chicago in October 1859, is one of the best of the photographs of a beardless Lincoln. Courtesy of the Abraham Lincoln Library and Museum, Harrogate, Tennessee.

LINCOLN'S RISE TO THE PRESIDENCY

William C. Harris

University Press of Kansas

Published by the University Press of Kansas (Lawrence, Kansas
66045), which was organized by the Kansas Board of Regents and is
operated and funded by Emporia State University, Fort Hays State
University, Kansas State University, Pittsburg State University, the
University of Kansas, and Wichita State University

ISBN 978-0-7006-1520-9

Printed in the United States of America

Book Club Edition

CONTENTS

Contents

ILLUSTRATIONS

ACKNOWLEDGMENTS

I AM VERY grateful to many colleagues and others who provided assistance to me as I was researching and writing this book. Alexander J. De Grand of North Carolina State University read the manuscript and offered many helpful suggestions, often while bemoaning the fate of the Chicago Cubs in baseball. Former colleague John David Smith, now in the Department of History, University of North Carolina at Charlotte, carefully read the manuscript, pointed out numerous ways to improve it, and gave unfailingly good advice. Michael Burlingame, peerless in his knowledge of Abraham Lincoln, reviewed most of the manuscript, made substantive recommendations, and generously sent me material from his forthcoming multivolume biography of the sixteenth president. Joe A. Mobley read some of the manuscript and advised me on the illustrations. I am also grateful for the valuable critique of the work supplied by two anonymous readers for the University Press of Kansas. Paul Betz carefully formatted the original manuscript.

Norene Miller and Mary Ellis in the Department of History, North Carolina State University, provided useful assistance in the preparation of the manuscript. The staff of the University's Interlibrary Loan Section, D. H. Hill Library, as always, went the extra mile to obtain materials for me. Darby Orcutt, collection's manager of the D. H. Hill Library, was especially helpful in acquiring newspapers on microfilm and other materials for the book. The library staffs at the University of North Carolina at Chapel Hill, Duke University, William and Mary, Ohio State University, the University of Illinois at Urbana-Champaign, the University of Alabama at Birmingham, and the Library of Congress also aided in the research. Tammy Ingram of my son Nelson's law office made copies of the manuscript.

Illustrations for the book were provided by Kenneth Johnson of the Photographic Services Section, Library of Congress; Michael Lynch of the Abraham Lincoln Library and Museum, Harrogate, Tennessee; Jane Ehrenhart, Roberta Fairburn, and Mary Michals of the Abraham Lincoln Presidential Library, Springfield, Illinois; Cindy Van Horn of the Lincoln Museum, Fort Wayne, Indiana; and Jason Flahardy of the University of Kentucky Libraries, Lexington.

I am also greatly indebted to Fred Woodward of the University Press of Kansas for his support of the project and the sage advice that he gave me regarding the manuscript. In addition, Susan McRory and Susan Schott of the press rendered valuable assistance in the production of the book.

Acknowledgments

My wife, Betty, read some of the chapters for clarity and style and helped in numerous other ways. As always, she was a great source of support.

William C. Harris

October 2006

INTRODUCTION

ON JUNE 16, 1858, Abraham Lincoln rose in the chamber of the Illinois House of Representatives and announced to the assembled state Republican delegates: "'A house divided against itself cannot stand.' I believe this government cannot endure, permanently half *slave* and half *free*." He went on to say: "I do not expect the Union to be dissolved—I do not *expect* the house to fall—but I *do* expect it will cease to be divided." Lincoln predicted that "either the *opponents* of slavery, will arrest the further spread of it, and place it where the public mind shall rest in the belief that it is in course of ultimate extinction, or its *advocates* will push it forward, till it shall become alike lawful in *all* the States, *old* as well as *new—North* as well as *South*."[1] Because of the ominous message in this passage, the speech became known as Lincoln's "House Divided Speech."

The speech followed the Springfield lawyer's nomination by Illinois Republicans to oppose Stephen A. Douglas's reelection to the United States Senate. Predictably, Douglas and his Democratic supporters denounced the speech as a call for direct northern action against slavery in the South and charged that Lincoln was an abolitionist. Lincoln, however, adamantly denied that this was the case. He insisted that his party's approach to ending slavery was conservative and within the republic's constitutional and political tradition. At Columbus, Ohio, on September 17, 1859, Lincoln affirmed that the "chief and real purpose of the Republican party is eminently conservative. It proposes nothing save and except to restore this government to its original tone in regard to this element of slavery, and there to maintain it, looking for no further change, in reference to it, than that which the original framers of the government themselves expected and looked forward to."[2] This meant leaving slavery alone in the states where it existed, but preventing its expansion and thereby placing it en route to "ultimate extinction." This conservative strategy against slavery, Lincoln believed, would succeed, whereas radical attacks on the institution in the South would fail.

Most scholars, with the slavery issue in mind, have labeled Lincoln a moderate, which in a modern sense he was. They have failed, however, to consider Lincoln's rise within the context of the political ideas and divisions of the time or the distinctions that Lincoln and his contemporaries made in political affairs. Lincoln, by his own admission and despite his occasionally strong

I

rhetoric, was conservative in his political orientation. In his famous Cooper
Union, New York, address on February 27, 1860, he defined his conservatism
as an "adherence to the old and tried, against the new and untried." At
Leavenworth, Kansas, on December 3, 1859, Lincoln declared that he and
his fellow Republicans, unlike the Democrats, who, he claimed, rejected the
well-tested policies of the past, were true conservatives in that they were attempting to maintain "the peace of society, and the structure of our government" established by the Founders.[3]

Lincoln's conservatism was rooted in his background as a Henry Clay
Whig, his close association with border-state rural people, his cautious nature, and the racial and political realities that he faced in central Illinois. His
reverence for the Founding Fathers, the Constitution, the laws under it, and
the preservation of the republic and its institutions undergirded and strengthened his conservatism. Lincoln's fear of mob violence and anarchy if the laws
were violated reflected his conservative tendency early in his career and continued, even into his presidency, to influence his views and policies. In his
address to the Young Men's Lyceum in Springfield on January 27, 1838,
Lincoln warned that the greatest danger to liberty and the republic of the
Founders was a breakdown of law and order. Like a true Whig conservative,
he declared that the descent into mobocracy or anarchy, followed by tyranny,
could only be prevented by a popular commitment to "reason, cold, calculating, unimpassioned reason." Though his Lyceum address expressed the fears
of a young Whig, Lincoln reacted to secession in a similar manner. In his
inaugural address on March 4, 1861, he announced that "the central idea of
secession, is the essence of anarchy. A majority, held in restraint by constitutional checks [and the law], . . . is the only true sovereign of a free people.
Whoever rejects it, does, of necessity, fly to anarchy or despotism."[4] Lincoln's
efforts late in the war to bring about a quick restoration of the southern
states to the Union partly reflected his fear that unless civil governments were
soon reestablished, anarchy would follow the surrender of rebel forces.

Lincoln's conservatism took a very different path from two other political approaches common among northerners and westerners of his time. It
was neither the hidebound, reactionary response of Whig ultraconservatives
(Know Nothings), who opposed the influx of immigrants and immigrants'
rights, nor the yielding view of many northern Democrats who favored a
"don't care" policy toward slavery and were willing to compromise with the
South. Instead, it embodied a progressive spirit that placed a premium upon
equality of opportunity for all and viewed slavery as morally wrong. Lincoln's support of government aid for internal (material) improvements was
designed to foster equality of economic condition. Slavery, Lincoln came to
believe by the 1850s, was the great obstacle to the fulfillment of the Found-

ers' purposes for America. Lincoln also concluded that the Declaration of Independence's equality clause applied to blacks as well as whites, though in Illinois, where prejudice against blacks was strong, he stopped short of supporting civil rights for the race. Within this conservative context, Lincoln framed his political ambitions and his position on issues.

ABRAHAM LINCOLN has always fascinated scholars as well as the general public, and he continues to be a popular subject for study. In recent years new books on Lincoln have focused on his private life, state of mind, and sexual orientation. (For an extended account of these studies and other trends in the Lincoln literature, see the Bibliographical Essay at the end of this book.) Lincoln scholar Mark E. Neely, Jr., has warned that, although the preoccupation with Lincoln's personal life may be useful in understanding the man, it "has left his more important public life the victim of neglect."[5] Other scholars have sliced off pieces of the Lincoln story and made important contributions to our understanding of the sixteenth president. Doris Kearns Goodwin, for example, in *Team of Rivals: The Political Genius of Abraham Lincoln* (2005), has provided a revealing account of Lincoln's relationship with members of his cabinet and fascinating biographical information on them. The speeches of Lincoln have attracted the attention of several scholars, notably Harold Holzer (*Lincoln at Cooper Union: The Speech That Made Abraham Lincoln President*, 2004). Historians' understanding of Lincoln's antislavery policies as president has been significantly advanced by Allen C. Guelzo's *Lincoln's Emancipation Proclamation: The End of Slavery in America* (2004). Douglas L. Wilson, in *Honor's Voice: The Transformation of Abraham Lincoln* (1998), has eloquently described Lincoln's efforts as a young man to improve himself and gain distinction. And in *The Young Eagle: The Rise of Abraham Lincoln* (2001), Kenneth J. Winkle has studied the social and economic environment that produced Lincoln, providing new insights on this American icon's early struggles.

While building on the work of Wilson, Winkle, and other scholars, my book focuses on Lincoln's remarkable political rise from obscurity to his inauguration as president on March 4, 1861. During this period, Lincoln became an influential political leader, first as a Whig, then a Republican, and finally president-elect. His unique political understanding and skill, developed in Illinois, served as a solid foundation for his extraordinary leadership during the Civil War. I explain Lincoln's rise in the context of the times and provide fresh insights on his prepresidential career, examining questions that have often puzzled biographers and historians (for example, why Lincoln ran for the state House of Representatives in 1854, why he made the controver-

sial house-divided statement in his June 16, 1858, speech, and when he believed that he was a viable presidential candidate). Interwoven with the nar-
rative are descriptions of aspects of Lincoln's life that were an integral part
of his rise to political prominence. These include his law practice, his relationships with family members and associates, and, by no means least important, his personal qualities.

I also describe how Lincoln became the leader of the antislavery coalition
in Illinois and organized it into the Republican party, while retaining the
support of its diverse elements. Lincoln's success in this regard was fostered
by his decision to cease promoting the Whig economic agenda that he had
advocated for two decades. Lincoln realized that antislavery Democrats in
Illinois would abandon the party if he continued to proclaim the virtues of
the old Whig platform. At the same time, he cleverly worked to satisfy these
Democrats, led by Lyman Trumbull, that old Whigs, who constituted the majority in the antislavery movement, would not dominate the new party.

I believe this book also sheds new light on Lincoln's ongoing efforts, beginning in the mid-1850s, to bring conservative Whigs and Know Nothings
(nativists) into the antislavery coalition without alienating German Americans and other ethnic groups. The conservative Whig and Know-Nothing
vote for Millard Fillmore in the 1856 presidential election had enabled James
Buchanan and the Democrats to win the state and retain control of the presidency. The need to secure the relatively large Fillmore vote in the critical central counties determined Lincoln's strategy against Douglas in the senatorial
contest of 1858. This included Lincoln's consistent support of the odious federal Fugitive Slave Act of 1850 and his repeated denials that he was an antislavery radical.

I have not been uncritical of Lincoln. Lincoln made racist statements in
several of his speeches, and although some may view them as having been politically necessary in Negrophobic Illinois, they were nevertheless deplorable
and, to an embarrassing extent, contrary to his support for black equality.
Furthermore, Lincoln's advocacy of black colonization, in which he argued
that both races would benefit from separation, was clearly wrong. Lincoln's
contention that the southern states would abolish slavery without federal action if the institution was not permitted to expand into the territories was
unrealistic. Once the slavery issue had become polarized by the late 1850s,
no political body in the South, despite Lincoln's conservatism and expressions of goodwill toward southerners, would dare move against the institution. Lincoln also mistakenly concluded after his election as president that
the southern threat of secession was either a bluff to gain concessions or a
conspiracy by a small minority to leave the Union. He believed that by standing firm against compromise, the secession movement would collapse. It is

clear, however, that no compromise would have satisfied the lower southern states. Only after the fighting began did Lincoln fully understand that force was necessary to put down secession.

This book begins with a chapter on Lincoln's early life and entrance into politics, which is followed by an extended account of his rise to prominence in the Illinois Whig party during the 1840s and his controversial term in Congress, when he opposed the Mexican-American War. Considerable attention is given to Lincoln's political redemption after the passage of the Kansas-Nebraska bill in 1854, his leadership in the state antislavery coalition, and, beginning in 1856, his prominent role in the Illinois Republican party. Two chapters are devoted to Lincoln's historic campaign to unseat Senator Douglas in 1858. The next chapter describes Lincoln's emergence as a favorite among western Republicans despite his defeat by Douglas, and the extension of his anti-Douglas and antislavery campaign into nearby states and the Kansas Territory in 1859. The focus then turns to the political events leading up to Lincoln's presidential nomination and the election of 1860. The last three chapters treat Lincoln's role as president-elect, including the political difficulties he encountered in forming his cabinet, his role in forestalling a congressional compromise on slavery in the territories, and his circuitous twelve-day journey to Washington for the inauguration. The enthusiastic crowds that greeted Lincoln along the way to Washington reinforced his determination to sustain the federal laws and forts in the seceded states. The trip ended with Lincoln secretly slipping into the national capital in order to avoid a real assassination plot in Baltimore. An epilogue describes and analyzes Lincoln's anxiously awaited inaugural address on March 4, 1861.

An explanation regarding political labels is in order. Historians have usually described Lincoln's opposition to slavery as moderate. The word "moderate," however, was rarely used to describe a political position in mid-nineteenth-century America. Lincoln identified himself as a "conservative" because, as he explained, he favored a strong American commitment to the principles of the Founding Fathers, the Constitution, and the laws, which included opposition to the expansion of slavery. He did not think that the Democrats, including Douglas, were true conservatives. Their lack of principles and their corrupt practices, Lincoln believed, would likely bring down rather than sustain the republic of the Founders. The term "radical" was applied to those staunch antislavery men, a minority in the Illinois Republican party, who, in addition to resisting the expansion of slavery, called for the abolition of the institution in the District of Columbia, the repeal of the Fugitive Slave Act, and the enactment of personal liberty laws in the North to prevent the capture and return of blacks to the South. Radicals also tended, in contrast to Lincoln and other antislavery conservatives, to vilify southern slaveholders as evil people. In addition, many radicals favored civil rights for blacks in Illinois and in other states. Only a few radical Republicans in Lincoln's home state were outright militant abolitionists who demanded action against slavery in the South.

The Though Lincoln concluded that the radicals were too extreme to succeed politically, he believed that they were more nearly on the side of the angels than Douglas and the Democrats were. A conservative antislavery policy, Lincoln predicted, would win Illinois and the free states for the Republican party. Lincoln also maintained that it would lead to slavery's "ultimate extinction" without causing the irrepressible conflict that he warned against in his House Divided Speech of 1858. In the end, this conservative strategy did make possible the triumph of the Republican party in 1860, Lincoln's elevation to the presidency, and the destruction of slavery. But these successes came at a heavier price than Lincoln had ever anticipated. The price, of course, was secession and internecine war.

CHAPTER ONE

FROM LOG CABIN TO SPRINGFIELD

ABRAHAM LINCOLN was born on February 12, 1809, in the dead of winter in a one-room log cabin on Nolin Creek, 18 miles southeast of Elizabethtown, Kentucky. On this same day in faraway Shrewsbury, England, another giant of the nineteenth century was also born—Charles Darwin. Thomas Lincoln, the father of the future president, and Nancy Hanks Lincoln, the mother, both came from the rolling hill country of western Virginia. Brought to the Kentucky wilderness by their families while young, they had settled in the same pioneer community. Little is known about Lincoln's mother or her parents. Nancy Hanks was a tall, slender woman who could not write her name. Lincoln believed that she was the illegitimate daughter of a Lucy Hanks (there was more than one Lucy Hanks) and a Virginia farmer or planter. Whatever her origins, she was a good mother. Thomas Lincoln came from a more established family in Virginia. His father, whose name was Abraham, had served as a captain of Virginia troops in the American Revolution. When the elder Abraham moved with his family to Kentucky after the war, it was partly because he had been inspired by tales of the frontier that he had heard from his distant relative Daniel Boone. Within a few years the former captain acquired several thousand acres of virgin land. But in 1786, while planting corn with his sons, Mordecai and Thomas, he was killed by marauding Indians. The fifteen-year-old Mordecai dashed to the house, grabbed the family gun, and killed one of the Indians before he could attack Thomas. The story was repeated many times around the family fire, and Abe, several years before becoming president, wrote that it became "imprinted upon my mind and memory."[1] He took great pride in the fact that he was named after his grandfather.

Thomas Lincoln, barely literate but with great "native ability," struggled to make a living as a carpenter and farmer. By the time Abe was born, Thomas owned several hundred acres of land. Unfortunately, the confused record of property titles in the Bluegrass State meant that Thomas was always defending the right to his land in court. Because of this problem and "partly on account of slavery," as his son remembered, Thomas Lincoln moved his family to southern Indiana in late 1816, when Abe was seven years old.[2] The risk that Thomas took in moving the family overland and across the icy Ohio River in the middle of winter was great, but he knew the land would need to be cleared in time for spring planting. The Lincolns settled on public land in a densely wooded area in what is now Spencer County. Bears, wolves, wildcats, panthers, turkeys, deer, and other wild animals inhabited the forest. Panthers filled the night with screams, and bears preyed on the swine.[3] Thomas Lincoln hurriedly constructed a rude log cabin enclosed on three sides with logs and branches; the open side contained a place for a fire, which the family kept burning throughout the winter. Young Abe helped his father clear some of the land in time to plant corn. Though only a boy, Abe vigorously wielded an axe. He developed powerful muscles and arms that served him well in performing heavy chores for his father and neighbors. He also excelled in wrestling, a popular sport on the frontier and one that gained him the respect of the young men in the community.[4] Throughout his life, Lincoln remained physically strong.

Though he later took pride in his strength and his work on the farm, Lincoln never enjoyed physical labor. On one occasion he admitted to a friend that "his father taught him to work but never learned him to love it." He took no pleasure in hunting or fishing either, activities that were necessary to provide meat for frontier families and which most boys of his generation enjoyed and saw as important in becoming a man. Soon after the Lincolns' arrival in Indiana, Abe shot and killed a turkey near the cabin. Rather than being excited by his accomplishment, he felt remorse that he had killed a wild creature. Years later, he wrote that he never again "pulled a trigger on any large game."[5] His sensitivity toward living things would follow him throughout his life.

The family suffered a crushing blow in the late summer of 1818. An attack of sickness caused by the milk of cows that had eaten the poisonous snakeroot plant struck the family. First, Nancy's uncle and aunt died, and in October Nancy herself came down with the milk sickness, a deadly illness whose cause was unknown at the time. She lingered for several days before death took her. The winter that followed was the worst period in Abraham Lincoln's life. He and his sister Sarah were deprived of a mother, and with no adult female to cook and look after the domestic needs of the family, living conditions in the cabin became deplorable. Thomas Lincoln, a practical man, realized that something had to be done to save the family. About one year after Nancy's death, he returned to Kentucky to find a wife for himself and a mother for his children among the people he had known there. Good fortune crowned his effort. At Elizabethtown, Thomas found Sarah Bush Johnston, a kind and competent widow with three small children of her own. She had household goods that the Lincoln family desperately needed, and Thomas agreed to pay her debts. They were married, packed Sarah's belongings, and with her small children left for the Indiana wilderness.

The forlorn condition of Abe and his sister, who at twelve years of age had done the best that she could to cook and wash for the family since her mother's death, shocked the new stepmother. She set to work to improve the situation in the cabin and "dress up" Abe and Sarah to make them "more human" than they had been when she had met them. The task was monumental, given the fact that she was now responsible for eight people, including Dennis Hanks, Abe's mother's cousin, in a small, though comfortable cabin, with few resources except what she had brought from Kentucky and what sympathetic neighbors could provide. With assistance from her new husband and stepchildren, Sarah Bush Lincoln created a marvelous home environment for the family. She became devoted to the Lincoln children, and Abe quickly came to love her and to call her "Mama." Years later, referring to himself in the third person, he remarked: "She proved a good and kind mother to him." He also provided for her in old age. In September 1865, Sarah Bush Lincoln recalled that Abe was a bright, witty, and sensitive boy. He was a model child, and her ways and his always "seemed to run together," she said.[6] Indeed, Abe's stepmother came to prefer him to her own children.

Sarah Bush Lincoln encouraged Abe's thirst for learning. She arranged for the ten-year-old boy, along with his sister Sarah and the three other children in the home, to attend the nearby subscription school of Andrew Crawford, a semieducated justice of the peace. She probably paid for the children's schooling with farm commodities. Crawford closed the school after one term of about three months. The next year Azel W. Dorsey opened a school in the same cabin, and Abe attended it for about six months. Including a brief attendance at a school 4 miles from the Lincoln home, Abe's formal education had ended by age fifteen. Lincoln later characterized his education as "defective" and wrote that "the aggregate of all his schooling did not amount to one year." Yet this learning experience had motivated him to read and study what books he could borrow.

Thomas Lincoln at times became exasperated when his son, a healthy, strong teenager, neglected his work to read John Bunyan's *The Pilgrim's Progress*, Parson Mason Weems's *Life of George Washington*, or William Scott's *Lessons of Elocution*. Nonetheless, according to the boy's stepmother, Thomas understood the value of education and rarely interfered with his son's study.[7] Abe also read from the family Bible, though he never joined the Baptist church where his father was an active member. It was from Scott's *Lessons of Elocution*, which included orations from Shakespeare, that Lincoln began to develop a desire for public speaking. He sometimes practiced by mimicking the sermons at the church, much to the annoyance of his father, who would stop Abe and put him to work. Abe could also be heard making political speeches to the other children. Though father and son differed, in one important way Thomas had an influence on his son's development. He passed on to him an appreciation of humorous stories with a rustic, frontier flavor.[8] Abe's skill and confidence in telling these stories in a public forum owed something to his father's convivial and witty nature.

Abraham Lincoln wanted a broader world than his father's farm could offer. He desired an outlet for his gregarious and restless nature. By his late teens, he was seizing every opportunity to work away from home. He participated in house raisings, corn shuckings, timber loggings, hog killings, and firewood cuttings for passing steamboats on the Ohio River. Abe also split rails and plowed fields for neighbors. He enjoyed talking, telling jokes, and playing tricks on customers at James Gentry's nearby store. Like many teenage boys raised in a backwoods environment, he was shy around girls, which suggested to his stepmother that "he was not very fond of girls."[9] Awareness of his awkward appearance reinforced Lincoln's shy behavior toward the opposite sex.

At the age of nineteen, Lincoln was asked by Gentry to join his son Allen in taking a flatboat with goods to New Orleans for sale. Lincoln immediately jumped at the chance to float lazily down the river and visit the exotic queen city of the Mississippi.[10] On the historic square in New Orleans he probably saw the slave market, where thousands of blacks were sold every month. In his trip down the Mississippi, he certainly saw at first-hand the inhumanity of the institution that one day he would help to destroy.

Abe and Allen Gentry returned home on a steamboat. The twenty-four dollars that Abe had earned he turned over to his father, which before age twenty-one he was legally bound to do. Recurring sickness in the community, the death of Lincoln's sister Sarah in childbirth, and the struggle to succeed in the rugged wilderness of southern Indiana convinced Thomas Lincoln that he should again move the family. This time he chose the prairie of central Illinois, where the land was fertile and not dominated by trees that had to be removed before planting corn and other crops. Though Abe was now twenty-one and anxious to strike out on his own, he dutifully helped the family make the difficult move in March 1830. With wagons drawn by ox teams, the Lincolns trekked about 200 miles, crossing frozen streams and high water on the Wabash River. The family, which included Dennis Hanks and probably another cousin, John Hanks, settled on the banks of the Sangamon River in Macon County, about 10 miles northwest of Decatur. Abe aided in clearing the land, planting corn, and splitting rails to fence the crop.[11]

That summer, the twenty-one-year-old newcomer in the frontier community made his first political speech. He was invited to reply to two local politicians, including a Mr. Posey, who somehow had irritated "the sovereigns" (voters) by failing to provide them with alcoholic refreshments. In his speech, Lincoln urged navigation improvements on the Sangamon, which appealed to the interior farmers' "sense and reason." Much "to his great astonishment," the young man "found himself a prophet" in the new land; even "his titled fellow-orator cordially complimented his performance."[12]

WHEN SPRING CAME, Lincoln saw an opportunity to strike out on his own. Denton Offutt contracted with Lincoln, his stepbrother John Johnston, and John Hanks to build a boat and transport produce to New Orleans. In their descent down the Sangamon, they soon encountered an important obstacle that necessitated a delay, an event that would change the course of Lincoln's life. The boat became stuck on a milldam at the tiny hamlet of New Salem. Lincoln devised an ingenious method of balancing and freeing the boat, a feat that created something of a sensation among the small crowd that watched from the riverbank. Offutt was impressed with the young man and offered him a position as a clerk in his store to open in New Salem later in the year. Poor and with no other foreseeable means of support, Lincoln eagerly accepted the offer.[13]

Lincoln returned from New Orleans in July 1831. His ungainly and disheveled appearance attracted a great deal of attention in New Salem and made a lasting impression upon the residents. Rough looking and barefooted, with shirtsleeves rolled up to his elbows and homespun pants that were too short for him, the twenty-two-year-old future president looked like a bumpkin from the backwoods even to the people of New Salem, who still lived in log cabins and were only a step removed from the frontier. William Butler, a resident of the community who befriended the young man, later said Abe was "as ruff a specimen of humanity as could be found."[14]

But the villagers' initial impression soon gave way to respect and affection for Lincoln. His physical prowess, gregariousness, fair-mindedness, good humor, and intelligence made him popular. New Salem, which had been founded only two years before Lincoln's arrival, consisted of fewer than thirty families, almost all from the upper South and conservative in their political and social views. At Offutt's store, Lincoln quickly became acquainted with the people in the outlying areas, including rough frontier types like Jack Armstrong and the Clary's Grove boys. Lincoln competed in a wrestling match with Armstrong that attracted considerable local attention and ended in a draw; this endeared him to these young men, and they became strong supporters of Lincoln in his rise to distinction in the community. During his six-year stay in New Salem, Lincoln boarded at numerous places, including the Armstrongs' home.[15] Years later, in 1858, he successfully—and without charging a fee—defended Jack's son Duff in a famous murder trial. Lincoln never forgot his old friends, and when they visited Springfield and Washington, he reminisced with them and told humorous stories.

Less than a year after Lincoln's arrival in New Salem, the Black Hawk War broke out on the Illinois frontier, giving him another opportunity to advance his reputation in the eyes of his neighbors. Backed by the Clary's Grove boys, Lincoln was elected captain of the local volunteers and marched off with his men to fight Sac and Fox Indians. Led by Black Hawk, these Native Americans had recrossed the Mississippi River to reclaim their lands in Illinois. For Lincoln's unit, the war was more of a lark than a war. They encountered no hostiles during their three-month military service. Though the war was brief, Lincoln made valuable friends, including Major John Todd Stuart, who later encouraged him to study law and enter politics. Lincoln took great pride in his brief military career. In 1859, he admitted that his election as a captain of volunteers in the war "gave me more pleasure than any I have had since."[16] Lincoln's military service increased his popularity and thereby aided him in his political rise.

In New Salem, young Lincoln set out to improve himself. Years later, he expressed, by way of advice to his young law partner William H. Herndon, his own philosophy of how to succeed in life. "The way for a young man to rise," Lincoln wrote Herndon, "is to improve himself every way he can, never suspecting that any body wishes to hinder him."[17] New Salem society, though hardly refined by eastern standards, offered many opportunities for someone of Lincoln's intelligence and ambition to succeed. The village boasted several college graduates among its residents. These men saw something promising in Lincoln, despite his uncouth and awkward appearance, and they encouraged his self-education. The local schoolteacher, with the fitting name of Mentor Graham, provided books for Abe to study and recommended Samuel Kirkham's *English Grammar,* which could only be found in another community. Lincoln walked 6 miles to obtain a copy of the book. His absorption in learning the principles of the language enabled him, as he said in 1860, "to speak and write as well as he now does."[18] After a careful study of Lincoln's writings, Douglas L. Wilson has concluded that the future president's literary excellence can be traced to his fascination as a youth with words and meanings and his obsession with clarity, both in understanding and in being understood.[19] The frequent sight of Lincoln sitting and reading under a shade tree amazed his friends and became an appealing part of the Lincoln legend. Lincoln read all of the newspapers that came to the village and delighted in discussing their contents with local residents.

Lincoln also became an active participant in New Salem's literary and debating clubs. The village contained a number of religious skeptics who influenced the young man's thinking, leading him to deny, at least at this time, some of the basic tenets of Christianity. He believed in a remote God that did not interfere in the affairs of humankind. In 1846, when answering political charges that he scoffed at religion, Lincoln admitted that "in early life I was inclined to believe in what I understand is called the 'Doctrine of Necessity'—that is, that the human mind is impelled to action or held in rest by some power, over which the mind itself has no control." Though not a member of a Christian church, he claimed in 1846 that he had "never denied the truth of the Scriptures."[20] During the Civil War, Lincoln refined his religious views and concluded that God had certain purposes in history that humankind could not comprehend. Lincoln hoped—and in the case of the Union cause in the war seemed to believe—that his policies conformed to God's purposes.[21]

But Lincoln's life at New Salem, from 1831 to 1837, did not consist only of social activities and intellectual pursuits. Lincoln had to work and earn a living. Denton Offutt's store failed after a few months, leaving him "without means and without business," as he expressed it. He did odd jobs, such as working at the local milldam and harvesting crops. For a time, he considered becoming a blacksmith. In 1832, Lincoln, only twenty-three years of age but already confident in his political ability and encouraged by his New Salem friends, ran for the Illinois House of Representatives. He was motivated not only by an interest in politics but also by the need to have a means of support. In his brief campaign, Lincoln focused on the necessity for state aid to fund internal improvements, particularly the clearing of navigable streams, which had become a matter of great concern to the virtually landlocked people in his district. He also advocated the construction of "rail roads" for Sangamon County.[22] Railroads had first appeared in America during the late 1820s and would soon attract considerable interest in Illinois and elsewhere. Other candidates for the state House of Representatives in 1832 also proclaimed their support for transportation improvements. Since organized political parties did not exist in Illinois in 1832, no party labels were attached to candidates. Returning from the Black Hawk War during the summer, Lincoln hoped that his military service would propel him to victory in the election. Though he won 277 of the 300 votes cast in the New Salem precinct—a clear indication of his popularity with his neighbors—Lincoln lost the election.

Lincoln's first attempt to achieve political distinction taught him that local support was not sufficient for success in countywide or district elections. The 1832 campaign taught him about the rough-and-tumble nature of politics in an area where raw frontier conditions still prevailed. At a Pappsville political rally, he came to the rescue of Rowan Herndon, a New Salem friend and a cousin of William H. Herndon, who was attacked by the cronies of a man

Herndon had whipped earlier. The fight ended when Lincoln came down from the platform and tossed the main assailant into the crowd, after which he continued his speech.[23] This would not be the only time Lincoln's physical strength would come in handy in maintaining order at a political rally.

Lincoln soon had a chance to become a partner in a New Salem store, and he jumped at the opportunity. As a storekeeper, he talked with people and increased his understanding of the political interests and concerns of the community. Customers and others who gathered in the store gained an appreciation for the tall, intelligent young man. Like most village storekeepers, he stocked a variety of goods, from salt and sugar to clothes, shoes, and equipment for local farmers. The business, however, did not prosper, mainly because of New Salem's commercial decline. Navigation on the Sangamon River was inadequate to meet the needs of the growing area, and other towns replaced New Salem in the local trade. Even before the store "winked out," Lincoln in April 1833 sold out to his partner, William F. Berry. Nonetheless, along with Berry, he found himself saddled with legal suits for the payment of outstanding debts. The court ordered the seizure of Lincoln's personal property in partial payment, and when Berry died in 1835, the ambitious young man had to assume the whole debt, a huge sum of $1,100. Determined to pay what he called his "national debt," Lincoln finally settled the obligation in the 1840s.[24] His misadventure as a storekeeper had lasted for only a few months.

As before, Lincoln in 1833 found himself dependent on odd jobs to tide him over until he could secure regular employment. Fortunately, he had influential friends in New Salem who interceded with the administration of Andrew Jackson to obtain his appointment as the local postmaster. The fact that Lincoln was a supporter of Henry Clay, an opponent of Jackson, did not work against him. He later explained that the office was "too insignificant to make his politics an objection."[25] Though the pay was poor, he expressed delight with the appointment. In addition to providing Lincoln with a regular income, the postmaster's duties were not onerous and gave him an opportunity to read all of the newspapers delivered by mail. He also subscribed to the conservative *Louisville Journal,* the leading Whig newspaper in the West and an important influence on his early political views. He endeared himself to many country residents by extending to them what later would be called "rural free mail delivery," despite postal regulations requiring people to pick up their mail at the post office. Lincoln served as postmaster until 1836, when the post office was moved to Petersburg.[26]

Meanwhile, Lincoln had acquired a second job, as a surveyor in Sangamon County. During his two or three years as a surveyor, he laid out the nearby country roads and several small towns. Lincoln was a sociable young man, and while surveying he visited many people and shared experiences and stories with them. They found him witty and concerned about their problems. These personal contacts, like those Lincoln acquired during the Black Hawk War and as a storekeeper and postmaster, proved valuable in his political rise in the county.

In 1834, Lincoln, still in his mid-twenties and encouraged by friends, ran again for the state House of Representatives. The second American party system, succeeding the old Federalist and Jeffersonian parties, was forming under the leadership of President Andrew Jackson and Senator Henry Clay. Jackson and his supporters opposed national economic and banking measures, whereas Clay and his political associates advanced a federal program that included aid for internal improvements, the rechartering of the Bank of the United States, and tariff duties to protect American products against foreign competition. Members of Clay's party called themselves "Whigs" because, as they said, like their Revolutionary forebears they opposed a king, in this case "King Andrew" Jackson.

Reflecting the internal improvements needs of his community, Lincoln naturally supported Clay's positive agenda for economic development. He particularly favored state aid for canals, roads, river navigation, and public education. Though many Jacksonian Democrats had a similar background, Lincoln's life among the economically hard-strapped people of New Salem caused him to reject the Democratic idea of limited government in favor of an active government. The purpose of government, Lincoln later wrote, was "to do for a community of people, whatever they need to have done, but can not do, *at all* or can not, *so well do,* for themselves."[27] The Whig party's support for internal improvements and education reflected this view of government.

As a stump speaker, Lincoln had not yet developed the skill that would later become legendary. At this time his keenness on the issues and his wit compensated for his awkward style and poor dress. Lincoln preferred the personal touch, visiting and talking with voters in the county. On one occasion he met a group of men harvesting grain who informed him that they would not vote for a candidate who could not hold his own in the field. Whereupon Lincoln announced: "Boys if that is all, I am shure [*sic*] of your votes." He took a cradle scythe and led the way around the field with perfect ease. He not only won the votes of the "boys," he also won the election, despite the fact that the county was predominantly Democratic.[28]

Though victorious at the polls, Lincoln soon suffered a tragedy in his personal life—the death of Ann Rutledge on August 25, 1835. The story of his relationship with Ann Rutledge has long held a fascination for people interested in this great president's early life. It has become enshrouded in mystery and legend. Historians have joined in the debate, which is ongoing, over Ann's significance in Lincoln's life. Some historians claim that only a friendly relationship existed between the two young people; others contend that she was the great love of his life and that he never really got over her death. The preponderance of evidence, however, strongly suggests that although Lincoln had a romantic relationship with Ann, his despair at her death was relatively brief.[29]

Still, Lincoln did fall into a deep depression at her death. Friends, fearing for his sanity, came to his assistance and helped him to overcome his grief. Ultimately, Lincoln's relationship with Ann did not seem to have a lasting impact on his life. About one year after her death, he began courting Mary Owens, a relatively well-educated and wealthy Kentuckian who was visiting her sister near New Salem. The relationship was a troubled one from the beginning. The independent-minded and sensitive Mary, who was a few months older than Lincoln, found him "deficient in those little links which make up the great chain of womans [*sic*] happiness."[30] On his part, Lincoln resented Mary's superior attitude toward him, and he was quick to react defensively to her efforts to control him. By early 1838, Mary had broken off their relationship and returned to Kentucky; she never saw Lincoln again. He soon recovered from the rejection and forgot a promise to never marry. When he did marry, it was to Mary Todd—who, despite the well-known troubles in the relationship, provided the kind of social refinement and political support that Lincoln needed in his rise to prominence.

During the legislative campaign of 1834, John Todd Stuart (Mary Todd's cousin), the leading Whig in Sangamon County and also a candidate for the state House, had urged Lincoln to become a lawyer, a thought that had already occurred to him. After his election to the legislature, Lincoln borrowed books from Stuart and "went at it in good earnest," as he later wrote, adding, "When the Legislature met, the law books were dropped, but were taken up again at the end of the session."[31] He studied diligently Sir William Blackstone's *Commentaries on the Laws of England* (1765) and became enamored of the orderly conservative system of the law advanced by Blackstone. Lincoln read other legal treatises, in addition to the statutes of the state. In 1836, at the age of twenty-seven, Abraham Lincoln received a license to practice law, ending the speculation in New Salem as to his intention about a career. He had qualified for the profession by means of a diligent self-education and disciplined intellectual effort. For men of his generation and ambition, the practice of law usually made likely a career in politics.

Lincoln spent much of his first session in the legislature (1834–1835) learning the procedures and becoming acquainted with men from different parts of the state. He shared a room, as was common practice then, with Stuart at one of the boarding taverns in the state capital, Vandalia, a small town of fewer than 1,000 residents in the southern part of the state that still had many of the features of the frontier. Before leaving New Salem to take his seat in the state House of Representatives, Lincoln borrowed money to purchase a suit and to provide for living expenses until he could draw per diem. Though he identified with the Whigs, party organization was virtually nonexistent in the legislature when Lincoln took his seat. This gave him freedom—or so he thought—to vote with the Democrats, the majority, on numerous issues. Lincoln soon discovered that his Democratic colleagues did not return the favor for his votes on bills and on appointments to various positions. The first-term representative, however, made a strong impression on his colleagues in the House, most of whom were young men like himself. House members soon noted his knowledge of legal language and his precision in writing. Before the end of the session, they were asking Lincoln to draw up bills and resolutions for them to introduce on the floor. They also enjoyed his humorous stories, which he often told to make a point, both in debate and at the boarding house in the evenings.[32] His storytelling habit would follow him throughout his life.

In 1836, Lincoln won reelection to the House of Representatives, and when it met in December, he was chosen as the minority party (Whig) floor leader. Though only twenty-seven years of age, he was a man clearly on the rise. During this session, the Sangamon County delegation, the largest in the General Assembly, secured the removal of the state capital from Vandalia to centrally located Springfield. Known as the "Long Nine" because of their height, Lincoln and his Sangamon colleagues reputedly engaged in some shady dealings to secure the capital for Springfield. No doubt Lincoln, in addition to making practical arguments in favor of the relocation, participated in a logrolling maneuver to obtain votes for Springfield, agreeing to support local internal improvements measures for the capital removal bill. But there was no corrupt bargain involved in his efforts. The extension of public aid for projects designed to lace Illinois with roads, railroads, and canals and improve river transportation was popular, especially in Lincoln's Whig party. However, when the Panic of 1837—a severe national economic recession—occurred, the aid proved disastrous for the state's financial health and injured the reputation of the Illinois Whig party. In defending their role in the matter, Whigs, with limited success, argued that Democrats, including Stephen A. Douglas, the rising star in the party, supported the internal improvements bills and the state bank scheme that the General Assembly had enacted.[33]

Potentially more politically damaging for Lincoln was his cosponsorship with Dan Stone on March 3, 1837, of an antislavery protest in the House declaring that "the institution of slavery is founded on both injustice and bad policy." This protest followed a series of legislative resolutions denouncing the emerging abolitionist movement and asserting that "the right of property in slaves is sacred to the slave-holding States by the Federal Constitution, and that they cannot be deprived of that right without their consent."[34] Lincoln and Stone agreed that Congress had no power to interfere with slavery in the states and, as they announced, that abolitionist doctrines tended "rather to increase than to abate its evils." However, in protesting the House resolutions, they wanted to take a moral stand against the institution. Though a free state, Illinois was antiblack in sentiment and strongly opposed to antislavery agitation. The Stone-Lincoln resolution was overwhelmingly defeated in the legislature. Because the protest acknowledged the constitutional authority of state control of slavery—and Lincoln evidently made no further antislavery comments in the legislature—he escaped public censure on the issue. But it is conceivable that the germ of Lincoln's later antislavery sentiment was planted at this time.

Meanwhile, John Todd Stuart, who had served as Lincoln's mentor in the legislature, asked the young man to join him in a law partnership in Springfield, about 20 miles from New Salem. Lincoln leaped at the opportunity to become associated with a prominent attorney like Stuart in the new state capital. On April 15, 1837, he packed all of his possessions into two saddlebags, threw them on the back of a borrowed horse, said goodbye to his New Salem friends, and rode off to Springfield. He had no idea what the future would hold for him, but he was determined to succeed in the practice of law and to carve out a promising life for himself in Whig politics.

ABRAHAM LINCOLN's arrival in Springfield attracted little attention, unlike his appearance in New Salem six years earlier. He was one of many new people flooding into the central Illinois town that had been only a village a few years earlier. By 1840 Springfield's population would reach 2,579, which did not include the many transients conducting business in the state capital or seeking land in the area. Lincoln was overwhelmed by the newness of the town and by his own poverty.[35]

On his first day in Springfield, Lincoln found a place to stay. He went to a general store on the courthouse square to secure bedding material, and there he met Joshua Speed, the young partner in the store. Moved by a sincere and sorrowful expression on Lincoln's face, Speed, as he recalled many times later, offered to share his room and bed with him above the store. Lincoln

Joshua F. Speed, Lincoln's
closest friend after the
future president moved to
Springfield in 1837. Courtesy
of the Abraham Lincoln
Library and Museum,
Harrogate, Tennessee.

quickly accepted. Their sleeping arrangement was not unusual for men in the developing western country, where lodging was at a premium. William H. Herndon, who worked in the store and later became Lincoln's partner, and another clerk also stayed in the same room. When Lincoln was on the judicial circuit, he often shared a bed with another lawyer rather than sleep on the floor. The fact that he slept in the same bed with Speed did not mean that they had a sexual relationship, as a 2005 book by C. A. Tripp claims.[36]

Speed, three years younger than Lincoln and popular with the ladies, became the future president's best friend and eased his entrance into Springfield's society. Joshua Wolf Shenk has written that, though Lincoln and Speed were not homosexual, they "had an intimate friendship, buoyed by an emotional and intellectual connection."[37] The two young men, both Whigs, frequently discussed political affairs, but Speed was content to succeed in business rather than politics.[38] They roomed together until 1841, when Speed returned to Kentucky, where his family owned a large farm. Lincoln and Speed remained close friends, and Lincoln visited his home near Louisville. During the Civil War, Speed supported the Union but opposed Lincoln's antislavery policy.

In addition to Speed, Lincoln soon attracted an admiring group of young Springfield men—such as William H. Herndon, Milton Hay, editor Simeon Francis of the *Sangamo Journal* (Springfield), and James H. Matheny—who were intelligent, relatively well-educated, and interested in public affairs. His wit and good humor appealed to their youthful, exuberant spirits. They were all Whigs like Lincoln, and they provided important aid in his rise to prominence in Springfield.

Anxious for approval in the new society and politically ambitious, Lincoln seized an early opportunity to address the Young Men's Lyceum in Springfield. The Lyceum was a movement formed in the Northeast to provide a cultural and intellectual outlet for town residents, and by the late 1830s it had penetrated the West. On January 27, 1838, Lincoln delivered a carefully prepared oration to the local Lyceum. Entitled "The Perpetuation of Our Political Institutions," this speech, though ostensibly nonpartisan, expressed the Whig fear of mobocracy that plagued Jacksonian America. In the address, Lincoln avoided associating mob violence with the expansion of democracy during the 1830s, though at this time in his life he was deeply concerned about democratic excesses in society. Later, when his political thought had matured, Lincoln, while rarely using the word "democracy" except as it referred to the political party, put great faith in the power of the people at the polls on vital issues affecting the republic.

The most serious troubles during the 1830s had occurred in Mississippi, where both blacks and whites had been lynched; in St. Louis, where vigilantes had burned to death a black man; and in Alton, Illinois, where abolitionist editor Elijah P. Lovejoy had been murdered. In his Lyceum address, Lincoln contended that the descent toward mob rule threatened the republican and constitutional structure that the Founding Fathers had created. Men of Washington's generation, he declared, had established "a system of political institutions, conducing more essentially to the ends of civil and religious liberty, than any which the history of former times tells us." It was the grave duty of his and later generations, Lincoln said, to preserve this legacy.[39] Lincoln's appeal to the history of the Founders became a staple of his political argument.

The danger to America, Lincoln told his audience, would not come from overseas, as many believed, but from a breakdown of law and order incited by passion at home. Such a chaotic condition in society would inevitably lead to the rise of an ambitious and "towering genius" like Napoleon Bonaparte who would destroy liberty and the republic of the Founding Fathers. What could be done to prevent such a calamity? Lincoln asked. The descent into tyranny could only be checked by a popular commitment to "reason, cold, calculating, unimpassioned reason," he answered in the language of a true conservative. "Let those [materials] be moulded into *general intelligence, [sound] morality* and, in particular, *a reverence for the constitution and laws*" to secure and maintain "the proud fabric of freedom" in America. "Let reverence for the laws" become "the political religion of the nation," and "let every American pledge his life, his property, and his sacred honor" to protect this principle. Lincoln admitted that "bad laws" might exist; such laws, he declared, "should be repealed as soon as possible, still while they continue in force, . . . for the sake of example, they should be religiously observed."[40] Though he did not always follow his own advice to avoid passion in public discourse, Lincoln's reverence for the Constitution and the laws became a guiding principle in his long political career. It would especially infuse his positions on slavery and southern secession.

Some scholars have made quite a leap of faith in claiming that Lincoln in his Lyceum address foretold his own ambition to exceed the achievements of the Founding Fathers.[41] Lincoln, however, sought to protect the work of the Founders against demagogues who, by playing on the emotions of the people, would seek to gain power and undermine the Constitution and the rights under it.

As A PARTNER of John Todd Stuart, Lincoln had no trouble obtaining clients. But with his "national debt" to be paid off, he cleared only enough money to meet living expenses. Stuart, in order to pursue a political career, virtually turned over his cases to his ambitious and energetic young partner. After a bruising campaign in 1838, Stuart defeated Stephen A. Douglas for Congress. When his partner left for Washington, Lincoln wrote in the firm's account book: "Commencement of Lincoln's administration."[42]

However, he became increasingly unhappy with Stuart's inattention to business and his own inability to significantly improve his own financial prospects. With a growing interest in politics, he probably also wanted to be freer to engage in Whig party affairs. In April 1841, Lincoln, now age thirty-two, entered a partnership with Stephen T. Logan, another established Springfield lawyer, who was nine years his senior. This partnership proved successful but was amicably dissolved in 1844, when Logan brought his son into the firm. The three years of his association with Logan were important in Lincoln's development as an attorney. Logan helped his young partner understand the finer points of the law and taught him the importance of case research. It soon became clear that Lincoln was a quick learner. He prepared well, grasping all of the facts and precedents involved in a case. Such attention to research and preparation also became a characteristic of his political methods. Possessed with an extraordinary memory, and despite his lack of a formal education, Lincoln frequently placed his opponents, whether in court or on the stump, at a disadvantage.

Increasingly, Lincoln became captivated by politics, a field that offered a road to success for an ambitious and able young man, particularly one with his background of hard work, convivial personality, understanding of people, and speaking skills. In his rise as a Whig leader in the central counties of Illinois during the late 1830s and early 1840s, he received encouragement from his friends in the state capital and from the contacts he made on the judicial circuit as a lawyer. His ambition for political success became a driving force for him in an age when politics was the leading form of public entertainment and interest. While campaigning for the state legislature during this period, Lincoln honed his skills as an entertaining and captivating stump speaker. He recognized the powerful effect that backwoods humor and biting ridicule had on audiences, and he became a master of both techniques. Sometimes he resorted to a self-deprecating humor that was cleverly designed to ridicule his opponent, not himself.

Lincoln genuinely enjoyed debating local Democrats on the stump; the prospect of nailing them to the wall on issues that he thought important excited him. At times he became overzealous in his efforts to take the measure of the Democrats and advance his own and his party's standing in the community. Voters in the West, with their frontier traditions, expected such overkill from the candidates, and many hoped that it would lead to physical confrontations. On occasion Lincoln could become personal and cruel toward an opponent or toward those who attacked him. The most notable instance of this kind was the "skinning" of Jesse B. Thomas, Jr., who ridiculed Lincoln and his friends in a speech on July 20, 1840. After Thomas had finished his speech, Lincoln, who was in the audience, stepped to the platform and angrily lashed out at his antagonist. He mimicked Thomas's voice and the peculiar motions of his body as he walked. Mortified, Thomas fled the platform in tears. Lincoln later regretted his conduct and apologized to Thomas.[43] His behavior on that occasion reflected what Samuel C. Parks, a Springfield attorney, recalled about young Lincoln—that his "temper both as lawyer & politician was admirable. But when thoroughly aroused & provoked he was capable of terrible passion & invective."[44]

Like many politicians of the period, Lincoln routinely exaggerated the opposition's threat to the republic and to constitutional liberties. During the intense presidential campaign of 1840—the first in which Lincoln played an important role—his Whig friends admonished him to tone down his vituperative attacks on President Martin Van Buren and his local Democratic supporters. Lincoln dismissed their advice, reportedly with the comment, "It is all right; *we must fight the devil with fire; we must beat the Democrats, or the country will be ruined.*"[45] Inspired by his own youthful enthusiasm and the public passion generated by the political contests, Lincoln seemed genuinely to believe what he said about the Democrats and the threat that the party of Jackson and Van Buren posed for the country. He associated the

Democratic party with financial anarchy, disrespect for the law, and a too rigid commitment to states' rights, all of which were anathema to Whig conservatives. Only the Whigs, Lincoln concluded, stood in the way of the republic's disintegration. Lincoln held that economic growth, a virtuous citizenry, and adherence to the law were necessary to check the destructive forces let loose by the Jacksonians during the 1830s. For Lincoln, loyalty to the Whig party was a virtue to be religiously practiced.

THE "LOG CABIN" presidential campaign of William Henry Harrison in 1840 proved pivotal in Lincoln's emergence as an important Whig party leader in central Illinois. It also drew attention to him in other areas of the state. The Whigs conducted the first hoopla presidential campaign in American history, one in which organization and enthusiasm played a crucial role. Lincoln served as a Harrison elector and was on the five-member state committee that planned Whig strategy for the campaign. In addition, he edited a campaign newspaper, *The Old Soldier* (Harrison). He made numerous speeches for the Whig ticket and also in support of his own election to the state House of Representatives for a fourth term. Lincoln's canvass for Harrison took him into backwater villages of southern Illinois, among a people whose background and culture were similar to his. The frontier and farm work of his youth had prepared Lincoln for the rigors of travel and the primitive accommodations in the isolated communities of southern Illinois. Even after the coming of the railroads during the 1850s, many villages and counties could only be reached by traditional means of transportation—wagons, carriages, horseback, foot, and boats, or a combination of these.

Only a summary account of one of Lincoln's 1840 campaign speeches has survived. In this speech, at Tremont in central Illinois on May 2, 1840, Lincoln trumpeted Whig support for economic development and the rechartering of the Bank of the United States, policies that the Democrats opposed. He excoriated President Martin Van Buren, the Democratic candidate, for his earlier (alleged) support of black suffrage in New York and for his "Janus-faced policy" in regard to the War of 1812.[46]

The 1840 contest also saw the emergence of women, overwhelmingly on the Whig side, as participants in national political campaigns. Western party leaders, influenced by the public stirrings of women in the northeastern Whig heartland, encouraged local women to assist in the Log Cabin rallies. Though they could not run for office or vote, Whig women made banners, participated in parades, organized picnics, and brought a refreshing spirit to the Harrison campaign.[47] Democrats, who saw that the Whigs had gotten a jump on them in utilizing the talents of women in the campaign, ridiculed female participation in politics. It was not the sort of thing, Democrats said, that respectable women did.

One spirited Whig activist in 1840 was Mary Todd of Lexington, Kentucky, who was visiting her sister Elizabeth Edwards in Springfield. Well-educated and witty, Mary was the daughter of Robert Smith Todd, an affluent Whig businessman and lawyer in Lexington. She had grown up in Whig circles and had imbibed deeply in the party's politics. Her father was an associate of Henry Clay, and her sister's husband, Ninian Edwards, and his friends in Springfield were prominent Whigs. (Edwards later became a Democrat and a supporter of Stephen A. Douglas.) Since childhood, Mary had been interested in politics, and she had often said—probably half in jest—that she planned to marry a man who would become president of the United States. She did not expect that man to be Abraham Lincoln. When they first met in late 1839, apparently at an Edwards social function, Lincoln did not seem to have much potential as a husband, much less the presidency. Still, Mary became attracted to him and believed that he had good prospects as a lawyer-politician. They seemed an unlikely pair. Their backgrounds and personalities were different. Mary was high-strung, suffered from headaches, and was suspicious of others; she also was a stickler for the social graces. Lincoln, in contrast, was indifferent to social conventions and dress, experienced frequent bouts of depression ("melancholy," as his friends called it), and was often abstracted in thought. Yet they had important characteristics in common. Both were intelligent, inquisitive, and ambitious—and both were staunch Whigs.

The Abraham Lincoln–Mary Todd relationship blossomed during the 1840 presidential campaign, though mainly through correspondence, since he was usually on the road electioneering and she remained in Springfield. Their letters brought them together, and it soon seemed that they were destined for matrimony, a conclusion that Mary had evidently drawn. Meanwhile, Harrison had won the national election but narrowly lost Illinois, which was still a Democratic state. Lincoln, however, won a fourth term in the state legislature.

After returning home from campaigning, Lincoln realized that he had made a mistake by encouraging Mary to believe a romantic attachment existed. However, he hesitated to tell her this. The truth was that his attention had turned to Matilda Edwards, a young cousin of Ninian Edwards, who for a time was Mary's housemate.[48] Unfortunately for the lovesick young man, Matilda failed to show any interest in him. Lincoln finally decided to write a letter to Mary indicating that he did not love her. But Joshua Speed persuaded him to inform her in person, because, as he explained, it was the proper thing to do and perhaps would forestall her resentment. Mary, however, reacted severely to Lincoln's confession. Believing that he had promised to marry her, Mary charged Lincoln with deception and acting dishonorably toward her. The charge stunned Lincoln, who had always placed a high premium on upholding his honor and honesty in relationships. His anguish over Mary's reaction virtually overcame him; Ninian Edwards, Mary's brother-in-law, recalled that Lincoln "went crazy as a Loon," and Speed feared that his friend, whose periodic bouts of depression seemed to intensify, would commit suicide. Elizabeth Edwards later claimed that Lincoln left Mary standing at the altar on her wedding day. Though it became a part of the Lincoln legend, the altar story is pure fiction.[49]

His honor questioned and gravely depressed by the wrong that he had apparently done to Mary, Lincoln in 1842 began the slow process of reconciliation with her. Contributing to the restoration of the relationship was their collaboration in a series of anonymous "Rebecca" letters published in the *Sangamo Journal*. These letters specifically criticized Democratic State Auditor James Shields for his policy regarding depreciated Illinois state bank notes. The letters were satirical and designed to hurt Shields and his friends in the Auditor's Office. A letter on August 27, written by Lincoln, exceeded the accepted bounds of political ridicule, however, and attacked Shields's character. "Shields is a fool as well as a liar," Lincoln declared. "With him truth is out of the question, and as for getting a good bright passable lie out of him, you might as well try to strike fire from a cake of tallow."[50]

Such a personal attack could not go unchallenged by the offended party in the rough, honor-sensitive West of the 1840s. An infuriated Shields immediately demanded the authorship of the letter. Reluctantly, Simeon Francis, the editor of the *Sangamo Journal*, gave it to him, but only after securing Lincoln's permission. Shields demanded that his adversary issue a retraction of the "slander, vituperation, and personal abuse" contained in this and other "Rebecca" letters. If Lincoln did not comply, the aggrieved auditor said, there would be "consequences which no one will regret more than myself." Lincoln replied that Shields had made "so much assumption of facts, and so much of menace as to consequences," that he could not submit to the demand.[51]

A duel now seemed inevitable. Shields wasted no time in demanding satisfaction on the field of honor. Lincoln accepted, and, because dueling was illegal in Illinois, they agreed to meet, with their seconds, in Missouri across the Mississippi River from Alton. In accepting the challenge, Lincoln must have realized that in fighting a duel he risked not only his life but also his political future. In addition, the resort to an affair of honor violated his conservative respect for the law. Lincoln, however, knew that his honor was at stake in the affair, and he did not believe that he could back down. The frontier tradition of manly honor was still important in Illinois, as it was in the more notorious antebellum South. Lincoln would find it difficult to live in Springfield with the stigma of cowardice attached to his name; he valued too much the respect of his friends, as well as his own self-respect, to decline Shields's challenge.[52]

Lincoln, as the challenged party in the Shields affair, chose "Cavalry broad swords of the largest size" as the weapons for the duel.[53] Many historians have assumed that in selecting broadswords Lincoln intended to make the affair appear ludicrous, a comic-opera posturing designed to stop short of actual violence. But he was dead serious, and there was a method in his choice of the weapon. His long arms would give him an advantage in a fight with broadswords against Shields, who could not match Lincoln's size.

Fortunately for Lincoln's political future, and, indeed, for that of the nation, the duel was never fought. Both parties went to the designated ground fully prepared for the affair of honor. Lincoln, however, had written a note the night before informing Shields that his "Rebecca" letter of August 27 was intended "wholly for political effect. I had no intention of injuring your personal or private character, or standing as a man or a gentleman."[54] Lincoln's explanation distorted his purpose in the letter: He had not only wanted to hurt Shields politically, he had also sought to damage his personal reputation.

Nevertheless, after some complicated negotiations between the seconds on the field of honor, the matter was peacefully resolved, though without Shields's initial approval. The parties and a disappointed crowd of spectators returned home without incident. Soon after the event Lincoln told a friend that in the event that the duel had been fought, he had not intended to kill Shields, only to disarm him.[55] The incident greatly embarrassed Lincoln, and he refused to speak of it in the future. But he had learned a valuable lesson from the affair: Never again would he place himself in a similar position. Lincoln resolved to avoid the kind of personal abuse of his opponents that might lead to a violent confrontation. The Shields incident also contributed to Lincoln's determination as a politician and lawyer to attempt to settle differences among factions and individuals before they became harmful. He was not always successful, however, as his presidency would prove.

Having upheld his honor in the Shields affair, Lincoln sought to set things right with Mary Todd, who had been an important helpmate during this difficult period. He secretly began to court Mary in the fall of 1842 and discovered that his attraction to her exceeded the bounds of mere friendship. Sobered by the Shields incident—and by the fact that he was in his mid-thirties and still single—he gave serious thought to a future in which politics and the law would be balanced with family life. Lincoln wanted a shield, so to speak, from the stresses that he was enduring in his life, and Mary, he thought, could provide the aid that he needed in the restoration of his self-respect and

Mary Todd Lincoln, 1846, four years after her marriage to Abraham Lincoln.
Courtesy of Townsend Collection, Special Collections and Digital Programs,
University of Kentucky Libraries, Lexington.

in the fulfillment of his professional and political ambitions. Furthermore, he could now support a wife and family. Lincoln knew that Mary reciprocated his feelings for her; she had wanted to marry him all along.

Precisely when he and Mary made the decision to marry is unknown, except that it was sometime in late October or early November 1842. Not until the day of the ceremony, on November 4, did they announce the wedding.

Lincoln only notified his groomsman, James H. Matheny, at noon on that day.[56] (Joshua Speed had returned to the family home in Kentucky and had married.) There are numerous conflicting accounts of Lincoln's demeanor on his wedding day, most of which were recalled many years later. One story has Lincoln replying to a boy who asked him where he was going: "To hell, I reckon," was his answer. According to another story, told by Mary's sister Frances Wallace near the turn of the century, the bridegroom "was cheerful as he ever had been, for all we could see."[57] Latter-day critics of Mary, such as William H. Herndon, claimed that Lincoln had no real affection for the bride and married her to gain an important connection in Springfield society. According to this view, Lincoln's only true love was Ann Rutledge; he could never feel the same about Mary. This was hardly the case. On his wedding day, the thirty-three-year-old bridegroom gave Mary a gold wedding ring with the engraving "Love is Eternal," which probably expressed his true feelings for her. In his characteristic manner, Lincoln wrote a friend one week later: "Nothing new here, except my marrying, which to me, is a matter of profound wonder."[58] It was also a profound wonder to Mary's friends and family in Springfield, who found it difficult to believe that she would accept Lincoln's marriage proposal after he had rejected her earlier. Though we cannot know for sure, neither partner ever seemed to regret the decision to marry, and in retrospect, despite problems in the marriage, both were better off for it.

CHAPTER TWO

WHIG CONGRESSMAN FROM
THE PRAIRIE STATE

IN MARRYING MARY, Abraham Lincoln had taken an important step in his rise to prominence as a lawyer-politician. The marriage improved his social contacts and standing in Springfield, though this benefit probably was not a prime consideration for him in the relationship. It settled him into a middle-class lifestyle, particularly after the couple had children. Lincoln was fascinated by the intelligent, well-educated Mary and strongly attracted to her, and he probably realized that he had gained a companion who would contribute to his intellectual and cultural development. Ambitious for her husband's success, Mary took on the task of polishing his manners and improving his dress. Her efforts, which continued to the end of her husband's life, achieved only limited success.

Lincoln was not ashamed of his crude, hardscrabble background, contrary to what some biographers have claimed. Though he did not enjoy "farm work," as he admitted at the time, Lincoln was not embarrassed about his early life as a laborer. He did express regret about his lack of formal education, but he took pride in his determination and ability to overcome this handicap. Lincoln's rustic stories, which he never tired of telling even to sophisticated easterners during his presidency, not only reflected his confidence but also his nostalgia for the past and for the common people and companions who had helped him in his political rise.

A few of Lincoln's friends, however, questioned whether he was capable of true friendships. Ebenezer Peck, a close political associate, wrote in 1861 that Lincoln used "his best friends in order to lift himself a round higher on the ladder of ambition."[1] Even Judge David Davis, who managed his presidential nomination at Chicago in 1860, contended after the war that Lincoln had "no Strong Emotional feelings for any person—Mankind or thing. He never thanked me for any thing I did."[2] Both comments seriously distorted Lincoln's feelings for his old friends. Peck and Davis had been disappointed because of Lincoln's failure, as president, to award them with the offices they wanted. Peck's bitter criticism came soon after the president refused to support his application for a position in the new administration. Though Lincoln appointed him to the Supreme Court, Davis thought that he deserved to be selected as chief justice when Roger B. Taney died in 1864. It is reasonable to conclude, however, that Lincoln cherished his old friends, particularly those from his early days in New Salem and Springfield. In 1849, Lincoln wrote Joseph Gillespie that "the better part of one's life consists of his friendships," and he was sorely troubled that he had recently disappointed one of his friends.[3]

Philosophically, Lincoln associated his success as a lawyer and politician with the freedom and opportunity that existed in republican America. Overcoming adversity and educating oneself were accomplishments that most Americans, particularly in the developing West, could appreciate. Many of his associates had similar backgrounds, though most of them had not experienced the poverty, lack of formal education, and severe hardships that Lincoln had. Still, it was Lincoln's exemplary character and his success in law and politics, not his rustic origins and style, that attracted him to Springfield's emerging elite and sustained their approval of him.

Mary Todd, despite her learning and her father's affluence, had lived an uncertain and troubled life. Her mother had died when she was six, and her stepmother, unlike Lincoln's, had brought turbulence to her life. She later wrote that her childhood was "desolate" and that her home "was truly at a boarding school."[4] Mary's personality and temperament had been set by her early life, though a measure of stability in it occurred when she married Lincoln. Her sharp temper, often displayed when she had a headache, and her controlling nature led to her frequent upbraiding of her husband, who usually reacted in a passive manner. Sometimes neighbors and friends observed Mary, on the slightest pretext, scolding him in public. William H. Herndon's later claim, which many historians have accepted, that Mary was a "she wolf" who made Lincoln's life in Springfield "a domestic hell on earth" is an exaggeration; still, it had an important element of truth in it. Lincoln's respect for Mary and his devotion to her survived the outbursts and discord. In some cases, Lincoln simply walked away when abused (in at least two instances he was physically attacked by Mary) and returned when he knew that her "spell" would be broken.[5]

Lincoln was hardly faultless in the couple's marital problems. As Lincoln scholar Michael Burlingame has written, "The moody, introspective, emotionally withdrawn Lincoln was far from an ideal husband."[6] He suffered from periodic bouts of depression, though these were less severe after his marriage. At times he would withdraw within himself and become abstracted in thought. Given Mary's unstable emotional state, Lincoln's moods contributed to the stress in the family. Furthermore, his long absences from home riding the judicial circuit, a requirement for success as a lawyer, or engaging in political campaigns left household affairs almost entirely in Mary's hands. Although she realized the financial and political needs for him to travel, Lincoln's absences contributed to her emotional problems and affected their marital relations. Mary sadly commented to a neighbor that "if her husband had staid at home as he ought to that she could have loved him better."[7]

After their marriage, the Lincolns moved into a large room at an inn, the Globe Tavern, which they rented for $4 a week. Anticipating the birth of their first child nine months after the wedding, they rented a small frame house on Fourth Street. A boon for the Lincolns occurred when Mary's father visited Springfield and became fond of his son-in-law, who represented him in a local land case and whose politics were the same. Todd arranged for his daughter to receive $120 a year for the rest of his life.[8] The following year, Lincoln bought a somewhat larger house on the corner of Eighth and Jackson streets, and the family, including newborn Robert, moved into it. Enlarged and improved later, the house was the only one that Lincoln ever owned.

WITH A FAMILY to support, which in 1846 would include another baby, Edward, Lincoln continued to build his law practice while participating in Whig politics. After the amicable dissolution of his partnership with Stephen T. Logan in 1844, he invited "Billy" Herndon to join him and share equally the firm's proceeds. Herndon, like many of Lincoln's other friends, had been born in Kentucky, had moved to Illinois with his family when he was a child, and was a Whig in politics. He thought of himself as a southerner who nonetheless looked toward New England for his ideas; he often corresponded with eastern antislavery intellectuals, particularly Theodore Parker. Herndon later boasted that he was an abolitionist, which probably was not true. His opposition to slavery seemed to have been based mainly on the absurd fear that black slavery would lead to white servitude.[9]

Herndon's personality, temperament, and appearance differed markedly from Lincoln's. Herndon, nine years Lincoln's junior, was impulsive and idiosyncratic in some of his ideas. A strong temperance advocate, he led the successful, though temporary, fight for prohibition in Springfield during the 1850s. Lincoln, a teetotaler throughout his life, spoke at several temperance rallies in central Illinois, but in his argument against drinking, he avoided the self-righteous preaching characterized by most activists in the movement. Herndon later fell off the wagon and, after the Civil War, gained the reputation, at least among his enemies, as the town drunk. He also served as mayor of Springfield in 1855. Why Lincoln chose Herndon to be his junior partner remains a mystery. It might have been because Lincoln was tired of being a junior partner and wanted someone younger whom he trusted and who had considerable promise as a lawyer. In Lincoln's mind, Herndon met both re-

William H. Herndon, Lincoln's law partner for sixteen years and faithful recorder of Lincoln's prepresidential life. Courtesy of the Abraham Lincoln Presidential Library, Springfield, Illinois.

quirements for the job. Furthermore, Billy Herndon was popular among insurgent young Whigs whose support Lincoln needed to advance his political career.[10]

The Lincoln-Herndon relationship proved strong during the sixteen years of the partnership. Herndon, who had earlier clerked in the Logan-Lincoln office, admired his senior partner and always called him "Mr. Lincoln" out of respect. The formality was also an apparently unconscious acknowledgment that their relationship was not one of complete equality. Lincoln referred to Herndon as "Billy" and was clearly fond of him. Herndon had to endure silently some of Lincoln's strange personal characteristics and also Mary's dislike of him. An avid reader and talker on almost any subject, Herndon found Lincoln's practice of repeating his anecdotes to be irritating; on one occasion he noted that Lincoln told the same story three times during a three-hour period. He also found annoying his partner's habit of reading aloud and his failure to discipline the rowdy Lincoln children when they visited the office. While Lincoln handled business on the judicial circuit, Herndon usually tried cases in the Springfield area and did most of the legal research. Both men attended to the clerical work.[11] As Lincoln probably expected, Herndon provided political support for him.

Lincoln and Herndon opened their law office in the Tinsley Building where the United States District Court of Illinois met. Their office was near the state capitol and the Sangamon County courthouse. After a slow beginning, the partnership thrived. Their reputation as hard-working and able lawyers whose fees were modest—no more than $10 to $25 for representing a client in the circuit court—attracted almost more business than they could handle. Juggling more than 100 cases a year, many of them away from Springfield, the partners soon gained a reputation as one of the leading law firms in central Illinois. When on the judicial circuit, Lincoln often secured the assistance of local attorneys; indeed, they also sought out his help.[12] As Lincoln biographer David Donald has written, "Lincoln and Herndon took on whatever clients came their way. They defended persons charged with murder, burglary, assault, embezzlement, and almost every other kind of crime."[13] In 1847, Lincoln even served as the attorney for Kentucky slaveholder Robert Matson, who was seeking the return of a runaway slave. The court, however, ruled against Matson and the slave was freed.[14]

By the 1850s Lincoln had become a "lawyer's lawyer." In 1860 a correspondent of the *New York Herald* interviewed separately "three of the ablest jurists in the State" regarding Lincoln's standing with the bar in Illinois and his qualities as a lawyer. Two of the judges were political opponents of Lincoln. All of them indicated, according to this reporter, that Lincoln "has been among the leading practitioners of the State for many years, and probably not a judge or a member of the bar can be found . . . who will express a doubt as to his being a superior man. While he is exceedingly well informed upon all general subjects, he cannot be considered a learned man. . . . The learning which is applicable to the case in hand he understands," they said, and had acquired in "a practical way."[15]

Much has been written about Lincoln's success as a railroad attorney and its influence on his political career. Most of his legal work did not involve railroad corporations; nonetheless, his most lucrative cases were those in which he defended—or in some instances opposed—the state railroads. Lincoln's legal services for the railroads occurred mainly during the 1850s after he had established his prominence as an attorney and statewide political leader. The Illinois railroads were faced with numerous suits as they expanded and sought tax concessions and other advantages. They needed an able, well-connected lawyer at the state capital, and Lincoln was an obvious choice. He had "the common touch"; with his wit and reservoir of homespun

Springfield street scene, 1858. Lincoln's office in the Tinsley Building is at the end
of the first block and across from the American House. In the middle of the block
is the hardware store of Mary Lincoln's brother-in-law, Clark M. Smith, where in
a back room Lincoln drafted his inaugural address. Courtesy of the Abraham
Lincoln Presidential Library, Springfield, Illinois.

stories, he could diffuse the populist arguments hurled against the "moneyed" railroad corporations to influence the juries.[16]

Beginning in 1853, he was often on retainer for the Illinois Central Railroad, which ran north and south through the state. At one point, when he was not on retainer, Lincoln concluded that he had saved the Illinois Central half a million dollars, earning him, according to his calculations, a fee of more than $5,000. When the railroad refused to pay, he sued for the money. The company, however, only offered token resistance in court, and a jury awarded Lincoln the full amount, the largest fee that he ever received. The Illinois Central's resident director explained to the railroad's president why he did not bring the company's formidable powers to bear against the suit. The Illinois Central, he said, needed to retain the goodwill and services of a man who was "not only the most prominent of his political party" in the state, "but the acknowledged special adviser of the [William H.] Bissell administration" in Springfield. As was his policy, Lincoln shared the jury's award with Herndon. The suit did not end his relationship with the Illinois

Central; Lincoln soon was handling two important tax cases for the company.[17]

Lincoln's work for the Illinois Central became a political issue in his celebrated senatorial campaign of 1858 against Stephen A. Douglas. He had to fight off charges by Douglas that he had schemed to defraud the state of tax money owed by the Illinois Central. At Carthage on October 22, Lincoln vigorously refuted the charges and denied the Douglas claim that he was "on very cozy terms with the Railroad Company."[18] Actually, Douglas, who was in a strategic position in Congress to secure land grants and provide other favors for the railroad, had a closer relationship with the Illinois Central than Lincoln did. In 1858 the senator received the railroad's assistance in his campaign against Lincoln. George B. McClellan, the company's general superintendent and a future Union general, provided the senator with a private car for the campaign.[19]

LINCOLN'S SUCCESS AS a lawyer enabled him financially to engage in his great passion—politics. Still, Lincoln was not wealthy by modern American standards, or even by contemporary eastern standards. During the 1840s, his annual income from his law practice was between $1,500 and $2,500, a modest amount. Always frugal, Lincoln by 1849 had saved enough money to lend some of it at interest. During the 1850s, his average annual income increased to $3,000. By 1860 Lincoln had more than $9,000 invested in interest-bearing notes and mortgages, which constituted a risk in the West, where speculation in land, railroads, and other commercial enterprises often ran wild, producing financial failure. By a conservative estimate, his real estate, mainly his home, was worth $5,000.[20] Lincoln's income enabled him to devote time and energy to political organization, speech writing, and campaigning without sacrificing his family's well-being. Nonetheless, after the grueling senatorial campaign with Douglas in 1858, Lincoln complained, probably with some exaggeration: "I have been on expences so long without earning any thing that I am without money now for even household purposes."[21] His income during the 1850s provided Mary with the means to expand the size of their house and purchase the kind of furnishings the Lincolns needed to hold receptions for local people and dinners and meetings for political friends who came to the state capital. Mary, with servants and sisters to help, proved to be a marvelous hostess for her rising husband. On one occasion, she invited about 500 people to a reception at the house, but a drenching rain and a popular bridal party in nearby Jacksonville reduced the attendance to 300.[22]

It was a truism in the nineteenth century that lawyering and politics went together. This symbiotic relationship was nowhere more apparent than in the emergence of Abraham Lincoln in the two decades before the Civil War. His close association with lawyers on the huge Eighth Judicial Circuit, which included much of central and eastern Illinois, established ties in the Whig party (later Republican) that were crucial to his political success. Lincoln's wit, good nature, moderation, and skill in the courtroom and in expressing his political ideas after the day's business endeared him to his Whig colleagues and gained their political support. Though Lincoln proved to be a popular stump speaker, he depended upon local party leaders, many of whom he met in the county seats of the Eighth Judicial District, to provide him with intelligence on public opinion. Still, he was careful to draw his own conclusions from what he heard—and also from what he read in the partisan press. Gregarious by nature, Lincoln genuinely enjoyed riding the circuit and the camaraderie of fellow lawyers. One friend on the circuit, Judge David Davis, became his most important political associate. When in Springfield, the rising young lawyer could be found in the evenings in the library of the State House, where attorneys came to research the authorities for their cases. "I hardly ever knew an evening to pass without Mr. Lincoln putting in his appearance," visiting lawyer Elihu B. Washburne recalled. "He was a man of most social disposition, and was never so happy as when surrounded by congenial friends." His stories and personality made Lincoln the center of attraction among the lawyers who pursued cases in the state capital and aided him in cementing political alliances.[23]

In June 1844, Lincoln spoke at the state Whig convention in Peoria and defended the party's platform, which he had helped draft and which expressed the views of Henry Clay, the party's presidential candidate. The platform called for a "sound currency," the distribution to the states of the revenues from the sale of public lands, and a tariff on imports that would "afford equal protection and encouragement to every branch of American Industry." Reflecting the Whig anger following President John Tyler's disapproval of Senator Clay's favorite measures, the Peoria platform advocated a restriction on the veto power and a one-term limitation for presidents.[24] For young, stalwart Whigs like Lincoln, the bitter experience with Tyler, who had succeeded to the presidency upon William Henry Harrison's death in 1840, only to betray the party, would long remain a sore point. Years later, as president-elect, Lincoln announced that his "political education" as a Whig "strongly inclines me against a free use of any of [the] means by the Executive, to control the legislation of the country. As a rule, I think it better that congress should originate, as well as perfect its measures, without external bias."[25] During the Civil War, Lincoln backed off somewhat from this position; however, he still rarely opposed congressional actions or lobbied Congress. A notable exception was his veto of the 1864 Wade-Davis reconstruction bill,

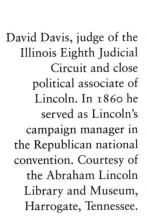

David Davis, judge of the Illinois Eighth Judicial Circuit and close political associate of Lincoln. In 1860 he served as Lincoln's campaign manager in the Republican national convention. Courtesy of the Abraham Lincoln Library and Museum, Harrogate, Tennessee.

which was designed to replace his lenient plan for southern restoration with a radical one.

His political prominence on the rise, Lincoln served as a presidential elector for Clay in 1844 and increased his standing as a Whig with an extensive speaking campaign for the party. Judge David Davis, even this early in Lincoln's career, praised him as "the best stump speaker in the State."[26] The *Springfield Register,* the Democratic newspaper organ in the state capital, took an uneasy notice of Lincoln by ridiculing his campaign performances. "Lincoln, another member of the [Whig] Junto . . . is our jester and mountebank," the *Register* announced. He "is a long-legged varmint [who] can make a speech which is all length and height like himself, and no breadth or thickness."[27]

Lincoln even campaigned in Indiana, where his support for "Harry of the West" (Clay) was fondly remembered when he ran for president in 1860. Lincoln went south to Perry County, visited with friends of his youth, and spoke to a large audience at Rockport.[28] Only a few brief accounts of his 1844 campaign speeches have been preserved. These reports indicate that Lincoln vigorously promoted the national Whig platform to aid economic development. In one speech, at Springfield on May 22, Lincoln, in support of Clay's position, opposed President Tyler's efforts to annex slaveholding Texas. He declared that the annexation was inexpedient at that time.[29] Lincoln apparently ignored the issue of the acquisition of slave territory, which concerned many upper northern Whigs. Like Clay, he argued that the annexation of Texas would cause a war with Mexico. Slavery was not an issue in the Illinois election.

One of the most memorable episodes in the 1844 campaign occurred in the Sangamon County courthouse during the evenings of March 20–25. There, after the day's business in court, several Democratic and Whig spokesmen debated the issues in the election. Lincoln entered the fray when Democratic champion Alfred W. Cavarly claimed that John Todd Stuart, a former Whig congressman and Lincoln's first partner, had admitted that the consumer paid for all tariff duties. Angered by what he considered to be a distortion of the effect of a protective tariff, Lincoln took the floor and promised to forfeit his ears and his legs if he could not demonstrate that protected goods had been cheaper since the passage of the tariff of 1842. The next evening, Lincoln debated his old friend John Calhoun, now a Democratic stalwart, and continued to defend the tariff, arguing that the duties "probably" fell upon the manufacturer, not the consumer.[30] Despite the vigorous efforts of Lincoln and other Whigs, Democrat James K. Polk, on a "Manifest Destiny" or expansionist and limited government platform, carried Illinois in the election and, in a close vote nationally, won the presidency.

By the mid-1840s Lincoln had set his sights on a seat in the U.S. House of Representatives. However, since the beginning of the second party system (Democrat and Whig) during the 1830s, the Whigs had controlled only one congressional district in the state, the seventh, where Lincoln and two other popular party leaders, John J. Hardin and Edward D. Baker, resided. All of them had claims on the party for the congressional seat. When the Whig district convention met at Pekin in 1843, Lincoln, at age thirty-four, was not ready to make his move for the congressional nomination, and Hardin was selected as the party's candidate. After the Hardin nomination, Lincoln, to avoid a divisive conflict and, not incidentally, to make probable his future success, secured the approval of Baker, though apparently not Hardin, for a policy by which they would alternate terms in the House. Lincoln deferred to Baker for the second term, and he was elected.

When Lincoln's time came for the Whig nomination in 1846, he heard disturbing reports that Hardin's friends were ignoring the "Pekin Agreement" and working to secure their man's return to Congress. Lincoln almost frantically opened correspondence with key district Whigs, including Hardin, claiming that he was due the nomination on the ground of "Turn about is fair play."[31] Other Whigs agreed, and backed by Baker, Lincoln received the nomination. Baker's fidelity to the "Pekin Agreement" cemented a strong friendship; Lincoln even named his second son, born that year, Edward Baker Lincoln.

Lincoln still faced a hard fight to win the congressional election. Baker had won by a narrow margin in 1844, and Democrats had high hopes of capturing the seat in 1846. To oppose Lincoln, the Democrats nominated Peter Cartwright, a famous circuit-riding Methodist minister who had served in the state legislature. Lincoln campaigned extensively, but only one report of a speech has survived, at Lacon on July 18. In this speech, he stressed the Whig argument for a tariff to protect American enterprise and farmers and, according to the report, "closed with some general observations on the Mexican war, annexation of Texas, and the Oregon [annexation] question." However, the account is silent on whether he took a stand on the war, which had begun in May.[32]

During the 1846 campaign, Lincoln had to defend himself from Cartwright's charge that he was an "infidel" and "an open scoffer at Christianity." This charge stemmed from his days in New Salem, when, along with other young men in the community, he had read Thomas Paine's *The Age of Reason* (1794) and imbibed the author's religious skepticism. At that time Lincoln reputedly drafted an essay challenging many points in the Bible, especially the concept of eternal damnation for the sinner. Fortunately for his political future, a friend persuaded him to destroy the essay.[33]

A few days before the congressional election, Lincoln decided to answer Cartwright's charge about his religious infidelity. In a handbill that appeared in Whig newspapers in the district, he admitted that he was "not a member of any Christian Church" but also said, "I do not think I could myself, be brought to support a man for office, whom I knew to be an open enemy of, and scoffer at, religion." He acknowledged that "in early life" he had believed in the " 'Doctrine of Necessity' — that is, the human mind is impelled to action, or held in rest by some power over which the mind itself has no control." But, he claimed, he had not argued for that position in more than five years. Lincoln contended that this was a doctrine "held by several of the Christian denominations" and implied that his view had not been heretical. Lincoln did not think that "any man has the right thus to insult the feelings, and injure the morals, of the community in which he may live." He condemned "those, whoever they may be, who [had] falsely put such a charge in circulation" against him. Lincoln, however, as his record in New Salem suggests, was somewhat disingenuous when he announced, "I have never denied the truth of the Scriptures." But Lincoln was apparently truthful when he said that he was not a "scoffer of religion."[34] It is still an open question whether Lincoln ever disputed the divinity of Jesus.

Lincoln won the election, and he believed that he would have been victo-

rious even if he had not responded to Cartwright's criticism.³⁵ His 1,511-vote
margin of victory out of 11,418 votes cast was the largest ever for any Whig
congressional candidate in the seventh district.

THE THIRTIETH CONGRESS did not convene for its first session until December 6, 1847, sixteen months after Lincoln's election. The long wait dimmed
the satisfaction that Lincoln had felt on winning the seat. He wrote his friend
Joshua Speed: "Being elected to Congress, though I am very grateful to our
friends, for having done it, has not pleased me as much as I expected."³⁶ In
the fall of 1847 Lincoln rented his home and with Mary and their two small
children left for Washington. They stopped at Lexington to visit Mary's
family. There the young congressman-elect heard his idol Senator Henry Clay
deliver a long speech attacking President James K. Polk for starting the war
with Mexico, which had become a standard Whig charge by 1847. Clay's
address was designed to win the support of antislavery Whigs in the upper
North, who were becoming increasingly disturbed by their leader's waffling
on the issue of slavery's expansion. At Lexington, Clay came out against the
institution's extension either as a result of the war or by the acquisition of
"foreign territory." The Kentucky senator probably stretched the truth when
he told his audience that he "had ever regarded slavery as a great evil."³⁷

Lincoln must have been influenced by Clay's speech and perhaps also by
political conversations with him and his associates in Lexington, including
his father-in-law, Robert Todd. Lincoln had earlier ignored or downplayed
the issue of slavery's expansion, which had been triggered by the annexation
of Texas. When Democrat James K. Polk won the 1844 presidential election,
Lincoln seemed more upset with "whig abolitionists of New York" who had
voted for the Liberty party candidate than with those who supported the expansion of slavery in the West. He wrote a friend in October 1845 that if
these New York Whigs, though a minority in the state party, "had voted with
us last fall, Mr. Clay would now be president, whig principles in the ascen-
dant, and Texas not annexed; whereas by the division, all that either had at
stake in the contest, was lost." Lincoln confessed: "I never was much interested in the Texas question. . . . I could never very clearly see how the annexation would augment the evil of slavery." "Slaves," he argued, "would be
taken there in about equal numbers, with or without annexation." Still, he
wrote, "I hold it to be a paramount duty of us in the free states, due to the
Union of the states, and perhaps to liberty itself (paradox though it may
seem) to let the slavery of the other states alone; while, on the other hand, I
hold it to be equally clear that we should never knowingly lend ourselves

directly or indirectly, to prevent slavery from dying a natural death—to find new places for it to live in, when it can no longer exist in the old."[38]

Lincoln and his family arrived in Washington in December 1847 and settled into Mrs. Ann Sprigg's boardinghouse (where the Library of Congress's Jefferson Building is now located). Lincoln was the only Whig congressman from his state, a circumstance that prompted the newspapers to refer to him as the "Lone Star of Illinois." He was also a junior member of a party with a narrow majority in the House of Representatives; Democrats, however, controlled the Senate. By the time that he took his seat, Lincoln had changed his views on the Mexican-American War. When the war began in May 1846, he seemed to have favored it. Along with Governor Thomas Ford and others, on May 30 he spoke at a nonpartisan rally in Springfield that proclaimed the necessity for immediate and united action in support of the war.[39] But influenced by Clay and other prominent Whigs who opposed it, the young Illinois congressman had come to view the conflict as unnecessary and waged for partisan purposes. Though a freshman representative, Lincoln planned to seize the first possible moment in the House and express his opposition to "Mr. Polk's war," which, he hoped, would earn him some political capital with the Whig leadership.

Lincoln must have known that a strong statement against the war in the House could hurt him back home; Illinois had sent more troops to the army than any other state except Missouri. But he was willing to take the political risk, inspired to a considerable extent by his zealous partisanship and ambition. American forces were on the verge of success in Mexico. They had already taken Mexico City, though news of the victory had not reached Washington. Lincoln probably also realized that his origins and mannerisms suggested to antislavery Whigs, like the new speaker of the House, Bostonian Robert C. Winthrop, that he was closely tied to the southern Whig faction. If he expected to gain influence in Washington and have an important role to play in the upcoming national election, Lincoln must disabuse northeastern Whigs of that notion. At the same time he could not afford to alienate upper South Whigs whose cultural and political roots were similar to those of his friends in central and southern Illinois. Lincoln had to establish a foothold in both camps. At Mrs. Sprigg's boardinghouse, he ate and discussed national affairs with such antislavery Whigs as Joshua R. Giddings of Ohio and proslavery Whigs like Daniel Moreau Barringer of North Carolina. Years later, Lincoln referred to Barringer as "my chum in Congress."[40]

The young congressman believed that unless the party's majority rallied around an antiwar and anti-expansion policy, radical Whigs would again bolt the party and cost it the 1848 presidential election. At any rate, he was determined to stake out a position placing the onus of the war on President Polk and the Democrats but avoiding the slavery issue in the territories. Lincoln thought that a middle-of-the-road or conservative position would gain the support of southern Whigs while satisfying the northern members of the party. To take the initiative on such a troublesome issue in Congress would be an audacious move for a first-term representative from a Democratic-controlled lower northern state. Lincoln, however, was no ordinary politician, as events would soon prove. In addition to being highly ambitious, he exuded youthful confidence in his intellectual ability—almost to the point of arrogance—and in his ability to express clearly and logically his position on issues.

On December 22, three weeks after taking his seat, Abraham Lincoln rose in the House and offered his famous (in retrospect) "Spot" resolutions. In a series of eight resolutions, he demanded that President Polk inform the House of Representatives the "spot" on American soil where the blood of U.S. troops had been shed creating the administration's justification for the war with Mexico. The accusatory tone of the resolutions obviously suggested that the territory between the Rio Nueces and the Rio Grande where American soldiers had been attacked in 1846, triggering Polk's war message, did not belong to the United States. Thus, the Illinois congressman suggested, the president had deliberately misled the American people into the war.

In his "Spot" resolutions, Lincoln kept his focus on the origins of the conflict and shrewdly side-stepped the issue of acquiring conquered territory from Mexico.[41] More importantly, he ignored the controversy over slavery's expansion that had been raised by the Wilmot Proviso. Introduced by Pennsylvania Representative David Wilmot in 1846, the proviso to an army appropriations bill called for the prohibition of slavery in any southwestern territories gained from the war. Sectional lines were immediately drawn on the issue, and some southerners, such as Senator John C. Calhoun of South Carolina, threatened disunion if the proviso became law. The proviso passed the House but failed in the Senate, where the South had an equal number of senators; however, some in both sections were willing to cross sectional lines on the question of slavery's expansion. Lincoln supported the Wilmot Proviso, though he admitted in an undated private document that he would do so only as long as it did not endanger "any dearer object"—specifically, the preservation of the Union.[42] The success of the Whig party, not the restriction on slavery, Lincoln believed at this time, was the best guarantor for sectional harmony and the future greatness of the republic.

Lincoln's "Spot" resolutions were laid on the table and not acted upon by the House. Less than two weeks later, on January 3, George Ashmun, a Whig representative from Massachusetts, proposed a resolution declaring that the war was "unnecessarily and unconstitutionally begun by the President of the United States." The Ashmun resolution passed by a strict party vote, with Lincoln joining Whigs from both North and South in supporting it.[43]

Inspired by Whig unity against the war and President Polk's own blundering effort to explain his policy in his annual message to Congress in December, Lincoln on January 12 delivered a stinging rebuke to the president. Polk, however, took no notice of the freshman representative's speech in the House.[44] Lincoln charged that the president had stooped to "the sheerest deception" by employing "every artifice to work round, befog, and cover up, with many words," to justify his flawed policy. Lincoln specifically contended that Polk had been inconsistent in his explanations of how the conflict began and how it was to be financed. "As to the mode of terminating the war, and securing peace, the President is equally wandering and indefinite. First, it is to be done by a more vigorous prossecution [*sic*] of the war in the vital parts of the enemies [*sic*] country." After "talking himself tired, on this point, . . . [Polk] tells us that 'with [the Mexican] people distracted and divided by contending factions, and a government subject to constant changes, by successive revolutions, the continued success of our arms may fail to secure a satisfactory peace.'" According to Lincoln, Polk said that it might be necessary to have the Mexican people desert their leaders and, protected by the American army, "set up a government from which we can secure a satisfactory peace." This approach also could fail, Polk acknowledged, whereupon the United States might have to take charge of affairs in Mexico, a prospect that deeply concerned Lincoln.

Lincoln claimed that the president's motive from the beginning was "to involve the two countries in a war." Polk trusted "to escape scrutiny, by fixing the public gaze upon the exceeding brightness of military glory—that attractive rainbow, that rises in showers of blood—that serpent's eye, that charms to destroy." He plunged the nation into a war that "has swept, *on* and *on*, till, disappointed in his calculation of the ease with which Mexico might be subdued, he now finds himself, he knows not where." Lincoln concluded that Polk, "his mind, tasked beyond it's [*sic*] power," was "a bewildered, confounded, and miserably perplexed man" who had led America into a needless and unfortunate war.[45]

Lincoln's "Spot" resolutions and his January 12 speech received little attention in Washington and in the national press. Prominent Whigs in Congress, such as Ashmun and Giddings, had made similar speeches, though not with Lincoln's precision of argument. Lincoln characterized an antiwar speech by "a little slim, pale-faced, consumptive man" from Georgia, Alexander H. Stephens, as the best one that he had heard. He was so moved by the speech of the man who would become vice president of the Confederate States that he immediately wrote William H. Herndon: "My old, withered, dry eyes, are full of tears yet." On the national level, attacks by Whig leaders on the Polk administration eclipsed Lincoln's effort. Only one member of the House, Democrat John Jamison of Missouri, took notice of Lincoln's speech on the floor of the chamber. Jamison found it "astonishing" that "the gentleman from Illinois" could make such an unpatriotic speech while troops from his state were fighting and dying in Mexico.[46]

Lincoln had raised a firestorm at home. The *Springfield State Register* belched forth vindictively against him. The editor of this Democratic newspaper, who had crossed swords with Lincoln for several years, sensed that he had found the Achilles' heel in the political armor of the rising Whig star of central Illinois. He saw not only a golden opportunity to destroy Lincoln but also to end Whig control of the Seventh Congressional District and reduce further the minority status of the Whig party in the state. Characterizing the "Spot" resolutions as treason, the editor of the *State Register* thundered that "the brand of [Benedict] Arnold is upon [Lincoln's] forehead, and the 'damned spot' will not [wear] out."[47] This editor printed numerous excerpts from Democratic newspapers in Illinois denouncing "spotty Lincoln" and declaring that, if he continued his traitorous course, he would have "a fearful account to settle" with the state's heroes when they returned from Mexico.[48] The *Peoria Democratic Press* predicted that "the miserable man of 'Spots' will pass unnoticed save in the execration that his treason will bring upon his name."[49]

Illinois Whigs also were displeased with their only representative in Congress. The war was popular in the state, and Whigs, particularly in the Seventh Congressional District, knew that Lincoln's antiwar stance could prove costly in the next election. Out of party and personal loyalty, they avoided public criticism, but reports soon reached Lincoln of their unhappiness with him. Herndon himself warned his law partner of the political troubles at home over his "Spot" resolutions and expressed his own disagreement with Lincoln's position that the war was wrong. He specifically questioned his law partner's vote for the Ashmun antiwar resolution.[50]

Lincoln responded to Herndon in two revealing letters. On February 1, Lincoln wrote that he regretted the disagreement, "not because of any fear we shall remain disagreed, . . . but because, if you misunderstand, I fear other good friends will also." The Ashmun resolution, Lincoln told Herndon, "affirms that the war was unnecessarily and unconstitutionally commenced by the President; and I will stake my life, that if you had been in my place, you would have voted just as I did." Lincoln maintained that he was "compelled to speak" against what he knew was a "lie" by Polk and his Democratic friends in Congress that the war was just and necessary. Despite Democratic claims, Lincoln declared that he, as well as almost all of the Whig members of Congress, had voted supplies for the army, and would continue to do so.[51]

Two weeks later, in his second letter to Herndon, Lincoln sought to refute another of his partner's contentions. This was, as Lincoln restated it, that "if it shall become *necessary, to repel invasion,* the President may, without violation of the Constitution, cross the line, and *invade* the teritory [sic] of another country; and that whether such *necessity* exists in any given case, the President is to be the *sole* judge." Lincoln argued that Herndon was incorrect. Polk's justification for war, Lincoln reminded his law partner, was not to repel an anticipated invasion, but to drive Mexican troops from soil that he wrongly claimed was America's.

Then Lincoln turned to the broader constitutional issue that Herndon had raised. He emphatically denied his junior partner's contention that the president could "invade a neighboring nation, whenever *he* shall deem it necessary to repel an invasion," and thus "make war at pleasure." If the president could launch such a preemptive strike, there would be no limit to his power of intervention. Lincoln gave this example: "If, to-day, [the president] should choose to say he thinks it necessary to invade Canada, to prevent the British from invading us, how could you stop him? You may say to him, 'I see no probability of the British invading us' but he will say to you 'be silent: I see it, if you don't.'" The Founding Fathers, Lincoln said, gave "the war-making power to Congress" because "kings had always been involving and impoverishing their people in wars, pretending generally, if not always, that the good of the people was the object." The Founders framed "the Constitution that *no one man* should hold the power of bringing this oppression upon us." Lincoln told Herndon that "your view destroys the whole matter, and places our President where kings have always stood."[52]

Meanwhile, in early 1848, Lincoln announced his support of General Zachary Taylor for president. Invited by a committee to attend a meeting in Philadelphia to nominate the general, on February 9 Lincoln replied, "I am decidedly in favor of General Taylor as the Whig candidate for the next Presidency." He boldly informed the committee that as the only Whig member of Congress from the state, "I think proper to say" that the overwhelming majority of Illinois Whigs supported Taylor. To a Virginia political friend, he gave his own reason for advocating Taylor's candidacy: "I am satisfied we can elect him, that he would give us a whig administration, and that we can not elect any other whig."[53] Lincoln wrote an Illinois Whig that "our only chance is with Taylor. I go for him, not because I think he would make a better president than Clay, but because I think he would make a better one than Polk, or Cass, or Buchanan, or any such [Democratic] creatures, one of whom is sure to be elected, if he [Taylor] is not."[54] He explained to another

Illinois associate that Taylor would be the ideal candidate in the state because, as a war hero, he could "take some democrats, and lose no whigs."[55]

Lincoln also probably thought that if he became a candidate for reelection to Congress, his support for Taylor would defuse much of the criticism hurled at him for his "Spot" resolutions on the war, and he could win on the general's coattails. Lincoln had told Herndon in January that he would seek a second term if it did not violate the fairness doctrine agreed to at Pekin in 1843 with John J. Hardin and Edward D. Baker.[56] The likelihood of this pledge still being in force was remote; Hardin had died a hero in Mexico, and Baker had moved to Galena, outside of the Seventh Congressional District, in the early spring after returning from the war. But by April, Lincoln realized that his opposition to the war would probably prevent his reelection, though he refused to admit it. He expressed to a friend a different reason for not running: "I can not become a competitor with others for the nomination. I have said I will not." He said there were "many others who will be quite as acceptable as myself."[57] Seventh district Whigs agreed. They nominated Stephen T. Logan, Lincoln's old law partner, for Congress.

With his political fortunes at home on the wane, Lincoln focused his attention on his congressional duties and on helping Taylor win the presidency. By campaigning for Taylor, he could expect political preferment if the hero of Buena Vista won the election. Earlier, in December 1847, Lincoln had joined an informal group of Whig congressmen, mainly southerners, who supported Taylor; they called themselves the "Young Indians" and included Alexander H. Stephens of Georgia and Daniel Moreau Barringer, Lincoln's friend from North Carolina. By avoiding the divisive issue of slavery in the territories to be gained from Mexico, the "Young Indians" were able to patch together a bisectional coalition in the House of Representatives. They concentrated on Whig economic principles (legislation to charter a national bank, raise the tariff on imports, and finance internal improvements); and they announced that General Taylor agreed with them. The "Young Indians" also denounced President Polk's war policies and claimed that Taylor favored, as Lincoln put it, a "defensive line policy" against further expansion in the Southwest.[58]

In March 1848, Lincoln drafted a list of mainly conservative suggestions that he hoped Taylor would follow. He recommended support for traditional Whig principles, including complete congressional authority in legislative matters, a position that reflected the party's opposition to the use of the veto by Presidents Jackson and Tyler. On the issue of slavery in the territories, Lincoln abandoned the position of his southern allies and expressed the hope that Taylor would adopt the antislavery principle contained in the Wilmot Proviso. Still, Lincoln would not close the door on southern territorial expansion, a position, he cleverly reasoned, that would retain crucial southern Whig support for the party while reassuring northern antislavery Whigs of Taylor's opposition to the expansion of the "peculiar institution." Lincoln wanted the general to announce that, though it might be necessary to take "some territory" from Mexico, the United States "shall not acquire any extending so far South, as to enlarge and agrivate [*sic*] the distracting question of slavery."[59] There is no evidence that the Illinois congressman's advice was ever sent to Taylor or circulated to Whig associates. Significantly, the draft indicated that Lincoln, who had avoided the issue of slavery's expansion in the past, was changing his view and beginning to think that the Whig party should oppose the institution's extension into the territories.

In June, Lincoln attended the national Whig convention in Philadelphia, but not as an official delegate to it. The delegates, after engaging in bitter factional conflicts in their state conventions, nominated "Old Rough and Ready" Taylor for president on a platform that ignored the slavery issue in the newly acquired "Mexican Cession." Antislavery northern Whigs opposed the platform and especially the nomination of a large slaveholder as president; they thought that the convention's actions had been dictated by proslavery southern Whigs. It appeared that many of these "conscience" Whigs, along with disgruntled Clay supporters, might bolt the party or at least go fishing on election day.[60] But not Lincoln; his candidate had received the nomination, and he believed that as a war hero, Taylor would be supported by many Democrats and by most Whigs. The general, Lincoln thought, would be particularly strong in Illinois, where Whigs needed a shot in the arm at the polls to overcome the Democrats. Though he objected to slavery's expansion, Lincoln refused to express displeasure with the Whig platform. His first priority was to win control of the federal government, after which Whig policies could be enacted and slavery's expansion checked. Lincoln set out to do all that he could to secure Taylor's victory in the fall and, not incidentally, revive his own sagging political fortunes in central Illinois.

Returning from the Republican convention, Lincoln spoke at a Taylor "ratification meeting" in Wilmington, Delaware, and later in the summer at Whig rallies in Seneca and Rockville, Maryland, both conservative slave states. In Wilmington, he cooled his antiwar rhetoric and admitted that the dispute with Mexico, as summarized in the *Delaware State Journal,* "could not have been settled in an amicable manner." Lincoln denied that the war was fought to expand slave territory, as many northerners believed; however, he faulted the Polk administration for seeking more territory than provided for in the treaty ending the war. The purpose of this expansion, he charged, was "to catch votes" for the "Locofoco party" (Democrats) in the 1848 election.[61] No account exists of Lincoln's speeches in Seneca and Rockville; however, he probably repeated what he had said in Wilmington.

Back in Congress, Lincoln delivered two long speeches, both of which had strong political overtones. These speeches sought to promote Taylor and the Whig party in the election. The first one, on June 20, 1848, argued in favor of federal aid for internal improvements, which the Whigs supported and the Democrats opposed. This address was technical and uninspiring; even Lincoln admitted that "nobody will read" it.[62] The second speech, on July 27, was more overtly political, defending Taylor and attacking Lewis Cass, the Democratic candidate for president. It sounded more like a Lincoln stump speech in Illinois than an address on the floor of Congress. Lincoln mixed stinging ridicule and humor with political rhetoric. He defended Taylor from the Democratic charge that he had no political views and that the Whigs had abandoned their principles, as well as their leader, Henry Clay, in nominating the general for president. Lincoln said that Taylor's platform was clear: He would "allow the people to have their own way, regardless of his private opinions." They would act through their representatives in Congress. Specifically, Taylor would defer to Congress on such Whig principles as federal aid for internal improvements. In contrast, Cass would ignore the wishes of the people and veto internal improvements bills. Taylor, Lincoln said, probably would not veto the Wilmot Proviso prohibiting slavery in the new territories gained from Mexico, though, he admitted, "I do not *know* it." Cass would certainly veto the proviso and would pursue a policy "leading to new wars, new acquisitions of territory [*sic*] and still further extensions of slavery."

Lincoln in his July 27 speech also defended the Whigs against the frequent Democratic charge that they were inconsistent in opposing the Mexican-American War and then nominating for president a commanding general of the conflict. He insisted that he saw nothing awkward or embarrassing about it. Lincoln explained that it was not unpatriotic to oppose the beginning of the war on grounds that it was unnecessary and unconstitutional, as stated in the Ashmun resolution. He maintained that during the war Whigs supported it, and many "worthy" Whigs fought and died in Mexico. General Taylor, "the noblest Roman of them all," was one of them. (Lincoln ignored the fact that Taylor did not cast his lot with the Whigs until after the war.) Whig representatives in Congress, Lincoln indicated, had consistently voted in favor of supplies for the army. The Democrats, he said, did not understand "the distinction between the cause of the President in beginning the war, and the cause of the country after it was begun." To them, "the President, and the country, seems to be all one." Whigs "see the distinction . . . clearly enough; and our friends who have fought in the war have no difficulty in seeing it also," Lincoln declared.[63] Thus, he announced, Whigs were un-troubled by the nomination of the "par excellence" hero of the war. Clearly, however, Lincoln's explanation for supporting Taylor rather than Clay for the presidency was strained.

AT THE END of the congressional session in August, William Schouler, editor of the *Boston Daily Atlas,* invited Lincoln to visit New England and speak at Whig rallies in behalf of Taylor and the party. Lincoln seized the opportunity to help the Whig party and advance his own political standing. He agreed, and, with his family, left Washington for New England on September 9. His reputation as the "Lone Star" representative of Illinois in the House and an able western stump speaker had preceded him. An element of curiosity about this "very tall and thin figure" from the raw prairie country also existed among New England Whigs. He arrived at Worcester, Massachusetts, on Sep-tember 12, the day before the state Whig convention met, and was invited to speak that evening to an assembly of delegates and other Whigs. Worcester was also in the heartland of the recently formed Free Soil party. This party consisted mainly of antislavery Whigs who had bolted their party after the slaveholder Taylor's nomination and selected former Democratic President Martin Van Buren as their candidate for the office. Van Buren had become alienated from the Democratic party by the Polk administration's shabby treatment of him and his friends. The free-soil movement, like the Liberty party in 1844, which Lincoln had blamed for his party's defeat in the presi-dential election, threatened to undermine the Whig cause in 1848. Greatly disturbed by this political development, Lincoln tailored his New England speeches to appeal to antislavery Whigs, allay their suspicions of General Taylor, and thereby reduce their support of the Free Soil party. This does not mean that only political calculations influenced Lincoln's speeches, or that he was the only Whig campaigning with these objectives in mind. Lincoln was experiencing a transformation from a politician who did not view slav-ery as a key issue in American expansion to a determined opponent of it in the new territories. In New England, he had a sympathetic audience for his antislavery views, however mild at this time, without having to pay a political price, as would have been the case in racially charged Illinois during the 1840s. Furthermore, he shared the platform and talked with Whigs who influenced him toward a stronger anti-expansionist position than before.

Lincoln's transformation on the issue of slavery's expansion had begun in Washington and would accelerate during the fall campaign. Earlier, Lincoln had been part of a broad antiwar movement, including southern Whigs, who opposed the Polk administration. Guided by political necessity at that time, he had soft-pedaled his opposition to slavery's expansion; but from the anti-slavery members in Congress, he had gained an appreciation of the moral and political arguments against the institution. In his New England tour, Lincoln combined his political purpose to check Whig defections to the Free Soil party and win support for Taylor by contending that the general opposed the extension of slavery. Lincoln's antislavery position would still be argued on conservative and constitutional grounds, which, he insisted, did not conflict with Whig national principles or with General Taylor's views.

At Worcester, in a speech that lasted for one and a half hours, Lincoln laid out his themes for his New England tour. He challenged the opposition's claim that Taylor had "no principles" and its contention that the Whig party had abandoned its history and creed by nominating him. Lincoln reminded his audience that earlier in the year the general had announced his support of the economic program of the Whig party favored by the people and free of presidential influence. "This was no new doctrine for Whigs," Lincoln said at Worcester. "It was the 'platform' on which they had fought all their battles, the resistance of Executive influence, and the principle of enabling the people to frame the government according to their will."

Lincoln announced that Taylor would neither encourage nor discourage slavery's expansion. He insisted, however, that the general would not veto the proposed Wilmot Proviso prohibiting slavery in the new territories, a measure that New England Whigs passionately supported. Regarding slavery in the southern states, Lincoln claimed—with some exaggeration—that "the people of Illinois agreed entirely with the people of Massachusetts on this subject, except perhaps that they did not keep so constantly thinking about it." "All agreed," he said, "that slavery was an evil, but that we were not responsible for it and cannot affect it in States of the Union where we do not live." The question of the expansion of slavery was different, he contended; it "is a part of our [national] responsibility and care, and is under our control"—and should be restricted. Lincoln argued that the Free Soil party, though opposed to expansion, would only take antislavery votes away from Taylor and thus insure the election of Cass, who as president would permit slavery in the new territories. Furthermore, even if the organizers of the Free Soil party "succeeded in electing Mr. Van Buren, they had no specific means to *prevent* the extension of slavery to New Mexico and California." Lincoln did not venture a reason why this would be the case. He also reminded Massachusetts Whigs that Martin Van Buren, an old "Locofoco" leader, had long been an anathema to their party.[64] Although Free Soilers and Democrats ignored his appearance at Worcester, Massachusetts Whig leaders and newspapers praised the speech of the "Lone Star" congressman of Illinois.

A few days later, Lincoln addressed the Boston Whig Club and continued the themes expressed at Worcester. According to the *Boston Daily Atlas,* "he pointed out the absurdity of men who professed Whig principles supporting Van Buren, with all his Locofocoism, while the Whigs were as much opposed to the extension of slavery as were the Van Buren party."[65] Lincoln then spoke at Whig rallies in nearby towns, returning to Boston on September 22. That evening he shared the platform at Tremont Temple with other Whig luminaries, including William H. Seward, the former governor of New York, who was the main speaker. Even cultivated Bostonian Whigs appreciated Lincoln's frontier humor and inimitable style; their approval had a great deal to do with his conservative anti-expansionist sentiments, which emphasized Whig unity in the face of the Free Soil party's threat. One Whig reported after Lincoln's speech at Tremont Temple: "The chief charm of his address lay in the homely [western] way he made his points. For plain pungency of humor, it would have been difficult to surpass his speech."[66] Henry J. Gardner, who would later become the governor of Massachusetts, recalled that Lincoln's "style and manner of speaking were novelties in the East. He repeated anecdotes, told stories admirable in humor and in point, interspersed with bursts of true eloquence, which constantly brought down the house."[67] Clearly, Lincoln had not adjusted his western style to conform to sophisticated New England rhetorical standards. At the same time, Lincoln's opposition to slavery's expansion expressed in his New England appearances contrasted with his public silence on the issue in Illinois.

Lincoln and Seward met in Boston for the first time. They stayed in the same hotel and discussed the slavery issue in the context of national Whig politics. According to Seward's son Frederick, Lincoln told his father, who leaned toward a radical antislavery position, "I have been thinking about what you said in your speech. I reckon you are right. We have got to deal with this slavery question, and got to give much more attention to it hereafter than we have been doing."[68] Though these may not have been the exact words that Lincoln spoke, the comment reflected his growing interest in the issue, deepened by his antislavery contacts in Massachusetts. Lincoln's campaign speeches, however, probably had little impact on the outcome of the election in that state. With most of its prominent leaders, such as Speaker of the House Robert C. Winthrop, and the main Whig newspapers remaining firm behind the party, Taylor won the state. Nonetheless, the Free Soil party received more votes than the Democrats did in Massachusetts, New York, and Vermont. Free Soilism, a militant stand against slavery's expansion, was the wave of the future in the upper North, which in turn threatened Whig strength in the nation.[69] Lincoln probably did not miss this important political point, but he knew that Illinois voters were not ready for an antislavery party in 1848, even one along conservative lines.

In October, Lincoln, along with his family, returned to Illinois via the Great Lakes. As expected, he campaigned for Taylor in the state. In the southern part of the Seventh Congressional District, a section that included Springfield, he received a cool reception because of his antiwar position in Congress. Furthermore, some members of his party were disappointed that he had supported Taylor rather than Clay for the Whig nomination. Lincoln's assurances to his New England audiences that General Taylor would not veto the Wilmot Proviso to prohibit slavery in the territories gained from the war went over poorly in central Illinois. Predictably, the Democrats lambasted Lincoln whenever he campaigned in their communities and charged him with "*misrepresenting* the wishes of the patriotic people of this district." After a debate between Lincoln and a Democrat at Jacksonville, the *Springfield Illinois State Register* told its readers that "Lincoln crouched in silence beneath the blows that fell thick and fast around him." This editor gleefully concluded, probably accurately, that Lincoln had "made nothing by coming to this part of the country to make speeches."[70] The embattled Whig congressman seemed to realize that he was a liability for Taylor in the Springfield area; he devoted the last weeks of the campaign to the northern parts of the congressional district, where he found a more friendly audience.[71]

In August, Illinois Whigs had received a premonition of what was to come in the November presidential election in their state when Whig candidate Stephen T. Logan lost his congressional contest with Democrat Thomas L. Harris, ending a decade of Whig control of the House seat. Whig activists in the district attributed Logan's defeat, as Judge David Davis recalled, to "Lincolns [*sic*] momentary unpopularity."[72] Lincoln preferred a different explanation for his former law partner's defeat. He wrote a friend that "a good many Whigs, without good cause, as I think, were unwilling to go for Logan." Lincoln noted that "Harris was a Major of the war, and fought at Cerro Gordo, where several Whigs of the district fought with him," and that these Whigs later worked for his election. However, he could not believe that there was "any political change in the district" and said that "the district must and will be found right side up again in November."[73]

As Lincoln predicted, Whigs won in the district in the fall presidential election. Taylor captured the presidency, but he lost Illinois to Lewis Cass and the Democrats. Martin Van Buren, the Free Soil candidate, carried eight northern counties; however, the antislavery Whig defections to his party were not decisive. Even if the disaffected Whigs had voted for Taylor in the election, he still would have lost the state to Cass.[74] Lincoln exulted in Taylor's election to the presidency, but he was disappointed that the Whigs had failed to loosen the Democratic grip on Illinois.

WHEN LINCOLN RETURNED to Washington in December for the second session of the Thirtieth Congress, debate over slavery in the Mexican Cession (today's Southwest) and in the District of Columbia had assumed paramount importance. The debate had been triggered by the antiwar controversy, the rise of the free-soil movement during the presidential campaign, and the strident proslavery reaction of southerners to the antislavery crusade. In this session, Lincoln took a more active role than before, though not a leading one, in support of the Wilmot Proviso. While cautious publicly, he had become increasingly aroused to the moral and political necessity for resisting slavery where the federal government had a constitutional right to act, namely, in the territories and in the District of Columbia. Lincoln did not believe that congressional legislation against slavery in the territories and in the District would lead to southern secession. Such federal action, Lincoln reasoned, would be peripheral to the security of slavery in the South and would not represent a threat to it, despite the ravings of radical southern rights men.

Nonetheless, he wrote a friend, it would be "arrogant—silly perhaps—to entirely disregard the opinions of the great and good men who think there is real danger" to the Union in the slavery controversy.[75] Lincoln, however, assumed that national leaders did not believe a crisis would occur if the Wilmot Proviso passed Congress. He understood that in Illinois support for the proviso would almost completely vanish if the Union was imperiled, and also that state Whigs, who were more in favor of the measure than the Democrats, would suffer politically.

It is difficult to determine precisely how many times Lincoln voted for the Wilmot Proviso because its nonexpansion principle regarding slavery appeared in different forms during his last session in the House. He later claimed that he voted for the proviso or its principle "at least forty times." Nonetheless, he did not speak in the contentious debates on the question. He was more interested in ending slavery and the slave trade in the District of Columbia than in prohibiting it in the territories. Still, compared to many antislavery northern Whigs, he took a conservative position on slavery in the District.

By the late 1840s, radical antislavery men had become increasingly offended by the presence of the barbarous institution in the national capital. They were deeply embarrassed that foreigners, who were eager to find flaws in the American creed of liberty and equality, witnessed slavery every day.

Motivated by the revival of the issue in the territories, antislavery proponents flooded Congress with petitions demanding emancipation in Washington. Several controversial bills and resolutions were introduced calling for the abolition of slavery and the slave trade in the District. A coalition of southerners of both political parties, joined by northern Democrats, defeated these measures. Lincoln opposed all antislavery bills that did not permit a vote by the District's (white) citizens, though he supported their objectives. In addition, he opposed a resolution introduced by Representative Daniel Gott of New York prohibiting the slave trade in the District of Columbia because he felt its preamble was unnecessarily provocative. The resolution passed in the House but did not receive the Senate's approval.[76]

Encouraged by Joshua Giddings, a radical antislavery Whig, Lincoln on January 10, 1849, announced his intention to introduce a comprehensive amendment to the Gott resolution that he hoped would be approved in both houses. His amendment would provide for the gradual, compensated emancipation of slaves in the District of Columbia and, by its nature, outlaw the slave trade there. The plan, however, would be contingent upon the approval of a majority of the voters in Washington and Georgetown. Lincoln's proposal also called for municipal authorities in the national capital "to provide active and efficient means to arrest, and deliver up to their owners, all fugitive slaves escaping into [the] District."[77] Lincoln believed that he had the approval of most Whigs, including William W. Seaton, the mayor of Washington and the conservative editor of the influential *Washington National Intelligencer,* for his amendment. He was soon disappointed. When Seaton and other conservative Whigs refused to support him, Lincoln did not formally introduce the plan. As he explained years later, upon "finding that I was abandoned by my former backers and having little personal influence, I *dropped* the matter knowing that it was useless to prosecute the business at that time."[78] Congress as a part of the sectional Compromise of 1850 abolished the slave trade in the District of Columbia. But slavery itself continued in Washington until the Civil War, when Congress, in April 1862, removed this stain on the national capital. As president, Lincoln signed the bill, which contained his original idea of compensation but without its submission to the voters.

In proposing a compromise solution to the controversy over slavery in the District of Columbia, Lincoln seemed to have conceded a great deal of moral weight on the issue. Joshua Giddings, however, thought otherwise. In 1860, this radical antislavery proponent supported the Illinois Republican for president and insisted that Lincoln, in advancing his plan to end slavery in the District, "took his position with those who were laboring in the cause of humanity." "I view it as one of high moral excellence, marking the heroism of the man," Giddings said.[79] At any rate, District voters would probably have rejected any emancipation scheme in 1848–1849. Most of the white residents held southern views on slavery and either had a vested interest in the institution or were fearful of emancipation's racial consequences. Lincoln's proposal was consistent with his subordination of the slavery issue to Whig party unity and to practical political realities. The prosperity and perpetuation of the Union, Lincoln believed, depended upon Whig success at the polls.

WHEN HIS TERM in Congress expired on the morning of March 4, 1849, Lincoln remained in Washington for Zachary Taylor's inauguration. Because of his early support of Taylor and his yeoman service in the 1848 campaign, he expected political preferment for himself and his associates. Even before the inauguration, Lincoln, like other Whig congressmen, began maneuvering for offices in the new administration. Lincoln focused his attention on obtaining positions for his political friends in Illinois; he especially recommended Edward Baker for a cabinet appointment. Despite widespread support for Baker in the West, the new administration ignored his claims, probably because of the opposition of the powerful Kentucky Whig John J. Crittenden.[80] Lincoln did not think that his own standing with the Whig leadership was strong enough for "a first class office"; and, he said, "a second class one would not compensate me for being snarled at by others who want it for themselves." Lincoln believed that he could have, "almost by common consent," the position of commissioner of the General Land Office, if he really wanted it. However, as he wrote Joshua Speed, there were other Illinois aspirants for the position, and he did not want to offend them by seeking it.[81]

Returning home in the spring, Lincoln renewed an earlier promise to support Cyrus Edwards for the General Land Office. But political and personal complications occurred, and it soon became clear to Lincoln and his friends that unless he sought the position of commissioner, this important political plum would go to Justin Butterfield, a favorite of the new secretary of the interior, Thomas Ewing. Butterfield had supported Clay against Taylor before the Whig convention and, according to Lincoln, had not worked hard for the party in Illinois and thus did not deserve the appointment. Declaring that the selection of Butterfield would "be an egregious political blunder [and] give offence to the whole whig party here," Lincoln flooded the mail with letters asking his supporters "to write General Taylor at once, saying that either I, *or the man I recommend* [Edwards], should . . . be appointed to that office, if any one from Illinois shall be." He acknowledged that the president might have in mind someone from another state, and added, "I do not ask to interfere with that."[82]

Lincoln exaggerated the Whig opposition against Butterfield. Evidence exists that Lincoln's appointment also would have divided Illinois Whigs, especially in his congressional district. His unpopular antiwar stand in 1847–1848, and his failure while in Congress to secure federal offices for a number of Whig activists, rankled many members of his party. Butterfield claimed that when he visited Springfield, he was presented with an unsolicited petition signed by "all the Whig county officers elected by the people, and also signed by the leading Whigs of the county," supporting him for commissioner of the General Land Office. "Mr. Lincoln's boasted 'overwhelming majority' [had] vanished into thin air," Butterfield wrote a friend. Even Springfield's "Whig mechanics" signed a petition expressing their dissatisfaction with Lincoln's course in Congress and, Butterfield said, recommended him for the position.[83] In the end, President Taylor permitted Ewing to make the choice. He selected Butterfield.

The episode clearly upset Lincoln. The fact that several of his friends had supported Butterfield particularly distressed him. Lincoln also deeply regretted that he had made a political enemy of Cyrus Edwards, the uncle of Mary Lincoln's brother-in-law Ninian Edwards and the father of Matilda, whose beauty had captivated him a few years earlier. Edwards believed that Lincoln had undercut his appointment as land commissioner. Lincoln told a friend that Edwards was "angry" with him: "He is wronging me very much," he said. "He wrote a letter against me & in favor of Butterfield." The future president sadly noted that his friendship with Edwards "was one of the most cherished" that he'd had, and that he had "not been false to it." Lincoln again insisted that he could "have had the office any time before the [Interior] Department was committed to Mr. Butterfield—at least Mr. Ewing & the President [said] as much." But he refused to be considered for it, "chiefly for Mr. Edwards' sake." Not until "the question was narrowed down to Mr. B. and myself," Lincoln insisted, had he sought the position.[84]

Despite the rancor over the appointment, Lincoln held no grudge, even against Butterfield and Secretary of the Interior Ewing. Probably feeling some guilt for the administration's treatment of Lincoln, Ewing offered him the position of secretary of the Oregon Territory and later the governorship, both of which Lincoln turned down. Ewing did appoint Whigs whom Lincoln had recommended to some minor offices, and this was probably a more important factor in Lincoln's reconciliation with the administration than the Oregon offers he received personally. The future president soon acknowledged that Ewing was "keeping faith with me in regard to my friends."[85]

Lincoln, however, still found President Taylor's delegation of important patronage decisions to Ewing and other cabinet members disturbing. He wrote Secretary of State John M. Clayton about the practice, but he directed his complaint to "the whole cabinet, and the President too." Taylor's procedure in the matter, Lincoln said, gave the "unjust and ruinous" appearance that the president was "a mere man of straw." "This must be arrested," he added, "or it will damn us all inevitably." Lincoln admitted that "the appointments need be no better than they have been, but the public must be brought to understand, that they are the *President's* appointments." Citing the example of President Jackson in taking responsibility for his actions, the brash former congressman told Clayton: "We dare not disregard the lessons of experience."[86] More than a decade later, Lincoln took that lesson with him to the White House.

LINCOLN'S TERM in Congress had been inauspicious and, in the minds of his constituents, marred by his opposition to the Mexican-American War. His experience in Washington, however, succeeded in terms of his political and personal growth. It broadened Lincoln's grasp of national issues, including the slavery issues; established his association with Whig leaders; and, despite his failures, increased his confidence in his own abilities. It also taught him the value of not getting ahead of Illinois voters and local party activists, as he had done with his antiwar stance and his emancipation proposal for the District of Columbia. Lincoln probably realized that if he expected to rebuild his political standing in Illinois, he must be patient and careful. The forty-year-old lawyer-politician could not have foreseen that the escalating sectional conflict over slavery during the next decade would be the avenue for his political redemption and ultimate rise to national prominence. But when Abraham Lincoln left Congress in March 1849, he seemed destined for political obscurity—an eventuality, however, that he refused to acknowledge. Still, disillusioned by the continued minority status of his party in the state and the failure of the Taylor administration to reward him adequately, Lincoln looked forward to returning to his law practice in Springfield and, for a time, disengaging from politics.

POLITICAL REVIVAL, 1850–1856

LINCOLN ADMITTED that after he left Congress in 1849 his law practice "almost superseded the thought of politics" for him because of "the hopelessness of the [Whig] cause in Illinois."[1] Since the beginning of the second party system in the 1830s (Whigs vs. Democrats), the Whig party had been in the minority in Illinois; because of its divisions over the war, the Wilmot Proviso, and presidential candidates (Taylor and Clay), it had lost more ground to the Democrats. When Lincoln was in Congress and involved in Whig presidential politics, Herndon had capably maintained the business of the firm. No longer drawing a congressman's pay, Lincoln now had to earn money, which meant focusing on the law. However, he did not completely abandon politics during the early 1850s, as some biographers have claimed.[2] Though only in his early forties, Lincoln's ambition for political distinction continued to burn fiercely. Despite the controversy over his brief congressional career, many Illinois Whigs still viewed him as a party leader and a highly desirable stump speaker. They expected Lincoln to play a key role in future political contests. Other matters, however, soon infringed on Lincoln's effort to reestablish his leadership position in the state Whig party.

During the early 1850s, Lincoln had to devote more attention to family affairs than he had earlier. Tragedy struck the Lincoln household in the winter of 1849–1850. Four-year-old Eddie became sick, and after a two-month bout with pulmonary tuberculosis, he died on February 1. Mary, in her grief, fled to her bedroom, and for weeks Lincoln had to attend to her and manage the house. When Mary recovered sufficiently, she became pregnant, and in December she gave birth to another son, whom the Lincolns named William Wallace in honor of a brother-in-law. The death of Eddie and the arrival of "Willie" led Lincoln, who perhaps felt guilty for his frequent absences from home, to become even more tolerant of his children's misbehavior than before, much to the dismay of Herndon and other friends, who found them virtually undisciplined. Joseph Gillespie, a close friend, later wrote: "He was the most indulgent parent I ever knew. His children literally [sic] ran over him and he was powerless to withstand their importunities."[3] Willie, whose personality was more like his father's than his brother Robert's was, became Lincoln's pride and joy and could often be seen in his company. Mary generally controlled domestic matters, and because of her husband's passivity at home, she provided a modicum of the discipline the children needed.

Meanwhile, Lincoln's father and stepmother were in dire straits in Coles County, Illinois. Thomas's health had declined, and his stepson John D. Johnston had proven virtually worthless as a provider for the family. On more than one occasion, Abe sent money to his father to save the farm and prevent the family's impoverishment. On May 25, 1849, John wrote Abe that his father was critically ill and not expected to live. The future president rushed to Coles County to visit him. While he was en route, a second message was sent to Springfield reporting that Thomas was out of danger.[4] Not having received this message, Abe arrived to find his father recovering from his illness. He spent three days with his father and stepmother before returning to Springfield.

The following winter, John sent another message to Abe to report again that Thomas was dying. He asked Abe to come or to write a word of comfort to his father. Only after receiving confirmation of his father's serious condition did he reply. Lincoln wrote his stepbrother that, though he had not been "uninterested," he "could write nothing which could do any good." "You already know I desire that neither Father or [sic] Mother shall be in want of any comfort either in health or sickness while they live," he said. Lincoln felt sure that John had "not failed to use [his] name, if necessary to procure a doctor, or any thing else for Father in his present sickness." "My business is such," he told John, "that I could hardly leave home now, if it were not, as it is, that my own wife is sick-abed," expecting a baby (Willie). "Say to him," Lincoln wrote, "that if we could meet now, it is doubtful whether it would not be more painful than pleasant." Knowing of his father's spirituality, Lincoln admonished him as he faced death "to remember to call upon, and confide in, our great, and good, and merciful Maker; who will not turn away from him in any extremity."[5] These were hardly the words of the same young man in New Salem who had expressed skepticism about the Bible.

On January 17, 1851, five days after Lincoln wrote this letter to John Johnston, Thomas Lincoln died. Only a few people attended the burial ceremony near his Coles County cabin; his son was not one of them.[6] Lincoln inherited 80 acres of land from his father and in turn sold it to his "brother" John for $1. Abe already owned 40 acres of the family farm, which he still held at his death in 1865.[7] In the spring, probably when he was in Coles County on the judicial court circuit, he visited his stepmother, apparently discussed her support with family members, and made entries in the family Bible.[8]

It has become customary for Lincoln biographers and others, with some justification, to criticize Thomas Lincoln for his failure to understand and encourage his talented son. They also emphasize that Abe, at an early age, sought desperately to escape from his father's uninspiring way of life. One scholar, however, went too far when he cavalierly asserted, "[Abraham] Lincoln, as we all know, hated his father."[9] Others have concluded that, at the least, as biographer Michael Burlingame has written, "Lincoln's relationship with his father was chilly." Based mainly on the fact that Lincoln rarely mentioned his father in his surviving written work, historian Richard N. Current wrote that "there must have been a real estrangement between him and his father." Biographer David Donald has written that Lincoln did not attend his father's funeral because he was "unable to simulate a grief that he did not feel or an affection that he did not bear." Lincoln "was not heartless," Donald insisted, "but Thomas Lincoln represented a world that his son had long ago left behind him."[10]

This view of a serious estrangement between father and son may be over-drawn. No doubt, like most ambitious young men, Lincoln naturally wanted to escape his father's control and the hard, unappealing labor of the farm. He struck out on his own and pursued a career and interests that were different from Thomas's. But this divergence did not necessarily mean that a complete estrangement occurred or that Lincoln had no affection for his father. Grown sons in "a man's society" like the rural West did not usually show the same affection for their fathers as they did for their mothers. Surviving Lincoln documents suggest that he thought enough of his father to have absorbed from him the family's history, and he retained the stories he had been told as a boy. Thomas handed down to his son his good humor and, to some extent, his skill as a storyteller, important traits that Abraham Lincoln cultivated and, indeed, found extremely effective in his political appeal to the rural people who constituted a majority in the state. Southwestern or frontier humor, both in print and in oral tradition, was immensely popular in the decades prior to the Civil War, and it resonated well with Lincoln's audiences.

As Abraham Lincoln became older and more successful, he thought more about his father's origins and family.[11] In an 1854 letter to Jesse Lincoln, a second cousin living in East Tennessee, he related the history of the family, mentioning his father several times and reporting the date of his death. (Ironically, when Lincoln was in Congress, another congressman and future president, Andrew Johnson, had provided him with information on his Tennessee relatives.)[12] In contrast, Lincoln showed little interest in the background of his mother or his stepmother. He believed that his mother's birth was illegitimate and that her family was shiftless—and he did not want to be reminded of it. In addition to his 1849 visit, Lincoln visited his father on another recorded occasion after he moved to Springfield, and it is reasonable to assume that he saw his father on other occasions when in Coles County on the judicial circuit.[13] His aging stepmother recalled in 1865 that Abe visited every year or so.[14]

His failure to see his family regularly did not mean that Lincoln had lost interest in his father and kin. The trip to Coles County during the 1840s took three days by buggy and was arduous. Lincoln could ill afford to leave his young family and law practice for a stay with his father and stepmother. A trip to Springfield would have been even more difficult for his aging father, who did not travel after settling in Coles County. Thomas never visited his son's home.

In 1850, close political associates wanted Lincoln to run for his old seat in Congress. Recognizing that his law practice and family obligations took precedence, Lincoln refused and supported Richard Yates. But there is no evidence that he participated in the campaign.[15] Lincoln must have been elated, however, when Yates recaptured the seat for the Whigs; victory also probably rekindled interest in his own political revival. The next year was a fallow political season in Illinois with no important offices subject to elections. Meanwhile, the congressional Compromise of 1850 had established a fragile peace on the slavery issue in the territories by approving the admission of California as a free state and permitting the organization of the vast New Mexico and Utah territories without restrictions on slavery. But the compromise had created a controversy in the North over one of its provisions—a harsh Fugitive Slave Act for the capture and return of fugitive slaves to the South. Radical antislavery Whigs, militant Free Soilers, and some northern Democrats refused to accept the law, and they prepared to make it an issue in the 1852 political contests. Lincoln was not one of them. Correctly from a political standpoint, Lincoln viewed the Fugitive Slave Act as essential to gaining southern acceptance of the compromise and to maintaining a unified, nonsectional Whig party, without which, he believed, the party would be destroyed and the Union placed in jeopardy. Lincoln also believed that, because the act was the law of the land, it must be obeyed until repealed or modified. Nonetheless, he thought that the law was too stringent and should be changed, for it might "likely . . . carry a free man into slavery," which, indeed, it sometimes did.[16]

In 1855, Lincoln wrote a letter to his proslavery friend Joshua F. Speed reminding him of the deplorable scene they had witnessed on the Ohio River in 1841, when they saw slaves "shackled together with irons." He lamented to Speed, who had returned to Kentucky, "that the sight was a continual torment to me; and I see something like it every time I touch the Ohio, or any other slave-border." But he acknowledged Speed's rights as a southerner "and *my* obligations, under the constitution, in regard to your slaves. I confess I hate to see the poor creatures hunted down, and caught, and carried back to their stripes, and unrewarded toils; but I bite my lip and keep quiet."[17]

In late 1851, Lincoln eased back into an active role in Whig party affairs. On December 22, he attended the state Whig convention in Springfield and served on the committees on resolutions and nominations for the 1852 campaign.[18] Then, on July 6, he delivered a eulogy at the memorial service of Henry Clay. The service for the great Whig leader, whom Lincoln had idolized, was as much a political event as it was a memorial. On that day, Springfield businesses closed and two memorial sessions occurred to honor the "Sage of Ashland." Lincoln delivered the main eulogy, which was held in the state Hall of Representatives following a processional from the Episcopal church. Citizens of both political parties crowded into the hall, and Lincoln made the most of the occasion to promote, though subtly, the Whig party and his own political restoration. He had carefully prepared a biographical sketch of Clay that emphasized the Kentucky Whig's love for the Union and liberty as well as his importance as a compromiser in the sectional controversies over slavery. Lincoln proclaimed that Clay, while willing to compromise to save the Union and the Constitution, "ever was, on principle and in feeling, opposed to slavery." As evidence of the Whig icon's antislavery sentiment, Lincoln cited Clay's support for gradual emancipation in Kentucky and voluntary black colonization to Africa.[19]

Though Lincoln exaggerated Clay's opposition to slavery, he believed the Kentuckian had genuine antipathy toward the "peculiar institution" of the South. Still, Lincoln had a larger political purpose in portraying Clay as antislavery. He sought to persuade Whigs in his district that an antislavery position was compatible with the conservative and national principles of the party of their fallen leader.

Lincoln's praise for Clay's black colonization plan also revealed something about his own thinking on slavery and race at this time. "Every succeeding year" since Clay had proposed his colonization scheme, Lincoln announced, "has added strength to the hope of its realization. May it indeed be realized! . . . If as the friends of colonization hope, the present and coming generations of our countrymen shall by any means, succeed in freeing our land from the dangerous presence of slavery; and, at the same time, in restoring a captive people to their long-lost father-land, with bright prospects for the future; and this too, so gradually, that neither races nor individuals shall have suffered by the change, it will indeed be a glorious consummation." If colonization occurred, then "none of [Clay's] labors will have been more valuable to his country and his kind."[20]

In closing the eulogy, Lincoln contended that, "in the providence of God," the great Kentuckian "was given us." The future president admonished his generation to "strive to deserve, as far as mortals may, the continued care of Divine Providence, trusting that, in future national emergencies, He will not fail to provide us the instruments of safety and security." Lincoln declared that while Clay lived, he was an instrument of national unity. A decade later, Abraham Lincoln would assume Clay's mantle as a national leader; and at that time he expressed the hope that, like Clay, he would be an "instrument of God" to preserve the Union.

Following Clay's example, Lincoln during the 1850s became involved in the black colonization movement that had become popular among whites in Springfield and elsewhere in Illinois. On the evening of August 30, 1853, he delivered a lecture on colonization at the First Presbyterian Church in Springfield.[21] Though apparently no copy of this address has survived, Lincoln probably endorsed Clay's proposal for voluntary colonization. He agreed to deliver a speech at the annual meeting of the Illinois State Colonization Society in Springfield on January 12, 1854, but sickness in the family prevented his participation. The purpose of this society was to purchase the freedom of slaves and colonize them in Africa, mainly in Liberia, which had been created by Americans in 1822 to facilitate black resettlement.[22] At Peoria in October, however, Lincoln expressed doubts about the practicality of the effort, announcing to his audience that "a moment's reflection" had convinced him "that whatever of high hope, (as I think there is) there may be in this, in the long run its sudden execution is impossible. If they were all landed there in a day, they would all perish in the next ten days; and there are not surplus shipping and surplus money enough in the world to carry them there in many times ten days."[23] Indeed, neither private nor public financial support proved adequate for such a large undertaking.

Lincoln and other advocates of colonization also failed to consider an equally important barrier to resettlement. Blacks did not want to leave their homes for "uncivilized" Africa; they sought freedom and opportunity in America. Lincoln did not try to find out if African Americans desired colonization. He assumed that, once freed, blacks would favor resettlement in Africa. If he had asked the opinions of the approximately 170 free blacks in Springfield, he probably would have learned that few of them wanted any part of colonization. Clearly, and particularly at this time, Lincoln saw the presence of African Americans in the United States as a major problem in securing racial and sectional harmony.

On January 4, 1855, Lincoln delivered the address to the Illinois State Colonization Society that he had promised for the previous annual meeting. Based on the outline for the speech in his *Collected Works,* Lincoln gave his audience a history of slavery, the foreign slave trade and its prohibition by Congress, and the 1787 ordinance prohibiting the institution in the Northwest Territory. Lincoln, according to his rough outline, sought to demonstrate that the American Colonization Society, founded in 1816, was antislavery and had as "its colateral [sic] objects—Suppression of Slave trade—commerce—civilization and religion." The outline of the speech does not reveal his arguments in support of these "objects."[24] At the society's annual meeting in January 1857, Lincoln was elected a director.[25]

Later in the year, in a political speech at Springfield in July, Lincoln made an argument for colonization that is offensive to latter-day racial sensibilities. He declared: "I have said that the separation of the races is the only perfect preventive of amalgamation. . . . Such separation, if ever effected at all, must be effected by colonization; and no political party, as such," including his own recently organized Republican party, "is now doing anything directly for colonization." He added, "Party operations at present only favor or retard colonization." Admitting that "the enterprise is a difficult one," Lincoln insisted that "when there is a will there is a way." He told his audience, "Will springs from the two elements of moral sense and self-interest. Let us be brought to believe it is morally right, and, at the same time, favorable to, or, at least, not against, our interest, to transfer the African to his native clime, and we shall find a way to do it." Remarkably, he compared the repatriation of blacks to Africa with the exodus of the Bible, citing the large number of Israelites under Moses' leadership who "went out of Egyptian bondage in a body."[26]

Lincoln in the same passage also contended that the Republicans believed "that the negro is a man; that his bondage is cruelly wrong, and that the field of his oppression ought not to be enlarged" by slavery's expansion into the territories. (Lincoln ignored the pro-black position of abolitionists, a tiny minority in Illinois, who not only advocated the end of slavery in the South but also civil equality for African Americans.) In contrast to the Republicans, Lincoln charged, the Democrats "deny [black] manhood; deny, or dwarf to insignificance, the wrong of his bondage; so far as possible, crush all sympathy for him, and cultivate and excite hatred and disgust against him; compliment themselves as Union-savers for doing so; and call the indefinite outspreading of his bondage 'a sacred right of self-government.' "[27]

For a time, however, Lincoln put aside his active support of colonization. During the war, partly in an effort to reduce opposition to emancipation, he revived his idea of voluntary black resettlement, not in Africa but in the Caribbean and Central America, and mainly financed by the federal government. Encouraged by Lincoln, an attempt was made to settle 453 blacks on an island off Haiti in 1863. The former slaves were dumped there without adequate shelter, food, or tools and under the control of a speculator named Bernard Kock. When Lincoln heard of their plight, he dispatched a steamer in March 1864 to evacuate the colony. This disaster finally persuaded him that African American colonization was a fantasy; before the end of the war, Lincoln envisioned freed blacks as equal partners with whites in America's future.[28]

But first, during the 1850s, the political conflict over slavery and party principles and alignments had to be fought. The election of 1852 found Lincoln campaigning, though not extensively, for still another Whig general for president—Winfield Scott. Selected by Illinois Whigs to serve as an elector, Lincoln was expected to canvass for Scott. Like many Illinois Whigs, he did not have much enthusiasm for the candidacy of "Old Fuss and Feathers." Only one of Lincoln's campaign speeches, at Springfield in August, has survived. In it, he defended Scott and Whigs in Washington from the far-fetched charge, made by Senator Stephen A. Douglas, that they were controlled by abolitionists.[29] Scott did not win the presidential election, losing in Illinois by a far larger margin than Taylor had four years earlier, despite the fact that Franklin Pierce, the Democratic victor, was virtually unknown in the state. Scott won only forty-two electoral votes in the national contest. The Democrats also gained control of Congress. For Lincoln and his fellow Whigs in Illinois, the political future continued to look bleak.

The year 1853, like 1851, was an off-year for political campaigns and elections, permitting Lincoln to concentrate on his growing law practice. After all, without funds in the bank he could not afford to maintain a high level of political activism. Few Illinois attorneys were in greater demand than Lincoln, not only by clients but also by fellow lawyers to assist them with their cases. Lincoln spent weeks on the judicial circuit and in federal and state courts in Springfield and Chicago where he made valuable political contacts with Whig lawyers, editors, and other party activists who encouraged him to play a leading role in future political contests.

Meanwhile, Lincoln had improved his understanding of grassroots political sentiment and concluded that the Whig party and its conservative principles still had broad, though not majority, support in the state. He had largely recovered from the decline in his public standing that had occurred after his ill-advised "Spot" resolutions in Congress opposing the Mexican-American War. A wiser and more politically mature Lincoln by 1854 had reemerged as the leading Whig in central Illinois and had gained important friends in the northern part of the state. Illinois Whigs, including Lincoln, recognized that the central counties held the key to their ascendancy in the state. They were a majority in northern Illinois, while the Democrats, led by Senator Douglas, dominated the southern counties and held the edge in the central belt. The Democratic counties had been settled mainly by southerners who favored the states' rights and limited government policies of Douglas's party as a check on the growing antislavery movement among northern Whigs. A dramatic turn of events, however, would soon occur, and Lincoln and his associates would be the beneficiaries. These events would inspire them, along with friends in other states, to organize a political coalition that would transform northern politics.

It all began in January 1854 when Stephen A. Douglas introduced into the Senate one of the most controversial bills in American history. The measure provided for the organization of the Nebraska Territory (later split into Kansas and Nebraska) on the basis of popular sovereignty regarding slavery, or letting the people of the territory decide the question. Senator Douglas's bill explicitly provided for the repeal of the Missouri Compromise line of 1820 (36 degrees, 30 minutes north latitude) separating free from slave territory in the western lands that extended to the eastern range of the Rocky Mountains. Implicitly, the Kansas-Nebraska bill gave slavery an opportunity to expand, particularly into Kansas, which lay adjacent to the slave state of Missouri. Protests against the bill immediately erupted in the North, including in northern Illinois. Effigies of Douglas were burned in the villages and towns of the northern part of the state. Protestant ministers thundered from their pulpits against the "Nebraska Bill" and joined other clergymen in written protests opposing the repeal of the "sacred" Missouri line.[30] Despite the growing opposition in the North to the bill, it passed Congress in May, with many northern Democrats, along with southerners, voting for it. The bill received Democratic President Franklin Pierce's signature.

The Kansas-Nebraska bill and the troubling events that followed in Kansas and in Congress led to the rise of the Republican party in the North during the mid-1850s and increasingly polarized the nation along North-South lines. These developments eventually divided the Democratic party and destroyed the Whig party, which had no platform on the territorial issue that could satisfy both northern and southern Whigs. The Republican party, based on its opposition to the expansion of slavery and to the perceived aggression of the slave power, claimed the allegiance of most old Whigs and a minority of Democrats. By 1860, it had become the majority party in the North. The Republican success in the 1860 presidential election with Lincoln as the party's standard-bearer plunged seven southern states into secession, created political uncertainty in the other slave states, and posed the threat of civil war.

This sequence of events is well known today, but Lincoln and his contemporaries could not have foreseen the future in the 1850s. Indeed, despite some Republican talk of an "irrepressible conflict" between North and South over slavery, Lincoln and other antislavery opponents of the Kansas-Nebraska bill minimized the danger to the Union in their opposition to the expansion of slavery. For two years after the enactment of the controversial measure, Lincoln, a loyal Whig, thought that his party, not the radical Republican party organized in upper North communities in 1854, should lead the state's "anti-Nebraska" forces. Like many northerners, Lincoln expressed moral outrage at the repeal of the Missouri Compromise line. However, he assumed that the success of the anti-Nebraska coalition under Whig party leadership in Illinois depended on an antislavery platform that would appeal to conservatives. Lincoln concluded that the need for a "conservative" (today's moderate) approach was especially true for the central counties, where many Whigs, like himself, were natives of the border slave states and had fundamentally conservative political instincts. Furthermore, Lincoln believed, a limited antislavery position, one that avoided condemning southerners, while charging a Douglas-slavocracy conspiracy to expand slavery and violate the antislavery intentions of the Founding Fathers, would sustain the Whig party as a national organization. He did not foresee that any northern Whig opposition to slavery's expansion, no matter how conservative, would prevent southern Whigs, including those in the border states, like Kentucky, from continuing to cooperate in the national party. By 1856, the Whig party had collapsed as a national organization, and Lincoln and other antislavery Whigs in Illinois finally conceded that they had to abandon their dream of a Whig resurgence, become Republicans, and work for the adoption of a conservative antislavery platform by the new party, a platform that, they believed, the majority of the voters would approve.

Lincoln first entered the anti-Nebraska lists as a stump speaker and adviser to Whig Richard Yates in his effort in 1854 to win back his central Illinois seat in Congress. On September 4, Lincoln announced his own candidacy for the state House of Representatives. Historians disagree on why Lincoln sought election to the legislature, particularly in view of the rapid growth of the anti-Nebraska movement in the state and his own bright prospects to replace his old antagonist James Shields in the U.S. Senate. When he ran for the Illinois House, Lincoln must have known, according to biographer David Donald, that the Illinois constitution prohibited the General Assembly from selecting one of its own for the Senate. Lincoln's election to the state House therefore would have served to dash his hopes to secure the Senate seat when the legislature met. Anguished by the effect that it would have on his political future, Lincoln, according to David Donald, agreed to run for the legislature only after it became clear that his refusal could cause the defeat of Yates and other Whigs in Sangamon County.[31] Historian Don E. Fehrenbacher concluded that in announcing his candidacy for the state House of Representatives Lincoln had overlooked the constitutional prohibition. According to Fehrenbacher, Lincoln did not get the senatorial bug until after the anti-

Nebraska coalition, consisting mainly of Whigs and a small minority of Democrats, won control of the legislature in the fall, placing them in a position to elect the next U.S. senator.[32]

It is reasonable to assume that Lincoln's moral outrage against the Kansas-Nebraska bill, which he passionately expressed in a speech at Peoria in October, along with his desire to help win the Seventh Congressional District seat for the Whigs, influenced his decision to seek election to the legislature. Prospects for an anti-Nebraska victory were not clear when he agreed to run for the state House of Representatives. As the 1854 campaign progressed and Whig prospects brightened, Lincoln received reports that the anti-Nebraska coalition might win, and he would be its likely choice for the Senate.[33] Lincoln probably reasoned, however, that if he withdrew as a candidate for the legislature in order to qualify for the Senate, it would cost the coalition a critical seat and the Douglas Democrats would retain a majority. He was unwilling to take a chance for his party on the outcome of the legislative contests. Lincoln later claimed that he "took the stump" in 1854 "with no broader practical aim or object that [than?] to secure" Yates's election to Congress. His decision to run for the state House came later. Nonetheless, Lincoln admitted that his ambition for the Senate seat had been whetted by the fact that early in the campaign his speeches "attracted a more marked attention than they had ever before done," and "he was drawn to different parts of the state" to canvass for the anti-Nebraska cause.[34]

Lincoln's campaign appearances focused increasingly on criticism of the Kansas-Nebraska bill and less on an appeal for voters to support Yates. On August 28 at the small village of Winchester southwest of Springfield, Lincoln denounced "the great wrong and injustice of the repeal of the Missouri Compromise, and the extension of slavery into free territory."[35] He continued his attack at Carrollton, Jacksonville, and Springfield, and then went north, outside of the Seventh Congressional District, to speak at rallies in Bloomington (twice), Chicago, and Peoria.[36]

At Peoria on October 16, Lincoln, as agreed to by Douglas, followed a three-hour speech by the senator with a long address that covered all of the issues in the Kansas-Nebraska conflict. The Illinois Whig press reported Lincoln's speech, and it clearly established the Springfield lawyer as the leader of the anti-Nebraska forces in the state. The speech laid out the position on slavery that he would maintain until the Civil War. Significantly, Lincoln's Peoria address and his later speeches ignored references to old Whig economic and financial policies (Henry Clay's American System). In disregarding economic issues, Lincoln was probably influenced by the likelihood that many Democrats, traditional advocates of limited government, who supported the anti-Nebraska coalition would seriously object if he trumpeted the Whig platform. For Lincoln, the controlling political issue since the passage of the Kansas-Nebraska bill was slavery, an issue that had a moral dimension to it and, in addition, had created unusual public concern in Illinois. Lincoln not only reflected this concern, he also wanted to sustain it for both political and ideological reasons. Beginning in 1854, Lincoln's campaign rhetoric would be devoted to the slavery question. This Lincoln characteristic of focusing on an overriding issue would be repeated during the Civil War, when his emphasis as president would be on preserving the Union and ultimately ending slavery, the source of the republic's disruption.

Lincoln began his Peoria address with a history of the slavery question as it related to the territories. In recounting this history, he denied the claim of Senator Douglas that the Founding Fathers did not seek to restrict the expansion of the institution. As he would do repeatedly in later campaign speeches, Lincoln cited the Northwest Ordinance of 1787 as unassailable evidence that the Founders had wanted to prevent slavery's extension and had only permitted it elsewhere as a "necessity" to secure southern support for the Union. Lincoln stressed "the wrong" in the Kansas-Nebraska bill's repeal of the Missouri Compromise line. He contended that the repeal was "wrong in its direct effect, letting slavery into Kansas and Nebraska—and wrong in its proscriptive principle, allowing it to spread to every other part of the wide world where men can be found inclined to take it." Lincoln expressed his hatred of Americans' "*declared* indifference [and] covert *real* zeal for the spread of slavery," adding, "I hate it because of the monstrous injustice of slavery itself. I hate it because it deprives our republican example of its just influence in the world—enables the enemies of free institutions, with plausibility, to taunt us as hypocrites—causes the real friends of freedom to doubt our sincerity, and especially because it forces so many really good men amongst ourselves into an open war with the very fundamental principles of civil liberty—criticising the Declaration of Independence, and insisting that there is no right principle of action but *self-interest*."[37]

Though he opposed slavery and its expansion, Lincoln denied that he had any "prejudice against the Southern people." "They are just what we would be in their situation," he said. "If slavery did not exist amongst them, they would not introduce it. If it did now exist amongst us, we should not instantly give it up." Lincoln informed his Peoria audience that "when southern people tell us they are no more responsible for the origin of slavery, than we; I acknowledge the fact." Because he had no solution to the problem of slavery where it existed, Lincoln announced that he did not blame the southern people for not knowing what to do with the institution. Admitting that the sudden colonization of slaves was impractical, he inquired, "What then? Free them all, and keep them among us as underlings?" He doubted that this kind of freedom would better their condition.[38]

In an effort to distance himself and other opponents of the Kansas-Nebraska Act from antislavery radicals in northern Illinois and elsewhere, Lincoln told his race-conscious Peoria audience that equality for blacks was impossible. "Free [blacks], and make them politically and socially, our equals?" he asked. He continued: "My own feelings will not admit of this; and if mine would, we well know that those of the great mass of white people will not. Whether this feeling accords with justice and sound judgment, is not the sole question, if indeed, it is any part of it. A universal feeling, whether well or ill-founded, can not be safely disregarded. We can not, then, make them equals. It does seem to me that systems of gradual emancipation might be adopted; but for their tardiness in this, I will not undertake to judge our brethren of the south."[39]

Lincoln went on to acknowledge the constitutional rights of southerners to hold slaves, "not grudgingly, but fully, and fairly; and I would give them any legislation for the reclaiming of their fugitives." But he objected to a law whose "stringency" would be "likely to carry a free man into slavery." The future president ignored the fact that the Fugitive Slave Act of 1850, whose repeal he opposed, had already opened the door for slave catchers to seize free blacks in the North, claim them as slaves, and take them to the South. He insisted that the willingness to respect the rights of white southerners "furnishes no more excuse for permitting slavery to go into our own free territory, than it would for reviving the African slave trade by law."[40]

Lincoln repeatedly expressed his moral indignation against slavery in this address while maintaining a conservative position on the laws protecting the institution and on the issue of black equality. This approach was designed to build a bridge between the antislavery Whigs in northern Illinois and the conservative Whigs and free-soil Democrats of central and southern Illinois, who were reluctant to associate with extreme antislavery men. Lincoln spoke to the conservatives when he announced:

> Some men, mostly whigs, who condemn the repeal of the Missouri Compromise, nevertheless hesitate to go for its restoration, lest they be thrown in company with the abolitionist. Will they allow me as an old whig to tell them good humoredly, that I think this is very silly? Stand with anybody that stands RIGHT. Stand with him while he is right and PART with him when he goes wrong. Stand with the abolitionist in restoring the Missouri Compromise; and stand AGAINST him when he attempts to repeal the fugitive slave law. . . . In both you stand on middle

ground and hold the ship [of state] level and steady. In both you are national and nothing less than national. This is good old whig ground.[41]

He told his Peoria audience that what he particularly objected to was "the NEW position which the avowed principle of the Nebraska law gives to slavery in the body politic. I object to it because it assumes that there CAN BE MORAL RIGHT in the enslaving of one man by another. . . . I object to it because the fathers of the republic eschewed, and rejected it," and only tolerated it because "they found the institution existing among us, which they could not help." Lincoln argued that instead of treating slavery as a necessity, the Kansas-Nebraska bill had transformed it into a "sacred right" and placed "it on the road to extension and perpetuity." Once established in a territory, slavery could not be eradicated, Lincoln declared. "Let no one be deceived," Lincoln warned, "the spirit of seventy-six and the spirit of Nebraska, are utter antagonisms; and the former is being rapidly displaced by the latter."[42]

Clearly, Lincoln announced, the main villain in the Kansas-Nebraska affair was Senator Douglas. He contended that Douglas, nicknamed "the Little Giant," differed with him and many northerners on the question of the basic humanity of blacks. Lincoln told his Peoria audience that "the Judge has no very vivid impression that the Negro is a human; and consequently has no idea that there can be any moral question in legislating about him. In [Douglas's] view, the question of whether a new country shall be slave or free, is a matter of as utter indifference, as it is whether his neighbor shall plant his farm with tobacco, or stock it with horned cattle." In contrast, Lincoln claimed, "the great mass of mankind," including himself, "take a totally different view. They consider slavery a great moral wrong." Such a sentiment against slavery "lies at the very foundation of their sense of justice; and it cannot be trifled with. It is a great and durable element of popular action, and, I think, no statesman can safely disregard it."[43]

For the first time in a public forum, Lincoln in the 1854 campaign had expressed his moral outrage at the institution of slavery. At the same time, he did not call for its end in the South, and he stopped far short of endorsing black equality and rights. For Lincoln to proclaim his support for these radical positions would have meant certain defeat for the anti-Nebraska coalition in Illinois and would have insured the continuation of the Douglas Democratic hegemony in the state.

The eminent biographer David Donald wrote that it would be "a mistake to attempt to palliate Lincoln's racial views by saying that he grew up in a racist society or that his ideas were shared by many of his contemporaries. After all, there were numerous Americans of his generation—notably many of them abolitionists—who were committed to racial equality." However,

Donald said, "Lincoln fortunately escaped the more virulent strains of racism."[44] He never engaged in the kind of racist harangues that characterized the campaigns and editorials of Douglas Democrats. It should also be noted that those abolitionists who supported full racial equality—and most of them probably did not—with a few exceptions lived outside of Illinois and were largely free of the political realities that Lincoln faced in a state with strident antiblack laws backed by public opinion. Still, within four years Lincoln had begun to proclaim that, though the African American was not his equal in certain respects, he was his equal in the enjoyment of the natural rights expressed in the Declaration of Independence, including the right to enjoy the fruits of his labor.

Lincoln's Peoria speech attracted considerable attention and, along with a similar address at Springfield, completed his reemergence as a person to be reckoned with in Illinois politics. Even radicals in the northern counties, despite Lincoln's support of the Fugitive Slave Act and his refusal to condemn slaveholders, praised his strong moral opposition to the "peculiar institution." Lincoln's skill on the stump in raising anti-Nebraska opposition also gained the attention of the radicals. Led by Owen Lovejoy, whose brother Elijah was lynched by a proslavery mob at Alton in 1837, and Ichabod Codding, Illinois radicals in 1854 were attempting to organize the Republican party in the state, a grassroots party that had rapidly emerged in the upper North in reaction to the Kansas-Nebraska bill. To be successful, they needed someone of Lincoln's political stature to give the new party credibility, especially in the central and southern counties and among old Whigs.

The Illinois radicals during the fall of 1854 appointed Lincoln, without his consent, to the recently formed Republican state central committee. When Codding, a Congregational minister, asked him to attend a November 17 meeting of the committee in Chicago, Lincoln sharply replied that he was "perplexed . . . why my name was placed on that committee." He acknowledged that "my opposition to the principle of slavery is as strong as any member of the Republican party"; but, he explained, "the extent to which I feel authorized to carry that opposition, practically, was not at all satisfactory to that party." Lincoln reminded Codding that "the leading men" of the radical movement had heard him speak at Springfield on October 4 when they had unsuccessfully attempted to organize the party. At that time, he said, Codding and his friends "had full opportunity to not misunderstand my position." Lincoln wanted to make it clear that his conservative antislavery strategy was different from theirs and would more likely succeed in uniting all of the antislavery elements in the state.[45] Both Lovejoy and Codding, while expressing their disappointment with Lincoln's unwillingness to endorse black equality, as well as with his support of the Fugitive Slave Act,

eventually admitted the political necessity for Lincoln's position on these issues in Illinois.

By the time Lincoln wrote to the (radical) Republican state central committee on November 27, the antislavery forces had won a stunning victory at
the polls. They had gained control of the Illinois General Assembly, and Lincoln himself had won election to the state House of Representatives. The coalition had also captured five of the nine congressional seats, though Richard
Yates had been defeated in the Springfield district. Lincoln knew that the new
legislature might elect a Whig to the U.S. Senate, and he knew that he was
the leading candidate. In order to qualify, he notified the governor of his decision to decline the election to the legislature.[46] Lincoln realized that if he
had accepted the radical Republicans' invitation to serve on their central
committee, support for his bid for the Senate seat would have been seriously
reduced among the Whig legislators of central and southern Illinois. Recalling the harmful political effects of earlier free-soil parties, Lincoln also believed that a competing antislavery party in northern Illinois would have
drawn off support from the anti-Nebraska coalition and undercut its control
of the new legislature. For these reasons, as well as because of his loyalty to
the Whig party, Lincoln had rejected the Republican committee's invitation
in November to join them. By implication, he criticized their effort to organize a separate anti-Nebraska party in Illinois.

With the encouragement of friends, Lincoln quietly began seeking support
for the Senate seat immediately after the November election—and even before he had declined the election to the House. The new state legislature was
slated to make the decision in early 1855. He wrote to influential local anti-
Nebraska men and legislators, announcing, "I have got it into my head to try
to be [a] U.S. Senator"; and he asked for their support.[47] For use in promoting his candidacy, Lincoln compiled and provided key supporters with a list
of members of the General Assembly and their political affiliation.[48] By his
count, 57 of the 100 members were anti-Nebraska men, but 18 of these were
Democrats and would probably find it difficult to support an old Whig for
the Senate. Lincoln believed that altogether more than 22 anti-Nebraska
members had not committed themselves to him.[49]

On the first ballot, most of the uncommitted Whigs and a handful of
the anti-Nebraska Democrats, along with Lincoln's loyal Whig supporters,
voted for him. He led on this ballot with 45 votes; James Shields, the incum-
bent Democrat, received 41. Unfortunately for Lincoln, five anti-Nebraska
Democrats—precisely the number of uncommitted members he needed to
win—voted for Lyman Trumbull, a former member of the Illinois state supreme court, whose Democratic antecedents were the same as theirs. Lincoln
had already concluded that he could never get three of these votes.[50] As ex-

pected, they refused to switch to Lincoln even when the Nebraska (Douglas) Democrats abandoned Shields for the popular governor Joel Matteson, a move that, according to Lincoln, had been secretly planned before the balloting began. As Matteson's support rose, the anti-Nebraska members, believing that Lincoln could not be elected, swung toward Trumbull. When two or three Whig supporters of Lincoln threatened to switch to Matteson, Stephen T. Logan urgently informed his former law partner that the Nebraska forces would probably win on the next ballot. Rather than see the Democrat Matteson elected, Lincoln was "determined to strike at once," as he expressed it; "and accordingly advised my remaining friends to go for" Trumbull, which they did. His action secured Trumbull's election.[51]

Lincoln wrote Congressman Elihu B. Washburne of Galena that he could have won "had it not been for Matteson's double game—and his defeat now gives me more pleasure than my own gives me pain." He told Washburne, "On the whole, it is perhaps as well for our general cause that Trumbull is elected."[52] Lincoln probably meant that his willingness to step aside and secure the election of an antislavery Democrat would strengthen the anti-Nebraska movement and reduce the opposition to Whig leadership in the coalition. Though his decision disturbed some of his staunch Whig friends, he had gained for himself the future support of antislavery Democrats, including the five Trumbull men who had refused to vote for him. One of these Democrats, Norman B. Judd of Chicago, became an important lieutenant of Lincoln's in his rise to the presidency. Many former Whigs in the antislavery coalition never forgave Judd for his role in their favorite's defeat in 1855 for the Senate, and the Chicagoan's support of Trumbull later became a source of serious division in the Republican party. Lincoln, however, did not hold it against him.

Still another obstacle appeared in the path of anti-Nebraska unity in 1855. This was the Know-Nothing, or nativist, movement that swept across areas of the North and the border South during the decade. Know Nothingism sprang largely out of Protestant Whig fears of Catholic and immigrant influence, especially that of Irish newcomers who seemed to threaten traditional American values and republican institutions. Primarily because of widespread Whig support for the Know-Nothing movement, Irish Catholic immigrants overwhelmingly voted for Democratic candidates who, in turn, denounced religious intolerance and naturalization restrictions. In many northern urban communities, the influence of the Catholic Church, according to historian Michael Holt, "seemed far more menacing and immediate to voters than did the threat of slavery's spread onto the distant plains of Kansas" or other territories.[53] Know-Nothing Whigs in the North, though generally opposed to slavery's expansion and to Democrats, believed that the

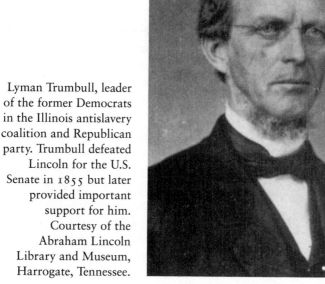

Lyman Trumbull, leader of the former Democrats in the Illinois antislavery coalition and Republican party. Trumbull defeated Lincoln for the U.S. Senate in 1855 but later provided important support for him. Courtesy of the Abraham Lincoln Library and Museum, Harrogate, Tennessee.

nativist movement had a greater chance for national success than an anti-slavery, sectional party like the Republican party. These Know Nothings concluded that the South, particularly the border slave states, and probably the lower North would reject an antislavery party and support their conservative movement.

Know Nothingism greatly disturbed Lincoln because of the threat that it posed to the success of the antislavery coalition in Illinois and also because of its bigotry. The fact that many of his old personal and political friends, such as James H. Matheny and John Todd Stuart, associated with the movement seemed incomprehensible to him. "Of [Know-Nothing] principles, I think little better than I do of those of the slavery extentionists [*sic*]," he wrote Owen Lovejoy. "Indeed, I do not perceive how any one professing to be sensitive to the wrongs of the Negroes," as many Know Nothings claimed, "can join in a league to degrade a class of white men."[54] Lincoln later repeated his indignation to Joshua Speed: "How can any one who abhors the oppression of negroes, be in favor of degrading classes of white people?" he wrote his Kentucky friend. He added: "Our progress in degeneracy appears to me to be pretty rapid. As a nation, we began by declaring that '*all men are created equal.'* We now practically read it 'all men are created equal, *except negroes.'* When the Know-Nothings get control, it will read 'all men are created equal, except negroes, *and foreigners, and catholics.'* When it comes to this I should prefer emigrating to some country where they make no pretence of loving liberty—to Russia, for instance, where despotism can be taken pure, and without the base alloy of hypocracy [*sic*]."[55]

Lincoln biographers and historians, however, have usually failed to point out that the future president, while privately expressing his opposition to nativism, warned his antislavery friends against alienating the Know Nothings. "Until we can get the elements of this organization" into the antislavery tent, he informed Lovejoy in the summer of 1855, "there is not sufficient materials to successfully combat the Nebraska democracy" led by Senator Douglas. Without a substantial number of Know Nothings in the antislavery movement, the successes of the anti-Nebraska coalition in 1854 would be reversed. "Know-nothingism has not yet tumbled to pieces; . . . and I fear an open push by us now, may offend them, and tend to prevent our ever getting them," he told Lovejoy.[56] Lincoln's failure to denounce the movement publicly caused Democrats to claim during the Lincoln-Douglas senatorial campaign in 1858 that he had been a nativist and a member of a Know-Nothing lodge. In a speech at Meredosia in October 1858, Lincoln angrily—and truthfully—denied that he had ever been connected with the Know-Nothing movement.[57]

By the summer of 1855, developments in Kansas were causing great concern in the North. The aggressive and illegal methods of "border ruffians" from Missouri to carry the election of a territorial legislature for slavery outraged northerners, including many people who had not earlier opposed the Kansas-Nebraska bill.[58] The young Republican party became the political beneficiary of the Kansas troubles. By 1856, Republicans had put down solid roots in the upper North and seemed destined to spread throughout the free states, at the expense mainly of the old Whig party.

Despite their early failure to persuade Lincoln to join them, Lovejoy, Codding, and other northern Illinois radicals continued to press him to affiliate with the new Republican party. However, Lincoln resisted their efforts, informing Lovejoy on August 11, 1855, that "the political atmosphere is such just now, that I fear to do any thing, lest I do wrong."[59] He clung to the unlikely notion that the Whig party could survive the sectional division over slavery and rally the party faithful against their Douglas Democratic adversaries on a conservative antislavery platform. "I think I am a whig," he wrote Joshua Speed on August 24, 1855, "but others say there are no whigs, and that I am an abolitionist. . . . I now do no more than oppose the extension of slavery" into Kansas and other western territories.[60]

Events in Kansas had intensified Lincoln's dislike of slavery and increased his resolve to resist the spread of the institution. Lincoln had become convinced that slavery threatened the very existence of the republic created by the Founding Fathers for the purpose of maintaining constitutional liberty, individual opportunity, and national unity. The Kansas-Nebraska bill, he wrote Speed, "was conceived in violence, passed in violence, is maintained in violence, and is being executed in violence." Lincoln took it for granted that "Kansas will form a Slave Constitution, and with it ask to be admitted to the Union." He vowed to oppose Kansas' admission as a slave state and said he would demand "the restoration of the Missouri Compromise" line prohibiting slavery in Kansas and in other northern territories. Lincoln also said that he was reluctant "to withhold my assent to the enjoyment of property *acquired,* or *located,* in good faith; but I do not admit that *good faith,* in taking a negro to Kansas, to be held in slavery, is a *possibility* with any man."[61]

In his gloom, Lincoln suggested to a correspondent that, regardless of what happened in the territories, slavery had become a permanent feature in the South. He wrote George Robertson, a Kentucky acquaintance and professor of law at Transylvania College: "So far as peaceful, voluntary emancipation is concerned, the condition of the negro slave in America, scarcely less terrible to the contemplation of a free mind, is now as fixed, and hopeless of change for the better, as that of the lost souls of the finally impenitent. The Autocrat of all the Russias [*sic*] will resign his crown, and proclaim his subjects free republicans sooner than will our American masters voluntarily give up their slaves."[62] Such a pessimistic view contrasted with Lincoln's later argument that if slavery were contained in the South, it would eventually be abolished by the southern states without federal intervention.

Apparently at some time in early 1856, Lincoln concluded that the fusion of all antislavery elements into the Republican party had become a necessity. Already established in the northern states, the new party was in the process of forming a national organization to challenge the Democrats in the fall elections. Though avoiding the label "Republican" because of its radical and sectional implications, in February Lincoln took a giant step toward becoming involved in the new party's organization when he accepted an invitation to attend a meeting of antislavery editors at Decatur to prepare for an "Anti-Nebraska" state convention. He was the only prominent politician to attend. The Decatur meeting, as historian Don E. Fehrenbacher has pointed out, "in every way except formal name" marked "the launching of the state Republican party."[63]

Introduced as "our next candidate for the U.S. Senate," Lincoln spoke for half an hour to the antislavery editors at Decatur. He announced his approval of the meeting's resolutions, which he had helped to write, condemning slavery's expansion into Kansas and Nebraska. The resolutions, as he had hoped, avoided radical antislavery proposals. Lincoln, however, must have been uneasy about a resolution denouncing Know Nothingism.[64] He realized that if the "Anti-Nebraska" party was to garner their support, the Illinois Know Nothings, most of Whig antecedents, would have to be treated gently. In addition to avoiding public criticism of the Know Nothings, the new party would have to maintain a conservative antislavery position. The party, Lincoln insisted, should endorse the odious Fugitive Slave Act and reject any federal policy interfering with slavery in the South and in the District of Columbia. Lincoln concluded that the new party could not depend on moral persuasion alone to succeed; it had to develop a constitutional and historical rationale for opposing the expansion of slavery, one that expressed the intentions of the Founding Fathers and would appeal to the state's conservative voters. Meanwhile, Lincoln continued to keep quiet in public about his opposition to nativism and hoped that political events would swing his Know-Nothing friends into the crusade against slavery's expansion.

As had been agreed to at Decatur, the convention of the "Anti-Nebraska party of Illinois"—soon to be called the Republican party—met in Bloomington on May 29, 1856. Enthusiasm for the new party reached a high among the hundreds of delegates at the convention. News of several incidents —the violent attack by South Carolina Representative Preston Brooks on antislavery Senator Charles Sumner at his desk in the Senate chamber; the proslavery sacking of Lawrence, Kansas; and the destruction of a newspaper office in Leavenworth—angered the delegates at Decatur and contributed to an emotional atmosphere that resembled the fervor of a Protestant tent revival.[65]

Lincoln gave the main speech at the convention. It was a powerful indictment of slavery, the violence over Kansas, and the national Democratic party's role in producing the troubles.[66] The applause for Lincoln was deafening. The address is known to history as the "Lost Speech," reportedly because the journalists in attendance were so carried away by Lincoln's rhetorical passion that they forgot to take notes. We only have a brief summary of the speech. Some delegates remembered it as Lincoln's greatest speech prior to the Civil War. Clearly, the new state party, whatever it called itself, now had its undisputed leader—one who was capable of uniting the disparate antislavery elements in the state—in Lincoln.

William E. Gienapp, the leading authority on the rise of the Republican party in the North, has written that, because of its strategic location in the West, Illinois was "the most important state in which the Republican party organized during the first half of 1856."[67] It was also the most difficult western state to secure a fusion of the antislavery elements. Lincoln more than anyone understood the difficulties that the new party faced in the state. Though he played the key role in the success of the Republican party in Illinois, Lincoln did not refer to himself as a Republican until late 1856. He still feared the radical implications of the name among his political friends in central Illinois. By the fall campaign, Lincoln, having cast his lot with the Republican party, had concluded that the new party—with its national organization and based on conservative antislavery principles, particularly in his state—was the wave of the future.

The Bloomington convention in May also nominated a state ticket for the fall election with William H. Bissell, an anti-Nebraska Democrat, as the gubernatorial candidate. Lincoln, with his ambition set on the U.S. Senate and a growing determination to unseat Douglas in 1858, did not express any desire to be governor. He also believed that only a former Democrat could win the position.

Despite the enthusiasm of the delegates at Bloomington, the Republican party had an uncertain beginning in 1856 as it faced its first major election. Lincoln realized that the party was little more than a coalition of old Whig conservatives, many of them with nativist leanings, and Democratic opponents of Douglas, and he knew these factions could founder on former political divisions. He expressed this fear to Senator Lyman Trumbull when he wrote that "a good many whigs, of conservative feelings, and slight proslavery proclivities [were] inclining to go for" James Buchanan, the Democratic candidate for president. "Nine tenths of the Anti-Nebraska votes have to come from old whigs," Lincoln told Trumbull, a former Democrat, and he warned him that if this element was disregarded and a radical platform adopted, the antislavery party would fail in Illinois.[68]

Lincoln was not alone among anti-Nebraska Whig leaders in seeing the danger to the new party in moving toward an ultra-antislavery position, specifically one that included the repeal of the Fugitive Slave Act and the abolition of slavery in the District of Columbia. Orville H. Browning, a Lincoln associate, declared that it was essential "to keep the party in this State under the control of moderate men, and Conservative influences." He predicted that "if rash and ultra counsels prevail, all is lost."[69] In addition, the *Springfield Illinois State Journal*, the organ of the old Whig party, announced that it would support the new party only so long as it did not succumb to antislavery radicalism. When Lincoln learned that Owen Lovejoy had been nominated for Congress by a Republican district convention in northern Illinois, he told a friend that "it turned me blind." But upon reflection, he said, "I really think it best to let the matter stand."[70] Indeed, Lincoln later went to Princeton, Lovejoy's hometown, and spoke on the same platform with the radical.

Owen Lovejoy,
northern Illinois
congressman and
leader of the radical
wing of the state
Republican party.
Lovejoy later modified
his radical views and
supported Lincoln.
Courtesy of the
Abraham Lincoln
Library and Museum,
Harrogate, Tennessee.

Lovejoy soon moderated his antislavery rhetoric, probably owing in part to Lincoln's insistence that the new party could not succeed if it refused to acknowledge conservative Whig concerns. Nonetheless, in central Illinois several prominent Whigs, including the ultraconservative John Todd Stuart, Lincoln's first law partner and Mary's cousin, announced that they could not support a party that had an "abolitionist" (Lovejoy) on its ticket.[71] When

Stuart and other old political friends established the *Springfield Conservative* to promote the third-party presidential candidacy of Millard Fillmore, a former Whig who had been president in 1850–1853, Lincoln angrily told Herndon: "These men are stool pigeons for the Democracy—bought up like cattle and hogs in the market." He erroneously charged that "the *Conservative* is run by the Democrats in fact."[72]

Lincoln had good reason to be angry about the organization of the Fillmore party. Assuming the name "American party," it adopted a watered-down nativist platform that, on the one hand, denounced the Democrats for permitting slavery in Kansas and, on the other, attacked the Republicans for creating a sectional party that, it claimed, if successful would precipitate southern secession. Fillmore's candidacy threatened to divide the antislavery vote and undercut the Republican effort to attract Know Nothings to their party. Leaders of the American party, Lincoln realistically feared, would influence old Whigs to vote for Fillmore on the dubious ground that he was as good as anyone in opposing slavery's expansion while at the same time avoiding the presumed radicalism of the Republican party.[73]

Meanwhile, Lincoln's political leadership in the Illinois antislavery movement did not escape the notice of Republicans beyond the state. When the Republicans met in Philadelphia in June 1856 to form a national party, draw up an anti-Nebraska platform, and nominate candidates for president and vice president, Lincoln received 110 votes in an informal balloting for vice president. The convention, however, nominated William L. Dayton of New Jersey for the second place on the party's ticket. In a strange move, the delegates selected the egotistical and rash John C. Frémont, whose exploits as the "Pathfinder" in the West had been greatly exaggerated. Lincoln, who did not attend the convention, had preferred conservative U.S. Supreme Court Justice John McLean of Ohio for the presidency. McLean, he believed, would have had greater appeal for the conservative antislavery element in Illinois and in other lower northern states.[74]

Despite his disappointment that McLean did not receive the nomination, Lincoln vigorously campaigned for Frémont. He later claimed to have made more than fifty speeches in which he sought to persuade voters that the Republican party was the only one that opposed slavery in the territories. Furthermore, despite the fact that almost all of the Republican votes would come from the northern free states, Lincoln contended that his party was neither a sectional party nor a threat to the Union. He insisted that Fillmore could not win the presidency, and that a vote for him was in reality a vote for Democrat James Buchanan. Lincoln flooded the mails in September and October with a form letter to conservative and nativist Whigs pleading with them not to be misled into supporting Fillmore. "Fillmore has no possible chance to carry Illinois," he told them. "Be not deceived. *Buchanan* is the

Millard Fillmore,
Whig president,
1850–1853, and
American or
Know-Nothing
candidate for
president in 1856.
Fillmore was popular
among Illinois
conservatives in
Lincoln's former
party. Courtesy of the
Library of Congress,
Washington, D.C.

hard horse to beat in this race. Let him have Illinois, and nothing can beat him" in the presidential election; *"and he will get Illinois,* if men persist in throwing away votes upon Mr. Fillmore." Lincoln told Whigs that "this is as plain as the adding up of the weights of three small hogs."[75]

Many former Whigs did not take Lincoln's advice; they voted for Fillmore. Frémont lost the state by a margin of about 9,000 votes and lost the national election when he failed to carry Illinois and other key states of the lower North. He won the upper North, where opposition to slavery's expansion and to the slavocracy was strong. Fillmore received 37,444 votes in Illinois, and it is safe to say that the overwhelming majority of these would have been cast for Frémont had the former president not been a candidate. As Lincoln had feared, the antislavery-expansionist vote—mainly old Whig—had been divided, thereby handing the election to Buchanan, who supported the proslavery government in Kansas. Lincoln must have been especially disappointed by the fact that Buchanan won both Sangamon County and Springfield, though it was not unexpected, since both were Democratic strongholds.[76] In the county, Fillmore's third-party vote exceeded that of Frémont. Even Mary Lincoln did not support the Republican candidate. She indicated to a sister that if she could have voted, her ballot would have been cast for Fillmore. Mary, who held nativist sentiments, was upset by the influx of "wild Irish" into Springfield and the difficulties that, as she put it, "we housekeepers are sometimes called upon" in dealing with them.[77]

The election of Republican gubernatorial candidate William H. Bissell, supported by Fillmore men as well as Frémont voters, provided Lincoln and his Republican friends with an important source of hope for their party's future in Illinois. For Lincoln, who had emerged as the leader of the Illinois Republicans, the object now was to continue the effort to draw erstwhile nativists (Know Nothings) and conservative Whigs into his party. But he would have to do this without offending immigrant voters, especially Germans, whose numbers were growing in the state. (With some exceptions, the Irish, who were often the targets of nativist Whigs, routinely voted for Democrats, a pattern that Lincoln did not think he could change.) The organization of the diverse antislavery elements into the Republican party had demonstrated Lincoln's formidable political skills, abilities that had been forged in the highly competitive partisan wars in central Illinois over the previous two decades. Events would soon place him on a larger political stage than Illinois. In 1858, his inspired effort to unseat Senator Stephen A. Douglas in a key battleground state would provide the springboard for his national emergence and ultimately to the presidency.

CHAPTER FOUR

"HE IS AS HONEST AS HE IS SHREWD"

INTENSE POLITICAL excitement gripped the prairie towns and rural communities of Illinois in 1858. Important state elections and the U.S. Senate seat were at stake, contests that had national implications. Senator Stephen A. Douglas, who had recently broken with the Democratic administration of President James Buchanan and his southern rights supporters over the proslavery Lecompton constitution for Kansas, faced reelection. If the Little Giant did not win, his presidential ambitions, harbored since the early 1850s, would be dead, and his controversial doctrine of popular sovereignty, which was designed to decide the question of slavery in the territories, would be repudiated. Furthermore, Illinois, along with Pennsylvania and Indiana, was a key lower northern state that the Republican party had failed to carry in 1856 in its first attempt to win the presidency. The party needed to win these states in 1860 in order to capture the executive branch of the national government and sustain the party's momentum. A poor showing by the Republicans in Illinois would likely revive the injurious divisions between party radicals and conservatives throughout the lower North. A Republican victory, however, would provide a dramatic boost to the antislavery movement in the free states.

Abraham Lincoln was the man that the Illinois Republicans were depending on to lead them to victory in 1858. His own political ambition was also at stake in the election. Douglas, despite his break with President Buchanan, was still a powerful and skillful political leader as well as a dynamic campaigner. He was hardly the "dead lion" that Lincoln wishfully labeled him in the beginning of the campaign.[1] Indeed, most observers outside of the partisan Republican ranks in Illinois expected Douglas to win, especially because, with his opposition to the Lecompton constitution, he seemed to be moving toward a nonexpansionist position on slavery in the territories.

During the 1850s, the Prairie State had risen to prominence in the West. Illinois had passed the pure frontier stage, though it was still overwhelmingly rural, and like Lincoln, many of its older citizens upheld frontier traditions while adjusting to the rapid growth of their society. Only Chicago, with about 100,000 people, could claim to be a city; Peoria was a distant second in size with a population of 14,000 in 1860. Springfield, the state capital, had only about 9,000 residents. In 1850 the population of the state was 851,470;

by the end of the decade it had doubled—to 1,711,951. Much of the increase had come from overseas, particularly from the German states and Ireland. Settlers from other northern states and natural increase also contributed to this tremendous growth. The southern population that had dominated the state's development during its formative period slowed to a trickle during the 1850s, and its influence, centered in southern and central Illinois, had declined in importance.

The agricultural and commercial economy of Illinois also grew during the decade. This expansion owed a great deal to the crisscrossing of the state with railroads and, to a lesser extent, the improvement of roads and waterways. When the decade began, Illinois had only 110 miles of railroad track, fewer even than South Carolina and three other slave states. By 1860, Illinois' railroad mileage had climbed to 2,868, and only Ohio in the United States could claim more track. The most important railroad was the Illinois Central. Construction on this road began in 1851, and when completed to Cairo in 1856, it provided a direct line from Chicago through the relatively isolated east-central counties to the southern tip of the state. The Illinois Central and other railroads opened markets for farmers and contributed immensely to the growth of towns and communities along their routes. During the 1850s, the Chicago, Alton, and St. Louis Railroad, with short east-west rail connections, provided convenient access to Springfield for lawyers, politicians, and others with state and legal business to conduct, important contacts to be made, and political meetings to attend. Lincoln found himself at the center of these activities. Furthermore, he benefited from the relative ease and quickness of travel by rail from Springfield to Chicago and to the many other towns that would have taken days to reach in an earlier time. Before the 1850s, Lincoln rarely traveled to Chicago, but with the coming of the railroads and the rise in importance of this city, he made numerous trips there during the decade to attend federal and state courts and political meetings.

The importance of the railroad system in the U.S. senatorial campaign of 1858 can hardly be exaggerated. Though Lincoln and Douglas also used traditional forms of transportation—boat, buggy, wagon, and horseback—the railroads made possible the widespread canvass of the state by candidates and party activists. It also meant that thousands of people, including journalists, could take excursions and regularly scheduled trains from Chicago, Peoria, Springfield, and Bloomington and even from outside the state to attend the political rallies and speeches.

Despite the state's changing demographics and economy, politically Illinois retained much of its early conservatism, an orientation based on its rural southern roots and the people's reverence for the republican and constitutional heritage of the Founding Fathers. Though by no means limited to trans-planted southerners, prejudice against blacks greatly influenced the political response of Illinois whites to the antislavery crusade of the 1850s. Whites feared that the success of the antislavery movement in the North would lead to an influx of freed African Americans into Illinois and create racial con-flict.[2] They also believed that radical antislavery leaders like Owen Lovejoy had as their ultimate objective black political and social equality. Senator Douglas and the Democratic press increasingly—and often successfully—played the white race card in their campaign against the Republicans.

In his rise to prominence as a Republican leader, Lincoln understood ra-cial sentiment in the state and the need to keep the antislavery movement within conservative political bounds.[3] By stating his antislavery sentiments within the context of the Founders' intentions and the U.S. Constitution (for example, the constitutional provision for the return of persons escaping ser-vice or labor in another state), he framed his position in a way that would not conflict with the basic conservatism of the people. His continued support of black colonization in the tradition of Henry Clay and other early leaders was also designed to persuade Illinois whites that antislavery sentiment had historical roots. In his argument for black colonization, Lincoln was hardly the conniving racist that black writer Lerone Bennett and other modern crit-ics have labeled him.[4] In the context of racial sentiment in Illinois and the lower North in the 1850s, Lincoln's brand of racial prejudice was mild and open to change, unlike the racism of most of his fellow citizens. The political turbulence in Kansas and the threat to the nation's republican principles posed by the aggressive slavocracy, Lincoln assumed, would persuade conser-vatives as well as others that the Democrats had abandoned the principles of the Founders and that they should support the Republican party regardless of their racial views. Still, Lincoln pressed his position almost to its limits in Illinois with his strong moral opposition to slavery and his acknowledgment that the equality clause in the Declaration of Independence, however lim-ited in practice and in his mind, applied to blacks. Only radical Republicans like Lovejoy and militant abolitionists expressed publicly a commitment to greater racial equality.

Lincoln correctly believed that a radical stance by Illinois Republicans calling for the abolition of slavery in the South or the repeal of the Fugitive Slave Act and other provisions of the Compromise of 1850 would dash the hopes of his party in Illinois. The perceived threat to the Union posed by radicals had caused many conservatives and others with mild antislavery views—including many who had supported the anti-Nebraska coalition in 1854–1855—to oppose the young party. They seemed ready to either vote for Douglas or for a third-party candidate, as so many had done in 1856, when they supported the American party. Lincoln's success in leading his party to victory in the 1858 elections and winning the Senate seat would depend upon his skill in uniting conservatives, mainly former Whigs, with the radical Republicans of the northern part of the state. Radical converts in northern Illinois were increasing with every transgression by the slavocracy and their Democratic allies in the North. Many of the Illinois radicals were recent German and Scandinavian immigrants who opposed a political association with conservative, old Whig nativists and Know Nothings in the central and southern counties. Lincoln's task of bringing these elements together to win control of the new legislature—and thus election as the next U.S. senator—would challenge his political skill and campaigning ability.

It would be wrong to assume that Lincoln's senatorial ambition was the only or even the governing motive behind his fervent involvement in the 1858 campaign. His correspondence and political actions since the passage of the Kansas-Nebraska bill in 1854, followed by the proslavery aggression in Kansas and the caning of Republican Senator Charles Sumner in the Senate chamber, clearly indicate that he had become passionately aroused to new heights in his opposition to the Democrats. He viewed Democratic leaders like Douglas and President James Buchanan as men who had no moral scruples about slavery or its extension into the territories. Indeed, Lincoln had come to believe that these northern Democrats, whom he had opposed in earlier campaigns and on other issues, including the Mexican-American War, had become part of a conspiracy to nationalize slavery, subvert the antislavery purposes of the Founding Fathers, and undermine free society. Despite his fervor and strong rhetoric, Lincoln remained consistent in his conservative strategy to win the state for the antislavery cause and advance his own political position.

The U.S. Supreme Court decision in the Dred Scott case in 1857, providing judicial legitimacy for the expansion of slavery and denying any black claim to equality, had greatly reinforced Lincoln's fear that the republic of the Founding Fathers was in grave danger. He was incensed, as he declared in a June 1857 speech in Springfield, that the decision did "obvious violence to the plain unmistakable language of the Declaration" of Independence declaring all men equal. Still, in the same speech, Lincoln took care not to alienate important conservative elements that were concerned about slavery but unwilling to accept a radical doctrine of racial equality. He maintained that "the authors of that noble instrument," the Declaration of Independence, "did not intend to declare all men equal *in all respects*. They did not mean to say all were equal in color, size, intellect, moral developments, or social equality." The Founders meant that all men were created equal with "certain inalienable rights, among which are life, liberty, and the pursuit of happiness." They believed, Lincoln said, that in proclaiming the right of equality, "the enforcement of it [would] follow as fast as circumstances should permit." The Founders sought "to set up a standard maxim for free society, which should be familiar to all, and revered by all; constantly looked to, constantly labored for, and even though never perfectly attained, constantly approximated, and thereby constantly spreading and deepening its influence, and augmenting the happiness and value of life to all people of all colors everywhere." The Dred Scott decision, Lincoln declared, repudiated this doctrine. However, he announced that this bad decision should not be defied, but instead should be overruled when the antislavery forces gained control of the national government.[5]

By 1858 Lincoln's stature as the recognized leader of the antislavery forces in Illinois made him the logical choice for the Senate if the Republicans won control of the legislature in the fall elections. But disturbing reports from the East soon reached Lincoln and Illinois Republicans. Some eastern Republicans, principally Horace Greeley of the influential *New York Tribune,* had approached Senator Douglas about an alliance with their party. This flirtation with their old enemy followed the Little Giant's denunciation of the proslavery Lecompton constitution of Kansas that was supported by President Buchanan. Greeley's purpose was to cultivate the emerging split between Douglas and Buchanan and thereby divide the national Democratic party. In a patronizing fashion, Greeley advised Illinois Republicans to clasp hands with Douglas and not challenge his reelection to the Senate. Even prominent Republican Senators William H. Seward of New York and Henry Wilson of Massachusetts cultivated the wily Douglas's goodwill and cooperation. Seward and Wilson met with Douglas and agreed to let him take the lead in Congress in opposing the Lecompton constitution.

From Washington, Illinois Senator Lyman Trumbull warned Lincoln that the eastern intrigues with the Little Giant posed a threat to the Republicans and their principles. "Some of our friends here," Trumbull wrote, "act like fools in running after & flattering Douglas. He encourages it & invites [them] to come & confer with him & they seem wonderfully pleased to go." The eastern Republicans hoped that Douglas would join their party and become a leader in the antislavery cause, the Illinois senator reported. "The idea is preposterous," he told Lincoln. Douglas, he said, had "done nothing to commend him to any honest Republican. He still endorses the Dred Scott decision & no man who does so ought to be thought of as deserving Republican support." Was Douglas "to be rewarded by us for bringing the country to the verge of civil war & stirring up a sectional strife which has nearly dissolved the Union?" Trumbull asked. He further contended that if the courtship of Douglas continued, the effect would be to undermine the Republican cause in Illinois. Trumbull pointedly informed Lincoln that in the forthcoming senatorial election in the state, he would labor for "that *Friend* who was instrumental in promoting my own" for the Senate.[6] He meant Lincoln.

Though pleased by Trumbull's promise to aid him, Lincoln reacted in cold fury to the eastern Republican effort to win over the Little Giant to their side. "What does the New-York Tribune mean by it's [*sic*] constant eulogizing, and admiring, and magnifying [of] Douglas?" Lincoln angrily asked Trumbull. "Have they concluded that the republican cause, generally, can be best promoted by sacraficing [*sic*] us here in Illinois? If so we would like to know it soon; it will save us a great deal of labor to surrender at once." Lincoln feared "if the Tribune continues to din [Douglas's] praises into the ears of it's [*sic*] five or ten thousand republican readers in Illinois, it is more than can be hoped that all will stand firm."[7]

Taking their cues from Trumbull and Lincoln, Illinois Republican leaders denounced eastern meddling in their affairs.[8] The *Chicago Tribune* told its readers: "There seems to be a considerable notion pervading the brains of political wet-nurses at the East, that the barbarians of Illinois cannot take care of themselves."[9] John H. Bryant, a Republican editor in northern Illinois and a brother of William Cullen Bryant, the eminent poet and editor of the *New York Evening Post,* expressed a similar sentiment in a letter to Lincoln. "I am not willing," Bryant told Lincoln, "that we republicans of Illinois who have received so much abuse at [Douglas's] hands should now turn round and endorse his traitorous course by giving him the highest office in our hands." Bryant feared that the Little Giant's men in the state might dupe some conservative friends into voting for Douglas's candidates for the legislature and thereby insure his reelection.[10] Lincoln agreed that the confusion would play into the hands of the Douglas forces. In addition to a few thousand Republicans, Lincoln worried, conservatives who had supported Fillmore for president in 1856 might be influenced by Douglas's anti-Lecompton stand to think that the Democratic senator provided a less radical and less threatening opposition to slavery in the territories than the Republican party.[11]

Lincoln and most Illinois Republicans knew that Douglas was not really antislavery. Nor did they believe that he opposed the slavocracy's purposes in Washington. They were convinced that "Dug" had no real qualms about the expansion of slavery or about the morality of holding people in bondage. After a tour of the state in April, William Herndon wrote Senator Trumbull that Republicans "see that Douglas is not, and *will not be a Republican*," despite his opposition to the Lecompton constitution and to President Buchanan. "If Mr Douglas honestly intends to be a Republican," Herndon asked, "why are he and his friends getting up, and now organizing a Douglas Convention" to meet later in the month? He wanted Trumbull to "let people—Senators—Representatives—or Editors from NY or Mass." know to "keep their hands clean off—aloof, in our Senatorial election. If they want our respect, or confidence, or support, now or *in the future,* they probably should sit still, and not interfere in our affairs." State Auditor Jesse Dubois told Trumbull, "Our Republican friends at Washington may make what trades they chose [*sic*]," but Douglas would not be accepted by the state's Republicans "with all his sins yet unrepented." Ebenezer Peck sent a similar message to Trumbull and informed the senator that Lincoln was the clear choice of Illinois Republicans to run against Douglas.[12]

Eventually, the outrage of Illinois Republicans over eastern dictation caused Seward, Thurlow Weed, a power-broker in New York, and other leaders, but not Greeley, to cease their glorification of Douglas and announce that they had no intention of interfering in the Senate election in Illinois.[13] The end of their courtship of the Little Giant was also facilitated by the action of the state Democratic convention that met in Springfield on April 21. Controlled by the Douglas forces, the convention adopted resolutions endorsing popular sovereignty in the territories and pledging the party's support for their hero's reelection to the Senate. The delegates called for a fair vote in Kansas on the Lecompton constitution and mildly censured President Buchanan for his dismissal of Douglas supporters from office. They refused, however, to take a position against the expansion of slavery or the immorality of the institution, both key principles for the Republicans. Despite an effort to conciliate Buchanan supporters in the convention, the "Buchaneers" (also called "Danites") bolted the party and formed the state "National Democracy."[14]

Lincoln could not contain his delight at the split in the state Democratic party. He wrote a friend: "I was in Springfield during the sittings of the two democratic conventions, [and] say what they will, they are having an abundance of trouble. Our own friends were also there, in considerable numbers from different parts of the State. They are all in high spirits, and think, if we do not win, it will be our own fault."[15]

A bitter resentment toward the party's eastern elite continued when the Republican delegates met in county conventions to prepare for the state convention. Almost all of these conventions passed resolutions proclaiming their unqualified support for Lincoln in the Senate race.[16] They instructed their delegates to the state convention to pledge the Illinois party to support Lincoln—and no one else—for the Senate.

When the state Republican convention met in the chamber of the House of Representatives in Springfield on June 16, enthusiasm for Lincoln ran high. Deafening cheers from the 1,200 delegates greeted the mention of their favorite's name. During the afternoon, Charles L. Wilson, editor of the *Chi-*

cago Journal, offered this motion: "Resolved, That Abraham Lincoln is the first and only choice of the Republicans of Illinois for the United States Senate, as the successor to Stephen A. Douglas." Virtually as one, the delegates thundered their agreement to the resolution.[17] This unprecedented show of support meant that Republican members of the new legislature, though not legally bound, were emphatically instructed by the state party to cast their votes for Lincoln in the senatorial election. Furthermore, it meant that the convention's endorsement of Lincoln "turned the legislative election into a senatorial contest and thus cleared the way for his historic debates with Douglas."[18] It was only the second time in American history that a senatorial candidate had been endorsed by a state party convention.

The Republican convention also nominated candidates for state treasurer and superintendent of public instruction, the only state offices to be filled in the fall election. It adopted a "Declaration of Principles" (platform) that denounced the proslavery Dred Scott decision, called for the prohibition of slavery in the territories, and condemned the Buchanan administration. The delegates disclaimed "all intention of attempting, either directly or indirectly, to assail or abridge the rights of any members of the confederacy guaranteed by the Constitution, or in any manner to interfere with the institution of slavery in the States where it exists." In an obvious effort to attract Fillmore supporters and uncommitted Whigs, the platform called for federal aid to improve "our harbors and rivers which freight the commerce of the West to market, and the construction of a central highway to connect our trade with the Pacific States." Finally, the Republicans denounced the speculators in western lands and demanded that the public domain be made available only to bona fide settlers.[19]

That evening the Republican delegates assembled in the stifling hot House of Representatives chamber to hear a speech from their senatorial candidate. The address, known in history as the "House Divided Speech," became the most controversial of Lincoln's long career.

Lincoln began his speech by reminding the delegates to the state Republican convention that "we are now far into the *fifth* year, since a policy was initiated, with the *avowed* object, and *confident* promise, of putting an end to slavery agitation." But the "agitation" spawned by the Kansas-Nebraska bill had not ceased; it had "*constantly* [been] *augmented.*" "It *will not* cease," Lincoln predicted, "until a *crisis* shall have been reached, and passed." Citing a biblical injunction that he had used at Bloomington in 1856, Lincoln declared: "'A house divided against itself cannot stand.' I believe this government cannot endure, permanently half *slave* and half *free.* I do not expect the Union to be *dissolved*—I do not expect the house to *fall*—but I *do* expect it will cease to be divided. It will become *all* one thing, or *all* the other." He described what might happen. "Either the *opponents* of slavery, will arrest the further spread of it, and place it where the public mind shall rest in the belief that it is in course of ultimate extinction; or its *advocates* will push it forward, till it shall become alike lawful in *all* the States, *old* as well as *new—North* as well as *South*."[20]

Lincoln asked his audience, "Have we no *tendency* to the latter condition?" He answered by referring to the "now almost complete legal combination" that had imposed the Kansas-Nebraska doctrine of "squatter sovereignty" in the territories and the proslavery Dred Scott decision on the nation. He asserted that since the introduction of the Kansas-Nebraska bill, the "chief bosses" in Washington—Senator Douglas and Presidents Franklin Pierce and James Buchanan—had served the proslavery cause. Though Lincoln admitted that Douglas had opposed Buchanan on the Lecompton constitution issue, it was a "squabble" merely over whether the people of Kansas had had "a fair vote" on the document. The two Democratic leaders differed little on the subject of slavery, Lincoln argued. He reminded his listeners that in the Lecompton debate in the Senate, Douglas had declared that "he cares not whether slavery be voted down or voted up." "How can he oppose the advances of slavery?" Lincoln asked. "He don't *care* anything about it. His avowed mission *is impressing* the 'public heart' to *care* nothing about it."[21]

Indeed, Lincoln charged in his House Divided Speech that Douglas, Pierce, and Buchanan, joined by Chief Justice Roger B. Taney, the author of the Dred Scott decision, had conspired to lull the northern people to sleep on slavery, preparatory to the nationalization of the institution. Taney's majority opinion in the Dred Scott case invalidated the Missouri Compromise line on slavery and denied congressional authority over slave property in the territories. Slavery would be extended into the North, Lincoln feared, because Taney's federal judiciary would permit "the courts of any slave state" to decide where a master could take his slaves in the United States. "We may, ere long, see . . . another Supreme Court decision, declaring that the Constitution of the United States does not permit a *state* to exclude slavery from its limits." He contended: "Such a decision is all that slavery now lacks of being alike lawful in all the States." The nationalization of the institution would surely happen "if the doctrine of 'care not whether slavery be voted *down* or voted *up*,' shall gain upon the public mind sufficiently to give promise that such a decision can be maintained when made." Lincoln declared that "we shall *lie down* pleasantly dreaming that the people of *Missouri* are on the verge of making their State *free;* and we shall *awake* to the *reality,* instead, that the *Supreme Court* has made *Illinois* a *slave* State."[22]

The underlying purpose in Douglas's Nebraska doctrine and in Taney's Dred Scott decision, Lincoln claimed, was "to *educate* and *mould* public opinion, at least Northern public opinion, to not care whether slavery is voted *down* or voted *up*." He admitted,

> We can not *know* that all these exact adaptations are the result of pre-concert. But when we see a lot of framed timbers, different portions of which we know have been gotten out at different times and places and by different workmen—Stephen, Franklin, Roger and James,[23] for instance—and when we see these timbers joined together, and see they exactly make the frame of a house or a mill, all the tenons and mortices exactly fitting, and all the lengths and proportions of the different pieces exactly adapted to their respective places, and not a piece too many or too few, . . . we find impossible not to *believe* that Stephen and Franklin and Roger and James all understood one another from the beginning, and all worked upon a common *plan* or *draft* drawn up before the first lick was struck.[24]

The only way to prevent the nationalization of slavery, Lincoln told the state Republican delegates—and Illinois voters—was to meet and overthrow "the power of the present political dynasty" in Washington. Douglas was still a part of this dynasty, he declared, and he should not be returned to the Senate. Lincoln directed his final remarks in the speech to conservative antislavery men in the state who believed that the Little Giant was "the aptest instrument there is" to check the expansion of slavery. "They remind us that *he* is a very *great man*, and that the largest of *us* are very small ones." But, Lincoln exclaimed, " 'a *living dog* is better than a *dead lion*.' Judge Douglas, if not a *dead* lion for *this work*, is at least a *caged* and *toothless* one." Lincoln asked, "How can [Douglas] oppose the advances of slavery," since he had no moral scruples about the institution? Lincoln charged that Douglas would not even oppose the reopening of the foreign slave trade that "is approaching" consideration by Congress: "For years [Douglas] has labored to prove it a *sacred right* of white men to take Negro slaves into the new territories. Can he possibly show that it is *less* a sacred right to *buy* them where they can be bought cheapest? And, unquestionably they can be bought *cheaper* in *Africa* than in *Virginia*." He insisted that the Little Giant was "not *now* with us—he does not *pretend* to be—he does not *promise* to *ever* be." Lincoln closed on an upbeat note. "We shall not fail—if we stand firm." Though "wise councils may accelerate or mistakes delay it, . . . sooner or later the victory is sure to come" over the forces of slavery.[25]

The radical nature of Lincoln's House Divided Speech has long puzzled historians. They have interpreted it as uncharacteristic of his cautious approach to the political realities that the antislavery cause and the Republican party faced in Illinois. Historians have pointed out that Lincoln had been warned by his Republican associates, who had a preview of his speech, to tone down his radical pronouncements, particularly the house-divided metaphor and the famous sentence that followed: "I believe this government cannot endure, permanently half *slave* and half *free.*" In an urgent meeting with him before the address, Lincoln's friends warned that the Republican party and his own political prospects would be severely damaged in the critical central region of the state if he included such a radical statement in his speech. But Lincoln refused to budge. "With some degree of emotion," as John Armstrong, a witness to the meeting, recalled, Lincoln told his friends, "I have thought about this matter a great deal—have weighed the question well from all corners; and am thoroughly Convinced [*sic*] the time has come when it should be uttered & if it must be that I must go down because of this speech then let me go down linked to truth—die in the advocacy of what is right & just. This nation cannot live on injustice—a house divided against itself cannot stand &c I say again & again."[26]

Despite its strong rhetoric, Lincoln's House Divided Speech, when viewed in its totality, did not contradict his earlier conservative position on slavery. Unlike the radical antislavery proponents, he had never challenged the southern states' constitutional right to have slavery; nor did he propose the involuntary abolition of slavery in the District of Columbia, federal interference with the interstate slave trade, or the violation of the Fugitive Slave Act. Lincoln's emphasis in the speech was on his claim that the national Democratic leaders, not rank-and-file Democrats, were plotting to make slavery a national institution. For Lincoln to have singled out Democrats generally as villains in the slavery controversy would have unnecessarily alienated many former supporters of the party in Illinois who had reluctantly affiliated with the Whigs in the Republican party. Lincoln's main objective in the speech was not to move the state Republican party toward a radical antislavery position, but to draw a sharp distinction, both moral and political, between himself and Douglas. Lincoln sought to persuade important conservatives, especially confused antislavery Whigs and Know Nothings who had supported Fillmore for president in 1856, that he, not Douglas, was the only one who stood against the aggressive slave power. He also wanted to demonstrate to eastern Republicans that Douglas's views on slavery were antagonistic to the antislavery cause, and that they should therefore cease their unseemly courtship of the Little Giant.

As Lincoln's friends had warned, the Douglas Democrats seized upon the house-divided part of the speech and painted the Republican candidate as an abolitionist who would destroy the Union in order to rid it of slavery. During the campaign, Douglas himself never tired of quoting from the speech in his attacks on Lincoln. At least one of Lincoln's close political associates, Leonard Swett, believed that it cost his friend the election.[27] Lincoln seemed surprised "that any part of it should be construed so differently from any thing intended by me." In a letter to Republican editor John L. Scripps, he insisted that nothing in the speech "asserts, or intimates, any power or purpose, to interfere with slavery in the States where it exists." Lincoln told Scripps that he had "declared a thousand times, and now repeat that . . . neither the General Government, nor any other power outside of the slave states, can constitutionally or rightfully interfere with slaves or slavery where it already exists." However, he informed the editor that "whenever the effort to spread slavery into the new teritories [sic], by whatever means, and into the free states themselves, by Supreme court decisions, shall be fairly headed off, the institution will then be in course of ultimate extinction; and by the language used" in the speech, "I meant only this."[28]

In the summer of 1859, when dining with intimate friends at Bloomington, the subject of the House Divided Speech was again raised. Lincoln's friends insisted that he had blundered in making such a radical pronouncement. But Lincoln defended it, declaring: "Well Gentlemen, you may think that Speech was a mistake, but I never have believed it was, and you will see the day when you will consider it was the wisest thing I ever said."[29] Perhaps in the long run of history he was correct in this prediction, but in 1858 the House Divided Speech damaged his prospects for defeating Douglas.

Soon after the state Republican convention adjourned, Lincoln wrote Senator Lyman Trumbull that "the signs look reasonably well" for the success of the state ticket, but that he deplored "the advantages" the Democrats already had in the holdover members. Eight of the thirteen holdover senators were Democrats. "We shall be very hard run to carry the Legislature," he informed Trumbull.[30]

Concluding that they had an uphill battle to win control of the legislature, some Republicans intrigued with disgruntled "Buchaneers" or "Danites" to defeat Douglas's candidates. On the floor of the U.S. Senate, the Little Giant charged that there was a plot between Republicans and Buchanan Democrats to divide his party in Illinois. Lincoln denied that any alliance existed or that any "concession of principle on either side, or furnishing of sinews, or partition of offices, or swopping [sic] of votes" had been made.[31] Though technically correct, his denial was misleading. Several Republican leaders, including Lincoln, later met with prominent Buchaneers and encouraged them to oppose Douglas, but no alliance was proposed. During the campaign, when the senator persisted in charging that there was a Republican-Buchanan conspiracy against the regular Democrats in the state, Lincoln at Galesburg on October 7 angrily declared: "I defy the Judge to show any evidence that I have in any way promoted that division, unless he insists on being a witness himself in merely saying so." By this time it was clear that the Buchaneers had little support among Illinois Democrats; indeed, in the election, their candidates won only 2 percent of the votes.[32]

The future president opened his campaign for the Senate at Chicago on July 10. The preceding evening, Douglas, after a triumphant journey from Washington, had spoken from the balcony of the Tremont House in the city. Lincoln probably timed his visit to coincide with Douglas's return to the state in order to hear him speak and learn his campaign strategy. He also wanted to be able to respond immediately and establish that he was capable and eager to take on the Little Giant. By invitation, Lincoln sat near Douglas when he spoke at the Tremont.

On this occasion, as on so many others throughout the campaign, Douglas attempted to undercut Lincoln on the issue of slavery in the territories. Speaking in an area where opposition to slavery's expansion was strong, Douglas emphasized his fight against the proslavery Lecompton constitution, labeling it "a fraud" upon the people of Kansas and upon his own doctrine of popular sovereignty. The constitution's defeat, the Little Giant boasted, was a "great moral victory" for the "principle of self-government," which he misleadingly credited to his own efforts; he ignored the fact that the Republicans in Congress provided most of the opposition to it. Douglas claimed that the rejection of the Lecompton constitution heralded the triumph of popular sovereignty "as a permanent rule of public policy in the organization of territories and the admission of new states" to the Union. In a thrust at Lincoln's position, he declared that "it is no answer . . . to say that slavery is an evil and hence should not be tolerated. You must allow the people to decide for themselves whether it is a good or an evil." He announced his approval of the Dred Scott decision, arguing that it did not violate the principle of popular sovereignty since the people, through their territorial legislature, could pass laws that did not protect slave property. Without security for their chattels, slaveholders would not take them into the territories. Popular sovereignty would thereby be sustained.[33]

Not unexpectedly, Douglas castigated his opponent's House Divided Speech as an inflammatory declaration that, if Lincoln had his way, it would lead to the North making war upon the South to end slavery and to impose national uniformity upon its institutions. Douglas, in a flight of fancy, charged that Lincoln was "for uniformity in our domestic institutions, for a war of sections, until one or the other shall be subdued. I go for the great principle of the Kansas-Nebraska Bill, the right of the people to decide for themselves." The senator declared that, unlike Lincoln, he "opposed any step that recognizes the Negro man or the Indian as the equal of the white man." The

American government, he told his Chicago audience, "was made by the white man, for the benefit of the white man, to be administered by white men, in such manner as they should determine." Finally, Douglas repeated his accusation that Illinois Republicans and Buchanan supporters had formed "an unholy, unnatural alliance" against him.[34]

The next evening, Lincoln spoke from the same balcony and replied to the senator. An estimated 9,000 people heard the Republican candidate launch his own campaign for the Senate.[35] Speaking without notes, he defended his House Divided Speech and told his audience that nothing in the address suggested he was in favor of northern interference with slavery in the southern states. "I only said what I expected would take place. I made a prediction only—it may have been a foolish one perhaps." The misunderstanding regarding his meaning in the speech, he explained, was due to the fact that "I am not a master of language. I have not a fine education; I am not capable of entering into a disquisition upon dialectics," a somewhat startling pronouncement in view of his skill in the use of language and his long, enviable experience on the stump and in the courtroom. "But I don't care about a quibble in regard to words. I know what I meant . . . in the use of that paragraph" in the House Divided Speech.[36]

Lincoln then explained to his Chicago audience what he meant. Prior to Douglas's introduction of the divisive Kansas-Nebraska bill in 1854, he said, the country had "endured" half slave and half free. Earlier, "the public mind did rest, all the time, in the belief that slavery was in course of ultimate extinction." By permitting slavery's spread, the Kansas-Nebraska bill had undermined this belief, Lincoln asserted: "I have always hated slavery, I think as much as any Abolitionist, . . . but I have always been quiet about it until this new era of the introduction of the Nebraska Bill began." Peace on the issue, he contended, could not be restored until "the public mind should rest [again] with the belief that it is in course of ultimate extinction," and this could only occur by the successful resistance to its spread.[37] But, Lincoln argued, the Supreme Court in the Dred Scott case, which Douglas supported despite his "Squatter Sovereignty" doctrine, had ruled that "the people of a territory have no right to exclude slavery."[38] Lincoln did not press Douglas for an explanation of the inconsistency between his doctrine and the decision of the Supreme Court; he would do this later, however, at Freeport and elsewhere.

He also responded to Douglas's claim that he and his fellow Republicans sought the political and social equality of the races. He said that no one would deny that the government "was made for white men," but that "the Judge goes into his passion for drawing inferences that are not warranted. I protest, now and forever, against that counterfeit logic which presumes that because I do not want a Negro woman for a slave, I do necessarily want her for a wife." Lincoln's Chicago audience greeted this remark with laughter and cheers, according to a newspaper report. Lincoln maintained that because "God made us separate, we can leave one another alone and do one another much good thereby. There are white men enough to marry all the white women, and enough black men to marry all the black women, and in God's name let them be so married." But, Lincoln went on to say, "let us discard all this quibbling about this man and the other man—this race and that race and the other race being inferior." We should unite on the Declaration of Independence principle that "all men are created equal, [and] let it be as nearly reached as we can."³⁹ This comment reflected Lincoln's progressive brand of conservatism, one that held out hope in the eventual fulfillment of the Founders' republican ideals, even for blacks.

Returning to Springfield, Lincoln confidently told his friends that he had won the first battle in the campaign against Douglas. "By his rampant indorsement of the Dred Scott decision," Lincoln reported, his opponent at Chicago "drove back a few republicans who were favorably inclined towards him." His tactics for the campaign, Lincoln concluded, were "to make it appear that he is having a triumphal entry [and] march through the country; but it is all as bombastic and hollow as Napoleon's bulletins sent back from his campaign in Russia." Lincoln also said that his audience, though not as large as that of the senator, was "five times as enthusiastic."⁴⁰

Others seemed surprised by the strength of Lincoln's performance at Chicago and the fervor of the crowd's response. Republican editors, who were concerned about the inflammatory passage in the House Divided Speech, hailed Lincoln's success. Even Horace Greeley's *New York Tribune,* which had been opposed to Lincoln's candidacy, praised the Chicago speech as "admirable and thoroughly Republican."⁴¹ Greeley privately expressed dismay that Illinois Republicans had not cooperated in the eastern Republican effort to bring Douglas into the antislavery party. "You have taken your course [and] have repelled Douglas, who might have been conciliated, and attached to our side," Greeley wrote Joseph Medill of the *Chicago Press and Tribune* in a letter that Lincoln saw and copied. "Instead of helping us in other states, you have thrown a load upon us that may probably break us down," Greeley continued. "You knew what was the almost unanamous [*sic*] desire of the Republicans of other states; and you spurned and insulted them. Now go ahead and fight it through. You are in for it, and it does no good to make up wry faces." Greeley doubted that Lincoln would "stand on the broad Anti-Slavery ground" during the campaign. "You have got your Elephant," Greeley indignantly told Medill, "now shoulder him!"⁴²

Outsiders who heard Lincoln for the first time gained a generally favorable impression of him at Chicago but concluded that he would be no match for the aggressive Little Giant in the campaign. Lillian Foster, an eastern travel writer and Douglas supporter, wrote to a friend that Lincoln was "tall and awkward; in manner, ungainly. His face is certainly ugly, but not repulsive; on the contrary, the good humor, generosity and intellect beaming from it, makes the eye love to linger there until you almost fancy him good-looking. He is a man of decided talents. On the stump, ready, humorous, argumentative, and tells an anecdote with inconceivable quaintness and effect. He is honest as a man; and enthusiastic as a politician." Foster, however, did not believe that Lincoln could defeat Douglas and thought that his career as a politician would be short-lived. "He is an able lawyer," she wrote, "and that is the true field of his fame."[43]

Foster was not the only outsider who underestimated "Long Abe's" political skill and his ability on the stump. A correspondent to the *Vincennes Sun* wrote: "Lincoln is popular—the strongest man the opposition have—is nearly fifty years old—six feet two—slightly stoop-shouldered—very muscular and powerful—dark eyes—a quizzical, pleasant, raw-boned face—tells a story better than anybody else—is a good lawyer—and is what the world calls a devilish good fellow. . . . But in dignity, intellect and majesty of mind it is not pretended that he is Douglas's equal."[44] Still, this correspondent believed that Lincoln, "a remarkably able man," would give the Little Giant the fight of his life.[45]

Even Douglas admitted that he would be in the fight of his life in the campaign. Lincoln, the senator wrote an eastern friend, "is the strong man of his party—full of wit, facts, dates—and the best stump-speaker, with droll ways and dry jokes, in the West. He is as honest as he is shrewd, and if I beat him my victory will be hardly won."[46]

Much has been written about the seven debates between Lincoln and Douglas, often to the neglect of the campaign generally. The candidates' tactics and many of their points of attack, however, were largely laid out at Chicago before the debates began. As the campaign progressed, it attracted attention throughout much of the nation, especially in the political circles of the North, but little in the deep South. William Cullen Bryant's paper, the *New York Evening Post,* proclaimed Illinois "the battleground of the year." This newspaper announced that "the results of this contest are held to be of the highest importance to the welfare of the country and the success of the great contending parties."[47] Labeling Lincoln "the champion of anti-slavery in the North," the *Louisville Democrat,* a newspaper that supported Douglas, described the contest as "the ablest and the most important that has ever taken place in any of the States, on the great question which has long agitated the country" —slavery."[48]

As Lincoln had predicted, Douglas's movement south after launching his campaign in Chicago was highlighted by an elaborate and well-organized display of his candidacy. His purpose was to create a steamroller effect on the voters. The Little Giant traveled on a special train with flags and the large words "S. A. Douglas, the Champion of Popular Sovereignty" emblazoned on each car. A flat car on the train carried a brass six-pound cannon that Douglas's entourage fired when within hearing distance of the towns. The two main trunklines, the Chicago, Alton, and St. Louis Railroad and the Illinois Central, provided the senator with special favors and his supporters with reduced excursion rates. Virgil Hickox, a staunch Douglasite and the general agent for the St. Louis, Alton, and Chicago line, lamely denied the Republican charge that his railroad extended special accommodations to Democratic excursionists and free campaign posters for Douglas.[49]

Born in Vermont in 1813, the "Little Giant" was just five feet four inches tall. He had settled in Jacksonville, central Illinois, as a young man, and had served in the Illinois House of Representatives during the 1830s. It was there that he apparently first met Lincoln. Douglas was appointed as a Democrat to the state Supreme Court in 1841. The fact that he had secured the legislature's approval of the expansion of the court, allowing him to be appointed to it, led Lincoln, in derision, to refer to him as the "Judge." In 1843, Douglas won election to the U.S. House of Representatives, where he became a staunch supporter of President James K. Polk and the Mexican-American War. In 1847, he married the daughter of a southern planter who later inherited a plantation in Mississippi with more than a hundred slaves. Douglas became the administrator of the estate and reaped profits from it. At about the same time, the Illinois General Assembly elected him to the U.S. Senate, and he moved to Chicago. Despite the fact that the senator now resided in Chicago and many of the party faithful in the North had abandoned him, at least temporarily, over the Kansas-Nebraska bill, Douglas remained a "lion" to central and southern Illinois Democrats. His support for limited government—except for federal and state aid to railroads—for American expansion ("Manifest Destiny"), and for a militant white supremacy appealed to these Democrats.

Both Lincoln and Douglas realized that the election would be decided in the central counties. After a speech at Bloomington on July 16, which Lincoln attended, Douglas rushed to Springfield to speak at a huge Democratic rally the next day. He admitted that his opponent was personally popular in his hometown. "Mr. Lincoln," he said, "is a kind-hearted, amiable, good-natured gentleman, with whom no man has a right to pick a quarrel. . . . He is a fine lawyer, possesses high ability, and there is no objection to him, except the monstrous revolutionary doctrines with which he is identified and which he conscientiously entertains, and is determined to carry out if he gets

Stephen A. Douglas, the "Little Giant." Douglas was a Democratic senator and Lincoln opponent in the 1858 senatorial campaign and in the 1860 presidential election. Courtesy of the Abraham Lincoln Library and Museum, Harrogate, Tennessee.

the power." Again, Douglas charged a conspiracy in Lincoln's attempt to win the Senate seat. "He has one element of strength upon which he relies to accomplish his object," the senator declared, "and that is his alliance with certain men in this state claiming to be Democrats, whose avowed object is to use their power to prostrate the Democratic nominees" for the legislature. Douglas claimed that Lincoln, in order to obtain the votes of the Buchaneers, "does not say a word against the Lecompton constitution," which the president's men supported.[50]

Though no conspiracy existed, on July 8, Lincoln had "had a conversation" with John Dougherty, the Buchaneer leader, on the political situation in the state. When Dougherty informed him that the National Democrats (Buchaneers) planned to run legislative candidates in every county and district of the state, Lincoln declared, "If you do this, the thing is settled"—that is, Douglas was sure to lose. Though Republicans offered encouragement to the National Democrats, Lincoln, according to Herndon, made no agreement with them. "That kind of thing does not suit his tastes," Herndon told Trumbull.[51] Furthermore, at Chicago one week earlier, Lincoln had attacked the Lecompton constitution, which the Buchaneers supported, as a violation of the rights of the people of Kansas, a fact that the Little Giant must have known but ignored.[52]

After the Douglas rally on July 17 at Springfield, Lincoln spoke to a large Republican crowd that evening. In his speech, Lincoln assumed the role of the underdog against Douglas and announced that Republicans—and by implication his own candidacy—labored under the disadvantage of a legislative apportionment made in 1852 "when the proportion of the population was far greater in the South (as compared with the North) than it now is; and inasmuch as our opponents hold almost entire sway in the South, and we a correspondingly large majority in the North, the fact that we are now to be represented as we were years ago, when the population was different, is to us a very great disadvantage." Lincoln, however, admitted that the legislature had recently passed a reapportionment bill that was presumably based upon a new census; but, he argued, it was still unfair to Republican districts. Southern Illinois, where the Democratic party was strong, retained a disproportionate number of seats in the General Assembly. As a result, Republican Governor William H. Bissell had vetoed the bill.[53]

When the bill passed that Bissell disapproved, no organized Republican party existed in the state. The majority in the legislature consisted of anti-Nebraska men of both old parties, some of whom still considered themselves to be Democrats and conceivably could return to the party fold. Lincoln was correct in noting that of the thirteen state senators who did not face reelection in 1858, eight were Democrats, giving Douglas a two-member advantage from the start.[54]

Lincoln then called the attention of his Springfield audience to "another disadvantage under which we labor." This was "the relative position" in political strength of himself and Douglas. "Senator Douglas is of world wide renown," Lincoln declared. "All the anxious politicians of his party . . . have been looking upon him as a certainty, at no distant day, to be President of the

United States. They have seen in his round, jolly, fruitful face, postoffices, landoffices, marshalships, and cabinet appointments, chargeships and foreign missions, bursting and sprouting out in wonderful exuberance ready to be laid hold of by their greedy hands." Lincoln contended that, despite "the little distraction" on slavery that had taken place in the Democratic party, these office-seekers "have been gazing upon this attractive picture so long," they cannot "give up the charming hope" of rewards at Douglas's hands: "With greedier anxiety they rush about him, sustain him, and give him marches, triumphal entries, and receptions" as never before. "On the contrary," he added, "nobody has ever expected me to be President. In my poor, lean, lank, face, nobody has ever seen that any cabbages were sprouting out."[55]

"Long Abe," as many called him during the campaign, devoted most of his Springfield speech to explaining his differences with Douglas on slavery. As he had done at Chicago, Lincoln riveted the attention of his audience on his opponent's inconsistencies in supporting the proslavery Dred Scott decision while continuing to preach the doctrine of popular sovereignty in the territories. He also attempted to persuade conservative antislavery voters that it was the Republican members of Congress—not Douglas, as claimed—who had defeated the proslavery Lecompton constitution. Douglas's vote opposing the Kansas constitution was his only antislavery action in the Senate, Lincoln cleverly informed his audience. "Does he place his superior claim to credit," he asked, "on the ground that he performed a good act which was never expected of him," while the Republicans bore the main burden in the Lecompton battle?[56]

Lincoln again sought to clarify the controversial remarks made in his House Divided Speech on June 16. "What is there in the language of that speech," he asked, that "I invite a war of sections; that I propose all the local institutions of the different States shall become consolidated and uniform" as Douglas had charged? "I have again and again said that I would not enter into any of the States to disturb the institution of slavery." Lincoln insisted that he "meant no more [than] that the institution of slavery ought to be placed in the very attitude where the framers of this Government placed it, and left it. I do not understand that the framers of our Constitution left the people of the free States in the attitude of firing bombs or shells into the slave states." Regarding the passage in his June 16 speech where he had said, "I believe that this Government cannot endure permanently half slave and half free," Lincoln explained that he had "simply expressed my *expectation,* not a wish or a *purpose*" to see the country divided. He elaborated on what he had said at Chicago: A sectional division would not occur if the spread of slavery was arrested and the institution "placed where the public mind shall rest in the belief that it is in the course of ultimate extinction; [then] we shall have peace on the slavery question." The Republican candidate told his Springfield audience that "the public mind did rest on that belief up to the introduction of the Nebraska bill" in 1854 by Douglas. The Dred Scott decision of 1857, which Douglas supported, had gone even further than the popular-sovereignty doctrine "in the direction of making [slavery] perpetual and national."[57] The future president renewed his earlier charge that Judge Douglas was a party to a proslavery "conspiracy" and to a "deception for the sole purpose of nationalizing slavery."[58]

In his July 17 Springfield speech, Lincoln again contested Douglas's claim that he proposed "to make Negroes perfectly equal with white men in social and political relations." He knew that, in addition to the House Divided Speech, his inclusion of blacks in the Declaration of Independence equality creed had created dismay among old Whig conservatives in central and southern Illinois, many of whom had been born and raised in the border slave states. Furthermore, Lincoln realized that many antislavery Democrats who had broken with Douglas over the Kansas-Nebraska Act might conclude that the Republicans were too radical for them; the senator's opposition to the proslavery Lecompton constitution was tempting them to return to their old party. Early in the campaign, he had received a report that some antislavery Democrats had indicated their intention to support Douglas candidates for the legislature. At that time, however, Lincoln wrote to a friend that he did not find "republicans from the old *democratic* ranks more inclined to Douglas than those from the old whig ranks." "Indeed," he said, "I find very little of such inclination in either class."[59] But Lincoln knew that Democratic fusion with antislavery Whigs had always been tenuous and could change during the course of a heated campaign, when old political animosities could resurface.

Lincoln in his Springfield speech sought to reassure conservative Whigs and antislavery Democrats that he had been "misrepresented" on the issue of black equality. He said: "I do not understand the Declaration to mean that all men were created equal in all respects. They are not our equal in color; but I suppose that it does mean to declare that all men are equal in some respects; they are equal in their right to 'life, liberty, and the pursuit of happiness.'" Also, "in the right to put into his mouth the bread that his own hands have earned," he said, a black man "is the equal of every other man, white or black." Lincoln then told his race-conscious audience: "All I ask for the Negro is that if you do not like him, let him alone. If God gave him but little, that little let him enjoy."[60] The race issue, as distinct from the immediate question of slavery's expansion, haunted Lincoln throughout the campaign, impelling him, for political reasons, in the fourth debate with Douglas, at Charleston, virtually to refute his earlier theoretical support for black equality.

Sometime in July, Lincoln made elaborate and detailed calculations, based on the 1856 election returns, concerning the possible results of the state House and Senate candidates in each district. Lincoln's computations, comprising six printed pages in his *Collected Works,* reveal the importance that he attached to the central counties. They also demonstrate a well-informed and careful mind at work in making detailed political analysis and projections, a trait that would serve Lincoln well in the election of 1860 and as president. Lincoln listed seventeen House districts in southern Illinois as hopeless for the Republicans and therefore as ones that should be ignored. He labeled twenty House districts, mainly in the central counties, "as doubtful, and to be struggled for." Nonetheless, Lincoln concluded that in the worst-case scenario, the Republicans, with their strength centered in the north, would win the House by a margin of three seats; at best, they would win by nineteen. In the state Senate campaign, Lincoln projected that the Republicans were virtually assured of nine districts, but "must struggle" for six other districts. He recorded no possible totals for the Senate elections.[61]

The Democratic press bombarded conservative voters in the critical central counties with allegations that Lincoln was closely linked with Owen Lovejoy and the "ultra-abolitionism" of northern Illinois. The *Springfield Illinois State Register* thundered, "Mr. Lincoln is for the abolition of slavery, [even] if it cost the sacrifice of the Union." This newspaper predicted that he would not succeed in his effort "to engulf his old whig friends" into the vortex of abolitionism and sectional conflict.[62]

Illinois Democrats also warmed over the old chestnut of "Mr. Lincoln's spotted record" in opposing the Mexican-American War and the claim that he had voted against supplies for the troops. The *Chicago Times* reached demagogic heights when it told its readers that Lincoln had voted against "the purchase of medicines and the employment of nurses to attend the sick and dying American soldiers in the hospitals and camps of hot and burning Mexico."[63] Unable to shake himself free from this old charge, Lincoln answered the Democratic "lie" through his friends in the Republican press. He acknowledged that he had opposed the war, but he insisted that "there is not a word of truth in the charge" that he had opposed provisions for the army. Lincoln explained to Joseph Medill of the *Chicago Daily Democratic Press,* soon to merge with the *Chicago Tribune* to form the *Chicago Press and Tribune,* that he had reexamined the journal of the House of Representatives and could find nothing in his votes suggesting that he had denied any support for the troops in the field. "The real origin" of the Douglas press's "blind rage to assail me," Lincoln angrily wrote, was its assigning to him his predecessor's vote against a provisioning bill. "I scarcely think any one is quite vile enough to make such a charge in such terms, without some slight belief in the truth of it," he lamented.[64]

Medill and other Republican editors immediately came to Lincoln's defense. The *Springfield Illinois State Journal* characterized the Mexican-American War accusations by the Democrats "as a black-hearted falsehood and base misrepresentation" illustrated with "vile epithets and cowardly billingsgate to bolster up Mr. Douglas' waning fortunes."[65] Though Lincoln himself soon concluded that "the more respectable" Democratic newspapers "have been compelled to take it back and acknowledge that [the charge] was a lie," Democratic attacks on Lincoln's war record continued throughout the campaign.[66] In Egypt (southern Illinois), a Lincolnite reported that Democratic orators, including congressional candidate John A. Logan, later a major general in Sherman's army and the Republican nominee for vice president in 1884, were digging up "the skeletons of all those who died on the plains of Mexico and attempting to prove by the use of Volcanic thunder—ignoring sound arguments—that they all died at the hands of Abe Lincoln."[67]

By late July, Douglas had seized the initiative in the senatorial campaign. Belatedly, in order to refute the Little Giant's charges, Lincoln began speaking in the towns of central Illinois immediately after the senator's rallies. The Democratic press had a field day with the "abolitionists' candidate's" tactic, claiming that it was the only way he could attract a crowd. The *Chicago Times* gleefully announced: "The cringing, crawling creature [Lincoln] is hanging at the outskirts of Douglas's meeting, begging the people to come and hear him." This newspaper impishly suggested that if the Republican candidate wanted a crowd for his speeches, his managers should make arrangements for him to talk at "two very good circuses and menageries traveling through the State; these exhibitions always draw good crowds. In this way, Lincoln could get good audiences, and his friends would be relieved from the mortification they all feel at his present humiliating position."[68] Lincoln and his friends took all of this "billingsgate" in stride; after all, it was part of the political culture in mid-nineteenth-century America and had great entertainment value for partisans. Though such ridicule spurred popular interest in the campaigns, how much difference it made at the polls is impossible to determine.

Sensing that Douglas had gained an important step on him, Lincoln went to Chicago on July 21–22 to confer on campaign strategy with Norman Judd, chair of the Republican state central committee, and other associates. All agreed that, because he was the underdog—and also partly to avoid the embarrassment of following his opponent around the state—Lincoln should challenge Douglas to a series of debates. On July 24, he proposed to the senator that they make an arrangement "to divide time, and address the same audiences during the present campaign."[69] Lincoln did not specify how many joint appearances should be scheduled; the wording, however, clearly suggested that he wanted to engage the senator at every campaign stop.

Douglas at first was reluctant to accept the challenge. The Little Giant figured that because of his opposition to the Lecompton constitution he had regained much of his popularity in the state; he did not want to give Lincoln, whom he feared as an able debater, a boost by sharing the platform with him. But he knew that he would lose face with the voters if he rejected the challenge. Furthermore, Douglas believed, joint debates would check Lincoln's practice of speaking after him in the towns where he campaigned and would give him an opportunity for an immediate rebuttal. Still, the senator had no desire to be tied to Lincoln throughout the campaign. Pleading that his schedule prevented him from taking part in an extensive series of debates, Douglas informed his Republican challenger that he would "accommodate" him with joint appearances "at one prominent point in each congressional district," except in the Chicago and Springfield districts. In these two districts, Douglas reminded his opponent, "we have both spoken, and in each of which cases you had the concluding speech," a point that Lincoln disputed but to no avail. He then listed, for Lincoln's consideration, the towns in the seven districts where the debates should be held. Though disappointed that Douglas had agreed to only seven debates, Lincoln drafted a letter accepting the proposal. In an accidental meeting with the senator on the prairie near Monticello, Lincoln offered, then and there, to compare his draft with the senator's letter and write out his final acceptance. Douglas, however, accompanied by a long line of festive supporters, refused to wait and went on to his next speaking engagement. Lincoln returned to Springfield and mailed his acceptance to Douglas.[70]

The first debate, at Ottawa in northern Illinois, was not scheduled until August 21. Meanwhile, Lincoln prepared for the debates, corresponded with local Republican leaders about political prospects in their counties, and conducted his legal business. He received reports of local political and personal rivalries that threatened to undermine the election of Republican legislative candidates in several counties. On a number of occasions, Lincoln intervened to avert serious divisions. In the central counties, the division among radicals and conservatives posed an even greater threat to the party's success. Lincoln warned his followers in these and adjacent northern counties to avoid nominating radical antislavery men for the legislature lest the party lose the support of Fillmore Whigs.[71]

In some northern counties where "abolitionists" were a strong minority in the party, a quid pro quo was arranged. Here, Lincoln activists, probably with his endorsement, agreed to the nomination of radicals for county offices in exchange for their support of conservative antislavery candidates for the General Assembly. A major fear of Lincoln associates was that the radical Owen Lovejoy, now in Congress from a northern Illinois district, would appear on the platform at Republican rallies in their communities. Judge David Davis of Bloomington excitedly warned Lincoln to keep Lovejoy out of central Illinois. "For God's sake," Davis told Lincoln, "don't let Lovejoy go into Tazewell." Tazewell was a key county in the district that had been settled by Kentuckians who had supported Fillmore and the American party in 1856. "Any man that has the taint of abolition about him must not go to Tazewell," Davis told Lincoln; otherwise, all would be lost.[72]

Though Lovejoy had promised Lincoln that he would temper his radicalism for the good of the party, his candidacy for reelection triggered an important Republican defection in the area. Theophilus Lyle Dickey, a prominent former Whig who had campaigned with Lincoln for John C. Frémont in 1856, announced that he would support Douglas for the Senate and run for Congress against Lovejoy.[73] In the end, Dickey's candidacy took away Whig and American votes from the Republicans in several north-central Illinois counties and insured a victory for Douglas legislative candidates there. Lovejoy, however, defeated Dickey in his northern congressional district.

On August 10, Lincoln started his movement north for the first debate at Ottawa, speaking at small towns along the route. At last, as an anxious friend remarked, Lincoln was prepared to "throw some of his hot shot into the Douglas camp, and charge home upon the doughface [Douglas]."[74] At Beardstown and Havana, along the Illinois River, he followed Douglas rallies by one day, adding to the Democratic complaint that the "abolitionist candidate" was using the Little Giant's coattails in order to gain an audience. Though this was partly true, Lincoln in his movement toward Ottawa did break away from Douglas's path to speak at several Republican rallies.[75]

The festive air, parades, rowdy crowds, and stirring speeches along the route of the senatorial candidates provided a dramatic dress rehearsal for the Great Debates. Newspaper accounts of the Douglas and Lincoln rallies predictably reflected the political bias of the publications. On the Republican side, the *Chicago Press and Tribune* reported from Beardstown, Lincoln's first stop on the Illinois River, that "an enormous crowd from this [Cass] and the adjoining counties of Schuyler and Morgan" heard him speak. When Lincoln arrived at Beardstown on the steamboat *Sam Gaty* in the morning, 300 or 400 supporters met him and escorted him to his hotel. Almost all of the committee members managing the event were old Whig friends of Lincoln's. The plan to fire the local cannon in his honor failed, however, because, as the *Press and Tribune* claimed, "the valorous Democracy," after using it the pre-

Illinois in 1858 Showing Where Lincoln Spoke in the Senatorial Campaign

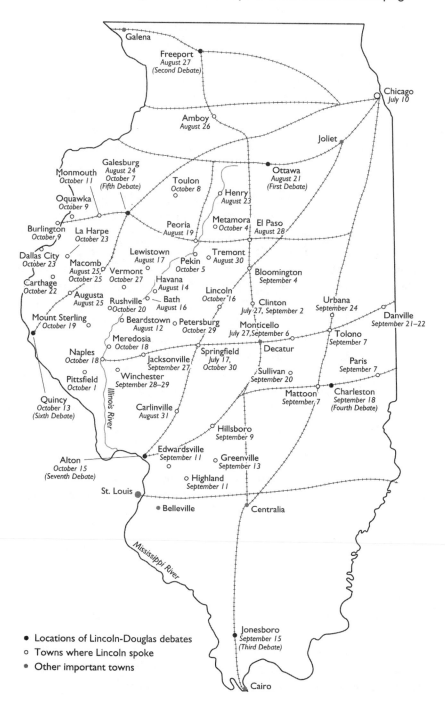

Galena

Freeport
August 27
(Second Debate)

Chicago
July 10

Amboy
August 26

Joliet

Galesburg
August 24
October 7
(Fifth Debate)

Monmouth
October 11

Toulon
October 8

Ottawa
August 21
(First Debate)

Oquawka
October 9

Henry
August 23

Burlington
October 9

La Harpe
October 23

Peoria
August 19

Metamora
October 4

El Paso
August 28

Dallas City
October 23

Lewistown
August 17

Tremont
August 30

Macomb
August 25,
October 25

Pekin
October 5

Bloomington
September 4

Carthage
October 22

Vermont
October 27

Havana
August 14

Lincoln
October 16

Urbana
September 24

Danville
September 21–22

Augusta
August 25

Rushville
October 20

Bath
August 16

Clinton
July 27, September 2

Mount Sterling
October 19

Beardstown
August 12

Petersburg
October 29

Monticello
July 27, September 6

Tolono
September 7

Meredosia
October 18

Springfield
July 17,
October 30

Decatur

Naples
October 18

Jacksonville
September 27

Sullivan
September 20

Paris
September 7

Pittsfield
October 1

Winchester
September 28–29

Mattoon
September 7

Charleston
September 18
(Fourth Debate)

Quincy
October 13
(Sixth Debate)

Carlinville
August 31

Hillsboro
September 9

Illinois River

Edwardsville
September 11

Greenville
September 13

Alton
October 15
(Seventh Debate)

Highland
September 11

St. Louis

Belleville

Centralia

Mississippi River

Jonesboro
September 15
(Third Debate)

Cairo

● Locations of Lincoln-Douglas debates
○ Towns where Lincoln spoke
● Other important towns

vious day to welcome Douglas, had spiked it "with pounded brick" to prevent the Republicans from discharging it. Fortunately, the Republicans "had two fine bands of music, two military companies—the 'Beardstown City Guards' and 'Independents'—and a cavalcade of forty horsemen to supply the deficiency and add to the éclat of the reception." Banners were stretched across the streets with such inscriptions as "Abe Lincoln against the Field"; "Freedom National, Slavery Sectional"; and "Liberty and Union, now and forever, one and inseparable." The *Press and Tribune* boasted, probably with some exaggeration, that "there was less noise, less liquor and fewer street fights" than during the Democratic rally on the previous day. It concluded that "Old Abe's" speech "dwarfed the Douglas harangue of yesterday into *nothing.*"[76]

The report in the Democratic *Chicago Times* predictably gave an entirely different version of Lincoln's reception as he moved northward on the Illinois River. Cleverly employing ridicule, it reported that "not fifty people" came to the boat landing at Havana to meet him; "as Lincoln was about leaving the boat, the American flag was run up on board, but, as if indignant at being raised in honor of such a man, it displayed itself at mast head, Union Jack down." Lincoln, the *Times* said, "is failing rapidly, but he has lost none of his awkwardness. He is all legs and arms, and his constant efforts to hide the extreme length of these members by keeping them twisted up when not in use, makes his movement very kinky and uncertain. His gestures when speaking, are positively painful, and while listening to him we are constantly uncomfortable, because you cannot divest yourself of the idea that he is suffering from an attack brought on by an imprudent indulgence in unripe fruit."[77]

Typical of the Democratic press's Negrophobic campaign against Lincoln was the *Times*'s report of his speech at Havana. This newspaper told its readers that Lincoln "clings to Negro equality," though at Havana he had "diluted the dose, no doubt thinking that down in this more southerly climate there were weaker stomachs [than] in Chicago," when he spoke on July 10. Having asserted that the Declaration of Independence's equality clause applied to blacks, "he was at loss to know what to do with them, and where to put them, that they might exercise it." "Lincoln," the editor of this Democratic newspaper scornfully declared, "admitted that [blacks] were not physically equal to the white race, but thought they were equal under the law, and that it was our duty to bring them to a state of social equality with ourselves."[78]

The Democratic line of attack on Lincoln—and by extension on Republican candidates for the legislature—had been clearly established before the first debate at Ottawa. It would rely heavily on an appeal to white racism and to the presumed threat that Lincoln and the Republicans posed to sectional harmony and the Union. Lincoln's support for black equality and his House Divided Speech, however rationalized by him, would be the centerpiece of this Democratic strategy. Douglas men sought to brand Lincoln as a radical in the minds of Illinois voters, who were overwhelmingly conservative on issues of race and slavery, despite their opposition to the "peculiar institution's" expansion. Lincoln would be on the defensive to counter the Democratic strategy while seeking ways to take the offensive against Douglas in the debates and in other campaign appearances. All of his political astuteness and platform skill would be tested in the effort against one of the best stump speakers of the 1850s and the most renowned public figure of his day. The table thus had been set for the most famous debates in American history; these dramatic political encounters, along with other events relating to the 1858 senatorial campaign, would go far toward determining the course of American history.

CHAPTER FIVE

THE GREAT DEBATES

"THE PRAIRIES are on fire" with political fervor, a correspondent of the *New York Evening Post* reported in the late summer from the scene of the debates between Lincoln and Douglas. "It is astonishing how deep an interest in politics this people take."[1] The enthusiasm reflected the youthful exuberance and confidence of the people of the West. Reporters from several major newspapers, from as far west as St. Louis and as far east as New York, covered the Great Debates. Their accounts almost invariably reflected the political biases of their newspapers. The leading state newspapers provided stenographers—probably for the first time in American history for a political campaign—to make verbatim transcripts of the speeches.[2] Small-town Illinois newspapers printed debate summaries based on extended reports taken from their party's main state publications—the *Chicago Press and Tribune* (Republican) and the *Chicago Times* (Democrat). Southern newspapers, except for the border slave states, virtually ignored the debates; they professed to find little to distinguish between the two candidates.

Political newspapers, aided by telegraphic reports and improved transportation, had exploded on the American scene in the early nineteenth century and had become a powerful instrument of partisan warfare by the 1850s. Some, like the *New York Tribune* and the *New York Herald,* had gained national reputations. Arguably, by mid-century newspapers had eclipsed the pulpit and political pamphlets as shapers of public opinion. The political press also contributed significantly to the rise of sectional divisions as partisan editors inflamed the passions of the people on the issues associated with slavery and, paradoxically, the preservation of the Union. Many prominent men of the 1850s in their early political careers had served as editors of their local party newspaper. Most of them continued to write articles for their party paper. The editors of the political press, despite their denials and their condemnation of partisan and sectional politics, existed to promote their party and tear down the opposition. Reporting the news was secondary.

Every town of any size could claim to have a newspaper for each party; most depended upon subsidies from their party and income from public printing in order to survive. State capitals like Springfield and rising cities like Chicago often had more than two newspapers and, in the North, a German-language paper. With an increasingly educated public to serve, and interest in political affairs growing, newspaper circulation expanded, aided by the coming of the railroads. Major eastern dailies like the *New York Tribune* and the *New York Herald* were delivered to towns along the railroad lines. In Illinois, the *Chicago Press and Tribune* and the *Chicago Times* could be found in most towns, and they served as a source of political commentary for the local party press.

The *Chicago Press and Tribune,* along with the *Springfield Illinois State Journal,* in 1858 had become virtual organs for Lincoln. They would contribute significantly to his political rise not only in the state but also in the greater West. From an early age, Lincoln had recognized the importance of newspapers, and he had read them avidly for political information and ideas. Beginning in the 1830s, he had frequently written anonymous articles for the Whig newspapers and later the Republican ones in Springfield, though, as in the case of his "Rebecca" letters in 1842, his identity did not always remain a secret.[3] He maintained a close relationship with the editors of his party's newspapers, and when in their communities, he often discussed political affairs with them. In 1859–1860, Lincoln briefly financed a German-language newspaper for the purpose of securing the support of this important ethnic group.

The first of the seven debates between Lincoln and Douglas opened at Ottawa in northern Illinois on August 21. Ottawa, with a population of about 6,000, located on the Chicago and Rock Island Railroad, overflowed with visitors anxious to participate in the political festivities. Men, women, and children, old and young, came from the nearby rural communities, from adjacent counties, and from distant towns; they came by every means of conveyance—foot, wagon, carriage, horseback, railroad, and boat. A journalist reported that throughout the morning, mule and horse "teams, trains and processions poured in from every direction like an army with banners. National flags, mottoes and devices fluttered and stared from every street corner. Military companies and bands of music monopolized the thoroughfares around the Court House and the public square. Two brass twelve-pounders banged away in the center of the city and drowned the hubbub of the multitude with their own higher capacities for hubbub. Vanity Fair never boiled with madder enthusiasm." By late morning, 12,000 people had assembled in a chaotic mass to participate in or observe the procession for each candidate and to hear the afternoon debate.[4]

About noon, Lincoln arrived at the Rock Island depot accompanied by seventeen cars full of cheering supporters from the Chicago and Joliet area. The Republican champion "was placed in a carriage beautifully decorated with evergreens and mottoes by the young ladies of Ottawa." A lively procession formed to escort him to the home of Mayor Joseph O. Glover, where he ate lunch before the debate. "Enormous crowds blocked the streets and side-walks through which the procession moved, and the shouts of the multitude rolled from end to end, around the street corners and across the bridge, in a continuous tumult," according to the *Chicago Press and Tribune* reporter.[5] Douglas arrived soon after Lincoln and reportedly was met by a similar demonstration and procession.[6]

About one o'clock, the crowd began to gather at the Ottawa courthouse square for the debate. Nothing went right at first. "The speaking stand had been foolishly left ungarded [*sic*]," according to an observer, "and was so crowded with people — that half an hour was consumed in a battle to make room for the speakers and reporters. . . . Two or three times the surge of people on the platform nearly drove the reporters off, and half a dozen clowns on the roof broke through some of the boards and let them down on the heads of the Reception Committees." The situation was made worse by the fact that the day was hot and the few trees on the square provided little relief for the crowd.[7]

After considerable confusion, the debate got underway in mid-afternoon. Still, many in the "vast concourse of people," Lincoln later reported, "could not [get] near enough to hear."[8] As agreed earlier, Douglas opened with an hour-long speech; Lincoln followed with a one-and-a-half-hour reply, and the senator concluded with a half-hour rejoinder. The sequence for speaking would be alternated in the seven debates. Both men spoke without a prepared text, though each sometimes read from printed passages to make a point against his opponent.

In his opening speech, Douglas wasted no time in seeking old Whig support by branding Lincoln an antislavery radical who posed a threat to the Union. Because some Democrats loyal to President Buchanan seemed determined to run legislative candidates against him, the Little Giant had concluded that he needed the votes of Whig conservatives to insure his reelection. To attract these conservatives, many of whom had supported Fillmore in 1856, Douglas realized that he had to deflect the harsh criticism he had faced over the Kansas-Nebraska bill and, at the same time, demonstrate that his popular-sovereignty doctrine was still a proper solution to the slavery controversy in the territories. He argued the historical similarity of Whig and Democratic positions on slavery and the Union as contrasted to Lincoln's (presumed) radicalism. The two parties, he contended, though differing on national financial issues, had always agreed on slavery and had jointly approved the compromise measures of 1850. Douglas claimed that his Kansas-Nebraska bill of 1854 had been based on the compromise principle advanced by Whig icon Henry Clay. He told his audience that at the time, the Illinois House of Representatives, with Whigs and Democrats voting unanimously for it, had endorsed the Kansas-Nebraska measure, a claim that Lincoln later disputed.

Taking the offensive, Douglas announced that Lincoln, in league with apostate Democrats like Lyman Trumbull, believed in black equality and was a disturber of sectional peace. Lincoln and Trumbull, Douglas charged, had "entered into an arrangement" in 1854 to dissolve the state Whig and Democratic parties and "connect the members of both into an Abolition party under the name and disguise of a Republican party." The terms of the agreement between the two Republican leaders "were that Lincoln should have [James] Shields' place in the U.S. Senate" in 1855 and "Trumbull should have my seat when my term expired." Douglas claimed that "Lincoln went to work to abolitionize the Old Whig party all over the state, pretending that he was then as good a Whig as ever; and Trumbull went to work in his part of the state preaching abolitionism in its milder and lighter form, and trying to abolitionize the Democratic party." In pursuance of the arrangement, the two parties met at Springfield in October 1854 and adopted an abolition platform for the new Republican party.[9]

Douglas then read from a set of resolutions, which he announced had been adopted by the state Republican party in the 1854 meeting. They called for the repeal of the Fugitive Slave Act, the abolition of slavery in the District of Columbia, and a prohibition on the admission of any more slave states into the Union. The senator told his Ottawa audience, "my object in reading these resolutions, was to put the question to Abraham Lincoln this day, whether he now stands and will stand by each article in that creed and carry it out." Noting that the "Black Republicans" of northern Illinois in the crowd had cheered approvingly as he read the radical resolutions, Douglas wanted Lincoln "to answer these questions, in order that when I trot him down to lower Egypt I may put the same questions to him." The Little Giant doubted that "Mr. Lincoln's principles will bear transplanting from Ottawa to Jonesboro" in southern Illinois ("Egypt") where the third debate would be held.[10] Douglas promised that when they met at Jonesboro he would "bring him [Lincoln] to his milk," an obscure colloquial expression designed to make an adversary appear weak and in need of nourishment.[11]

Predictably, Douglas turned to Lincoln's House Divided Speech and cited it as evidence that Lincoln's position was "revolutionary and destructive of this government." It was pure "abolition doctrine," the senator charged. "I believe that this new doctrine preached by Mr. Lincoln and his party will dissolve the Union if it succeeds. They are trying to array all the Northern states in one body against the South, to excite a sectional war between the free states and the slave states." Douglas reaffirmed his own commitment to the principle of popular sovereignty on the issues of slavery and blacks in the states and the territories. He declared: "I do not hold that because the negro is our inferior . . . he ought to be a slave. . . . I hold that humanity and Christianity both require that the Negro shall have and enjoy every right, every privilege, and every immunity consistent with the safety of the society in which he lives."[12] This was as much as Douglas would ever concede on the issues of black freedom and rights; he refused to make the same concession when he trotted down to Egypt, where racial prejudice was strong.

The predominantly Republican crowd at Ottawa roared its support when Lincoln stood to speak. Lincoln chose to devote most of his speech to a defense of the charges that Douglas had raised. He emphatically denied that he had anything to do with the radical resolutions adopted by the first Republican convention in 1854: "My friend Mr. [Owen] Lovejoy, who is here upon this stand, had a hand in it, . . . and I think if he will remember accurately, he will be able to recollect that he tried to get me into [the convention], and I would not go in." Indeed, Lincoln said, "I went away from Springfield when the Convention was in session, to attend court in Tazewell County. It is true they did place my name, though without authority, upon the [new party's] Committee, [but] I never had anything to do with that organization."[13]

Lincoln then denounced Douglas's charge that he had conspired with Trumbull in 1854 to "abolitionize" the Whig and Democratic parties. He reminded his audience that he had initially sought to maintain the Whig party as the proper conservative organization to oppose Douglas and the Kansas-Nebraska bill. As evidence of this political commitment, Lincoln said that in 1854–1855, Lovejoy, the Republican party's candidate for the Illinois House of Representatives, "complained of me that I had told all the old Whigs in his district that the old Whig party was good enough for them, and some of them voted against him because I told them so." Lincoln denied that he was determined to establish an abolitionist party in the state. He read an extended passage from his October 1854 speech at Peoria in which he declared that, though he hated slavery, he acknowledged the constitutional rights of southerners to own slaves, the validity of the Fugitive Slave Act, and his opinion that blacks were not the political and social equal of whites. He told his Ottawa audience, "This is the whole of it, and anything that argues me into [the] idea of perfect social and political equality with the Negro, is but a specious and fantastic arrangement of words, by which a man can prove a horse chestnut to be a chestnut horse."[14]

Lincoln went on to argue: "There is a physical difference between the two [races], which in my judgment will probably forever forbid their living together upon the footing of perfect equality, and inasmuch as it becomes a necessity that there must be a difference, I, as well as Judge Douglas, am in favor of the race to which I belong, having the superior position. I have never said anything to the contrary." Modern-day critics of Lincoln, who cite this statement as clear evidence of his deep-seated racism, ignore the comment that immediately followed: "But I hold that notwithstanding all of this, there is no reason in the world why the Negro is not entitled to all the natural rights enumerated in the Declaration of Independence, the right to life, liberty and the pursuit of happiness. I hold that he is as much entitled to these as the white man." The black man, Lincoln insisted, was the equal of the white man "in the right to eat the bread, without leave of anybody else, which his own hand earns."[15] This was a small concession to racial equality, but it was an important one in Negrophobic Illinois.

Lincoln's pronouncement on black inferiority was made in northern Illinois where strong antislavery sentiment existed; presumably, the people in his audience held relatively tolerant views of blacks. However, he understood that he could not be seen as supportive of true racial equality even in the antislavery northern districts where most of the people were either natives of the Northeast or immigrants. Furthermore, he knew that his remarks would be printed and circulated in central Illinois, where he was seeking to reassure former Whigs and Fillmore supporters that his antislavery position did not threaten their conservative racial views or their strong desire for national harmony.

Lincoln denied that in using the house-divided metaphor he sought to inflame the sectional controversy and cause a war between the North and the South: "I had no thought in the world that I was doing anything to bring about a war between the free and slave States," he told his Ottawa audience. "My main object was to show . . . the people of the country, what I believed was the truth—that there was a *tendency,* if not a conspiracy among those who have engineered this slavery question for the last four or five years, to make slavery perpetual and universal in this nation." The Republican candidate refuted a Douglas claim that he favored the "dead uniformity" of all local institutions to prevent the American house from dividing. Lincoln argued that "the great variety of the local institutions in the States, springing from differences in the soil, differences in the face of the country, and in the climate, are bonds of Union. They do not make 'a house divided against itself,' but they make a house united. If they produce in one section of the country what is called for by the wants of another section, and this other section can supply the wants of the first, they are not matters of discord but bonds of union, true bonds of union." But, Lincoln exclaimed, slavery was not one of those bonds of union; it was, "on the contrary, . . . an apple of discord and an element of division in the house." As he had said before, the solution was "to arrest the further spread of [slavery], and place it where the public mind shall rest in the belief that it is in the course of ultimate extinction." Then, Lincoln assured his audience, "the crisis would be past and the institution might be let alone for a hundred years, if it should live so long, in the States where it exists."[16]

The Republican *Chicago Press and Tribune,* in a typical partisan fashion, reported that when Lincoln concluded his speech at Ottawa, Douglas, "livid with passion and excitement," sprang to his feet to reply. "All his plans had been demolished, himself placed in the criminal's box to answer to an indictment, and to make head against a mountain of damning testimony heaped up against him by his antagonist," this newspaper told its readers. "We have never seen a face so distorted with rage. He resembled a wild beast in looks and gesture, and a maniac in language and argument. He made no adequate reply to the heavy charges brought against him, save to call everybody 'liars' who alleged or believed them."[17]

The *Springfield Illinois State Register* gave an entirely different account of the Little Giant's rebuttal. This Democratic newspaper reported that Douglas "riddled Lincoln's sophistries, ridiculed his evasions, and nailed him fast to the [radical] platform of '54, which Lincoln endeavored to creep out of. Lincoln withered before the bold, lucid and eloquent argumentation, and writhed under the sharp invective of Douglas." Lincoln had "the look of a boy who had 'let a bird go.'" The *Chicago Times* reported that the Little Giant's "excoriation of Lincoln was so severe, that the Republicans hung their heads in shame." The "abolition" candidate "alternately burn[ed] with fever, and then suddenly chilled with shame, his respiratory organs [became] obstructed, his limbs got cold, and he was unable to walk."[18]

Actually, Douglas's rebuttal at Ottawa was mainly a rambling and fiery summarization of the charges he had made against Lincoln in his opening address. Douglas insisted that Lincoln had failed to answer any of his questions about his views on slavery and black rights, which was hardly the case. The senator also angrily denied the charge that he had been part of a plot to nationalize slavery, exclaiming, "Mr. Lincoln has not character enough for integrity and truth merely on his own *ipse dixit* [assertion] to arraign President Buchanan, President Pierce, and nine judges of the Supreme Court, not one of whom would be complimented by being put on an equality with him." During the course of the rebuttal, Lincoln reportedly interrupted Douglas on three occasions, only to be restrained by his friends.[19] On another occasion, Mayor Glover, the Republican chair of the Ottawa debate, had to remind Lincoln supporters to cease their heckling of the Little Giant.[20]

After the debate, Lincoln's and Douglas's friends rushed the platform and triumphantly escorted their respective heroes through the crowd. Lincoln, with his legs dangling, was carried from the stand on the shoulders of his supporters, creating an amusing scene that the Douglas newspapers gleefully embroidered. "Such an exhibition as the 'toting' of Lincoln from the square to his lodgings," the *Chicago Times* delightedly reported, "was never seen at Ottawa before. It was one of the richest farces we have ever witnessed, and provoked the laughter of all, Democrats and Republicans."[21] The Republican press described no such ludicrous scene. The *Chicago Daily Journal* reported that the enthusiasm was so great for Lincoln that when the debate ended, his friends "rushed up to the stand, took him upon their shoulders, and bore him in triumphal procession to the house of Mayor Glover, where he stopped." That night, a throng of supporters, preceded by a musical band, escorted Lincoln to the courthouse, where the Republicans proclaimed a great victory over the Douglas forces. Owen Lovejoy "made a telling speech" against the Democrats. Later, they formed "a grand torchlight procession, and paraded the streets, with loud 'hurrahs for Lincoln.' "[22]

Naturally, both sides claimed victory in the first of the seven classic encounters between the "Little Giant" and "Long Abe." And each party exaggerated the failure of the opposition candidate. Both parties saw the importance of impressing voters with the success of their candidate in the first debate. They realized that public interest would probably be greater in the Ottawa encounter than later, and they knew that first impressions lingered. A correspondent of the *Chicago Press and Tribune* reflected this strategy when it reported from the scene: "It is universally acknowledged that Stephen A. Douglas is a used up man"; Lincoln " 'chewed him up' completely. I doubt if there is a Douglasite in town who witnessed the manner in which his idol was slain, who does not inwardly feel that the contest in this State is already practically ended—that, Douglas cannot be returned to the U.S. Senate, unless by an interposition of divine providence."[23] The *Springfield Illinois State Register,* in contrast, pronounced the Ottawa encounter "a most overwhelming overthrow of Mr. Lincoln." It continued, "It places him in his true attitude before the people of the state, which no shuffling or pettifogging dodging can get him out of." The paper predicted that Lincoln would "be forced to stand square up to his abolition platform or back clear down" in the subsequent debates.[24] The correspondent of the *St. Louis Morning Herald,* in a prediction dipped deep in irony, reported after the debate: "Lincoln may as well hang up his hat, take a back seat, and wait until 1860, as Douglas will then be President; and then Mr. Lincoln may make another effort for an election to the United States Senate, without having a Douglas to contend with."[25]

Lincoln, however, seemed pleased with his performance at Ottawa. He wrote a friend: "Douglas and I, for the first time this canvass, crossed swords here yesterday; the fire flew some, and I am glad to know I am yet alive."[26]

State Republican leaders told him that he had upstaged Douglas in the debate. Senator Trumbull wrote Lincoln: "In manner, temper, spirit, eloquence & every thing else you have obtained a complete triumph over the little pettifogger. . . . The debate at Ottawa ought to be sufficient to decide the contest with all intelligent men." L. D. Whiting, a party leader in northern Illinois, informed Lincoln that "every Republican I have heard express himself, think you in most respects proved yourself [Douglas's] superior." Nonetheless, the enthusiasm of his friends was tempered by their belief that Lincoln had not been sufficiently aggressive against "Dug" at Ottawa, and that he should be in an attack mode when he met the Little Giant at Freeport in the next debate.[27]

Believing that he needed advice on how to respond to the questions that Douglas had asked at Ottawa, Lincoln summoned Ebenezer Peck and Norman B. Judd of Chicago to meet and consult with him before the Freeport debate. He admonished them "to keep the matter to yourselves, and meet me at Freeport without fail."[28] Stirred to action, Peck and Judd hurriedly assembled three other Lincoln friends, including Joseph Medill of the *Chicago Press and Tribune,* and they met without Lincoln—evidently in Chicago—on the evening before the debate. When Lincoln arrived at Freeport the next day, Medill gave him a note outlining their suggested answers, which, however, he only partly followed in the debate. His friends mainly proposed "a few ugly questions" for Douglas, including how he could reconcile his "vaunted popular Soveignty [*sic*] in Territories since the Dred Scott decision" provided for the protection of slave property there. They also advised Lincoln not to "act on the defensive at all [or] refer to your past speeches. . . . Remember that you have good backing to day [in Freeport], and the more saucy you are the better. For once leave modesty aside. You are dealing with a bold, brazen, lying rascal & you must 'fight the devil with fire.' "[29]

The political festivities at Freeport, near the Wisconsin border, largely repeated the scene six days earlier at Ottawa. A crowd estimated at 15,000, mainly Lincoln supporters, descended upon the town. Most of the people came in crowded railroad cars from nearby northern towns as political delegations and clubs. One train arriving on the Galena and Chicago Union Railroad consisted of sixteen cars carrying more than a thousand people. They were on a mission to generate enthusiasm and rally support for their candidate. These partisans understood both the state and national implications of the senatorial contest, and they wanted to make the most of the opportunity that the debates provided to show the strength of their standard-bearer. For western people whose primary form of mass entertainment was attending large political gatherings, the Lincoln-Douglas debates had become the most exciting public event in their lives. As outlets for competitive spirit, political rallies were like today's football games between rival universities. The fan fervor was similar. Angry shouting and scuffles among partisans—more than a few intoxicated—frequently broke out and created moments of tension in the crowds. Fortunately, in the Lincoln-Douglas debates, when physical confrontations occurred, order was quickly restored.

Lincoln arrived by train in mid-morning at Freeport and reportedly was met by 5,000 enthusiastic supporters. Escorted to his lodgings at the Brewster House, he was called out on several occasions to make brief speeches to arriving delegations. At two o'clock Lincoln took a seat at the rear of a Conestoga wagon, drawn by six white horses, for the short trip to a large vacant lot behind the hotel. The Democratic press found the scene amusing. "Mr. L. was placed in or near the rear of the box on the wagon, and his legs extended forward several feet, and resembled the skeleton of some grey-hound," the local Democratic newspaper reported. "He is as queer looking as he is queer spoken. If [P. T.] Barnum could procure him in the style he so beautifully represented on his way to the stand from the Brewster House, then would Mr. L.'s fortune soon be made, for a more ridiculous and laugh-able show has never been presented to the American people."[30] Lincoln's long legs and awkwardness had become a favorite target of Democratic ridicule.

Lincoln opened the speaking at Freeport. Better prepared than he had been at Ottawa, he began by answering several "interrogatories" raised by Doug-las in the first debate. The Little Giant had asked whether Lincoln supported the Fugitive Slave Act. Lincoln answered, "I do not now, nor ever did, stand in favor of the unconditional repeal" of the law. However, he added, "I think it should have been framed so as to be free from some of the objections that pertain to it, without lessening its efficiency. . . . As we are now in an agita-tion in regard to an alteration or modification of the law, I would not be the man to introduce it as a new subject of agitation upon the general questions of slavery."[31] Lincoln's position on the act was consistent with what he had said earlier. However, many antislavery radicals in the audience, who not only demanded the law's repeal but also supported state personal-liberty leg-islation to prevent its enforcement, must have been dismayed by his answer.

Regarding Douglas's question about whether he opposed the admission of any more slave states, Lincoln answered that he "would be exceedingly sorry ever to be put in a position of having to pass upon that question." How-ever, "if slavery shall be kept out of the Territories," he said, and then the people "do such an extraordinary thing as to adopt a Slave Constitution, un-influenced by the actual presence of the institution among them, I see no alternative . . . but to admit them into the Union."[32] In this response, as in his response about the Fugitive Slave Act, Lincoln had expressed a conservative position, shrewdly taking an approach that was necessary to ensure the success of the state Republican party in 1858. He believed that the likelihood of a territorial convention approving a state constitution providing for slavery if no slaves had been permitted in the territory was remote. In conceding the point, Lincoln perhaps had the example of California in mind. The California convention, uninfluenced by the presence of slavery, had adopted a free-state constitution in 1849 that was approved by Congress as a part of the Compromise of 1850.

In his reply to Douglas's question about slavery in the national capital, Lincoln announced that he would be "exceedingly glad to see" the institution abolished there, provided the change was gradual, that it was approved by a majority of the District's voters, and that owners were granted compensation. This position was similar to his 1849 proposal for the emancipation of slaves in Washington. On the question raised by Douglas regarding the abolition of the interstate slave trade, Lincoln admitted that he had not given much thought to the issue: "I must say, however, that if I should be of opinion that Congress does possess the Constitutional power to abolish the slave trade among the different States, I should still not be in favor of the exercise of that power unless upon some conservative principle as I conceive it."[33] He did not explain what he meant by "some conservative principle."

Lincoln confidently told the Freeport crowd that he had defeated Douglas's intention in asking his questions. The senator, he explained, "had flattered himself that I was really entertaining one set of opinions for one place and another set for another place." In a statement that did not prove completely true when he went south, Lincoln declared, "What I am saying here . . . to a vast audience as strongly tending to Abolitionism" was the same as what he would say elsewhere in the state. He had mainly directed his conservative responses to old Whigs, especially in the central counties, who were virtually certain to read or hear about his Freeport speech. Reflecting this purpose, the *Springfield Illinois State Journal,* the main Republican newspaper in the central region, in several issues printed Lincoln's answers to Douglas's queries at Freeport. The column in each issue carried the heading "Lincoln Stands on the Old Whig Platform" and proclaimed it the same one that Henry Clay and Daniel Webster had supported.[34]

After completing his responses to Douglas's questions, Lincoln propounded his own "interrogatories" for "the Judge" to answer. The most famous of these questions was, "Can the people of a United States Territory, in any lawful way, against the wish of any citizen of the United States, exclude slavery from its limits prior to the formation of a State Constitution?"[35] In asking the question, Lincoln sought to show the contradiction between his opponent's advocacy of popular sovereignty and his approval of the Dred Scott decision providing for the right of slaveholders to take their slave property into the territories. Douglas's answer has become known as the Freeport Doctrine, and it has assumed widespread importance in American history.

The senator began his response by remarking, with exaggeration, that "Mr. Lincoln has heard me answer a hundred times from every stump in Illinois, that in my opinion the people of a territory can, by lawful means, exclude slavery from their limits prior to the formation of a State Constitution." Douglas explained that "it matters not what way the Supreme Court may hereafter decide as to the abstract question whether slavery may or may not go into a territory under the Constitution, the people have the lawful means to introduce it or exclude it as they please, for the reason that slavery cannot exist a day or an hour anywhere, unless it is supported by local police regulations." These regulations, he said, "can only be established by the local legislature, and if the people are opposed to slavery they will elect representatives to that body who will by unfriendly legislation effectually prevent the introduction of it into their midst. If, on the contrary, they are for it, their legislation will favor its extension. Hence, no matter what the decision of the Supreme Court may be on that abstract question, still the right of the people to make a slave territory or a free territory is perfect and complete under the Nebraska bill."[36]

In historical lore, the Freeport Doctrine won the senatorial election for Douglas because it separated him from the southern sympathizers in the Democratic party by demonstrating how the Dred Scott decision could be legally negated and slavery excluded from the territories if it was the will of the people. The doctrine, according to this interpretation, also divided the national Democratic party into northern and southern wings and ensured the election of a Republican for president in 1860, a purpose that Lincoln supposedly had in mind when he posed the question to Douglas. This explanation, however, ignores the fact that the Little Giant, as he acknowledged at Freeport, had earlier stated the substance of the doctrine in campaign speeches when asked how he could square popular sovereignty with the Dred Scott decision.[37] Furthermore, his opposition to the Lecompton constitution had already alienated him from the proslavery forces—a conclusion that Lincoln himself had earlier drawn—and made probable the sectional division of the Democratic party in the 1860 election, though it did not insure a Republican victory. Lincoln had written a friend on July 31, 1858, that Douglas "cares nothing for the South—he knows that he is already dead there." The senator's object, the Republican candidate insisted, was "to hold on to his chances in Illinois."[38] Douglas's plan, Lincoln believed, was to delude Illinois voters, particularly conservatives, into thinking that his popular-sovereignty strategy, which the Freeport Doctrine reaffirmed, would forestall slavery's ex-

pansion without the adoption of the Republican party's antislavery platform
or the election of its legislative candidates.

For many Illinois conservatives, Douglas's Freeport Doctrine, along with
his earlier opposition to the Lecompton constitution, tended to blur the profound differences between him and Lincoln over slavery. Many historians
have also failed to see these differences clearly.[39] But it was these differences,
both moral and political, that Lincoln sought to exploit at Freeport and elsewhere during the campaign. He argued that Douglas's position on slavery,
despite his clever attempt to reconcile the Dred Scott decision with popular
sovereignty, was a recipe for the expansion of slavery and a violation of the
Founding Fathers' promise of a free America. Lincoln wanted to make this
distinction clear in his often-ignored third and fourth "interrogatories" at
Freeport. He asked in number three: "If the Supreme Court of the United
States shall decide that States can not exclude slavery from their limits, are
you in favor of acquiescing in, adopting and following such decision as a rule
of political action?" In the fourth question, Lincoln asked Douglas if he was
"in favor of acquiring additional territory, in disregard of how such acquisition may affect the nation on the slavery question."[40] Both questions owed
their existence to Lincoln's repeated charge that Douglas and other national
Democrats, working through the instrumentality of the Supreme Court, conspired to expand and perpetuate slavery throughout the nation.

In his answer to the third question, Douglas emphatically denied that a
conspiracy existed to make slavery national, though he admitted that the
Washington Union, the newspaper organ of the Buchanan administration,
"did put forth that doctrine." "No such thing is possible," he declared.
"Mr. Lincoln's object" in making the charge, he added, was "to cast an imputation upon the Supreme Court" and its authority. (Lincoln later pointed
out that his opponent and national Democrats had no such qualms during
the Jacksonian period of the 1830s about criticizing the Supreme Court and
denying its authority.) With his northern Illinois audience in mind, Douglas
announced that a decision to nationalize slavery "would be an act of moral
treason that no man on the bench would ever descend to." Douglas remarked
that Lincoln's fourth question about future acquisitions of slave territories
was "very ingeniously and cunningly put." He responded to the question by
trumpeting American expansionism and asserting that he was in favor of acquiring more territory "without reference to the question of slavery." Douglas would leave "the people free to do as they please, either to make it slave
or free territory, as they prefer."[41] The senator ignored the part of question
four on how such territorial acquisitions would affect the sectional conflict
over slavery.

The Little Giant, instead of defending his own role in the slavery contro-versy, returned to his old political stock-in-trade tactic. This was a racist as-sault on the "Black Republicans" and Lincoln's ties to radicals like Owen Lovejoy and presumably to black spokesman Frederick Douglass. Douglas claimed that he had earlier seen Douglass in Freeport riding in a "magnifi-cent" carriage, driven by the white owner, with "a beautiful young lady" sit-ting outside on the box seat. The senator exclaimed to the Freeport crowd, "if you, Black Republicans" in the audience, "think that the negro ought to be on a social equality with your wives and daughters, and ride in a car-riage with your wife, whilst you drive the team, you have a perfect right to do so, . . . and of course will vote for Mr. Lincoln."[42] Republican newspapers denied that Lincoln or the state party had anything to do with Frederick Douglass or that the black spokesman had visited Freeport.

Douglas also renewed his charge that Lincoln and Trumbull "had formed a scheme to abolitionize the two parties and lead the Old Line Whigs and Old Line Democrats captive, bound hand and foot into the Abolition camp." "[Joshua] Giddings, [Salmon P.] Chase, Fred. Douglass and Lovejoy were here to christen them whenever they were brought in," the senator told the Freeport crowd.[43] As he did throughout the campaign, Douglas contended that Lincoln's House Divided Speech threatened a war between the North and the South.

The day after the Freeport debate, Lincoln went south to campaign in central Illinois before meeting the senator in the third debate at Jonesboro in Egypt. Large and exuberant crowds, resembling in enthusiasm those at Ottawa and Freeport, greeted the Republican contender wherever he spoke. At Bloomington, 6,000 people crowded into the square to hear him. The fact that "an imposing array of German Republicans" led Lincoln to the speaker's stand suggested that this important ethnic group was aligning with the Re-publicans.[44] He spoke for two hours or more in villages with names like Paris, Monticello, and Mattoon as well as in larger towns like Blooming-ton, Clinton, and Hillsboro.[45] Lincoln sought to satisfy his uneasy old Whig friends and other conservatives on the issue of black citizenship and rights without repudiating his support for the inherent equality of all people as ex-pressed in the Declaration of Independence. Furthermore, he attempted to reassure them that his House Divided Speech was not a call for a war on slavery against the South. From the fragmentary reports of these speeches that appeared in the press, it seems that Lincoln neither backed away from his earlier positions nor plowed new ground in his arguments.[46]

Except for his debate with Douglas at Jonesboro, Lincoln apparently made no speeches south of the small village of Highland below Edwardsville. Based on past election returns, Lincoln probably concluded that the southern third of Illinois was Douglas country and to campaign there would be a waste of valuable time. (See map on page 109.)

On the evening of September 14, Lincoln arrived in Jonesboro for the debate to be held the next day. In contrast to the people of Ottawa and Freeport, the citizens of Jonesboro had little enthusiasm for the debate. Jonesboro, a village of about 800 people in the heart of Egypt, had no railroad connection; the nearest station was at Anna about 2 miles away. The most excitement in the town occurred on the night before the debate when a brilliant comet appeared in the sky. Enthralled by the heavenly phenomenon, Lincoln sat with his friends for an hour or more in front of the small hotel watching the comet. Rumors had circulated that proslavery Kentuckians and Missourians planned to descend on the town and "put down" the "Black Republican" candidate. But no such incursion occurred.[47]

Only about 1,400 people braved the hot weather to attend the debate, which was held in a grove at the edge of town. About half of the audience favored Douglas, and the remainder divided about equally between Lincoln supporters and the Buchaneers.[48] The senator spoke first and mainly restated what he had said earlier in the campaign. As before, he charged that Lincoln and Trumbull had conspired to "abolitionize" the old parties and win seats for themselves in the Senate. Douglas announced that he now had evidence to support his charge. He read an extract from an 1856 speech by James H. Matheny, a Lincoln associate and groomsman in his wedding, who claimed that a deal had been struck between the two antislavery leaders for Lincoln to be elected senator in 1855 and Trumbull to obtain Douglas's seat in 1859. In his speech, Matheny angrily contended that Trumbull had broken the "bond" when he maneuvered to secure the Senate seat in 1855. Lincoln was thus, in a "most perfidious manner," cast aside. Douglas claimed that Lincoln, "after he was shoved off track . . . began to mope . . . until the Abolitionists coaxed and flattered him back by their assurance that he should certainly be a Senator in Douglas's place." The Matheny statement, which surprised Lincoln, clearly caused him discomfort when Douglas read it. A Republican reporter at Jonesboro wrote that Lincoln looked "as if he had not a friend on earth."[49]

The Little Giant in the Jonesboro debate continued his assault upon Lincoln and castigated the "Black Republican" party for its support for "negro" equality. Douglas declared that the Republicans—and Lincoln by extension—had a different platform on slavery and blacks for the northern and southern parts of the state. The senator asserted that in the northern districts Republicans had adopted resolutions demanding a prohibition on the admission of slave states to the Union, the unconditional repeal of the Fugitive Slave Act, the abolition of slavery in the District of Columbia, and an end to the inter-state slave trade. "All of these principles," Douglas charged, "aimed at a war-fare on the part of the North against the South." As the Republicans moved south, their principles, Douglas said, "became bleached and grew paler just in proportion as public sentiment moderated and changed in this direction." Members of the party "were Republicans or Abolitionists in the north, anti-Nebraska men down about Springfield, and in this neighborhood [Egypt] they contented themselves with talking about the inexpediency of the repeal of the Missouri Compromise" regarding slavery in the territories and refer to themselves as the "*free democracy.*"[50] Douglas ignored the fact that the state Republican platform, approved in Springfield in June, did not include the radical provisions that he claimed.

The Little Giant also shaded his position as he moved south, but Lincoln failed to take advantage of the inconsistency. At Jonesboro, Douglas vigor-ously defended the Dred Scott decision without mentioning his method (the Freeport Doctrine) for reconciling it with the principle of popular sover-eignty in the territories. In this bastion of southern rights and slavery sympa-thizers, Douglas avoided any reference to his assertion at Freeport that it would be immoral for the Supreme Court to render a decision legalizing slav-ery in the free states. He falsely claimed that Lincoln's support for black equality meant that Negroes should be given all of the rights of citizenship, a policy that Illinoisans strongly opposed. Continuing his criticism of Lin-coln's House Divided Speech, the Little Giant assured his Jonesboro audience that the Union could "exist forever divided into free and slave states as our fathers made it . . . if each state will carry out the principles upon which our institutions were founded, to wit: the right of each state to do as it pleases, without meddling with its neighbors." By acting on that principle, he said, "this Union will not only live forever, but it will extend and expand until it covers the whole continent, and make this confederacy one grand ocean-bound republic."[51] This position fitted in nicely with the state sovereignty and "manifest destiny" sentiments of the great majority of the people of Egypt; it also had a powerful appeal in central Illinois and to some extent in northern Illinois.

In his reply at Jonesboro, Lincoln sought to disarm the hostile audience by announcing, "There is very much in the principles that Judge Douglas has here enunciated that I most cordially approve." However, Lincoln mentioned only one point in which he agreed with the Little Giant: "that all the States have the right to do exactly as they please about all their domestic relations, including that of slavery." Lincoln criticized the senator for repeatedly plac-ing him in the wrong on the issue, "in spite of all that I can tell him."[52] Later, in 1859, Lincoln made the startling statement that "Massachusetts is a sov-

ereign and independent state." He did not mean that Massachusetts or any
state could flaunt the Constitution and laws of the United States, much less
exercise its sovereignty by seceding from the Union.[53] He meant that a state
had control over its domestic institutions—in the Massachusetts case, a proposed constitutional provision restricting foreign-born political participation. Still, Lincoln said he disapproved of the Massachusetts measure. At
Jonesboro, Lincoln refused to be goaded by Douglas into repeating his statements on black equality, thereby sidestepping the senator's contention that he
had become "bleached" on the issue when he moved south.

Lincoln, again in defense of his House Divided Speech, declared that the
specter of a sectional conflict had arisen because of the efforts of Douglas and
his associates to expand slavery. He reiterated, "When this government was
first established it was the policy of its founders to prohibit the spread of
slavery into the new Territories of the United States, where it had not existed." "But Judge Douglas and his friends," Lincoln declared, "have broken
up that policy and placed [slavery] upon a new basis by which it is to become
national and perpetual. All I have asked or desired anywhere is that it should
be placed back again upon the basis that the fathers of our government originally placed it upon. I have no doubt that it *would* become extinct, for all
time to come, if we but re-adopted the policy of the fathers by restricting it
to the limits it has already covered."[54]

In advocating this peaceful solution to the conflict over slavery, Lincoln
was overly sanguine. White southerners, including nonslaveholders, for a variety of reasons had become virtually united by the late 1850s in defense of
slavery, and they routinely denounced the antislavery "incendiaries" in the
North. While still largely supportive of the Union and the protection that the
Constitution gave to the institution, southerners would not tolerate any interference, whether local or national, with slavery in their states. The issue
had become so emotional that no southern candidate for the legislature or for
a state convention, which had the authority to regulate slavery and race relations, would dare to favor emancipation publicly, even by a gradual process
with compensation to the slaveholders and colonization for the freed blacks.
Even strongly Unionist East Tennessee opposed any movement toward abolition.

Lincoln mistakenly—and probably sincerely—thought that southerners
themselves would abolish slavery after it became clear that the institution
could not expand into fresh lands. He believed that slavery would then become an economic and social liability in their states and that the effort it
would take to retain it would become burdensome. Though the process of
eliminating the institution would take time, perhaps lasting into the twentieth century, Lincoln thought that his view would satisfy antislavery conser-

vatives and others in Illinois who opposed the radical policies of the Love-joy wing of the Republican party. This indirect approach to ending slavery would also appeal to those who were concerned about the expansionist slave power as well as to anyone concerned about a Republican party threat to sectional harmony. Lincoln and his Republican friends refused to face the hard reality that by the late 1850s, if not before, slavery's destruction depended upon armed intervention, a conclusion they finally reached during the Civil War. At Jonesboro and elsewhere in the 1858 campaign, Lincoln gave credence to the myth that slavery would eventually die out if it were prohibited from expanding. Even after the Civil War, some people continued to think that slavery would have died a natural death if expansion of the institution could have been prevented; in fact, this interpretation of history had considerable support between the world wars and still finds favor in some circles today.

The debate at Jonesboro was not always focused on important topics like slavery, however. Neither Lincoln nor Douglas was above pursuing personal matters that had little to do with the serious issues of the campaign. In concluding his rebuttal at Jonesboro, Lincoln took issue with the senator's claim in a speech at Joliet that he had trembled in his knees after the Ottawa debate and had to be carried from the platform. Lincoln read a newspaper report of Douglas's speech contending that his Republican opponent was "laid up" for seven days after the event while he consulted "with his political physicians"—Lovejoy and other leaders of the "Abolition party"—on how he should respond to the questions that he had been asked at Ottawa. Lincoln told his Jonesboro audience, "I have really come to the conclusion that I can explain [Douglas's account] in no other way than by believing the Judge is crazy. . . . There was not a word of truth in it." From his seat on the platform, Douglas shouted, "Didn't they carry you off [at Ottawa]?" Lincoln immediately shot back: "There; that question illustrates the character of this man Douglas, exactly," implying that the Judge did not know what had happened after the Ottawa debate and thus had given a false account in his Joliet speech. "I don't want to quarrel with him—to call him a liar—but when I come square up to him I don't know what else to call him."[55]

Though Lincoln scored some points against Douglas at Jonesboro, he did not win many converts to his cause; all of the counties in Egypt voted Democratic in the election. The next debate, at Charleston, Coles County, in east-central Illinois, would be far more important to Republican chances in the election. The area bordered Egypt and had been settled mainly by Kentuckians, including the Lincoln family. Most of the leading men were conservatives "of the old Henry Clay Whig stamp," many of whom had supported Fillmore in 1856.[56] In Coles County itself, 28 percent of the voters had cast their ballots for the former president in the 1856 election. By 1858, despite their concern about what they perceived to be the Republican party's radical tendencies regarding race and slavery, some of Lincoln's old Whig friends had organized the party in the area. Conservatives, including free-soil or anti-slavery Democrats as well as Fillmore men, were the swing voters who, Republicans reasoned, would determine the fall election in the district and perhaps also in the state. Lincoln needed to reassure these voters that he was no Attila the Hun hammering at the gates of the American Union and white supremacy.

In early afternoon, September 18, an enthusiastic crowd of between 12,000 and 15,000 people assembled at the Coles County fairgrounds in Charleston to hear the debate. Lincoln spoke first. After appealing to the partisan throng for "profound silence" so the speakers could be heard, Lincoln launched into a description of his views on black equality. Consisting of a long paragraph in his *Collected Works,* the statement would be Lincoln's most detailed pronouncement on the issue—and his most controversial. Lincoln began by explaining that he had not planned "to say much on that subject," but "at the hotel to-day an elderly gentleman called upon me to know whether I was really in favor of producing a perfect equality between the Negroes and white people. . . . As the question was asked me I thought I would occupy perhaps five minutes in saying something in regard to it." Despite his disclaimer that he had not intended to talk about the issue, Lincoln's decision to explain his view at Charleston owed a great deal to the increasing pressure on him in central Illinois to take a strong public stand against black equality. Many of his old Whig friends in this critical area of the state wanted some assurances that his endorsement of the Declaration of Independence's equality clause did not mean that he favored "a perfect equality" between the races. The elderly gentleman's question in the hotel, probably asked in the presence of others who also sought an answer, impelled Lincoln to reply in the debate.

Lincoln quickly came to the point. "I am not now, nor ever have been in favor of bringing about in any way the social and political equality of the white and black races," he announced. He continued:

I am not nor ever have been in favor of making voters or jurors of Negroes, nor of qualifying them to hold office, nor to intermarry with white people; and I will say in addition to this that there is a physical difference between the white and black races which I believe will for ever forbid the two races living together on terms of social and political equality. And inasmuch as they cannot so live, while they do remain together there must be the position of superior and inferior, and I as much as any other man am in favor of having the superior position assigned to

the white race. [Still,] I do not perceive that because the white man is to
have the superior position the Negro should be denied everything.

Lincoln went on to say that "because I do not want a Negro woman for a
slave I must necessarily want her for a wife. My understanding is that I can
just let her alone." He maintained that it "was quite possible for us to get
along without making either slaves or wives of negroes." Ignoring his support for the inherent equality of blacks that he had expressed in northern
Illinois, Lincoln claimed that he knew of no one in the state "who was in
favor of producing a perfect equality, social and political, between negroes
and white men." Furthermore, he said, "I do not understand there is any
place where an alteration of the social and political relations of the negro and
the white man can be made except in the State Legislature—not in the Congress of the United States—and as I do not apprehend the approach of any
such thing myself, and as Judge Douglas seems to be in constant horror that
some such danger [as black equality] is rapidly approaching, I propose as the
best means to prevent it that the Judge be kept at home and placed in the
State Legislature to fight the measure." According to an observer, "uproari-
ous laughter and applause" greeted Lincoln's remarks.[57]

The Republican candidate had struck the right racial chord with his Charleston audience. He had reassured many conservatives who heard and read his
speech that he was far from being a radical on the issue of black equality.
Lincoln, however, seemed uncomfortable in discussing what he considered a
moot question and an unnecessary diversion from the immediate issues of the
campaign—the expansionist designs of the slavocracy, aided and abetted by
the Democratic party and the "demagogue" Douglas. The threat posed by
national leaders like Douglas to the ideals of the Founding Fathers and to the
perpetuation of a united country was Lincoln's fundamental concern in the
election.

In the 1858 campaign, Lincoln's ambition for the Senate seat became
closely intertwined with his determination to defeat the political forces arrayed against the Republicans. Though his sharp denial of full equality for
freed blacks expressed a strong racist feeling—the harshest on his record—it
should be remembered that Lincoln could not appear to equivocate on the
issue in central Illinois. As he saw it, the political and, paradoxically, moral
stakes were too high for him to repeat in this critical area his belief that the
Declaration of Independence equality clause applied to blacks as well as
whites. Lincoln also had to demonstrate that he agreed on the issue with
former Whigs who were running for election to the legislature on a mild,
free-soil platform. These conservative Whigs had disavowed any association
with the "abolitionists" of northern Illinois. Simply put, the Republicans

needed their support to defeat Douglas. Continued public confusion in the central counties over the position of the party's standard-bearer could cost the Republicans control of the General Assembly and thus the senatorial election. After Charleston, despite his advocacy of black colonization until 1863, Lincoln never again made a blatant racist appeal. Indeed, after issuing the Emancipation Proclamation during the Civil War, Lincoln warmed to the notion that support for black equality went well beyond the theoretical principle expressed in the Declaration of Independence. Near the end of his life, he announced his support for black political rights, though he believed they should be qualified and enacted by the state Union governments in the South.[58]

Lincoln devoted the remainder of his hour at Charleston to an elaborate account of Senator Trumbull's charge that Douglas had plotted with proslavery forces in Congress in 1856 to prevent a vote by the people of Kansas on a state constitution, even though he claimed to support popular sovereignty and had made it the key element in his slavery policy. Though a modern audience might have walked out on this mind-numbing recitation, the crowd seemed delighted with Lincoln's detailed account of the Little Giant's presumed inconsistency.[59] Lincoln could reach oratorical heights when expressing the nation's republican and democratic ideals, as he had done at Bloomington in May 1856 and would do so again at Gettysburg in November 1863. But he could also descend into the dull and uninspiring language of a lawyer's brief in a complex legal case, as he did at Charleston in his effort to brand Douglas a proslavery conspirator against the voting rights of the people of Kansas.

In his response, Douglas feigned outrage that Lincoln had ignored "the political questions that now agitate the whole country." He denounced as "a lie" Trumbull's accusation that he had plotted to deny Kansans a vote on their constitution. The senator claimed that Lincoln's real purpose in repeating the charge was "to carry this election for the Black Republicans by slander, and not by fair means." "Mr. Lincoln's speech this day is conclusive evidence of the fact," he added.[60]

Douglas was not to be outdone by Lincoln in airing conspiracy accusations at Charleston. He repeated in detail his old charge that Lincoln and Trumbull had plotted to "abolitionize" the Whig and Democratic parties in the state in order to satisfy their ambition for the Senate. Douglas again tried to tie Lincoln to abolitionists whom, he said, two-thirds or more of the people of the state found highly objectionable. He accused Lincoln of vacillating on slavery and black equality depending on the political and social geography of the state. To please the radicals of northern Illinois, Douglas said, Lincoln had spoken in favor of black equality, but as he moved south, he had assumed a different position. The senator suggested that Lincoln's antiblack statement in the Charleston debate was only a political ploy to gain conservative support in central Illinois. He wanted to know where his opponent really stood on black citizenship and voting rights.[61]

On the defensive, Lincoln replied to Douglas that he did not favor black citizenship. He declared that even if the state of Illinois had "the power to make a negro a citizen under the Constitution of the United States," which it did not, according to the Dred Scott decision, "I should be opposed to the exercise of it." Furthermore, Lincoln denied the senator's claim that he had expressed "a very different cast of sentiment at the different points" in the state on black equality. "I will not charge upon Judge Douglas that he wilfully [sic] misrepresents me, but I call upon every fair-minded man to take these speeches and read them, *and I dare him to point any difference between my printed speeches north and south*." This denial was clearly a stretch of the truth by Lincoln—and he must have known it. As before, Lincoln at Charleston defended his House Divided Speech and rebutted Douglas's charge of a Trumbull-Lincoln conspiracy to "abolitionize" the Republican party and share the state's seats in the Senate.[62]

Republicans, especially in the central counties, praised Lincoln's performance at Charleston. Judge David Davis of Bloomington wrote him, "Your concluding speech on Douglass [sic] at Charleston was admirable," but admitted that radicals in northern Illinois had expressed concern about his strong rejection of black equality and his willingness to accommodate to the views of conservatives.[63] Lincoln, however, made believers out of some Democrats like Lew Wallace of nearby Indiana, a future Civil War general and author of the popular novel *Ben Hur* (1880). Wallace, who had favored Douglas, witnessed the debate and could not understand in the beginning how an "unattractive man" like Lincoln could be "the centre of regard by so many people" and compete with the renowned Little Giant on the stump. "I inwardly laughed" at Lincoln, he said, but ten minutes into Lincoln's speech, this changed: "I quit laughing. He was getting hold of me," Wallace reported. Wallace remembered that Long Abe's "voice was clear without being strong. He was easy and perfectly self-possessed." By the end of the speech, Lincoln had persuaded Wallace that slavery was a great threat to the republic and to freedom. The Indianan did not mention Lincoln's statement at Charleston denying that he favored black equality. Instead, he said: "While Mr. Lincoln had been the advocate of Freedom, Mr. Douglas, with all his genius for discussion, had not been able to smother the fact that he was indirectly and speciously acknowledging all the South claimed for slavery." Wallace came away wondering "how many of the unbelieving" like himself had been "converted to [Lincoln's] thinking" by the debate.[64]

The next debate, at Galesburg, did not take place until nineteen days after the Charleston event. Meanwhile, both candidates campaigned separately, but with Lincoln following Douglas to three speaking sites, Sullivan, Danville, and Urbana. Lincoln wrote a Danville friend, "My recent experience shows that speaking at the same place the next day after D. is the very thing—it is, in fact, a concluding speech on him."[65] Such a campaign tactic, however, not only invited renewed ridicule from the Democrats but also incited violent confrontations between passionate and sometimes intoxicated supporters of the two candidates. At Sullivan a brief melee broke out when a procession escorting Lincoln to the Republican rally attempted to march, with brass band blasting, through the grounds where the Little Giant was speaking.[66]

An immense crowd of as many as 20,000 poured into Galesburg in west-central Illinois on October 7 for the fifth debate between the senatorial contenders. Following the pattern established at Ottawa and Freeport, excursion trains brought numerous party delegations and clubs into the town; others arrived on horseback, in wagons and carriages, and on foot. Despite a fierce autumn wind that blew throughout the day, ripping apart many banners and signs, political excitement in Galesburg was high. This was Lincoln country, and banners predicted the triumph of "Long Abe," "the Living Dog," over "Douglas the dead Lion." Several inscriptions derided the Little Giant's earlier boast that he would "bring Lincoln to his milk" in southern Illinois. One banner proclaimed: "The dose of milk Abe gave Dug down in Egypt made him very sick."[67]

Douglas spoke first at Knox College, the site of the Galesburg debate. He devoted more than one-third of his one-hour speech to a defense of his Kansas-Nebraska bill and to his role in opposing the Lecompton constitution.[68] Douglas told his audience that the Republican party was the first political organization in American history that was not national. It was a sectional party whose leaders, he declared, appealed to northern passion and prejudice against the South. As he had done at Jonesboro and Charleston, Douglas charged that Lincoln's position on slavery and blacks was inconsistent, depending on the political geography of the state. Lincoln found it was "extremely difficult to manage a debate in the center part of the state, where there is a mixture of men from the North and the South," the senator said, while in the northern counties he had no problem in proclaiming the "Abolitionism" of Lovejoy and others of that ilk. Douglas declared that in the southern counties Lincoln had "nothing whatever to do with Abolitionism, or Negro equality, or Negro citizenship." The senator again denounced the doctrine of black equality as "a monstrous heresy" and repeated his opinion that the government created by the Founding Fathers "was made by white men for the benefit of white men and their posterity forever." Though the black man "ought not to be a citizen, it does not follow by any means that he should be a slave," he stated; instead, his status should be decided by the white people of the states and territories. Lest his comment suggested support for blacks, Douglas quickly reminded his audience that Illinois had already made its decision that "the Negro shall not be a slave, nor shall he be a citizen."[69]

Lincoln began his rejoinder at Galesburg by announcing that "a very long portion of the speech which the Judge has addressed to you has previously been delivered and put in print." Therefore, he saw no need to respond to most of the accusations that Douglas had expressed in his opening address. He could not, however, let several of his opponent's thrusts pass without challenging them. Having ignored the Declaration of Independence's equality creed in the south, Lincoln felt politically safe in his rebuttal to raise it again in the north. He charged that the Judge had slandered the authors of the Declaration when he insisted blacks were not included within the meaning of the document's equality clause. He argued that no American president, member of Congress, or "any living man upon the whole earth ever said" that the Declaration of Independence did not apply to blacks "until the necessities of the present policy of the Democratic party, in regard to slavery, had to invent that affirmation."[70] Such an assertion by Lincoln was surely a distortion of white racial attitudes in the early republic. Furthermore, no attempt had been made by the Founders of the republic to exclude slavery south of the Ohio River. After four years of grounding his antislavery arguments in what he perceived to be the intentions of the Founders, Lincoln probably had convinced himself of the Revolutionary generation's opposition to the expansion of slavery and its support for the inherent equality of blacks.

Richard J. Carwardine argued in his fine biography of Lincoln, published in 2003, that in the 1858 campaign the future president combined appeals to the Founders' natural rights philosophy with aspects of evangelical Protestantism.[71] However, in reality, Lincoln in his moral opposition to slavery at this time appealed to American history and the Declaration of Independence's natural rights philosophy, not to the Protestant or New Testament creed favored by evangelical abolitionists. Later, in the crucible of a devastating civil war, his moral aversion to slavery would converge with that of the northern Protestant clergy. He would view the institution as a violation of man's natural rights and a terrible offense against God. Lincoln came to believe that Providence had made him an instrument to end the inhumane institution and to purge America of this great sin.[72] Lincoln in 1858 might have viewed slavery as contrary to God's purposes, but he probably realized that an emphasis upon scriptural morality in his antislavery appeal would alienate immigrant groups who were already suspicious of the Know-Nothing, nativist element in the Republican party.

Lincoln informed his Galesburg audience that, despite Douglas's charge, he had been consistent during the campaign in his support for the fundamental equality of blacks. Declaring that he understood from the beginning his speeches "would be put in print and all the reading and intelligent men in the community would see them," Lincoln said that he had been careful to avoid "any conflict whatever between them. But the Judge will have it that if we do not confess that there is a sort of inequality between the white and black races, which justifies us in making them slaves, we must, then, insist that there is a degree of equality that requires us to make them our wives." Lincoln announced that he had "all the while [made] a broad distinction" on the issue and said that a reading "of the speeches will show that that distinction was made." While again contending that "a perfect social and political equality . . . was an impossibility," he affirmed that in the right to " 'life, liberty and pursuit of happiness,' as proclaimed in that old Declaration, the inferior races are our equals."[73]

As Douglas had insisted, Lincoln was not completely straightforward in claiming consistency in his position on black equality. Neither at Jonesboro nor at Charleston—nor in Republican rallies in central Illinois in which a record of his speeches exists—had Lincoln indicated his support for fundamental black equality. An exception was a tepid statement that he made near the end of his long speech at Springfield on July 17 when he argued that he stood by the Declaration of Independence's equality creed for all men. Still, at that time, Lincoln declared, "I do not understand the Declaration to mean that all men were created equal in all respects."[74] This remark had followed Douglas's criticism of the relatively strong position that Lincoln had taken on black equality at Chicago on July 10. Though Lincoln announced that he had not advanced "hypocritical, and deceptive, and contrary views in different portions of the country," he admitted that he was not "entirely free from all error in [his] opinions" on the issue.[75]

At Galesburg, Lincoln insisted that "the real difference between Judge Douglas and his friends, and the Republicans . . . is that the Judge is not in favor of making any difference between Slavery and Liberty. . . . Consequently every sentiment he utters discards the idea that there is any wrong in Slavery." The Little Giant "don't care whether Slavery is voted up or voted down." Lincoln declared that, in contrast, he belonged "to that class in the country who contemplate slavery as a moral, social and political evil, having due regard for its actual existence amongst us and the difficulties of getting rid of it in any satisfactory way, and to all the constitutional obligations which have been thrown about it." Unlike Douglas, he "look[ed] hopefully to the time when as a wrong it may come to an end."[76]

Despite his promise to avoid issues that earlier debates had covered, Lincoln could not resist pointing out again Douglas's unpersuasive effort to reconcile the Dred Scott decision with his popular-sovereignty doctrine for the territories. Lincoln revived the charge that unless the national elections went against the Democrats, the next Supreme Court decision on slavery would declare property rights in blacks to be national and perpetual. He claimed that by advancing his "don't care" policy regarding slavery, Douglas was "in every possible way preparing the public mind" for its permanence. Finally, Lincoln denounced the "Judge" for his support of the acquisition of more southern territory. Such a policy, he insisted, would give encouragement to American filibusters such as William Walker who at that time were trying to seize and spread slavery into Latin America, further inflaming sectional and political passion.[77]

The debates had reached a climax at Galesburg, and much that followed would be repetitious and a refinement and defense of earlier arguments. Before meeting Douglas at Quincy on October 13 for the sixth debate, Lincoln carried his campaign to west-central Illinois. Crowds of several thousand gathered at small communities like Oquawka and Monmouth to hear the Republican contender. While in the area, Lincoln crossed the Mississippi River and spoke for two hours to a large audience in Burlington, Iowa, where he was the guest of Republican Governor (and soon to be Senator) James W. Grimes. He spent the next day, a Sunday, at Grimes's home and prepared his speech to be delivered at Quincy.[78]

Arriving at Quincy on the morning of the debate, Lincoln received the now typical large escort to where he was staying, in this case the home of his friend Orville H. Browning. This west-central Illinois district had usually voted Democratic, but by only a small margin; Douglas had represented it in Congress during the 1840s. Lincoln and the Republicans hoped to win the area in 1858. As in many central counties, conservative Whigs, who generally had supported the American party in 1856, were the key to Republican success. The Lincoln procession in Quincy on the day of the debate reflected the Republican need to win the Whig vote. A raccoon—the symbol of the old party—was placed in front of the parade, and several banners and floats depicted Whig slogans. Not to be outdone by Lincoln enthusiasts, Douglas organizers had circulated handbills in Missouri calling on Democrats from this slave state to cross the Mississippi River and provide ardent support for their champion. Several river packets carried hundreds of Missouri and Illinois Democrats upriver to Quincy, and one boat brought a large Lincoln delegation downriver from Keokuk, Iowa. Partisans of both parties also crossed the Mississippi on ferries to hear the debate. Between 8,000 and 12,000 people crowded Quincy's public square for the afternoon debate. A near tragedy occurred before the speakers arrived when part of the speakers' stand collapsed; several people received minor injuries.[79]

Lincoln spoke first at Quincy. With area conservatives foremost in his mind, he insisted that he was no radical, despite the persistent efforts of the Democrats in the area to distort his record and brand him as an abolitionist and a promoter of sectional strife. Lincoln began by again denying the Little Giant's repeated charge that he had had a hand in the adoption of the radical resolutions approved by early state and local Republican meetings. He took aim at Douglas's frequent assertion that he was "guilty of a species of double-dealing with the public" in that he made "speeches of a certain sort in the North, among the Abolitionists," particularly at Ottawa, which he "would not make in the South," and vice versa. Lincoln insisted that his comments at Ottawa were "very nearly" the same as those "delivered by me down in Egypt" (he probably meant Charleston). However, he noted that "by some sort of accident," the reporters at Ottawa "passed over" his statement on black inequality, "and it was not reported."[80]

The Republican candidate's anger over Douglas's repeated misrepresentation of his record reached a boil in the Quincy debate. He had seethed over the Little Giant's charge, first expressed at Ottawa, that he and Trumbull had entered into a corrupt bargain to "abolitionize" the two old parties. Lincoln, whose honesty and consistency in what he said and in his dealings with others had always been of great importance to him, lashed out at his opponent for questioning his integrity in the debates. Douglas "impeaches my honor, my veracity and my candor, and because *he* does this, I do not understand that I am bound . . . to keep my hands off of him," Lincoln declared. Still, he informed his Quincy audience, "it really hurts me very much to suppose that I have wronged anybody on earth," and he hoped that at the end of the campaign the two men would "at least part without any bitter recollections of personal difficulties."[81]

The Republican contender reminded voters that the critical difference between the two parties in this election was that they took opposing views of slavery. "The Republican party," Lincoln exclaimed, "think it wrong—we think it is a moral, a social and a political wrong. We think it is a wrong not confining itself merely to the persons or the States where it exists, but that it is a wrong in its tendency, to say the least, that extends itself to the existence of the whole nation. Because we think it wrong, we propose a course of policy that shall deal with it as a wrong, . . . and so deal with it that in the run of time there may be some promise of an end to it." In remarks directed at antislavery conservatives in the Quincy area, Lincoln reiterated what he had said many times before: "We have a due regard to the actual presence of it amongst us and the difficulties of getting rid of it in any satisfactory way, and all the constitutional obligations thrown about it." He specifically mentioned that "we have no right at all to disturb it in the States where it exists." However, he declared, Republicans "go further than that" in accommodating to southern sensitivities. For example, "we don't propose to disturb [slavery] where, in one instance, we think the Constitution would permit us" to act—in the District of Columbia. Lincoln announced that in the case of the Dred Scott decision, though Republicans deplored it as a wrong, they did not oppose it "in any violent way." But "we propose so resisting it as to have it reversed if we can, and a new judicial rule established" that would prevent the extension of slavery into the territories and forestall the court's laying "the foundation for spreading that evil into the [free] States themselves."[82]

"The central idea of the Democratic party," Lincoln insisted at Quincy, was that slavery did not constitute a wrong. To support this point, he said that Douglas, the national leader of the party, had never said slavery was immoral. It could not be a wrong in the senator's mind, he charged, when he proclaimed that he "don't care whether slavery is voted up or voted down." Furthermore, he added, Douglas and other prominent Democrats claimed that there was no place where the evils of slavery should be discussed, whether in politics or the pulpit, in the South or in the North. Lincoln called on people who agreed with the Republicans "to stand and act with us in treating [slavery] as a wrong—then, and not till then, I think we will in some way come to an end of this slavery agitation."[83]

In his response, Douglas, despite Lincoln's proddings, refused to take a stand on whether slavery was morally right or wrong. He evaded the issue by declaring that "every state of this Union has a right to do as it pleases on the subject of slavery. In Illinois we have exercised that sovereign right by prohibiting slavery within our own limits. . . . It is none of our business whether slavery exists" in other states. Therefore, he did not choose to discuss "a question that we have no right to act upon."[84]

Douglas charged that Lincoln had failed to give straight answers to the questions that he had raised in the earlier debates. He wanted to know whether as a senator Lincoln would vote for the admission of any more slave states to the Union, even if the people (for example, in New Mexico) wanted slavery. Lincoln "would not answer my question directly, because up north, the Abolition creed declares that there shall be no more slave states, while down south, in Adams County [Quincy], in Coles, and in Sangamon, he and his friends are afraid to advance that doctrine. He gives an evasive and equivocal answer, to be construed one way in the south and another way in the north."[85] Douglas also repeated his jabs at Lincoln's House Divided Speech. The Little Giant risked some political support when he announced that if the slavery issue were let alone, "Mr. Lincoln will find that this republic can exist forever divided into free and slave states." By this time a large number of Illinois voters, even in the central counties, did not accept the chilling prospect that the institution might be perpetual, despite their willingness to accord southerners their constitutional rights regarding slavery.[86]

The day after the Quincy debate, both Lincoln and Douglas boarded the river packet *City of Louisiana* for Alton, the scene of the last debate. Arriving early in the morning on the day of the debate, October 15, Lincoln was joined by Mary, who had come on an excursion train from Springfield. The trip to Alton apparently was Mary's only campaign appearance outside of Springfield. A crowd estimated at between 4,000 and 6,000 attended the Alton debate, including several hundred from St. Louis, which was only 25 miles downriver. However, less hoopla preceded the speaking than in the earlier debates, with the exception of the one at Jonesboro. A reporter for the *Cincinnati Gazette* attributed the relative lack of enthusiasm to the fact that "the novelty had worn off and the full reports of the previous debates had partially satisfied the public curiosity. Little that was new could now be expected on either side."[87] Furthermore, both candidates had spoken earlier in the county, and by the time of the Alton debate farmers were busy harvesting and marketing their crops and unable to attend the event.

At Alton, the Little Giant clearly showed the effects of the long and grueling campaign. His energy was sapped; and he was also losing his voice. In conversations on the platform, he talked only in a whisper. When addressing the audience, Douglas managed to make himself understood only by the people in the inner circle of the crowd. Lincoln, in contrast, a man of greater physical strength and stamina, seemed energized by the intensity of the campaign and could be heard at the outer limits of the audience. A *New York Tribune* correspondent confidently reported that "if the intelligence and enlightened sentiment of the people shall prevail, then Mr. Lincoln is as sure to be successor of Mr. Douglas in the Senate of the United States as there is a sun in the Heavens, and the probabilities are now working very strongly in this way."[88] After the Alton debate, Lincoln also expressed "a high degree of confidence that we shall succeed" in the election.[89]

Lincoln had been buoyed late in the campaign by Senator Trumbull's vigorous canvass on behalf of the Republican legislative candidates. He assumed that Trumbull, a former Democrat who lived in Belleville, could swing important Democratic voters in the south-central area to the Republican cause. At least one prominent out-of-state Republican campaigned for Lincoln: Governor Salmon P. Chase of Ohio, also a former Democrat, spoke in Chicago to antislavery stalwarts. In addition, German Americans, who had earlier favored the Democrats because of their opposition to nativism, were falling in line behind Lincoln and the Republican candidates. In July, Lincoln had written Gustave P. Koerner, a native of Frankfurt-am-Main and a leading Republican of Belleville, encouraging him and Dr. Theodore Canisius to "set a plan on foot that shall gain us accession from the Germans, and see that, at the election, none are cheated in their ballots." Koerner took to the stump and later claimed to have spoken in every major town in the state. Canisius's *Alton Freie Presse,* which Koerner secretly owned, responded to Lincoln's plea by launching a vigorous newspaper campaign among the relatively large German population in the area. After the election, Canisius was brought to Springfield, where Lincoln financed the establishment of the *Illinois Staats-Anzeiger.*[90]

Important German American assistance to Lincoln and the Illinois Republican cause was also provided by twenty-nine-year-old Carl Schurz. A refugee from the revolutions of 1848–1849 in Germany, Schurz had arrived in America in 1852 and settled in Wisconsin. A vigorous advocate of democracy and an opponent of slavery, he joined the Republican party after its organization and soon found himself in great demand as a speaker in both German and English. In 1858, Schurz accepted an invitation by the state Republican committee to come to Illinois and campaign for the party. He spoke in Chicago and in the interior of the state, mostly to German audiences. Meeting Lincoln on the train to Quincy, he was "startled" by the future president's uninspiring appearance. "On his head he wore a somewhat battered 'stove-pipe' hat," Schurz later recalled. "His neck emerged, long and sinewy, from a white collar turned down over a thin black necktie. His lank, ungainly body was clad in a rusty black dress coat with sleeves that should have been longer. . . . His black trousers, too, permitted a very full view of his large feet." Schurz's first impression of Lincoln was similar to that of other strangers upon meeting him. "I had seen, in Washington and in the West, several public men of rough appearance," he wrote, "but none whose looks seemed quite so uncouth, not to say grotesque, as Lincoln's."[91]

After being received by Lincoln "like an old acquaintance," Schurz sat down with him on the train and they had a long conversation about the campaign. The Republican candidate, who was keenly aware of the importance of the dynamic young man to his campaign, probably talked about the German vote and Schurz's own role in securing it for the Republicans. Schurz was flattered by the fact that Lincoln repeatedly asked him his political opinion. He recalled that Lincoln "interspersed our conversation with all sorts of quaint stories, each of which had a witty point applicable to the subject in hand. . . . He seemed to enjoy his own jests in a childlike way, for his unusually sad-looking eyes would kindle with a merry twinkle, and he himself led in the laughter."[92] Though their cultural backgrounds were strikingly different, and Lincoln's politics were not radical like Schurz's, the German American saw something special and refreshing in Lincoln.

During the two weeks remaining in the campaign after the debate at Alton, Lincoln took to the stump with renewed vigor. He spoke to crowds in central Illinois that ranged from 2,000 at Dallas City to 8,000 at Bloomington. Though they could not vote, women, in the Whig tradition, turned out in relatively large numbers to parade, assist in the local arrangements, and hear Lincoln speak. At Carthage in Hancock County, 2,000 women were among the 6,000 people who attended a Lincoln rally on October 22. Altogether in the 1858 campaign, Lincoln made sixty speeches, seven of which were delivered in the rain.[93]

In a last-minute effort to sway undecided and wavering conservatives to vote Republican, Lincoln sought to demonstrate anew that his position on slavery coincided with that of Henry Clay.[94] He ignored the fact that his Whig hero, a Kentucky slaveholder, never really took a moral stand against the institution. Furthermore, unlike Lincoln, Clay had never claimed that the Declaration of Independence equality clause applied to blacks as well as whites. Old Whigs who remembered Clay's history of compromise on slavery were, to say the least, probably amused by Lincoln's effort, however conservative, to link their deceased champion with the Republican party's antislavery cause.

Lincoln's appeal to Illinois Whigs who had voted for Fillmore received a blow from a late October report in the *St. Louis Republican* (which, despite its name, leaned Democratic) that Senator John J. Crittenden of Kentucky had written Lincoln on July 29 expressing his support for Douglas. Earlier, Lincoln had complained to Crittenden, Clay's heir as the border-state Whig leader, that he had heard rumors that the senator was "anxious for the reelection of Mr. Douglas" and had promised "to write letters to that effect to [his] friends in Illinois." Lincoln warned Crittenden not to take a public position in the campaign, telling him that his Whig friends in the state "would be mortified exceedingly by anything of that sort from you." Crittenden in his July 29 letter promised not to write any statement for publication. But the Kentucky senator also informed Lincoln that he had privately written several old Illinois associates who had asked him for his preference in the election. In each case, Crittenden told Lincoln, he had praised Douglas because of his opposition to the Lecompton constitution.[95] Crittenden failed to mention, at least in his letter to Lincoln, his concern about the antislavery implications of the Republican candidate's success in the election.

Unfortunately for Lincoln, "a gentleman of St. Louis" saw a copy of the

July 29 letter that was in Crittenden's possession and informed the *St. Louis Republican* of its contents. On the eve of the election, the newspaper published the substance of the letter. Two days after the election, Lincoln wrote Crittenden lamenting that, though he did not blame him for the letter's disclosure, "the use of your name contributed largely" to his loss in the contest.[96] "The emotions of defeat," as Lincoln characterized his mood at the time, probably caused him to exaggerate the importance of Crittenden's letter in his loss. It was true that the letter hurt him in counties across the Mississippi where the *St. Louis Republican* circulated. But the issue of whether the Douglas press in the state's interior picked up on the report in time to give it wide circulation remains problematical. Lincoln admitted that he did not see a copy of it until two days before the election. Nonetheless, well before the election some old Fillmore Whigs knew of the Kentucky senator's support for Douglas and voted against Lincoln's candidates for the General Assembly.

The Democratic "colonization" of Irish voters in counties along and near the railroads created another concern for Lincoln on the eve of the election. In late September, Lincoln began receiving reports that immigrant Irish workers, who constituted a cheap labor force for the railroads, had been sent by the pro-Douglas officials of the Illinois Central Railroad to do "ballasting" work on the roadbed in several counties. This was a ruse, according to Lincoln's Republican informants. The real purpose, Republicans claimed, was to place Irish workers in communities where they could vote for Democratic candidates on election day.[97]

Lincoln in mid-October observed at first hand the "ballasting" ploy of another railroad company when he encountered "about fifteen Celtic gentlemen, with black carpet-sacks," at Naples in west-central Illinois. Local Republicans informed him that "about four hundred of the same sort were to be brought" into an adjoining county. Upset by what he saw and heard, Lincoln wrote Norman B. Judd, chair of the state Republican committee, that the party's candidates could be "over-run with fraudulent votes to a greater extent than usual." He told Judd that the Irish interlopers would appear at the polls, "swear to residence, and thus put it beyond our power to exclude them." They would be guilty of perjury, but it would be impossible to convict them because they would leave the county after the election. Lincoln had "a bare suggestion" for Judd on how this Democratic tactic might be turned to the advantage of the Republicans. "When there is a known body of these voters, could not a true man, of the *'detective'* class be introduced among them in disguise, who could, at the nick of time, control their votes?" he asked. "It would be a great thing," he added, "when this trick is attempted upon us, to have the saddle come up on the other horse." Lincoln expressed confidence that "if we can head off the fraudulent votes we shall carry the day."[98]

He was overly sanguine in believing that the "trick" could be turned against the Democrats. Irish American voters could not be so easily influenced to abandon their allegiance to Douglas's party and support Republican legislative candidates whom they believed were nativists. Lincoln himself doubted that most Irish American voters could be brought into the Republican ranks.

Lincoln from the stump imprudently denounced the colonization of "Celtic gentlemen" by the Democrats. In a speech at Meredosia, he reported his sighting of the Irish colonists at Naples. According to the Democratic *Jacksonville Sentinel,* Lincoln told his audience that the Irishmen "had been imported expressly to vote him down." The *Sentinel* and other Democratic newspapers immediately seized on Lincoln's charge and used it along with his support for black equality to stroke the racial prejudices of white immigrants. "Mr. Lincoln entertains a holy horror of all Irishmen and other adopted citizens who have sufficient self-respect to believe themselves superior to the negro," the *Sentinel* declared. "What right have adopted citizens to vote Mr. Lincoln and his negro equality doctrines down?" it derisively asked. The "Black Republican" candidate "would doubtless disfranchise every one of them if he had the power. His reference to the danger of his being voted down by foreigners was a cue to his followers . . . that under the pretext of protecting their rights, they should keep adopted citizens from the polls."

Lincoln's ill-advised comment, at least as reported by the partisan *Sentinel,* opened him to the false charge that he was a part of the old Know Nothing–Whig nexus. The *Sentinel* claimed that "an influential German," having heard Lincoln speak at Meredosia, had announced his support for the Democrats, and another local German leader "expressed the opinion that Mr. Lincoln was a know-nothing." Though Lincoln had blundered in publicly accusing the Democrats of "colonizing" Irish immigrants in the state, it was only a minor misstep. It came late in the campaign when almost all of the voters had already made up their minds on the candidates. Most German Americans, having escaped oppression in Europe, supported the antislavery candidates despite their uneasiness in voting with nativists in the Republican party.[99]

Lincoln ended his campaign on October 30 with a long and forceful speech at a huge Republican rally in Springfield. In an emotional appeal to his neighbors, he reaffirmed his position on the issues and made a rare personal statement. "I have borne a laborious, and, in some respects to myself, a painful part in the contest," he told his friends. "Through all, I have neither assailed, nor wrestled with any part of the constitution. The legal right of the Southern people to reclaim their fugitives I have constantly admitted. The legal right of Congress to interfere with their institution in the states, I have constantly denied. In resisting the spread of slavery to new teritory [*sic*], and with that, what appears to me to be a tendency to subvert the first principle of free government itself my whole effort has consisted." Despite what had been charged, even by old friends, he said, "I have labored *for,* and not *against* the Union. As I have not felt, so I have not expressed any harsh sentiment towards our Southern bretheren [*sic*]. I have constantly declared, as I really believed, the only difference between them and us, is the difference of circumstances." Lincoln added that he had "cultivated patience, and made no attempt at a retort" to those who had "bespattered" him "with every imaginable [*sic*] odious epithet."[100]

In a remarkable bit of self-revelation for a man whom historians have judged reluctant to reveal his inner self and motivations, Lincoln denied that personal ambition was a primary consideration in challenging Douglas.[101] "God knows how sincerely I prayed from the first that this field of ambition might not be opened," he declared. "I claim no insensibility to political honors; but today could the Missouri [line] restriction be restored, and the whole slavery question replaced on the old ground of 'toleration' by *necessity* where it exists, with unyielding hostility to the spread of it," he would "gladly agree, that Judge Douglas should never be *out,* and I never *in,* an office" as long as both of them lived.[102] But as Lincoln had frequently said, one cannot prove a negative, in this case that he never would have opposed the Little Giant during the 1850s if Douglas had not introduced his popular-sovereignty doctrine for the territories. After all, Lincoln and Douglas had long been leaders in competing state political parties—Whigs and Democrats— and had clashed over partisan issues stretching back into the 1830s. Young Lincoln, as Douglas Wilson and other scholars have written, was ambitious for political distinction and, by his own admission, had early set his sights on the U.S. Senate seat that the Democrats had held. (Trumbull was an anti-Nebraska Democrat when elected to the Senate in 1855.)

It is reasonable to assume that at some point during the 1850s, Lincoln would have challenged Douglas even if the latter had not reopened the slavery controversy in the territories, though without the moral fervor and determination that the issue of slavery's expansion provided him. It is also reasonable to believe that Lincoln was honest in his statement at Springfield in October 1858 that personal ambition was not the most compelling motivation for him in opposing the Little Giant. His differences with Douglas over the moral aspects of slavery and the threat that the institution posed to the republic of the Founding Fathers had become increasingly important to Lincoln during the mid-1850s, climaxing in the senatorial campaign. His outrage at Douglas's moral neutralism on slavery, and his concern that Democratic policies, including the Dred Scott decision, were rapidly leading to the perpetuation of the institution, became a powerful force in his desire to defeat Douglas, whom he also considered an unscrupulous demagogue.

Despite the radical implication of his House Divided Speech, Lincoln sought throughout the 1858 campaign to demonstrate his fundamental conservatism on slavery, which in part could be traced to his earlier Whig conservatism. His repeated calls for the continuance of the abominable Fugitive Slave Act were designed to some extent to distinguish him from the radical wing of the Republican party. Lincoln's moral concerns regarding the law became submerged in his long-standing conservative commitment to its enforcement on constitutional grounds as well as on the need for northerners to retain southern goodwill. Political necessity in Illinois also dictated Lincoln's support for the Fugitive Slave Act. Still, unlike Douglas, Lincoln expressed the hope that the law would be amended to provide protection for free blacks and others caught up in the web of its enforcement. He believed that Republican success in the Illinois elections in November would be an important step in this direction.

Lincoln's political standing grew over the course of the campaign, particularly in the American West. Some of his western friends heralded his emergence and the national implications for him and his party if he won. "Mr. Lincoln's efforts in this canvass have made for him a splendid national reputation," the *Chicago Press and Tribune* announced four days before the election. "Identified all his life long with the old Whigs party, always in a minority in Illinois, his fine abilities and attainments have necessarily been confined to a very limited sphere," this emerging western newspaper declared. "He entered upon the canvass with a reputation confined to his own state—he closes it with his name a household word wherever the [Republican] principles he holds are honored, and with the respect of his opponents in all sections of the country." The *Press and Tribune* announced that even if "Mr. Lincoln shall fail of an election to the Senate, his fame is already secure."[103]

But for the moment, Republican concern was for a victory in Illinois, one that would give the party control of the General Assembly, defeat Douglas, and send Lincoln to the U.S. Senate, where he could fight against those who sought to expand and perpetuate slavery in America. Republican success would probably remove Douglas from the presidential sweepstakes and deal a blow in the free states to the Democratic senator's insidious "don't care" policy regarding slavery and his illusory popular-sovereignty doctrine for the territories. The Little Giant's defeat would drive an even larger wedge into

Democratic ranks and make a Republican victory in the 1860 election more likely.

A cold, steady rain fell on election day, November 2, turning many prairie roads and streets into quagmires. In some areas, farmers could not get to the polls. Still, the turnout was 13,000 more voters than in the presidential contest of 1856. Illinoisans realized that much of the nation was anxiously awaiting their decision at the polls.

When the votes were counted, Republicans had won the state offices of treasurer and superintendent of public instruction, the only statewide contests decided in the election. They polled 125,430 votes to 121,609 for Douglas Democrats and 5,071 for Buchanan Democrats. But Lincoln had lost his bid for the Senate. Douglas candidates captured fifty-four seats in the legislature to Lincoln's forty-six. Democrats won most of the central districts, including Sangamon, Lincoln's home county. Contributing to Douglas's victory was the fact that Democrats already held eight of the thirteen state Senate seats that were not subject to election in 1858. As expected, Republicans won all of the northern Illinois counties and, conversely, lost all of the counties in Egypt.[104] Democrats also captured five of the nine seats in Congress. In other northern states, however, Democrats suffered severe losses in the congressional elections. Many of these losses occurred in the battleground states of the lower North and in New York, increasing Republican prospects for a victory in the 1860 presidential contest.[105] These victories brought little comfort to Lincoln and Illinois Republicans.

Though Douglas had been wounded by the Kansas-Nebraska bill and its aftermath, he had recovered much of his political influence among Illinois Democrats with his Freeport Doctrine. Douglas's position, however contrived his argument, seemed to favor a middle ground on the territorial issue, one that would avoid the presumed radicalism of the Republicans and the proslavery demands of the South. Many ultraconservative Whigs and Know Nothings, fearing the implications for the Union of Lincoln's House Divided Speech, agreed and reluctantly voted for the legislative candidates of their old adversary, Douglas. Nonetheless, the Republicans garnered more statewide votes than the Democrats, clearly suggesting that Lincoln's conservative antislavery strategy was working and that his party was on track to win control of Illinois.

The Democrats preferred to see only a silver lining in the election. They trumpeted the Little Giant's success and gloated over the defeat of the "Black Republican" contender. The *Springfield Illinois State Register* proclaimed: "The efforts of combined abolitionism and traitorous democrats have failed to defeat . . . the noble champion of sound democratic principles." This newspaper was especially pleased that "the old whig stronghold" in the central

counties "did sad work for Mr. Lincoln and his new friends. The old whigs
would not be 'merged' " with the abolitionists of northern Illinois.[106] Douglas
himself hailed his triumph over "the combined forces of the Abolitionists
and the federal [Buchanan] office holders."[107]

Illinois Republicans naturally sought explanations for their defeat. They
did not blame Lincoln, who, as one supporter expressed it, "has done [his]
duty nobly." Like Henry Clay, Lincoln was "too good and Great to advance."[108] Republicans placed some blame on "the railroad interest" that had
"colonized" Irish Democratic voters in doubtful districts. A Pike County Republican complained that the colonization of Irish in his district had increased the Democratic vote by more than 4,000, probably an inflated number. Others charged that the Douglasites had bought votes and dispensed
whiskey to carry the election in their communities, a tactic that the Republicans used on a smaller scale. Judge David Davis bitterly wrote Lincoln that
the defection of Theophilus Lyle Dickey, and Senator Crittenden's letter supporting Douglas, had influenced "the Pharisaical old Whigs in the Central
counties, who are so much more righteous than other people," to vote Democratic.[109]

Many Republicans, including Lincoln, believed that the arbitrary apportionment of legislative seats had favored the Democrats and contributed to
their failure to win a majority in the new General Assembly. Some Lincoln
biographers have also partly blamed Democratic reapportionment for the future president's defeat.[110] But the Republican party did not exist in 1852
when the apportionment bill was enacted, and in 1854 the anti-Nebraska
(antislavery) coalition had won control of the state legislature and elected
Trumbull to the Senate. It is debatable whether legislative apportionment
played a decisive role in Lincoln's defeat. Democrats had only a slight advantage in the distribution of seats; the apportionment might not have made a
difference on a joint ballot in the General Assembly. As expected, Douglas
men in the legislature, with an eight-vote majority, reelected their leader to
the Senate in early 1859.[111]

Finally, some Republicans blamed Horace Greeley and eastern party leaders for their candidate's defeat, saying they had blurred the distinction between the senator and Lincoln by identifying Douglas with the antislavery
cause. Even after the election, Illinois Republicans noted that Greeley's *New
York Tribune* focused its attention on Douglas's "hard-won, brilliant, conclusive triumph" and ignored Lincoln's superb contribution to the success of
their state ticket. William H. Herndon reflected this anger when he wrote an
eastern friend: "Greeley never gave us one single, solitary, manly lift. On the
contrary, his silence was his opposition. This our people felt." Greeley, Hern-

don concluded, "is a natural fool," a sentiment that Lincoln probably shared with his partner.[112]

Lincoln, understandably, keenly felt the loss. He lamented to a friend that in his home county, as well as other areas of central Illinois, "nearly all the old exclusive silk-stocking whiggery is against us. I do not mean nearly all the old whig party; but nearly all of the nice exclusive sort." He explained that "there has been nothing in politics since the Revolution so congenial to their [Whig] nature, as the present position of the great democratic party."[113] In expressing his disappointment with his old friends, Lincoln probably exaggerated the class division among the Whigs in the election. After all, a number of "silk-stocking" Whigs in the area, including John T. Stuart and James H. Matheny, both leaders in the 1856 Fillmore movement, had cast their lot with Lincoln in 1858. Furthermore, many Whig voters, especially natives of Kentucky and other southern states, regardless of class, agreed with Democrats that the Republican party was a dangerous antislavery organization and that Lincoln's inflammatory House Divided Speech suggested a sectional war over slavery.

In the aftermath of his defeat, Lincoln wrote a friend that, "though I now sink out of view, and shall be forgotten, I believe I have made some marks which will tell for the cause of civil liberty long after I am gone."[114] He took some solace in the fact that the Republicans garnered more votes than Douglas's party had in the statewide election and that he would have won if the Senate election had been based on popular votes. "We have some hundred and twenty thousand clear Republican votes," he wrote Norman Judd. "That pile" of votes, he said, was "worth keeping together" because it would elect a state treasurer two years hence. "In that day," he predicted, "I shall fight in the ranks, but shall be in no ones [sic] way for any of the places." He added that he was "especially for Trumbulls [sic] reelection" in 1860.[115] He probably meant for that last statement to reassure Trumbull that he posed no threat to him, expecting that Judd would tell him what he had written. Such an assurance would also reduce the fears of former Democrats about an old Whig domination of the Republican party.

After the grueling senatorial contest, Lincoln in late 1858 and early 1859, out of financial necessity, turned his attention to earning money. He had ended the campaign in debt. As he reported to Judd, "I have been on expenses so long without earning any thing that I am absolutely without money now for even household purposes."[116] He threw himself back into his law practice, perhaps with a temporary sense of relief to be free from the pressure of political conflict, as had been the case after his retirement from Congress in 1849. Lincoln's holiday from politics again would be brief. The Springfield lawyer was no longer merely a state and local politician. He was a rising Republican star in the West who had been thrust into the galaxy of national politics, and he would be in great demand to speak and aid his party outside as well as inside Illinois. Despite his misgivings immediately after the election, Lincoln would soon accept the reality and the promise of his new political position; and his ambition to advance his party's cause and his own prospects would be rekindled in a dramatic way. In retrospect, the cauldron of Illinois politics, in which his political instincts had been honed—highlighted by the extraordinary senatorial campaign of 1858—had prepared Abraham Lincoln well for the unprecedented role that he would play on the American political stage.

REPUBLICAN CHAMPION OF THE GREAT WEST

TWO DAYS AFTER THE 1858 senatorial election, the small-town *Lacon Illinois Gazette* emblazoned its editorial column with the words "Abraham Lincoln for President in 1860." The *Gazette* editor, Jeriah Bonham, exuberantly announced that Lincoln deserved the Republican nomination because of "the masterly manner in which he conducted the [late] canvass," a performance that "has attracted the attention of the whole country . . . and marks him as the leading statesman of the age."[1] On November 5, a day after Bonham's editorial appeared, a meeting of Republicans in Mansfield, Ohio, also proclaimed their support of Lincoln for president.[2] In December, the *Reading* (Pennsylvania) *Journal* declared that, though unsuccessful in the senatorial campaign, "Mr. Lincoln has made for himself a reputation as a great statesman and popular debater, as extensive as the country itself." Lincoln's name, the *Journal* announced, "has been mentioned in various parts of the country in connection with the highest post in the gift of the people. . . . At the proper time, his friends should present an unbroken front for the ablest statesman of the West, and the East will delight to honor the man whose integrity and adherence to principle are as proverbial as his mental endowments have rendered conspicuous in the brilliant canvass through which he has now just passed."[3]

Illinois Republicans happily noted the national acclaim that Lincoln received, including in remote New England and upstate New York communities. Young Horace White, who had reported the 1858 campaign for the *Chicago Press and Tribune,* confidently wrote Lincoln: "Your popular majority in the state will give *us* the privilege of naming our man on the national ticket—either President or Vice Pres't. Then, let me assure you, Abe Lincoln shall be an honored name before the American people."[4] From Washington, Illinoisan Josiah M. Lucas informed Lincoln, with prideful overstatement, that "many of the leading papers of the country" were proclaiming him "the leading spirit of the great west," adding, "Such sentiments I find not only in the press, but also amongst the Politicians of all classes and shade of party."[5] In late December, Jesse W. Fell of Bloomington, Illinois, secretary of the state Republican central committee, returned from a trip to the East and reported to Lincoln, also with apparent exaggeration, that "everywhere I hear you talked about." Republicans, Fell told Lincoln, praised his brilliant performance against Douglas and wanted to know more about him.[6]

Encouraged by such reports, several Lincoln friends held a meeting on January 6, 1859, in the library of the state capitol. There they discussed a proposal "to bring out Abraham Lincoln as a candidate for President."[7] Lincoln, who was present, immediately objected; he questioned his fitness for the presidency, a sentiment that he might have believed at the time. Whatever they thought about Lincoln's qualifications for national leadership, Republicans at the meeting knew that an announcement of their support for his candidacy would be premature. It could backfire and likely undercut any future movement to promote him for the presidency. Such a push, Lincoln's associates concluded, would be viewed by the party faithful, many of whom in 1859 had other candidates in mind, as unseemly and opportunistic coming so soon after the 1858 senatorial campaign and their friend's emergence from relative obscurity. On March 29, 1859, the *Chicago Press and Tribune,* whose editors were friends of Lincoln's, made it clear to Illinois Republicans that "the day for the nomination of the Republican candidate has not yet arrived. There is harm in premature discussion. The hour and the man will come together" at the right time.[8]

Though Lincoln had gained national exposure in his debates with Douglas, and despite claims of his widespread popularity, the Springfield lawyer had not yet attracted presidential attention in the major eastern Republican newspapers. Several candidates, including presumed frontrunner William H. Seward of New York, had already been put forward for the presidency by eastern Republicans. Indeed, the Republican *New York Times,* which was beginning to challenge Greeley's *New York Tribune* and the *New York Herald* for circulation in the region, seemed willing to endorse Douglas for the office. This newspaper concluded, notwithstanding contrary evidence, that the Little Giant's position was essentially the same as that of most Republicans and that his candidacy on an antislavery platform would guarantee the party's success in 1860.[9]

Meanwhile, Lincoln, though temporarily demoralized by his defeat for the Senate, took steps in Illinois to keep the issues of the 1858 campaign before the people. He also sought to maintain his leadership of the state party, keep Republicans from backsliding, and work for the defeat of the Democrats in 1860. Out of a sense of historical interest, or for his own reference in future campaigns—probably both—Lincoln began soon after the 1858 election to collect materials for a scrapbook on the campaign. He secured copies of his speeches from the *Chicago Press and Tribune* and of Douglas's from the *Chicago Times,* the Democratic newspaper that had covered the debates. With mixed results, Lincoln also wrote local politicians for their speeches.[10] In

March 1859, he decided to seek a publisher for the scrapbook, but with the stipulation that he would not receive any profits from it.[11]

Convincing someone to publish the scrapbook proved much more difficult than Lincoln had anticipated. Sufficient interest in its publication did not materialize until his successful speaking campaign in Ohio before the fall 1859 election in the state. After the election, the Ohio Republican central committee and prominent Buckeye Republicans, such as Governor-elect William Dennison, sensing the scrapbook's importance as a campaign document for 1860, secured Lincoln's approval for its publication by the state party at the committee's expense. Lincoln told the Ohio Republicans that he wanted "the whole to be accurately done, but especially let there be no color of complaint, that a word, or letter in Douglas' speeches has been changed."[12]

The book finally saw the light of day shortly before the Republican national convention in May 1860. It probably served to bring Lincoln to the greater attention of the delegates to the convention and in a small way helped to secure his nomination for president, though he hardly had this purpose in mind when he launched the project. Published by Follett, Foster and Company of Columbus, Ohio, the book became a best-seller after Lincoln's nomination. By mid-June, 30,000 copies had been sold, and by the end of the year the book had gone through four printings.[13]

Despite Lincoln's efforts to do justice to Douglas's speeches, the senator, after seeing the book, protested "against the unfairness of this publication, and especially against the alterations and mutilations in the Reports of my speeches." "The original reports as published in the Chicago Times," he told the publishers, "altho' intended to be fair and just, were necessarily imperfect and in some respects erroneous." Douglas complained that, unlike Lincoln, he did not have an opportunity to revise and correct his copy before publication.[14] Actually, in compiling the book, Lincoln had made only typographical corrections to the *Press and Tribune*'s copies of his speeches. Furthermore, in fairness to Douglas, Lincoln had deleted the parenthetical references to applause by his supporters.[15] The Illinois senator's real concern was that Lincoln had gotten the jump on him in the publication of campaign material and that the book would demonstrate that the Republican contender had won the debates.

Lincoln had learned from experience that personal contacts with party leaders and activists provided a more effective means than the printed word in securing political influence. Throughout 1859, he maintained an active correspondence on political matters with Senator Lyman Trumbull and other Illinois Republicans. Lincoln knew that his leadership of the Illinois party and Republican unity depended on his having a good relationship with Trumbull, who represented the old Democratic wing of the state's antislavery coa-

Chapter Six

lition. The two men had been political adversaries before 1854 and had never been intimate. Their relationship was almost strictly political. Trumbull's controversial election to the Senate over Lincoln in 1855 created lingering antagonism among friends of the two men. (After the election, Mary Lincoln, but not her husband, never again spoke to Trumbull's wife Julia, an old friend and bridesmaid at her wedding.[16])

As was true in most northern state parties during this period of political transformation, age-old factional rivalries and suspicions threatened Republican unity in Illinois. Factionalism could also hamper Lincoln's rise to national prominence. His chances for the Republican nomination hinged on a unified state party committed to backing him at the national convention. Splits along old Whig and Democratic party lines, especially in the powerful Chicago Republican organization, could undermine any hopes he might have for an endorsement by the state Republican convention, which was scheduled to meet before the national convention. A spillover of Chicago factionalism into other areas of the state could also occur and negate the gains that the state Republican party had made in 1858.

The Chicago conflict erupted in December 1858 when the popular but erratic "Long John" Wentworth began a series of articles in his *Chicago Democrat* (a Republican paper) attacking Norman B. Judd, chair of the state Republican central committee, and other former Democrats in the party hierarchy. He claimed that the Judd faction had not worked hard enough for Lincoln in his campaign against Douglas because of past political differences. Wentworth also revived the old charge that Judd in 1855 had conspired against Lincoln to win the Senate seat for Trumbull; in addition, he accused Judd of corruption. Though Long John was a former Democrat, the assault on Judd and associates, including the editors of the rival *Chicago Press and Tribune,* dealt more with the struggle for Republican supremacy in Chicago than with a division between old Whigs and old Democrats. Judd wrote Trumbull informing him of Wentworth's first article and declaring that his adversary was motivated by a hatred of "both yourself and Lincoln"; he added, however, that Wentworth's "policy" was "to conceal his dislike of Lincoln" by reopening old political wounds. Trumbull saw the attack as a back-door assault on him by Wentworth's former Whig supporters, two of whom, Judge David Davis and William Herndon, were close Lincoln associates. Trumbull wrote Lincoln complaining that Long John's purpose was "to stir up bad feeling between Republicans who were formerly Whigs, & those who were Democrats; and more especially to create prejudice against myself and the Democratic portion of the party." He told Lincoln that "friends like you and I should not permit any person whatever his motive to stir up un-

Norman B. Judd, former Democrat and controversial chairman of the Illinois Republican central committee. Judd became a close associate of Lincoln and nominated him for the presidency at the national convention of 1860. Courtesy of the Abraham Lincoln Library and Museum, Harrogate, Tennessee.

founded suspicions and bad feelings between our friends," and he suggested that both of them act to prevent it.[17]

Stunned by Trumbull's letter, Lincoln immediately wrote the senator and expressed his dismay at the possibility that the Chicago feud could cause a major breach just when the party seemed poised to win control of the state. He assured Trumbull that, though he had not read Wentworth's articles, "any effort to put enmity between you and me, is as idle as the wind. I do not for a moment doubt that you, Judd, [Burton C.] Cook, [John M.] Palmer, and the republicans generally, coming from the old democratic ranks, were as sincerely anxious for my success in the late contest, as I myself, and the old whig republicans were." Lincoln also reaffirmed an earlier promise to Trumbull. "Beyond all possible cavil," he told the senator, "you can scarcely be more anxious to be sustained two years hence" for reelection to the Senate "than I am that you shall be so sustained. I can not conceive it possible for me to be a rival of yours, or to take sides against you in favor of any rival." Lincoln promised that he would work to prevent any division between "the old democratic and whig elements in our party."[18]

Nonetheless, Lincoln, ever cautious in such personal and factional matters, was reluctant to intervene in the dispute between Wentworth and Judd. He found himself in a difficult political situation. Although Herndon and other close friends took the side of Wentworth, the main troublemaker in the affair, Lincoln knew that Judd had become an important ally and one that he could not offend because of his ties to Trumbull. For a time, he tried to avoid involvement in the feud, hoping that it would go away. However, by late 1859, the conflict, fueled by almost daily editorial sniping in the Chicago newspapers, had virtually careened out of control. Lincoln's presidential aspirations clearly were now at stake.

When Judd filed a libel suit for damages against Wentworth, both men called on Lincoln to sustain them. Wentworth cleverly asked the Republican leader to defend him in court, which Lincoln refused to do. He also demanded that Lincoln put down the Judd faction in the party.[19] Judd likewise told Lincoln that "there is only one mode of replacing [restoring?] the harmony of the party, and that is John Wentworth is to be driven out or silenced" and his "lying associates kicked into the kennel with the rest of the curs. The first branch I will undertake and the last belongs to you and your friends." The fiery Judd soon regretted the implied threat in his letter. Ten days later he wrote Lincoln that he did not find fault with him, explaining that at the time he had been overwrought by the "effects of the falsehoods."[20]

Lincoln replied with a soothing message, probably hoping that Judd would send the letter to his friend Trumbull. He assured Judd that he did not believe Wentworth's charge that he had intrigued against him in 1855. Furthermore, "I do not understand Trumbull & myself to be rivals. You know I am pledged to not enter a struggle with him for the seat in the Senate now occupied by him; and yet I would rather have a full term in the Senate than in the Presidency." Lincoln clearly favored Judd over the ambitious and volatile Wentworth.[21] Meanwhile, Lincoln asked for and obtained a letter from three prominent Chicago businessmen and old-Whig Republicans requesting a statement from him testifying to Judd's loyalty and his faithfulness to his duties as chair of the state committee. Lincoln shrewdly took this roundabout way because, as he explained to Judd, "I would rather not seem to come before the public as a volunteer" for the statement; he wanted to retain the mantel of neutrality in the affair.[22] After Judd complained about Herndon's attacks on him, Lincoln also secured a promise from his law partner to cease his criticism.[23]

Concerned that Judd's libel suit would result in an irreparable division in the party at the highest level, state Republicans by late 1859 demanded that Lincoln take a more direct role in settling "the war of the Roses" in Chicago.

"You can command in this matter," one worried Republican wrote Lincoln. "As the acknowledged leader of the party, you can enforce the peace."[24] David Davis also encouraged Lincoln to intervene and offer a judicious solution to the affair. Faced with an intraparty crisis virtually on the eve of the state Republican convention in which Judd hoped to be nominated for governor, in February Lincoln at last took matters in hand. He proposed a settlement that the antagonists essentially accepted. It provided that the Wentworth and Judd newspaper organs cease their warfare; that Long John take back his corruption charge against Judd; and that Judd drop his libel suit against him. Both parties reluctantly accepted the terms. Lincoln also wrote Wentworth cautioning him to say nothing to others about the squabble. "There may be men who wish the breach between you and Judd to be widened; and if there be, they will naturally look with an evil eye at any one who tries to heal it."[25]

Lincoln already knew that some of Wentworth's friends were casting "an evil eye" toward him for siding with Judd in the affair. Long John himself complained to Lincoln that his recent letters "show how friendly you are to Judd," though he continued to profess his loyalty to Lincoln.[26] By February 1860, Lincoln had begun to see himself as a viable presidential candidate, and he expected Judd to repay him for his support in the Wentworth affair. He wrote Judd that "your assailants are most bitter against me; and they will, for revenge upon me, lay to the [Edward] Bates [presidential] egg" in southern Illinois "and to the Seward egg" in the northern part of the state. Thus his critics would "go far towards squeezing me out in the middle with nothing." Lincoln asked Judd: "Can you not help me a little in this matter, in your end of the vineyard?" He professed that it would not "hurt much for me to not be nominated on the national ticket; but I am where it would hurt some for me to not get the Illinois delegates."[27]

Judd, as chair of the state Republican committee, did not fail Lincoln in tending the political vineyard for him. In the party's state convention in May, Judd worked for the delegates' endorsement of Lincoln for president. Furthermore, as the state's representative on the national Republican committee, he had managed to secure the national convention for Chicago—in Lincoln country. (Lincoln at the time did not put much importance in the selection of the site.[28]) Historian Don E. Fehrenbacher has concluded that in the Judd-Wentworth feud Lincoln "displayed the ability to act forcefully and yet impartially as the leader of his party, holding its disparate elements together."[29] Actually, Lincoln had wisely favored Judd, whose association with Trumbull and the old Democratic wing of the party was essential to Republican success. Without his close connections and powerful influence in the party, Lincoln could not have succeeded in restoring harmony among Illinois Republicans and preventing the derailment of his presidential candidacy. Lincoln had tended his own political vineyard in a masterly way.

Although he was aware of his popularity among western Republicans as a result of his valiant fight against Douglas in 1858, Lincoln in 1859 doubted that he had emerged as a presidential contender or even that he wanted the office. He had long desired to be a U.S. senator, a position, he believed, that was congenial to his political skills and experience. As a successful four-term member of the state House of Representatives during the 1830s and early 1840s, and a member of the U.S. House of Representatives in 1847–1849, Lincoln had enjoyed the debate and political maneuvering characteristic of the legislative branch of government. Furthermore, his "beau ideal," Henry Clay, owed his influence and greatness to his service in the Senate. As Lincoln admitted on occasion, a seat in the Senate was the height of his ambition.

Lincoln's lack of much formal education sometimes bothered him and probably caused him to wonder if he could hold his own as president in the world of well-educated men from the East and elsewhere. He had never held an executive office and had little interest in administrative matters except as they pertained to the specific cases of his clients. His introspective and relatively passive personality did not lend itself to a high executive position that carried with it constant public pressures. Lincoln's bouts of melancholy, though not as severe as before his marriage, probably also contributed to his concern regarding the presidency. Moreover, the presidential field was already crowded with men who had been in the national spotlight for many years, a point that he made to Jesse W. Fell, secretary of the state Republican central committee, who raised the question of the presidency with him during the winter of 1858–1859.[30]

The list of Republican aspirants for the office included Senator William H. Seward of New York, the acknowledged leader; Governor Salmon P. Chase of Ohio; Senator Simon Cameron of Pennsylvania; Associate Justice John McLean of Ohio; and Edward Bates of Missouri. All had been put forward by the press and their supporters as candidates. Bates had never clearly identified with the Republican party but was a favorite among old Millard Fillmore voters. Many observers, including Lincoln, correctly believed that this group of voters held the key to Republican success in winning the critical states of the lower North in 1860.

On April 13, 1859, Thomas J. Pickett, editor of the *Rock Island* (Illinois) *Register,* wrote Lincoln that he wanted to have a "talk" with him about "announcing your name for the Presidency." Pickett proposed to write other Illinois Republican editors to suggest that they all make a similar announcement. Lincoln immediately replied, repeating the position he had told his friends on January 6 at Springfield regarding his candidacy. "I must, in candor, say I do not think myself fit for the Presidency." He told Pickett: "I certainly am flattered, and gratified, that some partial friends think of me in that connection; but I really think it best for our cause that no concerted effort, such as you suggest, should be made." He admonished Pickett: "Let this be considered confidential," which suggested that he wanted to leave the door cracked for a possible candidacy.[31]

Whatever reservations he had about his candidacy, Lincoln knew that influential and friendly state Republican newspapers like the *Chicago Press and Tribune,* and also Senator Trumbull and his friends, were not yet prepared to support him. The old biblical adage "nothing good can come out of Nazareth" applied at this time to the views of some Illinois Republicans regarding Lincoln's qualifications for national leadership. A local Republican activist in Union County wrote Trumbull on February 4, 1860, "Our friend Lincoln is a good amiable and talented gentleman, but is not in my opinion the man for the times."[32] Some Illinois Republicans favored Trumbull as the state party's candidate for president because of his stand in the Senate against Douglas and the slavocracy. Others preferred Bates of nearby Missouri because they believed he could win the critical Know-Nothing and Fillmore vote. Some Republican radicals in northern Illinois, despite Seward's unpopularity in the state, favored the senator in view of his strong antislavery stand and the fact that he was already the frontrunner.[33]

As late as February 1860, only three months before Lincoln received the Republican nomination, two prominent state Republicans, the ailing Governor William H. Bissell and Orville H. Browning, cast serious doubts on a Lincoln candidacy. On February 4, Bissell wrote Salmon P. Chase informing him "that our folks have recently taken a notion to talk up Lincoln, [and] he is everything that we can reasonably ask in a man, and a politician. Still, I do not suppose that many of our friends seriously expect to secure his nomination as candidate for the Presidency. In fact they would be very well satisfied, probably, if he could secure the second place on the ticket."[34] Bissell, who died before state Republicans met to select delegates to the national convention, understated Lincoln's support for the presidency among Illinois Republicans.

About the same time, Browning, an ultraconservative Republican, had a long conversation with Lincoln in Springfield and bluntly told his friend that he favored Bates for the party's nomination. Browning asked Lincoln to support the Missourian. Lincoln, according to Browning, agreed and commented that Bates, as a staunch conservative and former Know Nothing, "can get votes even in this County that he [Lincoln] cannot get—and that there is a large class of voters in all the free States that would go for Mr. Bates."[35] Lincoln, however, doubted that Bates could ultimately win the nomination, despite the fact that he was a favorite of former Fillmore men. Bates never really endorsed Republican principles except for the right of Congress to control slavery in the territories; moreover, he had opposed antislavery agitation and was ultraconservative on other issues regarding slavery.[36] Furthermore, Lincoln knew that Bates, because of his Know-Nothing, nativist background, would be unlikely to win the critical votes of German Americans and other newcomers, whose numbers had increased dramatically in Illinois and elsewhere during the decade.

Lincoln, as well as many western Republicans, believed that the party should nominate a candidate from the lower North and, in particular, one from Illinois, Indiana, or Pennsylvania, states that John C. Frémont had lost in 1856. Such a candidate, Lincoln thought, had to hold conservative antislavery views in order to serve as a strong counterweight to Douglas, the presumed Democratic nominee. The Little Giant's popular-sovereignty doctrine, despite its deceptiveness on slavery, appealed to many voters in the region who wanted a check on the slavocracy but feared for the Union if a radical like Seward or Chase became president. Lincoln received reinforcement for his conservative antislavery position in an *Indianapolis Daily Journal* article sent to him in early 1859. The writer argued that "the doubtful, conservative states would not venture upon a man got up under the dictation of the ultra Free Soilers of the east, and they never will. Defeat will follow defeat under such leadership, and the national power remain forever in the grasp of our political foes" in the Democratic party. He contended that "the next Republican candidate for President must, to be successful, carry Pennsylvania, Indiana, and Illinois; he must reside in one of those States; and he must be . . . a true Republican." This writer listed Lincoln as one of the preferred candidates from the West.[37]

When the off-year election campaigns began in 1859, Lincoln, with his star on the rise, received numerous invitations to speak for the Republican party and its candidates in western states and as far away as upstate New York and New Hampshire. He accepted only a few of these invitations because of his financial problems and the need to maintain an active law practice after neglecting it during the 1858 campaign. As he wrote in turning down one invitation: "It is bad to be poor. I shall go to the wall for bread and meat, if I neglect my business this year as well as last."[38] Lincoln might not have been in such desperate financial circumstances as he claimed, though he probably sincerely felt the pressure of a declining income and the need to continue entertaining for professional and political reasons. Mary obviously shared her husband's concern about his reduced income, and she probably repeatedly reminded him of their financial situation. It is doubtful that Lin-

coln, while maintaining a comfortable middle-class lifestyle, had achieved by
the end of the 1850s the high level of affluence that some biographers have
claimed.[39]

In taking the stump again, Lincoln was motivated by a deep desire to defeat Douglas and his Democratic supporters. Personal ambition still played a
role in Lincoln's motivation, but arguably not to the extent that it did during
his early years in politics. Douglas and the Democrats, Lincoln was convinced, had undermined the virtuous republic of the Founding Fathers by
permitting, if not encouraging, the extension of slavery and refusing to take
a moral stand against the institution. The intention of the Founders, Lincoln
repeatedly said, had been to place slavery en route to ultimate extinction by
preventing its expansion. Slavery, he insisted, was the main flaw in the American republican experiment in liberty and the greatest obstacle to national
progress. Though Lincoln's approach to resisting slavery was fundamentally
conservative, he expected that, given the passage of time, and the repudiation
of Douglas's invidious "don't care" policy toward the institution, the republic would again be placed on the progressive road of freedom and equality
that the Founders had envisioned for it.

His party's cause had become Lincoln's mission. "For my single self," he
wrote a Pennsylvanian on November 1, 1859, "I have enlisted for the permanent success of the Republican cause; and, for this object, I shall labor faithfully in the ranks, unless, as I think not probable, the judgment of the party
shall assign me a different position."[40] Recognizing his new political clout,
Lincoln in 1859 advised Republicans, both inside and outside the state, that
victory would be theirs if they stood firmly behind the party's antislavery
platform and avoided the siren call of Douglas's popular-sovereignty doctrine. With remarkable foresight, he predicted in a letter to Senator Trumbull
in December 1858 that the Democrats meeting in their national convention
at Charleston, South Carolina, in 1860 would divide along sectional lines,
and that Douglas would find himself powerless to prevent the adoption of a
slave-code platform for the territories. "He will bolt at once," Lincoln told
Trumbull, "turn upon us, as in the case of Lecompton, and claim that all
Northern men shall make common cause in electing him President as the best
means of breaking down the Slave power." In that case, "the struggle in the
whole North will be, as it was in Illinois last summer and fall, whether the
Republican party can maintain it's [sic] identity, or be broken up to form the
tail of Douglas's new kite. Some of our great [eastern] Republican doctors
will then have a splendid chance to swallow the pills they so eagerly prescribed for us last Spring. . . . The truth is, the Republican principle can, in
no wise live with Douglas; and it is arrant folly now, as it was last Spring, to
waste time, and scatter labor already performed, in dallying with him."[41]

Here Lincoln was preaching to the choir. Trumbull's eastern colleagues in Congress clearly understood the Little Giant's political game and, having learned their lesson in 1858, had no intention of cooperating with him.

At the same time, Lincoln warned against "the temptation to lower the Republican Standard in order to gather recruits" for the party. Such a move, he told a Kansas associate, "would open a gap through which more would pass *out* than pass *in.* And this would be the same, whether the letting down should be in deference to Douglasism [popular sovereignty], or to the Southern opposition element. Either would surrender the o[b]ject of the Republican organization—the preventing the *spread* and *nationalization* of slavery. This object surrendered, the organization would go to pieces." Lincoln informed his Kansas friend that he would accept a southerner on the national Republican ticket, provided it could be done "with *safety* to the Republican cause."[42] This evidently was an oblique dismissal of the ultraconservative Edward Bates as the southern candidate for the nomination.

Wherever he spoke in 1859, Lincoln preached the immorality of slavery and called for Republican unity on that principle. "This matter of slavery," he exclaimed at a Chicago Republican gathering on March 1, "is a moral, political and social wrong, and ought to be treated as a wrong, not to let anything minor or subsidiary to that main principle and purpose make us fail to cooperate." He said that "the Republican principle [was] the profound central truth that slavery is wrong and ought to be dealt with as a wrong" and that members of his party "should never for a moment" lose sight of this. Still, Lincoln wanted to make clear that he was not an antislavery radical. "I suppose," he informed the Chicago Republicans, slavery "may long exist, and perhaps the best way for it to come to an end peaceably is for it to exist for a length of time. But I say that the spread and strengthening and perpetuation of it is an entirely different proposition. There we should in every way resist it as a wrong, treating it as a wrong, with the fixed idea that it must and will come to an end." He insisted that the antislavery cause and Republican victory were assured "if we do not allow ourselves to be allured from the strict path of our duty by such a device as shifting our ground and throwing ourselves into the rear of a leader [Douglas] who denies our first principle, denies that there is an absolute wrong in the institution of slavery." "All you have to do," he advised fellow Republicans, "is to keep the faith, to remain steadfast to the right, to stand by your banner . . . and victory complete and permanent is sure at the last."[43] The only practical application of Lincoln's moral opposition to slavery was for Republicans to stand firm against its expansion. Nonetheless, the fact that Lincoln took a strong moral position against slavery, along with his house-divided pronouncement, made him a relatively easy target for Democrats, who sought to brand him as an abolitionist and a threat to the Union.

While proclaiming slavery a great wrong, Lincoln expressed his deep concern that the adoption of radical antislavery resolutions by Republicans would reverse the party's momentum in Illinois and elsewhere in the lower North and cause its defeat in the 1859 and 1860 elections. When Lincoln read in the newspapers in June 1859 that the state Republican convention in Ohio had approved a resolution demanding the repeal of the Fugitive Slave Act, he excitedly wrote Governor Salmon P. Chase to denounce the action, claiming that it was "already damaging us here." He informed Chase that "the cause of Republicanism is hopeless in Illinois, if it be in any way made responsible for that plank" in the Ohio party platform. "I hope that you can, and will, contribute something to relieve us from it." Furthermore, "if that plank be even *introduced* into the next Republican National convention, it will explode it. Once introduced, its supporters and it's [sic] opponents will quarrel irreconcilably."[44]

Chase, in response, offered Lincoln no hope for relief from the radical Ohio resolution. He wrote that "a declaration in favor of the repeal of the Fugitive Slave Act of 1850 was indispensable" because the law was "unnecessarily hard & severe, and almost absolutely useless as a practical measure of reclamation." Chase told Lincoln: "I trust that our friends in Illinois will, if not already prepared to take same ground, soon be educated up to it." Lincoln must have resented the Ohio governor's patronizing comment. He must also have recoiled at Chase's reminder that he (Lincoln) had taken an extreme antislavery position "in that noble speech of yours at Springfield which opened the campaign last year in Illinois."[45] Chase referred to Lincoln's House Divided Speech.

Lincoln chose not to let the issue die. In a letter to Chase on June 20, he repeated his prediction that "the introduction of a proposition for repeal of the Fugitive Slave law, into the next Republican National convention, will explode the convention and the party." Lincoln also reminded Chase of the constitutional requirement that fugitives from states "*shall be delivered up*"; the Constitution, he said, "expressly empowered" Congress to legislate a fugitive slave act.[46] Chase remained unmoved by Lincoln's arguments. However, in 1860 the national Republican convention, mindful of the need to win conservative votes, ignored the hopes of Chase and other radicals for a plank in the platform calling for the repeal of the Fugitive Slave Act of 1850. In fact, the delegates did not even debate the issue.[47]

Soon after his exchange with Chase on the Fugitive Slave Act, Lincoln received a letter from Samuel Galloway, another prominent Ohio Republican, complaining about Chase's radicalism and contending that "we cannot have [him] or any man representing his ultra ideas as our Candidate for 1860." Galloway said that Lincoln would be an acceptable candidate and asked the Illinois Republican for his views on the matter. Lincoln replied that he had "a kind side for him [Chase]. He was one of the few distinguished men of the nation who gave us, in Illinois, their sympathy last year. I never saw him, suppose him to be able, and right-minded; but still he may not be the most suitable as a candidate for the Presidency." Lest this comment appear designed to advance his own presidential candidacy at Chase's expense, Lincoln quickly remarked, as he had done earlier, when Thomas J. Pickett and other Illinois friends had raised the issue with him: "I must say I do not think myself fit for the Presidency." Still, Lincoln wanted to keep the door open for the nomination if the other candidates faltered, and, probably with this in mind, he sought to cultivate a close relationship with Ohio Republicans, particularly the conservative opponents of Chase who might soon be in a position to control the state party. "As you propose a correspondence with me, I shall look for your letters anxiously," Lincoln wrote Galloway.[48]

Lincoln increased his efforts during the summer and fall to prevent the adoption by Republicans of either radical or ultraconservative resolutions that could divide the party and defeat it at the polls. He insisted that Republicans must stand united on a conservative antislavery platform while recognizing the regional political concerns of state and local parties. He warned Schuyler Colfax, a rising Republican leader in Indiana, that the "point of danger" for the party in the 1860 election was "the temptation in different localities to '*platform*' for something which will be popular just there, but which, nevertheless, will be a firebrand elsewhere, and especially in a National convention." "In every local convocation of Republicans," Lincoln lectured Colfax, "a point should be made to avoid everything which will distract republicans elsewhere." He referred not only to resolutions for the repeal of the Fugitive Slave Act, but also to "the movement against foreigners in Massachusetts" associated with the state party's fusion with the nativist Know Nothings. That state's fusionists had recently secured the legislature's initiation of a constitutional amendment requiring a two-year residency after naturalization before immigrants could vote. Lincoln sadly informed Colfax: "Massachusetts republicans should have looked beyond their noses; and then they could not have failed to see that tilting against foreigners would ruin us in the whole North-West," which, Lincoln believed, the Republicans could not win without German immigrant votes.[49]

Lincoln had had ample warning from German American Republicans in Illinois of the danger to the party if it did not repudiate the proposed Massachusetts amendment. Gustave P. Koerner, the state's most prominent German American, called on Lincoln to use his influence to get the state party's central committee to condemn the Massachusetts measure. He wrote Lincoln that it was *"necessary* for our future success, that we should speak out on this subject. It is time that we should quit the absurd hope of gaining converts from the Knownothings by a tenderfooted course."[50] Actually, Lincoln privately had already proposed to the state Republican central committee that it denounce the Massachusetts provision, an action that it soon took.[51]

Meanwhile, Theodore Canisius, the editor of the *Illinois Staats-Anzeiger,* a newspaper that Lincoln had financed, asked him to make a statement for publication regarding his position on the proposed Massachusetts amendment and his view of fusion with the Know-Nothing element. Under pressure from the growing German American community to denounce the Massachusetts movement, on May 17 Lincoln replied in a letter that Canisius printed. It subsequently received wide circulation in the state press. After noting that "Massachusetts is a sovereign and independent state and it is no privilege of mine to scold her for what she does," Lincoln announced that he disapproved of the adoption of any nativist provision "in Illinois, or in any other place, where I have a right to oppose it."[52]

Aware that he risked the loss of Know-Nothing support, Lincoln went on to explain to Canisius that, "understanding the spirit of our institutions to aim at the *elevation* of men, I am opposed to whatever tends to *degrade* them. I have some little notoriety for commiserating the oppressed condition of the Negro; and I should be strangely inconsistent if I could favor any project for curtailing the existing rights of white men, even though born in different lands, and speaking different languages from myself." On the question of Republican fusion with Know Nothings, Lincoln was less definite. "I am for it, if it can be had on republican grounds; and I am not for it on any other terms. A fusion on any other terms, would be as foolish as unprincipled. It would lose the whole North, while the common enemy would still carry the whole South."[53] He meant that a fusion with Know Nothings on nativist terms would undercut the Republican effort to win the immigrant vote in critical northern states, such as Illinois, while gaining nothing in any of the southern states, where the anti-Republican parties were almost certain to win. The problem, in short, was how to avoid offending German American voters but still gain the support of conservative Know Nothings who were mildly antislavery and traditionally anti-Democratic. It was a difficult political tightrope to walk in the North of the 1850s. Lincoln, however, had become a master at pursuing pragmatic politics while maintaining his core values of cultural tolerance and moral opposition to slavery.

Lincoln also warned Republicans against any deviation from the party's antislavery focus. When asked by a Pennsylvanian for his views on the tariff—

a subject dear to the industrial interests in the Keystone State—Lincoln an-swered that as an old Whig he had long supported "a moderate, carefully adjusted protective tariff." But, he cautioned, "it is my opinion that just now, the revival of that question, will not advance the [Republican] cause itself, or the man who revives it. I have not thought much upon the subject recently; but my general impression is, that the necessity for a protective tariff will, ere long, force its old opponents to take it up; and then it's [sic] old friends can join in, and establish it on a more firm and durable basis." Probably to avoid the use of his statement against him and his party in the West, which was largely low tariff, Lincoln asked the Pennsylvanian to keep his remarks con-fidential.[54]

In August, Lincoln made his first out-of-state trip to aid fellow Republi-cans in the 1859 elections. He went to Council Bluffs, Iowa, ostensibly for the purpose of examining land that Norman B. Judd wanted to deed to him as security for a debt. While in town, he delivered an address at the Council Bluffs Concert Hall. A local Democratic newspaper provided the only report of the speech. This partisan newspaper admitted that Lincoln "was listened to with much attention, for his Waterloo defeat by Douglas has magnified him into quite a lion here." Essentially, Lincoln exhorted Iowa Republicans to maintain party unity and avoid fusion with non-Republican elements.[55]

Then, in September, Lincoln accepted two invitations to speak in Ohio. Though still considered a western state, Ohio bridged the mid-Atlantic, espe-cially Pennsylvania, and the newer states farther west, mainly Indiana and Illinois. Lincoln needed no one to tell him that his party must continue the momentum in Ohio and the West that it had established in the 1858 elec-tions in order to win the presidency, capture the lower northern state govern-ments, and then gain control of Congress in 1860. Republicans had won the Buckeye State in 1856 and had placed Chase in the governor's chair. But the state Republican convention's adoption of a radical platform had damaged the party in Ohio and threatened Republican gains elsewhere in the lower North.[56] The upper North, with perhaps the exception of New York and Connecticut, seemed safe for the Republicans; all of these states had voted for John C. Frémont in 1856.

Anxious to take advantage of the Republican troubles in Ohio, Senator Douglas, who had announced his candidacy for president, scheduled major addresses in Columbus and Cincinnati in September. The Little Giant's ap-pearances came just after the publication of an important though ponderous article he had written for *Harper's Magazine*. In the article, Douglas went to great lengths to defend his doctrine of popular sovereignty and, as Lincoln had predicted, to portray himself as the moderate alternative to proslavery Democrats, including Buchanan supporters, on one side, and the "Black Republicans," on the other. Douglas repeated the far-fetched argument he had expressed in the Freeport Doctrine—that the people in the territories had the authority to determine the status of slavery despite the Dred Scott decision giving judicial sanction to slave property there. Clearly in an effort to distance himself from the slavocracy and win support among antislavery conservatives in the North, the Illinois senator took a page from Lincoln's claim regarding the national implications of the Dred Scott ruling. Like Lincoln, he contended that if the Supreme Court, as indicated in the Dred Scott case, could validate slave property in the territories, it also could do so in the free states, thereby precipitating the "irrepressible conflict" between the South and the North that Republicans had predicted. Only the Democratic policy of letting the people decide on slavery in the states and in the territories could prevent such an eventuality, Douglas wrote.

The Little Giant also argued that the Founding Fathers and their successors had established the principle that the people, not the federal government, should determine the slavery issue. Thus the Republicans—he meant Lincoln specifically, who had made a strong historical case against slavery's expansion and perpetuation—erred in assuming that the federal government could have a hand in controlling the institution. Douglas mainly repeated his *Harper's* article in his Columbus and Cincinnati speeches.[57]

The Ohio Republicans' invitations to Lincoln pointedly explained that they needed him in the state to counter Douglas. In effect, Lincoln's appearances would be a continuation of his 1858 campaign against the senator. "There is no man in the Union who under the circumstances can do so much good in Central & Southern Ohio as you can, and more especially to follow Douglas," one invitation read. "Do not fail us. We depend much upon you." Informing him that they would pay all of his expenses, the Ohio Republicans promised Lincoln that he would have large audiences at Columbus and Cincinnati and at other places where he might speak. Lincoln leaped at the opportunity to once more cross swords with the Little Giant. The Republican champion immediately agreed to follow Douglas to Columbus and Cincinnati, but said that he could do no more in the state.[58]

Accompanied by Mary and Tad, Lincoln left Springfield for Ohio on September 15 and spoke the next day in Columbus. With only a week to publicize Lincoln's appearance and in competition with the county fair, local Republicans were unable to bring out the large crowd that they had promised. Governor Chase did not attend; he was campaigning for the party in the northern part of the state. Some of Chase's radical friends were cool to Lincoln's appearance because of his criticism of the state party platform calling for the repeal of the Fugitive Slave Act. They also saw the Springfield lawyer as a threat in the West to their favorite's presidential candidacy.[59] Still, a great deal of curiosity attached to the arrival in the Ohio capital of "the man who had outmatched the Little Giant" on the stump in Illinois. Lincoln's "tall form, striking features, expressive mouth and tawny complexion" reportedly appealed to the people who saw him in Columbus.[60]

The crowd that attended the Republican rally on the State House terrace heard Lincoln "pitch hot shot" into Douglas. Lincoln, having seen copies of Douglas's *Harper's* article and his Columbus speech, mounted a spirited rebuttal of the senator's arguments.[61] Lincoln also drew upon material that he had used against Douglas in the 1858 debates. Indeed, at times during the speech it seemed that he was again debating Douglas on the same platform. Lincoln pointed out the insidious nature of Douglas's popular-sovereignty doctrine and his "don't care" position on slavery. He lambasted the senator for his contention in the *Harper's* article that the Founding Fathers had approved the principle of federal nonintervention regarding slavery in the territories, thereby leaving it to the people to decide the issue. The Democratic leader, Lincoln declared, "selects parts of the history of the United States upon the subject of slavery, and treats it as a whole." Douglas, Lincoln noted, had conveniently omitted Congress's action in passing the Northwest Ordinance of 1787 prohibiting slavery in that territory, and the Missouri Compromise of 1820 excluding it above the latitude of 36 degrees, 30 minutes north. Much to the delight of his overwhelmingly Republican audience, Lincoln repeatedly mocked Douglas's "great essay in Harper's Magazine" or his "copy-right essay."[62]

Lincoln gave his own version of the history of slavery in the early republic, contrasting it with Douglas's account in *Harper's*. Lincoln announced: "History shows that they [the Founders] decided in the cases actually brought before them, in exactly the contrary way" that Douglas claimed. "Not only did they so decide at that time" against the preservation of slavery, "they stuck to it during sixty years, through thick and thin, as long as there was one of the revolutionary heroes upon the stage of political action. Through their whole course, from first to last, they clung to freedom," Lincoln insisted. During this period, "the whole Union" had acquiesced in slavery's existence in the states out of necessity, while looking forward "to the ultimate extinction of the institution." Douglas's popular-sovereignty doctrine and his "don't care" attitude toward slavery, Lincoln told his audience, had upset this expectation and undermined the antislavery intentions of the Founders.[63] As before, Lincoln exaggerated the Founders' antislavery commitment in his argument against Douglas's noninterference doctrine.

As in the 1858 campaign, Lincoln asserted that if Douglas's policy and attitude prevailed, slavery could become a national phenomenon and the foreign slave trade could reopen. In reality, neither of these results was likely to occur. Even the Taney Supreme Court, despite its ruling that slavery in the territories fell under the Constitution's property rights provision, would hardly have handed down a decision protecting slavery in the North. Such a court ruling would have created tremendous resistance in the free states and would have insured Republican success at the polls, an eventuality that Taney himself wanted to avoid. Moreover, the foreign slave trade had been outlawed by Congress after December 31, 1807, and it was highly unlikely that it would be reopened. A proposal by a few southern extremists during the mid-1850s to repeal the prohibition failed in the House of Representatives by an almost unanimous vote. However, antislavery proponents, including Lincoln, continued to raise the issue, particularly after 1858–1859 when reports circulated that piratical landings of slave vessels were occurring on the southern coast. Most of the reports were false; actually, there was only one documented landing of slaves at this time. The ship, the *Wanderer,* had been seized by federal authorities, and some members of the crew had been prosecuted but subsequently freed.[64] Lincoln and fellow Republicans saw these events as part of a slave-power conspiracy, a fear fueled by Douglas's insidious policy on slavery, which they maintained would extend the "peculiar institution" throughout America.

At Columbus, Lincoln renewed his criticism of Douglas's exclusion of blacks from the Declaration of Independence equality clause and the senator's appalling description of them as brutes, not men. Lincoln, however, denied that the Republicans sought black political and social equality. "Negro equality!" he wrote in notes that he apparently made for his Ohio trip. "Fudge! How long, in the government of a God, great enough to make and maintain this Universe, shall there continue knaves to vend, and fools to gulp, so low a piece of demagougeism [*sic*] as this."[65] Lincoln insisted that the "chief and real purpose of the Republican party is eminently conservative. It proposes nothing save and except to restore this government to its original tone in regard to this element of slavery, and there to maintain it, looking for no further change, in reference to it, than that which the original framers of the government themselves expected and looked forward to."[66]

Leaving Columbus on September 17, Lincoln arrived late in the afternoon in Cincinnati, the largest city in the West with a population of about 160,000. At the depot "a large concourse of persons had assembled to greet the champion of Freedom in the 'Sucker State,'" the Republican *Cincinnati Gazette* reported. "The reception must have reminded him of his tour through his own state when, as here, the guns thundered welcome, music greeted [him], and people cheered at each place" along the route to his hotel.[67] Across the Ohio River lay slaveholding Kentucky, which consisted mainly of old Whig conservatives and Douglas Democrats. A radical stigma attached to the Republicans in Cincinnati and in nearby Kentucky. Anti-slavery men in the area found it necessary to refer to their organization as the "Opposition party" rather than the "Republican party."[68] With this name, they hoped to win over the conservative Whigs who had been longtime opponents of the Democrats and had supported Fillmore for president in 1856. Aware of this delicate political situation, Lincoln in his Cincinnati speech generally expressed the conservative sentiments of the anti-Democratic element in the area.

Lincoln's appearance that evening at the "Opposition" rally in Cincinnati seemed to confirm his popularity among the area's antislavery forces. Escorted by men on horseback to the portico of a building on Market Square where he was to speak, Lincoln found a huge cheering crowd assembled to hear him. Giant bonfires and fireworks shooting across the sky illuminated the area.[69] Having been advised that a light touch would play well with his southern Ohio audience—and set the northern Kentuckians at ease—Lincoln laced his remarks with humor. Democrats, however, were not amused by his levity. The *Cincinnati Enquirer,* Douglas's organ in the city, reported that "OLD ABE's" speech was full of jokes—well calculated to reduce to less than nothing the reputation of their utterer as a man of truth and candor." His efforts to please the crowd, the *Enquirer* remarked scornfully, reflected "the habits of the boor and the vocabulary of the ruffian as best adapted to his taste and his capacity."[70]

Though he recognized the need to satisfy conservative sentiment in the area, Lincoln refused to back down from the antislavery position he had expressed at Columbus and elsewhere. Speaking directly to the Kentuckians in his Cincinnati audience and across the river, he said that he was "what [you] call, as I understand it, a 'Black Republican.' I think Slavery is wrong, morally, and politically. I desire that it should be no further spread in these United States, and I should not object if it should gradually terminate in the whole Union." While he was not calling for federal interference with slavery in the southern states, Lincoln insisted that the United States "must have a national policy in regard to the institution of slavery, that acknowledges and deals with that institution as being wrong." "You, Kentuckians," he said, "differ with me upon this proposition; that you believe Slavery is a good thing; that Slavery is right; that it ought to be extended and perpetuated in this Union." Lincoln facetiously advised those who felt this way to support the nomination of "my distinguished friend Judge Douglas" for the presidency because Douglas agreed with them on the slavery issue. The Judge "is as sincerely for you, and more wisely for you, than you are for yourselves," he said.[71]

Lincoln then continued his unrelenting assault on Douglas, who had spoken a week earlier in the city. He took particular aim at the Little Giant's recent comment at Memphis that "in all contests between the negro and the white man, he was for the white man, but that in all questions between the negro and the crocodile he was for the Negro." He ridiculed Douglas's notion that the black man was little better than the crocodile, which implied, according to Lincoln, that "the white man may rightfully treat the negro as a beast or a reptile." "If there was a necessary conflict between the white man and the negro, I should be for the white man as much as Judge Douglas; but I say there is no such necessary conflict. I say that there is room enough for us all to be free, and that it not only does not wrong the white man that the negro should be free, but it positively wrongs the mass of the white men that the negro should be enslaved." Lincoln did not explain how whites were wronged by slavery except that it was a threat to free labor in the territories.[72] The *Chicago Press and Tribune,* in reporting the speech, concluded that Lincoln had given the lie to "the absurd notion that Mr. Douglas has any concern for the extension and perpetuation of free institutions," as many of his northern supporters claimed.[73]

While visiting the next day, a Sunday, with Mary's cousin and her family in Cincinnati, Lincoln received an invitation to address a Republican rally in Indianapolis. Delaying his plans to return to Springfield, he accepted the invitation. Along with Mary and Tad, he left Cincinnati on Monday and arrived that afternoon in the Indiana capital. Weary from his trip, "Old Abe" still spoke for two hours in the evening to an enthusiastic crowd, including the governor, at the Masonic Hall.[74] He mainly repeated his Ohio criticisms of Douglas. Lincoln based his strategy on the belief, as he wrote Chase, that "Douglasism . . . is all which now stands in the way of an early and complete success of Republicanism."[75]

The next day, Lincoln returned home, evidently without speaking en route. Eight days later, he left for Milwaukee to fulfill an earlier invitation to address the Wisconsin Agricultural Fair. In his written speech, which ostensibly was nonpolitical, Lincoln discussed the importance of agricultural fairs (a growing national phenomenon during the 1850s) as well as the value of both free labor and education in elevating the people. Although he did not relate the issue of free labor directly to the controversy over slavery in the territories, he clearly meant that white labor would be denigrated by the expansion and perpetuation of slavery. Free labor, Lincoln contended, "opens the way for all—gives hope to all, and energy, and progress, and improvement of condition to all. If any continue through life in the condition of the hired laborer, it is not the fault of the system, but because of either a dependent nature which prefers it, or improvidence, folly or singular misfortune."

Lincoln contended that those who supported what he called the "mud-sill" theory of society "conclude that all laborers are necessarily either *hired* laborers, or *slaves*. They assume that whoever is once a *hired* laborer, is fatally fixed in that condition for life; and thence again that his condition is as bad as, or worse than that of a slave." Furthermore, Lincoln said, supporters of the "mud-sill" theory argued "that labor and education are incompatible; and any practical combination of them impossible"; indeed, they suggested that "the education of laborers, is not only useless, but pernicious, and dangerous." But Lincoln confidently asserted "that the people of Wisconsin prefer free labor, with its natural companion, education," to the "mud-sill" theory.[76]

The Illinois Republican did not accept the view of some free-labor advocates that, as he put it, "labor is prior to, and independent of, capital; that, in fact, capital is the fruit of labor, and could never have existed if labor had not *first* existed—that labor can exist without capital, but that capital could never have existed without labor." "Hence," he said, "they hold that labor is the superior—greatly the superior—of capital." Lincoln suggested that labor and capital were not mutually exclusive; their interests, he contended, could coexist: "The prudent, penniless beginner in the world, labors for wages awhile, saves a surplus with which to buy tools or land, for himself; then labors on his own account another while, and at length hires another new beginner to help him." This arrangement, Lincoln argued, "is free labor— the just and generous, and prosperous system, which opens the way for all— gives hope to all, and energy, and progress, and improvement of condition to all." Lincoln concluded with his vision of America's future. "Let us hope," he declared, "that by the best cultivation of the physical world, beneath and around us; and the intellectual and moral world within us, we shall secure an individual, social, and political prosperity and happiness, whose course shall be onward and upward, and which, while the earth endures, shall not pass away."[77]

Lincoln was not alone, particularly in the developing West, in expressing this vision of economic opportunity and progress as a result of the free labor system. Lincoln's faith in free labor as the cornerstone of the American economic system, which basically was a nineteenth-century conservative doctrine, undergirded his opposition to slavery in any form and his belief that there should be no artificial weights placed on any people in their efforts to rise in society. Though unwilling, at least during the 1850s, to accept blacks into an equal partnership in the social and political order, Lincoln believed that they should be free to reap the rewards of their labor and skill.

After addressing the Wisconsin Agricultural Fair, Lincoln talked to a Republican meeting in Milwaukee. The next day, he spoke to Republicans in Beloit and Janesville. The brief newspaper reports of his Wisconsin political speeches indicated that Lincoln continued the conservative antislavery and anti-Douglas themes expressed in his Ohio campaign.[78]

Lincoln returned to Springfield in early October via Chicago, where he stopped to consult with Norman B. Judd and other close political associates. At home, he waited anxiously for the results of the October elections in Ohio and other free states. In the Buckeye State, the Republicans swept to victory, gaining control of all branches of the state government. They also won in other northern states where contests occurred. Lincoln had gone to Clinton to attend court when the news arrived of the Republican triumphs. That evening he spoke at a rally in town called to celebrate the party's victories. The elections, he told the festive crowd, demonstrated that "the good doctrines of the fathers of the Republic would yet again prevail, and become the rule of action of the Government." When he returned to Springfield, enthusiastic supporters marched to his home and persuaded him to come to the state capitol and speak to a Republican gathering celebrating the victory.[79]

Grateful Republicans in Ohio and in the other states where Lincoln had campaigned for the party showered him with praise for his contribution to their success. They reported to Lincoln that his speeches had shattered Douglas's popular-sovereignty "humbug" and had driven a stake into the heart of the Little Giant's presidential ambitions. (This was a premature conclusion on their part, however.) In addition to having been heard by several thousand Buckeyes, Lincoln's speeches had been printed and distributed throughout Ohio and neighboring states. The state Republican executive committee generously attributed the party's 1859 victory "in large measure to the influence of Lincoln's speeches." The committee soon received the future president's permission to publish a book containing his 1858 debates with Douglas along with his Columbus and Cincinnati speeches.[80] As indicated above, the book appeared in time for the 1860 presidential campaign. Even Chase praised Lincoln's effort in Ohio, though he must have realized that the Illinois Republican had emerged as a serious rival in the West.[81] Samuel Galloway of Columbus told Lincoln, "Your visit to Ohio has excited an extensive interest in your favor," and he advised him to "treat kindly and respectfully all requests for the use of your name" for president.[82]

The test of presidential electability was working in Lincoln's favor by the end of 1859. The Springfield lawyer had emerged as the Republican champion of the Great West. Seward, the frontrunner for the party's nomination, appeared vulnerable because of the perception that he was radical on the slavery issue. A decade earlier he had opposed the Compromise of 1850 on the grounds that "a higher law than the Constitution" required the exclusion of slavery from the territories. Then, in 1858, the New York senator had predicted an "irrepressible conflict" between the North and the South over slavery. These two pronouncements served to stigmatize him as an extremist whose nomination would probably doom the party in the West. Westerners, as well as people elsewhere, simply did not want to believe that the division over slavery was irrepressible or that there was a higher law than the Constitution. Furthermore, many western Republicans, especially in Illinois, resented Seward's earlier dalliance with Douglas on the Lecompton issue. The New York senator's strength, most Republican activists concluded, lay in the upper North and particularly the Northeast. Lincoln and other Republicans recognized that Seward had little support in the key lower western states. His support in the critical state of Pennsylvania (which, with twenty-seven electoral votes, was second only to New York), where Senator Simon Cameron held sway and intrigued for the nomination, was also low.

John Brown's raid on Harpers Ferry, Virginia, on October 16 to free and arm slaves had further damaged Seward's commanding lead in the Republican presidential sweepstakes. The strong reaction in the North, as well as in the South, against "Old Brown's invasion" created deep concern among Republicans that the party could not win the conservative lower North if the New York senator headed the ticket. The Democratic charge that Brown had acted out Seward's "irrepressible conflict" declaration caused many northerners to fear for the Union and the prospects for maintaining peace between the free states and the slave states if the Republicans nominated the senator. A few days after the raid, Charles H. Ray, proprietor of the *Chicago Press and Tribune,* reported to Lincoln how the incident had affected the mood in his city: "We are damnably exercised here about the effect of Old Brown's wretched fiasco in Virginia, upon the moral health of the Republican party! The old idiot—the quicker they hang him and get him out of the way, the better." Lincoln observed firsthand the harmful effects that Brown's attack had on the party. In a November special congressional election in the Springfield district, Democrat John A. McClernand easily defeated Republican John M. Palmer, a Lincoln supporter. Illinois Republicans attributed the Democratic success in the election to the reaction to the Harpers Ferry incident.[83] A Pennsylvanian writing to Lincoln about the prospects for Seward as the party's nominee said, "Since the Humbug insurrection at Harpers Ferry, I presume Mr Seward will not be urged"; he assumed Seward would be forced to give way to Cameron in his region.[84]

Republican setbacks in New York following Brown's abortive raid—a development that has not received the attention from historians that it deserves—confirmed the belief among Lincoln's friends in the West that Seward's frontrunner status was in jeopardy.[85] Mark W. Delahay, a Kansas Republican leader and an old Lincoln associate in Illinois, wrote his friend on November 14 that the New York election would be "referred to as an index of strength, or rather weakness of Mr Seward in his own State." Delahay reminded Lincoln that he had won more popular votes than Douglas in 1858, a point noticed by many Republicans. Lincoln, according to his Kansas friend, would be the ideal candidate to capture the critical lower North in the presidential election. Delahay admonished Lincoln to "discard a little modesty, strike boldly for the next 6 months," and he would win the prize. "You have always distrusted your own ability too much, the only advantage that Douglas ever possessed over you," he said.[86] Josiah M. Lucas, Lincoln's Illinois friend in the national capital, wrote him that "late developments have certainly damaged [Seward], and the timid or wavering portion of our friends regard him as a dead weight, and in doubtful districts he would loose [*sic*] instead of gaining us votes—hence it is presumed that Mr. S will not be the nominee." Lucas confidently told Lincoln that "his friends were legion" in Washington and suggested that he visit the city during the winter in order to take advantage of his growing prospects.[87] Even if Lincoln had been tempted to make the trip, to have gone to Washington would have appeared opportunistic.

By late 1859, in the aftermath of "Old Brown's wretched fiasco," as Charles H. Ray had characterized the incident, lower northern Republicans —and many in the upper North as well—in their determination to win the presidency and destroy "Douglasism," began to search for an alternative candidate to the radical Seward. They wanted someone who could retain the states won by John C. Frémont in 1856 and capture what some politicians and editors referred to even then as the "battleground states." Lincoln's stock as the alternative to Seward had risen, but he and his Illinois friends had to promote his candidacy more aggressively and boldly. Still, Lincoln, in keeping with American political tradition that the office sought the man, not the other way around, could not appear to campaign for the nomination. Simeon Francis, an old associate, told Lincoln two weeks after the Ohio election and Brown's raid: "You are the man for the times; and your friends should present your name to public attention in a manner that will make the people believe they are in earnest."[88] Lincoln grasped the message; soon he would take a dramatic step of his own to obtain support for the Republican nomination, though ostensibly to promote the political fortunes of his party. He took his campaign to Seward's heartland, the Northeast.

CHAPTER SEVEN

"HONEST ABE" FOR PRESIDENT

THE OPPORTUNITY FOR Lincoln to advance his national political prospects in the Northeast began when, returning from attending court in Clinton, Illinois, on October 15, 1859, he read a telegram inviting him to speak on or about November 29 at Henry Ward Beecher's famous Plymouth Church in Brooklyn. The message indicated that Lincoln could talk on any subject he chose and he would be paid the handsome sum of $200.[1] William H. Herndon and other Lincoln friends in Illinois believed correctly that the invitation, sent by James A. Briggs, a Salmon P. Chase supporter, represented a movement by prominent New York Republicans to undercut Senator Seward for the Republican nomination. The eastern Republican sponsors of the address sought to advance either Chase, Edward Bates, or Simon Cameron as alternatives to Seward. Some belonged to a Whig, now Republican, faction that long had fought Seward and his alter ego Thurlow Weed of the *Albany Evening Journal* for control of the New York party. Members of this faction believed that Weed's reputation for questionable political dealings in the state would undermine the corruption charges against the Buchanan administration that Republicans expected to be an important issue in the election. Many, such as Briggs and William Cullen Bryant, were former Democrats, and they favored Chase because he could be promoted as an incorruptible founder of the Republican party and an advocate of free trade, which New York commercial interests supported.

Eastern Republicans who opposed Seward recognized that the senator's "irrepressible conflict" speech had made him vulnerable in the battleground states of the lower North. Furthermore, Seward's opposition to nativism had alienated conservative former Whigs whose votes for Millard Fillmore had doomed the Republicans in the presidential election of 1856. In any case, the leaders of the Fillmore voters in Pennsylvania, Indiana, and Illinois had let it be known that they could not support Seward. The sponsors of the Lincoln invitation, including Horace Greeley, had already brought Frank Blair of Missouri, who was managing Bates's campaign, and the colorful Cassius M. Clay of Kentucky to New York to promote the party's cause, thereby clouding the political waters for Seward. Thomas Corwin, a well-known Ohio orator, soon would follow Blair and Clay.

When they issued the invitation to Lincoln, the eastern Republicans prob-

William H. Seward, New York senator and frontrunner for the Republican nomination for president in 1860. After the election, Lincoln appointed him secretary of state. Courtesy of the Library of Congress, Washington, D.C.

ably did not consider him a serious alternative to Seward. Except for Greeley, they had praised Lincoln's valiant senatorial campaign against the Little Giant in Illinois and, more recently, his Ohio canvass in behalf of the party. Nonetheless, although some Republicans in key western states began to tout him for the presidency, eastern party leaders knew that Lincoln lacked a strong base of support in their region. They perceived him as a popular, rather exotic westerner who would bring an anti-Douglas message to New York, provide the party faithful with an antidote to Seward's radicalism, and help their own candidate (Chase, Bates, or Cameron) against the controversial senator.

In late 1859 and early 1860, Pennsylvania Republicans dangled the vice presidential nomination before Lincoln in an effort to gain his support and through him western backing for Cameron. Lincoln refused to take the bait.[2] Even the Seward camp, with western delegates in mind, sought to cultivate the Springfield lawyer's support, though without any promises. Immediately after the resounding Republican success in the Ohio election, in which Lincoln had had a hand, Thurlow Weed sent an urgent dispatch to Norman Judd in Chicago. "Send Abram Lincoln to Albany immediately," Weed bluntly demanded. Judd seemed puzzled by the message, and when forwarding it to Lincoln, told his friend, perhaps as a warning: "I take it that Thurlow Weed is not so green as to think he can get you into a combination with his pet Seward and it must be something else and probably of importance."[3] Whatever the New York intriguer had in mind (perhaps the vice presidency), Lincoln wisely ignored the request to visit Albany.

However, Lincoln accepted the invitation to deliver an address at Beecher's church in Brooklyn. He was not altogether enthusiastic about the event and expressed some reluctance to speak before an audience of eastern sophisticates. The trip would be arduous and would take him away from his law practice at a crucial time. Though he could build on the political arguments and themes he had used in Ohio, Lincoln knew that for the well-educated audience he would need to prepare a learned lecture. The sponsors of the speech and Lincoln agreed on a late February 1860 date for the address instead of November, and unbeknownst to Lincoln until he arrived in New York, the site of the event was changed from the Brooklyn church to Cooper Union in Manhattan.

Did Lincoln view the eastern trip as an opportunity to advance his presidential ambitions? In his study of the Cooper Union address, Harold Holzer contended that the invitation ignited the spark in Lincoln's ambition that carried him to the presidency. David Herbert Donald, in his magisterial biography of Lincoln, maintained that the alacrity with which he accepted the invitation reflected his already developing interest in seeking the presidential nomination. Lincoln, Donald wrote, saw the speech as an opportunity to advance his candidacy.[4] William Baringer, in contrast, in his 1937 study of Lincoln's nomination, downplayed the invitation's importance in stoking Lincoln's presidential ambitions. Lincoln, this historian suggested, knew that a speech, even in the New York area, could not make him Seward's leading challenger for the nomination. "Practical politics, not speeches, win nominations," Baringer wrote. Thus, Lincoln went to New York with only the vaguest notion of what effect his appearance might have. Though he was determined to do well, he was surprised to find himself "the lion of the hour" after the Cooper Union address and in great demand to speak elsewhere in the East.[5] Whatever Lincoln's thinking in accepting the invitation, historians have agreed that eastern support for his candidacy grew as a result of his Cooper Union address and his subsequent campaign swing through New England.

Lincoln must have realized that his speech in New York, as well as other appearances in the region, would give him an opportunity to meet influential eastern Republicans and disabuse them of the notion that he was only a provincial western Republican leader. By giving him national exposure, Lincoln's trip to New York would enhance his reputation as a national party leader and strengthen both the party and the antislavery cause in Illinois against the Democrats. Lincoln may even have hoped that if Seward faltered in the Northeast, he could become a contender for the Republican nomination. Friends like Orville Browning, however, still considered Lincoln only a state or regional leader and favored Bates for the nomination. Radicals in the upper West, including northern Illinois, supported Seward, though not with much enthusiasm. Lincoln needed the virtually unanimous support of Illinois Republicans in order to mount a serious challenge to Seward in the national Republican convention. Support for Seward in the upper North, and for Cameron, Chase, and Bates in the lower North, would also have to erode in order for Lincoln to acquire a national following substantial enough to propel him into the Republican nomination.

BEFORE LEAVING FOR New York, Lincoln traveled to Kansas to assist Republicans in that disputed territory in their campaign to elect antislavery state officers and a congressman under the proposed free-state constitution adopted at Wyandotte and ratified by the voters on October 4.[6] This election, scheduled for December 6, was the final step in what Republicans hoped would be congressional approval of statehood for the territory that had been in the center of the sectional storm since the mid-1850s. A fragile peace had been achieved on the turbulent Kansas-Missouri border, and antislavery men were optimistic that they would win the election. But this was before their old antislavery avenger, John Brown, struck in Virginia on October 16 and revived passions along the border. Two Kansas editors, Lincoln's friend Mark Delahay of the *Leavenworth Times* and Daniel Wilder of the *Elwood Free Press,* issued an urgent call for the western Republican champion to bring his conservative antislavery message to the territory. Lincoln accepted the invitation, as he told his Kansas friends, out of a sense of duty "to your country and our common cause." Lincoln might also have concluded that his appearance in Kansas was timely from a personal political standpoint, especially since it would follow his Ohio success and attract Republican attention outside as well as inside the territory. Though the trip would be a drain on his finances, in agreeing to make the visit Lincoln announced that he felt "an eternal debt of gratitude" to "the friends of Freedom in Kansas."[7]

Lincoln packed his carpetbag, though somehow he failed to include a winter coat, and left for Kansas on November 30. The journey, undertaken in cold weather, would become one of the most arduous of his career. However, Lincoln's robust physical condition and experience with harsh winter conditions as a youth and as a lawyer riding the judicial circuit had prepared him for such trips. At Quincy, Lincoln took the ferry downriver on the Mississippi to Hannibal, Missouri, the hometown of young riverboat pilot Samuel Langhorne Clemens (Mark Twain). A crowd followed him as he walked the streets of Hannibal; but apparently Clemens was on the river and did not see Lincoln.[8] At Hannibal, Lincoln boarded a train for an uncomfortable ride to St. Joseph on the Missouri River, where Delahay and Wilder met him. The three men went to the riverbank and waited in the cold wind on a log for the ferry to take them to Elwood, a small Kansas town.[9]

Tired after the hard two-day trip and feeling ill upon his arrival at Elwood, Lincoln still spoke to a group of about forty men in the local hotel's dining room. Wilder reported the speech in his *Elwood Free Press*. Lincoln referred to the strife and bloodshed in Kansas that had grown out of "the new policy" for the territories enacted in the Kansas-Nebraska bill. Conceding that both parties had been guilty of outrages in the territory, he declared that a new age had dawned for Kansans with the adoption of the free-state constitution. He predicted that Kansas would soon take its place "in the brotherhood of States." As before, Lincoln stressed the Founding Fathers' antislavery intentions for the nation. He concluded with what evidently was his first public statement on John Brown and "the Harper's Ferry Affair." Lincoln asserted that Brown's attack was wrong for two reasons. "It was a violation of law and it was, as all such attacks must be, futile as far as any effect it might have on the extinction of a great evil." He told his Elwood audience that the proper means for expressing antislavery sentiment was through the ballot box, not through "violence or crime." Lincoln admonished "all to go out to the election on Tuesday [December 6] and to vote as became the Freemen of Kansas."[10] He meant that they should cast their ballots for the Republican candidates for state offices and for Congress.

After spending the night in Elwood, Lincoln took a cold buggy ride across the prairie to Troy. Along the 30-mile route, Henry Villard, a young New York newspaper correspondent, met the shivering Lincoln and lent him a buffalo robe to keep warm. A small group of dedicated Republicans turned out at the primitive courthouse in Troy to hear Lincoln speak. He went on to Doniphan, a frontier community, and to Atchison, where he spoke at the Methodist Church in the evening. (It was also the day that Virginia authorities hanged John Brown.) In each place, he spoke for almost two hours to audiences that never exceeded 200. Lincoln reportedly told a Kansas friend who apologized for the lack of a large turnout: "I never stop to inquire as to the character or numbers of those likely to hear me. To accomplish a little good is more gratifying to me than to receive empty applause."[11] Though the three speeches were not reported in the press, eyewitnesses remembered that Lincoln repeated the themes that he had expressed at Elwood.[12]

The next morning, December 3, Lincoln took a jolting carriage ride of 20 frozen miles to Leavenworth, where a crowd of supporters greeted him and escorted him to his hotel. That evening Lincoln made his major Kansas address, which was to a large gathering of free soilers at Stockton Hall. The thrust of this speech did not substantially differ from his talk at Elwood. In addition, Lincoln took pains to dispute the Democrats' claim that they were conservative and the Republicans radical. "What is conservatism?" he asked. "Preserving the old against the new," he answered. "Possibly you [the Democrats] mean you are conservative in trying to maintain the existing institution of slavery." Republicans were true conservatives, he said, in that they were attempting to maintain "the peace of society, and the structure of our government" established by the republic's Founders. This required that "we should let [slavery] alone" in the states where it existed but prevent its expansion.[13]

Responding to the Democratic charge that the Republicans had raised the slavery issue to greater prominence than before and had thereby precipitated the sectional crisis, Lincoln, as on other occasions, turned the tables on his adversaries. The Democrats, he argued, had ignited the slavery controversy with the Kansas-Nebraska bill and subsequently had raised the threat of secession if a "Black Republican" were elected president. Republicans, in contrast, had submitted peacefully to the election of a Democratic government under James Buchanan. Then, in a promise that, if indeed he had made it, proved prophetic, Lincoln reportedly told southern rights advocates that if the Republicans were successful in electing a president, "it will be our duty to see that you submit," even to the extent of "deal[ing] with you as old John Brown has been dealt with" by Virginia. Still, he said, "we hope and believe that in no section will a majority so act as to render such extreme measures necessary." While denouncing southern rights radicals or "fire-eaters," Lincoln also sought to disassociate his party from John Brown–type extremism: "Old John Brown has just been executed for treason against a state. We cannot object, even though he agreed with us in thinking slavery wrong. That cannot excuse violence, bloodshed, and treason. It could not avail him nothing that he might think himself right."[14]

Two days later, in a second speech at Leavenworth, Lincoln contended that Brown was insane, and he claimed that he had yet to find the first Republican who supported the Harpers Ferry raid to free slaves. Lincoln, however, told his audience that the institution of slavery fostered such uprisings. Though he repeated the Republican position that slavery was wrong, Lincoln declared, according to the newspaper report of the speech, that he wanted to keep the races separate. The "flimsy diatribes" about racial amalgamation "were perpetrated by the Democracy to divert the public mind from the real issue—the extension or the non-extension of slavery—its localization or its nationalization." The only solution to the troubles over slavery was the restoration of the Founders' policy to contain the institution and thereby put it en route to extinction.[15]

Clearly, in his Kansas speeches in late 1859 Lincoln recognized the racially charged atmosphere in the border country after John Brown's raid. Despite the fact that Kansans had ratified the free-soil constitution promulgated at Wyandotte, Lincoln and local Republican leaders worried that the reaction to the Harpers Ferry assault would cause a defeat for their party candidates at the polls on December 6 and undermine their efforts for statehood. Anxious about the outcome, Lincoln remained in Leavenworth for the election.[16] The Republicans won the election for state offices, but southerners in Congress, joined by some northern Democrats and ultraconservatives, in February 1860 voted down a statehood bill for the territory. Not until early 1861, after the lower South had withdrawn from the Union, did Congress admit Kansas as a state under the free-soil Wyandotte constitution.

RETURNING FROM KANSAS on December 8, Lincoln for the next two months busily attended to legal matters, including appearances before the state supreme court and the federal circuit court in Springfield. He also continued to referee the feud between John Wentworth and Norman B. Judd, the resolution of which was essential to Republican unity in Illinois and his own political fate. Lincoln discovered that support for his presidential nomination as a western alternative to Seward had grown since the October and November elections and John Brown's raid. One year earlier, Jesse Fell had asked Lincoln for an autobiography for distribution, but it had not been forthcoming. Now, in late December 1859, in view of the boomlet for his candidacy, Lincoln complied with the request. Referring to his autobiography as "a little sketch," which it was, Lincoln remarked, in a comment that has become legendary for understatement, "There is not much of it, for the reason, I suppose, that there is not much of me." He specifically told Fell "not to go beyond the material" in the sketch or reveal that he had written it. Fell sent the sketch to a Pennsylvania friend, who, despite Lincoln's instructions, elaborated on the material before having it published in the *Chester County Times* on February 11. Other Republican newspapers immediately copied it. This would be the first of several lives of Lincoln to appear in 1860; others were published after his nomination in May and would be true to the genre of "campaign biographies."[17]

Lincoln's decision to write the autobiographical sketch for Fell, like his renewed efforts to secure the publication of his 1858 debates with Douglas, meant that he had determined to pursue the nomination, albeit with due caution. In early 1860 (probably January), a number of prominent Illinois Republicans, including chairman Judd and other members of the state party central committee, met with Lincoln in the office of Illinois Secretary of State Ozias M. Hatch. According to Jackson Grimshaw, a participant, they "asked him if his name might be used at once in Connection with the coming Nomination and Election." Lincoln, Grimshaw later wrote, "with his characteristic modesty," expressed doubt about "whether he could get the Nomination even if he wished it." But Lincoln told them that he would give his answer the next morning. It was reasonable to assume that during the evening he carefully discussed the matter with Mary, who probably encouraged him to give the answer that his friends wanted—and probably that he also wanted. When the group met the next day, he authorized them "to consider him and work for him . . . as a Candidate for the Presidency."[18]

Though the state party central committee made no public announcement of support, a number of Republican newspapers in the state soon fell into line behind Lincoln. On January 14, the *Springfield Illinois State Journal* declared that the people of Illinois would place Lincoln's name before the Republican convention for the presidency. "They do it because they . . . have confidence in him as a man for the times; because with him in the Presidential chair, the rights of the people of all the States will be secured, respected and maintained; because he interprets the constitution as did our fathers who made it and illustrated it in their acts; because he is a conservative National Republican," the editor wrote. Furthermore, he predicted that Lincoln could easily win the critical western states in the election. On January 18, the anti-Republican *Louisville Journal* noted that newspapers beyond Illinois, particularly in the West, were proclaiming Lincoln as their choice for president. "We do not concur with him in some of his views, but there is much good in Abraham's bosom," the *Journal* announced.[19]

The *Chicago Press and Tribune,* much to the dismay of many Lincoln supporters, hesitated in its endorsement of Lincoln mainly because Joseph Medill, one of its editors, had privately favored Chase. But on February 16, this influential western newspaper, a few days before Lincoln left for New York to speak, proclaimed its support for the Springfield lawyer, justifying its decision primarily on the ground that he could win the key states of the lower North.[20] The *Press and Tribune* explained that Lincoln was "more certain to carry Illinois and Indiana than any one else, and his political antecedents are such as to commend him heartily to the support of [pro-tariff] Pennsylvania and New Jersey." His record, the newspaper insisted, was "right" for attracting old Fillmore Whig supporters, whose votes would be crucial in the 1860 election. As "an Old Line Whig of the Henry Clay school," Lincoln's antislavery principles would never lead him to violate his "constitutional conservatism" and his "respect for existing institutions and laws." Furthermore, the paper said, Lincoln was "a gentleman of unimpeachable purity of private life. His good name is not soiled by a single act, political, social, moral or religious, that we of his friends need blush to own as his." With considerable insight, the *Press and Tribune* also declared that Lincoln was a man of "great breadth and great acuteness of intellect. Not learned, in a bookish sense, but master of great fundamental principles, and of that kind of ability which applies them to crises and events."[21]

Inspired by the growing support in early 1860, Lincoln realized that his trip to New York in February could further his candidacy. With that in mind, as well as a strong desire to promote his party's antislavery principles in the East, Lincoln set to work preparing his "lecture." His themes would be the same ones that he had emphasized in his 1859 political speeches in Ohio, Wisconsin, Kansas, and Illinois, namely the Republican commitment to the antislavery principles of the Founding Fathers and the Democrats' violation of those principles. Lincoln would seek to refute Douglas's version of the history of slavery as put forward in his *Harper's Magazine* article. Because he would be speaking to a more cosmopolitan audience in New York than in the West, and because his address would be a "lecture," not a campaign speech, Lincoln felt compelled to pay greater attention than before to specific points. This meant intensive research in government documents and other relevant publications available in Springfield. Indeed, Lincoln went to work like a historian with the materials in the state capitol library, searching printed federal documents, the *Debates in the Federal Convention of 1787*, and the published papers of George Washington and James Madison. Herndon remembered that, despite Lincoln's thorough preparation, when he left for New York on February 23, "we had many misgivings—and he not a few himself—of his success in the great metropolis."[22] The local Democratic newspaper could not resist making a satirical comment in reporting Lincoln's departure to deliver the lecture: "Subject [of his speech], not known. Consideration, $200 and expenses. Object, presidential capital. Effect, disappointment."[23]

Lincoln's trip to the East in the dead of winter required more than two days and three nights of travel on five different trains, along with transfers that meant waiting in cold railroad stations. Lincoln arrived unheralded in New York on Saturday, February 25, and took a room at the Astor House. He was not to speak until Monday. New York was a city in ferment, which must have shocked Lincoln's small-town sensibilities. After reading in the newspaper that his lecture had been changed from Beecher's church in Brooklyn to Cooper Union in Manhattan, Lincoln expressed his concern to Richard C. McCormick that the lecture, though political, was designed for a church audience and presumably might not appeal to a broader group. Lincoln told McCormick, a member of the executive committee of the Young Men's Republican Union, which had assumed the sponsorship of the event, that he would need time to revise the speech to fit the Cooper Union audience. (McCormick's organization, despite its name, was dominated by older and prominent New York Republicans.) Lincoln spent much of his first day in New York revising the manuscript and making appropriate changes.[24]

The next day, Lincoln took the ferry across the East River to attend Henry Ward Beecher's church and hear the powerful antislavery minister's sermon. Back at the Astor, still anxious about his lecture, he continued to revise it. On Monday—before the event at Cooper Union, which was to be in the evening—he held court for Republicans who wanted to know more about this strange western leader and also to invite him to speak elsewhere. At some point during the day, Lincoln decided to tour Manhattan and visit the studio of the renowned photographer Mathew Brady on Bleecker Street. In the studio, he not only had what he called his "shaddow" recorded for posterity— and for the political campaign of 1860—he also met George Bancroft, the most distinguished historian of his day. Bancroft, though a staunch political opponent of the Republicans, cordially greeted Lincoln. Richard McCormick recalled that "the contrast in the two men was most striking—the one courtly and precise in his every word and gesture, with the air of a trans-Atlantic statesman; the other bluff and awkward, his every utterance an apology for his ignorance of metropolitan manners and customs."[25]

FIFTEEN HUNDRED PEOPLE, who paid twenty-five cents apiece for their tickets, turned out that night in the Great Hall of Cooper Union to hear Lincoln speak.[26] The Great Hall, a red-brick building, still stands in Manhattan. Three-fourths of the seats in the hall's basement auditorium were filled for Lincoln's address. Many in the audience expected "something weird, rough, and uncultivated" in the speaker's performance. Though he had bought a new black suit for the occasion, at a cost of $100 (one-half the amount of the honorarium), Lincoln's initial appearance at the podium did not immediately change the audience's preconceived notions about him. One listener, recalling his first impression of the Illinois Republican, noted "the long, ungainly figure, upon which hung clothes that, while new for the trip, were evidently the work of an unskilled tailor; the large feet; the clumsy hands, of which . . . the orator seemed to be unduly conscious; the long, gaunt head capped by a shock of hair that seemed not to have been thoroughly brushed out." Others rendered a similar description of the speaker. Introduced by the distinguished poet-editor William Cullen Bryant, Lincoln began awkwardly. His obvious nervousness in the beginning and his high-pitched voice caused many in the audience to fear that the Young Men's Republican Union had hoodwinked them into attending an awful performance.[27]

But once Lincoln relaxed and began to present his arguments, the audience realized that, despite his awkward and unattractive appearance, this westerner was something special. When he reached his subject, one observer noted, "he straightened up, made regular and graceful gestures; his face lightened as with an inward fire; the whole man was transfigured." Another person remarked that, though "his manner was to a New York audience a very strange one, . . . he held the vast meeting spell-bound. . . . I think I never saw an audience more carried away by an orator."[28] The Cooper Union audience, the *New York Tribune* reported, "frequently rang with cheers and shouts of applause" as Lincoln spoke. "One of nature's orators," the *Tribune* noted, Lincoln used "his rare powers solely and effectively to elucidate and convince, though their inevitable effect is to delight and electrify as well."[29]

Harold Holzer, in his highly acclaimed book on the Cooper Union address and the events associated with it, contended that the speech was a rousing antislavery appeal. Though implicitly conservative in one passage in order "to fend off Southern charges that Northerners [were] destructive," Holzer argues, the speech was actually a radical call to save "popular government and personal liberty" from the perpetuators of slavery. "In truth," Holzer wrote, "there is nothing conservative about it by 1860 standards."[30] However, not all historians have shared Holzer's view. In fact, despite Lincoln's occasional forceful rhetoric, a close reading of the speech reveals that it largely reaffirmed the conservative approach to slavery that he had expressed in his 1858–1859 public appearances. Lincoln by now no doubt hoped to persuade eastern Republicans that he was a conservative alternative to Seward and Chase for the presidency. A radical appeal in New York would not have served this purpose. If indeed he did want to win New Yorkers over to his side for the nomination, he was partly successful. Despite the contention of Holzer and others that the Cooper Union address was "the speech that made Lincoln president," it proved only one step—albeit an important step—toward his securing the nomination. The speech was probably less significant in the long run than his campaigns against Douglas in 1858–1859. Political considerations and developments—some of Lincoln's own making—still had to come together before he could become the alternative to Seward.

From the beginning to the end of the address, Lincoln demonstrated his mastery of the antislavery political argument that these eastern Republicans held dear—an argument that other speakers had failed to adequately illuminate. The depth of his research, and the precision with which he developed the history of the slavery question, impressed the educated elite in the audience, who did not expect such an intellectual triumph from the "backwoods" lawyer. Focusing on the Founding Fathers' policies and intentions regarding the institution, Lincoln appealed to the New Yorkers because he avoided both the radicalism of Seward and Chase and the violent extremism of John Brown. The logic in his historical and constitutional reasoning against slavery made good political sense to them. They also applauded Lincoln's denunciation of slavery on moral grounds and the clarity with which he contrasted his view with the Douglas and Democratic "don't care" policy toward the institution.

Lincoln began his speech with an attack on Douglas's argument in *Harper's Magazine* that the Founding Fathers had left the matter of slavery for the local citizens to decide without federal interference. The Illinois Republican leader in effect was continuing his debate over slavery with Douglas, which had begun in 1854. The Cooper Union address began the final chapter in the epic struggle between Lincoln and Douglas. In his speech, Lincoln argued that the Little Giant's history of the actions and intentions of the Founders regarding slavery was specious. He told his audience that, contrary to what Douglas had claimed, nothing in the Constitution framed by the Founders "forbid *our Federal Government* to control as to slavery in *our Federal Territories.*" Lincoln then traced the record of the thirty-nine signers of the Constitution, beginning with their prohibition of slavery in the Northwest Territory and continuing with their position on the territories and states formed out of the 1803 Louisiana Purchase. Though Congress never banned slavery in the Southwest, he argued, it did "take control of it" in a number of ways, including a prohibition on the foreign importation of slaves into the territories. Lincoln provided statistics on how the signers of the Constitution acted on all of the issues relating to slavery that were debated in Congress during the three decades after ratification. He concluded that "twenty-three out of our thirty-nine fathers who framed the Government under which we live" did not express opposition to congressional authority over the institution in the territories. The remaining sixteen, Lincoln said, "so far as I have discovered, have left no record of their understanding upon the direct question of federal control of slavery in the federal territories."[31]

Senator Douglas, Lincoln informed the Cooper Union audience, "has no right to mislead others, who have less access to history, and less leisure to study it, into the false belief" that the framers forbade the federal government from controlling slavery in the territories. In his version of history, Douglas had substituted "falsehood and deception for truthful evidence and fair argument." Lincoln contended, as he had done many times before, that the Founders marked slavery "as an evil not to be extended, but to be tolerated and protected only because of and so far as its actual presence among us makes that toleration and protection a necessity."[32]

Lincoln then addressed "a few words to the Southern people," who, he admitted, would probably not listen. He also intended his remarks for southern sympathizers in the North. "[Southerners] say we are sectional. We deny it," Lincoln declared. The burden of proof was upon them, he said. "The fact that we get no votes in your section, is a fact of your making, and not of ours," he continued, because southerners could not "show that we repel you by some wrong principle or practice." "If our principle, put in practice, would wrong your section for the benefit of ours, or for any other object, then our principle, and we with it, are sectional, and are justly opposed and denounced as such." But Republicans based their policy of preventing slavery's expansion on what the Founders, including Washington, "thought so clearly right" to adopt, and this restriction did not hurt either section. Lincoln asked: "Could George Washington himself speak, would he cast the blame of . . . sectionalism upon us, who sustain his policy, or upon you who repudiate it?"[33]

He next turned to a refutation of the southerners' claim that they were "eminently conservative—while we are revolutionary, destructive or something of the sort." Republicans, he asserted, unlike southern rights advocates (and Douglas Democrats), subscribed to the true definition of conservatism, which was "adherence to the old and tried, against the new and untried," a point that he had made in Kansas and probably on other occasions. Lincoln told Republican opponents that "we stick to, we contend for, the identical old policy" on slavery adopted by the Founders, "while you with one accord reject . . . and spit upon that old policy, and insist upon something new." Furthermore, he said, Republicans denied southerners' claims that "we have made the slavery question more prominent than it formerly was." Southerners, Lincoln argued, had caused the controversy by discarding "the old policy of the fathers" that prohibited the expansion of slavery and the foreign slave trade.[34] "We resisted, and still resist, your innovation" of the policy of the Founders. This was true conservatism, in Lincoln's mind.[35]

At Cooper Union, as in Kansas, Lincoln defended Republicans from the charges that they had been involved with John Brown and that they encouraged slave uprisings in the South. "John Brown was no Republican," he said, pointing out that no one had implicated "a single Republican in [Brown's] Harper's Ferry enterprise." Still directing his remarks at southerners as a rhetorical device, Lincoln contended that his party's "doctrines and declarations" did not lead to violence against them. Republican statements, he insisted, "are accompanied with a continual protest against any interference whatever with your slaves, or with you about your slaves." In common with the Founding Fathers, he said, "[we] declare our belief that slavery is wrong; but the slaves do not hear us declare even this" unless by "your misrepresentations of us, in their hearing," they became aware of it. Lincoln reminded southerners that "slave insurrections are no more common now than they were before the Republican party was organized." "In the present state of things in the United States," he said, "I do not think that a general, or even a very extensive slave insurrection is possible. The indispensable concert of action cannot be attained. The slaves have no means of rapid communication; nor can incendiary freemen, black or white, supply it," as southerners feared. "John Brown's effort was peculiar. It was not a slave insurrection. It was an attempt by white men to get up a revolt among slaves, in which the slaves refused to participate."[36]

Lincoln reassured southerners that the federal government would protect them against servile insurrections, and he emphasized that it had no power under the Constitution to emancipate the slaves. "Under all these circumstances, do you really feel yourselves justified to break up this Government" if a Republican were elected president? he asked. "In that supposed event, you say, you will destroy the Union; and then, you say, the great crime of having destroyed it will be upon us. That is cool. A highwayman holds a pistol to my ear, and mutters through his teeth, 'Stand and deliver, or I shall kill you, and then you will be a murderer!'"[37]

Finally, Lincoln directed "a few words" to Republicans. "Even though much provoked," he admonished his fellow party members, "let us do nothing through passion and ill temper. Even though the southern people will not so much as listen to us, let us calmly consider their demands, and yield to them if, in our deliberate view of our duty, we possibly can." Lincoln asked, "What will satisfy them?" and answered, "Simply this: We must not only let them alone, but we must, somehow, convince them that we do let them alone. This, we know by experience, is no easy task." "We have been trying to convince them from the very beginning of our organization," he said, that Republicans who were against the expansion of slavery wished only to let the South alone, "but with no success." Lincoln told his audience that southerners would only be convinced if "we cease to call slavery *wrong*, and join them in calling it *right*. And this must be done thoroughly—done in *acts* as well as

in *words*. . . . The whole atmosphere must be disinfected from all taint of opposition to slavery, before they will cease to believe that all their troubles
proceed from us." Lincoln asked, "In view of our moral, social, and political
responsibilities, can we do this?" The answer was no. "Let us stand by our
duty, fearlessly and effectively," by preventing slavery's "spread into the National Territories" and keeping it from overrunning "us here in these Free
States," while acknowledging "the necessity arising from its actual presence
in the nation." Lincoln warned against "a policy of 'don't care' on a question
about which all true men do care." He ended his ninety-minute peroration
with what has become a classic Lincoln statement. "Let us have faith that
right makes might, and in that faith, let us, to the end, dare to do our duty
as we understand it."[38]

  With these words, the Cooper Union audience erupted with shouts and
the waving of handkerchiefs and hats. One eyewitness remembered that the
hall "broke out in wild and prolonged enthusiasm. . . . The cheering was tu-
multuous." Years later, newspaperman Noah Brooks quoted a friend who
was so electrified by the speech that he called Lincoln "the greatest man since
St. Paul."[39] William Cullen Bryant's *New York Evening Post* praised the
speech and declared that Lincoln's emphasis on the antislavery position of the
Founding Fathers "strikes us as particularly forcible."[40] The *New York Tribune* immediately printed the speech and made it available for other newspapers. Lincoln later supervised the preparation of his acclaimed speech in
pamphlet form.[41]

LINCOLN LEFT the next day for Providence, Rhode Island, en route to visit his
son Robert at Phillips Exeter Academy in New Hampshire. His growing
reputation as a Republican spokesman, enhanced by his Cooper Union address, preceded him, and Lincoln found himself in great demand to speak.
The reception that the Illinois Republican received in Providence, where he
next spoke, was typical of the twelve days that he spent in New England.
"Railroad Hall was filled to overflowing . . . to welcome and to hear the
great champion of Republicanism in Illinois," the *Providence Journal* reported. After the address, many in the audience gathered around him for
"the pleasure of a personal introduction to the distinguished orator."[42]

  Lincoln wrote Mary that he had difficulty making speeches in New England "before reading audiences, who have already seen all my ideas in
print."[43] In his nine New England speeches, Lincoln largely repeated the
main points that he had made at Cooper Union. An exception was at Hartford and New Haven, where he noted the ongoing strike of Massachusetts
shoemakers and ridiculed Senator Douglas's claim that it arose from the "sec-

tional warfare" that had reduced the demand for New England products. Lincoln told his listeners, "You have not lost that trade; orders were never better than now!" Douglas's contention, the Illinois Republican insisted, was simply "another bushwhacking contrivance" by the senator and his southern friends in Congress to frighten northerners into ceasing their support of the Republicans. "I am glad to know," Lincoln declared, "that there is a system of labor where the laborer can strike if he wants to! I would to God that such a system prevailed all over the world."[44] In supporting collective action by workers he was taking a political risk in the America of the 1850s, which considered labor organizations a conspiracy against property rights. But although he probably sincerely believed in the workers' right to strike, Lincoln did not pursue this issue elsewhere. Returning to the issue would have diverted attention from the central issue of slavery, both in Lincoln's thinking and in his political strategy.

Leaving Providence on February 29, Lincoln traveled to Exeter, where he met Robert and members of a Republican committee from Concord, New Hampshire. The committee secured his promise to speak in their town the next day. After addressing Concord Republicans, Lincoln, accompanied by Robert and his classmate George Latham of Springfield, went on to Manchester, where he addressed enthusiastic crowds. Later Lincoln spoke at Dover and then at Exeter. He spent Sunday, March 3, with Robert and his friends at the Exeter Academy. Writing from Exeter, Lincoln complained to Mary that he was tired and anxious to go home. "I have been unable to escape the toil," he said. "If I had foreseen it I think I would not have come East at all."[45]

Despite his desire to go home, Lincoln still had speaking engagements to keep, especially in Connecticut, where important state elections would take place in a few weeks. Hartford Republican O. R. Post had written Lincoln that "our opponents are moving 'heaven and earth' to cut down our small majority, knowing full well that this is their last chance for breaking the Republican front in New England." Post, along with other state Republicans, "earnestly entreated" Lincoln to come to Connecticut and campaign for the party. Though Massachusetts Republicans wanted him to speak in their state, they told Lincoln that "the Connecticut people need you more & have more right to claim you. The cause is strong in Massachusetts, & Connecticut is suffering."[46]

Lincoln agreed. Bidding farewell to Robert, he went to Hartford, Meriden, and New Haven to speak, and he also crossed the state line to Woonsocket in Rhode Island. He made his final New England appearances at Norwich and Bridgeport, Connecticut.[47] At each place, "earnest Republicans," with bands playing and placards waving, greeted the western hero and escorted him into town. When Lincoln spoke at night, they formed torchlight processions and accompanied him to the place appointed for the speech, where crowds waited to hear him. (The political organization and campaign activities associated with his New England speaking tour, though on a smaller scale, were similar to those in Illinois.) The Republican press in the towns he visited naturally praised his speeches as the most important heard in their communities in many years. The *New Haven Palladium* asserted that Lincoln's address in their town "was the most powerful and convincing argument for Republican principles we ever listened to."[48]

At home, political friends seized eagerly on the eastern Republican acclaim for Lincoln's speaking efforts in the region. The *Chicago Press and Tribune* proudly reported that "the Republican journals of New Hampshire and Rhode Island speak of [Lincoln's] progress through those States as something like the march of a conqueror. . . . We hazard nothing in saying that no man has ever before risen so rapidly to political eminence in the United States." Lincoln's thorough preparation and his mastery of the subject matter, the *Press and Tribune* said, set him apart from other politicians and contributed much to his success in the East.[49] Despite the praise, no New England newspaper joined the Illinois Republican press in proclaiming Lincoln its candidate for president. Even Lincoln's hometown Republican newspaper admitted that Seward remained "unquestionably the choice of a majority of the Republican party for the Presidency," a conclusion that the *Press and Tribune* also drew.[50]

Nonetheless, his triumphant tour, including his appearance at Cooper Union, brought Lincoln to the attention of eastern Republican activists in a dramatic way and made it possible for them to support him if Seward could not win the nomination. Connecticut Republicans particularly appreciated the aid that Lincoln gave their candidates in the hard-fought spring elections that they won, an important point that historians have missed in their accounts of Lincoln's northeastern trip.[51] The vote was close in Connecticut, prompting fears among state Republicans that they could not succeed if the "radical" Seward of "irrepressible conflict" notoriety was the party's presidential candidate. James F. Babcock, editor of the *New Haven Palladium*, wrote Lincoln that "since the election, I have heard your name mentioned more freely than ever in Connection with the Chicago nomination." Some who favored other candidates, he said, "speak of you as their next preference, and their belief that we can carry this State for you by 5000 to 7000 majority. . . . I have written to some of our friends in Washington to that effect." Lincoln agreed that the close election in Connecticut and also in Rhode Island signified "a drawback upon the prospects of Gov. Seward." He was careful, however, not to speculate on how these elections might affect his own presidential prospects.[52] As it turned out, Lincoln's New England campaign probably proved more important than his historically acclaimed Cooper Union address in making him acceptable in the Northeast as an alternative to Seward.

ON MARCH 12, after a brief return to New York, Lincoln took the northern route home, arriving in Springfield two days later. He received the "earnest congratulations" of his friends for his eastern success, discovered that a number of Republican newspapers in the state had announced their support for his candidacy, and found encouraging letters that he needed to answer. One letter came from Mark W. Delahay in Kansas, who wanted Lincoln to provide him with $100 to finance his trip to the national convention in Chicago, where he would work for his old friend's nomination. He also wanted "a small loan of money" to aid his own election to the Senate. Lincoln gently replied that he wished him elected but that he had already "abundantly manifested" his friendship by campaigning with him in Kansas, and he could not lend the money. Delahay also suggested that Lincoln use money to advance his presidential candidacy. "I can not enter the ring on the money basis," Lincoln wrote, "first, because, in the main, it is wrong; and secondly, I have not, and can not get, the money. I say, in the main, the use of money is wrong; but for certain objects, in a political contest, the use of some, is both right, and indispendable [sic]." Lincoln probably meant that it was appropriate to raise money for the publication and distribution of campaign literature and also to pay the expenses of stump speakers. But he refused to offer money to secure votes. Lincoln informed Delahay that "with me, as with yourself, this long struggle" in the antislavery cause "has been one of great pecuniary loss." However, he promised Delahay, "If you shall be appointed a delegate to Chicago, I will furnish one hundred dollars to bear the expences [sic] of the trip." Delahay was not a delegate to the convention, but Lincoln still provided the one hundred dollars for him to travel to Chicago, where the Kansas politician lobbied for his friend's nomination.[53]

By late March Lincoln had gained a fair understanding of the lay of the land regarding the Republican presidential nomination. He learned from Samuel Galloway, his astute political friend in Columbus, that the Ohio delegation would probably support Governor Chase on the first ballot in the national convention but not on subsequent ballots. "There will be but little fervent attachment to Mr Chase in the Ohio delegation" because of his radicalism, Galloway reported. "No one intelligent as to general sentiment even *imagines* that he can be nominated. He could not be elected, if nominated." Galloway told Lincoln that "the predominant feeling demands a Candidate of Conservative Character." Seward's recent speech in the Senate in which he trimmed his radical sails "was significant proof of this fact." The New York senator, Galloway said, "will doubtless enter the Convention with the largest plurality vote. He cannot however be nominated unless Pennsylvania & New Jersey give him their votes—as the West and the North West, excepting Wisconsin & Minnesota will give him but few if any votes." Galloway informed Lincoln that "the concurrent opinion of our most intelligent politicians is that either you or Bates will be nominated," with the critical choice coming from the Pennsylvania and New Jersey delegations.[54]

Lincoln found Galloway's report encouraging. Richard M. Corwine of Cincinnati and Edwin A. Parrott, a member of the Ohio legislature, had written him to the same effect. Parrott said that "you have a great many friends in this Genl Assembly, as a candidate for the Presidency." They proposed to form a Lincoln club for the purpose of circulating campaign literature.[55] On March 24, Lincoln wrote Galloway that "I am gratified to know I have friends in Ohio who are disposed to give me the highest evidence of their friendship." He added, "If I have any chance, it consists mainly in the fact that the *whole* opposition [to the Democrats in the North] would vote for me if nominated. . . . I suppose I am not the *first* choice of a very great many." Most of the Republican delegates were committed to Seward, Bates, Chase, or Cameron, at least on the early balloting. "Our policy, then, is to give no offence to others—leave them in a mood to come to us, if they should be compelled to give up their first love," Lincoln said. Such a strategy, he informed Galloway, would deal "justly with all" and leave "us in a mood to support heartily whoever shall be nominated." He asked his Ohio friend to follow these "suggestions" in seeking support for him among Ohio Republicans. However, Lincoln admonished Galloway "to do no ungenerous thing towards Governor Chase, because he gave us his sympathy in 1858, when scarcely any other distinguished man did."[56] No doubt he was sincere, but Lincoln could have had another reason for his advice that the governor be treated kindly. He might have felt he would need the support of Chase delegates to defeat Seward if the balloting for the presidential nomination became extended in the national convention.

The month of April saw a greater surge in support for Lincoln. Douglas's expected nomination for president by the Democrats, who were to meet in Charleston, South Carolina, in late April, placed a premium upon the selection by the Republicans of a westerner with a growing national reputation who could defeat the Little Giant in the battleground states. To his friends, Lincoln remained the ideal candidate to oppose Douglas. He had built his national reputation on campaigning against Douglas and had skillfully emphasized the differences between his conservative antislavery position and

Douglas's "don't care," popular-sovereignty doctrine regarding slavery in the territories. Furthermore, except for his House Divided Speech, Lincoln had little ideological or political baggage that could work against him among Know Nothings and other nativists, on one side of the political spectrum, or among German Americans, on the other. His support for the Fugitive Slave Act concerned radical antislavery men in the upper West, including northern Illinois.[57] But they constituted a minority in the Republican party, and their desire to defeat Douglas and the Democrats would overcome any reservations they might have about Lincoln. Judge David Davis wrote Lincoln on the eve of the state Republican convention in early May that if the Democrats nominated Douglas, "your chances will be excellent."[58]

Both Davis and Lincoln recognized that the proceedings in the Illinois state convention, which would be meeting one week before the national convention, could seriously complicate his presidential candidacy. For Lincoln, the state convention posed something of a dilemma. On the one hand, as Davis warned him, he could alienate some of his supporters and risk losing the convention's overwhelming presidential endorsement if he interfered in the selection of the party's nominees for state offices. On the other hand, Norman B. Judd, chair of the state Republican committee and a former Democrat, expected Lincoln to "quietly shape the destinies of the [Illinois] party" at the convention. Judd specifically told him that he should interfere to ensure that "the State ticket [would] not be made up exclusively of men of Whig antecedents." With his own gubernatorial candidacy in mind, Judd said that "some prominent place must be reserved for our branch" of the party. He even suggested that many former Democrats in the Republican party would vote for their old leader, Douglas, if slighted in the selections.[59] Lincoln, however, wisely took Davis's advice, not Judd's, and refrained from intervening in the state nominations.

Then, virtually on the eve of the state Republican convention, an unexpected problem confronted Lincoln. A late movement was afoot in the West to advance the aging associate justice of the U.S. Supreme Court, John McLean of Ohio, as a compromise candidate. His supporters argued that McLean could appeal to all political elements and geographic divisions in the party. Joseph Medill of the *Chicago Press and Tribune*, whose newspaper had already endorsed Lincoln, wrote Senator Trumbull on April 16 that "an impression is gaining ground that the Chicago Convention *dare* not nominate Seward, Bates or Lincoln," and that McLean, a conservative Republican who had dissented in the infamous Dred Scott decision, could "harmonize and unite all segments of the opposition" to the Democrats. Medill dangled before Trumbull the prospect of the vice presidential nomination on the McLean ticket with the expectation that the elderly McLean would die in office and he would become president.[60] (Medill's prediction that McLean would not survive a term in office proved true; he died on April 4, 1861.)

Senator Trumbull probably was not interested in giving up his Senate seat for the vice presidency on the chance that McLean, if elected, would die and that he would succeed him. But the Republican senator was sobered by Medill's report that Lincoln did not appear to be the strongest candidate for westerners to support. After consulting with his Republican friends in Washington, Trumbull, on April 24, wrote Lincoln that, though he supported his candidacy, "this McLean movement is daily gaining strength, & even now looks formidable." Trumbull told Lincoln that McLean was the best alternative to Seward, who could not win Pennsylvania and other key states. The implication was clear: Lincoln should stand aside for McLean. Concerned, however, that he might alienate Lincoln and damage his own political standing in Illinois, Trumbull asked him for his views on the McLean movement.[61]

The senator's letter upset Lincoln. The news about a McLean boomlet, if true, threatened to undercut the momentum that his candidacy had received in Illinois on the eve of the state Republican convention. Without the undivided support of that body and the delegation to be sent to the national convention, Lincoln knew that he had no chance against Seward in Chicago. On April 29, he wrote a carefully worded response to Trumbull that had undertones of anger and an implied threat. It revealed a rare, hard side of Lincoln. "I will be entirely frank," Lincoln told him. "The taste is in my mouth a little," he said, and he warned the senator to "write no letters which can possibly be distorted into opposition, or quasi opposition to me" for the nomination. "There are men on the constant watch for such things out of which to prejudice my peculiar friends against you." As for a McLean candidacy, Lincoln wrote, "I hear no objection to [him], except his age; but that objection seems to occur to every one; and it is possible it might leave him no stronger than the others." Lincoln assured Trumbull that, "while I have no more suspicion of you than I have of my best friend living, I am kept in a constant struggle against suggestions of this sort." He also told the senator "that by no advice or consent of mine, shall my pretentions [*sic*] be pressed to the point of endangering our common cause."[62] Though he must have resented the dictation and the tone of the letter, Trumbull grasped the message: He ceased to promote McLean and instead rallied his friends in the party behind Lincoln's candidacy. David Davis, who in the past had been inclined to believe the worst about Trumbull, now assured Lincoln that the senator was true to him.[63]

On May 2, one week before the state Republican convention was to meet and two weeks before the national convention, Lincoln sized up his strength among the delegates based on the reports that he had received. In a letter to

Richard M. Corwine of Ohio, he predicted that "the Illinois delegation will be unanamous [*sic*] for me at the start; and no other delegation will." He believed that "a few individuals in other delegations would like to go for me at the start, but may be restrained by their colleagues. . . . The whole of Indiana might not be difficult to get." Lincoln acknowledged that he was not the first choice in Ohio but said, "Yet I have not heard that any one makes any positive objection to me. It is just so everywhere so far as I can perceive."[64] The state Republican conventions in Iowa, Wisconsin, and Minnesota had met early in the year, before Lincoln's candidacy had achieved momentum, and had selected Seward delegates for the national convention. Many of these delegates, despite their commitment to Seward, now favored Lincoln and could be expected to swing to him after the first ballot, Lincoln said.[65] Still, much depended on Republican unity in the Illinois state convention. A bitter division over the gubernatorial nomination, which seemed a good possibility, could lead to discord in the selection of national delegates and in their instructions. Conceivably, the convention could select some Seward delegates from northern Illinois, where the senator had radical friends.

THE ILLINOIS STATE Republican convention that met on May 9 played a surprisingly important role in American political history. It had the potential to prepare the way for Lincoln's presidential nomination or defeat his prospects. More than 600 enthusiastic delegates convened in a flimsy tent anchored precariously to a building in Decatur. Most of them had to stand during the proceedings. Besides the delegates, hundreds of other ardent Republicans from throughout the state elbowed their way into the tent, and many more could not find space inside of what they called the "Wigwam."

Lincoln arrived on May 8 and took a seat in the back of the Wigwam. Informed of his presence, the crowd shouted his name, and several sturdy men hoisted all six feet four inches of him onto their shoulders. They brought him to the platform. Richard J. Oglesby of Decatur, who was destined to become a major general in the Union army, a three-term governor of Illinois, and a U.S. senator, cried out that an "old Democrat" of the county had something he would like to give to the delegates. The crowd responded with shouts of "Receive it! Receive it!" Immediately from the back of the Wigwam, John Hanks, a cousin of Lincoln's mother, and Isaac Jennings, a friend, marched to the front carrying two fence rails and a banner that read: "ABRAHAM LINCOLN THE RAIL CANDIDATE FOR PRESIDENT IN 1860, Two Rails From a Lot of 3,000 Made in 1830 by John Hanks and Abe Lincoln."[66] Cheers rocked the tent and a call rang out for Lincoln to speak. In what might have been the most thrilling moment in his illustrious political career,

Lincoln, though somewhat embarrassed, stepped up to the speaker's stand and told the crowd that he did not know whether he had split those two rails, but he did know that he "had mauled many and many better ones since he had grown to manhood."[67] When he sat down, the cheers exploded again. This old-Whig-style convention with its Wigwam, reminiscent of William Henry Harrison's "hard cider" presidential campaign of 1840, gave Lincoln the sobriquet the "Rail Splitter," an appellation that inspired his followers but probably had little influence on his prospects in the national Republican convention in Chicago.

Before proceeding to a resolution on Lincoln's candidacy and the selection of delegates to Chicago, the state convention considered the party's candidate for governor. Norman B. Judd, who had intrigued for the nomination, led on the first ballot, with Leonard Swett second and Richard Yates third. But John Wentworth's friends, as well as former Whigs who still believed that Judd had conspired in 1855 to prevent Lincoln's election to the Senate, denied him the nomination. On the second and third ballots, Swett's supporters swung toward Yates, and on the fourth ballot this former Whig congressman won the nomination. Nominees for other state offices were also chosen, including a German American for lieutenant governor. Judd defused a potentially tense and divisive situation in the convention when, in a speech to the delegates, he gracefully accepted defeat and called for Republican unity in the campaign.[68] He continued as chair of the state Republican committee and in the national convention at Chicago nominated Lincoln for president.

Having resolved the question of the gubernatorial nomination, the convention next considered a resolution that declared Lincoln as the state party's "first choice of Illinois for the Presidency" and instructed the delegation "to use all honorable means for his nomination by the Chicago Convention, and to cast their vote as a unit." According to the *Chicago Press and Tribune*, "a warm and earnest debate sprang up" over an amendment that would release the delegates to vote their individual preferences if Lincoln could not win. The debate did not reflect opposition to Lincoln but rather the delegates' strong disagreement over the other candidates as a second choice. It was clear that the Illinois delegates had to vote for Lincoln on the first ballot regardless of the political situation they found when they arrived in Chicago and also until they were certain that he had no chance for the nomination. The convention enthusiastically approved the resolution, with the amendment.[69]

The state Republican convention at Decatur gave Lincoln an important role in the selection of delegates to the national convention. It permitted him to choose those at large and gave him influence in the choice of the district delegates. The twenty-two delegates selected included all elements of the party. Reflective of the importance of the German American voters, Lincoln chose Gustave Koerner as a delegate at large. Koerner, the leading German American in Illinois, worked tirelessly for Lincoln's nomination at Chicago. Lincoln did not seem to object to the selection of several delegates from northern Illinois districts who leaned toward Seward but proved willing to follow the convention's instructions to support Lincoln. Long John Wentworth was an obvious omission from the list of delegates, despite the fact that he was the mayor of Chicago. Though David Davis appealed to Lincoln on Wentworth's behalf, Lincoln rejected him because he viewed him as a troublemaker who would inevitably clash with his rival, Judd, at Chicago. Lincoln had chosen Judd as a delegate at large. Finally, the state convention adopted a platform supporting the admission of Kansas under its free-state constitution, passage of the free Homestead bill in Congress, and economy in government; by no means less important, it also declared the convention's opposition to any change in the liberal naturalization laws. The latter plank upset some nativists in the party, but it was necessary to include it in order to secure the German American vote, especially since the antislavery coalition in Massachusetts had alienated German Americans by seeking political restrictions on immigrants.[70]

ONE WEEK AFTER the state convention, national Republican delegates met in Chicago in a huge barn-like structure. Like the tent in Decatur, it was called the Wigwam, but it was designed to accommodate 10,000 people. Two or three days before the convention began, campaign managers for the presidential candidates arrived in the city and moved into rooms in the Tremont House and other hotels. Their purpose was to lobby and intrigue for their candidate's nomination. David Davis led the Lincoln forces, which also included Koerner, Judd, Orville Browning, Jesse K. Dubois, William Butler (an old Springfield friend), Leonard Swett, and Lincoln's former law partner Stephen T. Logan. Mark W. Delahay of Kansas, formerly of Illinois, whose expenses Lincoln paid, joined the group in Chicago. On the advice of his friends at the national convention, Lincoln did not go to Chicago. He explained in his inimitable—and political—way: "I am a little too much a candidate to stay home and not quite enough a candidate to go." However, he kept in contact with the Illinois delegation through letters and messages delivered by friends. Lincoln occasionally provided guidance. For example, he instructed Delahay to lobby the Iowa and Minnesota delegations, warning him—and perhaps other managers as well—to be "careful to give no offence, and keep cool under all circumstances."[71] He also admonished the Illinois delegates to refrain from agitating the tariff issue or "any subject" in the convention.[72] Lincoln also probably sent the Illinois delegation a letter he had received from Richard M. Corwine of Ohio. Corwine had written, "It is obvious to me that we can not elect extreme men. Moderation in their past life & their present views, must mark them, or we can not elect." Of the candidates for the nomination, only Lincoln, Corwine insisted, could pass this test.[73]

The influential *Chicago Press and Tribune* provided important aid to Lincoln's cause at the convention. It greeted the Republican delegates with a long editorial on why Lincoln should be the party's standard-bearer in the election. Disclaiming any hostility toward the other "eminent gentlemen" seeking the presidency, and playing down any "feeling of State pride or Western sectionalism," this newspaper declared that Lincoln's "unexceptionable record, his position between the extremes in the party, his spotless character as a citizen, and his acknowledged ability as a statesman, will, in the approaching canvass, give him an advantage before the people which no other candidate can claim." The editor explained that, though Lincoln supported "all the fundamentals of Republicanism, [his] nature has given him that wise conservatism that has made his action and his expressed opinions so conform to the most mature sentiment of the country on the question of slavery." Perceptively, the editor contended that Lincoln's "avoidance of extremes has not been the result of ambition which measures words or regulates acts, but the natural consequence of an equable nature and [a] mental constitution that is never off its balance. . . . He occupies the happy mean between that alleged radicalism which binds the older Anti-Slavery men to Mr. Seward, and that conservatism which dictates the support of Judge Bates." Furthermore, Lincoln, as a former Henry Clay Whig, would favor federal aid for internal improvements and a favorable tariff, which "is all that Pennsylvania and the West have a right to demand." "Without a stain of Know-Nothingism on his skirts, he is acceptable to the mass of the American party," the *Press and Tribune* asserted. Though admitting that most delegations favored Seward or the other contenders, this newspaper claimed that all would approve of Lincoln as their second choice and support him as a compromise candidate.[74]

Even before the opening session in the Chicago Wigwam, Lincoln's campaign managers were greatly encouraged by their talks with other delegates. The strategy of giving offense to no one while emphasizing Lincoln's broad appeal—and the conviction that he could win the election—struck a favorable political chord with western and eastern delegates alike. Illinois delegates reported to Lincoln that many New England delegates could not be counted on to support Seward. Former Democrat Gideon Welles, the chair of the Connecticut delegation, who could not forget his old partisan battles with Thurlow Weed's "Albany Regency," went about urging opposition to the New York senator.[75] Equally encouraging for Lincoln's managers was the knowledge that bad blood existed between the New Yorkers and Senator Simon Cameron's large Pennsylvania delegation. The Pennsylvanians believed that Seward's men had undercut Cameron's candidacy; furthermore, they concluded that Seward's opposition to nativism could cause the defeat of Republicans in Pennsylvania and in other lower northern states.

The formation of the Constitutional Union party at Baltimore on May 9 reinforced the view of the Pennsylvania delegation that a Seward candidacy would put Republican victory in jeopardy. The new party, consisting primarily of former Whigs, nominated Senator John Bell of Tennessee for president and the eminent Edward Everett of Massachusetts for vice president. This party denounced both the Republican and Democratic parties and adopted a simple platform of support for the Union and the Constitution. Primarily a border-state movement, the Constitutional Union party hoped to win the support of old Fillmore men and Know Nothings at the expense of the Republicans in the North and the Democrats in the South.

On the day that the Republican convention opened, May 16, a Pennsylvanian —apparently a delegate—wrote a public letter, which the *Chicago Press and Tribune* gladly published, warning delegates against the nomination of anyone opposed by the "doubtful states" of Pennsylvania, New Jersey, Indiana, and Illinois. The writer was clearly referring to Seward. Such a nomination, he contended, would "drive the Fillmore vote" of 1856 over to John Bell and "must necessarily prove fatal to the Republican ticket." The Pennsylvanian demonstrated his case by citing the voting statistics for the 1856 election in the four doubtful states. Each had given Fillmore a large vote, thereby enabling Democrat James Buchanan to win. In Pennsylvania, for example, the former Whig president had captured 82,175 votes as compared to Buchanan's 230,710 and Republican candidate John C. Frémont's 147,510. The letter writer asked the delegates, "Is the convention going to nominate a candidate without [the] consent" of the Republicans of the battleground states?[76] Lincoln's managers were confident that, though the Pennsylvania delegation would go for Cameron on the first ballot, when the choice came down to their candidate and Seward—an eventuality that they expected—the Keystone State delegates would throw their support to Lincoln.[77]

Aiding Lincoln's cause in an indirect way was busybody Horace Greeley, who told all who would listen in the hotel lobbies that Edward Bates could win New York in the election. Greeley's continued support for Bates, Lincoln's men believed correctly, was only a ruse to undermine his old enemies, Seward and Weed, in New York politics. Greeley had his eyes on the U.S. Senate seat that would be filled by the New York legislature in early 1861. Weed's "Albany Regency" was certain to oppose his election, and their effort would be strengthened if Seward won the presidential nomination. Seward's friends at the Chicago convention could often be heard using expletives to refer to Greeley.[78] Greeley's lobbying for Bates created further doubt about Seward's strength.

Lincoln's lieutenants at Chicago did not believe that the other candidates, with the exception of Bates, posed a threat, even if the balloting for president became extended. They knew that Cameron, who had a shady national reputation, could expect little support outside of his own Pennsylvania delegation. After all, one of the key promises of the Republicans was to end the corruption of the Democratic administration in Washington. Republicans could not afford to nominate a state political boss like Cameron who was tainted with corruption himself. Lincoln's managers also knew that the Ohio delegation—the third largest in the convention—was not united behind favorite son and state Republican founder Salmon P. Chase. Indeed, several Ohioans planned to vote for Lincoln on the first ballot, while others threatened to support John McLean or Senator Benjamin F. Wade. Though rumors had swirled around McLean as a compromise candidate, the aging justice lacked support and was easily dismissed as a contender at Chicago. Bates, a more serious candidate, had the solid backing of the Missouri delegation and a scattering of delegates from other border states. However, only if the convention became deadlocked, which Lincoln's men did not expect, could Bates prevail as a compromise candidate.[79]

On the eve of the convention, Lincoln's managers sanguinely concluded that Seward at best could only receive a plurality of the votes on any of the ballots. David Davis and his associates believed that after the first ballot, in which Seward would lead, the swing from the other candidates in almost every case would be toward Lincoln, though they could not be certain about it. Seward's managers, despite a show of confidence, also realized that their candidate's strength would decline after the first ballot. Thurlow Weed, Seward's wily campaign manager, approached Lincoln's friend William Butler through a subordinate on the day before the convention began with a confidential offer that, if accepted, would insure a Seward victory on the first ballot. The proposition, as Butler related it to Lincoln in a letter written on the same day, provided that the "Rail Splitter" would be nominated on the Seward ticket as the vice presidential candidate, and that money would be "placed in the proper hands" to carry Illinois and Indiana in the election. By inference, the delegations of these two states would vote for Seward on the first ballot. Butler replied immediately that "under no circumstances could [Lincoln's] name be used in a second place on the ticket." He told Lincoln that he feared Weed would use the offer, despite its rejection, to undercut Lincoln's presidential candidacy; he could ruin Lincoln's chances simply by telling other delegations that negotiations were underway to nominate him

Thurlow Weed, crafty leader of the "Albany Regency" and William H. Seward's alter ego. Courtesy of the Abraham Lincoln Library and Museum, Harrogate, Tennessee.

for vice president on the Seward ticket.[80] Though Weed and his New York associates had a reputation for such political skullduggery, they discreetly dropped the matter.

Meanwhile, Chicago, a booming city of 112,000 in 1860, had come alive for the Republican convention with the arrival of delegates and political hangers-on. Thirteen train-car loads of Seward supporters alone came from New York. Cannons thundered out a welcome for the arriving delegations and party enthusiasts, or "Wide Awakes," as the predominantly young Republican zealots were called. At night, rockets lit up the sky and brilliant illuminations could be seen everywhere in the city. Alcohol kept the crowds loud and boisterous well into the morning hours. As many as 25,000 people crowded into the downtown area, packing the hotels and taking any space where they could sleep. On the night before the convention, 1,500 visitors crammed into the elegant Tremont House, making it virtually impossible for people to move and talk. Many of the powers that be in the Republican party could be seen at the Tremont or at the nearby Richmond House. The candidates and congressmen, who were in session in Washington, were absent. Political intrigue was as thick as tobacco smoke in the hotel rooms, though its importance has been overstated by many historians.[81] Hard arguments regarding the candidates' electability, not promises of offices and favors, eventually determined the outcome of the Republican presidential nomination at Chicago.

On the morning of May 16, the delegates—some not altogether sober—assembled in the Wigwam for the opening gavel. Though the Wigwam could accommodate as many as 10,000 people, reportedly not one-fifth of those who sought entrance gained admission. More than 4,000 Republican enthusiasts had to stand during the proceedings; those outside of the Wigwam held their own meetings and repeatedly shouted support for their favorites. The delegates elected an able presiding officer in George Ashmun of Massachusetts, who quickly brought a measure of order to the massive gathering.[82]

The issue of seating "bogus" delegates from Virginia, Kentucky, Maryland, and Texas created a mild controversy because some were nonresident proxies and represented virtually no constituency. Causing additional concern was the fact that Virginia's delegation alone contained one more member than the Illinois delegation. Weed and his assistants expected these southerners to vote solidly for Seward, in view of the fact that he had cultivated their support, having promised to dispense federal patronage to them after winning the presidency. Rather than admit, by rejecting the delegates, that the Republican party did not seek southern support, and thus was a sectional party, the convention seated all of the contested delegations. To deny seats to these delegates could have especially hurt the Republicans among Whig conservatives in the critical lower North who otherwise might vote for John Bell, the Constitutional Union candidate.

The greatest debate occurred over the platform on the second day of the convention. When the Committee on Resolutions reported the platform, David K. Cartter of Ohio rose and called for the previous question, that is, a vote on it without debate. The venerable Joshua R. Giddings, also a member of the Ohio delegation and a radical antislavery man, immediately demanded the right to offer an amendment affirming the party's commitment to the natural rights creed or equality clause in the Declaration of Independence. Not wanting to open the floor to numerous amendments, Cartter insisted on the previous question and frankly told Giddings that his (Cartter's) purpose was to shut off debate. Whereupon the Ohio radical walked out of the convention, a dramatic action that deeply affected many in the Wigwam, prompting the delegates by a two-to-one margin to reject Cartter's call for the previous question. Almost on cue, Giddings then returned to the convention. George W. Curtis, a prominent eastern editor, gained the floor and offered an amendment similar to the one Giddings had proposed. His eloquent speech in its favor "took the convention by storm," and the delegates approved the Declaration of Independence clause. However, the final version of the amendment was not explicitly tied to black equality, and therefore it fell short of what the radicals, a minority in the convention, had originally wanted.[83]

Without further debate, the convention approved the party's platform. Of the seventeen planks, only five directly referred to slavery. The platform denounced the Democratic party for attempting to force the Lecompton constitution upon the people of Kansas, and it called for the immediate admission of that state under its free-state, or Wyandotte, constitution. One plank criticized "the new dogma" advanced by Douglas, though it did not mention his name, which claimed that the Constitution sanctioned the extension of slavery into the territories. Such a doctrine, the Republican platform proclaimed, "is a dangerous political heresy, at variance with the explicit provisions of the instrument itself [and] is revolutionary in its tendency, and subversive of the peace of the country." In addition, the platform denied the authority of Congress or the territorial legislatures "to give legal existence to slavery" in the territories. It branded "the recent re-opening of the African slave trade, under the cover of our national flag, aided by perversions of judicial power, as a crime against humanity and a burning shame to our country and age." The Republicans called upon Congress "to take prompt and efficient measures for the total and final suppression of the execrable traffic." Many of the Republicans in the convention must have known that the foreign slave trade had not been reopened, despite violations of the 1808 prohibition and an attempt by some proslavery extremists to revive it.[84]

The Republican platform reassured conservatives that the party was committed to the "inviolate" rights of the states. In a reference to John Brown's actions, it denounced "the lawless invasion by armed force of the soil of any State or Territory, no matter under what pretext, as among the gravest of crimes." The platform avoided any mention of the Fugitive Slave Act, which many radicals and abolitionists wanted repealed or revised, because taking any side on this controversial issue would have hurt the party in key northern states. The question of slavery in the District of Columbia was also ignored. These issues were not even debated in the convention lest a division occur that the Democrats could exploit. Also, to prevent a divisive debate Republicans refused to consider the subject of voluntary black colonization, even though Senator Benjamin F. Wade of Ohio and other Republicans had recently proposed a bill on the matter in Congress and wanted it incorporated into the platform.[85]

In an effort to gain German American support in key states like Illinois and Pennsylvania, the Republicans at Chicago announced their opposition "to any change in our Naturalization Laws or any State legislation" that would impair the rights of immigrants. The plank was a reference to the Massachusetts proposal to restrict these rights. Though the proposal had already failed in the state legislature, the Republicans feared that German American voters would still associate their party with it. Another important ethnic group, the Irish Americans, were almost solidly Democratic and could not be expected to switch to the Republican party in any case. Although the immigration rights plank in the Chicago platform upset Know Nothings, the Republicans hoped they would vote with them in 1860 rather than with their opponents.

The Republicans at Chicago, consisting of a large number of old Henry Clay Whigs, included in their platform measures that they had long advocated. However, they were careful in their wording not to offend former Democrats in the party who had opposed federal economic legislation. The platform included support for internal improvements (aid for river and harbor improvements and a railroad to the Pacific), free homesteads for bona fide settlers—a plank that many Democrats also supported—and, without using the controversial term "tariff," an adjustment of "imposts [duties] to encourage the development of the industrial interests of the whole country." Finally, the Republicans called for economy, accountability in the federal government, and an end to "the systematic plunder of the public treasury by favored partisans" of the Buchanan administration. In truth, Abraham Lincoln could have written the Republican platform.

HAVING ADOPTED what they believed was a winnable platform, the Republican delegates eagerly turned to the presidential nomination. Throughout the night before the balloting, intense hotel room discussions and delegation caucuses occurred. Lincoln's managers at Chicago, led by David Davis, labored tirelessly to fend off an aggressive Seward effort to win a majority on the first ballot. As expected, Thurlow Weed and his New Yorkers made promises of campaign contributions and offices to gain support for their candidate.[86] Concerned that the tactics of the Seward forces would succeed, Mark W. Delahay sent an urgent message to Lincoln that he must give his friends the authority to "fight the devil with fire" and make promises to influential delegates in critical states. Lincoln, however, sent instructions to Davis and his associates to *"make no contracts that will bind me"* if successful.[87] Still, many historians have concluded that Davis and Lincoln's other friends at Chicago ignored their candidate's order and made promises.[88] Pennsylvanians and lukewarm Seward delegates from the West wanted assurances that if they supported Lincoln on the second ballot, he would not be "proscriptive" against those who had earlier opposed him and, specifically, that he would deal justly with them in appointments to federal offices. After consulting with Davis, fellow Illinois delegate Leonard Swett, who had been contacted on the issue, later reported to Lincoln that he "gave them the most solemn assurances I am capable of giving, that they should not only not be proscribed but that by-gones should be by-gones & and they should be placed upon the same footing as if originally they had been your friends." Swett indicated to Lincoln that these delegates expressed satisfaction with his promise. Lincoln, who often remarked that he believed in short statutes of limitations in politics, reaffirmed this promise soon after the convention adjourned, a pledge that would be honored after the election.[89]

When visiting the delegations on the night before the balloting, Lincoln's managers, without the authority to make promises of office, focused on their old argument that Seward could not win the battleground states of the lower North. Henry S. Lane, the Republican candidate for governor in Indiana, provided the Illinois delegation with important aid in countering the Seward offensive. Throughout the night he went from one caucus room to another maintaining that if the New York senator were nominated, he (Lane) would lose overwhelmingly in his state's October election, a result that could very well foretell the outcome of the presidential and other elections in November.[90] Lincoln's men, as well as the Pennsylvania delegates, predicted a similar scenario for the October gubernatorial election in the Keystone State if Seward received the nomination. In Pennsylvania, gubernatorial candidate Andrew G. Curtin faced a strong Democratic threat and needed conservative and Know-Nothing votes to win.

When the sun rose over Lake Michigan on the day the Republican presidential nomination would be decided, the Seward forces believed that their night's work had achieved the desired results—a first-ballot victory. Even their New York enemy, the erratic Horace Greeley, a few hours earlier had dispatched a telegram to his newspaper reporting that "from all that I can gather tonight, . . . the opposition to Gov. Seward cannot concentrate on any candidate, and . . . he will be nominated."[91] Most Republicans who had gathered in Chicago for the convention agreed with Greeley. It would not be the first time, or the last, that the *Tribune* editor would be wrong. Meanwhile, in the Tremont House, Lincoln's managers were quietly confident that they had turned back the Seward tide and that the New York senator could not receive the necessary majority on the first ballot. Judge Davis wired Lincoln: "Am very hopeful; dont [*sic*] be Excited; nearly dead with fatigue."[92] It soon became clear that Davis and associates had done their work well.

Not an extra space could be found in the Wigwam when Chairman Ashmun gaveled the convention into session. Jesse W. Fell and other Lincoln friends had made a special effort to pack the Wigwam with his supporters. Fell actually had duplicate tickets printed to insure the admission of a large number of Lincolnites. Seward's forces, while also well represented and active among the 10,000 people in attendance, including women, were not quite as loud as Lincoln's western followers. Outside, the "Rail Splitter's" supporters could be heard shouting for their hero. Anxiety and excitement gripped the Republicans in the building when Ashmun finally called for nominations. The distinguished New York lawyer William M. Evarts nominated Seward, and then Norman B. Judd nominated Lincoln. Bates, Chase, Cameron, and a scattering of favorite sons also were nominated. Loud yells of support punctuated the nominations of Seward and Lincoln as both sides tried to outdo the other; the other nominations received a less enthusiastic response.

Murat Halstead of the *Cincinnati Commercial* has left a vivid account of the dramatic reaction to the Seward and Lincoln nominations. "The shouting was absolutely frantic, shrill and wild," he reported. "Hundreds of persons stopped their ears in pain." Viewing the scene from the stage, Halstead could see nothing "but thousands of hats—a black, mighty swarm of hats— flying with the velocity of hornets over a mass of human heads, most of the mouths of which were open" and shouting. The Lincoln demonstration had an added attraction. Henry S. Lane, the Indiana gubernatorial candidate, "leaped upon a table, and swinging hat and cane, performed like an acrobat." Though "his mouth was desperately wide open," Lane's voice "was lost in the aggregate hurricane" of noises.[93]

Clearly, much was at stake for Lane and other Republicans in the decision of that May day in Chicago and, as at no other national convention during their lifetimes, they were caught up in the excitement and passion of the moment. Their main concern was for the selection of a candidate who would win the fall election, purify the government in Washington after years of what they rightly considered to be Democratic misrule and corruption, and make the Republican party the dominant force in America. Republicans viewed themselves as the redeemers of the virtuous republic of the Founders, not as a lightning rod for sectional discord and southern secession. As Henry Lane put it, Republicans by their actions had "sternly rebuked the disunion spirit which now disgraces the politics of the United States." They should proudly "burn hissing hot into the brazen front of southern democracy the brand of disunion."[94] Though Lane's inflammatory words belied his party's commitment to sectional peace, the Republicans' opposition to slavery was conservative and designed to appeal to a broad electorate in the free states and perhaps even to some voters in the border slave states. Their platform and the maneuvering to secure an acceptable presidential nominee reflected this political reality.

The roll call for president began with the New England states, and it was evident to some in the Wigwam from the first votes that Seward was in trouble in states that he had been expected to win easily. The combined votes of Maine and New Hampshire went for Lincoln, and Rhode Island and Connecticut gave a scattering of votes to other candidates, but none to Seward. Senator Jacob Collamer, Vermont's favorite son, received all of the state's votes. To some extent, this was an anti-Seward vote, which became clear on the second ballot when Lincoln won all of Vermont's votes. The hopes of Seward supporters were revived when Massachusetts cast twenty-one of its twenty-five votes for their candidate; Lincoln received the other four. As expected, New York's delegation, by far the largest in the convention, gave all their seventy votes to their favorite son.

But a blow to Seward's hopes soon occurred from an unlikely place—and one that historians have heretofore missed. In one of the many ironies associated with the Civil War era, a southern delegation—Virginia's—played a key role in the balloting on the first roll call. Seward's managers had expected "the rotten borough" delegations from the South to vote overwhelmingly for the senator in exchange for promises of federal patronage in their states. Probably sensing that the New York senator could not win the fall election and fulfill the promises, Virginia's delegation, which included members from what later became the state of West Virginia, surprised the convention when it cast fourteen of its twenty-three votes for Lincoln. Kentucky immediately followed Virginia's action with a scattering of votes in which Lincoln and Chase received more support than Seward. The New York senator received only three votes from the border slave states of Delaware and Maryland; Bates obtained the remaining fourteen. As expected, Missouri's eighteen votes went for favorite-son Bates. Of the other slave states in the convention, only Texas, with six votes, gave a majority to the New York senator. A final blow to the Seward forces' hopes for a first-ballot victory—and, as it turned out, the nomination—occurred when Lincoln won all of Indiana's twenty-six votes.[95] At the end of the first balloting, the tally stood: Seward, 173; Lincoln, 102; Cameron, 50; Chase, 49; Bates, 48; and the remainder among seven other candidates.[96] Despite Seward's impressive plurality (he needed 233 to win), the vote was deceiving. The delegates and the nation soon would discover why.

The Lincoln men had achieved their objective of denying Seward a majority on the first ballot, and their hopes for a victory soared. The convention immediately moved to the second ballot. When Vermont's ten votes switched from Collamer to Lincoln, and Pennsylvania abandoned Cameron for the "Rail Splitter," the mood of Seward's managers became gloomy. However, most of Bates's and Chase's support remained firm, and neither Lincoln nor Seward could obtain a majority on the second ballot. Seward had picked up eleven votes but still fell far short of the necessary majority for the nomination. The count now stood at 184 for Seward and 181 for Lincoln.

As soon as the second balloting was completed, it dawned upon the throng in the Wigwam that Lincoln would win. They realized that Bates's conservative delegates, as well as Ohioans who had been committed to Chase—but had wanted Lincoln from the beginning—would now go overwhelmingly for the Illinois Republican rather than for Seward. With excitement mounting, the roll call for the third ballot began. New England's switch to Lincoln continued; but it was Ohio's twenty-nine votes for him (Chase retained fifteen) that brought Lincoln within two votes of victory. At this point, David K. Cartter of Ohio rose and dramatically announced the change of four more Ohio votes to Lincoln. Bedlam broke out in the Wigwam. "The entire crowd rose to their feet, applauding rapturously, and ladies waving their handkerchiefs, the men waving and throwing up their hats by the thousands, cheering again and again," the *Chicago Press and Tribune* reported. "Stout men wept like children." Staunch Seward delegates were crestfallen, but in the name of party unity, they called for all Republicans to rally around Lincoln in the election. Once Ashmun had restored a semblance of order, delegation chairmen "corrected" their states' votes by casting all of them for Lincoln. Illinois delegates brought a life-size photograph of "Old Abe" to the platform, precipitating another outburst of cheering in the Wigwam. Outside, a roar went up from the crowd at the announcement and a cannon fired a salute to the decision.[97]

After such tension and excitement, the selection of a running mate for Lincoln was naturally anticlimactic. Several candidates were put forward, including Senator Hannibal Hamlin of Maine and Cassius M. Clay of Kentucky, the leaders on the first ballot. The Illinois delegation supported Andrew H. Reeder of Pennsylvania, perhaps as a token of goodwill toward the state's large delegation that had swung its votes to Lincoln on the second ballot. The Illinois delegates' support for Reeder also suggested that neither they nor Lincoln had any control over the choice for vice president, because the Pennsylvanian did not receive the nomination. On the second ballot, Hamlin won; as a former Democrat and an easterner, he brought political and geographic balance to the ticket. Neither Lincoln nor Hamlin remembered having met, though both had served in Congress at the same time—Hamlin in the Senate and Lincoln in the House of Representatives.[98]

MEANWHILE, LINCOLN waited anxiously in his Springfield office for news from Chicago. To Christopher C. Brown, a fellow lawyer, he seemed "nervous, fidgety—intensely excited." To relieve the tension, Lincoln told stories. Finally, unable to work, he stepped outside and played a game of "ball" with several friends. The game involved hitting the ball with the hands against a wall, the rules of which remain obscure. When he received a telegraphic dispatch conveying the results of the first ballot, Lincoln seemed pleased and expressed the opinion that Seward could not get the nomination. The next message giving the results of the second ballot decided the issue, Lincoln told his friends. The last telegram of the morning brought the news that he had won. Rising from his seat, he read the message and remarked: "When the second ballot came I knew that this must Come." He received the news "with apparent coolness from the expression playing upon his Countenance," according to a friend. "However a close observer Could detect, Strong emotions from within." After spending a few moments in accepting congratulations, Lincoln looked toward home and said, "Well gentlemen there is a little woman at our house who is probably more interested in this dispatch than I am; if you will excuse me I will take the dispatch up and let her see it."[99]

In Washington, members of Congress also anxiously awaited reports from Chicago. They expected Seward to be the nominee, and when a bogus telegram circulated in the capitol chambers that the senator had won, Democratic and Republican reactions reflected their views of their parties' prospects in the election. "On the Democratic side," Representative Schuyler Colfax wrote Lincoln, "they were joyous & hopeful; for every one of them had insisted that we would nominate the New York Senator, & did not conceal their desire that we should" select him as the Republican candidate. Democrats believed that they could win the necessary electoral votes with the radical Seward heading the Republican ticket. After receiving the first report, "the Republican side of the House looked gloomy and desponding, with but few exceptions," Colfax reported.[100]

As Lincoln and others had predicted, the national Democratic party was in the process of dividing largely along sectional lines. Northern Democrats and a smattering of southerners supported Douglas and his popular-sovereignty platform as the only hope for maintaining an undivided Union. Southern Democrats overwhelmingly demanded the federal protection of slavery in the territories and denounced the Little Giant as a traitor to southern rights. Douglas and northern Democrats had excoriated Seward as the epitome of

"Black Republicanism" for several years, and they believed that he would be an easy target as a candidate in the lower North. Moreover, they thought the Democrats and conservatives would unite against the Republicans if he won the nomination. Despite the schism in the party at Charleston in April, Douglas was on course to become the Democratic nominee for president when the mainly northern wing of the party met in June at Baltimore. Though the Douglas Democrats were overly sanguine in believing that southerners would see a difference between Seward and any other Republican candidate, they no doubt would have had a good chance of winning the lower North if Seward had been nominated.

The mood of Republicans and Democrats in Congress changed dramatically in the afternoon when a genuine dispatch arrived from Chicago reporting Lincoln's nomination. "It was so unexpected we could hardly believe it," Illinois Congressman Elihu B. Washburne wrote Lincoln. "The countenances of our republicans were lighted up with joy, and all felt that a nomination had been made which would ensure success. The locofocos [Democrats] who had puckered up their mouths for Seward, now could not even laugh out of the other corner. Many of them were frank enough to admit that they had been deceived" into believing that Seward would be nominated, "and that there was no use talking, the nomination was a strong one." Colfax reported to Lincoln, "I do not think there were a dozen out of our 112 [Republicans] who did not join in the rejoicing" at the news of the nomination. Even New York's Republican delegation in Congress, Lyman Trumbull informed Lincoln, expressed delight, and "old Ben Wade" of Ohio "said the election was settled—that our success was certain," a view that Trumbull endorsed "as a fixed fact."[101]

Senator Douglas, Colfax wrote Lincoln, "surprised every one" in Congress "by the hearty & eulogistic manner in which he spoke of you." The Democratic leader told a friend that the selection by the Republicans "was the strongest nomination that could have been made, that no man could get as many votes . . . in the North West as [Lincoln]." Congressman R. W. Thompson, the leader of the Constitutional Union movement in Indiana, expressed his admiration for Lincoln and indicated that the nomination had placed him in a quandary as to what to do in the election. Colfax suggested to the Republican nominee that he should write Thompson and cultivate his goodwill. At least two prominent southern senators and future Confederate cabinet members, Judah P. Benjamin of Louisiana and Robert Toombs of Georgia, spoke kindly of Lincoln. Though acknowledging his disagreements with Lincoln, Benjamin told Trumbull that he had recently read Lincoln's 1858 debates with Douglas and was surprised to find him "so conservative a man." "These men," Trumbull wrote Lincoln, "see the hand writing on the wall."[102]

Throughout the North, Republicans celebrated Lincoln's nomination with enthusiastic displays the likes of which had probably never been seen before in the history of national political contests. In Springfield, a large Lincoln demonstration occurred the night of the nomination at the state capitol, highlighted by a cannonade of one hundred rounds and a march to Lincoln's home. The candidate made an appearance, gave a brief speech, and invited as many as possible into his house.[103] In Chicago, 2,000 Republican Wide Awakes, accompanied by a crowd of citizens, held a torchlight parade through the streets, shouting for "Honest Old Abe." A huge bonfire was set in front of the Tremont House, a blaze that could be seen for miles. In addition, Wide Awakes placed a cannon on the top of the Tremont, where it fired a thirty-three-gun salute representing all of the states in the Union. Even the Massachusetts delegation, which had held firm behind Seward until the end, joined in the festivities. The Bay State delegates, with their brass band playing, paraded through the streets, hurrahing for Lincoln and calling at the headquarters of the other delegations.

In Philadelphia, several thousand people gathered in Independence Square and marched through the main streets, "cheering and hurrahing for honest old Abe." In Boston, Republicans fired a 100-gun salute to Lincoln on the Commons and scheduled "a ratification meeting" for four days later. In New York, Indianapolis, Detroit, Columbus, and in small towns across the free states the pattern of Republican celebrations was the same, with the thundering of cannon, mass meetings, illuminations, and processions. Remarkably, many people did not seem to know Lincoln's first name. The *New York Times* announced "Abram Lincoln" as the Republican nominee for president.[104] Even in Illinois confusion existed regarding his name. The *Peoria Transcript* wanted to know, "Is it Abraham or is it the shorter name of Abram?"[105] Sidney George Fisher, a prominent Philadelphia conservative and writer on constitutional issues, cryptically noted in his diary that the Republicans "had nominated a Mr. Lincoln for President. I never heard of him before."[106]

Western Republicans exuded delight at the decision in Chicago. Like Henry Lane of Indiana, they had feared defeat not only in the presidential election but also in state and local elections in the fall if Seward was the party's standard-bearer. The *LaPorte* (Indiana) *Herald* hailed Lincoln as a man of the West, born into poverty and obscurity, who, "by the most intense labor and application, has risen to his high position" and become "a tower of strength" in the region. The *Davenport* (Iowa) *Gazette* declared that "the people of the West will feel in voting for him as though they were elevating from their own ranks one who thoroughly understands their interests and will faithfully represent them."[107] In Indianapolis, Benjamin Harrison, a young Republican candidate for reporter of the state Supreme Court who one day also would become president, echoed these themes to an enthusiastic crowd, adding that Lincoln represented "the free labor principle, which is the prominent feature of the Republican creed."[108] Even St. Louis Republicans—Missouri was a slave state, but with a relatively large German American population—held a "Great Ratification Meeting" for the Lincoln nomination. Frank Blair, the "People's candidate" for Congress in the St. Louis district, proclaimed the "Rail Splitter's" western virtues to the crowd.[109]

Some Republicans, particularly staunch Seward supporters, needed reassurance that the party's choice of Lincoln was wise. Henry J. Raymond of the *New York Times,* who visited Springfield the day after the Chicago convention adjourned, wrote that "no one doubts that [Lincoln] has all the intellectual ability, the honesty of purpose, and the fixedness of political principle essential" for the presidency. "The only apprehension which any of his friends entertain is, that he may lack the iron firmness of will and the practical experience of men and factions, which the passing crisis will render indispensable in a Republican President."[110]

The *Springfield* (Massachusetts) *Republican* explained to Senator Seward's "aggrieved friends" in the East that the choice of the Chicago convention "could not have been otherwise. The States that must be carried to secure a Republican triumph did not dare to assume Mr. Seward, and the forcing upon them a name that would weaken them . . . would have been neither wise nor fair." The *Republican* reassured Seward supporters that Lincoln was "a positive man" who "matches well with the platform" of the party. The *Concord* (New Hampshire) *Statesman* echoed this sentiment, saying, "The question at Chicago was not who [was] most worthy of our consideration, but what suitable candidate can we present with the strongest probabilities of success." The *Boston Courier and Enquirer* declared that, though Seward, "the first great representative of Republican principles has been defeated, we have in the nomination of Mr. Lincoln no expediency candidate, but one who early embraced the Republican cause, has always labored consistently for its successes—has from the beginning stood, and stands now, fair and square on its national and conservative platform." Lincoln's sterling reputation for honesty, as expressed in the sobriquet "Honest Abe," had worked to his advantage over Seward and other candidates in an election that many Republicans believed would be partly fought over Democratic corruption. The *Courier and Enquirer* called on all Republicans to rally around Lincoln and go to work to defeat "the sectional and corrupt Democracy." The *Boston Daily Advertiser,* also pro-Seward, reminded its readers of Lincoln's Whig antecedents and noted that he would be able to secure the critical support of the "conservative element of the Middle States." Even Thurlow Weed's *Albany Evening Journal,* while expressing disappointment with the nomination, had similar advice for Seward supporters, declaring that Lincoln's selection would be regarded "as the very next [best] choice of the Republicans of New York."[111]

Many abolitionists, who generally had little faith in political parties, expressed dismay at the work of the Chicago convention. William Lloyd Garrison, writing in *The Liberator,* was more upset with the Republican platform than with the party's nomination of Lincoln, which he noted without comment. Garrison denounced the platform because "it takes no issue with the Dred Scott Decision, or the Fugitive Slave Act, or with slavery as it exists in the District of Columbia; and, by omission at least, surrenders its old nonextension of slavery policy."[112] In a speech to the New England Anti-Slavery convention on May 30, 1860, Wendell Phillips, the silver-tongued abolitionist orator, characterized Lincoln as a "county court advocate" and a "huckster in politics," whose only recommendation for the nomination was that "his past is a blank."[113] Phillips never changed his negative view of Lincoln.

At the other extreme of the northern political spectrum, the Democratic press, not surprisingly, ridiculed Lincoln's selection by the Republicans. The *Boston Herald,* a Douglas newspaper, admitted, however, that "the nomination in many respects is a strong one, and will be difficult to defeat." Another Boston newspaper, the *Post,* told its Democratic readers that "the Chicago sectional Convention—a thorough geographical body—has crowned its work by nominating a mere local politician" and asked when "Abraham Lincoln [had] shown ability to warrant this distinction over his competitors." The *New York Herald,* which claimed to be politically independent but usually supported Democrats, remarked derisively: "The conduct of the Republican party in this nomination is a remarkable indication of small intellect, growing smaller. They pass over Seward, Chase and Bates, who are statesmen and able men, and they take up a fourth-rate lecturer, who cannot speak good grammar," as was evident, the *Herald* claimed, when Lincoln spoke at Cooper Union three months earlier. The *Buffalo Daily Courier* commented that Lincoln was "lacking in culture" and announced that vice presidential candidate Hannibal Hamlin was "a man of much higher order of ability than Mr. Lincoln."[114] Predictably, like Phillips, most of the Democratic newspapers never changed their harsh, negative opinions of Lincoln during his lifetime.

Not to be outdone by the Democratic press in other states, the *Chicago Times* and the *Springfield Illinois State Register* provided their own scornful commentary on the nomination of their fellow Illinoisan. The choice of Lincoln, the *Times* charged, was "the result of a conspiracy by Greeley and the

Blairs, aided by some men from Pennsylvania, to prevent the nomination of the great statesman of New York." (If Seward had been nominated, the *Times* surely would have brought its editorial guns to bear against him instead.) This newspaper told its readers that "the nomination of Lincoln (and we intend to say nothing unkind or disrespectful of him) will be regarded by all who know him, as a degradation of intellectual worth for mere purposes of crafty personal hatred towards others, and not because of any fitness on his part for the office."[115] While admitting that it was "gratified" the nomination had been conferred on a citizen of its town, the *Springfield Illinois State Register* lambasted Lincoln as an ultraradical candidate who subscribed to the sectional "irrepressible conflict" doctrine. Both the editor of the *Times* and the *State Register* proclaimed Lincoln the candidate of "Negro equality" and predicted that the Little Giant in the presidential election would easily repeat his 1858 success over the "Black Republican."[116] Their prediction of victory was a case of whistling through a dark cemetery; these editors probably understood that Lincoln's candidacy virtually assured a Republican victory in Illinois and perhaps throughout the critical lower North.

Southerners generally ignored Lincoln's nomination. When southern editors commented on the Republican candidate, they, like Illinois Democrats, usually dismissed Lincoln as no different from Seward or any "Black Republican." Southern newspapers mainly devoted their columns to the impending Democratic convention in Baltimore and the earlier nomination of John Bell by the Constitutional Union party. The *Richmond Daily Dispatch* claimed that Lincoln's nomination resulted from the efforts of the "vindictive philosopher of the *Tribune*" (Horace Greeley) to throw Seward "underfoot by the rough backwoodsman of the West [Lincoln], a flat boatman, a mauler of rails, and, worse than all, a man suspected of being 'honest.'" The *Dispatch* found little to choose between Lincoln and Seward, except "Lincoln is an uneducated man, possibly more honest, but also more violent in his anti-slavery language than Seward, less cool, cautious and circumspect, and therefore more likely to adhere to the [Republican] principles if elected, and to be rash and imprudent in carrying them out."[117]

The *New Orleans Bee* expressed a more sober and more realistic judgment of the Republican decision at Chicago. The editor of this newspaper declared that in their choice of a candidate, "the Black Republicans have furnished a signal manifestation of their determination to avoid extremes. . . . We predicted long ago the defeat of Seward in the Chicago Convention. We saw that he was opposed by two redoubtable antagonists—first, the conservative element of his party, and next, the power and influence of the West." Republicans believed that Seward could not succeed "in the doubtful States" without conservative and western support, the *New Orleans Bee* editor explained. As an old Whig from a key western state, Lincoln was "but slightly tinctured with anti-slavery notions. . . . The nomination of Mr. Lincoln was a master stroke of political craft." This editor told southerners that the Illinois rail splitter was "a formidable competitor for the Presidency" in the election and called on Democrats at Baltimore to unite behind Douglas.[118] The implication was clear: only Douglas could prevent the election of the "Black Republican" candidate.

THE DAY FOLLOWING the Republican convention, a committee headed by George Ashmun arrived in Springfield to notify Lincoln officially of his nomination. After Lincoln greeted the Republican committee in the parlor of his home, Ashmun made a few remarks and delivered the official letter notifying Lincoln of his nomination and also gave him a copy of the party's platform. The Republican nominee responded to the committee with a brief statement, saying he was "deeply, and even painfully sensible of the great responsibility" that had fallen upon him. Lincoln informed Ashmun that he would write and send him his official acceptance in a few days. Ashmun, who had known Lincoln in Congress, then introduced each of the committee members to Lincoln, who, according to Henry J. Raymond of the *New York Times,* "made some brief remarks—generally humorous or complimentary—to each—told two or three anecdotes, and seemed anxious that every one should consider himself perfectly at home." After socializing for about thirty minutes, the visitors returned to their hotel for supper before leaving on the midnight train for Chicago.[119]

The members of the Republican committee, most of whom had not met Lincoln, clearly were impressed with him. They were also relieved that the eastern and Democratic image of Lincoln as an uneducated, crude product of the western frontier did not fit the man. Ashmun, a Massachusetts congressman who had supported Seward, admitted as such in an account of the meeting written that night for his hometown newspaper. "Those who had never seen him, and were troubled with some apprehension of awkwardness, or rawness, were at once set at ease on that score," he wrote. "No diplomatic interview could have been conducted with more becoming propriety." Initially, Lincoln seemed unimpressive or "bronze" to Ashmun; but then, "at the instance of speaking," his face was "lighted up by a fire of intellect, [and] the warmth of a great heart shone out in every feature."

Neither did Lincoln's lifestyle suggest an uncouth westerner to the Republican committee. Ashmun happily reported to his eastern friends that Lincoln's "house is a style and character exactly suited to his position in life." He specifically mentioned that "the furniture, without pretension to show, was neat, and in admirable keeping with what is understood to be his moderate pecuniary ability. Everything seemed to represent the home of a man who has battled hard with the fortunes of life, and whose hard experience has taught him to enjoy whatever of success belong to him, rather in solid substance than in showy display." Ashmun also set at ease his friends who might be concerned about Mary Lincoln's social capabilities. "I shall be proud, as an American citizen," Ashmun wrote, "when the day brings her to grace the White House."[120] His account was designed, at least in part, to dispel the image, which Republican opponents were sure to exploit, that the Lincolns did not have the background or capacity to conduct the duties of the presidency.

Ashmun and his fellow Republicans had nominated Abraham Lincoln at Chicago because he could capture the critical states of the lower North; they did not believe that Seward, whom they assumed had greater leadership abilities, could win. The legendary appeal associated with the "Rail Splitter" image of Lincoln played only a minor role, if that, in the Republican convention's choice, though it probably helped him in the election. Republicans calculated that Lincoln, a former Whig and a conservative in the antislavery movement, could satisfy all the northern political elements needed for their party's success in the fall. These constituencies included staunch antislavery men, former Know Nothings and Fillmore men, German immigrants, antislavery Democrats, and Pennsylvanians of all parties who demanded tariff duties to protect their growing industries. Neither Seward nor any other of the Republican contenders for the nomination could secure the support of this procrustean bed of opponents of Douglas and southern Democrats. No promises of offices or favors were necessary for the Republicans to make the hardheaded decision to nominate the Illinois lawyer-politician, and Lincoln made none except that as president he would treat all Republicans fairly.

Years later, Carl Schurz, a German American leader and Seward supporter in the Republican convention, shrewdly noted the reason for Lincoln's nomination. "Much has been said about the superior volume and fierceness of the shouting for Lincoln in the packed galleries and its effect upon the minds of the delegates," Schurz wrote. "But that is mere reporters' talk [as well as that of many historians]. The historic fact is, [the convention] had no other alternative than to select Lincoln as the man who satisfied the demands of the earnest anti-slavery men without subjecting the party to the risks inseparable from the nomination of Seward." Though "the popular demonstrations for Lincoln in and around the Convention were, indeed, well planned and organized, . . . they were by no means a decisive factor. Without them the result would have been the same," Schurz concluded.[121]

Little did the Republican delegates at Chicago know that, out of the welter of candidates, they had chosen the best person to lead America through its greatest crisis. In nominating Lincoln, the Republicans, as historian Don E. Fehrenbacher has rightly written, "did not compromise themselves or their principles. In fact, without fully realizing it, they had selected a man whose moral fiber was tougher than Seward's" or, Fehrenbacher could have said, that of any of the candidates.[122] After the Ashmun notification committee left the Lincoln home on May 19, Pennsylvania delegate William D. ("Pig Iron") Kelley reportedly commented to a fellow Republican, "We might have done a more brilliant thing, but we could hardly have done a better thing."[123] History would judge that the Republicans of 1860 did both.

CHAPTER EIGHT

CAMPAIGN AND ELECTION

THE ACTION OF the Republican national convention changed Lincoln's life forever. Immediately, the demands on his time became enormous. By mid-June 1860, Lincoln was receiving hundreds of letters daily, and visitors from throughout the country poured into Springfield to see him. His law practice soon fell victim to the burden of his new status. Though he appeared in federal court on four occasions in June, Lincoln realized that it was impossible to concentrate on the cases, and he turned over his workload to Herndon. Afterward, he collected several unpaid fees, but his income suffered. His friends raised $500 to help meet his expenses.[1]

In early June, Lincoln hired a young German American, John G. Nicolay, to serve as his private secretary with a salary of $75 per month. Nicolay had come to the United States with his parents at the age of six; as a teenager he had gone to work for a Whig newspaper in Pittsfield, Illinois. He eventually owned the newspaper, but he had sold it in 1856. Nicolay was clerking in the office of Ozias M. Hatch, secretary of state for Illinois, when Lincoln appointed him secretary. He would ably fill the position until the end of Lincoln's life.[2] Primarily assigned the tasks of sorting the correspondence and replying to requests for information, Nicolay brought order into the affairs of a man who had never been very organized as a lawyer. Lincoln himself prepared form letters for Nicolay to send to people seeking biographical information and asking for his political views. In the first instance, Nicolay told correspondents that it was "simply impossible" to answer the numerous requests for biographical sketches and, in the second, that Lincoln had determined "to write nothing upon any point of political doctrine."[3]

One of Nicolay's first tasks was to copy an autobiography that Lincoln had prepared for John L. Scripps of the *Chicago Press and Tribune*. After some confusion about publication, Scripps produced a brief, disappointing campaign biography of Lincoln based on the autobiography. Nicolay became involved during the summer in arranging, after a "wrangle" over authorization, for the publication of a more substantial Lincoln biography written by William Dean Howells and published by Follett, Foster and Company of Columbus, Ohio.[4]

Governor John Wood graciously provided Lincoln with a reception room on the second floor of the State House in Springfield. Daily, throughout the hot summer, Lincoln patiently received visitors from all walks of life and from all areas, many in groups who pressed into the crowded and unkempt room to scrutinize and shake hands with "Old Abe." Committed to the republican tradition that public figures should make themselves available to the citizens, Lincoln denied admission to no one. In these meetings, he revealed little about himself or his plans; he spent most of the time reminiscing, telling stories, and listening to his callers. Well-wishers showered upon him a veritable museum of farm implements befitting his "Rail Splitter" image. As Nicolay recalled, "Mr. Lincoln used the axes, wedges, log-chains, and other implements as texts for explanations and anecdotes of pioneer craft; thus making them serve a double purpose in amusing his visitors and keeping the conversation away from politics."[5] Ironically in view of what happened on April 14, 1865, Lincoln's visitors, according to a Nicolay memorandum written at the time, "nearly always . . . expressed hope that he would not be so unfortunate as were [Presidents] Harrison & Taylor, to be killed off by the cares of the Presidency—or as is sometimes hinted by foul means." Nicolay also revealed that "a great many letters have been written to Mr. Lincoln on the [same] subject."[6]

The meetings with the public soon caused Lincoln to be "bored—bored badly," Herndon reported. A welcome break in the routine occurred when intimate Illinois associates such as Orville H. Browning came for a visit. Lincoln usually insisted that they remain after the well-wishers and curiosity seekers had departed. Then he relaxed and, as Browning wrote after a June 12 visit, "fell into his old habit of telling amusing stories, and we had a free and easy talk of an hour or two."[7]

Republican leaders or their agents and journalists who came to Springfield received a warm welcome, which often included long discussions with Lincoln and invitations to dinner. No visit attracted more attention than that of Thurlow Weed, Seward's right-hand man, who had been invited to Springfield by David Davis and Leonard Swett immediately after the Chicago convention. Davis and Swett hoped to gain the support of the Albany Regency for the campaign. Arriving in Springfield on May 24, "the Wizard of the Lobby" conferred with Lincoln for five hours, mainly about the campaign in the East. The meeting went extremely well. Weed made no demands except for a vague request for fair play by Lincoln, which was agreed to. Lincoln expressed surprise to Senator Trumbull that Weed "showed no signs whatever of the intriguer. He asked for nothing; and said N.Y. is safe, without condition." On his part, Weed left Springfield pleased with the Republican candidate, particularly his political sagacity, and he promised to throw his influence behind Lincoln in the East.[8] Lincoln must have understood that Weed and his New Yorkers wanted to arrange an amiable political accommodation with him,

despite their bitter disappointment at Seward's defeat—a disappointment
Weed readily admitted to Swett and probably to Lincoln also. They did not
want to be left out after the election when the new president dispensed patronage and needed guidance. Like Lincoln with his promise of fair play,
Weed proved as good as his word. He worked diligently for Lincoln's success
in the campaign and kept the presidential candidate informed of the political
situation in the East.[9]

Soon Seward himself shook off his despair and abandoned an early decision to retire after the completion of his senatorial term. He received appeals
from Republicans to take to the stump in behalf of the party. After a conference with Weed and other New York associates, Seward reluctantly agreed to
a barnstorming tour of New England and the West. Charles Francis Adams
of Massachusetts noted after a meeting with Seward that the senator expected to wield considerable influence in the administration if Lincoln won
the election. Seward's travels in the West took him briefly through Springfield, where he had an awkward twenty-minute meeting with Lincoln at the
train station and told a crowd of 2,000 to 3,000 that he supported their
townsman.[10] The Albany Regency, joined by Governor Edwin D. Morgan,
helped Lincoln in New York, New England, and the upper West (Michigan,
Wisconsin, and Minnesota), but, except for New York, the electoral votes
of these staunch Republican areas were virtually assured for him anyway.
Though divided in state Republican politics, the major Republican newspapers in New York City—Greeley's *Tribune,* Raymond's *Times,* and Bryant's
Evening Post—united behind their party's candidate.[11]

No newspaper had a larger national circulation or was "more powerful
for mischief" than the *New York Herald,* a self-proclaimed independent paper owned by the imperious James Gordon Bennett. Realizing that Bennett
would probably not endorse Lincoln for the presidency, Norman Judd and
other Illinois Republicans visited "His Satanic Majesty" during the summer
in an effort to at least "spike his gun" in the campaign. Joseph Medill, a
member of the delegation, reported to Lincoln that Bennett did not seek an
office in the administration but wanted social distinction when he visited
Washington and the White House. Medill suggested that this pledge had
been given to Bennett. The *Herald* proprietor seemed agreeable. Bennett predicted a Lincoln victory and believed that he "would make a good president," provided he rejected the advice of Seward and the radical antislavery
elements in the party. Within a few days after the interviews with the Illinois
Republicans, Medill wrote Lincoln that the *Herald* had begun to give "the
Democrats some hard blows, and treats you rather tenderly than harshly."[12]
Bennett, however, did not endorse Lincoln for president; instead, fearing
the calamitous disunion implications of a Republican administration domi-

nated by Seward, particularly on New York's financial interests, he supported Douglas. Bennett hoped that somehow a fusion of Douglas Democrats and other anti-Republicans could be achieved.[13]

In August, the *Herald* dispatched a "special correspondent" to Springfield to talk to Lincoln and gain the opinion of his neighbors. The journalist found that Lincoln was "universally regarded as a plain, unassuming man, possessing strong common sense, wedded to a quickness of perception that detects the right from the wrong and winnows chaff from the wheat" on issues. Even local Democrats admired him for his honesty and his "sociability." The *Herald* reporter was cordially received at the Lincoln home. " 'Old Abe' and your correspondent took a chair together," he wrote, "and talked upon almost every topic now attracting the attention of the public." Lincoln reaffirmed his position on slavery, declaring that "it was his principle not to touch [slavery] where it exists, but to prevent its spread into Territories now free. He spoke of slavery as an institution that did not meet the universal sanction of the Southern people." Lincoln said that "public opinion is not always private opinion." Citing the French Revolution, when leading revolutionaries privately opposed the execution of King Louis XVI but "were publicly obliged to declare in favor of that deed," Lincoln argued that it had been the same with the people of the South regarding slavery. "They were obliged to sustain slavery, although they secretly abhorred the institution," Lincoln apparently told the correspondent.[14]

If the correspondent quoted him correctly, Lincoln in fact had a false understanding of white southern opinion on slavery. Such a notion could have contributed to his view that "the people of the South," as he wrote a friend on August 15, "have too much of good sense, and good temper, to attempt the ruin of the government."[15] As their private letters and diaries indicate, white southerners, even in border slave states like Kentucky where Mary Todd Lincoln's family owned slaves, overwhelmingly supported the institution. They bitterly resented northern antislavery agitation, despite its conservative form as expressed by Lincoln and his party's Chicago platform. They saw the "Black Republicans" as a threat to their social and economic system, to race control, and to the peace of their communities, especially after John Brown's October 1859 raid on Harpers Ferry.

After years of controversy and propaganda, proslavery southerners rejected outright Republican expressions of goodwill toward the South. The issue for these southerners, if Lincoln was elected, was how best to protect themselves and their communities. Should they stay in the Union and wait and see what Lincoln would do, or should they secede before the Republicans had a chance to impose an antislavery regime upon them? In the same interview with the *Herald* correspondent in which he denied a strong southern attachment to slavery, Lincoln acknowledged the southern outrage toward his party, but he refused to admit that it might lead to secession upon his election. "The Southern mind," he said, was "laboring under the delusion that the Republicans were to liberate the Slaves, who were to apply firebrands to the fields and dwellings of their masters, massacre old and young, and produce a state of anarchy and bloodshed in the South." Lincoln told the *Herald* reporter that he would "like to go South and talk to the Southerners on this topic, [but that] the minds of some were so inflamed against him that they would not listen to his reasoning." Indeed, according to the *Herald* correspondent, Lincoln said that southerners "might be inclined to inflict Lynch law upon his person should he appear before him."[16] When criticism erupted over the "Lynch law" comment, Lincoln insisted that it was only made in jest.[17] Nonetheless, he did not visit Kentucky or any southern state to reassure southerners about slavery and his candidacy. Indeed, he would have risked physical harm if he had crossed the Ohio River to speak.

LINCOLN, UPON the advice of Senator Trumbull, David Davis, and other prominent Republicans, made no campaign speeches whatsoever; nor did he write public letters seeking support for his election. William Cullen Bryant, the venerable editor of the *New York Evening Post*, wrote Lincoln that he expressed "the wish of the vast majority of your friends when I say that they want you to make no speeches, write no letters as a candidate, enter into no pledges, make no promises, nor even give any of those kind words which men are apt to interpret into promises."[18] At that time, in fact, it was not customary for presidential candidates to campaign. Lincoln wrote an Ohio friend that "in my present position, . . . by the lessons of the past, and the united voice of all discreet friends, I am neither [to] write or speak a word for the public."[19] Lincoln concluded that public statements on the issues would be used against him, jeopardizing his favored position in the election.

From the beginning, Lincoln's friends throughout the North expressed confidence, both publicly and privately, that he would win.[20] After the Democrats made their final split at Baltimore on June 18 into twin branches, nominating Douglas (northern branch) and John C. Breckinridge (southern branch), Lincoln also believed that victory would be his in November. He found it "an amusing fact" about the Little Giant's southern opposition that after all that had been said about Republican sectionalism, "I had more votes from the Southern section at Chicago, than he had at Baltimore! In fact, there was more of the Southern section represented at Chicago, than in the Douglas rump concern at Baltimore!!"[21] Despite his confidence in victory, Lincoln became concerned that a fusion of the anti-Republican elements (supporters of Douglas, Breckinridge, and Bell) could defeat him, particularly in Indiana and Pennsylvania.

The Lincoln campaign was carried on at the state and local level in the North by a vast array of Republican activists. Republican Wide Awake clubs and, to a lesser extent, "Lincoln Young Americas" were formed. Emphasizing old Whig campaign tactics, they built wigwams, raised flagpoles, displayed Lincoln fence rails, exploded fireworks, ignited bonfires, and held torchlight parades in hundreds of villages, towns, and cities.[22] Lincoln's "Rail Splitter" image, while not decisive in his nomination at Chicago, carried an important symbol of democracy and opportunity for all classes in the West and for farmers and workingmen in eastern areas like central and western Pennsylvania that the Republicans needed to win. The evangelical-type rallies culminated in stirring speeches by Republican politicians. A multitude of party newspapers lent their voices to the crusade to sweep the Democrats and the proslavery South from power. Despite the fervor of their rhetoric, Republicans still proclaimed that their message was national, not sectional. Republicans avowed that their party posed no threat to the South or to its constitutional rights, and they emphasized the charges of corruption against the Buchanan administration. The Democrats organized a similar campaign, but except in some areas of the lower North, their parades and rallies never approached the Republicans' high level of organization and intensity.

In Springfield, where the political parties were about equal in strength, processions and rallies by Lincoln Wide Awakes and other Republicans as well as by Democratic Hickory Clubs (named after Democratic icon Andrew Jackson) occurred almost daily. At his room in the State House, Lincoln paid little attention to the political excitement below him in the streets, though at night, at home on the corner of Eighth and Jackson Streets, he greeted the Wide Awakes and other supporters, who often serenaded him.[23] By remaining away from the rallies, he sought to avoid the pressure to deliver a campaign speech. However, there was one grand Republican rally, on August 8, that Lincoln could not miss—and probably did not want to miss—for it exceeded anything that Springfield or Illinois had seen in any previous campaign.

At dawn on that day, cannon boomed out the signal for the people to begin to assemble in the streets of the state capital. Many had arrived the day before, as they had before the Lincoln-Douglas debates two years earlier. Throughout the morning, special trains chugged into Springfield carrying not only Lincoln Wide Awakes but also supporters of other Republican candidates, including Senator Trumbull, whose fate would be determined by the legislative elections in the fall. (Lincoln wrote a friend that it "would be a great disaster" if Trumbull lost the election; "please do not let it fall upon us," he said.[24]) Republican clubs came not only from inside the state but also from as far away as Hannibal and St. Louis, Missouri. Nearby counties sent large delegations of more than a thousand each. Republican organizers set up a telegraphic transmitter in the cupola of the State House to notify the twenty-five marshals on the ground of the arrival of visiting delegations.

The procession of about 4,000 revelers began in the morning and wound through the streets of Springfield, stopping at the Lincoln home, where "the cheers of the marchers made an incessant roar." Not until two o'clock did the procession reach the Fair Grounds, where a throng liberally estimated at 50,000 or 60,000 gathered to hear the orators. Wide Awakes paraded with floats heralding Lincoln's frontier origins and his early struggles as a rail splitter, laborer, and flat boatman. One large wagon, driven by twenty-three yoke of oxen, contained blacksmiths, wheelwrights, and rail splitters busy at their work. A steam-powered loom, courtesy of the Springfield Woolen Mills, had been mounted on another float, where spinners and a tailor were preparing a pair of pantaloons "to encase the limbs of the future President."[25] In reporting the rally on August 9, the *Springfield Illinois State Journal* headed its columns with an elephant holding in its trunk a banner proclaiming "WE ARE COMING!" and "CLEAR THE TRACK!" This might have been the first use of the elephant as a symbol of the Republican party.[26]

Prominent Republicans from Illinois and other western states, recognizing the state's importance in the election, appeared on the platform at the Fair Grounds and spoke to the enthusiastic crowd. The political leaders also came to Springfield to see Lincoln and hopefully gain a coattail effect back home from their association with the party's presidential candidate. The main speakers were Senator James Doolittle of Wisconsin, who spoke for one and a half hours, and Lincoln's friend Orville H. Browning. Both were conservatives, though Browning, unlike Doolittle and Lincoln, followed an ultraconservative path. Wisely, the Republican organizers balanced the speakers' list with John Wilson, the former Know-Nothing and American party leader in the state, and Gustave Koerner, the German American spokesman. Wilson had been a delegate to the Constitutional Union convention that had nominated John Bell for president, but he swung his support to Lincoln during the summer.[27]

While the rally was in progress, Lincoln arrived in a carriage. A crowd of men immediately rushed forward, lifted the gangly Lincoln to their shoulders, and carried him to the platform. The presidential nominee announced that he had "no intention of making a speech." He explained: "It has been my purpose, since I have been placed in my present position, to make no speeches." After his brief comments, Lincoln mounted a horse and slipped away before his fanatical supporters knew that he had left. That night, the rally continued with a torch-light parade, punctuated by the igniting of Roman candles. It ended with typical campaign festivities under the stars at the local wigwam.[28]

BY MIDSUMMER, the Douglas forces had resurrected all of the old charges against Lincoln in an attempt to win important conservative votes in Illinois and other lower northern states. One charge placed Lincoln earlier in a Know-Nothing lodge in Quincy, Illinois. Abraham Jonas, a Quincy friend, wrote Lincoln that local Democrats were gathering affidavits to publish in Washington saying he had been present at the lodge in 1854. Their object, Jonas said, was to alienate German American voters. Lincoln immediately provided Jonas with a detailed account of his visit to the town at that time, and he vehemently denied that he had ever attended a Know-Nothing meeting. "I spoke at some Hall there," he said, but it was not to a nativist meeting, and he declared that his recollection "could be easily proved, by respectable men, who were always in the lodges and never saw me there." Ever mindful of the need to remain circumspect in his effort to maintain party harmony, Lincoln asked Jonas to keep his explanation confidential. "Our adversaries think they can gain a point," he said, "if they could force me to openly deny this charge, by which some degree of offence would be given to the Americans [Know Nothings]. For this reason, it must not publicly appear that I am paying any attention to the charge."[29] German Americans remained unmoved by the charge; they dismissed it as a desperate Democratic campaign ploy, which it was. Lincoln's opposition to the Massachusetts effort to restrict the voting rights of new citizens had cemented his relationship with German Protestants. At the same time, many German Catholics, like Irish Catholics, continued to support the Democratic party because they considered Douglas's party untainted with evangelical nativism.

The Democratic press, particularly in Illinois, revived the old claim that Lincoln as a congressman had failed to support the troops in the Mexican-American War. The *Springfield Illinois State Register,* joined by the *Chicago Times* and local Democratic newspapers, led the attack.[30] After distorting his record in Congress on the war, the editor of the *State Register* professed to "leave it to Mr. Lincoln and his abolition, disunion black republican presses and stump speakers to excuse or palliate . . . his treasonable resolutions, speeches, and votes . . . as best they may." The *Cairo Gazette* descended to a new low in vilification when it called on Mexican war veterans to remember Lincoln at the polls "not only because he sought to stigmatize you as murderers, but because when you were almost reduced to starvation, and forced to grind upon hand mills the grain for your own bread, he, with fanatics of kindred stamp, refused to promptly send you supplies. . . . Such a man . . . asks to be made president of the United States by the hands of a people he has signally outraged, and the glory of whose military achievements he has sought to convert into shame and burning disgrace."[31] A Galesburg friend, Clark E. Carr, wrote Lincoln early in the campaign that many of the old soldiers believed the charge: "Our democratic friends are making capital of it," Carr said.[32] Lincoln and the state Republican press, however, ignored the attack lest it provide the Democrats with an excuse to keep the matter alive. In the end, the war issue had no appreciable effect on the election, except perhaps to reinforce stalwart Democratic opposition to Lincoln in his home state.

The main Democratic thrust against Lincoln was that his antislavery policy would inevitably result in southern secession and black equality. Democrats repeatedly claimed that he was the real "disunion candidate" in the election and often cited his 1858 House Divided Speech as proof. "Lincoln and his followers," the *Springfield Illinois State Register* declared, "assisted in sowing the seeds of this fell [foul?] spirit of abolitionism, the effects of which have stunned the country." Though he was attempting "to wiggle out of his declarations in favor of negro equality," the paper said, Lincoln could not "expect to evade responsibility for the inevitable results which follow his teachings." In addition to driving the South out of the Union, Lincoln's antislavery policies, Democratic propagandists charged, would bring blacks into the free states and produce African American political equality. In Lincoln's view, "the negro slave is to be elevated, and the white freeman degraded," the *State Register* contended.[33]

The *New York Herald,* the Douglas newspaper with the largest circulation, came out on the eve of the election with an unabashedly racist assault against the Republicans. If Lincoln was elected, the *Herald* predicted, "hundreds of thousands" of fugitive slaves would "emigrate to their friends—the Republicans—North, and be placed by them side by side in competition with white men. . . . African amalgamation with the fair daughters of the Anglo Saxon, Celtic, and Teutonic races will soon be their portion under the millennium of Republican rule."[34] This harsh pronouncement anticipated racist fears that emerged during the Civil War among northerners who worried that if emancipation became a reality, interracial sex and marriage would follow soon thereafter.

Douglas, in a break with tradition for a presidential candidate, spoke extensively, beginning in New England and extending into the South and the West. Everywhere, the Little Giant proclaimed that he was the only national candidate and that Breckinridge and Lincoln represented sectional extremes that would split the nation if elected. Douglas repeated what he had said earlier about his opponent. Lincoln, he declared, was "a very clever fellow—a kindhearted, good natured, amiable man. I have not the heart to say anything against Abe Lincoln; I have fought him so long that I have a respect for him."[35] But, Douglas contended, Lincoln supported Seward's "irrepressible conflict" doctrine over slavery. Douglas waved the black-equality flag against Lincoln and the Republicans in an effort to unite Democrats and conservatives behind his candidacy. He argued that of the three opposition candidates —Breckinridge, Bell, and himself—he was the only one who could derail the "Black Republican" train. Speaking at Chicago a few days following Seward, Douglas brazenly announced that the radical New York senator would dominate a Lincoln administration and would labor to make blacks the equal of white men in Illinois and elsewhere.[36]

Though Lincoln did not leave Springfield until after the election, he played an active behind-the-scenes role in the Republican campaign. He often called on Republicans to provide reports on the campaign in their states.[37] A steady stream of party leaders or their representatives visited him in Springfield and discussed the course of the canvass. Some visitors expressed their amazement with Lincoln's understanding of politics in their states. A Republican of Oneida County, New York, reported after a meeting with Lincoln: "He sat down beside me on the sofa and commenced talking about political affairs in my own State with a knowledge of details which surprised me."[38]

Lincoln or his secretary, John G. Nicolay, provided Republicans in New York and other states with information on the campaign. But Lincoln refused to answer questions about policies, except to provide Senator Simon Cameron of Pennsylvania with some earlier notes on his support for tariff duties to aid industry. When T. Apolion Cheney of Cherry Creek, New York, wanted to know his position on the Fugitive Slave Act, which Lincoln had consistently supported, he declined to answer, replying that "it would be both imprudent, and contrary to the reasonable expectation of friends for me to write, or speak anything upon doctrinal points now. Besides this, my published speeches contain nearly all I could willingly say. *Justice and fairness to all,* is the utmost I have said, or will say."[39]

AS THE CAMPAIGN entered its most intense phase during the late summer, Lincoln and the Republicans faced a serious threat as their opponents attempted to merge, or "fuse," their electoral votes in the battleground states of the North. The most important fusionist efforts occurred in Indiana and Pennsylvania, states that would be decisive in the election. Lincoln's nomination at Chicago had hinged on the Republican belief that as an antislavery conservative who had never supported the Know-Nothing movement, he could win the combined forty electoral votes of these two critical states. Both Indiana and Pennsylvania were scheduled for gubernatorial elections on October 9. It was clear to contemporaries (and later to historians) that the results of the two elections would foretell the outcome of the presidential contest in November. If successful in Indiana and Pennsylvania, the fusion movement could spill over into New York, Illinois, and other states, causing Lincoln to be defeated.

Lincoln therefore wisely focused his attention on the Indiana and Pennsylvania campaigns. Calling on the national Republican committee to aid the cause in these two states, he wrote to Governor Edwin D. Morgan of New York, chair of the committee, that "the whole surplus energy of the party throughout the nation, should be bent upon that object up to the close of the election." Morgan had written Lincoln that he had received a disturbing report that the Republicans might not win control of the Illinois legislature and return Lyman Trumbull to the Senate. Lincoln informed Morgan that "no one thing will do us so much good in *Illinois*" or elsewhere "as the carrying of *Indiana* [and Pennsylvania] in the October election."[40] In Illinois a group of John Bell supporters meeting in Decatur on August 16 had formed a "National Union" ticket and nominated John Todd Stuart for governor. The new conservative party, however, rejected fusion with the Democrats.[41] The Illinois National Union party proved to be only a shadow of the old Whig and American parties; most former Clay conservatives now favored the Republican party, and particularly Lincoln.

Lincoln worried most about Indiana, a state that was staunchly conservative on the slavery issue and where the Know Nothings, though a minority, still had an effective organization that could rally the faithful against the Republicans. However, soon after his nomination, he received information that Richard W. Thompson might be persuaded to support him. Thompson was the leader of Indiana's Know Nothings, who were soon to be organized as the Constitutional Union party (with Bell as their nominee). Though Thompson disliked the "Dutch" plank in the Chicago platform opposing restrictions on immigrants, he felt that "Indiana must not be carried by the Democracy; and that he expected to oppose the formation of any Bell Electoral ticket," according to his friend Schuyler Colfax. Lincoln realized that such a ticket, if formed, could give the election to Douglas in Indiana. He immediately dispatched a friendly letter to Thompson complimenting him and recalling their service together as Whigs in Congress.[42]

In his reply, Thompson told Lincoln that he had not decided how to vote. However, he reaffirmed that his "primary object was to beat the Democracy by holding off" Know-Nothing opposition "in the doubtful northern states," thereby letting Lincoln carry them. He declared that "this will close the career of the monster [Douglas]." If he was elected, Lincoln would have the opportunity to "inaugurate a Conservative & national administration, which, the slavery question out of the way, would bring about the restoration of Whiggery," Thompson wrote.[43] In a subsequent letter, he expressed a desire to meet Lincoln—but only in secret—in order to avoid charges of collusion before the state Constitutional Union convention met in August to determine the issue of fusion with the Douglas forces. He explained to Lincoln that the need for secrecy did not "arise out of a want of confidence felt in you, but from the strong feelings existing in particular localities between some of *our* men & the Republicans." These old Fillmore conservatives, he said, still had to be convinced "that you, if elected, will not suffer yourself to be led into ultraism by Radical men; but [that] your administration will be national."[44]

Thompson believed that, given time, he could succeed in persuading his Indiana supporters of Lincoln's conservatism, and thereby thwart a Know-Nothing fusion with the Democrats. Lincoln, he said, must understand the "exceeding delicacy" of the matter, especially since, from Lincoln's standpoint, a public meeting with a prominent Know Nothing like Thompson would create concern among his German American friends both in Illinois and in Indiana.

Discreetly, Lincoln dispatched John G. Nicolay to meet with Thompson at Terre Haute. His instructions to Nicolay were simple: "Tell him my motto is 'Fairness to all,' but commit me to nothing," a position that Lincoln had taken when he met with Thurlow Weed and other political leaders. The interview with Thompson went well, and Nicolay reported that the Indianan "did not even hint at any exaction or promise as being necessary to secure the 'Know Nothing' vote for the Republican ticket."[45] Encouraged by Thompson's position, Lincoln in late July wrote Caleb B. Smith, a Republican leader in Indiana, that "from present appearances we might succeed in the general result [election], without Indiana, but *with* it, failure is scarcely possible."[46]

Despite Thompson's goodwill toward Lincoln and his efforts to prevent fusion in his state, great pressure was brought by prominent Kentuckians, Know Nothings, and men of Whig antecedents in Indiana to support the Douglas ticket. Senator John J. Crittenden, George Prentice of the *Louisville Journal,* and former Governor Charles S. Morehead—all Clay Whigs—bombarded conservatives across the Ohio with the argument that only the success of Douglas could prevent disunion. Speaking at Louisville on August 2, Crittenden, in an address that the Democratic press in Indiana and Illinois eagerly reported, declared that "Mr. Lincoln may be a very worthy, upright and honest man." But if elected president, "he must be governed by the political influence and voice of his party. Mr. Lincoln is at the head of the great anti-slavery party, a purely sectional party, which, according to all its antecedents, threatens the existence of slavery everywhere. . . . Although the leaders and wise men of that party may not proclaim such sentiments, there are enough among them in their camp who do hold and proclaim such abolition doctrines as must make every man south feel uneasy in his condition and in his property." Crittenden, who had sought Lincoln's defeat in the 1858 senatorial election, insisted that "the mere fact of Mr. Lincoln's election would be, therefore, a great calamity to the country, though he never should do an act positively offensive or injurious to any interest of the country. His election would create and continue an alarm that would keep the country agitated and unhappy, if not create an opposition and resistance to the government itself." With the typical border-state fear of being caught in the middle of a clash between North and South, Crittenden predicted that if Lincoln won, the antislavery effort "would go further than it has yet gone, and cause still greater dangers to the peace and security of the south."[47]

When the Indiana Constitutional Union convention met in Indianapolis on August 15, Morehead spoke and appealed to the delegates to support Douglas as the only viable alternative to the "disunionist" Lincoln. Thompson, however, told the delegates that, though he preferred Bell for president, only Lincoln could win the election, and that therefore no bargain should be struck with either Douglas or John C. Breckinridge Democrats (the southern rights candidate). The convention partly agreed; it endorsed Bell for president, but rejected fusion with the Democrats.[48] Lincoln's popularity in his boyhood state, along with traditional Whig opposition to the Democrats, contributed to the willingness of many conservatives who had voted for Fillmore in 1856 to oppose fusion in 1860.

Kentuckians and their Indiana supporters of fusion, however, did not give up the fight in their state. They changed their tactics and launched a campaign to defeat Republican Henry S. Lane in the crucial gubernatorial election in October. Their target was Lincoln, they admitted, rather than Lane. As most political observers believed, a defeat for Lane, as well as a loss for Republican gubernatorial candidate Andrew G. Curtin in Pennsylvania at the same time, would crush Lincoln's hopes in the November election. Kentuckians appealed to old Whigs of Indiana to go to the polls and vote for Democrat Thomas A. Hendricks for governor, who they thought could rally conservatives to his standard. The Indiana Democratic party, however, was bitterly divided between Douglas men and supporters of Senator Jesse D. Bright. Despite Hendricks's popularity in the party, Bright, embittered by his feud with Douglas, proclaimed his support for Lane for governor and Breckinridge for president.[49]

Five days before the October 9 state election, Thompson, upset by the intrigues of the Kentuckians, issued a printed circular called *To the Conservative Men of Indiana* announcing that he would vote not only for Lincoln but also for Lane. He reminded conservatives that both Lincoln and Lane were old Whigs who would restore the principles of that party to state and national government.[50] Thompson dispatched a copy of the circular to Lincoln and also provided for its immediate distribution in Indiana. Lincoln must have realized that Bright's apostasy and the Thompson circular, barring a political catastrophe, sealed the fate of the Democratic candidates in the Indiana elections.

In Pennsylvania, the Republican cause became extremely complicated because of factionalism in the state party and the strength of the Know Nothings among conservatives. Moreover, influential Philadelphia merchants feared that Lincoln's election would induce southern secession and upset their financial interests in the South. Because of their party's radical image and the need to attract conservatives to their cause, Republicans in the state officially called themselves the "People's Party." Lincoln's nomination on a conservative antislavery platform and support for legislation "to encourage the development of the industrial interests of the whole country" (code language for a protective tariff), however, made the word "Republican" palatable to an increasing number of anti-Democrats in the state. The Pennsylvania Republican party's division was mainly along personal lines between friends loyal to Senator Simon Cameron and those devoted to gubernatorial candidate Andrew G. Curtin.[51]

Factionalism among Pennsylvania Democrats ran even deeper than in the state Republican party. It owed its origins to Douglas's opposition to President Buchanan's pro-southern Kansas policy and the proslavery Lecompton constitution. Buchanan, a native of the state, had long controlled the state Democratic organization, and in the 1860 presidential election he threw his support behind Breckinridge, his vice president. But faced with the "Black Republican" threat to the Union (after all, Pennsylvania lay just north of Maryland, which was a slave state), and realizing the importance of the state in the national election, Democrats could conceivably swallow their mutual antagonisms and agree to fusion. The wild-card factor in the campaign was the position of those who had voted for Fillmore in 1856. Most of the 82,175 Fillmore voters, or 17.8 percent of the total cast in the state, were Know Nothings who objected to Resolution Fourteen, or the "Dutch plank" in the national Republican platform, which opposed restrictions on the rights of immigrants. Soon after his nomination, Lincoln's friends had advised him to ignore the Dutch plank lest he lose the large Know-Nothing vote in Pennsylvania and elsewhere. He took the advice to heart and remained silent on the controversial resolution.[52]

At the same time, Lincoln intervened to promote harmony in the Pennsylvania party. In July, he received reports that Curtin supporters, who controlled the state central committee, were questioning the party loyalty of members of the Cameron faction and ignoring them in the campaign. The powerful Cameron forces threatened to organize "an auxiliary" to the state committee. Such a parallel organization, Lincoln feared, would inevitably divide the party and weaken Curtin's prospects in the critical October election. Lincoln wrote Leonard Swett, who had important contacts in the state, that the situation "pains me. I am afraid there is a germ of difficulty in it. Will not the men thus suspected [of disloyalty] make a dangerous explosion?" Lincoln wanted Swett to write Joseph Casey, an influential friend in the Cameron faction, and "suggest to him that great caution and delicacy of action, is necessary in that matter." He also asked Swett and David Davis to go to Pennsylvania and help resolve the difficulty.[53]

Davis, without Swett, visited the state and talked to Republican leaders; he also met with party luminaries in New Jersey and New York. On August 4, Davis spent the day with Cameron. Later he reported to Lincoln that the senator had agreed that the gubernatorial election in October was too important nationally for Pennsylvania Republicans to be divided in their support of Curtin. Davis had given Cameron notes on the tariff that Lincoln had written in 1847, and the Pennsylvania Republican leader expressed his delight with Lincoln's unambiguous support of a tariff to protect the state's industry. Buoyed by what he heard from Cameron and other state Republican leaders, Davis sanguinely wrote Lincoln that Pennsylvania was safe for the party in the election.[54]

A few days later, political craftsman Thurlow Weed met with Cameron in Philadelphia. He reported to Lincoln that the senator "was well pleased with the visit of Judge Davis, and will go to work earnestly" for the cause in the state. New York's "Wizard of the Lobby" reminded Lincoln that Cameron was "by far the strongest man and best worker in the State," strongly suggesting that he should continue to cultivate the goodwill of the Pennsylvania senator. Though he had misgivings about Cameron's reputation as a political spoilsman, Lincoln needed no reminder from Weed of the senator's importance to his success in the Keystone State. When John M. Pomeroy, a friend of both Cameron and Curtin, wrote him to say that the controversy over the control of the party's state committee had been settled, Lincoln assured him that he had always been "slow to listen to criminations among friends, and never expose [sic] their quarrels on either side." His wish, he told Pomeroy, was "that both sides . . . allow by-gones to be by-gones, and look to the present & future only."[55]

Meanwhile, bitter factionalism in the Pennsylvania Democratic party worked decidedly to Lincoln's advantage in the state. The state Democratic central committee, which was controlled by the Buchanan faction, met in Philadelphia on July 2 and reaffirmed a previously agreed upon policy of a single Democratic presidential electoral ticket. Under this fusionist arrangement, electors would cast all of their votes for the Democratic candidate, Douglas or Breckinridge, whoever had the better chance of success after the election results in other states were known. This plan proved unacceptable, however, to Douglas leaders, who foresaw that Breckinridge would win most of the South and, with the backing of Buchanan officeholders, probably the Democratic vote in Pennsylvania as well. They thus could find themselves in the untenable position of supporting the southern rights candidate. "No true friend of Douglas," Democrat John W. Forney of the *Philadelphia Press* announced, "can touch an electoral ticket which contains upon it the single name of a Breckinridge Disunionist."[56]

Forney, who had supported Douglas's war on Buchanan, was hardly a friend of the Little Giant. Pennsylvania Republicans reported to Lincoln that this powerful Democratic editor and publisher had seen the handwriting on the wall in national politics and was now intriguing to win the state for the Republicans. Forney also owed his recent election as clerk of the U.S. House of Representatives to Republican votes.

The Philadelphia editor later admitted that he had worked for Lincoln's victory in Pennsylvania in 1860 by fueling his party's divisions and denouncing any fusion with the Breckinridge "seceders." His efforts succeeded. Douglas supporters meeting on July 26 adamantly rejected fusion with the Breckinridge faction and selected their own electoral ticket. David Wilmot, whose antislavery proviso to an army appropriations bill during the Mexican-American War had sparked a bitter sectional debate in Congress, joyfully reported to Lincoln from his home in Pennsylvania: "I cannot [now] feel a doubt of the results" of the presidential election. "The confusion of Bable [*sic*] has fallen upon the counsels of the Enemies of Freedom. They are doomed through their great iniquities, and by the inexorable moral law of Heaven, to defeat, shame & humiliation. The moral and political power of the party of Slavery is broken, and no patched up arrangements of its leaders, were such a thing possible, can save it from its just doom."[57]

Despite the optimism of Wilmot, Davis, and others, the Pennsylvania gubernatorial election in October held serious pitfalls for the Republicans. A Republican failure in the state would reverse the party's momentum throughout the lower North and also in New York. Curtin, the Republican candidate, was a weak stump speaker, and members of the Cameron wing of the party grumbled about his lack of leadership in the campaign. Furthermore, the threat of a Douglas Democratic fusion with supporters of presidential candidate John Bell of the Constitutional Union party created concern among some Republican leaders both inside and outside of the state. The possibility of such a coalition was particularly real in Philadelphia, where voters were upset that Curtin's campaign committee had gone to the money markets of New York for support. Russell Errett, Republican editor of the *Pittsburgh Gazette,* wrote Joseph Medill of the *Chicago Press and Tribune* that "this indiscretion has wounded Phila. sensibility in its tenderest point. The idea of begging New York to carry a Phila. election is repulsive to every Philadelphian." It could also give the merchant class, in addition to their fear of southern secession if Lincoln won in November, another reason to support the anti-Republican fusion movement in the October gubernatorial election.[58]

Fortunately for the Republicans, the factional conflict in the Pennsylvania Democratic party, as in Indiana, spilled over into the gubernatorial campaign. In its July 2 meeting, the Democratic state central committee had endorsed Henry D. Foster for governor, a candidate who, it was believed, could obtain the support of both factions of the party. Keenly aware of the significance of the gubernatorial contest to the presidential election in November, Forney, still claiming to be a Democrat while aiding the Republicans, set out to sabotage Foster's chances. In the columns of the *Philadelphia Press,* Forney demanded that Foster announce which Democratic candidate he supported for president.[59] Forney cleverly believed that if Foster said he favored Breckinridge, he would lose the Douglas vote—and vice versa. Having been endorsed by the Buchanan-dominated state central committee that supported Breckinridge, Foster refused to indicate a preference for president or denounce the "disunionists" in the party as Douglas activists insisted. Many friends of the Little Giant concluded that Foster was playing a double game at their expense by remaining friendly with Breckinridge and the southern rights faction. The division between the Breckinridge (Buchanan) and Douglas forces in the state inevitably meant that Foster could not expect a full party vote in October. Many Douglas supporters would either go fishing on election day or vote for Curtin.

Thus, the situation in Pennsylvania was similar to the situation in Indiana. The possibility that the Bell vote would be thrown to Foster in the gubernatorial election proved a greater concern to Republicans than a unified Democratic vote. In early September, a virtual panic gripped Pennsylvania Republicans when reports reached them that Bell leaders in Philadelphia were poised to reach an agreement with Democrats to support Foster. Philadelphia had been a center for the American party, where as many as 25,000 votes had been cast for Fillmore in 1856. Alarmed Republicans concluded that if Foster received a majority of these votes, he would win the election. Because of Lincoln's Whig antecedents, including support for a protective tariff, national Republican leaders believed that Lincoln, not Bell, would win the bulk of the Fillmore vote in November. But they feared that the "prestige" of Foster's success in the Pennsylvania gubernatorial election "would be bad for us in other states."[60] To counter the threat, Republican orators flooded Pennsylvania to campaign for both Curtin and Lincoln. Though minuscule by modern standards, money for campaign literature and outside speakers—such as German American spokesman Carl Schurz—was provided by northeastern Republicans.[61] As the gubernatorial campaign climaxed in the late summer, Senator Cameron reassured Lincoln that Pennsylvania was safe for Curtin. The wily senator predicted that old political enmities between the Democrats and Bell leaders in Philadelphia could not be bridged. He was correct. In the negotiations with the Democrats, Bell supporters insisted upon "the sacrifice of certain democrats running for Congress as a quid pro quo," which Foster's forces refused to give. By the first of October, it was clear to Pennsylvania Republicans that Curtin would carry Philadelphia and, with it, the election.[62]

Though confident that his party would win the important October state elections in Indiana and Pennsylvania, Lincoln could not be sure. Soon after midnight on election day, October 9, telegraphic reports revealed that the Republicans had swept these states and also Ohio, a state that had never been in doubt. The next day, Lincoln wrote Herndon in Petersburg, Illinois, where he was campaigning for the party, that Republicans had handily won all three states. Herndon was speaking at a rally in the courthouse when he received the note from Lincoln. Pandemonium broke out as he read it to the crowd. Herndon recalled, "I never finished that speech. The crowd yelled—screamed—threw up their hats—ran out of doors—made bonfires—&c. &c."[63] Similar Republican demonstrations occurred throughout the North. "The doubts and fears of the Republicans of the nation are dispelled," the *Chicago Press and Tribune* exclaimed. Republican "labor is rewarded by the prospect of a triumph which will be both splendid and enduring." This editor jubilantly predicted that "with steadiness and firmness for yet one [more] month [the labor] is done, and on the fourth of March, the country . . . will, under the lead of that pure patriot and honest man ABRAHAM LINCOLN, enter upon a career of freedom and prosperity" after years of Democratic corruption and "reckless Legislation for the interest of slavery."[64]

Far away in Washington, Stephen A. Douglas received the election news with dismay. The Indiana and Pennsylvania results had destroyed his hopes for a victory in November and, he believed, foretold an ominous future for the republic. The Little Giant told his secretary, "Mr. Lincoln is the next President. We must try to save the Union. I will go South," which he did, only to be greeted with insults.[65]

Lincoln's pleasure in his party's October successes quickly turned to the realization that the heavy weight of the presidency would soon be on him. His old concern about his fitness and desire for the office that he had expressed to friends when first approached about the presidency now returned to trouble him. On October 25, he earnestly told Benjamin Welch, commissary general of New York: "I declare to you this morning General—that for personal considerations I would rather have a full term in the Senate—a place in which I would feel more consciously able to discharge the duties required, and where there was more chance to make [a] reputation, and less danger of losing it—than four years in the Presidency."[66]

After the October elections, Lincoln's demeanor became sober and withdrawn, reflecting the anguish within him. The extreme depression, or "melancholy," of his youth, however, did not return, perhaps because he was almost constantly engaged with the public and preparing for his new responsibilities. Though congenial to visitors and his old associates, Lincoln, according to Judge Davis, "looked as if he had a heavy responsibility resting on him." Davis predicted that "the cares & responsibilities of office will wear on him. . . . The cormorants for office will be numerous & greedy." Politicians were entering Illinois to campaign for Lincoln and the Republicans, "now that the Presidential Election is settled," Davis wrote his wife. These "Speakers from abroad," he said, "wish to show their devotion & worship the rising sun" in order to gain favors from Lincoln.[67] The "cormorants," either directly or through important Republican friends, were approaching Lincoln about offices as if he had already won the election.[68] He made no commitments.

Anti-Republican forces in the East, particularly in New York, made a last, desperate effort at fusion to prevent Lincoln's election. James Gordon Bennett's *New York Herald* expressed to its readers the ominous meaning of the October 9 election in Pennsylvania. "The overwhelming defeat of Foster," this newspaper declared, "throws the whole weight of the Presidential battle upon New York. Pennsylvania is irretrievably lost—the great West presents no satisfactory signs of a rescue—the New England States have been abandoned to the enemy—our Northern conservative forces arrayed against Lincoln's election are, in fact, routed everywhere, except in New York, and New York is their forlorn hope."[69] The *Herald* reflected the alarm of businessmen in the East, who soon realized that southern talk of secession if Lincoln won was no mere bluff to gain concessions, as Republicans had argued. Following the October elections, New Yorkers with extensive interests in the South's agricultural economy received almost daily reports of the determination of southerners to leave the Union upon the election of Lincoln. Southern newspapers, even in upper South states like Tennessee and North Carolina, bombarded their readers with apocalyptic predictions of what Lincoln's victory would mean, sending chills through the commercial and financial halls of New York and among former American party men in the state, including Millard Fillmore, who was then in retirement in Buffalo.

Moderate southerners—most of whom had been associates of Fillmore Whigs and were now supporters of John Bell's Constitutional Union party— declared that the only hope remaining to avoid the "evil day" was a unified stand against the Republicans in New York. That state's thirty-five electoral votes, if cast against the Republicans along with southern votes, would throw the election into the House of Representatives, even if Lincoln won the other northern states. In the House, according to this reasoning, either Breckinridge, Douglas, or Bell would be chosen president. "New York," the *New Orleans Daily Crescent* contended, "has it in her power to avert" the election of the "Black Republican" and prevent the secession of the southern states. "Upon the great Empire State, alone, the hopes of the South now rest for the preservation of the peace, the security, and . . . the Union of the States," it said.[70] Caught in the middle of the crisis, border-state Unionists, with New York in mind, also frantically called for a coalition of the Bell and Douglas forces to defeat the "disunionist" candidates, Lincoln and Breckinridge. "Men of the American Union," the *Louisville Journal,* edited by the influential George D. Prentice, cried out, "if you would have your consciences and your names free from the ineffaceable and damning stain of liberticide, defeat the Republican candidate for the Presidency together with his Seceding accomplice, and bury the two in one common pit of ruin and of shame."[71]

Prior to the Indiana and Pennsylvania elections, an attempt to bring about a fusion of the anti-Republican elements in New York had floundered. In a letter to Thurlow Weed in August, Lincoln predicted that "the most extraordinary effort ever made to carry New-York for Douglas" would be made by those attempting to throw the old Fillmore vote to the Little Giant. The critical importance of the American party and Know-Nothing vote for the Republicans in central Illinois during the mid- and late 1850s had conditioned Lincoln to be anxious about any threat from this political quarter, whether in Illinois, Indiana, Pennsylvania, or New York, in the presidential contest. Weed and other New York Republicans, however, assured Lincoln that, except for diehard Fillmore conservatives, or "Silver Grays" who supported Bell, the fusion movement in New York would not succeed and he would win almost all the relatively large American party vote of 1856.[72] Lincoln was not so confident. On September 14, he wrote former Indiana senator John Pettit that he had received good news from New York, but he admitted that "it is from friends, and is one-sided, [and] it may be delusive."[73]

James O. Putnam, a former American party leader of upstate New York, reassured Lincoln on September 25 that the Fillmore vote in the area had been won over by his conservative position on slavery and the South. Putnam told Lincoln that he had lifted the Republican party "high and dry out of the abolition ruts, and brought into it a very strong conservative force, strong in numbers, strong in talent, strong in moral and social position."[74] It is doubtful that Lincoln's nomination as a conservative had achieved such a dramatic change in the character of the Republican party in the hotbed of antislavery sentiment in upstate New York. Antislavery men clearly viewed the "Rail Splitter" as a more acceptable candidate than Douglas and Bell, who, while claiming to be conservative, had no moral or political scruples about slavery.

After the October elections, diehard New York Silver Grays and apprehensive New York merchants, many of whom were also former Whigs, launched a final campaign to fuse the Bell, Douglas, and Breckinridge votes in the state. Supported by the *New York Herald*, they agreed to a fusion supporting Douglas, who was expected to win most of the anti-Republican popular vote in the state. The agreement provided that Douglas would receive a majority of the places on the anti-Lincoln electoral ticket. Claiming that the fusionists represented a true national position, in contrast to the sectional Republicans, the *Herald* referred to the fusion movement as the Union party.[75]

Concerned Republicans recognized that the fusionists were placing their hopes in New York City, where Irish immigrants had routinely voted for Democrats and where the merchant class was providing money and influence for the fusion ticket. Governor Morgan anxiously reported to Lincoln that "the enemy has been aided with money from men who really believe the Union is in danger, [and] in some cases alarmed our friends."[76] (New York merchants also dispatched money into New Jersey to aid a late fusion effort to win that state's seven electoral votes.) To counter the fusion threat in the city, Republican newspapers and orators repeatedly reminded Irish Americans and other immigrant groups of the Silver Grays' Know-Nothing background. Furthermore, Weed, who was directing his party's strategy from Albany, flooded New York City and other vulnerable places with speakers and Wide Awake activists. He persuaded Seward to attend a grand rally in the city and make a major speech reassuring New Yorkers that a Republican victory would not mean aggression against the slave states, southern secession, or the disruption of trade, as the fusionists claimed. On November 2, four days before the election, Seward delivered an address before a huge and enthusiastic crowd at the Palace Garden. It evidently had some effect. Though New York City gave the fusion ticket a 30,000-vote majority, this local victory was not as dramatic as observers had expected it to be. Upstate support for the Republicans proved overwhelming, and by an impressive margin of 50,000 votes, Lincoln won the Empire State's thirty-five electoral votes.[77]

Finally realizing in late October that fusion would fail and the "Rail Splitter" would be elected president, George D. Prentice of the *Louisville Journal* wrote Lincoln asking for a public letter "setting forth your conservative views and intentions" as president. Such a letter, this editor said, would be "calculated to assure all the good citizens of the South" of his goodwill and "to take from the disunionists every excuse or pretext for treason." Otherwise, he informed Lincoln, "almost as soon as the fact of your election shall be proclaimed, a desperate blow will be struck for the dismemberment of the Union." Prentice's statement that he had "the strongest confidence" in Lincoln's "personal and political integrity" but opposed his election "because I greatly fear its influence upon the peace of the country" did nothing to ingratiate him with Lincoln.

Lincoln angrily shot back that although Prentice did "occasionally speak" of him "in terms of personal kindness," he gave "no prominence" to his "oft-repeated expressions of conservative views and intention; but busy yourself with appeals to all conservative men, to vote for Douglas—to vote any way which can possibly defeat me—thus impressing your readers that you think, I am the very worst man living." Lincoln said that a public letter, if written, would do no good and would be used by "*bad* men," both North and South, "who are eager for something new upon which to base new misrepresentations—men who would like to frighten me, or, at least, to fix upon me the character of timidity and cowardice." Lincoln told Prentice, whose newspaper he had devotedly read as a young man, that, "if I were to labor a month, I could not express my conservative views and intentions more clearly and strongly, than they are expressed in our plat-form, and in my many speeches already in print, and before the public." Lincoln told the editor that even if he agreed to the request for a public letter, he had no reason to believe that Prentice would publish it in the *Journal*.[78]

Lincoln's refusal to agree to Prentice's request for a soothing letter was similar to his response to others who sought, both before and after the election, to obtain reassurance regarding his policy during the crisis.[79] Nothing Lincoln could have said would have changed the results of the election; however, a reaffirmation of his conservatism and his goodwill toward the South might have made a difference in the course of secession in states like Georgia, where the voters were divided. Furthermore, a careful statement by Lincoln, while not violating his commitment to the Republican platform, could have reinforced the Union position in the upper South and the border slave states.

ELECTION DAY, November 6, in Springfield was a day of tension and anticipation. No one in Lincoln's company, however, could sense that this was the most important day in his life. His demeanor was the same as it had been the evening before when someone at the post office had asked him how he planned to vote. He replied, "for Yates for Governor." How for president? "By ballot," he quipped, then told a funny story and walked away.[80] On the morning of the election, as had been his custom since May, Lincoln went to his office at the State House. Already the streets were filling with people from Springfield and nearby communities. Anticipating victory, Republican bands marched through the town, their music punctuated occasionally by the roar of cannon. About three o'clock, when he was told the way was clear to vote at the courthouse, Lincoln left his office to cast his ballot. As soon as he appeared on the street, "he was recognized and welcomed with such a cheer as no man ever received who has not the hearts as well as the voices of his people," a *New York Tribune* correspondent reported. "Every vestige of party feeling seemed to be suddenly abandoned. Even the distributors of the Douglas tickets shouted and swung their hats as wildly as the rest."[81] Arriving at the polls, Lincoln cut his name from the top of the ballot because it was customary—in a tradition that was not always adhered to—not to vote for oneself. He then deposited a straight Republican ticket into the ballot box. As he left the building, Lincoln greeted some of the people who crushed around him, then immediately returned to the State House. He had been gone for only about five minutes.[82]

That evening, crowds jammed into the downtown area. When the returns began to come in, Lincoln and a handful of close associates left his office at the State House and walked over to the Western Union telegraph office. Before midnight, telegraphic dispatches indicated that the western states and Pennsylvania were safe for Lincoln and the Republicans. But still no word came from New York. As the tension mounted, Lincoln and his small party crossed the street and entered a large second-story room on the public square where wives and daughters of prominent Springfield Republicans, apparently including Mary Lincoln, had prepared food and decorations. When he walked through the door, the women, in unison, greeted him, "How do you do, Mr. President!" Hardly had Lincoln sat down at the table when a dispatch arrived saying that he had carried New York. A tumult of rejoicing broke out in the room and on the street below, a scene that continued into the wee hours of the morning.[83] News also arrived that the Republicans had probably captured the Illinois state offices and the General Assembly. There was only one regret for Lincoln; by a narrow margin (forty votes) he had lost his home county, though he won Springfield. Traditional support for the Democrats and the fear of southern secession if the Republicans came to power were too strong in Sangamon County in 1860 for Lincoln to overcome at the polls. He also lost Sangamon in the 1864 election.[84] Thus Lincoln has the dubious distinction of being the only successful presidential candidate in two elections to fail to win his home county on both occasions.

The final election returns indicated that Lincoln had swept the West and the Northeast, except for New Jersey, where, in a peculiar state arrangement, he had shared electoral votes with Douglas. In all, he received 180 electoral votes to 72 for Breckinridge, 39 for Bell, and 12 for Douglas. Lincoln won 39 percent of the popular vote, which is still the smallest percentage of any winning presidential candidate. He captured 54 percent of the northern vote. With four candidates in the election, it was evident that the popular percentage for the winner would not be large. For all practical purposes, Lincoln was not on the ballot in the fifteen slave states. Only in the border slave states (Missouri, Kentucky, Maryland, and Delaware) and Virginia in the upper South did Lincoln receive any votes. Of the 26,390 Lincoln votes in these five slave states, 17,028 were polled in Missouri, mainly in St. Louis with its relatively large German and northern population. Even in the border slave states, it took an act of courage for Republicans to distribute Lincoln ballots; it was impossible in most of the South, where hostility to Republicans exceeded all political rationality. With more than 80 percent of the eligible voters casting ballots, the election was essentially two elections, one in the North (Lincoln versus Douglas or fusion) and one in the South (Breckinridge versus Bell).

Democrats at the time and some historians since then have claimed that if the fusion movement had been successful in all of the free states, Lincoln could not have won a majority of the electoral vote. Historian and Lincoln scholar Richard N. Current has pointed out that the election was closer than the electoral vote indicated. A shift of 2 percent, or 80,000 popular votes, in certain areas would have cost Lincoln a majority of the electoral votes.[85] The election then would have been thrown into the House of Representatives, where each state delegation would have had only one vote. Since the anti-Republican parties controlled a majority of the delegations, Douglas or one of the other two candidates would have been chosen as president. But William E. Gienapp and other scholars have challenged this interpretation. Even with fusion in the states where it was possible, Lincoln would have received twenty-seven more electoral votes than needed to win, according to Gienapp. "Only in New Jersey, California, and Oregon," this historian wrote, "did Lincoln's margin of victory result from the division of the opposition vote, and these provided him with only eleven electoral votes."[86]

Speculation aside, the likelihood of a successful fusion was slim in the key states because of the deep-seated antagonisms among the various anti-Republican elements. Lincoln's candidacy on his party's conservative antislavery platform, and his strong commitment to this platform, undermined much of the opposition's use of his 1858 House Divided Speech to portray him as a radical who sought a conflict with the South over slavery. As the delegates to the national Republican convention had recognized, the Illinois "Rail Splitter" proved acceptable to the majority of voters in the states where the election was decided. During the campaign, Republican newspapers and speakers, politically sensitive to northern white racism, refused to respond to the Democratic charges that Lincoln supported black equality. They riveted voter attention on their candidate's commitment to the republican principles of the Founding Fathers, on the national Democratic violation of these principles in Kansas, and on the corruption of the Buchanan administration. In the North, Douglas failed to overcome his reputation as a northern "dough-faced" demagogue in the service of the slave power, despite his late and futile effort to find a middle way between the antislavery and proslavery positions in the sectional conflict.

In addition, Republican newspapers, Wide Awake clubs, and other party activists effectively exploited Lincoln's "Rail Splitter" image as the symbol of a vibrant, egalitarian, democratic America and contrasted it in their speeches and campaign literature to the oligarchical, corrupt, and decrepit Democratic party. First-time voters, attracted by the enthusiasm and promise of a better America, overwhelmingly cast their ballots for Lincoln.[87] Though a commercial and industrial revolution had begun in the United States, the North still consisted primarily of rural and small-town communities centered on an agricultural economy. It was in these communities that the Republicans had their greatest success in 1860. While the opposition, whether Democratic or fusion, carried New York City, which cast 62 percent for the anti-Republican ticket, and other urban enclaves, Lincoln swept the rural North. (However, as expected, he won Chicago.) By emphasizing Lincoln's rural and heartland background, the Republican "Wigwam" campaign, reminiscent of the Whig "Log Cabin" campaign of 1840, had a powerful appeal to farmers and workingmen. They saw Lincoln as a champion of free white labor—and as opposed to the Democratic appeasement policy on slave labor—particularly in the territories, where they believed free land should be available for white settlers.

The Republican candidate's well-deserved reputation for political and private honesty, reflected in the oft-repeated sobriquet "Honest Abe," also gained Lincoln support. Lincoln's probity contrasted sharply with the corruption in the Buchanan administration that a recent congressional investigation had revealed.[88] Some members of both parties believed that the corruption issue was decisive in the election. "Our triumph was achieved more because of Lincoln's reputed honesty & the corruptions of the Democrats, than because of the Negro question," Republican Senator James W. Grimes of Iowa declared. August Belmont, a prominent New York Democrat, agreed. "The country at large had become disgusted with the misrule of Mr. Buchanan, and the corruption which disgraced his Administration," Belmont wrote a southern friend. "The Democratic party," Belmont said, "was made answerable for [Buchanan's] misdeeds. . . . This feeling was particularly strong in the rural districts."[89] Nonetheless, the underlying issue in the election for Lincoln and the Republicans was slavery and the threat posed by its expansion.

Regionally, the upper North, where opposition to the aggressive slavocracy was strong, voted overwhelmingly for Lincoln, though the election was relatively close in Michigan and Wisconsin. Abolitionists like William Lloyd Garrison of *The Liberator,* while uneasy over Lincoln's conservatism, particularly his support for the Fugitive Slave Act, cast their ballots for him. Though a small Radical Abolitionist party had been formed by Gerrit Smith and a handful of followers, Garrisonians generally realized that Lincoln was the only viable antislavery candidate in the contest. These abolitionists concluded that his election would be a step in the right direction against slavery. In an important sense, the abolitionists had contributed much to Lincoln's victory. Despite their small numbers, they had planted antislavery seeds and hostility to southerners in the North that bore fruit for Lincoln throughout the free states. Even the powerful abolitionist orator Wendell Phillips, who had referred to Lincoln as the "Slave Hound of Illinois" because of his approval of the return of fugitive slaves, gave Lincoln support, albeit tepid, in the election. On the day after the election, Phillips announced, with obvious overstatement, that "for the first time in our history, the slave has chosen a President of the United States." His favorable opinion of Lincoln, the Illinois "pawn on the political chessboard," as he also had referred to him, would be short-lived.[90]

Still, Lincoln probably would have lost the election had he failed to win the support of the 1856 Fillmore and American party voters in the critical battleground states of Indiana and Pennsylvania. The defeat of the anti-Republican fusion movement in those states—and possibly also in New York, where a late attempt at an anti-Republican merger fell far short of success—proved crucial in Lincoln's victory. The fact that Lincoln was an old Whig conservative who, unlike Douglas and other Democrats, had never fiercely attacked the Know Nothings made him acceptable to these voters. Know Nothings, the main element in the American party of 1856, would have preferred the less sectional candidate, John Bell, the border-state champion of the old Clay and Fillmore Whigs, but they realized that the Tennessean could not win the election. Despite their uneasiness with the plank in the Republican platform opposing restrictions on immigrants, these na-tivists, constituting a relatively large minority in the battleground states, re-jected fusion with the Democrats and voted for the candidate whom they considered the lesser evil—Lincoln.

While gaining the backing of the Know Nothings, Lincoln won the votes of most non-Catholic immigrants, especially Germans. These immigrants in 1856 had favored the Democrats in the key states and elsewhere in the North because of strong nativist sentiment among former Whigs in both the Ameri-can and early Republican parties. Irish American Catholics and some Ger-man American Catholics continued in 1860 to vote the Democratic ticket. Lincoln's support for a protective tariff, though perhaps not as significant as the procrustean alliance of Know Nothings and immigrants, also contributed to his success in Pennsylvania. His southern ancestry and southern Indiana roots helped him and his party in the Hoosier State and even in Egypt (lower Illinois), where he won a number of counties. In essence, Lincoln's majority in the electoral vote can be attributed to several factors, all of which were important to his victory.

THE ELECTION, despite Lincoln's denial of sectionalism, had brought a sec-tional party to power, producing the greatest crisis in American history. But for Republicans, Lincoln's victory meant a reaffirmation of the republican principles established by the Founding Fathers, principles that had been un-der constant attack since the introduction of the Kansas-Nebraska bill by Douglas in 1854. Typical of this view was a congratulatory letter written to Lincoln by George G. Fogg, secretary of the national committee, on the day after the election. "The deed is done. The victory of Republicanism over slave Democracy is won. The friends of constitutional liberty—of 'free speech, free labor, a free country, and free men'—have triumphed. To your hands are entrusted the destinies of the most important revolution of modern times," he wrote.[91] Even Salmon P. Chase, who no doubt thought that he was more deserving than Lincoln, sent his congratulations to his rival and happily noted: "The great object of my wishes & labors for nineteen years is accom-plished in the overthrow of the Slave Power. The space is now clear for the establishment of the policy of Freedom on safe & firm grounds. The lead is yours. The responsibility is vast."[92]

The unspoken question, one that Chase and many others probably asked themselves, was obvious: Could a man who had never held an executive of-fice, who had served only one term in Congress, who was viewed virtually as an enemy in the South, and who was opposed by 46 percent of northern vot-ers successfully manage the secession crisis that awaited him? Though James

Buchanan would be president until March 4 and, along with a politically divided Congress, would have to deal with the first shock of secession, Lincoln would immediately become the focus of attention both in the North and in the South. All of his political skills and moral and intellectual qualities, developed in his struggles to gain distinction for himself and dominance for his party in the highly partisan conflict of the past two decades in Illinois, would soon be tested at the national level. Abraham Lincoln's ability to meet the test of leadership in the volatile situation created by his election would determine the fate of the nation and his own place in history.

CHAPTER NINE

CABINET MAKING

ACCORDING TO Samuel Weed, on the day of the November election Lincoln remarked that "elections in this country were like big boils—they caused a great deal of pain before they come to a head, but after the trouble was over, the body was in better health than before." Lincoln expressed hope, Weed said, that the "bitterness of the canvass would pass away as easily as the core of a boil."[1] Lincoln believed that the southern threat of secession was either a bluff to gain concessions or a conspiracy by a few. Either way, he remained confident that loyalty to the Union and obedience to the Constitution would prevail in the South. It was wishful thinking on his part.

Yet Lincoln was not alone in taking such a sanguine view of the impact of his election on southerners. Western Republicans concluded that Lincoln's southern heritage, along with his fundamental conservatism, honesty, and good sense, would commend him to southerners as someone whom they could trust. Like Lincoln, they assumed that the South would acquiesce in his election. Though Lincoln supported the theoretical view of racial equality and believed that blacks should be permitted to enjoy the fruits of their labor, white southerners, western Republicans hoped, would realize that he was not a radical. After all, the western position on race and the veneration of the Constitution generally conformed to that of white southerners. Western Republicans mistakenly reasoned that southerners, despite the inflamed rhetoric, would recognize this mutual white kinship on race and conclude that Lincoln, a native of Kentucky, did not threaten their social system. These Republicans believed that Lincoln's appointments to his administration would prove his goodwill toward the South and his intention to rule fairly.[2]

In a speech at Springfield on November 20, Illinois Governor-elect Richard Yates reinforced the view that southern hostility to Lincoln would subside after he became president. Yates confidently predicted: "It will not be one year till the whole South, except the traitors bent on disunion any how, will hail the election of Mr. Lincoln as one of the greatest blessings" to the country. Under Lincoln, "the Federal Government will withhold support to slavery in the Territories, and oppose its extension, and the re-opening of the African slave trade," Yates told his audience. But southerners should not object to these policies, since they were those "which their own great statesmen inaugurated" after the Revolution. At the same time, slavery would be protected in the South, and southerners would "soon settle down in the enjoyment of all [their] constitutional rights."[3] These words were born of the delusion, propagated by the Republicans during the campaign, that it was the Democrats, not the Republicans, who constituted a threat to the Union. Yates and western Republicans claimed that their party, led by "Honest Abe" on a conservative platform, would purify the government and redeem the principles of the Founders. They expected that in the South a sober reality of the consequences of disunion soon would replace the political passion and threats generated by southern fire-eaters during the presidential contest.

Such wishful thinking ignored the hostility that had developed toward the Republicans since the rise of the antislavery party. The threat of southern secession was broad-based and real. White southerners bitterly viewed Lincoln's election as a northern endorsement of the antislavery crusade against their society, and they feared the consequences of a "Black Republican" regime. Reports to Lincoln from the South, though not in large number, made him aware of this strong feeling. William C. Smedes, a prominent "conservative man" of Mississippi, in February 1861 wrote Lincoln explaining why the majority of the people of the lower South, after years of agitation over slavery, had moved to dissolve their ties with the Union. "No one act" like the fall election "could have produced such a wide-spread & deep-seated conviction of so stern a necessity as the destruction of the Government, over whose ruins every man of sensibility must mourn deeply," he told Lincoln. Instead, "it was the profound conviction that had pervaded all classes of our people, & become fixed in their minds and hearts that their lives & property & their liberties were in jeopardy, & must be lost, if they allowed for one hour longer than it could be prevented, the agitation or public discussion of any question connected with the permanence, character or nature of their social & domestic institutions." The determination to leave the Union, this Vicksburg lawyer informed Lincoln, "roused, without the aid of politicians & against the judgments of many who had helped to precipitate the very issue, the entire masses of the people, men women & children." The feeling that "their very happiness and life itself" was at stake, Smedes wrote, "is not temporary, but is deeply rooted and determined." He expressed his hope for "a peaceful adjustment of our political difficulties & a reconstruction of the Union," but he remained doubtful for the future of the country.[4]

Immediately after the election, the *Augusta* (Georgia) *Chronicle and Sentinel* thundered: "The crisis which has been so long looked forward to with apprehension by the patriot has at length arrived. A Northern geographical party, completely sectional in every aspect, and largely fanatic in its views and tendencies, has succeeded by the numerical force of majorities in electing a President and Vice President. Against all the warnings of the South, and the labors of conservative men in the North, the Republicans have persisted in electing their candidates."[5] Though this editor stopped short of advocating immediate secession, preferring a "watch and wait" policy toward Lincoln, other lower South newspapers and politicians demanded action before the "Black Republican" took the oath of office and had an opportunity to launch his antislavery agenda. Led by South Carolina, "Cotton South" legislatures in November called for state conventions to meet for the purpose of considering "Federal relations," meaning secession. Texas, where Governor Sam Houston refused to convene the legislature into a special session, was the exception. Secessionists, however, ignored Houston and scheduled a state referendum on the issue for February 1.

Soon after Lincoln's election, disunion sentiment seemed destined to spread into the upper South states (Virginia, North Carolina, Tennessee, and Arkansas). David Schenck, a lawyer in western North Carolina, reflected sentiment in an area of the South not usually associated with the southern fire-eaters when he wrote: "Lincoln is elected. Sadness covers every countenance, and alarm pervades every walk of life. Every woman and child now talks of war and its consequences." Republican control of the federal government, Schenck lamented, endangered southern society "because the fundamental principle of the party was war on our property, and the object was the 'Equality of the Negro & the white man.' "[6] Even border slave states (Maryland, Kentucky, and Missouri) were not immune from the secession fever, particularly if it could not be checked farther south.[7]

True to form, the northern Democratic press blamed the Republicans for "this appalling danger upon our country." The cause of the secession excitement, the *Concord* (New Hampshire) *Democratic Standard* exclaimed, "is the war which has been waged by the fanatics and demagogues of the North upon the domestic institutions of the South, culminating at last in the election of a President upon the avowed principle of hostility to the South. It is the fruits of the crusade of Northern Abolitionism against Southern Slavery, carried on in violation of both the letter and spirit of the Constitutional compact under which both sections have agreed to live."[8] The editor of a lower South newspaper could have written this column.

Democratic newspapers almost gleefully reminded the northern people of their grim predictions during the presidential campaign that Lincoln's election would trigger a southern resort to separation from the Union. "The Republicans," the *Providence Daily Post* declared, "treated our statements and cautions with all the appearances of contempt. It was all done for partisan effect."[9] Remedying the crisis, the Democratic press contended, would require making concessions to the South and putting an end to antislavery agitation. The alternative to compromise was the disruption of the Union, an eventuality "too dreadful to contemplate, . . . unless justice and the Constitution is soon made to take the place of the excited and unjust feeling which now pervades the Abolition States," said the *Cleveland Daily National Democrat.*[10]

The Democratic *Albany Atlas and Argus* provided a more hopeful outcome for the crisis. While professing to understand southern resentment against the Republicans, its editor told southerners that if they did not act rashly, "we at the North will be able to take care of Republicanism, and in another short year, the crisis will have passed, and fanaticism will have burned out, and a healthful reaction will give renewed life and vigor to the body politic." Meanwhile, this editor claimed, Lincoln as president would be restrained by the Constitution and by the anti-Republican majority in Congress in the exercise of his antislavery policy. "Mr. Lincoln, as a matter of absolute necessity, . . . must execute the laws and obey the Constitution," the paper said; otherwise, "the curses of the present and future generations would brand him as a perjured traitor, and the Constitutional process of impeachment would expel him from the Presidential office."[11]

Outwardly, Lincoln seemed unperturbed by the threats from the South and the alarming pronouncements of many northern Democrats. Twenty-four hours after the election, a *New York Times* correspondent in Springfield reported that Lincoln, despite "the storm of desperate opposition that his election has occasioned in some quarters, preserves an equanimity that inspires confidence in his friends. It is not the apathy of the stoic, the inertia of one unconscious of danger, or the phlegmatic silence of a sluggish temperament. No, it is the calm and dignified self-reliance of a man who has marked out his course" in the tempest. Lincoln's plan, the *Times* correspondent concluded after talking to him, was "to act precisely as he would were there no secession threatened in consequence of his election." He seemed determined to remain silent regarding events in the South until his inauguration. According to this writer, Lincoln planned "to rely upon the support of intelligent men of all sections familiar with his oft-repeated declaration of principle" on slavery and avoid intruding upon President Buchanan's "business."[12]

Lincoln in fact did act as though the threat of secession was nonexistent, largely avoiding any appearance of concern. He continued to see hordes of visitors in his office at the State House. Lincoln biographer Benjamin P. Thomas has written that visitors "descended on him in such numbers that Springfield's hotels and boarding-houses were crammed and the overflow put up in sleeping cars."[13] As he had done during the campaign, Lincoln often managed with small talk and anecdotes to divert attention from the political issues convulsing the nation. The *New York Times* correspondent reported that "Mr. Lincoln's memory of persons is remarkable, and he seems to know the personal history of nearly all visitors." He "seems to recall readily the most unimportant details; the boundaries of farms, the peculiarities of maiden aunts, the hobbies of venerable farmers, . . . and he patiently hears the latest news on these subjects, while he tosses about carelessly the huge ax and wedges which are strewn on his table, and which manufacturers have sent him in case he should ever take to rail-splitting again."[14]

Caught in the middle of the secession furor, border-state leaders desperately demanded that Lincoln issue a statement reassuring southerners of his goodwill and his conservative policy on slavery. Soon after the election, Nathaniel P. Paschall, editor of the *St. Louis Missouri Republican,* a Democratic newspaper, wrote a letter to a friend in Springfield, Illinois, intended for Lincoln's eyes, insisting that the president-elect make a public declaration designed to soothe southern fears. Lincoln rejected the demand. On November 16 he informed Paschall, "I could say nothing which I have not already said, and which is in print and accessible to the public." Lincoln told the editor that "if I thought a *repetition* would do any good I would make it. But my judgment is it would do positive harm. The secessionists, *per se* believing they had alarmed me, would clamor all the louder." Lincoln used the occasion in his response to Paschall to issue a biting criticism of "papers, like yours, which theretofore have persistently garbled, and misrepresented what I have said." The president-elect wrote that "the true cure for any real uneasiness in the country that my course may be other than conservative" was for "your class of newspapers" to print the "copious extracts from my many published speeches" available in the Republican newspapers.[15]

Angered by Lincoln's response, Paschall wrote a long letter to Lincoln denouncing him for his inaction in the unfolding crisis. In this letter, which he published in his St. Louis newspaper, Paschall criticized the president-elect for his refusal to provide public guarantees to the South regarding slavery. "You are," the former Whig editor told Lincoln, "a *Sectional* President, elected by the Free States alone, . . . to accommodate the fanaticism of the peculiar elements composing the population of those States." Paschall, who probably knew that his letter would be reprinted in newspapers throughout the South and in Democratic sheets in the North, reminded Lincoln that a "little over two weeks have passed" since the election and already several southern states were laying plans to leave the Union. Lincoln, he charged, did not think that these states were in earnest; otherwise he would have given new assurances that Paschall believed were necessary to check the descent toward disunion. "The conservative States—Maryland, Virginia, North Carolina, Kentucky, Tennessee, and Missouri," he grimly warned, "will not stand idly by and see their sister States . . . trampled in the dust."[16]

In a private letter to Lincoln, Paschall told the president-elect that it was "hardly possible for us to keep Missouri in her conservative stand" for the Union "if something [was] not done to keep down the excitement now pervading the South."[17] Unwilling to satisfy the St. Louis editor, Lincoln refused to participate further in the correspondence.

After the election, eastern merchants and bankers, concerned about the financial impact of secession, also joined the demand for Lincoln to make a public statement to ease both southern and northern fears. Indeed, a severe financial panic had gripped New York and Philadelphia because of the political uncertainty. The *New York Herald* contended that Republican publication of extracts from Lincoln's speeches in the 1858 campaign against Douglas did not "meet the necessities" of the situation. "What we want is a letter or a speech from Mr. Lincoln now, on the present crisis in the South, embracing his views for the preservation of the Union" on a strictly conservative basis, the paper said. Such a statement, the writer hoped, would calm commercial jitters over secession.[18] Some alarmed eastern Republicans, knowing the president-elect's reluctance to speak out or write a public letter at this time, asked him to issue a conciliatory statement through an intermediary that could be published. Henry J. Raymond of the *New York Times* even proposed the wording of a "note" for publication outlining Lincoln's views. The note, Raymond assured the president-elect, would not retract anything that he had said; it would simply express his goodwill toward the South and ask southerners to defer judgment on him until his administration had the opportunity to demonstrate that their fears were unwarranted.[19] Lincoln, however, rejected the suggestion.[20]

Lincoln also rejected a similar appeal from Republican Truman Smith, a former Connecticut senator. Smith, who had served in Congress with Lincoln, thought that such a statement would calm eastern financial markets. "I am not insensible to any commercial or financial depression that may exist," Lincoln wrote Smith, "but nothing *is* to be gained by fawning around the '*respectable scoundrels*' who got it up. Let them go to work and repair the mischief of their own making; and then perhaps they will be less greedy to do the like again." Lincoln informed Smith, as he did Paschall and others who asked for a public statement, that he "could say nothing which I have not already said, and which is in print, and open for the inspection of all. To press a repetition of this upon those who *have* listened, is useless; to press it upon those who have *refused* to listen, and still refuse, would be wanting in self-respect, and would have an appearance of sycophancy and timidity, which would excite the contempt of good men, and encourage bad ones to clamor the more loudly."[21]

Some Republican luminaries agreed with the president-elect's determination to avoid public statements. Governor Edwin D. Morgan of New York wrote Lincoln on November 20 that "it has given me great pleasure to know that you have not felt called upon to respond by speech or by letter to the numerous requests that have been made. Instead of appeasing—either would create an appetite for more," he contended. Morgan, himself a New York merchant, told Lincoln that the crisis, "brought about by madmen North and South," should not affect his decision to remain silent. Members of the Illinois state Republican central committee, including Norman B. Judd and Gustave Koerner, met with Lincoln in mid-November and also urged him to stand firm and continue to refuse to make new public statements. Thurlow Weed, Judge David Davis, and George Ashmun of Springfield, Massachusetts, gave Lincoln similar advice. Ashmun, far from the storm center of the crisis, confidently wrote Lincoln that if he maintained his policy of "'masterly inactivity' in both word & deed, . . . the whole danger, as well as all fear of danger, will have passed away at the hour of your Inauguration."[22]

Lincoln, faced with mounting pressure from the border states and elsewhere, finally decided, more than two weeks after the election, to issue a brief statement, despite his belief that it would be misrepresented by his opponents. The statement would be delivered through an intermediary, Senator Lyman Trumbull, who agreed to insert Lincoln's message into a speech he was scheduled to deliver in Springfield on November 20. In reporting Trumbull's address, the press announced that the senator spoke "the sentiments of the president-elect."[23]

In his statement, Lincoln reaffirmed his promise to leave the southern states "in complete control of their own affairs respectively, and at as perfect liberty to choose, and employ, their own means of protecting property, and preserving peace and order within their respective limits, as they have ever been under any administration." He declared that "Disunionists *per se,* are in hot haste to get out of the Union, precisely because they perceive they can not, much longer, maintain apprehension among the Southern people that their homes, and fireside, and lives, are to be endangered by the action of the Federal Government. With such [men] '*Now, or never*' is the maxim." But such men did not represent the majority of southerners, he suggested. Remarkably, in the text he gave to Trumbull, Lincoln announced that he was "rather glad of [the] military preparation in the South," which had begun after John Brown's raid at Harpers Ferry in late 1859. The organization of state militias, Lincoln claimed, would "enable the [southern] people the more easily to suppress any [secessionist] uprisings there."[24] Though Lincoln wanted to put the best face possible on events in the South, he probably realized that the military preparations were designed to defend against the abolitionists and Republicans, not to prevent a secessionist coup d'état. Perhaps because of this unrealistic conclusion, Trumbull wisely did not include this part of Lincoln's statement in his speech.

Privately, Lincoln expressed his firm opposition to secession and declared that the "government possesses both the authority and the power to maintain its own integrity." But he admitted to friends that "the ugly point" in the matter "is the necessity of keeping the government together by force, as ours should be a government of fraternity."[25] He continued to think that southern goodwill toward the Union would assert itself after the passions of the election had died down, and that secession sentiment would be reversed.

Lincoln soon discovered, as he had expected, that the opposition press in the North and the border states had distorted his statement in Trumbull's speech, while newspapers in the upper and lower South virtually ignored it. Lincoln complained to Henry J. Raymond of the *New York Times* that not "a single newspaper, heretofore against us, urged that speech [upon its readers] with a purpose to quiet public anxiety." On the contrary, these newspapers "hold the same speech up to the South as an open declaration of war against them." Lincoln told Raymond: "This is just as I expected, and just what would happen with any declaration I could make. These political fiends are not half sick enough yet. 'Party malice' and not 'public good' possesses them." Lincoln's passage in Trumbull's speech, however, did have a temporary calming effect upon eastern financial markets.[26]

Having convinced himself that he could do no more until his inauguration in March to placate the South or calm fears in the North, in late November Lincoln turned his attention to the formation of his cabinet. He asked a few associates and Vice President–elect Hannibal Hamlin to meet him in Chicago to discuss cabinet positions. Lincoln also invited Joshua Speed and his wife, Fanny, to join him and Mary in Chicago; their presence would provide him with a social respite from the public receptions and political meetings he was certain to experience in the city.[27] For the first time since May, Lincoln left Springfield. Along with Senator Trumbull, two other friends, and Mary, on November 21 he boarded the Chicago, Alton, and St. Louis Railroad at the Springfield depot, where a large crowd gathered to witness the departure. From this point onward, everywhere Lincoln went he found himself surrounded by enthusiastic crowds. Some of the people simply sought an opportunity to shake his hand or obtain a glimpse of the man who would soon be president of the United States. Many, including Democrats, sought to encourage him in the difficult tasks ahead, hoping that he would provide the leadership to quiet the sectional furor and maintain the Union.

In Chicago, Lincoln and his party took rooms at the Tremont House and awaited Vice President–elect Hamlin's arrival. Receptions and serenades by local Wide Awakes occupied the remainder of the day. The next day, November 22, Hamlin arrived at the Tremont. After a brief conversation, the two Republican leaders accepted an invitation to visit the Wigwam, where they had been nominated, and the federal buildings in the city. Afterward, Lincoln returned to the Tremont, where he faced a constant stream of visitors. His usual wit and playfulness helped him to survive the ordeal, and his good humor bolstered his popularity.[28]

Meanwhile, Joshua and Fanny Speed arrived in Chicago and found Lincoln at a reception in the Tremont. Elated to see his old friends, Lincoln arranged to meet Joshua and Fanny in secret with Mary at the Speeds' room. At the hotel, as his friend remembered, Lincoln bluntly asked, "Speed, what are your pecuniary Conditions—are you rich, or poor[?]" Speed, who had never held a public office, quickly saw that the conversation was leading toward an offer of a position in the new administration. "Mr Presdt. [he probably said "Lincoln"] I think I Know what you wish. I'll speak Candidly to you—my pecuniary Conditions are good—I do not think you have any office within your gift that I can afford to take."[29] Four years later, Lincoln, having failed to bring Joshua Speed into his administration, appointed Joshua's older brother, James, as attorney general in his cabinet. Both Speeds, though reluctant to endorse Lincoln's antislavery policies, nevertheless proved vital supporters for the Union cause in Kentucky during the Civil War.

Somehow Lincoln found time between public appearances to discuss cabinet appointments with Hamlin, Trumbull, and other Republican associates, which was the purpose of the Chicago trip. Meeting at the home of Ebenezer Peck, north of the Chicago River, the Republican leaders agreed with Lincoln that the cabinet should be balanced politically between the former Whig and Democratic elements in the party. They also suggested that a major effort should be made to bring William H. Seward into the cabinet. Lincoln had already decided to ask Seward, his main rival in the party, to become secretary of state.[30] He recognized that a failure to appoint the powerful Seward, who had tempered his radicalism, would be viewed as an insult to New York Republicans, whose delegation at Chicago had voted unanimously for the senator's nomination. Perhaps recalling the bitter Whig divisions that followed the snub of party leader Henry Clay by presidents John Tyler and Zachary Taylor, Lincoln concluded, probably correctly, that his administration could not succeed without the active support of Seward and his friends. The support of this important eastern Republican faction could only be achieved, he believed, by Seward's presence in his cabinet.[31]

In addition to political balance, Lincoln wanted geographical balance. All major regions of the country, he believed—including the South—should be represented in the administration. Even before the Chicago meeting, Lincoln had decided to invite Edward Bates, his leading rival in the lower North, to join the cabinet. The appointment of the Missourian, he assumed, would provide the South with assurances that he did not intend to be a sectional president; furthermore, it would increase conservative support for his administration in the North.[32] As in the case of his other cabinet appointments, except for Seward, Lincoln had not determined what position Bates would hold.

Lincoln also wanted another southerner in his administration, one more closely associated with the South than Bates, who was a St. Louis resident. In the Chicago meeting, Lincoln mentioned James Guthrie of Kentucky, a respected railroad president and a former secretary of the treasury in the Pierce administration, as an excellent possibility. He may have hoped that the selection of Guthrie would bolster Wall Street's confidence in the new administration. The president-elect had also mentioned Guthrie to Speed as a prospective member of the cabinet. Guthrie had never associated with the Republican party, however, and after the Chicago talks Lincoln discovered that the Kentuckian was not interested in a cabinet position.[33]

Lincoln and his associates at Chicago agreed that Pennsylvania, whose delegation in the Republican convention arguably had made the difference in Lincoln's nomination, should have an important place in the cabinet. Senator Simon Cameron, the state's most prominent Republican, seemed a logical choice, but his reputation for dishonesty and political corruption caused concern among Lincoln's associates in the meeting. Other Pennsylvanians, including radical antislavery congressman Thaddeus Stevens, John M. Read, and David Wilmot, were mentioned as alternatives to Cameron.[34] Lincoln, however, decided to wait and give additional thought to the matter before making the Pennsylvania appointment.

New England, with its staunch Republican majority, also had to be accommodated in the cabinet. Because of its maritime tradition, it seemed reasonable that the position of secretary of the navy should go to that region. Lincoln had invited Hamlin to join the talks in Chicago; presumably he would be in a position to provide advice on New England's representative in the cabinet. Though several names evidently were put forward in the meeting, Hamlin was unable to make a recommendation. With other cabinet appointment priorities to be met, Lincoln did not move to fill the New England position until a month later. On December 24, he wrote Hamlin: "I need a man of Democratic antecedents from New England. I cannot get a fair share of that element in [the cabinet] without." He gave Hamlin three names to choose from; one was Gideon Welles, a former Democratic congressman of Connecticut.[35]

Lincoln had met Welles at Hartford in March during his speaking tour of New England and had had two long conversations with him. At that time, the New Englander had made a favorable impression upon the future president. Hamlin sensed, evidently from comments Lincoln had made in Chicago, that he favored Welles, who had led the Connecticut delegation in the Republican convention.[36] On December 29, Hamlin wrote Lincoln that Welles was "the better man for New England," despite the fact that he was opposed by Massachusetts Republicans in the Seward-Weed wing of the party. This faction urged the appointment of Charles Francis Adams, the son and grandson of former presidents.[37]

Lincoln, ever cautious, was still juggling prospective names for his cabinet into the new year and did not offer a position to Welles until the eve of the inauguration in March. Summoning Welles to Washington, Lincoln apologized for the delay and informed the New Englander that he would nominate him for a seat in the cabinet. Though Lincoln said that he preferred him in the Navy Department, he told Welles that, because he wanted to get the right mix for his cabinet, he might need to appoint him postmaster general. Welles did not know that on the previous day the president-elect had blocked an attempt by his northeastern opponents to prevent his elevation to the cabinet. On March 5, one day after the inauguration, Lincoln finally announced his decision on the position: He appointed Welles as secretary of the navy.[38] Honest, fundamentally conservative, and determined not to be driven by partisan concerns, Gideon Welles, who during the Civil War became known affectionately as "Old Neptune," proved to be one of Lincoln's best appointments.

The participants in the Chicago meeting in November also discussed the cabinet claims of Indiana, Ohio, and Illinois. Indiana Republicans, who had played a crucial role in Lincoln's nomination and election, were sharply divided between supporters of Caleb B. Smith and Congressman Schuyler Colfax for a seat in the cabinet. Smith, a four-term former Whig congressman, was an early Republican who had seconded Lincoln's nomination at Chicago. Colfax, in contrast, was a brilliant and rising young man who had been a Know Nothing before affiliating with the Republican party. For Ohio's representative, Lincoln seemed to favor Salmon P. Chase. He knew of Chase's important leadership in organizing the antislavery coalition after the passage of the Kansas-Nebraska bill and remembered that the Ohio governor, soon to be a senator, had been the only prominent Republican from another state to campaign for him in the 1858 senatorial contest. Some concern apparently was raised that Chase was too radical for an administration that promised to be conservative. Lincoln, however, kept his own counsel regarding the Indiana and Ohio appointments and deferred making a decision on them until he could sort out the other selections.[39]

Illinois Republicans also thought that their state deserved a position in the cabinet. In the Chicago meeting, they argued that Lincoln needed a close associate in Washington with whom he could confide on sensitive matters and who would have his interest foremost in mind. Lincoln rejected the idea, indicating that he was the state's representative in the administration.[40] The president-elect had just so many plums to distribute, and he realized that his home state could not be accommodated. Furthermore, the leading Illinois contenders for a cabinet post were Norman B. Judd and David Davis, who represented different factions in the state party. Davis was an ally of the volatile John Wentworth. If Lincoln had chosen either for the cabinet, the old Judd-Wentworth feud would have been reignited, seriously dividing the state Republican party.

Advocates for both Judd and Davis, however, continued to pester Lincoln. Jesse W. Fell of Bloomington, though a friend of Davis's, cautioned Lincoln not to succumb to the demands from either side. "By giving neither Judd nor Davis appointments," Fell told the president-elect, "you [will] not only have a better opportunity to satisfy the claims of other States but you will keep down a *vast deal of ill feeling here at home.*"[41] Lincoln agreed. After his inauguration, he named Judd minister to Prussia, and in 1862 he selected David Davis for the U.S. Supreme Court. Lincoln's closest associate, William Herndon, apparently never sought a federal office from his partner, preferring to remain at home and maintain the law practice.

Lincoln's top priority after the Chicago meeting in late November was to secure Seward's and Bates's agreement to serve in the administration. With that in mind, he sent a message to Bates requesting that he meet with him in St. Louis "about some points connected with the formation of [the] Cabinet." Bates confided to his diary, "I thought there was an unfitness in *his coming to me,* and that I *ought to go to him.*" Instead of St. Louis, the Missouri conservative went to Springfield and conferred with Lincoln on December 15.[42]

At that meeting, Lincoln, after a "very cordial" greeting, immediately informed Bates that since his nomination for president in May, he had determined to appoint him to his cabinet. The position would most likely be that of attorney general, though if Seward rejected a forthcoming offer to become secretary of state, then Lincoln would nominate Bates to head the State Department. Bates accepted the offer with the comment that in regard to his "private affairs, the Att.y. Genl.'s place is most desirable." According to John Nicolay, Lincoln's secretary, the Missourian said he was "inflexibly opposed to secession, and strongly in favor of maintaining the government by force if necessary."[43] While cheered by Bates's opposition to secession, the president-elect had not come to the conclusion that force might be required to preserve the Union.

After returning to St. Louis, Bates wrote Lincoln asking him to make his appointment public. He told the president-elect that an announcement would produce "a good effect . . . on the public mind—especially in the border slave States—by letting the people know (substantially) the relations which now subsist between us." Lincoln agreed and authorized a press statement saying that Bates had been offered and had accepted an undetermined position in the cabinet.[44] Despite Bates's ultraconservatism and the fact that he came from a slave state, Republicans generally expressed approval of the selection. Lincoln made no other public announcement of cabinet appointees until he became president.[45]

As Lincoln anticipated, the effort to bring Seward into the cabinet as secretary of state did not go smoothly. When reports reached the East that he planned to ask the New York senator to join his administration, irate opponents of Seward and the Albany Regency informed Lincoln of their displeasure. An elite group of New York City Republicans, headed by William Cullen Bryant and eminent lawyer William Curtis Noyes, with Horace Greeley's blessings, formed a committee to oppose the appointment. This group sought out Lyman Trumbull when he was in New York, laid out their anti-Seward case to him, and asked the Illinois senator to express their concerns to Lincoln. The main point these old Seward foes made was not that the senator himself was corrupt or incompetent. They argued that his alter ego, Thurlow Weed, would control the federal patronage of New York for the benefit of his dishonest friends in Albany. They also opposed Seward because of what seemed to be his willingness, despite his radical antislavery reputation, to make concessions to the southern secessionists.[46]

Though Trumbull objected to Seward's appointment, he reported to Lincoln without comment the New York committee's arguments against the senator. On December 8, Lincoln wrote Trumbull: "I regret exceedingly the anxiety of our friends in New-York, . . . but it seems to me the sentiment in that state which sent a united delegation to Chicago in favor of Gov. S. ought not, and must not be snubbed, as it would be by the omission to offer Gov. S. a place in the cabinet. I will, myself, take care of the question of 'corrupt jobs' and see that justice is done to all, our friends," including Seward's opponents.[47] Though keenly aware that Seward might attempt to dominate the new administration, Lincoln weighed this potential problem against the necessity of having him in the cabinet and not in the Senate, where he would be a source of Republican division. At any rate, Lincoln, who was gaining in his confidence to unite the Republican party and manage the government, chose to take his chances on a Seward "premiership." Still, he was not sure that the New York senator would accept a cabinet position from a man who lacked his national influence and experience and had defeated him for the party's nomination. Vice President–elect Hamlin reinforced this point when, reporting from Washington on December 4, he informed Lincoln that his "impression" was that Seward would "not desire a place in your Cabinet." "But he may," he added.[48]

On December 8—the same day that Lincoln wrote Trumbull—the president-elect sent two letters to Hamlin, both addressed to Seward and inviting him "to take charge of the State Department" in the new administration. The first one was a brief formal letter saying, "With your permission, I shall, at the proper time, nominate you to the Senate, for confirmation, as Secretary of State." The other was a longer, more personal letter to Seward assuring him that the offer was not tendered "as a compliment, and with the expectation that you would decline it," as "rumors" in newspapers had claimed. "I have said nothing to justify these rumors," Lincoln wrote. "On the contrary, it has been my purpose, from the day of the nomination at Chicago, to assign you, by your leave, this place in the administration. I have delayed so long to communicate that purpose, in deference to what appeared to me to be a proper caution in the case." Lincoln meant that he had delayed the offer because of the opposition to the appointment. But he told Seward that "nothing has been developed to change my view in the premises; and I now offer you the place, in the hope that you will accept, it, and with the belief that your position in the public eye, your integrity, ability, learning, and great experience, all combine to render it an appointment pre-eminently fit to be made." After these flattering words, Lincoln, remembering Seward's and Weed's patronage concerns, told the senator: "I have prescribed for myself the maxim, 'Justice to all'; and I earnestly beseech your co-operation in keeping the maxim good."[49]

Lincoln asked Hamlin to "consult with Judge Trumbull; and if you and he see no reason to the contrary, deliver the letter[s] to Governor Seward at once. If you see reason to the contrary, write me at once."[50] (Lincoln routinely referred to Seward by his earlier title as governor of New York.) Though Seward continued to deny that he was interested in a cabinet post, both Trumbull and Hamlin concluded that they should show him the letters from Lincoln. When he read the letter expressing the president-elect's good-will toward him, his strong desire to have him in the cabinet, and, apparently of equal importance, his commitment to deal fairly with his friends in patronage matters, Seward became excited and, turning to Hamlin, remarked: "This is remarkable, Mr. Hamlin. I will consider the matter, and, in accordance with Mr. Lincoln's request give him my decision at the earliest practicable moment." Seward wrote Lincoln indicating that he would reflect upon the offer and provide an answer in a few days. He also said he would have liked to meet with Lincoln on the "very anomalous condition of public affairs, . . . but I do not see how it could prudently be held under existing cir-

cumstances."[51] Congress had just met, and the senator expected to play a
leading role in the debate over the impending secession of South Carolina
and the other cotton states. His decision to forego a trip to Springfield was
probably also due to his reluctance to appear to be seeking an appointment
before the president-elect's offer was publicly known.

Instead, Seward immediately went to Albany to consult with Weed about
the secretary of state offer. He learned upon his arrival that his friend had an
invitation to visit with Lincoln to discuss political issues. This seemed fortui-
tous to both men. They agreed that Weed's trip to Springfield would provide
an excellent opportunity for them to ascertain Lincoln's views before Seward
accepted the appointment, which he was already inclined to do. By skillful
management, Weed might even succeed in influencing the president-elect to
Seward's way of thinking on the secession crisis and on the selection of the
remaining members of his cabinet, perhaps even as a condition of Seward's
acceptance. At any rate, Seward informed Lincoln that Weed had found it
convenient to go west. "He will be able to inform you of my present unsettled
views" on the appointment as secretary of state and also "concerning the
condition and prospect of public affairs," he wrote.[52]

While the New York senator waited at his home in Auburn, Weed met with
the president-elect, along with Judge David Davis and Leonard Swett, for several hours on December 20. As was usual in talks with Lincoln, the conversation was interspersed with his stories, which Weed professed to find amusing and "always and exactly suited [to] the occasion." "The liege lord of the
Albany lobby" began by showing Lincoln a December 17 editorial in his *Albany Evening Journal,* a copy of which, probably by prior arrangement, had
arrived the preceding day in Springfield. The editorial called for concessions
to the South as a necessity to save the upper southern and border slave states
for the Union. It specifically proposed the revival of the Missouri Compromise line to separate slavery from freedom in the territories, a measure that
border-state conservatives and others had advanced, but that no prominent
Republican had publicly advocated. The editorial, inspired by Weed, contended that the Republican victory in the fall election, and the anticipated
acceptance by Congress of Kansas' free-state constitution, had decided the
territorial issue. The question regarding slavery in the remaining territories, the editorial argued, could "now be safely left to natural laws" that
willed the Southwest unsuited for a slave economy. Why not, as an important
gesture and Union-saving compromise, give southerners the theoretical right
to carry their slaves into the territories below the old Missouri Compromise
line? The people in these territories, the editorial claimed, would choose to
enter the Union as free states. The newspaper also proposed legislation making the Fugitive Slave Act more "efficient, but not revolting" in its execution,

followed by the repeal of the personal-liberty laws in the northern states.[53] It is reasonable to assume that Seward, who was becoming fearful of the dreadful consequences of southern secession, had given tacit support to the *Evening Journal* editorial, since it appeared after his meeting with Weed in Albany. Weed would not have permitted the publication of the editorial if the senator had objected.

Two decades later, Weed vividly remembered Lincoln's reaction to the *Evening Journal* editorial. "After reading it very attentively, Mr. Lincoln said, 'This is a heavy broadside. You have opened your fire at a critical moment, aiming at friends and foes alike. It will do some good or much mischief.'" The president-elect, who opposed any deviation from the Republican platform against slavery in the territories, clearly thought that the proposal would do more mischief than good. Lincoln asked whether the New York Republicans agreed with this view. He probably wanted to ascertain whether Seward had approved the compromise proposal. Seeing that Lincoln was taken aback by the editorial, Weed cleverly answered that as a journalist he expressed his own views of affairs; "enlightened politicians," he added, "entertained similar views [but] would hesitate to express them" because of their natural caution. "Enlightened politicians" was clearly a reference to Seward. Lincoln remarked that he hoped his own apprehensions regarding southern secession were unfounded. Weed later wrote: "While there were some loud threats and much muttering in the cotton States, [Lincoln] hoped that by wisdom and forbearance the danger of serious trouble might be averted, as such dangers had been in former times."[54] The president-elect, faced with the greatest crisis since the birth of the republic, found it imperative to believe that southern goodwill would prevail and that the Union could be preserved without "serious trouble"—namely, civil war. Lincoln wanted to impress upon Weed and those Republicans who favored a compromise that his policy of firmness was the only way to success.

Probably to Weed's relief, the Springfield talks then turned to the issue of cabinet appointments, a matter that, Lincoln wryly noted, the New Yorker had some experience in and he did not. Weed assured him that his reputation as "a boss cabinet-maker" was unjustified; indeed, he said that Lincoln was the first president-elect he had met. Lincoln then asked him whether he had any suggestions of a general character to make regarding appointments. Weed replied that he believed it would be desirable for at least two cabinet members to be selected from the slaveholding states. Lincoln, who earlier had failed to bring James Guthrie of Kentucky into his cabinet, expressed doubt that he could find truly loyal southerners who would enforce the laws and sustain the government in an emergency. Eight days before meeting with Weed, the president-elect had written an anonymous editorial in the *Springfield Illinois State Journal* questioning whether "any [southern] gentleman of character would accept a position in the Cabinet." If so, "on what terms? Does he surrender to Mr. Lincoln, or Mr. Lincoln to him, on the political difference between them? Or do they enter upon the administration in open opposition to each other?"[55] Lincoln's skepticism was probably influenced by the failure of southern members in President Buchanan's cabinet to favor the Union as the secession crisis deepened in December.

Weed assured Lincoln that loyal southerners could be found who would support the government even if their states seceded. "Well," Lincoln demanded, "let us have the names of your white crows [who] you think fit for the cabinet." Weed named several prominent old Whigs from the upper and border South who, he insisted, were acceptable. Included in his list was congressman John A. Gilmer of North Carolina, whom Lincoln on December 15 had written in response to specific questions regarding his position on slavery.[56] The president-elect, however, refused to commit himself to a slave state appointment beyond that of Edward Bates of Missouri, who hardly qualified as a true southerner.

The Lincoln-Weed conference next turned to a discussion of northern prospects for the cabinet. Weed expressed his opposition to Chase as secretary of the treasury and Gideon Welles as secretary of the navy. Both of them were old Democrats and hostile to Seward. He indicated that he knew of several "gentlemen" whose selection would be more favorable to Republicans of his region. Lincoln immediately sensed that the New Yorker wanted to stack the administration with former Whigs acceptable to the Albany Regency. He reminded Weed that "the Republican party is constituted of two elements, and that we must have men of Democratic as well as of Whig antecedents in the cabinet." As a former Whig, Lincoln believed that he could be liberal to the segment of the Republican party that consisted of old Democrats, without whose votes he could not have been elected.[57]

Weed, however, did not concede the point that old Whigs should dominate the administration. When Lincoln told him that Montgomery Blair, a former Democrat of a prominent Maryland political family, had been suggested for the cabinet, the New Yorker expressed his disappointment (inwardly he was outraged) and recommended that Henry Winter Davis, a former Maryland Whig, should be substituted for Blair. Davis also had been an American party leader in his state and had supported the Constitutional Union party in 1860. Lincoln did not think that he could elevate Davis to the cabinet over Montgomery Blair, one of the founders of the Republican party. Davis, a combative and brilliant orator, never forgave Lincoln for slighting him in favor of the Blairs in Maryland politics, and, though a conservative Unionist in the secession crisis, he became a radical Republican opponent of the president during the war.

Weed reminded Lincoln that if the expected appointments of Chase, Welles, Blair, and Cameron occurred, the cabinet would stand four to three in favor of men of Democratic antecedents. (Seward, Bates, and Caleb B. Smith of Indiana would be the former Whigs.) "You seem to forget," Lincoln replied, "that *I* expect to be there; and counting me as one, you see how nicely the cabinet would be balanced and ballasted." Besides, Lincoln declared, "we could say of General Cameron, without offence, that he is 'not Democrat enough to hurt him.' I remember that people used to say, without disturbing my self-respect, that I was not lawyer enough to hurt me."[58]

Before ending the conversation, Weed renewed his appeal for a southerner in the cabinet. Davis and Swett agreed with Weed on this point. Lincoln finally yielded and said he would approach Gilmer, a Union Whig and large slaveholder of North Carolina, about joining his administration. According to Weed, the president-elect promised that if Gilmer accepted the appointment, he would exclude Blair from further consideration. Before "the Wizard of the Lobby" left town, Lincoln handed him a letter for delivery to Gilmer, then in Washington, that broached the matter of his appointment to the cabinet. Lincoln, in a separate letter, invited the North Carolinian to visit him in Springfield.[59] On December 29, Gilmer wrote Lincoln informing him that "such a visit would I apprehend not be useful to either of us, or the country." He blamed Lincoln for the rapid spread of secession sentiment by his failure to compromise on slavery in the territories, and he glumly predicted that a devastating civil war would follow. Implicit in Gilmer's refusal to pursue a seat in the cabinet was his recognition that he probably would be ostracized in North Carolina if he agreed to a "Black Republican" appointment.[60]

In the Springfield talks, Lincoln had thrown cold water on Weed's effort to establish a Seward "premiership" in Washington. The crafty New Yorker returned home having failed to gain any concessions on slavery in the territories. Moreover, he had not secured Lincoln's agreement for an old Whig majority in the cabinet, though if Gilmer had accepted an appointment, the members of the party of Henry Clay, not counting Lincoln, would have had a four-to-three edge in the administration. Realizing politically that Weed needed something tangible to take back to Seward, Lincoln drew up three tepid resolutions on slavery that most Republicans could support. He asked Weed to show Seward the resolutions and said it was his desire for the senator to introduce them into Congress, without revealing the name of their author.[61] (These resolutions and their fate are described in Chapter 10.)

Though he must have been disappointed by his inability to obtain Lincoln's approval of a compromise on slavery or an old Whig ascendancy in the administration, Weed publicly expressed his admiration for the president-elect and declared that his only regret was that "Mr. Lincoln could not have taken the helm of state as successor to Mr. Buchanan, on the first Monday of December."[62] He probably also conveyed the view to Seward, whom he met on the train at Syracuse, that Lincoln's political ability had been underestimated and that it was in his friend's interest to accept the position of secretary of state. A few days later, Seward wrote to Lincoln to accept the appointment.[63]

After word of the New Yorker's selection was leaked to the press by the senator's friends (Lincoln made no announcement of it), anti-Seward Republicans like Trumbull and George G. Fogg admitted that the appointment was probably a necessity. Fogg, an influential New Englander, absolving the president-elect from the "blame for making the offer of the post" to Seward, said, "I know that *almost* everybody thought it necessary."[64] Certainly Lincoln thought so.

Anxious to manage affairs in Washington during the secession winter, Seward pressed Lincoln for the names of his choices for secretary of war and secretary of the navy. He wanted them to come to Washington as soon as possible to confer with him on the crisis and to discuss actions that should be taken to protect the new government. Lincoln replied on January 3 that he could not make the appointments "until I can ascertain definitely whether I can get any suitable men from the South" to join the cabinet. Two weeks later, he still hoped that Gilmer would, "on a fair understanding with us, consent to take a place in the Cabinet." Lincoln rejected other candidates as not having "a *living* position in the South," or as not being "farther South."[65]

When it became clear that Gilmer could not be persuaded to join the cabinet, Lincoln gave up on the attempt to select someone from a southern state threatened by secession. He finally settled on Montgomery Blair of Maryland as the southern representative in the cabinet, despite the fact that, like Edward Bates of Missouri, he could only marginally qualify as a southerner. Blair descended from an old Democratic family that had helped organize the national Republican party; his venerable father, Francis P. Blair, Sr., had served as an important adviser to President Andrew Jackson and still had a powerful influence in border-state politics. Montgomery Blair's appointment, Lincoln knew, would please the anti-Seward faction in the party and, more importantly, provide an aura of Jacksonian firmness in dealing with southern secessionists. No-compromise Republicans like Trumbull, Senator Benjamin F. Wade, and the new governor of Ohio, William Dennison, wanted Blair as secretary of war, but the political need to satisfy Pennsylvania caused Lincoln in the end to select him for postmaster general.[66]

The appointment of a Pennsylvanian proved the most troublesome problem Lincoln faced in the selection of his cabinet. Making this choice would test his formidable ability to weigh and manage political rivalries and underlying divisions within his party. Because of the Keystone State's importance in the fall election, Pennsylvania, like New York, Lincoln believed, could not be ignored. The most likely candidate from that state was Senator Simon Cameron, despite his shady reputation extending back to the 1830s, when he was branded as the "Winnebago Chief" for the profits his bank received from a settlement he had negotiated with the Winnebago Indians in Pennsylvania. As Senator Kingsley Bingham of Michigan remarked, "Lincoln don't want a thief in his cabinet." Chicago editor Joseph Medill wrote the president-elect: "Simon Cameron and *Honest* Abe don't sound well together."[67] Other Republicans had a similar view.

When Lincoln returned home on November 26 from his meeting in Chicago, he found himself overwhelmed, as he wrote Hannibal Hamlin, "from very strong and unexpected quarters in Pennsylvania, urging the appointment of General Cameron to a place in the cabinet." The fact that the secession movement in the lower South was gaining momentum, and that South Carolina was on the verge of leaving the Union, seemed lost in the welter of correspondence regarding Cameron that Lincoln had received from Pennsylvania.[68]

Supporters of Cameron reminded Lincoln of Pennsylvania's crucial role in his success; they insisted that the state deserved a top cabinet position, preferably secretary of the treasury. Cameron was the only choice of the state's Republicans for this office, they said. "Any other selection," congressman James K. Moorhead of Pittsburgh warned, "would be disastrous and damaging" to the Republican party in the state. Andrew H. Reeder, former territorial governor of Kansas and chair of the Pennsylvania delegation at Chicago, wrote Lincoln that four-fifths of the state's Republicans supported Cameron for a cabinet seat. Joseph Casey, the senator's right-hand man, reminded Lincoln associate Leonard Swett of "conversations and understandings between you & Judge Davis on the one side, & myself, on the other, at the Tremont House, the night before the nomination." According to Casey, who probably stretched the truth, Swett and Davis at that time promised a cabinet seat for Cameron in exchange for the Pennsylvania delegation's support of Lincoln on the second ballot. This action, they argued, had turned the tide in Lincoln's favor. Swett sent Casey's letter to Lincoln in Springfield, with the clear implication that Lincoln owed Cameron a top position in his cabinet.[69]

In a visit with Lincoln, Reeder persuaded the president-elect to invite Cameron to Springfield for talks.[70] Lincoln had prepared for the meeting on December 30 by carefully compiling a list of Pennsylvania Republicans, including their political positions, who had written letters supporting Cameron. What he read and heard from Cameron convinced him that the corruption charges had been exaggerated by the senator's enemies and were probably related to old rivalries between former Whigs and Democrats in the state Republican party. The next day, Lincoln wrote Cameron a letter offering him a position in the cabinet. "I think fit to notify you now, that . . . I shall at the proper time, nominate you to the U.S. Senate, for confirmation as Secretary of the Treasury, or as Secretary of War—which of the two, I have not yet definitely decided."[71] The president-elect apparently handed the appointment letter to Cameron before he left Springfield; if he had sent it to him, he would have marked it "Confidential," as he did with other sensitive correspondence.

Leaked reports of the Cameron appointment immediately created a firestorm of dismay and opposition in powerful Republican circles. On January 2, Alexander K. McClure, chair of the Pennsylvania state Republican committee and an associate of Governor-elect Andrew Curtin, rushed to Springfield in an effort to persuade Lincoln to forego the appointment. For almost four hours, he laid out the charges of corruption and favoritism against Cameron. No doubt, in typical McClure fashion, he exaggerated the charges. The president-elect also heard from Republican leaders in Congress. Lyman Trumbull, Lincoln's main contact in the Senate, informed him that if the reports were true that Cameron had been appointed secretary of the treasury, "your truest friends in the Senate" believe that it "would be very detrimental to your administration. . . . Not a Senator I have spoken with, thinks well of such an appointment." Trumbull told Lincoln that "there is an odor about Mr. C." that would not go away. Hannibal Hamlin also wrote Lincoln, saying, "I do not believe one man can be found amongst all our friends in the Senate who will not say it will be ruinous to apt [sic] Cameron, whatever all the politicians in Pa may say." Hamlin advised Lincoln that "it would be better to take no one from Pa." Illinois congressman Elihu B. Washburne, a confidant of Lincoln's, provided a similar report from Washington. The news of the appointment, he declared, had "created intense excitement and consternation among all of our friends here." He continued: "I trust in God, it is not so. . . . Should the report prove true, it would do more than almost anything else to impair confidence in your administration. The best and strongest men in the Senate, & upon whom you must rely for support, are appalled at the apparent probability of the report being true."[72]

From outside of Washington, William Cullen Bryant, whose views Lincoln respected, expressed similar "consternation" upon hearing "the rumored intention" of Lincoln to appoint Cameron as secretary of the treasury. He hurriedly wrote the president-elect that "Mr. Cameron has the reputation of being [involved] in some of the worst intrigues of the democratic party a few years back. His name suggests to every honest Republican in this State no other than disgusting associations, and they will expect nothing from him when in office but repetition of such disgusting transactions." In the November election, Bryant reminded Lincoln, the Republican party had "struggled not only to overthrow the party that sought the extension of slavery, but also to secure a pure and virtuous administration of the government. The first of these objects we have fully attained, but if such men as Mr. Cameron are to compose the Cabinet, however pure and upright the Chief Magistrate may himself be, . . . we shall not have succeeded in the second."[73]

Shaken by the letters of powerful Republicans opposing the Cameron appointment, Lincoln sought the advice of his close Illinois associates who were in Springfield. Early on a cold Sunday morning, he knocked at the door of Gustave Koerner's hotel room and brusquely announced: "I want to see you and Judd. Where is his room?" While Koerner dressed, Lincoln retrieved Judd and brought him to his German American friend's room, where he said, "I am in a quandary; Pennsylvania is entitled to a cabinet office. But whom shall I appoint?" Both Judd and Koerner immediately answered, "Not Cameron." As Koerner remembered, their friend told them that he had received "delegation after delegation from Pennsylvania, hundreds of letters, and the cry is 'Cameron, Cameron!' They say, 'if you leave out Cameron you disgrace him.'" Koerner reminded him that "Cameron cannot be trusted; he has the reputation of being a tricky and corrupt politician." "I know, I know," Lincoln responded, "but can I get along if that State should oppose my administration?" His friends again protested against the nomination, whereupon he left the room "very much distressed" about the situation.[74]

Whether Lincoln realized it or not, he had used Judd and Koerner as a sounding board to help him work through a tough decision in the Cameron matter. Lincoln concluded that he could not afford to alienate powerful members of his party in Congress and elsewhere even before he took the oath of office. Despite his rule of never breaking a promise, he did just that on January 3 when he wrote Cameron revoking the appointment made four days earlier. Lincoln explained: "Since seeing you things have developed which make it impossible for me to take you into the cabinet." "You will say that this comes of [the] interview with McClure" in Springfield, he added, "and this is partly, but not wholly true. The more potent matter is wholly outside of Pennsylvania; and yet I am not at liberty to specify it. Enough that it appears to me to be sufficient." Lincoln, of course, was referring to the outrage expressed by leading Republicans to reports of the appointment. He bluntly asked Cameron to write him "declining the appointment, in which case I do not object to its being known that it was tendered to you. Better do this at once, before things so change, that you can not honorably decline, and I be compelled to openly recall the tender."[75]

Trumbull, Washburne, and most Republicans in Congress celebrated the news that Lincoln had revoked the offer to the Pennsylvania senator. Meanwhile, Cameron wallowed in self-pity. He confronted Leonard Swett in Washington, showed him Lincoln's January 3 letter, and complained that he had been treated badly in the matter. Swett, who had championed Cameron's appointment within Lincoln's inner circle, reported to the president-elect that the senator was particularly mortified by the letter's "imputation upon his character." Swett wrote that he had attempted unsuccessfully to persuade Cameron to follow Lincoln's advice and write a letter declining the nomination.[76] When Seward tried to console him, Cameron bitterly declared that neither Pennsylvania nor New Jersey should now have a place in the cabinet. Lincoln, Cameron insisted, owed him a letter of explanation that would preserve his honor in the affair.[77]

Meanwhile, the Pennsylvania congressional delegation, anxious to preserve the state's claim for a seat in the cabinet, met and recommended Thaddeus Stevens, a staunch antislavery congressman, for secretary of the treasury. Only after Cameron assured Stevens, according to the congressman's account, that "he had absolutely declined" to pursue a cabinet appointment, did Stevens permit the use of his name. Governor Andrew Curtin immediately wrote Lincoln endorsing Stevens for treasury secretary. He told Lincoln that Stevens "is one of the oldest and ablest of our Statesmen, possessing unquestioned personal and political integrity [who] would faithfully represent the vital interests of Pennsylvania in the General Government."[78]

But Cameron and his Pennsylvania supporters had no intention of conceding the fight to their enemies, who included Governor Curtin. From Washington, Trumbull warned Lincoln that "there may be more trouble in quieting Gen. C than I anticipated." A new wave of letters and messages flooded Springfield urging Lincoln to honor his original commitment to appoint Cameron. At least two of these letters came from influential Pennsylvanians who had played important roles in the Republican victories in the fall, Senator-elect Edgar Cowan and editor John W. Forney. Both asked Lincoln to select Cameron as secretary of the treasury because, they frankly admitted, he would protect the state's industries and workers if the economy was disrupted by secession and war. Their enthusiasm for the "Winnebago Chief" was clearly motivated by reports that Lincoln now favored Salmon P. Chase, a free-trader who opposed a protective tariff, for treasury secretary.[79] As political conservatives, Cowan and Forney also wanted to head off the boomlet for the radical Stevens. Forney, whose newspapers in Philadelphia and Washington would staunchly support Lincoln's policies during the Civil War, summed up his reasons for supporting Cameron's appointment. Cameron, Forney said, "is a tariff man and a conservative man, and all objections to him will subside before the fact that he stands by the industry and the interests of Pennsylvania."[80]

Cameron refused to decline Lincoln's offer of the cabinet appointment. When Thaddeus Stevens learned of Cameron's violation of his promise to him, he reacted in cold fury. In a letter to Washburne, which Washburne then sent to Lincoln, Stevens denounced Cameron "as a man destitute of honor and honesty"; he promised to make the senator's duplicity "a personal matter." Washburne warned the president-elect that "if Cameron now goes into the Cabinet, it will inaugerate [*sic*] an 'irrepressible conflict' in the party at the threshold of your administration which will break it down." Senator Trumbull echoed Washburne's warning and reported that Cameron "by his schemes has for the moment created an apparent public sentiment in Pa. in his favor. Many of the persons who are most strenuously urging his appointment are doubtless doing so in anticipation of a compensation." The opinion that they were creating in Springfield, Trumbull told Lincoln, "is not real." Senator William P. Fessenden of Maine reported to the president-elect that he had talked to "all of our leading men in the Senate, except Mr. Seward, and their unanimous & decided opinion is that such an appointment would not only be highly injurious, but disastrous in the want of confidence it would occasion."[81] Washburne, Trumbull, and other anti-Cameron men in Congress also dispatched George G. Fogg, secretary of the national Republican committee, to Springfield to counter efforts on behalf of the Pennsylvania senator.[82]

Cameron, however, had a powerful, though circumspect, ally in Senator Seward. Anti-Seward Republicans charged, probably with some truth, that the New York senator believed that if Cameron were in the cabinet, the two of them could dominate the administration.[83] Factions had developed in the Republican leadership that coalesced around Seward, Weed, and Cameron on one side, and Trumbull, Washburne, Judd, Greeley, and Bryant, on the other. Weed had created problems for Seward among many Republicans by publicly proclaiming his friend's "premiership" in the new administration. His editorial proposing a compromise on slavery in the western territories had also stirred controversy. Always seeking an opportunity to thwart Seward, the erratic but influential Horace Greeley of the *New York Tribune* had joined the anti-Seward coalition with a vengeance after Weed's Albany Regency prevented his election to the Senate. Leaders and spokesmen of both factions seemed genuinely to believe that their rivals supported policies and men that would undermine the Republican party and play into the hands of its Democratic foes in the North and the secessionists in the South.

While the controversy over Cameron within the Republican hierarchy raged, Lincoln concluded that political necessity required that he must offer the "Winnebago Chief" a seat in the cabinet, but not as secretary of the treasury, the second-ranking post in the administration and the one that the Pennsylvanian craved. In reconsidering the Cameron appointment, Lincoln had become convinced that if he placed Cameron in control of government finances, where he might fulfill the corrupt expectations of his critics, the Republican reaction in Congress would be too severe for the good of the party and his administration. But Lincoln realized that he must satisfy Pennsylvania Republicans by offering him the next ranking position—secretary of war. In view of the fact that some juggling of the seats in the cabinet was still under way, Lincoln decided to wait until he arrived in Washington before again approaching Cameron. In explaining his decision to Trumbull, he wrote that although Cameron could not be offered the treasury department because of the "very fierce opposition" to him, he had nevertheless been "more amply recommended for a place in the cabinet than any other man in the state." To satisfy "the protectionists of Pennsylvania," Lincoln said, Cameron "must be brought to co-operate" with the new administration, and "he would readily do this for the War Department."[84]

Lincoln already had someone else in mind for the treasury office, a man whose reputation for honesty and competence had never been questioned and who also came from a key northern state. This man was Salmon P. Chase, former governor of Ohio and senator-elect from that state. As an attorney in Cincinnati, Chase had been active in aiding slaves escaping to freedom. Though Lincoln and Chase disagreed on the enforcement of the Fugitive Slave Act, Chase's "ability, firmness, and purity of character," Lincoln informed Trumbull, "produce the propriety" lacking in Cameron; moreover, Lincoln said, "he alone can reconcile Mr. Bryant, and his class, to the appointment of Gov. S[eward] to the State Department."[85] The president-elect also knew that the Chase offer would go far toward reconciling Trumbull, arguably one of the most influential of Lincoln's supporters, to the Cameron appointment.

Chase's likely selection for the cabinet awakened old political rivalries in Ohio. Conservative Republicans in Ohio, mainly former Whigs, warned Lincoln against the choice, denying that the radical Chase had the support of most Republicans in the state. His selection, William M. Wilson wrote, would "hazard an explosion in our party" that would affect the conservative cause throughout the West. "If you have been led to believe that the Republican party of Ohio is ultra and aggressive, it is a misconception," he informed Lincoln. "A vast majority of the staid, moral, sober, religious, and intelligent classes of the community are with us," which included "seven eighths of the old Whig party . . . and a slice of the old democracy. In the nature of things, a party thus composed cannot be other than conservative," he said, and would react bitterly to a Chase appointment. With considerable insightfulness, Wilson acknowledged Chase's "great executive ability, so far as public affairs are concerned." But, he declared, Chase "lacks magnanimity to be a truly great man. Lacking this great quality, his intense desire of the Presidency makes him supremely selfish." As a member of the cabinet, Wilson predicted, Chase would seek to fulfill this ambition. In a similar letter, Ohio state senator John E. Cummins warned Lincoln that Chase's radical antislavery history would further alienate southerners and undermine Unionists in the upper South and border states.[86]

Seward and Weed joined conservative Ohio Republicans in their opposition to Chase. They opposed having such a talented and powerful former Democrat as Chase in the administration. Furthermore, as Weed wrote Leonard Swett, who forwarded the letter to the president-elect, "with the Treasury and Post Office Departments in the hands of radical Democrats," Lincoln "would either be compelled to interfere for the protection of his old Friends [Whigs], or see them every where ignored." Weed reminded Swett that, "in this State, the potential patronage of the Secretary of the Treasury is enormous, so enormous that when not discreetly dispensed, it tears a party to pieces." Former Whigs, who constituted two-thirds of the New York Republican party, Weed claimed, would find themselves out in the cold. Because of Chase's longtime advocacy of free-trade policies, Pennsylvania Republicans, with vital industries to protect, also vigorously fought the Ohioan's appointment as secretary of the treasury.[87]

Chase, however, had influential supporters, especially among old Democrats like Trumbull, George G. Fogg, and the Blairs. They saw Chase as a powerful counterweight to Seward in the cabinet.[88] Chase's strong presence in the cabinet, they believed, would be needed if Lincoln, influenced by Seward, wavered in his support of the Republican platform on slavery in the territories. Still, like the conservatives in the Republican party, Chase and the radicals, with few exceptions, acknowledged that under the Constitution slavery was a state institution and therefore that it should not be interfered with in the South.[89]

New York City merchants who, like Chase, favored free trade and the stability of the currency and bond markets also pressed Lincoln to choose Chase for the Treasury Department, arguing that his selection would restore confidence to the business community during the secession crisis. When Lincoln delayed in appointing the Ohioan, these businessmen rushed wealthy merchant and soon-to-be mayor George Opdyke and two other prominent citizens to Springfield to urge him to offer the treasury post to Chase immediately; "delay," Opdyke later wrote Lincoln, "would awaken sensibilities which would prevent [Chase's] acceptance."[90]

The preponderance of Republican opinion clearly favored the selection of Chase as secretary of the treasury, though perhaps in the minds of some, like Bryant, for no other reason than to prevent Cameron's appointment to this sensitive office. On December 31, Lincoln invited Chase to Springfield for "a conference" on "these troublous times." Arriving on January 5, the president-elect met Chase at his hotel. It was Lincoln's first meeting with him. Off and on for two days, the two men discussed both the composition of the cabinet and the secession crisis. On Sunday, Lincoln took Chase to church. Though the talks were cordial, Lincoln probably reached the same conclusion about Chase's ego that Senator Benjamin F. Wade had. Wade had quipped: "Chase is a good man, but his theology is unsound. He thinks there is a fourth person in the [Holy] Trinity," himself.[91] Whatever Lincoln's personal reaction, Chase reported to Opdyke that Lincoln wanted him to "take charge of the Treasy. Dept., but said that circumstances—& mainly the uncertainty whether the appt. wd. be satisfactory to Pennsylvania—prevented his present tender of the position to me."[92] Chase made it clear to the president-elect that he was reluctant to give up the Senate seat, to which he had recently been elected, to accept the appointment "of an subordinate one" in the administration. However, he promised to consider the offer if the Pennsylvania matter could be settled.

Despite the sense of urgency expressed by Opdyke and others to appoint Chase, Lincoln waited until he reached Washington in late February before resolving the Cameron question and completing his cabinet.[93] Soon after arriving in the capital, he asked each Republican senator to indicate his preference for one cabinet appointment, presumably that of secretary of the treasury. Of the nineteen senators who responded, eleven named Chase as their choice.[94] This settled the matter for Lincoln; Chase would be given the treasury portfolio and Cameron the war office. On March 1, three days before the inauguration, Lincoln summoned Cameron to Willard's Hotel, where he was staying, and offered him the position of secretary of war. (At the eleventh hour, he also selected Caleb B. Smith, arguably the leading Indiana Republican, over popular young congressman Schuyler Colfax for secretary of the interior and as that state's representative in the cabinet.) Though Cameron still wanted the treasury office, the War Department appointment satisfied his sense of honor enough to compensate for the early humiliation of having an offer withdrawn. While professing his reluctance to serve, Cameron accepted the appointment.[95]

The "Winnebago Chief's" acceptance permitted the soon-to-be president to complete his slate of cabinet officers, but not before the Seward forces, including the senator himself, made a bold attempt to have Lincoln drop Chase and Blair from consideration. Their objective was to secure an old Whig dominance of the administration and, under Seward's leadership, adopt a conciliatory policy toward the South. Such an approach to the secession crisis, they believed, would save the upper South and the border states and perhaps eventually restore the cotton states of the lower South to the Union. Joined by anxious Virginia Unionists, Weed and other Seward associates visited Lincoln at Willard's Hotel in late February in a last-ditch effort to persuade him against the Chase and Blair appointments. They had in mind former Whigs Thomas Corwin or Robert C. Schenck of Ohio in place of Chase, and Henry Winter Davis of Maryland instead of Blair. When Norman Judd, a member of the anti-Seward faction, heard a rumor that Davis would be chosen over Blair, he rushed to Lincoln's room and excitedly asked, "Is it true, Mr. Lincoln . . . that we are to have a new deal after all, and that you intend to nominate Winter Davis instead of Blair?" "Judd," the president-elect replied, "when that slate breaks again, it will break at the top."[96] In other words, Lincoln would make no changes in the list of cabinet nominations that he planned to send to the Senate after the inauguration.

Lincoln's refusal to replace Chase on his list greatly distressed Seward. The senator reportedly remarked that "there are differences between myself and Chase which make it impossible for us to act in harmony. The cabinet ought, as General [Andrew] Jackson said, to be a unit," which, Seward predicted, it would not be if both he and Chase were in it.[97] Seward also must have been humiliated by newspaper commentaries saying that Chase and Blair, "men of great energy, activity, tenacity and decision of character," as the *New York Herald* claimed, would dominate the administration.[98]

Seward's friends, who were in Washington for the inauguration, persuaded the senator to withdraw his acceptance of the State Department post. Such an action, they believed, would force Lincoln to reverse his decision on the Chase appointment rather than face a damaging embarrassment at the beginning of his administration. On March 2, two days before the inauguration, Seward sent Lincoln a cryptic note withdrawing his consent to serve in the cabinet. "Circumstances which have occurred," Seward dryly wrote, "render it my duty" to reject the appointment.[99]

Lincoln found startling the effrontery of the man who had just reviewed his inaugural address and had made several suggestions that he had accepted.

For two days, Lincoln pondered his response to the withdrawal note. On the morning of the inauguration, while the parade formed below his room at the Willard's, he drafted his response and remarked to John G. Nicolay, his secretary: "I can't afford to let Seward take the first trick."[100] Lincoln informed Seward that his note "is the subject of the most painful solitude with me; and I feel constrained to beg that you will countermand the withdrawal. The public interest, I think, demands that you should; and my personal feelings are deeply inlisted [*sic*] in the same direction." He asked Seward to answer by nine o'clock the next morning.[101]

Lincoln had succeeded in calling Seward's bluff in the Chase matter—and the New Yorker knew it. Seward, who all along had seen himself as the only man who could save the Union, had second thoughts about withdrawing from the cabinet at a time when the government faced the secession crisis. He realized that his withdrawal might not only damage the new administration; it would also greatly reduce his political influence. After the inauguration, Seward called at the White House, and the two men had a long and confidential meeting. The next day Seward sent the new president a note indicating that he would serve in the cabinet.[102]

On the same day, March 5, Lincoln forwarded the names of his cabinet members to the Senate for confirmation; all were immediately approved. Apparently only Seward, Bates, and Cameron knew beforehand that their names were on the list. Lincoln had been especially closemouthed about his cabinet choices, which left the door open for the press to circulate wild rumors regarding his selections. Even Chase, who had not talked privately to Lincoln since their January meeting in Springfield, did not find out that he had been appointed to head the Treasury Department until he had taken his seat in the Senate to begin his term. Having discovered that his name was on the list of nominations for confirmation, Chase hurried over to the White House to protest, only to be told by Lincoln that his rejection of the appointment would be embarrassing to the new administration and to the Union cause. Moved by the most "unpropitious and forbidding" circumstances facing the country, as he expressed it, Chase agreed to resign from the Senate and serve as secretary of the treasury.[103]

The cabinet, formed after careful deliberation, factional controversy, and frustrating negotiations, represented the balance of former Whigs (Seward, Bates, and Smith) and Democrats (Chase, Blair, and Welles) that Lincoln had wanted from the beginning. Though a former Democrat, Cameron had generally aligned himself with the Seward faction. Lincoln, like most political leaders of his day, realized that national political success and the ability to govern when in power required a sensitivity to state political alignments; in other words, state politics was also national politics. In forming his cabinet,

Lincoln had succeeded in selecting the most prominent Republicans from the key free states of New York, Pennsylvania, and Ohio. He had secured the appointment of two leading men from the border slave states (Bates and Blair), but he had failed in his effort to bring into the cabinet a well-known Unionist from the upper or lower South. Although his cabinet was chosen primarily to meet the need for political and geographic balance, Lincoln in fact selected several men with good executive skills to head what soon would be wartime departments. The notable exception was Cameron in the War Department, though the dire predictions by Trumbull, Fessenden, Bryant, and other members of their faction that the appointment would divide the party and embarrass the Lincoln administration in the eyes of the world did not occur. Cameron proved incompetent in dealing with the enormous problems associated with the preparations and prosecution of the Union war effort. In January 1862, Lincoln forced him out the cabinet. Caleb B. Smith, whose health deteriorated during his one-year tenure as secretary of the interior, also proved unequal to his responsibilities.

Seward correctly predicted that harmony could not be obtained in an administration that included men of such different personalities, ambitions, and views as himself and Chase; he could have added Blair as well. Despite the disagreements and in-fighting among its members, the cabinet under Lincoln's patient leadership functioned reasonably well during the republic's most critical period. Ironically, the cabinet member who proved most congenial and helpful to Lincoln during the four years of the Civil War was Seward, who had created considerable trouble for him in the early weeks of the new administration. Not until after the war began in April 1861 did Seward abandon his ambition to be the premier of the federal government. On June 5, Seward wrote his wife, "The President is the best of us"; he added that Lincoln "needs constant and assiduous cooperation."[104] He meant advice as well as cooperation, both of which Seward provided the president. As a result, the relationship between the two Republican leaders flourished in the crucible of war. Lincoln, who rarely revealed his plans, was the more practical and cautious of the two men. But Seward, an inveterate talker with considerable persuasive skills, mesmerized people, according to young Henry Adams, with "his grand, broad ideas that would inspire a cow with statesmanship if she understood our language."[105]

The president learned to appreciate his secretary of state's personal loyalty and political knowledge. At the same time, Lincoln provided the necessary restraint that enabled his impetuous and talented foreign secretary to make a major contribution to Union success in the Civil War. By 1863, Seward was praising the president to a fellow New Yorker as "the best and wisest man he has ever known."[106] The warm and productive relationship of the two former Republican rivals was one of the most remarkable stories of the Civil War era.[107]

Although the formation of the cabinet proved an important and difficult challenge, a greater and more momentous one gripped the nation. This, of course, was the secession crisis. Lincoln as president-elect and leader of the victorious Republican party inevitably served as the focal point of the national response to southern secession—and to the hopes of millions that somehow secession could be checked and a civil war prevented. Lacking any official authority for four months after his election, Lincoln was called on to influence congressional attempts to resolve the crisis during the winter of 1860–1861. Even his cabinet-making, as has been seen, partly reflected the need to establish northern and border-state unity behind a policy of preserving the Union and forestalling the secession of the upper southern and border states. Furthermore, Lincoln still hoped that cotton-state southerners would come to their senses and return to the Union. Never before or since has a president-elect faced such a daunting and uncertain task. Clearly, all of Lincoln's intellectual capacity, temperamental balance, and political wisdom would be tested in the historic effort to save the United States from dissolution.

CHAPTER TEN

"HOLD FIRM, AS
WITH A CHAIN OF STEEL"

ON DECEMBER 3, 1860, Congress assembled under the most ominous circumstances in American history. South Carolina and other cotton states were poised to leave the Union, and secession threatened to engulf the upper South. In less than three weeks, a state convention would meet in South Carolina and, as expected, take the Palmetto State out of the Union. Other lower southern states were almost certain to follow in January, though a minority in each wanted to wait and see what Lincoln and Congress would do before taking such a drastic step.

Lincoln, while disturbed by events, believed that secession was a lawless conspiracy of a minority of southerners whose real purpose was to extort concessions from the free states. He concluded that only a firm stand in Washington against compromising the Republican platform, particularly on the issue of the expansion of slavery in the territories, could check the conspirators and sustain Unionism in the cotton states. One day in December 1860, Lincoln told a *Philadelphia Bulletin* correspondent that, because southern charges against the Republicans were not "well defined [and] are so vague, . . . they cannot be long maintained by reasoning men even in the southern states."[1] Still, he did not say what he would do as president if "reasoning men" failed to sustain Union authority in the South and if South Carolina and other states seceded.

One "reasoning" man whom Lincoln hoped would be a bulwark against the secessionists was Georgian Alexander H. Stephens, a former Whig who had served with him in Congress in 1847–1849. After reading a newspaper account of a Union address by Stephens to the Georgia legislature in November, Lincoln asked him for a copy of the speech as revised for publication.[2] The diminutive Georgian replied that he had not prepared it for publication; the newspaper accounts, he said, were substantially correct. Lincoln, in a letter marked "*For your eye only,*" thanked Stephens for his response and took the opportunity to assure him that "I fully appreciate the present peril the country is in, and the weight of the responsibility on me." He attempted to put Stephens at ease regarding his position on slavery, pointedly asking, "Do the people of the South really entertain fears that a Republican administration would, *directly,* or *indirectly,* interfere with their slaves, or with them, about their slaves? If they do, I wish to assure you, as once a friend, and still, I hope, not an enemy, that there is no cause for such fears."[3]

Lincoln told Stephens that "the South will be in no more danger in this respect, than it was in the days of Washington. I suppose, however, this does not meet the case. You think that slavery is *right* and ought to be extended; while we think it is *wrong* and ought to be restricted. That I suppose is the rub. It certainly is the only substantial difference between us."[4] Lincoln probably concluded that Stephens was fundamentally conservative because, like himself, he revered the Founders, the Constitution, and the laws under it. There should be no need, Lincoln believed, for the conservative masses of the South to fear his presidency.

On December 30, Stephens replied that "personally, I am not your enemy—far from it; and however widely we may differ politically, yet I trust that we both have an earnest desire to preserve and maintain the Union." Then Stephens went to the heart of the matter, something that Lincoln had not admitted in his letter: "When men come under the influence of fanaticism, there is no telling where their impulses or passions will drive them. This is what creates our discontent and apprehensions, not unreasonable when we see . . . such reckless exhibitions of madness as the John Brown raid into Virginia, which has received so much sympathy from many, and no open condemnation from any of the leading members of the dominant party." Stephens was wrong in claiming that Lincoln and other prominent Republicans had failed to condemn Brown's assault. But some Republicans had praised Brown as a martyr to the antislavery cause, and white southerners had concluded that Lincoln, Seward, and other members of the Republican hierarchy agreed and would permit similar violence against their communities. Nonetheless, Stephens asked Lincoln to "do what you can to save our common country." He specifically said that "a word fitly spoken by you now would be like 'apples of gold in pictures of silver.'"[5]

The president-elect did not provide the "apples of gold" assurances that Stephens thought would help reverse the secessionist momentum in the cotton states. By this time—late December—it was unlikely that a statement by Lincoln reaffirming his intention to provide security for slavery in the South, or even one including concessions on the territorial issue, could have prevented the secession of Georgia and other lower southern states. These states, following the example of South Carolina on December 20, were primed to leave the Union in January. In February, Stephens would become vice president of the newly formed Confederate States of America.

LINCOLN WORRIED THAT Congress and President Buchanan, both lame ducks, would be driven by desperation to adopt a compromise policy undercutting the Republican platform and emboldening secessionists in the South. "The attention of the President-elect is now fixed on Congress," journalist Henry Villard reported on December 3. "He awaits the appearance of [Buchanan's] Message with great anxiety. The attitude likely to be assumed by Northern and Southern Congressmen are also a frequent theme of conversation with him."[6]

Lincoln had good reason to be anxious. In one of the strangest annual presidential messages in American history (equivalent to today's State of the Union Address), Buchanan announced that secession was illegal, but he maintained that he could do nothing about it. Without a word of censure for the southern fire-eaters or secessionists, he denounced the antislavery spirit in the North that had inflamed the South against the Union. "The long-continued and intemperate interference of the Northern people with the question of slavery in the Southern States," Buchanan asserted, "has at length produced its natural effects"—the election of an antislavery president. Many southerners, he declared, no longer felt secure in the Union. Buchanan, however, also said that Lincoln's election was no cause for "revolutionary resistance"; the election had been "held in strict conformity" with the Constitution and laws under it. "The stern duty of administering the vast and complicated concerns of this Government," Buchanan told southerners, "affords in itself a guaranty that [Lincoln] will not attempt any violation of a clear constitutional right" upon assuming office on March 4. The president proposed that Congress initiate a constitutional amendment protecting slavery in the southern states and also issue a call for a national convention to resolve any "existing evils" between the two sections.[7]

After he read a telegraphic synopsis of the message, Lincoln, according to Villard, "very severely gave vent" against Buchanan's attempt "to rest the whole responsibility of the secession movement on the free states." He calmed down after studying the complete message.[8] Still, Lincoln remained deeply concerned that Congress might adopt Buchanan's appeasement policy and agree to a shameful compromise.

He soon received reports from Washington tending to confirm his fears that some Republicans in Congress were leaning toward a compromise on slavery in the territories. Republican support, Lincoln knew, was crucial to the success of any compromise. On a visit to Washington, hard-line Republican George G. Fogg, with some exaggeration, reported to Lincoln that he "found great numbers of our friends afflicted with the secession panic, and almost ready to concede away the entire Republican platform to pacify the secessionists."[9] Lincoln did not agree with Buchanan and some Republicans in Congress, including Seward, that a constitutional amendment protecting slavery in the states was necessary. Such a proposed amendment, however, was not a central concern for him. It would be superfluous because neither he nor his party, Lincoln said, had ever challenged the constitutional right of southerners to control the institution in the South. An amendment affirming slavery's legitimacy, he believed, would suggest that the Republicans lacked firmness in the crisis. Furthermore, Lincoln opposed the idea of calling a national convention, concluding that its approval would also send a message to secessionists and their friends that Republicans were willing to abandon the platform on which he had been elected.

Lincoln's concern increased when the House of Representatives, immediately after the reading of Buchanan's message, set up a committee of thirty-three—one member from each state—to recommend a solution to the crisis. Conservative Republican Thomas Corwin of Ohio chaired the committee, which included sixteen members of his party. Two weeks later, the Senate also formed a committee, consisting of thirteen members, to propose a plan of adjustment between the disaffected slave states and the free states.[10] Though Lazarus Powell, a Democrat of Kentucky, chaired the Senate committee, his colleague John J. Crittenden, a seventy-four-year-old former Whig, was its leading member. Border-state Unionists viewed Crittenden as the inheritor of the Henry Clay mantel of sectional compromise, and they expected him to develop a plan to save the Union that would receive the approval of Congress. (Until the lower southern representatives withdrew, the Republicans did not have a majority in Congress. A smorgasbord of political party allegiances prevailed in Congress, though the Republicans were the main faction.)

The Senate Committee of Thirteen, as it was known, reflected the full range of sectional and political sentiment in America. In addition to Crittenden and Powell, the committee included Jefferson Davis of Mississippi, Stephen A. Douglas of Illinois, and William H. Seward of New York. The Senate "Union Saving Committee," as Seward facetiously called it, soon overshadowed the work of the House committee. It adopted a rule offered by Davis that only by a dual majority of the five Republicans and of the other eight members could a proposal receive the committee's approval. This meant that unless Lincoln, who was still in Springfield, signaled his support to the Republican members, it would be virtually impossible for the committee to approve a compromise package.

Lincoln, however, did not signal his approval for a compromise on the Republican platform's opposition to the expansion of slavery. Disturbed by the formation of the select committees on the crisis, on December 10 he wrote to Senator Trumbull. "Let there be no compromise on the question of *extending* slavery," he told Trumbull. If slavery was permitted to expand, "all our labor is lost, and, ere long, must be done again." Lincoln deplored reports that "some of our friends have a hankering to run" with Douglas's popular sovereignty in the territories as a concession to the South. "Have none of it," Lincoln demanded of Trumbull and other Republicans in Congress. "Stand firm. The tug has to come, & better now, than any time hereafter."[11]

Trumbull agreed with Lincoln. At the same time, he reaffirmed what Fogg had reported to the president-elect. "Not all of our Republican friends" in Congress, the Illinois senator wrote, were "as firm as I could wish. Some of them especially from the commercial portions of the country are talking of concessions & compromises." The "commercial embarrassment in the cities," caused by the threat of losing the southern trade, had alarmed them.[12] Trumbull named only one senator, James Dixon of Connecticut, as a potential defector who might break party ranks; many of his Republican colleagues, however, believed that Seward, whom Fogg and Trumbull distrusted, was in lockstep with Thurlow Weed in his call for concessions.

When William Kellogg, a member of the House Committee of Thirty-Three, asked for guidance on the issue, Lincoln warned him that "Douglas is sure to be again trying to bring in his 'Pop. Sov.' Have none of it." The instant the Republicans agreed to such a compromise, Lincoln wrote the Illinois congressman, "they have us under again, all our labor lost, and sooner or later must be done over." Whether the issue was the extension of the Missouri line or popular sovereignty, "it is all the same," he told Elihu B. Washburne, another Illinois congressman. "Let either be done, & immediately filibustering and extending slavery recommences. On that point hold firm, as with a chain of steel."[13] Lincoln informed Trumbull that "if any of our friends do prove false, and fix up a compromise on the territorial question, I am for fighting again—that is all." Still, he said, "I am for an honest inforcement [sic] of the constitution—fugitive slave clause included."[14]

Lincoln recognized that once a western territory had been conceded to slavery and slave codes adopted, it would be nearly impossible to eradicate the institution there. Such a concession also, as he said, would have been an invitation for slavery's further expansion. It is reasonable to assume that Lincoln was correct on this point. Though the West beyond East Texas might not be conducive to cotton cultivation, the western demand for slave labor to work in extractive industries, railroad construction, and grain production would have been strong if slavery received legal status in the territories. Furthermore, proslavery expeditions into Latin America during the 1850s, perhaps only temporarily checked by the execution of the notorious filibuster William Walker in Honduras on September 12, 1860, would receive a new lease on life by the opening of territories to the institution. But Lincoln's belief that southerners themselves would move to end slavery in their states if it could no longer expand into the fresh lands of the West was wishful thinking. Given the sectional polarization, white southerners' fears of the loss of racial control, and the bitter opposition to antislavery expressions in the South by the 1860s, no southern legislature or state convention would dare act to abolish the institution.

While congressmen dismissed the possibility of compromise, Lincoln responded to a letter from Thurlow Weed informing him of a conference of free-state governors scheduled for December 20 in New York. The Albany chief and several friends had invited the governors to meet "so that, if possible, there should be harmony of views and action between them" on the crisis. Only four eastern governors and Governor William Dennison of Ohio attended what Weed referred to as a "quiet and confidential" meeting.[15]

Though Lincoln had not been asked to write a statement for the New York meeting, he penned a "Private and confidential" letter to Weed conveying his views for the governors. "Tell them," Lincoln instructed Weed, "you judge from my speeches that I will be inflexible on the territorial question; that I probably think either the Missouri line extended, or Douglas' and Eli Thayer's Pop. Sov. would lose us every thing we gained by the election." Lincoln repeated his view that the adoption of either plan would revive "filibustering" operations "for all South of us," and the admission of slave states "would follow in spite of us." He also reaffirmed his belief that "all opposition, real and apparant [sic], to the fugitive slave [clause] of the constitution ought to be withdrawn" by those upper northern states that had enacted personal-liberty laws. Finally, Lincoln outlined to the governors his policy toward secession. Admitting that he had said little about the issue in his earlier speeches, he wrote, "My opinion is that no state can, in any way lawfully, get out of the Union, without the consent of the others; and that it is the duty of the President, and other government functionaries to run the machine as it is."[16]

A man who weighed his thoughts carefully before expressing them, Lincoln in his statement for the governors' conference clearly set forth his position on the compromise movement. The statement also foretold his general policy toward the seceded states after he became president. However, Lincoln did not indicate how he expected "to run the machine as it is" in the seceded states, nor did he suggest that he would use military force against the secessionists. The five governors meeting in New York agreed with Lincoln's position and promised to recommend it to their state legislatures.[17]

Weed probably had not received Lincoln's letter when he met with him in Springfield on December 20 and called the president-elect's attention to the compromise proposal in his *Albany Evening Journal*. As described in the preceding chapter, Lincoln found Weed's plan for a compromise regarding slavery in the territories "a heavy broadside" that inevitably would do "much mischief." Nonetheless, Lincoln drew up three resolutions for Seward to propose to the Senate Committee of Thirteen. The resolutions did not touch the territorial question because, as he told Senator Trumbull, he wanted a unanimous vote of "our friends" in Congress on the resolutions. Lincoln believed that the substance of his proposal, if approved, "would do much good" and would check any Republican movement toward concessions on the territorial issue. Lincoln's resolutions called for a fugitive slave law "with efficient provisions . . . for punishing all who resist it, and with the usual safeguards to liberty, securing free men against being surrendered as slaves." In addition, all state measures in conflict with the federal law "ought to be repealed" by the legislatures. Finally, Congress should pledge that "the Federal Union must be preserved."[18] Though Lincoln rejected a compromise solution on the territorial question, his proposed resolutions expressed his consistently conservative position on slavery.

Senator Seward, however, largely disregarded Lincoln's resolutions and instead offered three of his own. He explained to the president-elect that his (Seward's) resolutions had been approved by the other Republican members of the Committee of Thirteen. Seward told Lincoln that they "seemed to me to cover the ground of the suggestion made by you." However, only one, a recommendation that the free states repeal their personal-liberty laws, was also in Lincoln's. Otherwise, Seward's proposal provided that the Constitution should never be amended as to prohibit federal interference with slavery in any state. It also called for a change in the Fugitive Slave Act of 1850 to require jury trials for blacks apprehended under it.[19] The president-elect's proposal did not specifically provide for jury trials for fugitive slaves. Lincoln had no serious objection to either of these resolutions; however, he saw both as unnecessary and a distraction from the principal point—a congressional commitment to the preservation of the Union in its entirety. Seward's resolutions ultimately failed to win the approval of the Senate Committee of Thirteen. Jefferson Davis specifically objected to jury trials for fugitives from slavery. Despite Seward's assurances to Lincoln, a majority of the Republicans on the committee also opposed the resolutions, but for a different reason than Davis's—they did not like the idea of making a conciliatory gesture toward the South. Ironically, the soon-to-be Confederate president and these Republicans worked together to defeat Seward's proposal.[20]

THE MAIN ISSUE before the two "crisis committees" in Congress was the status of slavery in the territories. Senator Seward, like his alter ego Thurlow Weed, had become increasingly concerned about the cascading events in the South and, influenced by frightened New York merchants and border-state Unionists, would have accepted a partial compromise if not for the president-elect's adamant opposition to it.[21] In this position, Lincoln was backed by Senator Benjamin F. Wade of Ohio, Senator Trumbull, Chase, the Blairs, William Cullen Bryant, and most of the Republican governors. Like Lincoln, they believed that temporizing with secession would tend to give legitimacy to it in the cotton states and encourage disunionists in the upper and border South. On December 17, Wade made a powerful two-hour speech in the Senate in which he denounced those who would compromise the Republican platform on the territorial issue and exclaimed that to stand silent when the Constitution was "to be trampled under foot [was] akin to treason itself."[22] Increasingly, rank-and-file Republicans, particularly in the rural areas and small towns of the upper North, joined in the demand that their leaders in Congress reject any compromise on slavery in the territories, including Stephen A. Douglas's popular-sovereignty solution. They also insisted that the government stand firm against the surrender of federal property and forts in the seceded states.[23]

Unwilling to risk alienating himself from Lincoln and his party's mainstream, Seward voted on December 28 with his fellow Republicans on the Senate Committee of Thirteen to defeat a compromise package proposed by Senator Crittenden of Kentucky. (It was on that same day that Seward wrote Lincoln accepting the appointment as secretary of state.) The Crittenden Compromise, as it is known in history, consisted of six constitutional amendments and four supplementary resolutions. The critical provision that doomed the compromise in the committee was an amendment restoring the Missouri Compromise line (36 degrees, 30 minutes north latitude) in the West to guarantee federal protection of slavery in the territories below that latitude. The Crittenden Compromise also included a proposed constitutional amendment prohibiting any federal interference with slavery in a state where it already existed, and a resolution calling on the northern states to repeal their personal-liberty laws. Seward and the other Republican members on the committee endorsed both of these measures, but not the restoration of the Missouri line. Historian David M. Potter has pointed out that "only one of [the] ten items" in the Crittenden package "could be considered a concession to the antislavery element, a fact lending credence to Republican complaints that the whole thing was not a compromise but a surrender."[24] This was precisely Lincoln's conclusion, and he felt a sense of relief when the Senate committee rejected the Crittenden Compromise. Lincoln's relief, however, would be short-lived.

Senator Crittenden did not give up the fight for his compromise. In January, the Kentuckian took his plan to the Senate floor as a personal bill. By this time, Georgia, Florida, Alabama, Mississippi, and Louisiana were holding state conventions that before the end of the month would lead them to join South Carolina in severing their ties with the Union. Texas was almost certain to follow by means of a referendum that was to be held on February 1. A few days later, the seceded states would dispatch delegates to Montgomery, Alabama, to form the Confederate States of America. Furthermore, in a process that could easily lead to more states seceding from the Union, elections on calling conventions were scheduled for January and February in the upper South and in Missouri.

With the secession fever spreading, renewed pressure mounted for Congress to adopt Crittenden's border-state proposal or a similar compromise plan. Business and professional leaders of New York, including the venerable Peter Cooper and Republicans Moses Grinnell, Hamilton Fish, and William H. Aspinall, rushed to Washington to plead with northern members of Congress to support the Crittenden Compromise.[25] The *Philadelphia Press,* whose Democratic editor, John W. Forney, had supported Lincoln in the election, declared that "surely the Territorial question can be adjusted." The *Press* recommended: "Let us agree upon the principle which will leave the matter [of slavery] to the natural law that rules it under our system of self-government; or, by a safe anticipation, fix the line of demarcation, and so put this radical source of discontent at rest forever." In other words, Congress should either apply Douglas's popular-sovereignty principle or restore the Missouri Compromise line in the West. The *Press* reported that southerners "tell us that it is not the election of Lincoln that disturbs them, but the sentiment which that election manifests, which they take to be a determined hostility to their system of slavery. And against this danger they seek security." The newspaper announced that, in addition to guarantees regarding slavery in the South, the northern people must "strike the [antislavery] bone of contention out of our political platforms, and the anti-slavery sentiment among us would instantly fall into the category of moral suasion enterprises."[26] The *Press*'s recommendation expressed the voice of a middle-of-the-road element in the North, desperate to find a solution, however unrealistic, to the crisis that would be acceptable to southern secessionists.

Typically, Democratic newspapers raised the specter of civil war if the compromise effort failed. The *Allentown* (Pennsylvania) *Democrat* insisted that the politicians in Congress "should be forced by the pressure of public opinion to submit to the popular vote Crittenden's or some other set of acceptable resolutions." Otherwise, the editor predicted, "a catastrophe which must end in horrid scenes of suffering and blood" awaited the country. The *Democrat* told its readers that if Lincoln, Seward, and other Republican leaders "have a stomach for civil war, let them throw away their lives, . . . but they must not expect us to follow their foolish example."[27] The *Madison Wisconsin Daily Patriot* exclaimed: "Civil War is staring us in the face. Its horrors already menace our peace and safety.—The Southern fire-eaters will not yield.—the Northern fire-eaters are inexorable. Without a reconciliation, war is inevitable." Such a "revolution would be nothing milder than a bloody, internecine war," the *Patriot* editor somberly predicted. War "would enfeeble the people—eat out their substance—paralyze energies—break up their commerce—ruin their prosperity—and slaughter their fathers and sons." Writing on February 11, this editor declared that "unless something is done within the next ten days to satisfy the Border States, this Union, and all its blessings are lost forever," and that war would occur over the "mere abstraction" of slavery in the territories.[28] However, as the recent violent history of Kansas had demonstrated, the issue of slavery in the territories was no "mere abstraction."

Unionists in the upper South and border-slave states begged Lincoln to throw his weight behind the Crittenden Compromise and secure its passage before it was too late to save their states. Samuel T. Glover of Missouri informed Lincoln that "much of the union feeling in Mo is deceptive." "Disunionists put on the 'livery of the union' everywhere," he said, but unless the Crittenden plan was approved by inauguration day, they would join the secessionists and Missouri would leave the Union.[29] A clipping from an unidentified St. Louis newspaper, sent to Lincoln and found in his papers, called on him "to advise your political friends, in Congress, to give up their opposition to the measure of adjustment known as the Crittenden proposition." Failure to act on this plan, the editor predicted, "will lead inevitably to civil war—in which fifteen States will have to be subjugated before the shadow of peace can be restored."[30] John D. Defrees, a friend from Indiana, wrote Lincoln that, though the cotton states were lost, the Crittenden plan would keep the border and upper South in the Union. "Many Southern men," Defrees said, wanted Lincoln to speak out in support of the compromise.[31]

From Tennessee, Neill S. Brown, a former Whig governor, and Russell Houston of Nashville reported to Lincoln that "the whole southern states" were inflamed "to an extreme line of action." Though Brown and Houston professed to be "strongly attached to the Union," they said, "frankness compels us to admit that the period is approaching when union sentiments will be powerless to arrest the march of revolution." Only the immediate adoption of a compromise plan, they wrote, could save the Union. Brown and Houston told Lincoln: "You have the power, by virtue of your position, to speak peace to the troubled waves" and avert a civil war by giving your "moral" support to the Crittenden proposals. These two prominent Tennesseans held out an enviable place for Lincoln in the nation's history, next to George Washington, if he abandoned his no-compromise policy and took action to save the Union.[32]

Despite these pleas, most Republicans who wrote and visited Lincoln in early 1861 insisted that he remain steadfast and show no weakness in the face of the intense pressure for him to endorse the Crittenden plan. Old factional divisions between former Democrats and Whigs, radicals and conservatives, tended to disappear in the wave of advice that Lincoln received on this critical issue. His conservative friend Orville H. Browning and the Blairs joined Salmon P. Chase and other radicals in insisting that he "never consent, under any circumstances, to any concession which would lead to the recognition of slavery as a national institution," as Browning told Lincoln. Furthermore, Browning said, it was "the duty of the government to protect its property" and execute the laws in the seceded states. "The evils attending this course, great as they may be," he argued, "would be infinitely less than those which would inevitably follow the organization of separate confederacies."[33]

Senator James R. Doolittle, the conservative Republican of Wisconsin, wrote Lincoln that the "disease" of secession was "so deep seated that it must run its course. No compromise would stay it. An offer to do so would be treated with contempt as wrung from our fears." Doolittle exclaimed, "I will not consent, though the grave should open this very hour," to a compromise of Republican principles. "If God so wills it, that we must drink of the cup of civil war, be it so," Doolittle boldly declared.[34] The venerable Francis P. Blair, Sr., of Maryland informed the president-elect that "the adoption of Mr Crittenden's contrivance would probably satisfy the mass of Union men in the border states; but it would not tend even to reconcile the nullifiers [secessionists] of the border [upper South?] states, or any portion of the malcontents of the Cotton states."[35] Despite his advanced age, Blair's political mind remained sharp and his analysis of the effect of the compromise, if it passed Congress, had merit. He reasoned that no compromise by this time would satisfy the secessionists in the cotton states who were celebrating their easy success in withdrawing from the Union. Meanwhile, their supporters in the upper South, though not yet a majority, believed that history was on their side and that eventually, despite concessions, their states would separate from a North controlled by "Black Republicans."

LINCOLN NEEDED little Republican encouragement to oppose the critical provision in the Crittenden proposals—the restoration of the Missouri compromise line. His opposition went beyond the political need to establish and maintain control of his party in Washington, as some historians have suggested. Visiting Lincoln in January, George Sumner, the brother of Senator Charles Sumner of Massachusetts, reportedly heard Lincoln say that he "would sooner go out into his backyard and hang himself" than agree to the border-state compromise on the territories. "By no act or complicity of mine," he declared in his quaint way, "shall the Republican party become a mere sucked egg, all shell and no principle in it."[36] Lincoln told Congressman William Kellogg that he opposed any compromise that would bring "our system" of government "down to a level with the existing disorganized state of affairs in Mexico." But "this thing," he said, was "in the hands of the people; and if they desire" through Congress, as had been proposed, "to call a Convention to remove any grievances complained of, or to give new guarantees for the permanence of vested rights [slavery], it is not mine to oppose."[37] Lincoln, however, would not concede any territory to slavery in order to satisfy southern grievances.

Like Crittenden, Senator Seward had not given up on the idea of a compromise to save the Union. Despite his vote against the Crittenden plan in the Committee of Thirteen, Seward anxiously wanted a settlement that would satisfy most Republicans, gain the support of northern Democrats and southern Unionists, and disarm southerners who were contemplating secession. "Mad men North, and mad men South," Seward wrote his wife Frances, "are working together to produce a dissolution of the Union, by civil war. The present Administration and the incoming one unite in devolving on me the responsibility of averting those disasters." He told Frances that he sought "to gain time for the new administration to organize and for the frenzy of passion to subside." Seward insisted that he was "doing this without making any compromise whatever, by forbearance, conciliation, magnanimity."[38] However, many staunch Republican opponents of the Crittenden plan, including Senators Doolittle and Trumbull and Representative Washburne, believed that Seward would be willing as part of a compromise to surrender the far West to slavery and also any territories that might still be acquired from Mexico.[39]

On January 12, before a crowded gallery of anxious onlookers, Seward delivered a speech in the Senate that was designed to calm passions and reverse the secessionist impulse. He called for a moratorium on the debates over slavery in the territories and also on the coercion of the seceded states and other polarizing issues. Proclaiming that Americans were "a homogeneous people," Seward sang paeans to the common heritage and benefits of the Union. Like Lincoln and other Republicans, he denied that a state had a constitutional right to secede. The New York senator contended that unless secession could be checked, a destructive civil war would follow, creating chaos and even slave uprisings in the South.[40]

Seward then offered several recommendations for preserving the Union, including some contained in the Crittenden Compromise. He proposed a constitutional amendment prohibiting federal interference with slavery in the states, to be followed by a convention to deal with other sectional controversies. Seward also called for the repeal of northern personal-liberty laws that had been designed to prevent the enforcement of the Fugitive Slave Act. However, he recommended a provision in the federal act that would protect citizens from having to aid in the pursuit of fugitive slaves. The New York senator also proposed a federal law to prevent antislavery invasions of a state, as had occurred in John Brown's raid on Harpers Ferry in 1859. On the central issue of slavery in the territories, Seward attempted a clever circumvention that he thought would maintain his party's no-expansion principle while recognizing southern interests in the West. Adopting the suggestion of his friend Charles Francis Adams on the House "crisis committee," Seward recommended that, after the anticipated admission of Kansas as a free state, the remaining areas in the West should be organized into two huge territories and immediately admitted as states, with the possibility of later divisions.[41] Seward unrealistically believed that this solution would avoid the controversy over slavery in the territories. But it could also mean that New Mexico, where there were a handful of slaves, would come into the Union as a slave state, an eventuality that the New York senator would not admit.

Seward's Senate speech received mixed reviews. Southern Unionists and many northern Democrats praised its conciliatory tone while maintaining that it did not go far enough toward placating the South on the territorial issue. Washburne reported to Lincoln that the address gave "great satisfaction to the border State men who are with us."[42] Some Republicans, such as Adams and Thomas Corwin, chair of the House "crisis committee," applauded the speech. But most Republicans, while remaining publicly silent, deplored the one-sidedness of Seward's concessions. Even Frances Seward believed that her husband's address was too conciliatory. She wrote him that the speech's "compromises" put him "in danger of taking the path which led Daniel Webster to an unhonored grave ten years ago" because of his support of the Compromise of 1850.[43]

Lincoln at first preferred to think that the proposals outlined in Seward's speech did not violate the Republican platform. He wrote his secretary of state–designate: "Your recent speech is well received here; and, I think, is doing good all over the country." The president-elect also found encouraging a Seward report "that the secessionists are already in danger of [a] reaction" against them.[44] But he soon received disturbing news from Kellogg and Trumbull that Seward, in his role as "premier" of the administration, might agree to some form of compromise that would be completely unacceptable to Lincoln and most Republicans. The possibilities included his scheme for the immediate organization and admission as states of two large territories in the West. Seward himself gave credence to this view when he wrote Lincoln on

January 27 that the only alternative to a compromise was a long, destructive war.

Lincoln probably had not received this letter when he penned a note to Seward on February 1 saying he was "baffled" by Kellogg's and Trumbull's reports from Washington regarding concessions. Lincoln emphatically told Seward, "I say now, . . . as I have all the while said, that on the territorial question—that is, the question of extending slavery under the national auspices,—I am inflexible. I am for no compromise which *assists* or *permits* the extension of the institution on soil owned by the nation." Lincoln wrote that "any trick by which the nation is to acquire territory, and then allow some local authority to spread slavery over it, is as obnoxious as any other." In a gentle warning to Seward against his wavering, Lincoln reminded him that "the object of all these proposed compromises" was "to put us again on the high-road to a slave empire." However, as to fugitive blacks, slavery in the District of Columbia, the interstate slave trade, "and whatever springs of necessity from the fact that the institution is amongst us, I care but little, so that what is done be comely, and not altogether outrageous." Finally, Lincoln, in what appears to have been a remarkable concession in view of his adamant stand for freedom in the territories, informed Seward: "Nor do I care much about New-Mexico, if further extension" of slavery "were hedged against."[45] Lincoln probably believed that slavery could not exist in the New Mexico territory, which also included the present state of Arizona, despite the territorial legislature's adoption of a slave code in 1859. Though two prominent territorial officials held slaves, the federal census of 1860 did not list any bondsmen in New Mexico.[46]

The contents of Lincoln's message to Seward, though marked "Private and confidential," found its way to congressional Republicans. Lincoln's position on the Crittenden plan and other compromise proposals, according to journalist Henry Villard, provided "an infusion of backbone" to wavering members of his party.[47] Republicans now united to defeat the compromise effort. Seward also dropped his own plan for the creation of two territories in the West that would be admitted without reference to slavery. In the House, Seward's friend Charles Frances Adams had proposed a similar concession regarding New Mexico, but he abandoned it when he encountered opposition in his party.[48]

Meanwhile, the Virginia legislature, desperate to avoid secession and possible war, issued a call for a convention of the states to meet in Washington to recommend a compromise for Congress to enact. Lincoln must have believed that there was no end of efforts to undercut his firm policy against territorial concessions on slavery. He angrily told Orville H. Browning that "no good results would follow the border State Convention, but evil rather, as increased excitement would follow when it broke up without having accomplished any thing." Browning confided to his diary that Lincoln "agreed with me that no concession short of a surrender of every thing worth preserving, and contending for would satisfy the South." Furthermore, Browning said, Lincoln declared that "far less evil & bloodshed would result from an effort to maintain the Union and the Constitution, than from disruption and the formation of two confederacies."[49]

In what became known as the "Peace Conference"—or the "Old Gentlemen's Convention," because of the large number of former influential politicians who attended—delegations from twenty-one states assembled on February 4 in an annex of Willard's Hotel. Ironically, representatives from the seceded states met on the same day in Montgomery, Alabama, to form the Confederate States of America. On that day also, Virginia voters approved a convention to consider the state's position; however, of the 152 delegates who were elected, only 32 were immediate secessionists. Most of the majority were conditional Unionists who opposed secession as long as Lincoln did not adopt a policy of coercion against the lower South. Significantly, the Virginia election broke the secessionist momentum in the South; it was followed by more Unionist successes in elections in Tennessee, Arkansas, and North Carolina in February. The border slave states—Delaware, Maryland, Kentucky, and Missouri—proved even more resistant to the secessionist fever.

The success of the Unionists in the elections meant to Lincoln that the Republican policy of refusing to make concessions on slavery in the territories, combined with assurances to southerners that their constitutional rights would be protected, was working. Lincoln believed that the southern confederacy formed at Montgomery would be short-lived if Congress ceased its dalliance with appeasement. As he later announced to thousands of people along his route to Washington, he believed that "time, patience and a reliance on that God who has never forsaken this people" would save the Union.[50] Lincoln failed to understand, or did not want to admit, that much of the February success of the Unionists in the upper South hinged on his rejection of federal coercion after he became president.

Though Lincoln remained concerned that concessions would be made in Washington, the issue of a compromise on slavery in the territories was dead by late February. Nonetheless, the Peace Conference, after an acrimonious debate, adopted resolutions similar to the Crittenden proposals and submitted them to Congress for consideration. Congress rejected all but one of these resolutions, a proposed constitutional amendment forever prohibiting federal interference with slavery in the states. On inauguration day, March 4, the proposed amendment received the necessary two-thirds vote in Congress to initiate it. Forty-five Republicans voted for the amendment, knowing that Lincoln did not seriously object to it.[51]

Two weeks later, Lincoln, as president, dutifully sent the amendment to the states for approval, including those of the upper South that had adopted a "watch and wait" policy toward him.[52] The onslaught of war and northern resistance to any concession to the rebels forestalled state ratification of this version of the Thirteenth Amendment to the Constitution. Ironically, the Thirteenth Amendment that became a part of the Constitution in December 1865 did not guarantee slavery but instead abolished the institution that Lincoln had long realized was a blot on the American national fabric.

Lincoln's unwillingness to compromise on the question of slavery in the territories during the winter of 1860–1861 left him vulnerable to critics then and now. Some assert that his support of a compromise on this crucial point would have reversed secession and prevented the Civil War. It is highly unlikely, however, that any concessions by him or by Republicans in Congress on this or other issues would have checked secession in the lower South, prevented the formation of the Confederate States, or headed off an armed clash between the two sides. After more than a decade of intense conflict over slavery, the cotton states, led by South Carolina, had crossed the Rubicon on secession, and no matter what Lincoln and the Republicans conceded, they would not have voluntarily returned to a Union controlled by "Black Republicans" or countenanced the continued presence of federal forts and properties and the enforcement of federal laws in their states.

Still, Lincoln's acceptance of the Crittenden Compromise or the Peace Conference resolutions could have increased support for the Union cause in the border states and upper South. It might have also reduced somewhat the opposition in those states to his decision in April, after the bombardment of Fort Sumter, to use military force against the seceded states. However, Lincoln's willingness to restore the Missouri Compromise line, the centerpiece of the appeasement movement, would have violated the Republican platform and would have seriously divided his party between the hard-liners of the Chase-Trumbull majority faction and the compromisers of the Seward-Weed minority. Lincoln could not afford such a division, one that would have been a recipe for the failure of the new administration and the destruction of the Union. Seward and Weed eventually accepted Lincoln's position. But regardless of any compromise that Lincoln and his fellow Republicans might have made during the winter crisis, the upper southern states (Virginia, North Carolina, Tennessee, and Arkansas) probably would still have left the Union and joined the Confederacy when the war began.

A more difficult decision to defend was Lincoln's refusal after the fall election to issue a public statement reassuring white southerners of his fundamental conservatism. Lincoln's policy of public silence was influenced by his mistaken view that white southerners would read his old speeches and realize that he was far from being a radical threat to their liberties and rights. He also believed that such a declaration would be distorted by the opposition press in the North and ignored in the South. His enemies in the border and northern states, he declared on several occasions, would discredit any new pronouncement that he made. This is in fact just what occurred when he inserted a statement in Senator Trumbull's speech at Springfield in late November. But the reaction to Trumbull's message does not mean there was nothing Lincoln could have done to change the tide of secession at that point. A soothing public declaration by Lincoln could have conveyed to the general public what he was saying to visitors and friends in Springfield.

Lincoln's private statements affirmed his intention to protect southern constitutional rights, prevent antislavery violence, and appoint "no strangers" to federal offices in the South. Though it would have failed to appease the lower South, a carefully worded printed declaration, despite the risk of misrepresentation, could have had a salutary effect upon opinion in the upper and border South. Furthermore, a statement could have calmed growing fears in the North and increased confidence in Lincoln's ability to lead after he became president. He also could have used the press to refute erroneous reports like the one appearing in a *New York Herald* editorial on December 18, charging that he intended to force the seceded states back into the Union. The editor asserted that "Mr. Lincoln holds that there is no such thing as peaceable secession, which is equivalent to a declaration of war against a seceding State or States."[53] To friends and visitors in Springfield, Lincoln repeatedly denied that he had any intention of coercing the wayward states.[54] At any rate, an evaluation of Lincoln's reaction to the secession crisis of the fall and winter of 1860–1861 should take his policy of public silence into account because it was an important factor in the history of this uncertain period.

AS THE INAUGURATION APPROACHED, the security of the national capital and, indeed, Lincoln's own safety had become a major concern of General-in-Chief Winfield Scott and Republicans in Washington. "There is a feverish excitement here which awakens all kind of apprehensions of popular disturbance and disorders, connected with your assumption of the government," Seward reported to Lincoln in late December.[55] The Republican senator was in almost daily contact with the aging Scott, who at first believed that President Buchanan was ignoring the danger.

On January 4, Congressman Elihu B. Washburne informed Lincoln that "there now exists a formidable conspiracy to seize the capitol. In it are men of high position." On the same day, General Scott wrote Lincoln that Henry A. Wise, a former governor of Virginia, was "enrolling minute men pretty extensively" for the assault on the national capital to prevent the installation of the new government. President Buchanan, who had earlier refused to recognize any threat to a peaceful inauguration, finally became concerned by January. Along with his new secretary of war, Kentuckian Joseph Holt, he threw his support behind Scott's efforts to thwart the secessionist scheme to storm the capital. By February, owing mainly to his careful preparations, Scott no longer feared that the inauguration would be disrupted, though rumors of an assault on Washington continued to be heard.[56]

Lincoln put more credence in reports that anti-Republicans planned to block the congressional certification of his electoral vote than in the rumors of a secessionist-led plot to prevent the inauguration. On January 3, he wrote Seward that "the inauguration is not the most dangerous point for us." "Our adversaries have us more clearly at disadvantage," he said, on February 13, "when the [electoral] votes should be officially counted." Lincoln feared that Republican opponents would somehow prevent the two houses of Congress from meeting, "or meet without a quorum of each." If either occurred, "where shall we be?" he asked Seward. "I do not think that this counting is constitutionally essential to the election; but how are we to proceed in absence of it?" He informed his secretary of state–designate that "in view of this, I think it is best for me not to attempt appearing in Washington till the result of that ceremony is known."[57] On the day of the electoral count, General Scott stationed troops at the entrance of the Capitol, and the proceedings in Congress occurred without incident. Ironically, Vice President John C. Breckinridge, who later served as a Confederate general and secretary of war, presided over the count and officially announced that Lincoln had been elected president.[58]

Meanwhile, in Springfield, Lincoln busily prepared for his journey to Washington and the inauguration. Earlier, as the Republican nominee for president, he had received a letter from eleven-year-old Grace Bedell of Westfield in upstate New York telling him that if he grew whiskers "you would look a great deal better for your face is so thin. All the ladies like whiskers and they would tease their husband's [sic] to vote for you and then you would be President."[59]

Contrary to legend, Grace Bedell was not the only person advising Lincoln to grow a beard in order to improve his appearance. An anonymous group of "True Republicans" had written Lincoln noting that his campaign photographs were unflattering. They suggested that he would have a greater appeal at the polls if he had a beard and wore standing collars. Lincoln apparently did not reply to the "True Republicans," but he did to Grace Bedell. He wrote her that, "having never worn any [whiskers], do you not think people would call it a piece of silly affection if I were to begin it now?"[60]

Lincoln, however, perhaps wanting to give his face a more dignified and mature look befitting a national leader, took the advice of Grace Bedell and the "True Republicans" and began growing whiskers. By the time he left for Washington in February, he had a full beard. At least one Springfield resident thought that Lincoln's whiskers dramatically enhanced his appearance. Nineteen-year-old Anna Ridgely, who in November had criticized him as a man "without any polish of manners" and not fit to be president, attended Lincoln's farewell reception on February 6 and wrote in her diary that "Mr. L really looked handsome to me. His whiskers are a great improvement and he has such a pleasant smile I could not but admire him."[61]

In an effort to escape the hordes of admirers, on December 29 Lincoln moved his office out of the State House and took a pleasant room in the Johnson Building on the corner of Fourth and Washington streets. Leaving John Nicolay to manage the office, Lincoln spent most of his time at home. When out-of-state luminaries like Thurlow Weed, Salmon P. Chase, and Horace Greeley made their pilgrimage to Springfield, Lincoln went to their hotels to meet them.[62] Regardless of his location, office-seekers and their friends persisted in seeing him. Henry Villard has left a description of their unrelenting efforts to secure Lincoln's ear. The "visiting bores," this *New York Herald* correspondent reported, "will first endeavor to hunt him up and besiege him in his downtown office. If unsuccessful there, they will call at his private residence, and, if admission to the Presidential presence be denied to them upon the first application they never fail to make a second, third, etc., one, until their wishes are gratified by the object of their obtrusiveness." Villard wrote that these men were "hardly ever satisfied with the privilege of one interview. They either exact an invitation to call again by conversational tactics or persuade Mr. Lincoln to return their call at their hotels, where once got hold of, he is seldom able to cut himself loose without the loss of several hours' time." While faulting the "irrepressible impudence" of the visitors, Villard also blamed "Mr. Lincoln's inexhaustible good naturedness" for the charade.

Villard reported that the president-elect, as his time in Springfield grew to a close, found several "secret haunts" to escape the visiting bores. One place was the studio of the Cincinnati sculptor Thomas D. Jones, where he went "for sittings, but [also] to open and read his morning mail." Another "sanctum" was the *Springfield Illinois State Journal* office where he spent many quiet hours.[63] However, it was in "a dingy, dusty, and neglected back room" of Clark M. Smith's store on the Springfield square where, with complete privacy in late January, Lincoln wrote the first draft of his inaugural address and pondered what he wanted to say to the crowds en route to Washington. He had the *Illinois State Journal* office secretly print a few copies of the inaugural draft. After revising it, Lincoln again had it printed. When he reached Washington, he gave William H. Seward a copy to critique. He showed another copy to Orville H. Browning in Indianapolis. Both Seward and Browning made important suggestions to the address, which Lincoln accepted.[64]

On January 30, Lincoln slipped away to Coles County for an emotional visit to see his stepmother and other relatives, arriving late in the day at Charleston on a freight train. Accompanied by his cousin John Hanks, he spent the next day with his "Mother," visited the unmarked grave of his father, and arranged for a proper stone to be placed at the site. He also held a public reception at Charleston, where he shook hands and spoke briefly to old friends. Returning to Springfield the next day, Lincoln appeared to Nicolay's assistant, John Hay, "much refreshed" and with "renewed vigor" for his departure to the East on February 11.[65]

On the evening of February 6, the Lincolns held a farewell reception at their home. Two days earlier, he had placed an announcement in a local newspaper inviting "friends" to the reception. Villard described it "as the most brilliant affair of the kind witnessed here in many years. Hundreds of well-dressed ladies and gentlemen," including Democrats like Anna Ridgely and her family, "gathered at the Presidential mansion to spend a last evening with their honored hosts. . . . Every room both on the first and second floor was densely packed with a fashionable multitude."[66]

On February 8, after disposing of their household furnishings and renting their home, the Lincolns moved into the Chenery House in downtown Springfield. Villard noticed that as the day approached for the departure, Lincoln took on "a more sober, solemn expression than heretofore." Villard reported that "a certain sadness pervades his conversation and restrains the wonted outbursts of humor. . . . He loves to dwell on the cherished past in preference to the contemplation of the uncertain future."[67]

On Sunday, February 10, his last day in Springfield, Lincoln spent most of the time with close associates. He also had one important out-of-state visitor, Carl Schurz, whom he introduced to his friends as "the great German orator." Later, as Schurz prepared to leave, Lincoln locked the door of his room and read the draft of his inaugural address to him. Schurz wrote his wife that "after we had discussed it point by point," Lincoln turned to him and said: "Now you know better than any man in this country how I stand, and you may be sure that I shall never betray my principles and my friends."[68] Schurz apparently did not suggest any changes to the address.

That afternoon, Lincoln visited Herndon at the law office to discuss with his junior partner "some legal matters in which he still felt some interest." Herndon recalled that, after disposing of this business, Lincoln "threw himself on the old office sofa" and, with his face toward the ceiling, remained in deep thought for a few moments. Finally, he began to talk, reminiscing about their relationship and his life on the judicial circuit. When Lincoln started to leave, he turned to his partner of sixteen years and directed "Billy" not to take down their law-office shingle at the foot of the stairs. "Give our clients to understand," Herndon remembered Lincoln saying, "that the election of a President makes no change in the firm of Lincoln and Herndon. If I live I'm coming back some time, and then we'll go right on practicing law as if nothing had ever happened."[69] That evening at the Chenery House, Lincoln roped the family trunks and on a card wrote the delivery address: "A. LINCOLN, EXECUTIVE MANSION, WASHINGTON."[70]

Early the next morning, Lincoln took a carriage to the Great Western Railroad depot to begin a twelve-day, circuitous trip to the national capital. Mary and the younger boys planned to join the train en route. Waiting at the station to go with Lincoln were several close associates, including Browning, who would leave the entourage at Indianapolis; Norman B. Judd; Ward H. Lamon, a lawyer and a friend of Lincoln's; Richard Yates, the recently inaugurated Republican governor, who only went part of the way; two railroad officials; Lincoln's secretary, John G. Nicolay; Nicolay's assistant, John Hay, who covered the trip for the *New York World;* several other newspaper correspondents, including Henry Villard of the *New York Herald;* and three military aides—Major David Hunter, Captain John Pope, and Captain George W. Hazzard. A fourth officer, Colonel Edwin V. Sumner, along with Judge David Davis, boarded the train at Indianapolis. Hunter, Pope, and Sumner became major generals during the Civil War.[71]

A special train, consisting of the engine, three coaches, and a baggage car, had been arranged to take Lincoln and his party along eighteen railroad lines to Washington. Hundreds of local citizens, including Democrats, braved the cold, rainy weather to say goodbye to the friend who had been placed in the most critical position in the history of the republic. Lincoln stood bareheaded in the rain on the rear platform and made a few emotional, extemporaneous remarks to the crowd.

His impromptu "Farewell Address," of which there are three versions, has become an important part of Lincoln lore. As the train moved out of Springfield, Lincoln attempted to write down the remarks he had just made; part way through, he decided to dictate the remainder to Nicolay. According to this first written version, which is probably the most accurate one, he said: "My friends—No one, not in my situation, can appreciate my feeling of sadness at this parting. To this place, and the kindness of these people, I owe every thing. Here I have lived a quarter of a century, and have passed from a young to an old man. Here my children have been born, and one is buried. I now leave, not knowing when, or whether ever, I may return, with a task before me greater than that which rested upon Washington. Without the assistance of that Divine Being, who ever attended him, I cannot succeed. With that assistance I cannot fail. Trusting in Him, who can go with me, and remain with you and be every where for good, let us confidently hope that all will yet be well. To His care commending you, as I hope in your prayers you will commend me, I bid you an affectionate farewell."[72]

Lincoln was so filled with emotion that he could hardly finish his remarks. The editor of the *Springfield Illinois State Journal* reported the next day: "We have known Mr. Lincoln for many years; we have heard him speak upon a hundred different occasions; but we never saw him so profoundly affected, nor did he ever utter an address which seemed to us so full of simple and touching eloquence." Another old friend wrote, "Many eyes in the crowd were filled to overflowing."[73]

Like never before, Lincoln in his brief Farewell Address spoke to the people of their common dependence on the "Divine Being" for strength to overcome the problems that faced the nation. This religious affirmation was not merely a tactic on his part to gain public sympathy and support. Because of the ethnic diversity of the state and the use of religion against him in the 1846 congressional election, Lincoln had not appealed to the religious sentiments of voters in his political rise during the 1850s. However, with pressure mounting on him as he prepared to assume the leadership of a troubled country in three weeks, Lincoln seemed genuinely to believe that he needed God's blessing and assistance in order to succeed and save the republic of the Founding Fathers. Lincoln's spirituality and his search to know the will of the "Almighty" became even greater during the war, particularly after the battle of Gettysburg and culminating in his powerful second inaugural address on March 4, 1865.[74]

As the train pulled out from Springfield on February 11, 1861, to take Lincoln to Washington, the eyes of the nation were fixed on him. The border-state congressmen and the Peace Conference in Washington were still trying to put together a plan that would lure the lower South back into the Union— or at least save the upper southern states—and hopefully remove the threat of civil war. Realistically, however, the issue was no longer a sectional compromise, if it ever was possible. The question was, would or could Lincoln and the Republicans, when they assumed power in March, enforce federal laws and protect federal property in the South, including installations and forts, and restore the seceded states to the Union? When Lincoln began his trip to Washington, he had not decided what he planned to do about the "disaffected" South, though clearly he did not recognize the legitimacy of secession and assuredly would take a firmer stand than his predecessor against the secessionists. Lincoln soon found that the massive receptions and encouragement he received along the route would strengthen him in his determination to maintain the whole Union, even at the risk of civil war.

CHAPTER ELEVEN

TRAIN TO WASHINGTON

ALL ALONG the train route to Washington, crowds of men, women, and children turned out to catch a glimpse or shake the hand of the man who held the destiny of the country in his hands and to hear him speak. The *New York Times* reported that the nation expected the president-elect's departure for Washington "a fit occasion for breaking the silence he has hitherto so resolutely maintained on the state of public affairs. He is no longer simply a private citizen, but is on his way to an assumption of duties and responsibilities more grave and momentous than have ever before devolved upon any of his predecessors."[1]

The purpose of the circuitous twelve-day journey across the western heartland and into the mid-Atlantic states, however, was not to disclose a specific policy toward the seceded states; it was to reveal Lincoln to the citizenry and urge national unity under his leadership. The route chosen, evidently by Lincoln in consultation with railroad officials, would take the president-elect, by invitation of the legislatures, to the capitals of the lower northern states (Indianapolis, Columbus, Albany, Trenton, and Harrisburg) and to major centers in these states (Cincinnati, Cleveland, Pittsburgh, Buffalo, New York City, and Philadelphia). In the selection of the itinerary, some consideration also was given to communities that had extended invitations for Lincoln to visit en route to Washington.[2] Because of time limitations and geographic inconvenience, Lincoln omitted New England from the itinerary.

BEFORE LEAVING SPRINGFIELD, Lincoln had told all within hearing distance that he did not recognize secession. John G. Nicolay reported him as saying: "The right of a state to secede is not an open or debatable question. It was fully discussed in [President] Jackson's time, and denied not only by him, but also by a vote." He was referring to the congressional action that took place when South Carolina threatened to leave the Union over the tariff of 1828. Lincoln, however, did not indicate what action he would take as president if the seceded states defied his authority, except to say, as he informed Nicolay, that "it is the duty of a President to execute the laws, and maintain the existing government."[3]

By February 11, when Lincoln began his journey toward Washington, the flash point in the secession crisis clearly had become the control of the federal forts and properties in the South. Lincoln sanguinely hoped that his pursuit of a firm though patient policy toward the seceded states would prevent a clash over these possessions. At the same time, he remained closemouthed on the broader question of using military force to restore the states to the Union. However, according to journalist Henry Villard, the president-elect remarked to several visitors in November that "no coercion will be used in case of secession, unless by special act of Congress," which seemed unlikely.[4]

South Carolina's secession on December 20 immediately raised Lincoln's ire. The next day, he sent a confidential message to General Winfield Scott informing him "to be as well prepared as he can to either hold, or retake, the forts, as the case may require, at, and after the inauguration [sic]."[5] A few days later, when reports reached Springfield that President Buchanan would surrender Forts Moultrie and Sumter in Charleston harbor, Lincoln angrily wrote Senator Trumbull, "I can scarcely believe this; but if it prove true, I will, if our friends at Washington concur, announce publicly at once that they are to be retaken after the inauguration [sic]. This will give the Union men a rallying cry."[6]

Actually, the War Department had only given Major Robert Anderson, commander of the forts, permission to transfer his troops from Fort Moultrie to Fort Sumter. The Buchanan administration reasoned that Sumter, which was surrounded by water, occupied a more defensible position in case of an expected assault by South Carolinians. Republicans in Congress soon dropped their objection when they learned that the move to Fort Sumter was an effort to reinforce federal authority in Charleston harbor.[7] President Buchanan immediately followed this action with the appointment of Joseph Holt, a Kentuckian who firmly opposed the surrender of Fort Sumter and Fort Pickens in Pensacola harbor to the secessionists, as secretary of war.

Under the circumstances, Senator Trumbull advised Lincoln that "your true course I have no doubt is to remain quiet, & not loose [sic] your equanimity let what will happen."[8] Naturally cautious anyway, Lincoln backed off of his threat to issue a declaration to sustain the Charleston forts. He wanted to wait until he arrived in Washington and consulted with Republican and military leaders before deciding on a course of action. In a January 14 note to the venerable General John E. Wool, who had written him giving his views on the crisis, Lincoln admitted that he was unclear what role the military should play in maintaining the Union. He told Wool, who commanded the Department of the East: "As to how far the military force of the government may become necessary to the preservation of the Union; and, more particularly, how that force can be directed to the object, I must rely chiefly upon Gen. Scott and yourself."[9] However, Wool, who like Scott had served in the army since the War of 1812, did not become an important military adviser of the new president.

With policy making put on hold for the moment, the slow progress of the president-elect's train across the heartland in February gave thousands of people their only chance to see Abraham Lincoln, a moment that would become etched in many memories. Along the route, anxious citizens waved flags and handkerchiefs, cheered, and offered encouragement to Lincoln in his task to preserve the Union. Henry Villard, reporting for the *New York Herald,* said the road between Springfield and Indianapolis "was literally lined with male and female humanity" as the train carrying the Lincoln entourage chugged across the prairie. At numerous stops for the engine to receive water and fuel, hundreds gathered, clamoring "for a sight of Old Abe" and rendering "it impossible for him to leave their wishes ungratified."[10]

The president-elect's train arrived in Indianapolis late in the afternoon on the first day of the trip. There, Governor Oliver Morton and a thirty-four-gun salute welcomed Lincoln to the state capital. Placed in an uncovered carriage drawn by four white horses, Lincoln received a large, colorful escort to the Bates House, where state legislators and public officials awaited him. He had insisted that his appearances, not only in Indianapolis but elsewhere as well, should be nonpartisan and reflect his theme of national unity in the crisis. In the street below, a crowd estimated at 50,000 or more demanded that Lincoln make a speech, which he did from the balcony of the Bates House. It was his first important speech en route to Washington, and it was also one that left him open to sharp criticism.

With the seceded states in mind, Lincoln sought to explain to his Bates House audience the meaning of coercion and invasion. He asked a series of questions intending to demonstrate that neither word would apply to these states if the federal government "simply insists upon holding its own forts, or retaking those forts which belong to it." The collection of duties upon foreign imports, he said, would also not apply. To Lincoln, such a policy would be a conservative approach to the sectional crisis and should be understood by all reasonable people. "Would any or all of these things be coercion?" Lincoln asked. If supporters of the Union say so, Lincoln argued, "the means for the preservation of the Union they so greatly love, in their own estimation, is of a very thin and airy character. . . . In their view, the Union, as a family relation, would not be anything like a regular marriage at all, but only as a sort of free-love arrangement—to be maintained on what that sect calls passionate attraction." This comparison provoked prolonged laughter from the crowd. However, given the gravity of the situation at hand, Lincoln's lighthearted metaphor left him vulnerable to serious criticism. Lincoln closed by declaring that he was "deciding nothing" on the matter of coercion, "but simply giving something for you to reflect upon" so that his audience could "decide for yourselves, if you choose, when you get ready."[11]

If Lincoln had designed his statement as a trial balloon on the issue of coercion, he soon received a response that disappointed him and prompted further reflection on his part. Republicans generally ignored or played down his disconcerting remarks at Indianapolis.[12] The opposition press in the North paid close attention to the speech, denouncing it as provocative and suggesting that he intended to make war on the seceded states. The *Cleveland Plain Dealer,* a leading Democratic newspaper, declared that the excitement surrounding his reception in Indianapolis so affected Lincoln that it "carried away all his reserve, waked the 'old war horse' in him and he made a regular stump speech, instead of delivering a diplomatic Presidential address."[13] The *New York Herald* lamented that Lincoln "will reclaim, by force of arms, all that have been lost before resorting to conciliation to secure the States in danger. Thus, in the very outset of his official journey to our federal capital, the President elect proclaims a line of policy adverse to union and to peace, and eminently adapted, not only to enlarge, strengthen and consolidate the new Southern republic, but to destroy the hopes and law and order of the North in a wasting civil war."[14]

The border-state press expressed a similar foreboding view of Lincoln's speech in the Indiana capital. The *Louisville Daily Courier* thundered that the speech was "a war proposition couched in language intended to conceal the enormity of the crime beneath pretexts too absurd to require exposure and fallacies too flimsy to deceive the most stupid." It meant "war without a declaration of war, waged under false pretenses, and justifiable only to that fanaticism of which Mr. Lincoln is at once the embodiment and representative," the *Courier* editor asserted.[15] The president-elect, according to the *St. Louis Daily Missouri Republican,* made clear that "the forts, arsenals, mint and custom-houses, in possession of the Seceding States must be *retaken,* and to do this the army must be called into requisition, as well as the navy, and so civil war begins—the North against the South, and the latter to be subjugated at all hazards."[16] Such criticism of the Indianapolis speech further reinforced southern suspicion of Lincoln's intentions, increased secessionist sentiment in the upper South, and created greater concern in the North.

Lincoln must have immediately grasped that his statements on coercion at Indianapolis were provocative. He had set out to promote unity while avoiding policy statements about the future as he moved toward Washington, and the speech had stirred only contention. After the Bates House speech, he ignored the issue of coercion until near the end of his trip, when he spoke to the New Jersey General Assembly on February 21. By that time, he had witnessed the hardening of northern attitudes toward the seceded states and the strengthening of support for the enforcement of the laws and the protection of federal installations in the South.

The day after his Bates House speech, which also was his fifty-second birthday, Lincoln and his retinue, which now included Mary, Willie, and Tad, left Indianapolis for Cincinnati, the largest city in the West. Arriving in the afternoon, "Old Abe" received an enthusiastic welcome from a crowd of perhaps as many as 150,000.[17] On the balcony of the Burnet House, where he was staying, Lincoln delivered a brief but stirring speech. He appealed to the people, regardless of political party loyalties, for their unqualified support of the Union, the Constitution, and its free institutions. Expressing pleasure that "all parties were united" in welcoming him, and that such unity "should ever be" the case "when any citizen of the United States is constitutionally elected President," he declared: "Although we have some threatening National difficulties now—I hope that while these free institutions shall continue to be in the enjoyment of millions of free people of the United States, we will see repeated every four years what we now witness" in Cincinnati. He admonished Ohioans to extend to their "fellow citizens" across the river in slaveholding Kentucky and throughout the South "a cordial good will when our present differences shall have been forgotten and blown to the winds forever." Repeating what he had said in his 1859 speech in Cincinnati, Lincoln told Kentuckians in the audience, "We mean to leave you alone, and in no way to interfere with your institutions." "There is no difference between us, other than the difference of circumstances," he added. Otherwise, he ignored the division over slavery. Lincoln had intended to cross the Ohio for a brief visit to Kentucky to give a speech, but probably because of security concerns, he did not go. He closed his Cincinnati address by appealing to "the good sense of the American people, on all sides of all rivers in America, under the Providence of God, who has never deserted us, [to] again be brethren, forgetting all parties."[18]

The following day, February 13, Lincoln went on to Columbus, making brief stops along the route to make short speeches. In Columbus, a crowd that far exceeded the town's population of about 20,000 welcomed the president-elect. Lincoln made two speeches at the state capitol, one inside to the legislature and the other on the steps of the building. In a more formal, though unwritten address to the Ohio lawmakers, he noted the criticism as well as the "credit" that had followed from his decision to maintain silence regarding his southern policy. Lincoln explained that "in the varying and repeatedly shifting scenes of the present, and without a precedent which could enable me to judge by the past, it has seemed fitting that before speaking upon the difficulties of the country, I should have gained a view of the whole field." Such a delay, he insisted, would leave him "at liberty to modify and change the course of policy, as future events may make a change necessary." Lincoln continued: "I have not maintained silence from any want of real anxiety. There is a good thing that there is no more than anxiety, for there is nothing going wrong. . . . There is nothing that really hurts anybody. We entertain different views upon political questions, but nobody is suffering anything. This is a most consoling circumstance, and from it we may conclude that all we want is time, patience and a reliance on God" to set things right again.[19]

Lincoln's statement that "nothing is going wrong" appeared designed to reduce public fears about the inevitability of disunion and civil war. The comment, however, created dismay in some northern circles and throughout the border states. The *New York Herald* told its thousands of readers that the president-elect "betrays at Columbus a most lamentable degree of ignorance touching the revolutionary evils of the day. . . . 'Nothing going wrong'? Why, sir, we may more truly say there is nothing going right."[20] Edward Everett, New England's most prominent conservative and the vice-presidential candidate for the Constitutional Union party in 1860, wrote a damning indictment of Lincoln after reading his remarks in Indiana and Ohio: "The President-elect," he confided to his diary, "is making a zigzag progress to Washington, called out to make short speeches at every important point. These speeches thus far have been of the most ordinary kind, destitute of everything, not merely of felicity and grace, but of common pertinence. He is evidently a person of very inferior cast of character, wholly unequal to the crisis."[21] Later, on that memorable day at Gettysburg, November 19, 1863, Everett shared the platform with Lincoln, and the following year he served as one of his electors in Massachusetts.

Lincoln's speech at Columbus caused some Republicans who had withheld judgment on his provocative remarks at Indianapolis to wonder if he might be out of touch with reality. Congressman Charles Francis Adams, the Massachusetts Brahmin whom Lincoln would soon appoint minister to Britain, recorded dismissively in his diary that the president-elect's speeches "betray a person unconscious of his position as well as the nature of the contest around him."[22]

EARLY THE NEXT MORNING, February 14, Lincoln's train rolled out of Columbus and toward Pittsburgh, stopping at numerous small towns on the way where he made brief remarks to the crowds that were waiting. Villard reported that "the journey of the President-elect" had become "a march of triumph."[23] At Xenia, Ohio, people jumped on top of the train, stormed the platform of Lincoln's car, and attempted to force the doors in an effort to meet "Old Abe." The mob devoured the food prepared by the Xenia welcoming committee before the president-elect and his party had an opportunity to eat. As usual, Lincoln took things in stride, responding to the bedlam with his usual wit.[24]

Suffering from a cold and exposed to winter weather at the many stops en route, Lincoln could barely speak when the train pulled into Pittsburgh late on the night of the fourteenth. Arriving in the rain, John G. Nicolay wrote Therena Bates, his fiancée, "We hardly expected to find a soul at the depot. It was a vain illusion. The depot and grounds were literally jammed full of people. We finally got Mr. Lincoln into a carriage; but . . . it looked for a while as if we would never get the carriage out of the crowd that was pushing and pulling and yelling all around us." Nicolay later wrote that in the "absolutely uncontrollable mele [*sic*] of moving wheels and hoofs, of noise and shouting," Lincoln's "immediate friends clustered about him to render all possible assistance, under the gravest apprehension of his safety" and of their own. Shaken by the mob scene at Pittsburgh, Nicolay lamented to his future wife that "it has been a serious task for us of his escort, to prevent his being killed with kindness. The expression may be anomalous, but it is nevertheless literally true."[25]

The next morning, from the balcony of Pittsburgh's Monongahela House, Lincoln spoke to a large gathering. He repeated what he had said at Columbus about the reason for remaining silent on his southern policy before the inauguration but admitted that "the condition of the country [was] an extraordinary one, and fills the mind of every patriot with anxiety and solicitude."[26] Having just said this, Lincoln then declared, "There is really no crisis except an *artificial one*!" He contended that the crisis was "such a one as may be gotten up at any time by designing politicians." He maintained that "if the great American people will only keep their temper, on both sides of the line, the troubles will come to an end, and the question which now distracts the country will be settled just as surely as all other difficulties of like character" in the past.[27] At Pittsburgh as well as elsewhere, Lincoln was trying to reduce sectional conflict until he had an opportunity to take office and demonstrate his peaceful intentions, reassurances that he hoped "disaffected" southerners would accept. But his remarks drew severe criticism, particularly the use of the word "artificial" to describe the crisis. His language added to the opinion of many people that Lincoln was naïve and did not understand the nature of the crisis or what should be done to save the Union.

Lincoln also raised, for the only time during his journey, an economic issue. Speaking where pro-tariff sentiment had contributed to his victory in Pennsylvania, the president-elect affirmed his support for the ambiguous tariff plank in the Republican platform. He confessed that he did not "understand this subject in all its multiform bearings" but added, "I promise you that I will give it my closest attention, and endeavor to comprehend it more fully." He said that any consideration of tariff policy should take into account "all the varied interests of our common country, so that when the time for action arrives adequate protection can be extended to the coal and iron of Pennsylvania, the corn of Illinois, and the 'reapers of Chicago.'" Tariff legislation, Lincoln suggested, was a matter for Congress, not the president, to decide. He alluded to the fact that the Morrill tariff bill, which would raise import duties, was pending in Congress.[28]

Significantly, in view of the Republicans' antislavery principles, Lincoln avoided at Pittsburgh and elsewhere on his trip to Washington his party's moral and political opposition to the "peculiar institution" of slavery, even in the territories. This avoidance was hardly surprising, because a large minority of Douglas Democrats and John Bell conservatives in the North and in the border states, as well as the overwhelming majority of white southerners, blamed Lincoln and his party's antislavery agitation for the secession crisis and the threat of civil war. Lincoln needed the support of northern and border-state Democrats and conservatives if he was to succeed in keeping the Union intact. He did not want to stir passions over the slavery issue and thereby defeat the unifying purpose of his appearances en route to Washington. However, Lincoln boldly announced to an audience in the hotbed of antislavery sentiment in the Western Reserve area of northern Ohio that his government would continue to enforce the Fugitive Slave Act.[29]

From Pittsburgh on February 15, the president-elect's train meandered through bitter winter conditions to Cleveland. The train was met outside of Cleveland by "myriads of human beings" waiting in a snowstorm to escort Lincoln into the city. To the deafening shouts of tens of thousands, according to Villard, "Honest Old Abe" stood in an open carriage and bowed and waved his hat to the crowds as the procession moved into Cleveland. At the end of the trek, Lincoln, speaking with a weak voice, briefly addressed the crowd, commending them for marching through the "snow, rain and deep mud" with him for what turned out to be a couple of miles. Their fortitude under the circumstances, he declared, was about something far greater than him personally. "You have assembled," he told them, "to testify your respect to the Union, the constitution and the laws." Lincoln then made a rhetorical point, perhaps predictable, that he would repeat almost everywhere he spoke: "And here let me say that it is with you, the people, to advance the great cause of the Union and the constitution, and not with any one man." With the support of communities like Cleveland, he said, "I am convinced that the cause of liberty and the Union can never be in danger."[30]

At nine o'clock the next morning, February 16, Lincoln's entourage left Cleveland and moved eastward toward Buffalo along Lake Erie. At each stop, the president-elect told the crowd that he had virtually lost his voice and could not make a speech. At Westfield, New York, near the Ohio border, he asked if Grace Bedell, the girl who had written him in October suggesting that he grow whiskers, was in the crowd. When she was identified in the audience, Lincoln left the train, went over to Grace, and "gave her several hearty kisses . . . amid the yells of delight from the excited crowd."[31]

At Dunkirk, New York, where 12,000 to 15,000 people had gathered, Lincoln spoke from "a platform around a flag staff, covered with velvet carpet."[32] Stepping forward, he grasped the staff from which the flag waved and exclaimed: "I stand by the flag of the Union, and all I ask of you is that you stand by me as long as I stand by it." Whereupon, "countless cheers rang out," and inside the cars, as the train moved away, "the company evinced a general disposition to intone hurrahs and sing patriotic songs out of tune."[33]

Prominent Republicans frequently joined the entourage when it traveled through their area. At Girard, Ohio, Horace Greeley, wrapped in his famous red and blue blanket, created a sensation when he unexpectedly appeared in the cars. The eccentric New York editor explained that he had mistaken the special for the general train, a circumstance, given Greeley's peculiarities, that might have been true, but nonetheless would have been highly unlikely. After a cordial, 20-mile ride with Lincoln, Greeley left the train at Erie, Pennsylvania.[34]

An estimated 75,000 people greeted Lincoln's arrival at Buffalo, including former President Millard Fillmore, who had opposed his election and would do so again in 1864. A chaotic scene occurred at the station. Thousands of men, John Hay reported, "endeavored to force an entrance to the depot, which was already packed to its utmost capacity. The President himself narrowly escaped unpleasant personal contact with the crowd." Major David Hunter and others suffered minor injuries in the melee. Nicolay later wrote that he "never saw anything to compare with the fearful rush of this crowd after the President as he was leaving the depot. It was awful." Finally, the local militia cleared a path to the carriages, though barely, for Lincoln, Fillmore, and other dignitaries. Along the route to the hotel, "the streets were densely thronged, the cheers unremitting, the stars and stripes waved everywhere."[35] Upon arriving at the hotel, Lincoln spoke briefly to the crowd in the street, repeating his call for "the devotion of the whole people to the Constitution, the Union, and the perpetuity of the liberties of this country."[36]

Leaving Buffalo on February 18, the "presidential train" moved eastward along the New York Central line. It stopped at Batavia, Rochester, Syracuse, Schenectady, and other towns where Lincoln spoke briefly to thousands of people from the platform of the train.[37] In turn, the crowds offered encouragement for him to stand by the union of all the states. Arriving in Albany in mid-afternoon, the president-elect encountered another wild scene that kept him in his car until a militia company cleared a path for him and his party. On the ride downtown to the state capitol, he stood upright in his carriage, "bowing and swaying like a tall cedar in a storm" as he acknowledged the shouts and cheers of the people.[38]

At the capitol, Lincoln, accompanied by Governor Edwin D. Morgan, addressed a joint session of the New York legislature. Repeating points he had made throughout the trip, he emphasized the necessity for a nonpartisan acceptance of the election results in November and the importance of supporting the preservation of the whole Union. "You have invited and received me without distinction of party," he said. "I cannot for a moment suppose that this has been done in any considerable degree with reference to my personal services, but that it is done in so far as I am regarded at this time as the representative of the majesty of this great nation." He continued: "[While] I hold myself without mock modesty, the humblest of all individuals that have ever been elevated to the Presidency, I have a more difficult task to perform than any one of them." Lincoln once again explained why he could not "speak at this time of the policy of the Government." "In the meantime," he said, "if we have patience; if we restrain ourselves; if we allow ourselves not to run off in a passion, I still have confidence that the Almighty, the Maker of the Universe, will, through the instrumentality of this great and intelligent people, bring us through this as He has through all the other difficulties of our country."[39]

After spending the night in Albany, Lincoln and his retinue left early on the morning of February 19 for New York City. There a large crowd of New Yorkers greeted the president-elect and his family at the station on Thirteenth Street, though, according to the *New York Herald,* with "none of those spontaneous outbursts of enthusiasm for which our people are noted."[40] Horace Greeley's *New York Tribune* saw it differently. "We but reflect the popular opinion," the *Tribune* reported, "when we say that the ovation was one of the grandest, and most soul-stirring we have ever witnessed." The crowds, this Republican newspaper intoned, showed "their implicit confidence in the coming man."[41] The city had voted overwhelmingly against Lincoln in November, and many of the people gathered at the station and watching from the streets and buildings did so simply out of curiosity to see the "Rail Splitter." New York City, unlike Buffalo and Albany, provided excellent police protection for Lincoln, however. Nicolay reported: "Broadway had been kept clear, so that the double line of carriages which made up the procession moved from the depot . . . to the Astor House," where Lincoln was staying, "in perfect order and with plenty of room." The preparations gave "the people, who crowded the side streets, doors, balconies, windows, and lined even the roofs of buildings with a continuous fringe of humanity, a clear view of the President-elect."[42]

At the Astor House immediately after his arrival, Lincoln began the obligatory ritual of receiving Republican delegations and public officials. When asked to make a speech in the hotel, Lincoln reminded the group that he had been "occupying a position, since the Presidential election, of silence, of avoiding public speaking, of avoiding public writing." He assured them that he had not kept silent "from any party wantonness, or from any indifference to the anxiety that pervades the minds of men about the aspect of the political affairs of this country. I have kept silence for the reason that I supposed it was peculiarly proper that I should do so until the time came when, according to the customs of the country, I should speak officially."[43]

The next day, February 20, Lincoln ate breakfast at the home of prominent New Yorker Moses Grinnell on Fifth Avenue. Members of the city's elite and state Republican luminaries like Thurlow Weed also attended. At eleven o'clock, Lincoln went to the City Hall for a ceremony officially welcoming him to New York. There, Mayor Fernando Wood, a vitriolic Democratic foe of the Republicans, gave an opening speech. In January, the mayor had proposed that the city sever its bonds with the state and become a free city because, he contended, "a dissolution of the Federal Union is inevitable" and to remain in it would wreak havoc upon New York's interests.[44] In welcoming Lincoln to the city, the mayor told the president-elect that he was "coming into office with a dismembered government to reconstruct and a disconnected and hostile people to reconcile." Wood cited New York as a particular case in point. "The present political divisions have solely afflicted her people," he said. "All her material interests are paralyzed. Her commercial greatness is endangered. . . . We fear that if the Union dies the present supremacy of New-York may perish with it." Wood informed Lincoln that New Yorkers looked to him "for a restoration of fraternal relations between the States—only to be accomplished by peaceful and conciliatory means."[45]

In his reply to Wood, Lincoln did not challenge the mayor's foreboding statement. Instead, he assured New Yorkers that "there is nothing that can ever bring me willingly to consent to the destruction of this Union, under which not only the commercial city of New York, but the whole country has acquired its greatness."[46] The purpose of such rhetoric was to rally support for his presidential leadership and to underscore his recognition of New

York's economic importance to the Union. The tremendous receptions that he received in New York and elsewhere, despite the warnings of Mayor Wood and Democratic newspapers, reinforced Lincoln's determination to pursue a hard-line policy against secession. Still, he understood that the support of Wood and other Democrats would crumble if the costs of preserving the Union became too high.

A public reception for the president-elect followed the ceremony at City Hall. For almost two hours a steady stream of people, estimated at 5,000, passed by Lincoln to receive "a hearty shake" of the hand in the popular western style. In the evening, while Mary hosted a reception of her own at the Astor House, Lincoln, accompanied by Judge David Davis and New York Alderman Charles G. Cornell, went to the Academy of Music to attend the opera *The Masked Ball*. Entering while the first act was in progress, Lincoln went unnoticed. But during the intermission, the audience discovered his presence and applauded him wildly. Though the audience wanted Lincoln to speak, he only bowed and listened while the building rang with patriotic songs. Lincoln and his friends, pleased with the reception but not with the opera, left after the second act.[47]

EARLY THE NEXT MORNING, Lincoln and his party boarded the ferry for New Jersey. They made brief stops in Jersey City, Newark, and other towns en route to Trenton. Arriving in Trenton at noon, Lincoln delivered two addresses, one to the state Senate and the other to the state's lower house, the General Assembly. In the Senate, he reflected on the struggles of the Revolution "for the liberties of the country." Lincoln recalled reading about the Revolutionary War as a child in Mason Locke ("Parson") Weems's *Life of George Washington*. None of the battles, he said, "fixed themselves upon my imagination so deeply as the struggle here at Trenton," where the Continental Army had achieved a stunning and badly needed victory over the British on December 26, 1776. He told the New Jersey state senators that the Revolution meant "something even more than National Independence." "That something," he declared, "held out a great promise to all people of the world to all time to come; I am exceedingly anxious that this Union, the Constitution, and the liberties of the people shall be perpetuated in accordance with the original idea for which that struggle was made, and I shall be most happy indeed if I shall be an humble instrument in the hands of the Almighty, and of this, his almost chosen people, for perpetuating the object of the great struggle."[48] In this passage, Lincoln came close to expressing the popular nineteenth-century idea of American exceptionalism as a God-given right. In a calculated effort to inspire support for the Union cause during the uncertain period ahead, Lincoln also appealed to his contemporaries' memory of the Revolutionary patriots and the higher principles for which they stood.

In his second address, the president-elect assured the members of the New Jersey General Assembly, most of whom were Democrats, that he would do everything in his power "to promote a peaceful settlement of all our difficulties." "The man does not live who is more devoted to peace than I am," he said, "but it may be necessary to put the foot down firmly" against the secessionists. At this point, the audience, according to the press report, "broke out into cheers so loud and long that for some moments it was impossible to hear Mr. L.'s voice." The response prompted Lincoln to declare that, though a majority of the assemblymen opposed him "in political sentiments," he trusted that he would "have their assistance in piloting the ship of State through this voyage, surrounded by perils as it is; for, if it should suffer attack now, there will be no pilot ever needed for another voyage."[49] From the legislators' reaction to his remarks, Lincoln likely concluded that even in a northern state controlled by the Democratic party he had strong popular support for a policy to enforce the laws in the South, protect the federal installations, and maintain the whole Union.

Approximately 100,000 people turned out to greet his arrival in Philadelphia later in the day. The next morning, February 22, the eleventh day of his grueling cross-country trip, Lincoln went to Independence Hall to participate in a flag raising to commemorate the admission of Kansas as a state. Before he went outside for the ceremony, he was asked to make a speech in the hall. Though "wholly unprepared," he professed, and "filled with deep emotion," he agreed to do so. Lincoln's comments on this occasion became a minor classic in Lincoln lore. "All the political sentiments I entertain," he began, "have been drawn . . . from the sentiments which originated, and were given to the world from this hall in which we stand. I have never had a feeling politically that did not spring from the sentiments embodied in the Declaration of Independence." Lincoln's history, however, suggests that the Constitution had been of a comparable influence on his political thinking and action. In a passage that has had a lasting significance, Lincoln declared at Philadelphia, "I have often inquired of myself, what principle or idea it was that kept this Confederacy so long together. It was not the mere matter of the separation of the colonies from the mother land; but something in that Declaration giving liberty, not alone to the people of this country, but hope to the world for all future time. It was that which gave promise that in due time the weights should be lifted from the shoulders of all men, and that *all* should have an equal chance." Lincoln affirmed that, "if this country cannot be saved without giving up that principle—I was about to say I would rather be assassinated on this spot than to surrender it."[50]

Then, in another frequently quoted passage from his Independence Hall speech, the president-elect announced, "There is no need of bloodshed and war, . . . and there will be no blood shed [sic] unless it be forced upon the Government." He assured his audience that "the Government will not use force unless force is used against it," a remark that produced prolonged applause and cries of "that's the proper sentiment."[51]

After the flag-raising ceremony, Lincoln and his party left for Harrisburg, where he was scheduled to speak that afternoon to the Pennsylvania General Assembly. Lincoln found the greetings of the people along the route and into the state capital, unlike elsewhere, noticeably restrained. The receptions, John Hay wrote, "seemed more the result of curiosity than enthusiasm. Even at Harrisburg, not one man in a hundred cheered. The crowds everywhere were uniformly rough, unruly, and ill bred. Mr. Lincoln was so unwell he could hardly be persuaded to show himself."[52] Except in Lancaster County, Republican congressman Thaddeus Stevens's home, the people in this area, near the Mason-Dixon Line, held strong Democratic sentiments, and they dreaded the consequences of Lincoln's no-compromise policy toward the South.[53] Speaking briefly at Lancaster, Lincoln gave a new reason, at least publicly, for remaining silent on his southern policy. "It is well known," he said, "that the more a man speaks the less he is understood—the more he says one thing, his adversaries contend he meant something else." Lincoln, as before, promised soon "to speak officially, and then I will endeavor to put my thoughts just as plain as I can express myself."[54]

As he inched closer to Washington and the inauguration, Lincoln's public remarks focused on the question of force to preserve the Union. In Trenton, Lincoln had announced that it might be necessary to put his "foot down firmly" against the seceded states. In Philadelphia, he had declared that there would be no bloodshed unless forced upon the government. But his statement at Trenton suggested that Lincoln was prepared to take the risk of an armed confrontation in order to enforce the laws and protect the federal installations in the South. It is reasonable to conclude, however, that he did not expect such a confrontation to result in a civil war, as Democrats and border-state men predicted.

At Harrisburg, Lincoln denied that he would be the aggressor if he found it necessary to use force to save the Union. The president-elect noted the presence of state military units lined up to welcome him to the Pennsylvania capital and expressed "the hope that in the shedding of blood their services may never be needed, especially in the shedding of fraternal blood." Lincoln announced that "it shall be my endeavor to preserve the peace of this country so far as it can possibly be done, consistently with the maintenance of the institutions of the country." In his address to the state General Assembly,

Lincoln recurred to this theme for the purpose of preventing any misunderstanding about his position. "It is not with any pleasure," he told the Pennsylvania legislators, "that I contemplate the possibility that a necessity may arise in this country for the use of the military arm." Though "exceedingly gratified to see the manifestation upon your streets of your military force" and the promise "to use that force upon a proper emergency, . . . I do most sincerely hope that we shall have no use for them." Lincoln promised that "if so painful a result shall in any wise be brought about, it shall be through no fault of mine." Lincoln thus projected responsibility for any future military action upon the recently seceded states. Loud applause and cheers in the chamber greeted his remarks.[55]

After addressing the Pennsylvania legislature, Lincoln, according to John Hay, was "completely exhausted [and] retired at 8 o'clock."[56] The president-elect, however, did not remain in his room. Secretly, under cover of darkness and with one companion, a heavily armed Ward Hill Lamon, he slipped out of Harrisburg and returned to Philadelphia for a midnight train ride to Baltimore. Lincoln had been told the previous day, when he was at the Continental Hotel in Philadelphia, of a plot to assassinate him in Baltimore, the last important stop on his journey to Washington. Even before Lincoln had left Springfield, army captain George W. Hazzard, who was familiar with the political turbulence in eastern Maryland, informed him that "the greatest risk your excellency will have to encounter on your way to the national capital will be in the city of Baltimore and on the road from that point to Washington." Baltimore lay along the most convenient train route to the capital and probably could not be avoided, Hazzard said. He recommended that Lincoln travel incognito through Baltimore on the night train from Philadelphia, then on to Washington before daylight. The captain suggested that he should be accompanied through the city by not more than five trusted friends.[57]

S. M. Felton, president of the Philadelphia, Wilmington, and Baltimore Railroad, also feared that an attempt might be made on Lincoln's life while he traveled on his line in Maryland. Felton earlier had hired Allan Pinkerton, head of a Chicago detective agency, to investigate plots by Maryland rowdies to sabotage the railroad's property. In the course of the investigation, Pinkerton and his men, working undercover, had discovered a conspiracy to kill the president-elect when he passed through Baltimore. The evening before the flag raising at Independence Hall, Pinkerton, accompanied by Felton, had informed Lincoln of the plot. Along with Norman Judd, they advised him to go immediately to Washington.

Pinkerton's story at first did not convince Lincoln of a serious plot; after all, he had received numerous threats against his life since the election and nothing had happened. But later that night, Frederick Seward, the senator's son, arrived in Philadelphia with independent intelligence from General Scott confirming that such a plot existed. He also brought a note from his father asking Lincoln "to reconsider your arrangement" to go through Baltimore.[58] Colonel Charles P. Stone, Scott's officer in charge of security in the Washington area, earlier had employed three New York detectives to investigate the activities of pro-secessionists in Baltimore. On the morning of February 21, while Lincoln was traveling south through New Jersey toward Philadelphia, the detectives had reported to Colonel Stone that "there is serious danger of violence to and the assassination of Mr Lincoln in his passage through that city should the time of passage be known." According to Stone, the detectives had heard "men declare that if Mr Lincoln was to be assassinated they would like to be the men." The colonel concluded that "the danger is one which the authorities & people in Baltimore cannot guard against." Stone, who had opposed Lincoln's election but nevertheless was determined to see him safely inaugurated, also recommended that the president-elect, along with a portion of his entourage, secretly take the night train through the city.[59]

Stone's report, conveyed through General Scott and in turn through Senator Seward and his son Frederick, convinced Lincoln that he and his party were in danger if they traveled openly through Baltimore. Judd told him that if he slipped incognito through the city, "the world will laugh at you," and you must be prepared "to meet the charge of cowardice. . . . But go you must." Lincoln agreed. He insisted, however, on meeting his "engagements" at Independence Hall in the morning and later at Harrisburg. "After these engagements are fulfilled," he informed Judd and Pinkerton, "you are at liberty to take such course as you please" in the matter.[60]

The next evening, after the ceremonies at Harrisburg, Judd and Lincoln met with David Davis and the military officers traveling with the party. When Judd revealed the plan for the night trip through Baltimore, Colonel Edwin V. Sumner, the senior officer, exploded. "That proceeding," Sumner exclaimed, "will be a d—d piece of cowardice"; he declared that he could organize a squad of cavalry "to cut our way to Washington." Davis turned to Lincoln and asked for his decision on the plan. The president-elect replied: "I have listened to this discussion with interest—I see no reason—no good reason to change the Programme" for the night trip through Baltimore. When Mary Lincoln was informed of the plan, she insisted that the burly Ward Hill Lamon accompany her husband rather than one of the military officers. The group agreed, and also that the others in Lincoln's retinue would come later.[61]

On a special train arranged by the superintendent of the Pennsylvania Central Railroad, Lincoln and Lamon left Harrisburg on the evening of February 22. Traveling incognito, Lincoln wore a shawl thrown loosely over his shoulders and a small black Kossuth hat that someone had given him in New York. The traditional account that he went carefully disguised in a long military cloak and a Scottish plaid cap was the invention of a newspaper correspondent for the *New York Times*. This story, in turn, was embellished in the telling by Lincoln's opponents and contributed to the ridicule hurled at him after his furtive midnight trip.[62]

Lincoln and Lamon arrived in Philadelphia too early to catch the eleven o'clock train to Baltimore at the depot. In order to avoid detection at the station, the party, now joined by Pinkerton, drove around the city in a carriage until it was time to enter the sleeping car for Baltimore. Occupying a berth ostensibly reserved for a "sick friend" of a railroad official, Lincoln had an uneventful, though sleepless, ride to the Maryland city. Arriving at the President Street station, Lincoln's car was tied to a team of horses for the required transfer to Camden Station. There, they had to wait in the dark for thirty minutes to take the Baltimore and Ohio train to Washington. Pinkerton recalled that, despite their anxiety, Lincoln, in a quiet voice to avoid notice, entertained the two men with "some jokes" while they waited.[63] When the Baltimore and Ohio train arrived from the west, Lincoln's car was coupled to it, and it chugged away toward Washington.

Dawn was breaking on February 23 when the train with the president-elect, along with Lamon and Pinkerton, arrived at the station on New Jersey Avenue and C Street in Washington. Only one person on the crowded platform recognized the distinguished traveler. Representative Elihu B. Washburne, who had been alerted by Frederick Seward of the president-elect's coming, was there to greet Lincoln. The congressman recalled that Lincoln "looked more like a well-to-do farmer from one of the back towns of Jo Davies's county [Illinois] than the President of the United States."[64] The men entered a carriage and quietly moved through the streets to Willard's Hotel, where Lincoln would stay until March 4. Seward, who had intended to meet the train but overslept, rushed to the hotel, where, with great relief, he greeted the next president.

LINCOLN'S MYSTERIOUS ARRIVAL created a sensation in Washington and elsewhere when the news went out over the telegraph wires. Though tired by his trip, Lincoln found that he had no time for rest. Seward took him under his wing and by the end of the morning had Lincoln at the White House to call upon President Buchanan, who was not aware that his successor had arrived in Washington. After a "pleasant interview," Buchanan escorted his visitor to another room, where the cabinet was meeting, and introduced him to each member. One of these men, Edwin M. Stanton, would later become Lincoln's secretary of war; another, Joseph Holt, would be appointed judge advocate general, an important post during the Civil War. After leaving the White House, Lincoln and Seward called upon General Scott at the War Department, but he was absent on official duties. When Scott returned, he immediately visited Lincoln at his hotel room, where he "expressed his great gratification at Mr. Lincoln's safe arrival." At four o'clock, the Illinois congressional delegation, including Senator Douglas, came to the hotel to pay their respects. Before the end of the day, Francis P. Blair, Sr., the old associate of Andrew Jackson, and his son Montgomery, who would become Lincoln's postmaster general, had also made an appearance.[65]

In the late afternoon or early evening, Mary and the boys arrived in Washington after a raucous but safe train trip through Baltimore. The tops and platforms of the cars, the *New York Tribune* reported, were "covered by a screaming, hooting, yelling crew, bent certainly upon insult and obstruction, probably upon violence" if Lincoln had been on board. "The spectacle, even as described in the Baltimore papers," the *Tribune* indicated, "tends very much to abate the condemnation which many were at first inclined to bestow upon Mr. Lincoln's advisers for changing his original programme."[66] In a book later ascribed to him but which he did not write, Ward Hill Lamon quoted Lincoln as saying, "You . . . know that the way we skulked into this city [Washington] . . . has been a source of shame and regret to me, for it did look so cowardly!" Congressman Washburne later gave a more reliable account of Lincoln's reaction to the night passage through Baltimore. He wrote: "I was the first man to see him after his arrival in Washington, . . . and I know he was neither 'mortified' nor 'chagrined' at the manner in which he reached Washington," as some people claimed. "He expressed to me in the warmest terms his satisfaction at the complete success of the journey," Washburne said. Washburne also insisted that "there can be no reasonable doubt" of a conspiracy in Baltimore to assassinate Lincoln.[67]

That evening, February 23, Lincoln ate dinner at the Sewards'. At nine o'clock he met with "old fossil" delegates to the Peace Conference, which included former President John Tyler and other prominent Virginians. When the delegates attempted to draw Lincoln out on his policy, he only repeated what he had said many times on the trip. As president he would preserve, protect, and defend the Constitution and laws made under it. One delegate, Daniel Moreau Barringer of North Carolina, Lincoln's desk-mate in Congress during the late 1840s, had a hopeful view of his old friend's intentions. The North Carolinian wrote his wife that Lincoln "does not know himself what his policies will be. But I think now it will be conciliatory &

for peace. This depends however upon the will of those into whose hands he may fall." Like many political observers, Barringer believed that Lincoln would not be his own man but would follow the lead of Seward and other powerful Republicans. The same evening, Lincoln's first day in Washington, members of Buchanan's cabinet returned his earlier call at the White House.[68] Thus ended Lincoln's long and eventful day; he had not slept since his stay at the Continental Hotel in Philadelphia two nights earlier.

Lincoln's circuitous twelve-day journey to Washington, except for its last day, had been a triumphal procession that a Roman emperor would have envied. It achieved Lincoln's purpose of rallying the northern people, including Democrats, to support a policy to enforce the laws and protect federal property in the seceded states. Lincoln wisely avoided announcing what specific measures he would take to preserve the government's authority in the South. Indeed, when Lincoln left Springfield, he did not know himself what he would do; he wanted to wait until he could evaluate the situation in Washington before determining a course of action. Statements of his specific intentions would have raised questions that Lincoln could not truthfully answer and would have created divisions undermining the unifying purpose of his trip and weakened confidence in his ability to lead. The outpouring of nonpartisan support that Lincoln received on his journey to the national capital reinforced his determination to stand firm against secession. At Harrisburg, he had painfully suggested that if peaceful efforts failed, he would use armed force to maintain "the institutions of the country" and federal laws in the South. Lincoln still assumed, as he indicated later in his July 4, 1861, message to Congress explaining his actions in the beginning of the war, that most southerners, except in South Carolina, were Unionists at heart.[69] When Lincoln arrived in Washington on February 23, he still wanted to believe that the application of force to preserve the Union presence in the seceded states would not trigger a civil war. The people in the South, including those in the border states, knew that he was grievously mistaken.

LINCOLN'S REMAINING DAYS before his inauguration were intense and filled with meetings, receptions, dinners, and visits from well-wishers and office-seekers. Lincoln told Henry Villard, who had come from New York for the inauguration, that the demands on him were "bad enough in Springfield, but it was child's play compared with this tussle here. I hardly had a chance to eat or sleep."[70] Lincoln turned down all demands for office, preferring to wait until after the inauguration before making appointments to mid-level and minor positions. He still had to complete his cabinet, including coaxing

Seward on the day of the inauguration to withdraw his letter declining the position of secretary of state.

On his second day in Washington, a Sunday, Lincoln attended church with Seward, partly to escape, at least for an hour or two, the hordes of visitors. After church, he gave the senator a copy of his inaugural address to critique. Seward spent the afternoon reviewing it and writing suggestions for revisions. The New Yorker recommended several important changes, as well as stylistic improvements, designed, as he wrote the president-elect, "to soothe the public mind." Seward strongly suggested that Lincoln delete the provocative second and third paragraphs declaring his intention to abide faithfully by the Republican party's platform. To retain these paragraphs, even in modified form, Seward warned, "will give such advantages to the Disunionists that Virginia and Maryland will secede, and we shall within ninety, perhaps within sixty, days be obliged to fight the south for this capital, with a divided North for reliance." Whether or not Lincoln believed this dire prediction, he deleted the paragraphs.

Seward told Lincoln that his argument in the message, presumably his position against secession, was strong and should not be changed. But, he said, Lincoln needed a passage "to meet and remove prejudice and passion in the South, and despondency and fear in the East. Some words of affection— some of calm and cheerful confidence"—should be included, he said. Notably, Seward drafted a closing paragraph designed to strengthen the bonds of Union.[71] Lincoln agreed but rephrased it into one of the most memorable passages in American history.

Almost to the last hour before delivery, Lincoln continued to refine his address. In addition to Seward's suggestion, he made an important change that Orville H. Browning recommended. In Indianapolis Lincoln had given his friend a copy of the address to review, and Browning, after returning home to Illinois, carefully read it and sent his critique to Lincoln in Washington. Browning suggested that he delete the passage pledging to use "all the power at my disposal . . . to reclaim the public property and places which have fallen" to the secessionists, but to retain the statement "to hold, occupy and possess the property and places belonging to the government, and to collect the duties on imports &c." Browning explained that "the declaration of the purpose of reclamation . . . will be construed into a threat, or menace, and will be irritating even in the border states. On principle the passage is right as it now stands. The fallen places ought to be reclaimed. But cannot that be accomplished as well, or better, without announcing the purpose in your inaugural?" Browning went on to advise that, "in any conflict which may ensue between the government and the seceding States, it is very important that the traitors shall be the aggressors, and that they be kept constantly and palpably in the wrong."[72] Lincoln agreed to delete the provocative passage in his inaugural address, but he did not follow Browning's recommendation that the secessionists be characterized as wrongful traitors.

The next day, February 25, the omnipresent Seward escorted Lincoln to the Capitol to visit both houses of Congress, a courtesy call by a president-elect that was unprecedented. Of the southern senators remaining in Washington, only Tennessee's Andrew Johnson greeted him in the Senate. Senator Thomas Bragg of North Carolina wrote in his diary, "Strange to say I was so much engaged that I did not see him," adding that he did not regret it. In the House, the Illinois "Rail Splitter" received a cordial greeting, reportedly even by some southern representatives. Lincoln and Seward moved on to the Supreme Court, where they met the justices, including Chief Justice Roger B. Taney of Dred Scott case infamy, who soon would unsuccessfully cross swords with Lincoln over presidential war powers.[73]

In an effort to persuade Lincoln to reject a policy of coercion and to seek compromise, Douglas, Bell, and Breckinridge, his three opponents in the fall election, visited him separately at Willard's. Their talks were cordial; however, Lincoln remained steadfast in his opposition to making concessions to the South. Douglas, who died three months later, remained a loyal critic of the administration, but Bell and Breckinridge cast their lots with the Confederacy after the war began. Virginia congressman Alexander R. Boteler called on Lincoln to urge him to use his influence to block the passage of a Republican bill in Congress authorizing the military suppression of the seceded states. The measure, if enacted, he said, would drive Virginia out of the Union. Boteler, who made notes of the meeting, quoted Lincoln as saying, "Well, I'll see what can be done about the bill you speak of. I think it can be stopped and that I may promise you it will be." When the congressman asked Lincoln if he could announce his position on the floor of the House, the president-elect replied: "By no means, for that would make trouble. The question would at once be asked, what right I had to interfere with the legislation of this Congress. Whatever is to be done in the matter must be done quietly." Lincoln clearly did not want congressional intervention in the crisis before he had an opportunity in his inaugural address to outline his policy and express his goodwill toward his "dissatisfied fellow countrymen." That night, evidently after he had "quietly" intervened, Congress disapproved the bill.[74] Congress, however, probably would have rejected the bill anyway.

On the evening of February 28, the Lincolns held "a levee" at Willard's for invited guests including members of Congress, army and navy officers, and the diplomatic corps. During the reception, the Marine Band and a large crowd of supporters gathered in front of the hotel. The band played "Hail to the Chief," and the crowd cheered and called for Lincoln. Finally, after numerous calls, the president-elect appeared and made brief remarks. He pointed out to the well-wishers that he had arrived in the national capital "under circumstances considerably differing from those under which any other man has ever reached it. I have reached it for the purpose of taking an official position amongst the [southern?] people, almost all of whom were opposed to me, and are yet opposed to me, as I suppose."[75]

For three days prior to the inauguration, Lincoln held private interviews on appointments and policies. He also received two delegations from Virginia seeking support for a compromise. At the same time, Lincoln continued to work on his inaugural address. On March 1, he attended a dinner hosted by the German minister of Bremen, and the next evening he dined with General Scott. On the evening before the inauguration, the Lincolns gave a dinner for cabinet members. Finally, after his guests had left the hotel, Lincoln retired to his room and prepared for the most important day of his public life, a day that his fellow Americans had anxiously awaited since November.[76] At last, on that day, Abraham Lincoln would reveal his policy toward the seceded states.

EPILOGUE: INAUGURATION

ON THE SURFACE, inauguration day, March 4, seemed little different from earlier inaugurations. Crowds gathered in the streets, citizens displayed placards and flags in profusion, bands played, and anticipation gripped the air. It was also a typical March day—windy, blustery, and cold. But an undertow of apprehension lingered over this city of 61,000 people, many of whom sympathized with the secessionists. Republicans and Union men still feared that pro-secessionists would try to prevent Lincoln's inauguration. Hundreds of Wide Awakes had descended upon the city to insure Lincoln's inauguration. They were not needed. In fact, these young Republicans increased the tension in the streets by their militant presence. Fortunately, General Winfield Scott, Colonel Charles P. Stone, and their officers had made careful preparations to insure against any effort to disrupt the proceedings or assassinate the new president. They marched troops in front of and behind the carriage of the outgoing and incoming presidents; assigned a small cavalry force to protect the procession from the side streets; placed riflemen on the roofs of strategic houses along Pennsylvania Avenue and in the windows of the Capitol; and finally, stationed a "flying" (mobile) artillery battery on Capitol Hill to guard the approaches to the east front of the building where the ceremony took place.[1]

Lincoln rose at five o'clock. After an early breakfast, he had his son Robert read the inaugural address to him, and the soon-to-be president reportedly added the final touches to it. He also spoke with Seward. At noon, President Buchanan arrived to escort Lincoln to the inauguration.[2] The two men entered an open carriage for the slow procession up Pennsylvania Avenue to the Capitol. District militiamen, soldiers, special policemen, and Wide Awakes could be seen everywhere. After attending the swearing-in ceremony for Vice President Hannibal Hamlin in the Senate chamber, Buchanan and Lincoln, arm in arm and along with other dignitaries, moved to a platform on the east front of the Capitol. In the nineteenth century, the inaugural address preceded the taking of the presidential oath. After his old friend Senator Edward Baker of Oregon introduced him, Lincoln stepped forward to the podium, faced a crowd estimated at between 25,000 and 30,000, and delivered his long-anticipated inaugural address.[3]

Lincoln began by informing southerners that "there has never been any reasonable cause" for their apprehension because of the accession of his administration. "Ample evidence" that their property, peace, and personal security would be safe in his hands, Lincoln announced, could be found in almost all of his published speeches. To emphasize this point, he quoted from one of them. "I have no purpose, directly or indirectly, to interfere with the institution of slavery in the States where it exists," Lincoln read. "I believe I have no lawful right to do so, and I have no inclination to do so." Lincoln then cited his party's 1860 platform affirming "the maintenance inviolate of the rights of the States, and especially the right of each state to order and control its own domestic institutions" and denouncing "the lawless invasion by armed force of the soil of any State or Territory, no matter under what pretext, as among the gravest of crimes." Lincoln said that this resolution "was a law to [Republicans], and to me." The last part of this resolution referred not only to John Brown–type raids into the South to free slaves but also armed proslavery incursions into the territories as had occurred in Kansas.[4]

Referring to the clause in the Constitution that required "the delivering up of fugitives from service or labor," Lincoln assured southerners that Republicans were bound by their oath to support "the whole Constitution." This included the return of fugitive slaves by federal and state authority. He stopped short of demanding that the free states repeal their personal-liberty laws and that their citizens aid federal officers in the apprehension of fugitive slaves. Lincoln, however, entered an important qualification to any enforcement of the fugitive slave law. "All the safeguards of liberty known in civilized and humane jurisprudence," he said, should be established "so that a free man be not, in any case, surrendered as a slave." Furthermore, provision should be made "for the enforcement of that clause in the Constitution which guarranties [*sic*] that 'The citizens of each State shall be entitled to all previleges [*sic*] and immunities of citizens in the several States.'" Here Lincoln apparently referred to the rights of slave owners, or their agents, to go north and without resistance secure the return of blacks bound to them under southern state laws.[5]

Lincoln provided an additional assurance to southerners and also to those opposed to him in the North. "I take the official oath to-day," he insisted, "with no mental reservations, and with no purpose to construe the Constitution or laws, by any hypercritical rules." He maintained that "it will be much safer for all, both in official and private stations, to conform to, and abide by, all those acts which stand unrepealed, than to violate any of them, trusting to find impunity in having them held to be unconstitutional."[6] Lincoln was restating the conservative position that he had always held: Bad laws should be obeyed until modified, repealed, or declared invalid by the courts.

Lincoln next turned to the secession crisis. He explained why secession was unacceptable to him. "I hold," he declared, "that in contemplation of universal law, and of the Constitution, the Union of these States is perpetual. Perpetuity is implied, if not expressed, in the fundamental law of all national governments. It is safe to assert that no government proper, ever had a provision in its organic law for its own termination." Lincoln maintained that the Union was not merely a contract that one party may break; it required all parties to the covenant "to lawfully rescind it." Furthermore, "the history of the Union itself" confirmed the perpetuity of the nation. The Union, he said, was formed by the "Articles of Association" in 1774 and "matured and continued by the Declaration of Independence," the Articles of Confederation, and finally, in 1787, by the promulgation of the Constitution. The latter had as a stated purpose "*to form a more perfect union.*" But if secession is "lawfully possible," Lincoln argued, "the Union is *less* perfect than before the Constitution, having lost the vital element of perpetuity." Thus, "no State, upon its own mere motion, can lawfully get out of the Union,—that *resolves* and *ordinances* to that effect are legally void; and that acts of violence, within any State or States, against the authority of the United States, are insurrectionary or revolutionary, according to circumstances."[7]

Lincoln announced, "To the extent of my ability, I shall take care, as the Constitution itself expressly enjoins upon me, that the laws of the Union be faithfully executed in all the States." However, he said, "there needs to be no bloodshed or violence; and there shall be none unless it be forced upon the national authority. The power confided to me, will be used to hold, occupy, and possess the property, and places belonging to the government, and to collect the duties and imposts; but beyond what may be necessary for these objects, there will be no invasion—no using of force against, or among the people anywhere." It was unrealistic for Lincoln to assume, as his statements suggest, that federal property, including military installations like Fort Sumter in Charleston harbor, could be indefinitely retained without provoking violence and bloodshed. Lincoln also promised not "to force obnoxious strangers" into federal offices "where hostility to the United States" was great.[8]

The new president admitted in his inaugural address that it would be futile to direct his remarks at those persons "who seek to destroy the Union at all events." But he asked other southerners—a majority in his mind outside of South Carolina—to think wisely "before entering upon so grave a matter as the destruction of our national fabric, with all its benefits, its memories, and its hopes." Lincoln told the assembled crowd that there had not been "a single instance in which a plainly written provision of the Constitution has ever been denied, [or] by the mere force of numbers" a majority had deprived, "a minority of any clearly written constitutional right." However, Lincoln admitted, "no organic law," including the Constitution, "can ever be framed with a provision specifically applicable to every question which may occur in practical administration." He mentioned, for example, the issue over which authority, federal or state, should return fugitive slaves, and also the question of whether Congress could prohibit or protect slavery in the territories. In such cases, Lincoln insisted, the will of the majority must prevail, "or the government must cease" and further divisions occur. "Plainly, the central idea of secession is the essence of anarchy. A majority, held in restraint by constitutional checks, and limitations, and always changing easily, with deliberate changes of popular opinions and sentiments, is the only true sovereign of a free people. Whoever rejects it, does, of necessity, fly to anarchy or to despotism."[9]

"One section of our country," Lincoln declared, "believes slavery is *right*, and ought to be extended, while the other believes it is *wrong*, and ought not to be extended. This is the only substantial dispute." The issues, he said, over the enforcement of the Fugitive Slave Act and the foreign slave trade "cannot be perfectly cured; and it would be worse in both cases after the separation of the sections, than before." Lincoln expected that if separation occurred, "the foreign slave trade, now imperfectly suppressed, would be ultimately revived without restriction, in one section; while fugitive slaves, now only partially surrendered, would not be surrendered at all, by the other." He acknowledged that many "worthy, and patriotic citizens are desirous of having the national constitution amended," and he would, "under existing circumstances, favor, rather than oppose, a fair opportunity [for] the people to act." He preferred "the convention mode" rather than congressional initiation because "it allows amendments to originate with the people themselves, instead of only permitting them to take, or reject, propositions, originated by others, not especially chosen for the purpose, and which might not be precisely such, as they would wish to accept or refuse." Lincoln, however, added that he did not object to the ratification of the proposed constitutional amendment recently initiated by Congress affirming that the federal government "shall never interfere with the domestic institutions of the States, including that of persons held to service."[10] This amendment, as indicated previously, was not ratified by the required three-fourths of the states.

Lincoln appealed to disaffected southerners to "think calmly and well, upon this whole subject. Nothing valuable can be lost by taking time. [You] still have the old Constitution unimpaired, and, on the sensitive point, the laws of your own framing under it; while the new administration will have no immediate power, if it would, to change either." He insisted that "no single good reason for precipitate action" existed. "Intelligence, patriotism, Christianity, and a firm reliance on Him, who has never yet forsaken this favored land," the new president declared, "are still competent to adjust, in the best way, all our present difficulty. In *your* hands, my dissatisfied fellow countrymen, and not in *mine,* is the momentous issue of civil war. The government will not assail you. You can have no conflict, without being yourselves the aggressors. You have no oath registered in Heaven to destroy the government, while I shall have the most solemn one to 'preserve, protect and defend' it."[11]

Lincoln closed with words that rendered his inaugural address a classic text in American political history. "We are not enemies, but friends," he announced in a voice filled with emotion. "We must not be enemies. Though passion may have strained, it must not break our bonds of affection. The mystic chords of memory, streching [sic] from every battle-field, and patriot grave, to every living heart and hearthstone, all over this broad land, will yet swell the chorus of the Union, when again touched, as surely they will be, by the better angels of our nature."[12]

After Lincoln finished the address, Chief Justice Roger B. Taney stepped forward and administered the oath of office to him. Ironically, the aging Taney, a frequent target of Lincoln's during the senatorial campaign of 1858, was the first to shake the new president's hand. Buchanan, Douglas, Chase, and others on the platform followed the chief justice in congratulating Lincoln. "A Southern gentleman," probably from Virginia, also seized the new president's hand and exclaimed, "God bless you, my dear sir; you will save us."[13]

Most southerners, however, including many in the border states, viewed Lincoln's inaugural address as a clarion call for the armed suppression of the secessionists. Republicans, in contrast, applauded the speech as properly firm but conciliatory. Many northern Democrats, including Douglas, and staunch border-state Unionists believed that Lincoln had set forth a pacific policy that rejected coercion.[14] They preferred not to confront the hard reality of how federal property, including Fort Sumter in Charleston harbor and Fort Pickens in Pensacola harbor, could be protected and the laws enforced in the seceded states without military coercion and civil war. The *Providence Daily Post* recognized the true meaning of Lincoln's refusal to recognize secession and his promise "to hold, occupy, and possess the property, and places belonging to the government, and to collect the duties and imposts." This pro-Douglas newspaper told its readers: "There stands secession—bold and palpable; and if we refuse to recognize it to-day, we shall have to recognize it, with [military] arms in our hands, to-morrow. It cannot long be dodged. There is an irrepressible conflict between the simple fact which stares us in the face when we look Southward, and the execution of the laws as proposed by the President."[15] Likewise, Edward Everett of Massachusetts wrote in his diary that Lincoln's tone in the address was "as conciliatory as possible," but that his intention to hold the forts and collect the duties in the seceded states would nevertheless "result in Civil War, which I am impelled to look upon as almost certain."[16]

AFTER THE INAUGURATION, the new president and his predecessor returned to their carriage for the procession down Pennsylvania Avenue to the White House. When they arrived at the mansion, Buchanan warmly shook Lincoln's hand and wished him well. Some of the crowd followed the new president into the White House, where he received them. Lincoln then went to bed.[17]

Before going to sleep—if indeed he slept—on his first day as president, Lincoln must have reflected on his remarkable rise from an unschooled wilderness boy to the presidency. If so, it is not unreasonable to conclude that he attributed his success mainly to the opportunities offered by an America based on the creed of equality. For Lincoln, the idea of equality and its handmaiden, liberty, given to the nation by the Founders and perhaps ordained by Providence, was a work in progress that eventually would know no racial, ethnic, or geographic bounds. America, he believed, was a republican model for the world, one that would succeed not by force of arms but by example.

Early in Lincoln's life, this vision of America's purpose had become ingrained in him. It owed a great deal to his origins, the nature of his self-education, and the optimistic western and nationalistic environment in which he grew to political maturity. Lincoln's leadership qualities had been forged in the politics of the 1840s and 1850s, a period of his life highlighted by the success of his conservative strategy in creating an antislavery party out of discordant political elements in Illinois, his challenge of Stephen A. Douglas for the U.S. Senate in 1858, and, as the Republican leader in a key lower northern state, his successful contest for the presidency in 1860. Along with his unusual political wisdom and personal integrity, Lincoln's finely honed intellect, his skill with words, and his attractive personality blended in well in the emerging West and by 1860 also proved appealing in the East. These qualities set Lincoln apart from other political leaders of his generation.

Lincoln's life and public career before March 1861 had prepared him for the Herculean task that he now faced as president of a divided nation. His legendary patience, pathos, good humor, and humanity as America's Civil War leader had become an important part of his character and personality before he arrived in Washington. Furthermore, the republican ideals that Lincoln expressed at Gettysburg in November 1863, and his hatred of slav-

ery, which led to the Emancipation Proclamation, had evolved as he rose to
political prominence in Illinois. Though America has too often fallen short
of his vision for it, Abraham Lincoln did end slavery, save the republic, advance the cause of democracy, and preserve the Founders' hopes of "a more
perfect union." This was his greatest legacy.

NOTES

ABBREVIATIONS

AL   Abraham Lincoln

CW   *The Collected Works of Abraham Lincoln,* ed. Roy P. Basler et al. 9 vols. and 2 supplements. New Brunswick, N.J.: Rutgers University Press, 1953–1955, 1974, 1990.

HI   *Herndon's Informants: Letters, Interviews, and Statements about Abraham Lincoln,* ed. Douglas L. Wilson and Rodney O. Davis, with the assistance of Terry Wilson. Urbana: University of Illinois Press, 1998.

PAL   Papers of Abraham Lincoln, Manuscript Division, Library of Congress, Washington, D.C. Available at http://www.papersofabrahamlincoln.org/.

PLT   Papers of Lyman Trumbull, Manuscript Division, Library of Congress, Washington, D.C.

INTRODUCTION

1. "A House Divided": Speech at Springfield, Illinois, June 16, 1858, CW, 2: 461–462. All emphases in the book are in the original quotations.

2. Speech at Columbus, Ohio, September 16, 1859, CW, 3: 404.

3. Speech at Leavenworth, Kansas, December 3, 1859; Speech at Cooper Institute [Union], February 27, 1860, CW, 3: 501, 537.

4. Address before the Young Men's Lyceum of Springfield, Illinois, January 27, 1838; First Inaugural Address—Final Text, March 4, 1861, CW, 1: 112–115, 4: 268.

5. Mark E. Neely, Jr., "Abraham Lincoln," in *The American Civil War: A Handbook of Literature and Research,* ed. Steven E. Woodworth (Westport, Conn.: Greenwood Press, 1996), 101.

CHAPTER ONE: FROM LOG CABIN TO SPRINGFIELD

1. AL to Jesse Lincoln, April 1, 1854, CW, 2: 217.

2. Autobiography Written for John L. Scripps [c. June 1860], CW, 4: 61–62.

3. For a description of the frontier in southern Indiana where the Lincolns settled, see Benjamin P. Thomas, *Abraham Lincoln: A Biography* (1952; reprint, New York: Random House, 1968), 8–9. For a comprehensive social history of Lincoln's early environment and the influences on him, see Kenneth J. Winkle, *The Young Eagle: The Rise of Abraham Lincoln* (Dallas: Taylor Trade Publishing, 2001).

4. Many of the main facts of Lincoln's ancestry and early life are well known and are described by his biographers. Some of the information Lincoln himself probably supplied, including material in an 1860 campaign biography by William Dean Howells, which is often ignored as a source for Lincoln's early life. This ninety-four-page

biography contains information provided by researcher James Q. Howard, who visited Springfield and conducted interviews. After the publication of the book, entitled *The Lives and Speeches of Abraham Lincoln and Hannibal Hamlin* (Columbus, Ohio: Follett, Foster, 1860), Lincoln read a copy owned by Samuel C. Parks, a political associate, and made more than a dozen corrections on its pages. In 1938, the Abraham Lincoln Association published a facsimile of the Parks copy of the Howells biography. However, the most important sources of information on Lincoln's early history are the interviews, letters, and statements collected by Lincoln's last law partner, William H. Herndon, after the president's death. Lincoln biographers and students owe Herndon a tremendous debt for his diligence in tracking down and obtaining information from people who had known the future president. These documents may be found in the Herndon-Weik Collection, Manuscript Division, Library of Congress, Washington, D.C. (also on microfilm). See *Herndon's Informants (HI)* for a marvelous—and convenient—compilation of many of these materials.

5. Autobiography Written for John L. Scripps [c. June 1860], *CW*, 4: 60.

6. Sarah Bush Lincoln interview with William H. Herndon, September 8, 1865, *HI*, 107.

7. Ibid.

8. Matilda Johnston Moore interview with William H. Herndon, September 8, 1865, *HI*, 110; Howells, *Lives and Speeches of Lincoln and Hamlin,* 20.

9. Sarah Bush Lincoln interview with William H. Herndon, September 8, 1865, *HI,* 108.

10. Autobiography Written for John L. Scripps [c. June 1860], *CW*, 4: 62.

11. Ibid., 4: 63; Howells, *Lives and Speeches of Lincoln and Hamlin,* 23.

12. Howells, *Lives and Speeches of Lincoln and Hamlin,* 23.

13. Thomas, *Abraham Lincoln,* 23–24.

14. Douglas L. Wilson, *Honor's Voice: The Transformation of Abraham Lincoln* (New York: Knopf, 1998), 53.

15. The best study of Lincoln's life in New Salem is ibid., chaps. 1–5.

16. AL to Jesse W. Fell, Enclosing Autobiography, December 20, 1859, *CW*, 3: 512.

17. AL to William H. Herndon, July 10, 1848, *CW*, 1: 497–498.

18. Howells, *Lives and Speeches of Lincoln and Hamlin,* 29–30; Autobiography Written for John L. Scripps [c. June 1860], *CW*, 4: 62.

19. Douglas L. Wilson, "They Said He Was a Lousy Speaker," *Time* 166 (July 4, 2005): 67. See also Wilson, *Lincoln's Sword: The Presidency and the Power of Words* (New York: Knopf, 2006), for Lincoln's fascination with words and their usage, beginning at an early age.

20. Wilson, *Honor's Voice,* 69–75; Handbill Replying to Charges of Infidelity, July 31, 1846, *CW*, 1: 382.

21. Richard J. Carwardine, *Lincoln* (London: Pearson, Longman, 2003), 220–221, 224–225; Allen C. Guelzo, *Abraham Lincoln: Redeemer President* (Grand Rapids, Mich.: William B. Eerdmans, 1999), 326–328.

22. Communication to the People of Sangamo County, March 9, 1832, *CW*, 1: 5–9.

23. J. Rowan Herndon to William H. Herndon, June 21, 1865, *HI,* 51.

24. Autobiography Written for John L. Scripps [c. June 1860], *CW*, 4: 65; Thomas, *Abraham Lincoln,* 37.

25. Autobiography Written for John L. Scripps [c. June 1860], *CW,* 4: 65.

26. Howells, *Lives and Speeches of Lincoln and Hamlin,* 32.

27. Fragment on Government [July 1, 1854?], *CW,* 2: 220–221.

28. J. Rowan Herndon to William H. Herndon, May 28, 1865, *HI,* 8.

29. For two studies that carefully reviewed the evidence and concluded that an intimate relationship existed between Lincoln and Ann Rutledge, see Wilson, *Honor's Voice,* 116–123; and John Y. Simon, "Abraham Lincoln and Ann Rutledge," *Journal of the Abraham Lincoln Association* 11 (1990): 13–34. A recent challenge to the romantic interpretation is Lewis Gannett, "'Overwhelming Evidence' of a Lincoln-Ann Rutledge Romance? Reexamining Rutledge Family Reminiscences," *Journal of the Abraham Lincoln Association* 26 (Winter 2005): 28–41.

30. Mary Owens Vineyard to William H. Herndon, May 23, 1866, *HI,* 256.

31. Autobiography Written for John L. Scripps [c. June 1860], *CW,* 4: 65.

32. Thomas, *Abraham Lincoln,* 43, 48; David Herbert Donald, *Lincoln* (New York: Simon and Schuster, 1995), 53–54; Wilson, *Honor's Voice,* 152. Paul Simon, a future U.S. senator, wrote an excellent account of Lincoln's legislative career (*Lincoln's Preparation for Greatness: The Illinois Legislative Years* [Norman: University of Oklahoma Press, 1965]). See especially pp. 25–32 for Lincoln's activities in the first session.

33. Donald, *Lincoln,* 60–62; Wilson, *Honor's Voice,* 159–164.

34. The legislative resolutions and the Lincoln-Stone protest can be found in *CW,* 1: 74–75.

35. AL to Mary S. Owens, May 7, 1837, *CW,* 1: 78. When Lincoln moved to Springfield, his relationship with Mary Owens had not ended.

36. Two leading Lincoln scholars, David Donald and Michael Burlingame, have effectively refuted C. A. Tripp's assertion that Lincoln was "predominantly homosexual." For Speed's and Herndon's relationships with Lincoln and the challenge to Tripp's account, see David Herbert Donald, *"We Are Lincoln Men": Abraham Lincoln and His Friends* (New York: Simon and Schuster, 2003), 29–39. Michael Burlingame's criticisms can be found in a response that he was permitted to include in Tripp's *The Intimate World of Abraham Lincoln* (New York: The Free Press, 2005).

37. Joshua Wolf Shenk, *Lincoln's Melancholy: How Depression Challenged a President and Fueled His Greatness* (Boston: Houghton Mifflin, 2005), 36.

38. Donald, *"We Are Lincoln Men,"* 33.

39. Address Before the Young Men's Lyceum of Springfield, Illinois, January 27, 1838, *CW,* 1: 108–110.

40. Ibid., 1: 112–115.

41. See especially George B. Forgie, *Patricide in the House Divided: A Psychological Interpretation of Lincoln and His Age* (New York: W. W. Norton, 1979), 85–86; and Dwight G. Anderson, *Abraham Lincoln: The Quest for Immortality* (New York: Knopf, 1982), 74.

42. Mark E. Neely, Jr., *The Abraham Lincoln Encyclopedia* (New York: McGraw-Hill, 1982), 292; AL to John T. Stuart, December 23, 1839, *CW,* 1: 158–159.

43. William H. Herndon and Jesse W. Weik, with an introduction by Horace White, *Abraham Lincoln: The True Story of a Great Life,* 2 vols. (New York: D. Appleton, 1892), 1: 188–189.

44. Samuel C. Parks to William H. Herndon, March 25, 1866, *HI,* 239.

45. As quoted in Wilson, *Honor's Voice,* 203.

46. Communication to the Readers of *The Old Soldier,* February 28, 1840; Speech at Tremont, Illinois, May 2, 1840, *CW,* 1: 203–205, 209–210.

47. Robert Gray Gunderson, *The Log-Cabin Campaign* (1957; reprint, Westport, Conn.: Greenwood Press, 1977), 136–139.

48. Wilson, *Honor's Voice,* 222. For testimony regarding Lincoln's romantic interest in Matilda Edwards, see Ninian Edwards interview with William H. Herndon, September 22, 1865, *HI,* 133.

49. My account of this episode in the Abraham Lincoln and Mary Todd relationship is mainly based on Douglas Wilson's careful study of it (*Honor's Voice,* 221–231). For the testimony of Joshua Speed and Elizabeth Edwards about the affair, see *HI,* 474–475, 477, 592.

50. The "Rebecca" Letter: Letter from the Lost Townships, August 27, 1842, *CW,* 1: 295.

51. The events associated with the Lincoln-Shields affair can be found in ibid., 1: 299–302 and notes.

52. For Lincoln's determination to uphold his honor in the Shields affair, see Wilson, *Honor's Voice,* chap. 9.

53. Memorandum of Duel Instruction to Elias H. Merryman [September 19, 1842], *CW,* 1: 300–301.

54. Ibid.

55. Wilson, *Honor's Voice,* 281.

56. James H. Matheny interview, August 21, 1888, *HI,* 666.

57. The quotations can be found in Wilson, *Honor's Voice,* 291–292.

58. AL to Samuel D. Marshall, November 11, 1842, *CW,* 1: 304–305.

CHAPTER TWO: WHIG CONGRESSMAN FROM THE PRAIRIE STATE

1. As quoted in David Herbert Donald, *"We Are Lincoln Men": Abraham Lincoln and His Friends* (New York: Simon and Schuster, 2003), 66.

2. David Davis interview, September 20, 1866, *HI,* 348.

3. AL to Joseph Gillespie, July 13, 1849, *CW,* 2: 57–58.

4. For Mary's childhood, see Jean H. Baker, *Mary Todd Lincoln: A Biography* (New York: W. W. Norton, 1987), chap. 2.

5. Michael Burlingame, *The Inner World of Abraham Lincoln* (Urbana: University of Illinois Press, 1994), 268, 271–274.

6. Ibid., xvi.

7. As quoted in David Herbert Donald, *Lincoln* (New York: Simon and Schuster, 1995), 108.

8. Ibid., 94–96.

9. Mark E. Neely, Jr., *The Abraham Lincoln Encyclopedia* (New York: McGraw-Hill, 1982), 145–147.

10. For the reasons that Lincoln might have selected Herndon for his partner, see Donald, *Lincoln,* 101.

11. Neely, *Abraham Lincoln Encyclopedia,* 145–147. For a fine biography of Herndon, see David Donald, *Lincoln's Herndon* (New York: Knopf, 1948). See also

Stephen B. Oates, *With Malice toward None: The Life of Abraham Lincoln* (New York: Harper and Row, 1977), 78–81, for the Lincoln-Herndon relationship and law practice.

12. The Lincoln Legal Papers project in Illinois, which has recently collected thousands of cases involving Lincoln, has dramatically increased interest in Lincoln's law practice during the years before he became president. Scholars as well as others have benefited immensely from the publication of *The Law Practice of Abraham Lincoln: Complete Documentary Edition,* ed. Martha L. Benner and Cullom Davis (Urbana: University of Illinois Press, 2000). An old but useful account of Lincoln as an attorney is John J. Duff's *A. Lincoln: Prairie Lawyer* (New York: Rinehart, 1960); it has recently been superseded by Mark E. Steiner, *An Honest Calling: The Law Practice of Abraham Lincoln* (DeKalb: Northern Illinois University Press, 2006).

13. Donald, *Lincoln,* 103.

14. The details of the Matson case can be found in Steiner, *An Honest Calling,* chap. 5.

15. *New York Herald,* October 20, 1860.

16. Duff, *Prairie Lawyer,* 170.

17. Ibid., 316–317; Don E. Fehrenbacher, *Prelude to Greatness: Lincoln in the 1850's* (Stanford, Calif.: Stanford University Press, 1962), 9 (quote).

18. Speech at Carthage, Illinois, October 22, 1858, CW, 3: 330–331.

19. Stephen W. Sears, *George B. McClellan: The Young Napoleon* (New York: Ticknor and Fields, 1988), 59; Horace White, *The Lincoln and Douglas Debates: An Address before the Chicago Historical Society, February 17, 1914* (Chicago: University of Chicago Press, 1914), 17.

20. The definitive account of Lincoln's financial condition is Harry E. Pratt, *The Personal Finances of Abraham Lincoln* (Springfield: Abraham Lincoln Association, 1943). See especially pp. viii, 123–124. Lincoln was worth more than $85,000 at his death, mainly owing to the amount accumulated from his $25,000 salary as president and invested in government bonds.

21. AL to Norman B. Judd, November 16, 1858, CW, 3: 337.

22. Baker, *Mary Todd Lincoln,* 112–114.

23. Elihu B. Washburne, "Abraham Lincoln in Illinois, Part I," *North American Review* 347 (October 1885): 311.

24. Resolutions Adopted by the Whig Convention at Peoria, Illinois, June 19, 1844, CW, 1: 338–340 and 340n.

25. Speech at Pittsburgh, February 15, 1861, CW, 4: 214.

26. Entry for April 3, 1844, *Lincoln Day by Day: A Chronology, 1809–1865,* ed. Earl Schenck Miers (Washington, D.C.: Lincoln Sesquicentennial Commission, 1960), 1: 227, quoting David Davis.

27. Entry for February 16, 1844, Miers, ed., *Lincoln Day by Day,* 2: 222–223, quoting the *Springfield Register.*

28. Washburne, "Abraham Lincoln in Illinois," 313; entry for October 30, 1844, Miers, ed., *Lincoln Day by Day,* 2: 238; Cyrus M. Allen to AL, November 8, 1860, PAL.

29. Entry for May 22, 1844, Miers, ed., *Lincoln Day by Day,* 2: 229.

30. Debates with John Calhoun and Alfred W. Cavarly in Springfield, Illinois, March 20–25, 1844, Miers, ed., *Lincoln Day by Day,* 1: 334–335. Unfortunately,

only two brief newspaper accounts of these debates exist. Later, in October 1860, a correspondent for the *New York Herald* in Springfield learned of the debates and provided the readers of his newspaper with a report of them. *New York Herald,* October 20, 1860. The report, which was read by many pro-tariff Pennsylvanians, probably aided Lincoln in the presidential election.

31. See, for example, his letters to Benjamin F. James, November 17, 1845; to Henry E. Dummer, November 18, 1845; and to John J. Hardin, January 19, 1846, *CW,* 1: 349, 350, 360–365.

32. Speech at Lacon, Illinois, July 18, 1846, *CW,* 1: 381–382.

33. Douglas L. Wilson provides a penetrating analysis of Lincoln's religious views, or lack thereof, at New Salem. See his *Honor's Voice: The Transformation of Abraham Lincoln* (New York: Knopf, 1998), 76–83. Another account, also cited by Wilson, said that Lincoln's friend Samuel Hill snatched the essay from him and threw it in the fire. Ibid., 81.

34. Handbill Replying to Charges of Infidelity, July 31, 1846, *CW,* 1: 382. After the election, Lincoln explained, for the record, the events leading to his issuance of the handbill. AL to Allen N. Ford, August 11, 1846, *CW,* 1: 383–384. The infidelity charge had clearly infuriated him.

35. AL to Allen N. Ford, August 11, 1846, *CW,* 1: 383.

36. AL to Joshua F. Speed, October 22, 1846, *CW,* 1: 391.

37. For an excellent account of Clay's Lexington speech and his purpose in it, see Michael F. Holt, *The Rise of the American Whig Party: Jacksonian Politics and the Onset of the Civil War* (New York: Oxford University Press, 1999), 279.

38. AL to Williamson Durley, October 3, 1845, *CW,* 1: 347–348.

39. Entry for May 30, 1846, Miers, ed., *Lincoln Day by Day,* 1: 273.

40. For Lincoln's recollection of his friendship with Barringer, see Septima M. Collis, *A Woman's War Record, 1861–1865* (New York: G. P. Putnam's Sons, 1889), 65–66.

41. "Spot" Resolutions in the United States House of Representatives, December 22, 1847, *CW,* 1: 420–422.

42. Mark E. Neely, Jr., "Lincoln's Theory of Representation: A Significant New Lincoln Document," *Lincoln Lore* (May 1978): 2.

43. Albert J. Beveridge, *Abraham Lincoln, 1809–1858,* 2 vols. (Boston: Houghton Mifflin, 1928), 1: 423–424.

44. In his comprehensive diary of his presidential term, President Polk makes no mention of Congressman Lincoln. One wonders, did the two men ever meet? Probably not, except perhaps in a reception line at the White House. *The Diary of James K. Polk during His Presidency, 1845 to 1849,* 4 vols., ed. Milo Milton Quaife (Chicago: A. C. McClurg, 1910).

45. Speech in United States House of Representatives: The War with Mexico, January 12, 1848, *CW,* 1: 431–442.

46. Donald W. Riddle, *Congressman Abraham Lincoln* (Urbana: University of Illinois Press, 1957), 50.

47. As quoted in ibid., 39.

48. Ibid., 36–38.

49. *Abraham Lincoln: A Press Portrait,* ed. Herbert Mitgang (Athens: University of Georgia Press, 1989), 58.

50. William H. Herndon and Jesse W. Weik, with an introduction by Horace White, *Abraham Lincoln: The True Story of a Great Life,* 2 vols. (New York: D. Appleton, 1892), 1: 265–267.

51. AL to William H. Herndon, February 1, 1848, *CW,* 1: 446–447.

52. AL to William H. Herndon, February 15, 1848, *CW,* 1: 451–452.

53. To Taylor Committee, February 9, 1848; AL to Thomas Flournoy, February 17, 1848, *CW,* 1: 449, 452.

54. AL to Jesse Lynch, April 10, 1848, *CW,* 1: 463.

55. AL to Usher F. Linder, February 20, 1848, *CW,* 1: 453.

56. AL to William H. Herndon, January 8, 1848, *CW,* 1: 430–431.

57. AL to Jesse Lynch, April 10, 1848, *CW,* 1: 463–464. Historian Mark E. Neely, Jr., writes that Lincoln chose not to run because he had become tired of serving in Congress and receiving little thanks in return from his constituents. Neely, "Lincoln and the Mexican War: An Argument by Analogy," *Civil War History* 24 (March 1978): 24.

58. Fragment: What General Taylor Ought to Say, *CW,* 1: 454. For the "Young Indians" movement, see Holt, *The Rise of the American Whig Party,* 285–290.

59. Fragment: What General Taylor Ought to Say, *CW,* 1: 454.

60. Holt, *The Rise of the American Whig Party,* 331–334.

61. Speech at Wilmington, Delaware, June 10, 1848, *CW,* 1: 475–476. "Locofoco party" refers to a radical faction of the Democrats in New York whose members detested banks and corporations. Locofocos were so named during the 1830s because of their use of "locofoco" matches to light candles after conservative Democrats turned off their gas lights in a meeting hall. Whigs derisively referred to all Democrats as "locofocos." Glyndon G. Van Deusen, *The Jacksonian Era, 1828–1848* (New York: Harper and Row, 1959), 95.

62. Speech in United States House of Representatives on Internal Improvements, June 20, 1848; AL to William H. Herndon, June 22, 1848, *CW,* 1: 480–490, 492.

63. Speech in U.S. House of Representatives on the Presidential Question, July 27, 1848, *CW,* 1: 501–516.

64. Speech at Worcester, Massachusetts, September 12, 1848, *CW,* 2: 1–5.

65. Speech at Boston, Massachusetts, September 15, 1848, *CW,* 2: 5.

66. Mitgang, ed., *Lincoln: A Press Portrait,* 65.

67. As quoted in Reinhard H. Luthin, "Lincoln and the Massachusetts Whigs in 1848," *New England Quarterly* 14 (1941): 626.

68. Frederick W. Seward, *Seward at Washington, as Senator and Secretary of State: A Memoir of His Life, with Selections from His Letters, 1846–1861* (New York: Derby and Miller, 1891), 80.

69. For the rise of the Free Soil party and its implications for the future of national politics, see David M. Potter, *The Impending Crisis, 1848–1861,* completed and edited by Don E. Fehrenbacher (New York: Harper and Row, 1976), 228–229.

70. Debate at Jacksonville, Illinois, October 21, 1848, *CW,* 2: 11–13.

71. Riddle, *Congressman Abraham Lincoln,* 138–140. Lincoln scholar Gabor S.

Boritt reaches a different conclusion regarding opposition to Lincoln in his district. He writes that there was little evidence of popular disagreement with his antiwar position except among Democrats. Boritt, "A Question of Political Suicide: Lincoln's Opposition to the Mexican War," *Journal of the Illinois State Historical Society* 67 (February 1974): 79–100.

72. David Davis interview, September 20, 1866, *HI*, 348.

73. AL to William Schouler, August 28, 1848, *CW*, 1: 518–519.

74. Riddle, *Congressman Abraham Lincoln*, 141.

75. Neely, "Lincoln's Theory of Representation," 1–2.

76. Paul H. Verduin, "Partners for Emancipation: New Light on Lincoln, Joshua Giddings, and the Push to End Slavery in the District of Columbia, 1848–49," *Papers from the Thirteenth and Fourteenth Annual Lincoln Colloquia, Galesburg, Illinois, September 26, 1998, and Springfield, Illinois, October 9, 1999* (Springfield: Lincoln Home National Historic Site and Lincoln Studies Center at Knox College, 2002), 75, 77.

77. Remarks and Resolutions Introduced in United States House of Representatives concerning Abolition of Slavery in the District of Columbia, January 10, 1849, *CW*, 2: 20–22.

78. Donald, *Lincoln*, 136–137; *CW*, 2: 22n (quote).

79. As quoted in Verduin, "Partners for Emancipation," 86.

80. AL to William Schouler, February 2, 1849; AL to Joshua Speed, February 20, 1849; AL to Zachary Taylor, February 27, 1849, *CW*, 2: 25, 28–29, 30.

81. AL to Joshua Speed, February 20, 1849, *CW*, 2: 28–29.

82. AL to Elisha Embree, May 25, 1849, *CW*, 2: 51. For Lincoln's letters expressing concern regarding Butterfield's appointment as commissioner, see ibid., passim.

83. Butterfield's letter to Caleb B. Smith, June 6, 1849, in Riddle, *Congressman Abraham Lincoln*, 209–210.

84. AL to Joseph Gillespie, July 13, 1849, *CW*, 2: 58.

85. AL to Josiah M. Lucas, November 17, 1849, *CW*, 2: 67.

86. AL to John M. Clayton, July 28, 1849, *CW*, 2: 60.

CHAPTER THREE: POLITICAL REVIVAL, 1850–1856

1. Autobiography Written for John L. Scripps [c. June 1860], *CW*, 4: 67.

2. For the historical interpretation that Lincoln took an extended holiday from politics during the early 1850s, see Albert J. Beveridge, *Abraham Lincoln, 1809–1858*, 2 vols. (Boston: Houghton Mifflin, 1928), 1: 493; Benjamin P. Thomas, *Abraham Lincoln: A Biography* (1952; reprint, New York: Random House, 1968), 130; Stephen B. Oates, *With Malice toward None: The Life of Abraham Lincoln* (New York: Harper and Row, 1977), 101. For the contrary interpretation, see Don E. Fehrenbacher, *Prelude to Greatness: Lincoln in the 1850's* (Stanford, Calif.: Stanford University Press, 1962), 21.

3. Joseph Gillespie to William H. Herndon, January 31, 1866, *HI*, 181.

4. Augustus H. Chapman to AL, May 24, 28, 1849, PAL. The Papers of Abraham Lincoln are conveniently available on the World Wide Web, thanks to a collaborative project by the Library of Congress, Manuscript Division, and the Lincoln Studies

Center, Knox College, Galesburg, Illinois (http://www.papersofabrahamlincoln.org/). Chapman was the husband of the daughter of Lincoln's second cousin Dennis Hanks and Elizabeth Johnston, Lincoln's stepsister.

5. AL to John D. Johnston, January 12, 1851, *CW*, 2: 96–97.

6. Beveridge, *Abraham Lincoln*, 1: 510.

7. Mark E. Neely, Jr., *The Abraham Lincoln Encyclopedia* (New York: McGraw-Hill, 1982), 62, 166.

8. Entry for May 17, 1851, *Lincoln Day by Day: A Chronology, 1809–1865*, ed. Earl Schenck Miers (Washington, D.C.: Lincoln Sesquicentennial Commission, 1960), 2: 54.

9. Michael Fellman, review of Brian R. Dirck, *Lincoln and Davis: Imagining America, 1809–1865*, in *Journal of Southern History* 69 (August 2003): 695.

10. Michael Burlingame, *The Inner World of Abraham Lincoln* (Urbana: University of Illinois Press, 1994), 38; Richard N. Current, *The Lincoln Nobody Knows* (1958; reprint, New York: Hill and Wang, 1963), 29–30; David Herbert Donald, *Lincoln* (New York: Simon and Schuster, 1995), 153.

11. AL to Jesse Lincoln, April 1, 1854; AL to Richard V. B. Lincoln, April 6, 1860; AL to John Chrisman, September 21, 1860, *CW*, 2: 217–218, 4: 37, 117.

12. AL to Jesse Lincoln, April 1, 1854, *CW*, 2: 217–218.

13. Entry for May 12, 1845, Miers, ed., *Lincoln Day by Day*, 1: 251. On this occasion, Lincoln assigned $35 to his father from a court judgment in favor of a client.

14. Interview with Sarah Bush Lincoln, September 8, 1865, *HI*, 108.

15. To the Editors of the Illinois Journal, June 5, 1850, *CW*, 2: 79; Miers, ed., *Lincoln Day by Day*, 2: 37–42 passim.

16. Speech at Peoria, Illinois, October 16, 1854, *CW*, 2: 256. The Compromise of 1850, really an armistice between the North and the South over slavery, also provided for the end of the interstate slave trade in the District of Columbia, the federal assumption of Texas's debt, and the Lone Star State's surrender of its claim to New Mexico territory.

17. AL to Joshua F. Speed, August 24, 1855, *CW*, 2: 320.

18. Entry for December 22, 1851, Miers, ed., *Lincoln Day by Day*, 2: 66.

19. Eulogy on Henry Clay, July 6, 1852, *CW*, 2: 121–132 and 121n.

20. Ibid., 2: 132.

21. Entry for August 30, 1853, Miers, ed., *Lincoln Day by Day*, 2: 104–105. For a fine account of the colonization movement in Illinois, beginning in the 1830s, see Kenneth J. Winkle, *The Young Eagle: The Rise of Abraham Lincoln* (Dallas: Taylor Trade Publishing, 2001), 254–256.

22. Entry for January 12, 1854, Miers, ed., *Lincoln Day by Day*, 2: 114.

23. Speech at Peoria, October 16, 1854, *CW*, 2: 255.

24. Outline for Speech to the Colonization Society [January 4, 1855?]; Drafts of Resolutions Recommending Amendment of the Kansas-Nebraska Act [January 4, 1855?], *CW*, 2: 298–299, 299n, 300–301, 301n.

25. Entry for January 26, 1857, Miers, ed., *Lincoln Day by Day*, 2: 189.

26. Speech at Springfield, Illinois, June 26, 1857, *CW*, 2: 409.

27. Ibid.

28. For an excellent survey of Lincoln's wartime support for colonization, see

Allen C. Guelzo's *Lincoln's Emancipation Proclamation: The End of Slavery in America* (New York: Simon and Schuster, 2004), 140–144.

29. Speech to the Springfield Scott Club, August 14, 26, 1852, *CW*, 2: 135–157. Lincoln delivered the first part of the speech on August 14 and the second part on August 26.

30. Arthur Charles Cole, *The Era of the Civil War, 1848–1870*, with a new introduction by John Y. Simon (1919; reprint, Urbana: University of Illinois Press, 1987), 122.

31. Donald, *Lincoln*, 171–172.

32. Fehrenbacher, *Prelude to Greatness*, 37–38.

33. William R. Randolph to AL, September 29, 1854; Richard L. Wilson to AL, October 20, 1854; Horace White to AL, October 25, 1854, PAL.

34. Autobiography Written for John L. Scripps [c. June 1860], *CW*, 4: 67.

35. Speech at Winchester, Illinois, August 26, 1854, *CW*, 2: 226–227.

36. Speech at Carrolton, Illinois, August 28, 1854; Speech at Springfield, Illinois, September 9, 1854; Speeches at Bloomington, Illinois, September 12, 26, 1854; Speech at Peoria, Illinois, October 16, 1854, *CW*, 2: 227, 229, 232–233, 234–240, 247–283, 283–284.

37. Speech at Peoria, Illinois, October 16, 1854, *CW*, 2: 247–255, 274. The quote is on p. 255.

38. Ibid., 2: 255–256.

39. Ibid., 2: 256.

40. Ibid.

41. Ibid., 2: 273.

42. Ibid., 2: 274–275.

43. Ibid., 2: 281–282.

44. Donald, *Lincoln*, 633n22.

45. AL to Ichabod Codding, November 27, 1854, *CW*, 2: 288.

46. AL to Noah W. Matheny, November 25, 1854, *CW*, 2: 287–288.

47. AL to Charles Hoyt, November 10, 1854; AL to Thomas J. Henderson, November 27, 1854; AL to Hugh Lemaster, November 29, 1854 (quote), *CW*, 2: 286, 288, 289.

48. List of Members of the Illinois Legislature in 1855 [January 1, 1855], *CW*, 2: 296–297.

49. AL to Elihu B. Washburne, January 6, 1855, *CW*, 2: 303–304.

50. AL to Richard Yates, January 14, 1855, *CW*, First Supplement, 26.

51. AL to Elihu B. Washburne, February 9, 1855, *CW*, 2: 304–306. For Logan's role, see Stephen T. Logan interview [1865–1866], *HI*, 467.

52. AL to Elihu B. Washburne, February 9, 1855, *CW*, 2: 305–306.

53. Michael Holt, "Making and Mobilizing the Republican Party, 1854–1860," in *The Birth of the Grand Old Party: The Republicans' First Generation*, ed. Robert F. Engs and Randall M. Miller (Philadelphia: University of Pennsylvania Press, 2002), 37.

54. AL to Owen Lovejoy, August 11, 1855, *CW*, 2: 316.

55. AL to Joshua F. Speed, August 24, 1855, *CW*, 2: 323.

56. AL to Owen Lovejoy, August 11, 1855, *CW*, 2: 316.

57. John M. Allen to Ozias M. Hatch, October 29, 1858, PAL; AL to Edward Lusk, October 30, 1858, *CW*, 3: 333, reporting his remarks at Meredosia.

58. William E. Gienapp, *The Origins of the Republican Party, 1852–1856* (New York: Oxford University Press, 1987), 170–171.

59. AL to Owen Lovejoy, August 11, 1855, *CW*, 2: 316.

60. AL to Joshua F. Speed, August 24, 1855, *CW*, 2: 323.

61. Ibid., 2: 321.

62. AL to George Robertson, August 15, 1855, *CW*, 2: 318.

63. Fehrenbacher, *Prelude to Greatness*, 44.

64. Speech at Decatur, Illinois, February 22, 1856, *CW*, 2: 333 and n.

65. Fehrenbacher, *Prelude to Greatness*, 46.

66. Speech at Bloomington, Illinois, May 29, 1856, *CW*, 2: 341.

67. Gienapp, *Origins of the Republican Party*, 286.

68. AL to Lyman Trumbull, June 7, 1856, *CW*, 2: 342–343.

69. As quoted in Gienapp, *Origins of the Republican Party*, 290.

70. AL to David Davis, July 7, 1856, in Willard L. King, *David Davis: Lincoln's Manager* (Cambridge, Mass.: Harvard University Press, 1960), 112–113.

71. *CW*, 2: 347n; King, *David Davis*, 113.

72. William H. Herndon, in *Recollected Words of Abraham Lincoln*, ed. Don E. Fehrenbacher and Virginia Fehrenbacher (Stanford, Calif.: Stanford University Press, 1996), 248.

73. AL to John Bennett, August 4, 1856; AL to Hezekiah G. Wells, August 4, 1856; AL to Lyman Trumbull, August 11, 1856, *CW*, 2: 358, 359–360.

74. AL to Lyman Trumbull, June 7, 1856, *CW*, 2: 342.

75. Form Letter to Fillmore Men, September 8, 1856, *CW*, 2: 374.

76. A convenient compilation of presidential election returns by counties for the Civil War era can be found in *Presidential Ballots, 1836–1892*, comp. W. Dean Burnham (Baltimore: Johns Hopkins Press, 1955). The county votes for Illinois appear on pp. 368–390. For the Springfield returns, see Paul M. Angle, *"Here I Have Lived": A History of Lincoln's Springfield, 1821–1865* (1935; reprint, New Brunswick, N.J.: Rutgers University Press, 1950), 223.

77. Mary Todd Lincoln to Emilie Todd Helm, November 23, 1856, *Mary Todd Lincoln: Her Life and Letters*, ed. Justin G. Turner and Linda Levitt Turner (New York: Knopf, 1972), 46; Winkle, *The Young Eagle*, 297.

CHAPTER FOUR: "HE IS AS HONEST AS HE IS SHREWD"

1. In his famous House Divided Speech, June 16, 1858, Lincoln referred to Douglas as a "dead lion" who, even if he wanted to, could do nothing to prevent the advance of slavery. Like the House Divided metaphor, the "dead lion" statement referred to a biblical passage. *CW*, 2: 467. The Republican editors and speakers repeated the "dead lion" metaphor throughout the 1858 campaign. Democrats, in contrast, ridiculed the characterization and declared that, unlike Lincoln, the Little Giant was very much a living lion politically.

2. The best study of racial attitudes and antiblack laws in the prewar North remains Leon F. Litwack, *North of Slavery: The Negro in the Free States* (Chicago: University of Chicago Press, 1961). For white hostility to blacks and the discriminatory laws in Illinois, see pp. 67, 69–70, 93, 277.

3. "Conservative" in the lexicon of mid-nineteenth-century politics meant a position that was not radical or extreme. The word "moderate" was rarely, if ever, used in this context.

4. Lerone Bennett, Jr., *Forced into Glory: Abraham Lincoln's White Dream* (Chicago: Johnson, 2000), passim; Thomas J. DiLorenzo, *The Real Lincoln: A New Look at Abraham Lincoln, His Agenda, and an Unnecessary War* (Roseville, Calif.: Forum, 2002), Foreword, x, and chap. 2.

5. Speech at Springfield, Illinois, June 26, 1857, CW, 2: 401, 405–406.

6. Lyman Trumbull to AL, January 3, 1858, PAL.

7. AL to Lyman Trumbull, December 28, 1857, CW, 2: 430.

8. John Wentworth to AL, April 19, 1858, PAL; Richard Allen Heckman, *Lincoln vs Douglas: The Great Debates Campaign* (Washington, D.C.: Public Affairs Press, 1967), 28.

9. As quoted in Don E. Fehrenbacher, *Prelude to Greatness: Lincoln in the 1850's* (Stanford, Calif.: Stanford University Press, 1962), 62.

10. John H. Bryant to AL, April 19, 1858, PAL.

11. AL to Owen Lovejoy, March 8, 1858; AL to Stephen A. Hurlbut, June 1, 1858, CW, 2: 435, 456.

12. William H. Herndon to Lyman Trumbull, April 12, 1858; Jesse Dubois to Trumbull, April 8, 1858; Ebenezer Peck to Trumbull, April 15, 1858, PLT.

13. Charles L. Wilson to AL, May 31, 1858, PAL; AL to Wilson, June 1, 1858, CW, 2: 457.

14. Heckman, *Lincoln vs Douglas,* 48–50. For the state Democratic platform, see the *Springfield Illinois State Register,* April 22, 1858. The name "Danite" was derived from the biblical prophecy of Jacob concerning one of his sons: "Dan shall be a serpent in the way," which is how the Douglas forces saw the supporters of Buchanan. David Zarefsky, *Lincoln, Douglas, and Slavery: In the Crucible of Public Debate* (Chicago: University of Chicago Press, 1990), 257n1.

15. AL to Thomas A. Marshall, April 23, 1858, CW, 2: 443.

16. Ibid., 2: 456n; AL to Lyman Trumbull, June 23, 1858, CW, 2: 472.

17. Heckman, *Lincoln vs Douglas,* 54; Fehrenbacher, *Prelude to Greatness,* 67.

18. Fehrenbacher, *Prelude to Greatness,* 68–69 (quote).

19. The state Republican platform can be found in the *Springfield Illinois State Journal,* June 17, 1858.

20. "A House Divided": Speech at Springfield, Illinois, June 16, 1858, CW, 2: 461–462.

21. Ibid., 2: 462–464.

22. Ibid., 2: 466–467.

23. Here Lincoln referred to Douglas, Pierce, Taney, and Buchanan.

24. "A House Divided": Speech at Springfield, Illinois, June 16, 1858, CW, 2: 464–466.

25. Ibid., 2: 467–469.

26. John Armstrong interview [February 1870], HI, 575.

27. Leonard Swett to William H. Herndon, January 17, 1866, HI, 163.

28. AL to John L. Scripps, June 23, 1858, CW, 2: 471.

29. Leonard Swett to William H. Herndon, January 17, 1866, *HI*, 163. See also John Armstrong interview [February 1870], *HI*, 575.

30. AL to Lyman Trumbull, June 23, 1858, *CW*, 2: 472.

31. Ibid., 2: 471–472.

32. Fifth Debate with Stephen A. Douglas, at Galesburg, Illinois, October 7, 1858, *CW*, 3: 227; Fehrenbacher, *Prelude to Greatness*, 113–114.

33. For an excellent account of Douglas's Chicago speech, see Robert W. Johannsen, *Stephen A. Douglas* (New York: Oxford University Press, 1973), 641–643. The speech, as reported in the *Chicago Times*, July 11, 1858, can be found in *Created Equal? The Complete Lincoln-Douglas Debates of 1858*, ed. Paul M. Angle (Chicago: University of Chicago Press, 1958), 12–25.

34. Heckman, *Lincoln vs Douglas*, 73.

35. *Collections of the Illinois State Historical Library, vol. 3, Lincoln Series, vol. 1, The Lincoln-Douglas Debates of 1858*, ed. Edwin Erle Sparks (Springfield: Illinois State Historical Library, 1908), 38–39. This collection is a convenient source of contemporary newspaper reports on the 1858 campaign.

36. Speech at Chicago, July 10, 1858, *CW*, 2: 491.

37. Ibid., 2: 492.

38. Ibid., 2: 487–488.

39. Ibid., 2: 498–501. The quotations are on pp. 498 and 501.

40. AL to Gustave P. Koerner, July 15, 1858, *CW*, 2: 502–503.

41. Heckman, *Lincoln vs Douglas*, 72, citing the *New York Tribune*, July 16, 1858; Sparks, ed., *Lincoln-Douglas Debates*, 39, 40.

42. Horace Greeley to Joseph Medill, July 24, 1858, PAL.

43. Lillian Foster, *Way-side Glimpses, North and South* (1860; reprint, New York: Negro Universities Press, 1969), 221.

44. Sparks, ed., *Lincoln-Douglas Debates*, 32, quoting the *Vincennes Sun*.

45. The quote is from the *New York Herald*, in Sparks, ed., *Lincoln-Douglas Debates*, 46.

46. As quoted in Johannsen, *Stephen A. Douglas*, 640–641.

47. Sparks, ed., *Lincoln-Douglas Debates*, 43–45, quoting the *New York Semi-Weekly Evening Post*.

48. Ibid., 42–43, quoting the *Louisville Democrat*.

49. Ibid., 49–50; Horace White, *The Lincoln and Douglas Debates: An Address before the Chicago Historical Society, February 17, 1914* (Chicago: University of Chicago Press, 1914), 17. For Virgil Hickox's unabashed support of Douglas, see Thomas F. Schwartz, "Money and Campaigns in the Lincoln Era," *For the People: A Newsletter of the Abraham Lincoln Association* 6 (Summer 2004): 1.

50. Sparks, ed., *Lincoln-Douglas Debates*, 65–66.

51. William H. Herndon to Lyman Trumbull, July 8, 24, 1858, PLT.

52. Speech at Chicago, July 10, 1858, *CW*, 2: 489.

53. Speech at Springfield, Illinois, July 17, 1858, *CW*, 2: 505.

54. Ibid., 2: 505–506.

55. Ibid., 2: 506.

56. Ibid., 2: 510.

57. Ibid., 2: 513–515.

58. Ibid., 2: 521.

59. Stephen A. Hurlbut to Lyman Trumbull, May 16, 1858, PLT; AL to Stephen A. Hurlbut, June 1, 1858, CW, 2: 456.

60. Speech at Springfield, Illinois, July 17, 1858, CW, 2: 520.

61. 1858 Campaign Strategy [July? 1858], CW, 2: 476–481. Lincoln's calculations were completed before July 16.

62. *Springfield Illinois State Register,* July 15, 1858.

63. *Springfield Illinois State Register,* July 16, 1858; *Springfield Illinois State Journal,* June 25, 1858, quoting the *Chicago Times.*

64. AL to Joseph Medill, June 25, 1858, CW, 2: 473–474. Lincoln's predecessor in Congress was John Henry, not Edward D. Baker as is usually assumed. Henry replaced Baker when the latter resigned to join the army.

65. *Springfield Illinois State Journal,* June 25, 1858.

66. Angle, ed., *Created Equal?* 271 (Lincoln quote).

67. O. R. Winters to AL, September 3, 1858, PAL.

68. As quoted in Sparks, ed., *Lincoln-Douglas Debates,* 56–58.

69. AL to Stephen A. Douglas, July 24, 1858, CW, 2: 522.

70. Angle, ed., *Created Equal?* 85–86; AL to Stephen A. Douglas, July 29, 1858, CW, 2: 528–530, 527n.

71. AL to Burton C. Cook, August 2, 1858; AL to Henry C. Whitney, August 2, 1858; AL to Joseph O. Glover, August 9, 1858, CW, 2: 532–533, 534–535 and note, 537.

72. David Davis to AL, August 3, 1858, PAL. See also Benjamin F. James to AL, August 25, 1858, PAL.

73. Henry C. Whitney to AL, August 7, 1858, PAL.

74. Entry for August 10, 1858, *Lincoln Day by Day: A Chronology, 1809–1865,* ed. Earl Schenck Miers (Washington, D.C.: Lincoln Sesquicentennial Commission, 1960), 2: 224. "Doughface" refers to northern Democrats like Presidents Franklin Pierce and James Buchanan and Senator Douglas who allegedly could be molded like dough into any shape that the proslavery proponents wanted.

75. For the Lincoln-Douglas canvass as they moved north toward Ottawa, see Angle, ed., *Created Equal?* 91–101.

76. Ibid., 93–94. An extended account of the Lincoln rally at Beardstown can be found in the *Springfield Illinois State Journal,* August 16, 1858.

77. Angle, ed., *Created Equal?* 96–97.

78. Ibid., 97.

CHAPTER FIVE: THE GREAT DEBATES

1. As quoted in Don E. Fehrenbacher, *Prelude to Greatness: Lincoln in the 1850's* (Stanford, Calif.: Stanford University Press, 1962), 101.

2. David Zarefsky, *Lincoln, Douglas, and Slavery: In the Crucible of Public Debate* (Chicago: University of Chicago Press, 1990), 54.

3. For Lincoln's practice of writing editorials as early as the 1830s, see James H. Matheny interview, November 1866, *HI,* 431. Michael Burlingame has ferreted out

"hundreds of anonymous and pseudonymous pieces" that the future president wrote for the *Springfield Illinois State Journal.* Burlingame, "Lincoln Spins the Press," in *Lincoln Reshapes the Presidency,* ed. Charles M. Hubbard (Macon, Ga.: Mercer University Press, 2003), 65–66.

4. *Collections of the Illinois State Historical Library,* vol. 3, Lincoln Series, vol. 1, *The Lincoln-Douglas Debates of 1858,* ed. Edwin Erle Sparks (Springfield: Illinois State Historical Library, 1908), 128–129, 133 (quote).

5. *Chicago Press and Tribune,* August 23, 1858, in Sparks, ed., *Lincoln-Douglas Debates,* 133–134.

6. Sparks, ed., *Lincoln-Douglas Debates,* 129.

7. Ibid., 134 (quote), 142.

8. AL to Joseph O. Cunningham, August 22, 1858, *CW,* 3: 37.

9. *Created Equal? The Complete Lincoln-Douglas Debates of 1858,* ed. Paul M. Angle (Chicago: University of Chicago Press, 1958), 103–105. In citing Douglas's speeches in the debates, I have chosen to follow Angle's edition, which was copied, with corrected typographical errors, from a scrapbook of the speeches that Lincoln had put together soon after the campaign. For Lincoln's speeches, his *Collected Works,* edited by Roy P. Basler and others, has been used. Harold Holzer has provided an intriguing edition of the debates based on the friendly press of each speaker, which, he contends, was not "sanitized" by the partisan press that Lincoln used and subsequent editors have copied. *The Lincoln-Douglas Debates: The First Complete, Unexpurgated Text,* ed. Harold Holzer (New York: HarperCollins, 1993). See Douglas F. Wilson's penetrating critique of Holzer's methodology in "The Unfinished Text of the Lincoln-Douglas Debates," *Journal of the Abraham Lincoln Association* 15 (Winter 1994): 70–84.

10. Angle, ed., *Created Equal?* 106–107.

11. Neither the transcription of Douglas's speech at Ottawa in Angle, ed., *Created Equal?* nor the *Collected Works of Lincoln* record the remark "bring him to his milk." The *Quincy* (Illinois) *Whig,* August 26, 1858, however, reported it in a summary of the Ottawa debate. It is possible that Douglas first used the phrase after the debate; nevertheless, it became a popular target of ridicule by both sides during the campaign. The *Quincy Whig* report is found in Sparks, ed., *Lincoln-Douglas Debates,* 144.

12. Angle, ed., *Created Equal?* 109, 112, 114.

13. First Debate with Stephen A. Douglas at Ottawa, Illinois, August 21, 1858, *CW,* 3: 13, hereinafter cited as First Debate.

14. Ibid., 3: 13–16.

15. Ibid., 3: 16.

16. Ibid., 3: 17–20.

17. As reported in the *Rockford Republican,* August 26, 1858, transcribed in the Illinois Historical Digitization Projects, Northern Illinois University Libraries, DeKalb, Illinois.

18. Sparks, ed., *Lincoln-Douglas Debates,* 140–141, 142–143.

19. Angle, ed., *Created Equal?* 131–137; Richard Allen Heckman, *Lincoln vs Douglas: The Great Debates Campaign* (Washington, D.C.: Public Affairs Press, 1967), 85.

20. First Debate, *CW,* 3: 30.

21. Sparks, ed., *Lincoln-Douglas Debates,* 143.

22. Ibid., 145.

23. As reported in the *Alton Weekly Courier,* August 26, 1858, transcribed in Illinois Historical Digitization Projects.

24. As reported in Sparks, ed., *Lincoln-Douglas Debates,* 141.

25. As reported in ibid., 133.

26. AL to Joseph O. Cunningham, August 22, 1858, *CW,* 3: 37.

27. Lyman Trumbull to AL, August 24, 1857 [1858]; L. D. Whiting to AL, August 23, 1858, PAL.

28. AL to Ebenezer Peck, August 23, 1858, *CW,* First Supplement, 32–33.

29. Joseph Medill to AL [August 27, 1858], PAL.

30. *Freeport Weekly Bulletin,* September 2, 1858, transcribed in Illinois Historical Digitization Projects.

31. Second Debate with Stephen A. Douglas at Freeport, Illinois, August 27, 1858, *CW,* 3: 40–41, hereinafter cited as Second Debate.

32. Ibid., 3: 41.

33. Ibid., 3: 41–42.

34. *Springfield Illinois State Journal,* September issues, 1858.

35. Second Debate, *CW,* 3: 43.

36. Angle, ed., *Created Equal?* 152.

37. Ibid.

38. AL to Henry Asbury, July 31, 1858, *CW,* 2: 530–531.

39. For an important challenge to the traditional view of the Freeport Doctrine, see Fehrenbacher, *Prelude to Greatness,* 108–109. Though my account differs in several particulars, Fehrenbacher has provided a fine analysis of the doctrine in Chapter 6 of his book of essays on Lincoln during the 1850s.

40. Second Debate, *CW,* 3: 43.

41. Angle, ed., *Created Equal?* 154–156.

42. Ibid., 156.

43. Ibid., 161.

44. *Springfield Illinois State Journal,* September 7, 1858.

45. Entries for August 30–September 13, 1858, *Lincoln Day by Day: A Chronology, 1809-1865,* ed. Earl Schenck Miers (Washington, D.C.: Lincoln Sesquicentennial Commission, 1960), 2: 226–228.

46. Accounts of these speeches are in *CW,* 3: 76–101.

47. *Springfield Illinois State Journal,* September 20, 1858; Sparks, ed., *Lincoln-Douglas Debates,* 213, 259–260; entry for September 14, 1858, Miers, ed., *Lincoln Day by Day,* 2: 228.

48. Sparks, ed., *Lincoln-Douglas Debates,* 262.

49. Angle, ed., *Created Equal?* 192–193, 196–197. The quotes are found on p. 197.

50. Ibid., 193.

51. Ibid., 200–203.

52. Third Debate with Stephen A. Douglas at Jonesboro, Illinois, September 15, 1858, *CW,* 3: 116, hereinafter cited as Third Debate.

53. Lincoln's comment on Massachusetts' sovereignty can be found in his letter to Theodore Canisius, May 17, 1859, *CW*, 3: 380.

54. Third Debate, *CW*, 3: 117.

55. Ibid., 3: 133–134.

56. Sparks, ed., *Lincoln-Douglas Debates,* 322–323.

57. Fourth Debate with Stephen A. Douglas at Charleston, Illinois, September 18, 1858, *CW*, 3: 145–146, hereinafter cited as Fourth Debate.

58. For Lincoln's support for black suffrage late in his life, see William C. Harris, *With Charity for All: Lincoln and the Restoration of the Union* (Lexington: University Press of Kentucky, 1997), 256–257. However, none of the Union governments in the South that Lincoln had created provided for black political rights.

59. Fourth Debate, *CW*, 3: 147–157.

60. Angle, ed., *Created Equal?* 247–255.

61. Ibid., 260–266.

62. Fourth Debate, *CW*, 3: 179.

63. David Davis to AL, September 25, 1858, PAL; Heckman, *Lincoln vs Douglas,* 114.

64. *Lew Wallace: An Autobiography,* 2 vols. (New York: Harper and Brothers, 1906), 1: 254–256.

65. Entries for September 20, 21, 23, 1858, Miers, ed., *Lincoln Day by Day,* 2: 229; AL to William Fithian, September 3, 1858, *CW*, 3: 84.

66. *Jacksonville Sentinel,* October 8, 1858, copying a report in the *Milwaukee News,* September 22, 1858, transcribed in Illinois Historical Digitization Projects.

67. *Galesburg Semi-Weekly Democrat,* October 9, 1858, transcribed in Illinois Historical Digitization Projects.

68. Angle, ed., *Created Equal?* 285–289.

69. Ibid., 290–295.

70. Fifth Debate with Stephen A. Douglas, at Galesburg, Illinois, October 7, 1858, *CW*, 3: 219–220, hereinafter cited as Fifth Debate.

71. Richard J. Carwardine, *Lincoln* (London: Pearson, Longman, 2003), 81–83.

72. William C. Harris, *Lincoln's Last Months* (Cambridge, Mass.: Belknap Press of Harvard University Press, 2004), 143–144.

73. Fifth Debate, *CW*, 3: 221–222.

74. Speech at Springfield, Illinois, July, 17, 1858, *CW*, 2: 520.

75. Fifth Debate, *CW*, 3: 221–222.

76. Ibid., 3: 225–226, 233.

77. Ibid., 3: 230–236. The quotes are on pages 231, 233–234.

78. For Lincoln's itinerary and receptions after the Galesburg debate, see entries for October 8–13, 1858, Miers, ed., *Lincoln Day by Day,* 2: 232. For his Burlington visit, see James W. Grimes to William H. Herndon, October 28, 1866, *HI,* 377–378.

79. Sparks, ed., *Lincoln-Douglas Debates,* 389–395, 446.

80. Sixth Debate with Stephen A. Douglas, at Quincy, Illinois, October 13, 1858, *CW*, 3: 246–249, hereinafter cited as Sixth Debate.

81. Ibid., 3: 254.

82. Ibid., 3: 254–255.

83. Ibid., 3: 256–257.

84. Angle, ed., *Created Equal?* 343–344.

85. Ibid., 339–342.

86. Ibid., 352.

87. Entries for October 14, 15, 1858, Miers, ed., *Lincoln Day by Day,* 2: 232. As in the case of the other debates, an excellent source of information for the Alton debate, though biased politically, is newspaper reports in Sparks, ed., *Lincoln-Douglas Debates,* 497–510.

88. Sparks, ed., *Lincoln-Douglas Debates,* 504–505. For a description of Douglas and Lincoln at Alton, see *Memoirs of Gustave Koerner, 1809–1896,* ed. Thomas J. McCormack, 2 vols. (Cedar Rapids, Iowa: Torch Press, 1909), 2: 67–68.

89. AL to Norman B. Judd, October 20, 1858, *CW,* 3: 329.

90. AL to Gustave P. Koerner, July 25, 1858, *CW,* 2: 524 and n; McCormack, ed., *Memoirs of Gustave Koerner,* 2: 68. Lincoln also arranged for the publication in German of his July 17 Springfield speech. Lincoln to Koerner, August 6, 1858, *CW,* 2: 537.

91. *The Reminiscences of Carl Schurz,* 3 vols. (New York: McClure, 1907–1908), 2: 90–91.

92. Ibid., 2: 91. For an excellent biography of Schurz, see Hans L. Trefousse, *Carl Schurz: A Biography* (New York: Fordham University Press, 1998).

93. Angle, ed., *Created Equal?* 403; Heckman, *Lincoln vs Douglas,* 45; entry for October 22, 1858, Miers, ed., *Lincoln Day by Day,* 2: 233.

94. AL to James N. Brown, October 18, 1858; Speech at Rushville, Illinois, October 20, 1858; Speech at Petersburg, Illinois, October 29, 1858, *CW,* 3: 327–328, 329, 333.

95. AL to John J. Crittenden, July 7, 1858, *CW,* 2: 483–484; John J. Crittenden to AL, July 29, October 27, 1858, PAL.

96. AL to John J. Crittenden, November 4, 1858, *CW,* 3: 335–336.

97. Clipping from *Chicago Herald,* September 22, 1858; Henry C. Whitney to AL, October 14, 1858, PAL.

98. AL to Norman B. Judd, October 20, 1858, *CW,* 3: 329–330.

99. Speech at Meredosia, Illinois, October 18, 1858, *CW,* 3: 328–329, as reported in the *Jacksonville Sentinel,* October 22, 1858.

100. Angle, ed., *Created Equal?* 406–407; Fragment: Last Speech of the Campaign at Springfield, Illinois, October 30, 1858, *CW,* 3: 334.

101. For a good account of Lincoln's reluctance to reveal his inner self, see Richard N. Current, *The Lincoln Nobody Knows* (1958; reprint, New York: Hill and Wang, 1992), chap. 1.

102. Fragment: Last Speech of the Campaign at Springfield, Illinois, October 30, 1858, *CW,* 3: 334.

103. As quoted in Angle, ed., *Created Equal?* 405.

104. For a map of the election results by county, see Heckman, *Lincoln vs Douglas,* 134.

105. Don E. Fehrenbacher, *The Dred Scott Case: Its Significance in American Law and Politics* (New York: Oxford University Press, 1978), 501–503.

106. *Springfield Illinois State Register,* November 4, 6, 1858.

107. As quoted in Fehrenbacher, *The Dred Scott Case,* 501.

108. G. W. Rives to Ozias M. Hatch, November 5, 1858, quoted in Zarefsky, *Lincoln, Douglas, and Slavery,* 206.

109. Sparks, ed., *Lincoln-Douglas Debates,* 536; David Davis to AL, November 7, 1858; M. M. Inman to AL, November 9, 1858; William A. Grimshaw to AL, November 11, 1858, PAL.

110. Benjamin P. Thomas, *Abraham Lincoln: A Biography* (1952; reprint, New York: Random House, 1968), 192; Stephen B. Oates, *With Malice toward None: The Life of Abraham Lincoln* (New York: Harper and Row, 1977), 173; William E. Gienapp, *Abraham Lincoln and Civil War America* (Oxford: Oxford University Press, 2002), 66; Carwardine, *Lincoln,* 85.

111. For the view that a fairer legislative apportionment would not have made a difference in the election, see Zarefsky, *Lincoln, Douglas, and Slavery,* 207–208; David Herbert Donald, *Lincoln* (New York: Simon and Schuster, 1995), 228; and Fehrenbacher, *The Dred Scott Case,* 501.

112. David Davis to AL, November 7, 1858, PAL; John M. Palmer to Lyman Trumbull, December 9, 1858, PLT; Harlan Hoyt Horner, *Lincoln and Greeley* (Urbana: University of Illinois Press, 1953), 156 (quote).

113. AL to Anson G. Henry, November 19, 1858, CW, 3: 339.

114. Ibid.

115. AL to Norman B. Judd, November 15, 1858, CW, 3: 337.

116. Ibid.

CHAPTER SIX: REPUBLICAN CHAMPION OF THE GREAT WEST

1. William Baringer, *Lincoln's Rise to Power* (Boston: Little, Brown, 1937), 52–53. The original of the editorial supporting Lincoln for the presidency has not been found, and some historians have doubted its authenticity. However, years later, in his book *Fifty Years Recollections, Illinois Gazette* editor Jeriah Bonham printed the editorial, presumably from his own newspaper's files. After applying the tests of historical evidence, historian William Baringer persuasively argues that it was authentic. Baringer provides his evidence in a note on pp. 53–54.

2. *Collections of the Illinois State Historical Library, vol. 3, Lincoln Series, vol. 1, The Lincoln-Douglas Debates of 1858,* ed. Edwin Erle Sparks (Springfield: Illinois State Historical Library, 1908), 581.

3. As copied in the *Chicago Press and Tribune,* December 16, 1858, *Abraham Lincoln: A Press Portrait,* ed. Herbert Mitgang (Athens: University of Georgia Press, 1989), 135.

4. Horace White to AL, November 5, 1858, PAL.

5. Josiah M. Lucas to AL, December 21, 1858, PAL.

6. Baringer, *Lincoln's Rise to Power,* 66–67.

7. Ibid., 68–69; Frances Milton Morehouse, *The Life of Jesse W. Fell,* University of Illinois Studies in the Social Sciences, vol. 5, no. 2 (Urbana: University of Illinois, 1916), 58.

8. *Chicago Press and Tribune,* March 29, 1859.

9. *New York Times,* November 5, 6, 1858. By 1860, the *Times,* edited by

Henry J. Raymond, had realized its mistake in promoting Douglas, and during the Civil War it loyally supported Lincoln.

10. AL to Henry C. Whitney, November 30, December 25, 1858, *CW,* 3: 343, 347; Whitney to AL, December 8, 1858; John Dougherty to AL, December 28, 1858; Ozias C. Skinner to AL, December 28, 1858, PAL.

11. AL to William A. Ross, March 26, 1859, *CW,* 3: 372-373.

12. Ohio Republican State Central Committee to AL, December 7, 1859; Samuel Galloway to AL, December 13, 1859, PAL; AL to Galloway, December 19, 1859, *CW,* First Supplement, 47-49 (quote).

13. AL to George M. Parsons and Others, December 19, 1859; AL to James W. Sheahan, January 24, 1860, *CW,* 3: 510, 515, and 374n; John G. Nicolay and John Hay, *Abraham Lincoln: A History,* 10 vols. (New York: Century, 1890), 2: 188-189.

14. Stephen A. Douglas to Follett, Foster and Company, June 9, 1860, PAL.

15. George M. Parsons to AL, January 30, 1860; James W. Sheahan to AL, January 21, 1860, PAL; AL to Sheahan, January 24, 1860, *CW,* 3: 515. Sheahan, editor of the *Chicago Times,* complained that the Ohio publishers had refused earlier to provide him with copies of Lincoln's speeches for his campaign biography of Douglas.

16. Mark M. Krug, *Lyman Trumbull: Conservative Radical* (New York: A. S. Barnes, 1965), 99-100.

17. Norman B. Judd to Lyman Trumbull, December 26, 1858, PLT; Trumbull to AL, January 29, 1859, PAL.

18. AL to Lyman Trumbull, February 3, 1859, *CW,* 3: 355-356.

19. John Wentworth to AL, November 28, December 21,1859, PAL.

20. Norman B. Judd to AL, December 1 (quote), 11, 1859, PAL.

21. AL to Norman B. Judd, December 9, 1859, *CW,* 3: 505.

22. AL to George W. Dole, Gurdon S. Hubbard, and William H. Brown, December 14, 1859; AL to Norman B. Judd, December 14, 1859, *CW,* 3: 507-508, 509.

23. AL to Norman B. Judd, February 5, 1860, *CW,* 3: 516 and n.

24. Nehemiah Niles to AL, December 16, 1859, PAL.

25. David Davis to AL, February 21, 1860, PAL; AL to John Wentworth, February 13, 1860, *CW,* First Supplement, 48. A tenuous peace occurred in the newspaper war when Judd's friends at the *Chicago Press and Tribune* gave support, albeit tepid, to Wentworth's election as mayor of the city. See issue of February 20, 1860.

26. John Wentworth to AL, February 7, 19, April 21, 1860, PAL.

27. AL to Norman B. Judd, February 9, 1860, *CW,* 3: 517.

28. AL to Norman B. Judd, December 14, 1859, *CW,* 3: 509.

29. Don E. Fehrenbacher, *Prelude to Greatness: Lincoln in the 1850's* (Stanford, Calif.: Stanford University Press, 1962), 151. Wentworth was clearly the loser in the affair. He was excluded from the state Republican committee and, owing to Lincoln's insistence, was not selected as a delegate-at-large to the national convention in Chicago. Krug, *Trumbull,* 157.

30. For Lincoln's statement to Fell, see William E. Barton, *President Lincoln,* with preface and the last three chapters by William H. Townsend, 2 vols. (Indianapolis: Bobbs-Merrill, 1933),1: 58.

31. Thomas J. Pickett to AL, April 13, 1859, PAL; AL to Pickett, April 16, 1859, *CW,* 3: 377.

32. Ben L. Wiley to Lyman Trumbull, January 10, 1860, PLT.

33. G. O. Pond to Lyman Trumbull, December 28, 1859; Jubal C. Brock to Trumbull, January 15, 1860, PLT.

34. William H. Bissell to Salmon P. Chase, February 4, 1860, in Baringer, *Lincoln's Rise to Power*, 144–145.

35. Entry for February 7, 1860, *The Diary of Orville Hickman Browning*, ed. Theodore Calvin Pease and James G. Randall, 2 vols. (Springfield: Illinois State Library, 1925–1933), 1: 395. For an excellent account of the Browning-Lincoln relationship, see David Herbert Donald, *"We Are Lincoln Men": Abraham Lincoln and His Friends* (New York: Simon and Schuster, 2003), chap. 4.

36. The erratic Horace Greeley of the influential *New York Tribune* declared that he supported Bates because "I want to succeed this time." Historian David M. Potter provides a good summary of the Missourian's candidacy. Potter, *The Impending Crisis, 1848–1861,* completed and edited by Don E. Fehrenbacher (New York: Harper and Row, 1974), 420–421.

37. Clipping in *Indianapolis Daily Journal*, n.d., from William H. Hanna to AL, January 26, 1859, PAL.

38. AL to Hawkins Taylor, September 6, 1859, CW, 3: 399–400.

39. See Stephen B. Oates, *With Malice toward None: The Life of Abraham Lincoln* (New York: Harper and Row, 1978), 113; and Thomas J. DiLorenzo, *The Real Lincoln: A New Look at Abraham Lincoln, His Agenda, and an Unnecessary War* (Roseville, Calif.: Forum, 2002), 15.

40. AL to William E. Frazer, November 1, 1859, CW, 3: 491.

41. AL to Lyman Trumbull, December 11, 1858, CW, 3: 345.

42. AL to Mark W. Delahay, May 14, 1859, CW, 3: 378–379. For a similar warning, see AL to W. H. Wells, January 8, 1859, CW, 3: 349.

43. Speech at Chicago, Illinois, March 1, 1859, CW, 3: 366, 368–370.

44. AL to Salmon P. Chase, June 9, 1859, CW, 3: 384.

45. Salmon P. Chase to AL, June 13, 1859, PAL.

46. AL to Salmon P. Chase, June 20, 1859, CW, 3: 386.

47. *Three against Lincoln: Murat Halstead Reports the Caucuses of 1860*, ed. with intro. by William B. Hesseltine (Baton Rouge: Louisiana State University Press, 1960), 152–158.

48. Samuel Galloway to AL, July 23, 1859, PAL; AL to Galloway, July 28, 1859, CW, 3: 394–395.

49. AL to Schuyler Colfax, July 6, 1859, CW, 3: 390–391.

50. Gustave P. Koerner to AL, April 4, 1859, PAL.

51. AL to Gustave P. Koerner, April 11, 1859, CW, 3: 376.

52. AL to Theodore Canisius, May 17, 1859, CW, 3: 380 and 381n.

53. Ibid., 3: 380.

54. AL to Edward Wallace, October 11, 1859, CW, 3: 486–487.

55. Speech at Council Bluffs, Iowa, August 13, 1859, CW, 3: 396 and 397n; Ralph Gary, *Following in Lincoln's Footsteps: A Complete Annotated Reference to Hundreds of Historical Sites Visited by Abraham Lincoln* (New York: Carroll and Graf, 2001), 201.

56. See Samuel Galloway to AL, July 23, 1859, PAL, for the damaging effect of the Ohio Republican platform of 1859 upon the party in the state.

57. Stephen A. Douglas's article in *Harper's Magazine* is reprinted in *In the Name*

of the People: Speeches and Writings of Lincoln and Douglas in the Ohio Campaign of 1859, ed. with an intro. by Harry V. Jaffa and Robert W. Johannsen (Columbus: Ohio State University Press, 1959), 58–125, hereinafter cited as Jaffa and Johannsen, eds., *Ohio Campaign of 1859.* This collection of documents contains a fine introduction by the editors as well as the Ohio speeches of Douglas and Lincoln and a rebuttal of Douglas's article by Jeremiah Black, Buchanan's attorney general.

58. William T. Bascom to AL, September 1, 9, 1859; Peter Zinn to AL, September 2, 1859, PAL; AL to Peter Zinn, September 6, 1859, CW, 3: 400.

59. *Chicago Press and Tribune,* September 19, 1859. For the cool reception Chase's supporters gave Lincoln, see Jaffa and Johannsen, eds., *Ohio Campaign of 1859,* 19–20.

60. *Chicago Press and Tribune,* September 19, 1859.

61. Joseph Medill to AL, September 10, 1859, PAL. After his speech on the State House terrace, Lincoln spoke briefly to the Young Men's Republican Club of Columbus. Entry for September 16, 1859, *Lincoln Day by Day: A Chronology, 1809–1865,* ed. Earl Schenck Miers (Washington, D.C.: Lincoln Sesquicentennial Commission, 1960), 2: 261.

62. Speech at Columbus, September 16, 1859, CW, 3: 400–425 passim.

63. Ibid., 3: 407–408, 413–417.

64. For an account of the feeble effort to reopen the foreign slave trade, see Don E. Fehrenbacher, *The Slaveholding Republic: An Account of the United States Government's Relations to Slavery,* completed and edited by Ward M. McAfee (New York: Oxford University Press, 2001), 180–183.

65. Fragments: Notes for Speeches, c. September 1859, CW, 3: 399.

66. Speech at Columbus, September 16, 1859, CW, 3: 404–405, 421–423.

67. As quoted in Jaffa and Johannsen, eds., *Ohio Campaign of 1859,* 21.

68. The anti-Democratic movement in the upper South and the border slave states consisted of former Whigs who were staunchly proslavery. They also called their movement the "Opposition party" at this time. Allan Nevins, *The Emergence of Lincoln,* vol. 2, *Prologue to Civil War, 1859–1861* (New York: Charles Scribner's Sons, 1950), 58–63. The Opposition party would become the Constitutional Union party in 1860.

69. For a description of the rally at Market Square, see Baringer, *Lincoln's Rise to Power,* 103; and Robert S. Harper, *Lincoln and the Press* (New York: McGraw-Hill, 1951), 41.

70. As quoted in Mitgang, ed., *Lincoln: A Press Portrait,* 142–143.

71. Speech at Cincinnati, Ohio, September 17, 1859, CW, 3: 440–441, 460.

72. Ibid., 3: 445–446.

73. *Chicago Press and Tribune,* September 21, 1859.

74. Baringer, *Lincoln's Rise to Power,* 107; entry for September 19, 1859, Miers, ed., *Lincoln Day by Day,* 2: 261.

75. Speech at Indianapolis, Indiana, September 19, 1859; AL to Salmon P. Chase, September 21, 1859, CW, 3: 463–470, 471.

76. Address before the Wisconsin State Agricultural Society, Milwaukee, Wisconsin, September 30, 1859, CW, 3: 477–480.

77. Ibid. Lincoln's concluding statement is on pp. 481–482.

78. M. A. Northrop to AL, September 14, 1859, PAL (quote); Speech at Beloit, Wisconsin, October 1, 1859; Speech at Janesville, Wisconsin, October 1, 1859, *CW,* 3: 482–486 and 482n, 484n.

79. Speech at Clinton, Illinois, October 14, 1859; Speech at Springfield, October 15, 1859, *CW,* 3: 487–489 and notes.

80. Nicolay and Hay, *Abraham Lincoln,* 2: 188–189.

81. Samuel Galloway to AL, October 13, 1859; William T. Bascom to AL, October 13, 1859; Republican Party of Ohio to AL, December 7, 1859; Salmon P. Chase to AL, September 29, 1859, PAL; *Chicago Press and Tribune,* September 19, 21, 1859.

82. Samuel Galloway to AL, October 13, 1859, PAL.

83. Charles H. Ray to AL, October 31, 1859; Lyman Trumbull to AL, November 23, 1859, PAL; Arthur Charles Cole, *The Era of the Civil War, 1848–1870,* with a new introduction by John Y. Simon (1919; reprint, Urbana: University of Illinois Press, 1987), 182. Ironically, Lincoln appointed both McClernand and Palmer as generals during the Civil War.

84. William E. Frazer to AL, November 12, 1859, PAL.

85. For a brief account of the Republican setbacks in New York after Brown's raid and Seward's reaction, see Glyndon G. Van Deusen, *William Henry Seward* (New York: Oxford University Press, 1967), 216.

86. Mark W. Delahay to AL, November 14, 1859, PAL.

87. Josiah M. Lucas to AL, January 26, 1860, PAL.

88. Simeon Francis to AL, October 29, 1859, PAL.

CHAPTER SEVEN: "HONEST ABE" FOR PRESIDENT

1. James A. Briggs to AL, October 12, 1859, PAL.

2. William E. Frazer to AL, November 12, 1859, PAL. See AL to Frazer, November 1, 1859, *CW,* 3: 491, for Lincoln's cool reaction to the courtship by Cameron's Pennsylvania supporters.

3. Thurlow Weed to Norman B. Judd, October 20, 1859; Judd to AL, October 21, 1859, PAL.

4. Harold Holzer, *Lincoln at Cooper Union: The Speech That Made Abraham Lincoln President* (New York: Simon and Schuster, 2004), 14; David Herbert Donald, *Lincoln* (New York: Simon and Schuster, 1995), 257.

5. William Baringer, *Lincoln's Rise to Power* (Boston: Little, Brown, 1937), 159.

6. For the important but often neglected Wyandotte constitution, see Nicole Etcheson, *Bleeding Kansas: Contested Liberty in the Civil War Era* (Lawrence: University Press of Kansas, 2004), 205–206.

7. A Kansas correspondent to the *New York Tribune,* August 30, 1860. The Lincoln quote in this letter is not included in Lincoln's *Collected Works.*

8. For Lincoln's brief visit in Hannibal, see Ralph Gary, *Following in Lincoln's Footsteps: A Complete Annotated Reference to Hundreds of Historical Sites Visited by Abraham Lincoln* (New York: Carroll and Graf, 2001), 256–257.

9. William E. Barton, *President Lincoln,* with preface and last two chapters by William H. Townsend, 2 vols. (Indianapolis: Bobbs-Merrill, 1933),1: 19–20.

10. Speech at Elwood, Kansas, December 1 [November 30?], 1859, *CW,* 3: 495–497, 497n.

11. A Kansas correspondent to the *New York Tribune,* August 30, 1860.

12. Baringer, *Lincoln's Rise to Power,* 124; Gary, *Following in Lincoln's Footsteps,* 205.

13. Speech at Leavenworth, Kansas, December 3, 1859, *CW,* 3: 500–502.

14. Ibid., 3: 502.

15. Second Speech at Leavenworth, Kansas, December 5, 1859, *CW,* 3: 503–504.

16. A Kansas correspondent to the *New York Tribune,* August 30, 1860; AL to Levant L. Jones, December 9, 1859, *CW,* 3: 504–505.

17. AL to Jesse W. Fell, Enclosing Autobiography, December 20, 1859, *CW,* 3: 511–512 and n.

18. Jackson Grimshaw to William H. Herndon, April 28, 1866, *HI,* 247. The meeting in Hatch's office should not be confused with the January 6, 1859, meeting in which Lincoln declined the request of his friends to use his name for the nomination.

19. The *Springfield Illinois State Journal,* January 14, 1860; and the *Louisville Journal,* January 18, 1860, as quoted in *Lincoln: A Press Portrait,* ed. Herbert Mitgang (Athens: University of Georgia Press, 1989), 144–145.

20. Joseph Medill to Lyman Trumbull, April 16, 1860, PLT.

21. *Chicago Press and Tribune,* February 16, 1860. In its March 6, 1860, issue, this newspaper elaborated on the argument that Lincoln, not Seward, could win the "Fillmore element" in the lower North.

22. For the books and printed documents that Lincoln consulted in preparing his New York lecture, see Holzer, *Lincoln at Cooper Union,* 51–54.

23. *Springfield Illinois State Register,* February 23, 1860.

24. Holzer, *Lincoln at Cooper Union,* 72–73.

25. Ibid., 88, 91, 92 (quote), 95, 97; Donald, *Lincoln,* 238.

26. Most historical accounts of the place of this important speech identify it as Cooper Institute. The editors of Lincoln's *Collected Works* also refer to it as Cooper Institute. Lincoln scholar Harold Holzer, however, proves that at the time it was called Cooper Union.

27. As quoted in Donald, *Lincoln,* 238. See also Baringer, *Lincoln's Rise to Power,* 154–155.

28. Both quotes derive from Holzer, *Lincoln at Cooper Union,* 113–114.

29. *New York Tribune,* February 28, 1860.

30. Holzer, *Lincoln at Cooper Union,* 134, 144.

31. Address at Cooper Institute, New York City, February 27, 1860, *CW,* 3: 522–531.

32. Ibid., 3: 535.

33. Ibid., 3: 536–537.

34. Though Congress had prohibited the foreign slave trade, American slavers, with virtual impunity, continued to ply the notorious Middle Passage across the Atlantic to Cuba and Brazil.

35. Address at Cooper Institute, New York City, February 27, 1860, *CW,* 3: 537–538.

36. Ibid., 3: 538–541.

37. Ibid., 3: 541, 546–547.

38. Ibid., 3: 547–550.

39. As quoted in Holzer, *Lincoln at Cooper Union,* 146.

40. As reported in the *Chicago Press and Tribune,* March 2, 1860. The *New York Times,* February 28, 1860, which gave an incomplete account of the speech, reported that when Lincoln finished, he received "three rousing cheers" from the audience.

41. *New York Tribune,* February 28, 1860. The manuscript of the speech is not extant, and the version printed in Lincoln's *Collected Works* was reproduced from the Lincoln-edited pamphlet. See *CW,* 3: 522n.

42. As quoted in *Lincoln, 1854–1861: Being the Day-by-Day Activities of Abraham Lincoln from January 1, 1854, to March 4, 1861,* ed. Paul M. Angle (Springfield: Abraham Lincoln Association, 1933), 322.

43. AL to Mary Todd Lincoln, March 4, 1860, *CW,* First Supplement, 49.

44. Speech at Hartford, Connecticut, March 5, 1860; Speech at New Haven, Connecticut, March 6, 1860, *CW,* 4: 7, 24–25.

45. AL to Mary Todd Lincoln, March 4, 1860, *CW,* First Supplement, 49.

46. O. R. Post to AL, February 24, 1860; John D. Candee to AL, February 28, 1860; E. A. Rollins to AL, March 2, 1860, PAL.

47. For Lincoln's New England itinerary, see entries for February 28–March 10, 1860, *Lincoln Day by Day: A Chronology, 1809–1865,* ed. Earl Schenck Miers (Washington, D.C.: Lincoln Sesquicentennial Commission, 1960), 2: 274–275.

48. As quoted in *Chicago Press and Tribune,* March 14, 1860.

49. Ibid., March 14, 17, 1860.

50. Ibid., March 15, 1860, citing the *Springfield Illinois State Journal.*

51. F. W. Northrop to AL, March 22, 1860, PAL.

52. James F. Babcock to AL, April 8, 1860, PAL; AL to Mark W. Delahay, April 14, 1860, *CW,* 4: 44.

53. Mark W. Delahay to AL, February 17, 19, 1860, PAL; AL to Delahay, March 16, 1860, *CW,* 4: 31–32.

54. Samuel Galloway to AL, March 15, 1860, PAL.

55. Edwin A. Parrott to AL, March 5, 1860; Richard M. Corwine to AL, March 24, 1860, PAL.

56. AL to Samuel Galloway, March 24, 1860, *CW,* 4: 33–34. See also AL to Richard M. Corwine, April 6, 1860, *CW,* 4: 36. Though Lincoln mentioned Parrott's report in his letter to Galloway, no record remains that he replied to him.

57. Alonzo J. Grover to AL, January 31, 1860, PAL.

58. David Davis to AL, April 23, 1860, PAL.

59. Ibid.; Norman B. Judd to AL, May 2, 1860, PAL.

60. Joseph Medill to Lyman Trumbull, April 16, 1860, PLT.

61. Lyman Trumbull to AL, April 24, 1860, PAL.

62. AL to Lyman Trumbull, April 29, 1860, *CW,* 4: 45–46.

63. David Davis to AL, May 5, 1860, PAL.

64. AL to Richard M. Corwine, May 2, 1860, *CW,* 4: 47.

65. Hawkins Taylor to AL, February 25, April 15, 1860; Horace Rublee to AL, February 13, 1860; A. S. Seaton to AL, April 24, 1860, PAL.

66. Baringer, *Lincoln's Rise to Power,* 183–185; _____ Johnson to William H. Herndon [1865–1866], *HI,* 462–463; *Chicago Press and Tribune,* May 10, 1860.

67. Remarks to Republican State Convention, Decatur, Illinois, May 9, 1860, *CW*, 4: 48.

68. *Chicago Press and Tribune,* May 10, 1860.

69. *Chicago Press and Tribune,* May 11, 1860.

70. Ibid.; David Davis to AL, April 23, 1860, PAL; *Memoirs of Gustave Koerner, 1809–1896,* ed. Thomas J. McCormack, 2 vols. (Cedar Rapids, Iowa: Torch Press, 1909), 2: 83–85.

71. Jesse K. Dubois and David Davis to AL, May 14, 1860, PAL; AL to Mark W. Delahay, May 12, 1860, *CW*, 4: 49. Lincoln's comment for not attending the convention appears in Mitgang, ed., *Lincoln: A Press Portrait,* 167.

72. AL to Edward Wallace, May 12, 1860, *CW*, 4: 49.

73. Richard M. Corwine to AL, April 30, 1860, PAL. This letter is in Lincoln's handwriting. Lincoln copied the letter for his file and evidently gave the original to one of his campaign managers (perhaps State Auditor Jesse K. Dubois) to take to Chicago and use in his behalf.

74. *Chicago Press and Tribune,* May 15, 1860.

75. Jesse K. Dubois to AL, May 13, 1860; Mark W. Delahay to AL, May 14, 1860; William Butler to AL, May 14, 1860; Amos Tuck to AL, May 14, 1860, PAL. For Gideon Welles's role in opposing Seward at the convention, see John Niven, *Gideon Welles: Lincoln's Secretary of the Navy* (1973; reprint, Baton Rouge: Louisiana State University Press, 1994), 292–298.

76. "Keystone," *Chicago Press and Tribune,* May 16, 1860.

77. William Butler to AL, May 14, 15, 1860, PAL.

78. Jesse K. Dubois to AL, May 13, 1860; Mark W. Delahay to AL, May 13, 14, 1860; William Butler to AL, May 14, 1860, PAL.

79. Orville H. Browning, who privately had supported Bates, but lobbied for Lincoln's nomination at Chicago, concluded that Bates had no chance of winning the nomination unless the balloting became extended. Entry for May 17, 1860, *The Diary of Orville Hickman Browning,* ed. Theodore Calvin Pease and James G. Randall, 2 vols. (Springfield: Illinois State Library, 1925–1933), 1: 407.

80. William Butler to AL, May 15, 1860, PAL.

81. For a vivid description of the scene at Chicago, see *Three against Lincoln: Murat Halstead Reports the Caucuses of 1860,* ed. with an intro. by William B. Hesseltine (Baton Rouge: Louisiana State University Press, 1960), 142–144.

82. I pieced together the proceedings of the Chicago convention from the following sources: journalist Murat Halstead's reports in Hesseltine, ed., *Three against Lincoln,* 143–177; the *Chicago Press and Tribune,* May 17–19, 1860; and the *New York Times,* May 19, 1860, as printed in Mitgang, ed., *Lincoln: A Press Portrait,* 167–173.

83. *Chicago Press and Tribune,* May 18, 1860; J. G. Randall, *Lincoln the President: Springfield to Gettysburg* (New York: Dodd, Mead, 1945), 1: 156–158.

84. The Republican platform appears in Hesseltine, ed., *Three against Lincoln,* 156–158; and Elting Morison, "Election of 1860," in *History of American Presidential Elections, 1789–1968,* 10 vols. (New York: Chelsea House, 1985–1986), 3: 1124–1127.

85. Congress never approved the Wade proposal. See the *New York Tribune,* March 13, 1860, for Republican support of this measure.

86. Hesseltine, ed., *Three against Lincoln,* 161–162.

87. Mark W. Delahay to AL, May 17, 1860, PAL; Endorsement on the Margin of the *Missouri Democrat* [May 17, 1860], *CW,* 4: 50 and n. E. L. Baker, the editor of the *Springfield State Journal,* delivered this message, written in pencil on the *Democrat,* to Lincoln's managers on the day before the nominations, apparently in response to Delahay's telegram and an earlier letter from Charles H. Ray of the *Chicago Press and Tribune.* Ray had written Lincoln that "a pledge or two may be necessary when the pinch comes." Ray to AL, May 14, 1860, PAL.

88. For the conclusion that Lincoln's managers ignored his instructions to make no promises, see Baringer, *Lincoln's Rise to Power,* 266–267; Reinhard H. Luthin, *The First Lincoln Campaign* (Cambridge, Mass.: Harvard University Press, 1944), 158; David M. Potter, *The Impending Crisis, 1848–1861,* completed and edited by Don E. Fehrenbacher (New York: Harper and Row, 1976), 428. For the contrary view, see Donald, *Lincoln,* 249.

89. Leonard Swett to AL, May 25, 1860, PAL. See AL to Swett, May 26, 1860, *CW,* 4: 55 and n; and AL to David Davis, May 26, 1860, *CW,* First Supplement, 54, for Lincoln's approval of the promise.

90. Hesseltine, ed., *Three against Lincoln,* 161–162.

91. Ibid., 160–161; *Boston Daily Advertiser,* May 19, 1860.

92. David Davis to AL, May 17, 1860, PAL. Punctuation added.

93. Hesseltine, ed., *Three against Lincoln,* 164–166.

94. Lane's statement appears in the *Chicago Press and Tribune,* May 19, 1860.

95. *Chicago Press and Tribune,* May 22, 1860; Hesseltine, ed., *Three against Lincoln,* 166–167.

96. For the votes, by states, on the ballots, see Hesseltine, ed., *Three against Lincoln,* 167–170. I have dropped the fractions in the delegates' votes.

97. *Chicago Press and Tribune,* May 19, 1860; Hesseltine, ed., *Three against Lincoln,* 170–172.

98. Hesseltine, ed., *Three against Lincoln,* 174–176; AL to Hannibal Hamlin, July 18, 1860, *CW,* 4: 84; Hamlin to AL, July 23, 1860, PAL.

99. Christopher C. Brown interview, 1865–1866; James Gourley interview, 1865–1866; Charles S. Zane statement, 1865–1866, *HI,* 438, 453, 490–491.

100. Schuyler Colfax to AL, May 18, 1860; Elihu B. Washburne to AL, May 19, 1860, PAL.

101. Elihu B. Washburne to AL, May 19, 1860; Schuyler Colfax to AL, May 18, 1860; Lyman Trumbull to AL, May 18, 1860, PAL.

102. Elihu B. Washburne to AL, May 19, 1860; Schuyler Colfax to AL, May 18, 1860; Lyman Trumbull to AL, May 18, 22, 1860, PAL.

103. *Chicago Press and Tribune,* May 19, 1860; Response to a Serenade, May 18, 1860, *CW,* 4: 50 and n.

104. *Chicago Press and Tribune,* May 19, 1860; *New York Times,* May 19, 1860; William Schouler to AL, May 23, 1860, PAL.

105. As quoted in Robert S. Harper, *Lincoln and the Press* (New York: McGraw-Hill, 1951), 54.

106. Entry for May 18, 1860, *A Philadelphia Perspective: The Diary of Sidney George Fisher Covering the Years 1834–1871,* ed. Nicholas B. Wainwright (Philadelphia: Historical Society of Pennsylvania, 1967), 353.

107. Both quoted in *Chicago Press and Tribune,* May 23, 1860.

108. *Chicago Press and Tribune,* May 24, 1860.

109. *Boston Daily Advertiser,* May 29, 1860.

110. *New York Times,* May 24, 1860.

111. These newspapers are quoted in *New York Times,* May 21, 1860.

112. *The Liberator,* May 25, 1860.

113. As reported in *The Liberator,* June 8, 1860.

114. These newspaper quotes appear in Harper, *Lincoln and the Press,* 56–58.

115. *Springfield Illinois State Register,* May 22, 1860.

116. *Springfield Illinois State Register,* May 19, 1860.

117. *Richmond Daily Dispatch,* May 24, 1860.

118. *New Orleans Bee,* May 21, 1860.

119. Reply to Committee of the Republican National Convention, May 19, 1860, *CW,* 4: 51; *New York Times,* May 24, 1860; *Chicago Press and Tribune,* May 24, 1860.

120. Clipping from the *Springfield* (Massachusetts) *Daily Republican,* May 23, 1860, in PAL. Ashmun sent his article to Lincoln.

121. *The Reminiscences of Carl Schurz,* 3 vols. (New York: McClure, 1907), 2: 184–185.

122. Don E. Fehrenbacher, *Prelude to Greatness: Lincoln in the 1850's* (Stanford, Calif.: Stanford University Press, 1962), 159.

123. *Reminiscences of Schurz,* 2: 188.

CHAPTER EIGHT: CAMPAIGN AND ELECTION

1. William Herndon to Lyman Trumbull, June 19, 1860, PLT; Harry E. Pratt, *The Personal Finances of Abraham Lincoln* (Springfield: Abraham Lincoln Association, 1943), 110; Anonymous newspaper correspondent, June 21, 1860, *Recollected Words of Abraham Lincoln,* ed. Don E. Fehrenbacher and Virginia Fehrenbacher (Stanford, Calif.: Stanford University Press, 1996), 4–5.

2. John G. Nicolay to Therena Bates, June 7, 1860, *With Lincoln in the White House: Letters, Memoranda and Other Writings of John G. Nicolay, 1860–1865,* ed. Michael Burlingame (Carbondale: Southern Illinois University Press, 2000), 1. Michael Burlingame's introduction, pp. xi–xxi, contains an excellent biographical sketch of Nicolay.

3. John G. Nicolay, "Lincoln in the Campaign of 1860," *An Oral History of Abraham Lincoln: John G. Nicolay's Interviews and Essays,* ed. Michael Burlingame (Carbondale: Southern Illinois University Press, 1996), 91–92.

4. John G. Nicolay to Messrs. Follett & Foster, June 15, 1860; Nicolay to James Q. Howard, June 19, 1860, Burlingame, ed., *With Lincoln in the White House,* 2–4; *CW,* 4: 60n; John L. Scripps to AL, July 11, 17, 1860, PAL.

5. Helen Nicolay, *Personal Traits of Abraham Lincoln* (New York: Century, 1912), 145, citing notes of John G. Nicolay.

6. "Memorandum, 16 October 1860," Burlingame, ed., *With Lincoln in the White House,* 6–7.

7. "Thomas Hicks," in *Reminiscences of Abraham Lincoln, by Distinguished Men of His Time,* ed. Allen Thorndike Rice (New York: North American Review, 1889), 596; William Herndon to Lyman Trumbull, June 19, 1860, PLT; entries for

June 12, 13, 1860, *The Diary of Orville Hickman Browning,* ed. Theodore Calvin Pease and James G. Randall, 2 vols. (Springfield: Illinois State Library, 1925-1933), 1: 415.

8. David Davis to AL, May 23, 1860; Lyman Trumbull to AL, May 31, 1860; Leonard Swett to AL, June 13, 1860, PAL; AL to Swett, May 30, 1860; AL to Trumbull, June 5, 1860, CW, 4: 57, 71. For Weed's reaction to Lincoln, see Glyndon G. Van Deusen, *Thurlow Weed: Wizard of the Lobby* (Boston: Little, Brown, 1947), 256.

9. See Thurlow Weed to AL, June 25, July 11, 27, 1860, PAL.

10. Glyndon G. Van Deusen, *William Henry Seward* (New York: Oxford University Press, 1967), 229, 231-233; CW, 4: 87n; Paul M. Angle, *"Here I Have Lived": A History of Lincoln's Springfield, 1821-1865* (New Brunswick, N.J.: Rutgers University Press, 1935), 251.

11. Edwin D. Morgan to AL, June 4, 1860; Lyman Trumbull to AL, June 8, 1860, PAL. Though he did not campaign for Lincoln, Edward Bates, at the urging of Orville H. Browning and other Republican friends, wrote a public letter supporting the "Rail Splitter." "I consider Mr. Lincoln a sound, safe, national man," Bates told a friend. "He could not be sectional if he tried." Marvin R. Cain, *Lincoln's Attorney General: Edward Bates of Missouri* (Columbia: University of Missouri Press, 1965), 116 (quote).

12. Joseph Medill to AL, June 19, July 5, 1860, PAL.

13. *Springfield Illinois State Register,* August 23, 1860.

14. The *Chicago Press and Tribune,* August 15, 1860, printed the correspondent's account that appeared in the *New York Herald* on August 13.

15. AL to John B. Fry, August 15, 1860, CW, 4: 95.

16. As reported in the *Chicago Press and Tribune,* August 15, 1860.

17. AL to George G. Fogg, August 16, 1860; AL to Samuel Haycraft, August 16, 1860, CW, 4: 96, 97.

18. William Cullen Bryant to AL, June 16, 1860, PAL.

19. AL to Samuel Galloway, June 19, 1860, CW, 4: 80.

20. Lyman Trumbull to AL, May 22, 1860; David Davis to AL, May 18, 1860, PAL.

21. AL to Anson G. Henry, July 4, 1860, CW, 4: 82.

22. James G. Randall, *Lincoln the President: Springfield to Gettysburg* (New York: Dodd, Mead, 1945), 1: 179-180; *Memoirs of Gustave Koerner, 1809-1896,* ed. Thomas J. McCormack, 2 vols. (Cedar Rapids, Iowa: Torch Press, 1909), 2: 98.

23. Angle, *"Here I Have Lived,"* 249.

24. AL to William Fithian, August 15, 1860, CW, 4: 95.

25. *Chicago Press and Tribune,* August 10, 1860; "Springfield Correspondence, 9 August 1860," *Lincoln's Journalist: John Hay's Anonymous Writings for the Press, 1860-1864,* ed. Michael Burlingame (Carbondale: Southern Illinois University Press, 1998), 3-6; Angle, *"Here I Have Lived,"* 246-247; and McCormack, ed., *Memoirs of Gustave Koerner,* 2: 99.

26. CW, 4: 91-92n; entry for August 8, 1860, Pease and Randall, eds., *The Diary of Orville Hickman Browning,* 1: 421.

27. Entry for August 8, 1860, Pease and Randall, eds., *The Diary of Orville Hickman Browning,* 1: 422. For Koerner's participation in the campaign, see McCormack, ed., *Memoirs of Gustave Koerner,* 2: 97-99.

28. Remarks at a Republican Rally, Springfield, Illinois, August 8, 1860, CW, 4: 91 and 91n; "Springfield Correspondence, 9 August 1860," Burlingame, ed., *Lincoln's Journalist*, 5–6; Angle, *"Here I Have Lived,"* 247.

29. Abraham Jonas to AL, July 20, 1860, PAL; AL to Jonas, July 21, 1860, CW, 4: 85–86.

30. *Springfield Illinois State Register*, June 2, 5, 1860.

31. As reported in *Springfield Illinois State Register*, August 21, 1860.

32. Clark E. Carr to AL, May 26, 1860, PAL.

33. *Springfield Illinois State Register*, July 14, 31, August 7, 1860.

34. As quoted in James M. McPherson, *Battle Cry of Freedom: The Civil War Era* (New York: Oxford University Press, 1988), 224.

35. For an excellent account of Douglas's campaign, see Robert W. Johannsen, *Stephen A. Douglas* (New York: Oxford University Press, 1973), 778–803.

36. Allan Nevins, *The Emergence of Lincoln*, vol. 2, *Prologue to Civil War, 1859–1861* (New York: Scribner's Sons, 1950), 295.

37. See, for example, AL to George G. Fogg, August 14, 1860; AL to James F. Simmons, August 17, 1860; AL to Amory Holbrook, August 27, 1860, CW, 4: 94, 97, 101.

38. As quoted in Doris Kearns Goodwin, *Team of Rivals: The Political Genius of Abraham Lincoln* (New York: Simon and Schuster, 2005), 264.

39. AL to T. Apolion Cheney, August 14, 1860, CW, 4: 93.

40. AL to Edwin M. Morgan, September 20, 1860, CW, 4: 116.

41. For the Bell meeting at Decatur, see the *Springfield Illinois State Register*, August 18, 1860.

42. Schuyler Colfax to AL, May 30, 1860, PAL (quote); AL to Colfax, May 26, 1860, CW, 4: 54. Lincoln's letter to Thompson has not been found, but the Indianan's reply to Lincoln, June 12, 1860, PAL, provides a summary of its contents.

43. Richard W. Thompson to AL, June 12, 1860, PAL.

44. Richard W. Thompson to AL, July 6, 1860, PAL.

45. Ibid.; "Lincoln in the Campaign of 1860," Burlingame, ed., *An Oral History of Lincoln*, 93–94; Instructions for John G. Nicolay [c. July 16, 1860], CW, 4: 83.

46. AL to Caleb B. Smith, [July 23,] 1860, CW, 4: 87–88.

47. John P. Usher to AL, August 18, 1860, PAL. A report of John J. Crittenden's speech can be found in the *Springfield Illinois State Register*, August 23, 1860.

48. John P. Usher to AL, August 18, 1860; John D. Defrees to AL, August 17, 1860, PAL.

49. John D. Defrees to AL, October 1, 1860; Leonard Swett to David Davis, October 1, 1860, PAL.

50. Richard W. Thompson, *To the Conservative Men of Indiana* (n.p., n.d.), in PAL.

51. James E. Harvey to AL, June 5, 1860; John M. Pomeroy to AL, August 27, 1860, PAL.

52. James E. Harvey to AL, May 21, 1860; Schuyler Colfax to AL, May 26, 1860; Elihu B. Washburne to AL, May 20, 1860; David Davis to AL, June 7, 1860, PAL.

53. John M. Pomeroy to AL, August 27, 1860, PAL; AL to Leonard Swett, July 16, 1860, CW, 4: 83–84 and 84n.

54. David Davis to AL, August 5, 1860; Davis to AL, August 12, 1860, PAL.

55. Thurlow Weed to AL, August 13, 1860; John M. Pomeroy to AL, August 27, 1860, PAL; AL to Pomeroy, August 31, 1860, *CW*, 4: 103.

56. Forney, quoted in Reinhard H. Luthin, *The First Lincoln Campaign* (1944; reprint, Gloucester, Mass.: Peter Smith, 1964), 204. For the bitter factionalism in the Pennsylvania Democratic party, see Edward L. Ayers, *In the Presence of Mine Enemies: War in the Heart of America, 1859–1863* (New York: W. W. Norton, 2003), 65–66.

57. Alexander K. McClure to AL, July 2, 7, 18, 1860; David Wilmot to AL, July 11, 1860, PAL.

58. John M. Pomeroy to AL, August 27, 1860; Russell Errett to Joseph Medill, July 24, 1860, PAL.

59. Joseph Medill to AL, July 29, 1860; Elihu B. Washburne to AL, September 5, 1860, PAL.

60. Russell Errett to Joseph Medill, July 24, 1860; Joseph Medill to AL, July 29, 1860; Alexander K. McClure to AL, September 12, 1860; Elihu B. Washburne to AL, September 5, 1860 (quote), PAL.

61. Luthin, *The First Lincoln Campaign,* 205; Willard L. King, *Lincoln's Manager: David Davis* (Cambridge, Mass.: Harvard University Press, 1960), 154–155.

62. AL to Joseph Medill, September 4, 1860, quoting Simon Cameron letter of August 29, 1860, *CW*, 4: 110–111; John W. Forney to Thurlow Weed, September 27, 1860 (quote); James E. Harvey to AL, October 6, 1860, PAL.

63. AL to William H. Herndon, October 10, 1860, *CW*, 4: 126 and note (Herndon quote).

64. *Chicago Press and Tribune,* October 10, 1860.

65. Johannsen, *Stephen A. Douglas,* 797–799.

66. John G. Nicolay Memorandum, Springfield, October 25, 1860, Burlingame, ed., *With Lincoln in the White House,* 7.

67. As quoted in King, *Lincoln's Manager,* 159.

68. R. B. Carter to AL, October 29, 1860, PAL; George A. Nourse to Lyman Trumbull, October 29, 1860, PLT.

69. *New York Herald,* October 11, 1860.

70. *New Orleans Daily Crescent,* October 13, 1860, as reported in *Southern Editorials on Secession,* ed. Dwight Lowell Dumond (New York: Century, 1931), 187–188. Dumond includes editorials on the dire consequences of a Lincoln victory in November that appeared in newspaper reports in the upper South after the Indiana and Pennsylvania elections, such as one from the *Nashville Union and American* on October 12, 1860, and one from the *Richmond Semi-Weekly Examiner* on October 26, 1860, on pp. 181–184, 191–195.

71. *Louisville Daily Journal,* October 30, 1860, as reported in Dumond, ed., *Southern Editorials on Secession,* 198.

72. AL to Thurlow Weed, August 17, 1860, *CW*, 4: 97–98; Weed to AL, August 13, 1860; George G. Fogg to AL, September 11, 1860, PAL.

73. AL to John Pettit, September 14, 1860, *CW*, 4: 115.

74. James O. Putnam to AL, September 25, 1860, PAL.

75. *New York Herald,* November 4, 5, 6, 1860.

76. Edwin D. Morgan to AL, November 1, 1860, PAL. See also Thurlow Weed to AL, October 28, 1860, PAL.

77. Luthin, *The First Lincoln Campaign,* 216–217; Van Deusen, *William Henry Seward,* 235.

78. George D. Prentice to AL, October 26, 1860, PAL; AL to Prentice, October 29, 1860, and endorsement on the back of the letter, *CW,* 4: 134–135.

79. Two days before he drafted his letter to Prentice, Lincoln wrote a similar reply to George T. M. Davis of Alton, Illinois, an old friend who had asked him to write a soothing public letter to businessmen for the purpose of preventing a southern plot to create a panic in northern financial circles upon his election. AL to Davis, October 27, 1860, *CW,* 4: 132–133.

80. As quoted in *Lincoln, 1854–1861: Being the Day-by-Day Activities of Abraham Lincoln from January 1, 1854, to March 4, 1861,* ed. Paul M. Angle (Springfield: Abraham Lincoln Association, 1933), 358.

81. *New York Tribune* correspondent, as quoted in Burlingame, ed., *An Oral History of Abraham Lincoln,* 105–106.

82. Ibid., 106; Angle, *"Here I Have Lived,"* 251.

83. Angle, *"Here I Have Lived,"* 252–253; John G. Nicolay to Therena Bates, November 8, 1860, Burlingame, ed., *With Lincoln in the White House,* 9.

84. Though the war issues were paramount in 1864, old party loyalties, with some realignment, persisted in the election. For the 1864 election, see my *Lincoln's Last Months* (Cambridge, Mass.: Belknap Press of Harvard University Press, 2004), chap. 1.

85. Richard N. Current, *The Lincoln Nobody Knows* (1958; reprint, New York: Hill and Wang, 1992), 212.

86. William E. Gienapp, "Who Voted for Lincoln?" in *Abraham Lincoln and the American Political Tradition,* ed. John L. Thomas (Amherst: University of Massachusetts Press, 1986), 62. In this essay (pp. 50–97), Gienapp provides a careful analysis of the 1860 election results. My conclusions, however, differ in some particulars.

87. For the support of young voters for Lincoln, see ibid., 77.

88. Professor James M. McPherson, *Battle Cry of Freedom,* 225–226, has an excellent account of the corruption in the Buchanan government and its importance in the 1860 contest.

89. Biographer Michael Burlingame has graciously provided me with a copy of chapter 16 in his forthcoming multivolume life of Lincoln that contains the Grimes and Belmont quotes.

90. For Wendell Phillips's position in the election, see Irving H. Bartlett, *Wendell Phillips: Brahmin Radical* (1961; reprint, Westport, Conn.: Greenwood Press, 1973), 222–223.

91. George G. Fogg to AL, November 7, 1860, PAL.

92. Salmon P. Chase to AL, November 7, 1860, PAL.

CHAPTER NINE: CABINET MAKING

1. Lincoln made this comment to Samuel R. Weed, a St. Louis newspaper reporter. *Recollected Words of Abraham Lincoln,* comp. and ed. Don E. Fehrenbacher and Virginia Fehrenbacher (Stanford, Calif.: Stanford University Press, 1996), 460.

2. A *New York Times* correspondent, reporting from Springfield on November 9, described the reasons westerners believed that Lincoln would be able to gain southerners' confidence and that the cry of secession would fade. The report was printed in the November 15, 1860, issue.

3. Yates's speech was printed in the *Chicago Tribune,* November 30, 1860. After the 1860 presidential election, the *Chicago Press and Tribune* reverted to its old name, the *Chicago Tribune.*

4. William C. Smedes to AL, February 4, 1861, PAL.

5. *Augusta Chronicle and Sentinel,* November 13, 1860, quoted in *Southern Editorials on Secession,* ed. Dwight Lowell Dumond (New York: Century, 1931), 231.

6. Entries for November 5, 8, 1860, David Schenck Diary, Southern Historical Collection, University of North Carolina Library, Chapel Hill, North Carolina.

7. Delaware was also a slave state, with 1,798 slaves in 1860. But its proximity to Philadelphia markets and northern neighbors mitigated against a secession threat in the state.

8. *Concord* (New Hampshire) *Democratic Standard,* November 24, 1860, quoted in *Northern Editorials on Secession,* ed. Howard Cecil Perkins, 2 vols. (1942; reprint, Gloucester, Mass.: Peter Smith, 1964), 1: 99.

9. *Providence Daily Post,* November 8, 1860, quoted in Perkins, ed., *Northern Editorials on Secession,* 1: 83.

10. *Cleveland Daily National Democrat,* November 19, 1860, quoted in Perkins, ed., *Northern Editorials on Secession,* 1: 94.

11. *Albany Atlas and Argus,* November 10, 1860, quoted in Perkins, ed., *Northern Editorials on Secession,* 1: 87.

12. *New York Times,* November 15, 1860. The correspondent's report was dated November 9.

13. Benjamin P. Thomas, *Abraham Lincoln: A Biography* (1952; reprint, New York: Random House, 1968), 231.

14. *New York Times,* November 15, 1860.

15. AL to Nathaniel P. Paschall, November 16, 1860, *CW,* 4: 139–140.

16. *St. Louis Daily Missouri Republican,* November 21, 1860, quoted in Dumond, ed., *Southern Editorials on Secession,* 258–260.

17. Nathaniel P. Paschall to AL, November 18, 1860, PAL.

18. William E. Baringer, *A House Dividing: Lincoln as President Elect* (Springfield: Abraham Lincoln Association, 1945), 32. See also the *New York Herald,* November 8, 1860.

19. Henry J. Raymond to AL, November 14, 1860, PAL. See also Henry S. Sanford to AL, November 15, 1860, and Schuyler Colfax to AL, November 27, 1860, PAL.

20. AL to Henry J. Raymond, November 28, 1860, *CW,* 4: 145–146.

21. AL to Truman Smith, November 10, 1860, *CW,* 4: 138.

22. Edwin D. Morgan to AL, November 20, 1860, PAL; *Memoirs of Gustave Koerner,* ed. Thomas J. McCormack, 2 vols. (Cedar Rapids, Iowa: Torch Press, 1909), 2: 104; Thurlow Weed to David Davis, November 17, 1860; George Ashmun to AL, November 13, 1860, PAL.

23. *Chicago Tribune,* November 22, 1860 (quote); *Lincoln on the Eve of '61: A Journalist's Story by Henry Villard,* ed. Harold Garrison Villard and Oswald Garrison Villard (New York: Knopf, 1941), 23–24. Henry Villard was a correspondent for the

New York Herald in Springfield. Though the *Herald* was hostile to Lincoln, Villard favored him. Some of Villard's dispatches, while printed in the *Herald,* were not included in the published book. The young correspondent indicated that he was frequently in Lincoln's company in Springfield and later during a trip to the East. He left the president-elect's train at New York.

24. Passage Written for Lyman Trumbull's Speech at Springfield, Illinois, November 20, 1860, *CW,* 4: 141–142.

25. John G. Nicolay, "Memorandum, Springfield, 15 November 1860," *With Lincoln in the White House: Letters, Memoranda and Other Writings of John G. Nicolay, 1860–1865,* ed. Michael Burlingame (Carbondale: Southern Illinois University Press, 2000), 10.

26. AL to Henry J. Raymond, November 28, 1860, *CW,* 4: 146; *New York Herald,* December 6, 1860. For the calming effect of the speech on eastern financial men, see John W. Forney to AL, November 22, 1860, PAL.

27. AL to Hannibal Hamlin, November 8, 1860; AL to Joshua F. Speed, November 19, 1860, *CW,* 4: 136, 141.

28. *Chicago Tribune,* November 24, 1860.

29. Joshua Speed interview [1865–1866], *HI,* 475.

30. For Lincoln's early intention to bring Seward into his cabinet, see his letter to Seward, December 8, 1860, *CW,* 4: 148, and John G. Nicolay, "Memorandum, Springfield, 15 December 1860," Burlingame, ed., *With Lincoln in the White House,* 18.

31. AL to Lyman Trumbull, December 8, 1860, *CW,* 4: 149.

32. Entry for December 16, 1860, *Diary of Edward Bates, 1859–1866,* ed. Howard K. Beale (Washington, D.C.: Government Printing Office, 1933), 164.

33. Harry J. Carman and Reinhard H. Luthin, *Lincoln and the Patronage* (1943; reprint, Gloucester, Mass.: Peter Smith, 1964), 12; Joshua Speed interview [1865–1866], *HI,* 475.

34. *New York Herald,* November 29, 1860.

35. AL to Hannibal Hamlin, December 24, 1860, *CW,* 4: 161.

36. George G. Fogg to AL, December 29, 1860, PAL, reminding the president-elect of his early preference for Welles.

37. John Niven, *Gideon Welles: Lincoln's Secretary of the Navy* (1973; reprint, Baton Rouge: Louisiana State University Press, 1994), 289, 313–317; Hannibal Hamlin to AL, December 29, 1860; Leonard Swett to AL, January 4, 1861, PAL.

38. Niven, *Gideon Welles,* 321–322.

39. *New York Herald,* November 29, 1860.

40. The *New York Herald,* November 26, 1860, reported that Lincoln had rejected the idea of an Illinoisan in the cabinet.

41. Republican Members of the U.S. Senate to AL, January 7, 1861; Lyman Trumbull to AL, January 7, 1861; Russell Errett to AL, November 21, 1860; Jesse W. Fell to AL, January 2, 1861, PAL.

42. Entry for December 16, 1860, Beale, ed., *Diary of Edward Bates,* 164.

43. Nicolay, "Memorandum, Springfield, 15 December 1860," Burlingame, ed., *With Lincoln in the White House,* 17–19.

44. Edward Bates to AL, December 18, 1860, PAL; AL to Bates, December 18, 1860, *CW,* 4: 154.

45. Salmon P. Chase to James Shepherd Pike, January 10, 1861, *The Salmon P. Chase Papers,* vol. 3, *Correspondence, 1858–March 1863,* ed. John Niven (Kent, Ohio: Kent State University Press, 1996), 47. George G. Fogg, an influential former Democrat of New England, wrote Lincoln that the country "will pronounce" Bates's appointment "a selection 'eminently fit to be made.'" Fogg to AL, December 22, 1860, PAL.

46. Lyman Trumbull to AL, December 2, 1860, PAL.

47. AL to Lyman Trumbull, December 8, 1860, CW, 4: 149.

48. Hannibal Hamlin to AL, December 4, 1860, PAL.

49. AL to William H. Seward, December 8, 1860, CW, 4: 148–149.

50. AL to Hannibal Hamlin, December 8, 1860, CW, 4: 147.

51. H. Draper Hunt, *Hannibal Hamlin of Maine: Lincoln's First Vice-President* (Syracuse, N.Y.: Syracuse University Press, 1969), 131 (quote); William H. Seward to AL, December 13, 1860, PAL.

52. Leonard Swett to Thurlow Weed, December 10, 1860; David Davis to Weed, December 10, 1860; *Life of Thurlow Weed, Including His Autobiography and a Memoir,* 2 vols. (Boston: Houghton, Mifflin, 1883), 1: 301–302; David M. Potter, *Lincoln and His Party in the Secession Crisis,* with a new introduction by Daniel W. Crofts (1942; reprint, Baton Rouge: Louisiana State University Press, 1995), 164–165; William H. Seward to AL, December 16, 1860, PAL.

53. *Life of Thurlow Weed,* 1: 603–604, 612; *Albany Evening Post,* December 17, 1860, as printed in the *New York Herald,* December 19, 1860. Reporting from Springfield, Villard provided the *Herald* with a colorful—and biased—account of Weed's visit. Issue of December 25, 1860.

54. *Life of Thurlow Weed,* 1: 604–605.

55. Editorial in the *Springfield Illinois State Journal,* December 12, 1860, CW, 4: 150.

56. *Life of Thurlow Weed,* 1: 605–606, 614; AL to John A. Gilmer, December 15, 1860, CW, 4: 151–152, 153n.

57. *Life of Thurlow Weed,* 1: 610.

58. Ibid., 1: 611.

59. Ibid., 1: 614. This letter is not extant. CW, 4: 153n.

60. John A. Gilmer to AL, December 29, 1860, PAL.

61. AL to Lyman Trumbull, December 21, 1861, CW, 4: 158.

62. As quoted in Glyndon G. Van Deusen, *Thurlow Weed: Wizard of the Lobby* (Boston: Little, Brown, 1947), 261.

63. William H. Seward to AL, December 28, 1860, PAL.

64. George G. Fogg to AL, February 5, 1861, PAL.

65. William H. Seward to AL, December 29, 1860, PAL; AL to Seward, January 3, 12, 1861, CW, 4: 170,173.

66. For the effort to secure Montgomery Blair's appointment as secretary of war, see Benjamin F. Wade to Preston King, November 20, 1860; Lyman Trumbull to AL, December 18, 1860; and William Dennison to AL, January 7, 1861, PAL. Even before Gilmer turned down his offer, Lincoln, in response to the lobbying effort on behalf of Blair, wrote Trumbull that "I expect to be able to offer Mr. Blair a place in the cabinet, but I can not, as yet, be committed on the matter, to any extent whatever." AL to Trumbull, December 24, 1860, CW, 4: 162.

67. Both quotes are in Joseph Medill to AL, December 18, 1860, PAL.

68. AL to Hannibal Hamlin, November 27, 1860, *CW,* 4: 145.

69. James K. Moorhead to AL, November 23, 1860; Andrew H. Reeder to AL, November 21, 1860; Joseph Casey to Leonard Swett, November 27, 1860, PAL. Numerous other letters supporting Cameron can be found in the Lincoln Papers, late 1860 and early 1861.

70. Andrew H. Reeder to AL, December 18, 1860, PAL. In a letter to Simon Cameron dated January 3, 1861 (actually written on January 13), Lincoln confirmed that he had asked the senator to come to Springfield. *CW,* 4: 174.

71. AL to Simon Cameron, December 31, 1860, *CW,* 4: 168.

72. *New York Herald,* January 5, 1861; Lyman Trumbull to AL, December 31, 1860; AL to Hannibal Hamlin, December 27, 1860; Elihu B. Washburne to AL, January 1, 1861, PAL.

73. William Cullen Bryant to AL, January 3, 4 (quote), 1861, PAL.

74. McCormack, ed., *Memoirs of Gustave Koerner,* 2: 114.

75. AL to Simon Cameron, January 3, 1861, *CW,* 4: 169–170.

76. Lyman Trumbull to AL, January 16, 1861; Elihu B. Washburne to AL, January 10, 1861; Leonard Swett to AL, January 8, 14, 1861, PAL.

77. William H. Seward to AL, January 13, 1861, PAL.

78. Thaddeus Stevens to Elihu B. Washburne, January 19, 1861; Andrew G. Curtin to AL, January 17, 1861, PAL.

79. Lyman Trumbull to AL, January 16, 1861; Edgar Cowan to AL, January 10, 1861; John W. Forney to AL, January 13, 1861, PAL.

80. John W. Forney to AL, January 13, 1861, PAL.

81. William P. Fessenden to AL, January 20, 1861, PAL.

82. John Allison to AL, January 16, 1861; Thaddeus Stevens to Elihu B. Washburne, January 19, 1861; Washburne to AL, January 20, 1861; Lyman Trumbull to AL, January 20, 1861; Henry Wilson to AL, January 19, 1861, PAL.

83. George G. Fogg to AL, February 5, 1861, PAL.

84. AL to Lyman Trumbull, January 7, 1861, *CW,* 4: 171.

85. Ibid.

86. William M. Wilson to AL, January 19, 1861; John E. Cummins to AL, January 18, 1861, PAL.

87. Thurlow Weed to Leonard Swett, January 20, 1861; Republican Members of Pennsylvania Senate to AL, January 1861; Republican Members of Pennsylvania House of Representatives to AL, January 1861; John J. Patterson to AL, January 19, 1861, PAL.

88. Henry Wilson to AL, January 19, 1861; Lyman Trumbull to AL, January 20, 1861; William Cullen Bryant to AL, January 22, 1861; Amos Tuck to AL, January 14, 1861, PAL.

89. For a revealing letter by Salmon P. Chase regarding his position on slavery and the sectional crisis, see Chase to Ruhaman Ludlow Hunt, his sister-in-law, November 30, 1860, Niven, ed., *The Salmon P. Chase Papers,* 35–36.

90. George Opdyke to AL, January 24, 1861, PAL.

91. Wade, quoted in entry for [July–August 1863], *Inside Lincoln's White House:*

The Complete Civil War Diary of John Hay, ed. Michael Burlingame and John R. Turner Ettlinger (Carbondale: Southern Illinois University Press, 1997), 77.

92. Salmon P. Chase to George Opdyke, January 9, 1861, Niven, ed., *The Salmon P. Chase Papers,* 45.

93. Lincoln had already decided that no subordinate offices would be filled until after the inauguration, which created confusion and uncertainty in the government at a time of national crisis. *New York Herald,* January 10, 1861.

94. List of Senators' Preferences for Cabinet Appointment [March 1? 1861], *CW,* 4: 248. Though the editors of the *Collected Works* suggest a March 1 date for Lincoln's listing of the preferences, it probably was compiled a few days earlier.

95. *New York Tribune,* February 28, March 2, 1861.

96. Ibid.; Baringer, *A House Dividing,* 322–324; John G. Nicolay and John Hay, *Abraham Lincoln: A History,* 10 vols. (New York: Century, 1890), 3: 370 (quote).

97. As quoted in Allan Nevins, *The Emergence of Lincoln,* vol. 2, *Prologue to Civil War, 1859–1861* (New York: Charles Scribner's Sons, 1950), 453.

98. *New York Herald,* March 2, 1861 (quote); *New York Tribune,* February 17, 1861.

99. William H. Seward to AL, March 2, 1861, PAL.

100. Nicolay and Hay, *Abraham Lincoln,* 3: 369–370.

101. AL to William H. Seward, March 4, 1861, *CW,* 4: 273. Though the note was written at Willard's, Lincoln headed it the "Executive Mansion," which he would occupy before the end of the day.

102. Nicolay and Hay, *Abraham Lincoln,* 3: 371–372.

103. Ibid.; Frederick J. Blue, *Salmon P. Chase: A Life in Politics* (Kent, Ohio: Kent State University Press, 1987), 132–133; John Niven, *Salmon P. Chase: A Biography* (New York: Oxford University Press, 1995), 237–238.

104. Frederick W. Seward, *Seward at Washington, as Senator and Secretary of State: A Memoir of His Life, with Selections from His Letters, 1846–1861* (New York: Derby and Miller, 1891), 590. For an excellent account of the Lincoln-Seward relationship, see David Herbert Donald, *"We Are Lincoln Men": Abraham Lincoln and His Friends* (New York: Simon and Schuster, 2003), chap. 5.

105. Henry Adams to Charles Francis Adams, Jr., December 9, 1860, *The Letters of Henry Adams,* vol. 1, *1858–1868,* ed. J. C. Levenson et al. (Cambridge, Mass.: Harvard University Press, 1982), 204.

106. As quoted in Donald, *"We Are Lincoln Men,"* 156.

107. My account of the Lincoln-Seward relationship was written before the appearance of Doris Kearns Goodwin's well-written though heavily anecdotal book *Team of Rivals: The Political Genius of Abraham Lincoln* (New York: Simon and Schuster, 2005).

CHAPTER TEN: "HOLD FIRM, AS WITH A CHAIN OF STEEL"

1. As quoted in *Recollected Words of Abraham Lincoln,* comp. and ed. Don E. Fehrenbacher and Virginia Fehrenbacher (Stanford, Calif.: Stanford University Press, 1996), 6.

2. AL to Alexander H. Stephens, November 30, 1860, CW, 4: 146.

3. AL to Alexander H. Stephens, December 22, 1860, CW, 4: 160, 160–161n.

4. Ibid.

5. Alexander H. Stephens to AL, December 30, 1860, in *Recollections of Alexander H. Stephens,* ed. Myrta Lockett Avary (New York: Doubleday Page, 1910), 60. This letter is not in the Lincoln Papers.

6. Villard's December 3, 1860, report appeared in the *New York Herald* on December 9.

7. *Messages and Papers of the Presidents,* comp. James D. Richardson, 20 vols. (New York: Bureau of National Literature, 1909), 7: 3157–3159, 3168.

8. *New York Herald,* December 10, 1860.

9. George G. Fogg to AL, December 17, 1860, PAL.

10. David M. Potter, *Lincoln and His Party in the Secession Crisis,* with a new introduction by Daniel W. Crofts (1942; reprint, Baton Rouge: Louisiana State University Press, 1995), 89–92.

11. AL to Lyman Trumbull, December 10, 1860, CW, 4: 149–150.

12. Lyman Trumbull to AL, December 14, 1860, PAL. See also George G. Fogg to AL, December 17, 1860, PAL.

13. AL to William Kellogg, December 11, 1860; AL to Elihu B. Washburne, December 13, 1860, CW, 4: 150, 151. "Filibustering" refers to the mid-nineteenth century effort of southerners and other Americans to seize territory in the Caribbean, Mexico, and Central America. One of the purposes of these armed expeditions was to expand slavery.

14. AL to Lyman Trumbull, December 17, 1860, CW, 4: 153.

15. Thurlow Weed to AL, December 11, 1860, PAL.

16. AL to Thurlow Weed, December 17, 1860, CW, 4: 154 and n.

17. Lyman Trumbull to AL, December 24, 1860, PAL.

18. Resolutions Drawn up for Republican Members of Senate Committee of Thirteen [December 20, 1860]; AL to Lyman Trumbull, December 21, 1860, CW, 4: 156–157, 158.

19. William H. Seward to AL, December 26, 1860, PAL.

20. For the fate of the Seward resolutions, see Potter, *Lincoln and His Party in the Secession Crisis,* 172–174.

21. For the conclusion that Seward would have voted for a compromise if Lincoln had not opposed it, see ibid., 184. My analysis of Seward's position differs somewhat from Potter's.

22. For Wade's December 17 speech, see Hans L. Trefousse, *Benjamin Franklin Wade: Radical Republican from Ohio* (New York: Twayne, 1963), 133–136.

23. For a particularly revealing letter regarding public sentiment in the northern heartland, see Carl Schurz to AL, December 18, 1860, PAL. See also Horace White to AL, December 22, 1860; and William H. Triplett to AL, January 28, 1861, PAL.

24. David M. Potter, *The Impending Crisis, 1848–1861,* completed and edited by Don E. Fehrenbacher (New York: Harper and Row, 1976), 531–532.

25. Albert D. Kirwan, *John J. Crittenden: The Struggle for the Union* (Lexington: University Press of Kentucky, 1962), 392. Crittenden believed that the Republicans in Congress, under pressure in the North, would agree to his key proposals.

26. As quoted in *Northern Editorials on Secession,* ed. Howard Cecil Perkins, 2 vols. (1942; reprint, Gloucester, Mass.: Peter Smith, 1964), 1: 243–244.

27. As quoted in ibid., 1: 249–250.

28. As quoted in ibid., 1: 271–272. For other examples of northern editorials calling for Congress to enact the Crittenden Compromise or a similar plan and predicting civil war if it failed to pass, see ibid., 1: 245–247, 252–254, 256–259.

29. Samuel T. Glover to AL, February 5, 1861, PAL.

30. Clipping from unidentified St. Louis, Missouri, newspaper, January 14, 1861 (probably the *St. Louis Missouri Republican,* an old Whig paper), in PAL.

31. John D. Defrees to AL, January 8, 1861, PAL.

32. Neill S. Brown and Russell Houston to AL, January 13, 1861, PAL. See also L. L. Gash to AL, January 14, 1861; D. F. Caldwell to AL, December 31, 1861; William H. Russell to AL, January 16, 1861; and Alexander H. H. Stuart to John T. Stuart, January 21, 1861, PAL. Gash and Caldwell were North Carolinians; Russell and Stuart were from Kentucky and Virginia, respectively.

33. Orville H. Browning to AL, January 15, 1861; Salmon P. Chase to Norman B. Judd, January 20, 1861, PAL.

34. James R. Doolittle to AL, January 10, 1861, PAL.

35. Francis P. Blair, Sr., to AL, January 14, 1861, PAL. See also Carl Schurz to AL, January 31, 1861; Salmon P. Chase to AL, January 28, 1861; and George G. Fogg to AL, February 5, 1861, PAL.

36. Fehrenbacher and Fehrenbacher, eds., *Recollected Words of Lincoln,* 436.

37. Remarks concerning Concessions to Secession [c. January 19–21, 1861], *CW,* 4: 175–176 and 176n.

38. William H. Seward to Frances Seward, January 23, 1861, in Frederick W. Seward, *Seward at Washington, as Senator and Secretary of State: A Memoir of His Life, with Selections from His Letters, 1846–1861* (New York: Derby and Miller, 1891), 497.

39. James R. Doolittle to AL, January 10, 1861; Elihu B. Washburne to AL, January 7, 1861, PAL. Though Republicans opposed the acquisition of Mexican territory, Democrats, especially southern Democrats, advocated further expansion into northern Mexico and also the acquisition of Cuba. Robert E. May, *The Southern Dream of a Caribbean Empire, 1854–1861* (1973; reprint, Baton Rouge: Louisiana State University Press, 2002), chaps. 6–7.

40. Potter, *Lincoln and His Party in the Secession Crisis,* 286–287; Daniel W. Crofts, *Reluctant Confederates: Upper South Unionists in the Secession Crisis* (Chapel Hill: University of North Carolina Press, 1989), 236.

41. Ibid.

42. Elihu B. Washburne to AL, January 13, 1861, PAL.

43. As quoted in Glyndon G. Van Deusen, *William Henry Seward* (New York: Oxford University Press, 1967), 245. See also Henry Adams to Charles Frances Adams, Jr., January 17, 1861, *The Letters of Henry Adams,* vol. 1, *1858–1868,* ed. J. C. Levenson et al. (Cambridge, Mass.: Harvard University Press, 1982), 222.

44. AL to William H. Seward, January 19, 1861, *CW,* 4: 176.

45. William H. Seward to AL, January 27, 1861, PAL; AL to Seward, February 1, 1861, *CW,* 4: 183.

46. *Dictionary of Afro-American Slavery,* ed. Randall M. Miller and John David Smith (Westport, Conn.: Greenwood Press, 1988), 803.

47. Henry Villard's letter of February 6, 1861, *New York Herald,* February 16, 1861.

48. Potter, *The Impending Crisis,* 533–534.

49. Entry for February 9, 1861, *The Diary of Orville Hickman Browning,* ed. Theodore Calvin Pease and James G. Randall, 2 vols. (Springfield: Illinois State Library, 1925–1933), 1: 453.

50. Address to the Ohio Legislature, Columbus, February 13, 1861, CW, 4: 204.

51. Potter, *The Impending Crisis,* 507–509, 545–547, 550–551, 564. For a good summary of the Washington Peace Conference, see *Encyclopedia of the American Civil War: A Political, Social, and Military History,* vol. 4, ed. David S. Heidler and Jeanne T. Heidler (Santa Barbara, Calif.: ABC-CLIO, 2000), 2071–2072.

52. See, for example, Lincoln's form letter to "The Governor of the State of North Carolina," March 16, 1861, Correspondence of Governor John W. Ellis, North Carolina Division of Archives and History, Raleigh.

53. *New York Herald,* December 18, 1860.

54. Henry Villard's letter of December 1, 1860, in *New York Herald,* December 6, 1860. Significantly, in its editorial policy, the *Herald* was rarely influenced by Villard's reports from Springfield. Indeed, whereas Villard tended to be sympathetic to Lincoln, editor James Gordon Bennett was hostile toward him.

55. William H. Seward to AL, December 28, 1860; Leonard Swett to AL, December 31, 1860, PAL.

56. Elihu B. Washburne to AL, January 4 (quote), 30, 1861; Winfield Scott to AL, January 4, 1861; Simon Cameron to AL, January 3, 1861; Thurlow Weed to AL, January 10, 1861, PAL.

57. AL to William H. Seward, January 3, 1861, CW, 4: 170.

58. Ronald C. White, Jr., *The Eloquent President: A Portrait of Lincoln through His Words* (New York: Random House, 2005), 40.

59. Grace Bedell to "A. B. Lincoln," October 15, 1860, CW, 4: 130n.

60. AL to Grace Bedell, October 19, 1860, CW, 4: 129; "True Republicans" to AL, October 12, 1860, PAL. We cannot know for certain whether these two letters prompted Lincoln to grow whiskers, but it is reasonable to assume that they had an influence on his decision.

61. As quoted in White, *The Eloquent President,* 10.

62. John G. Nicolay to Therena Bates, December 30, 1860, *With Lincoln in the White House: Letters, Memoranda and Other Writings of John G. Nicolay, 1860–1865,* ed. Michael Burlingame (Carbondale: Southern Illinois University Press, 2000), 21; *Lincoln on the Eve of '61: A Journalist's Story by Henry Villard,* ed. Harold Garrison Villard and Oswald Garrison Villard (New York: Knopf, 1941), 61.

63. Villard and Villard, eds., *Lincoln on the Eve of '61,* 56–58.

64. William H. Herndon and Jesse W. Weik, with an introduction by Horace White, *Abraham Lincoln: The True Story of a Great Life,* 2 vols. (New York: D. Appleton, 1892), 2: 188; CW, 4: 249n; Orville Browning to AL, February 17, 1861, PAL. The drafts of the inaugural address may also be found in the Lincoln Papers.

65. AL to John Hanks, January 28, 1861; Remarks at Charleston, Illinois, Janu-

ary 31, 1861, *CW,* 4: 181, 182; Herndon and Weik, *Abraham Lincoln,* 2: 190–191; *Lincoln's Journalist: John Hay's Anonymous Writings for the Press, 1860–1864,* ed. Michael Burlingame (Carbondale: Southern Illinois University Press, 1998), 22–23.

66. *New York Herald,* February 16, 1861.

67. Villard and Villard, eds., *Lincoln on the Eve of '61,* 67.

68. Carl Schurz to his wife, February 10, 1861, *Speeches, Correspondence, and Political Papers of Carl Schurz,* ed. Frederic Bancroft, 6 vols. (New York: Putnam, 1913), 1: 179.

69. Herndon and Weik, *Abraham Lincoln,* 2: 192–194.

70. White, *The Eloquent President,* 11.

71. *New York Times,* February 19, 1861; William Baringer, *A House Dividing: Lincoln as President Elect* (Springfield: Abraham Lincoln Association, 1945), 267.

72. Farewell Address at Springfield, Illinois [A. Version], February 11, 1861, *CW,* 4: 190. B and C versions are also included in *CW,* 4: 190–191. Henry Villard, who was on the train, later reported that he had asked Lincoln to write out the remarks he had made at the station. Villard and Villard, eds., *Lincoln on the Eve of '61,* 73.

73. Both quotes are found in White, *The Eloquent President,* 22.

74. For Lincoln's growing spirituality during the Civil War, see Richard J. Carwardine, *Lincoln* (London: Pearson Longman, 2003), 220–231, and my *Lincoln's Last Months* (Cambridge, Mass.: Belknap Press of Harvard University Press, 2004), 59–62, 142–144.

CHAPTER ELEVEN: TRAIN TO WASHINGTON

1. *New York Times,* February 13, 1861.

2. John Hay, Springfield correspondence, January 28, 1861, *Lincoln's Journalist: John Hay's Anonymous Writings for the Press, 1860–1864,* ed. Michael Burlingame (Carbondale: Southern Illinois University Press, 1998), 21.

3. John G. Nicolay, "Memorandum, Springfield, December 13, 1860", *With Lincoln in the White House: Letters, Memoranda, and Other Writings of John G. Nicolay, 1860–1865,* ed. Michael Burlingame (Carbondale: Southern Illinois University Press, 2000), 17.

4. Henry Villard's letter of December 1, 1860, *New York Herald,* December 6, 1860.

5. Lincoln sent the message to General Scott through Congressman Elihu B. Washburne. AL to Washburne, December 21, 1860, *CW,* 4: 159.

6. AL to Lyman Trumbull, December 28, 1860, *CW,* 4: 163.

7. James M. McPherson, *Battle Cry of Freedom: The Civil War Era* (New York: Oxford University Press, 1988), 265–266.

8. Lyman Trumbull to AL, December 27, 1860, PAL.

9. AL to John E. Wool, January 14, 1861, *CW,* 4: 175 and n.

10. *Lincoln on the Eve of '61: A Journalist's Story by Henry Villard,* ed. Harold Garrison Villard and Oswald Garrison Villard (New York: Knopf, 1941), 76. This work (pp. 75–100) and Burlingame, ed., *Lincoln's Journalist* (pp. 23–45) are the best contemporary accounts of Lincoln's trip to Washington. Lincoln students and scholars are indebted to Burlingame for tracking down John Hay's reports to the *New York*

World and other newspapers and making them available in book format. Burlingame located these articles among the scrapbooks in the John Hay Papers, Manuscript Division, Library of Congress, Washington, D.C. Ironically, neither Villard nor Hay agreed with the editorial policies of the newspapers that published their reports—for Villard, the *New York Herald,* and for Hay, the *World.* Villard left the train in New York and did not rejoin it for the final leg of the trip.

11. Speech from the Balcony of the Bates House at Indianapolis, Indiana, February 11, 1861, *CW,* 4: 195–196.

12. See, for example, the *Chicago Tribune,* February 13, 1861.

13. As quoted in Ronald C. White, Jr., *The Eloquent President: A Portrait of Lincoln through His Words* (New York: Random House, 2005), 36.

14. *New York Herald,* February 15, 1861.

15. *Louisville Daily Courier,* February 13, 1861, as quoted in *Southern Editorials on Secession,* ed. Dwight Lowell Dumond (New York: Century, 1931), 453.

16. *St. Louis Daily Missouri Republican,* February 15, 1861, as quoted in ibid., 460. This was a Democratic newspaper.

17. John Hay, Cincinnati correspondence, February 12, 1861, Burlingame, ed., *Lincoln's Journalist,* 27–28. Villard estimated that 100,000 people greeted Lincoln in Cincinnati. Villard and Villard, eds., *Lincoln on the Eve of '61,* 80.

18. Speech at Cincinnati, Ohio, February 12, 1861, *CW,* 4: 199. Lincoln prepared a five-page manuscript for a speech that he had planned to deliver in Kentucky. *CW,* 4: 201n.

19. Address to the Ohio Legislature, Columbus, Ohio, February 13, 1861, *CW,* 4: 204–205. In his remarks on the steps of the Ohio capitol, as at Cincinnati, Lincoln noted the nonpartisan nature of the crowd and assured Democrats that if Senator Douglas had been elected, the Republicans would have supported his government. Speech from the Steps of the Capitol at Columbus, Ohio, *CW,* 4: 205–206.

20. *New York Herald,* February 15, 1861.

21. As quoted in Paul Revere Frothingham, *Edward Everett: Orator and Statesman* (Boston: Houghton Mifflin, 1925), 415.

22. As quoted in White, *The Eloquent President,* 60.

23. Villard and Villard, eds., *Lincoln on the Eve of '61,* 82.

24. *New York Times,* February 18, 1861.

25. John G. Nicolay to Therena Bates, February 15, 1861, Burlingame, ed., *With Lincoln in the White House,* 27; "Some Incidents in Lincoln's Journey from Springfield to Washington," *An Oral History of Abraham Lincoln: John G. Nicolay's Interviews and Essays,* ed. Michael Burlingame (Carbondale: Southern Illinois University Press, 1996), 114.

26. Speech at Pittsburgh, Pennsylvania, February 15, 1861, *CW,* 4: 210.

27. Ibid., 4: 211.

28. Ibid., 4: 211–213.

29. Speech at Cleveland, Ohio, February 15, 1861, *CW,* 4: 215–216.

30. Ibid., 4: 215; Villard and Villard, eds., *Lincoln on the Eve of '61,* 86–87.

31. Remarks at Westfield, New York, February 16, 1861, *CW,* 4: 219. For Lincoln's brief remarks at stops on the Cleveland-Buffalo leg of the trip, see ibid., 4: 217–220.

32. *Philadelphia Inquirer,* February 20, 1861, report of Lincoln's remarks at Dunkirk, New York, February 16, 1861, *CW,* 4: 219–220.

33. John Hay, Buffalo correspondence, February 18, 1861, Burlingame, ed., *Lincoln's Journalist,* 33.

34. Ibid., 31; Villard and Villard, eds., *Lincoln on the Eve of '61,* 87.

35. John Hay, Buffalo correspondence, February 18, 1861, Burlingame, ed., *Lincoln's Journalist,* 33–34; Nicolay, "Some Incidents in Lincoln's Journey from Springfield to Washington," Burlingame, ed., *An Oral History of Abraham Lincoln,* 114–116.

36. Speech at Buffalo, New York, February 16, 1861, *CW,* 4: 220–221.

37. For his brief remarks at towns between Buffalo and Albany, see *CW,* 4: 221–224.

38. Villard and Villard, eds., *Lincoln on the Eve of '61,* 91–93.

39. Address to the Legislature at Albany, New York, February 18, 1861, *CW,* 4: 225–226.

40. *New York Herald,* February 20, 1861.

41. *New York Tribune,* February 20, 1861.

42. Nicolay, "Some Incidents in Lincoln's Journey from Springfield to Washington," Burlingame, ed., *An Oral History of Abraham Lincoln,* 118.

43. Speech at the Astor House, New York City, February 19, 1861, *CW,* 4: 230–231.

44. Allan Nevins, *The Emergence of Lincoln,* vol. 2, *Prologue to Civil War, 1859–1861* (New York: Charles Scribner's Sons, 1950), 363.

45. As quoted in the *New York Tribune,* February 21, 1861.

46. Reply to Mayor Fernando Wood at New York City, February 20, 1861, *CW,* 4: 232–233.

47. Nicolay, "Some Incidents in Lincoln's Journey from Springfield to Washington," Burlingame, ed., *An Oral History of Abraham Lincoln,* 118–119; *New York Tribune,* February 21, 1861.

48. Address to the New Jersey Senate at Trenton, New Jersey, February 21, 1861, *CW,* 4: 235–236.

49. Address to the New Jersey General Assembly at Trenton, New Jersey, February 21, 1861, *CW,* 4: 236–237.

50. Speech in Independence Hall, Philadelphia, Pennsylvania, February 22, 1861, *CW,* 4: 240–241.

51. Ibid.

52. John Hay, Harrisburg correspondence, February 22, 1861, Burlingame, ed., *Lincoln's Journalist,* 41–42.

53. The 1860 county election returns for Pennsylvania reveal the strength of the Republicans' opponents (Democrats and John Bell supporters) in the area along or near Lincoln's route to Harrisburg. For the election returns, see W. Dean Burnham, *Presidential Ballots, 1836–1892* (Baltimore: Johns Hopkins Press, 1955), 704–720.

54. *New York Tribune,* February 23, 1861; Remarks at Lancaster, Pennsylvania, February 22, 1861, *CW,* 4: 242.

55. Reply to Governor Andrew J. Curtin at Harrisburg, Pennsylvania, February 22, 1861; Address to the Pennsylvania General Assembly, February 22, 1861, *CW,* 4: 243–244, 245.

56. John Hay, Harrisburg correspondence, February 22, 1861, Burlingame, ed., *Lincoln's Journalist,* 42.

57. George W. Hazzard to AL [undated, but probably early February 1861], PAL.

58. Norman B. Judd interview [November 1866], *HI,* 433–434. Allan Pinkerton's report, with documents, is conveniently included in this volume (pp. 267–314). See

also Allan Pinkerton to William H. Herndon, August 23, 1866, *HI*, 317–324. These and additional documents, along with a fine introduction, can be found in *Lincoln and the Baltimore Plot, 1861, From the Pinkerton Records and Related Papers,* ed. Norma B. Cuthbert (San Marino, Calif.: Huntington Library, 1949).

59. Charles P. Stone Memorandum, February 21, 1861, PAL; Charles P. Stone, "Washington on the Eve of the War," *Battles and Leaders of the Civil War,* ed. Robert U. Johnson and Clarence C. Buel, 4 vols. (New York: Century, 1887–1888), 1: 22–23.

60. Norman B. Judd interview [November 1866], *HI*, 433.

61. Ibid., 434–435.

62. Allan Pinkerton to William H. Herndon, August 23, 1866, *HI*, 323; William E. Baringer, *A House Dividing: Lincoln as President Elect* (Springfield: Abraham Lincoln Association, 1945), 294–295.

63. Allan Pinkerton to William H. Herndon, August 23, 1866, *HI*, 323–324.

64. Ernest B. Furgurson, *Freedom Rising: Washington in the Civil War* (New York: Knopf, 2004), 44; Elihu B. Washburne, "Abraham Lincoln in Illinois, Part II," *North American Review* 347 (November 1885): 455.

65. For Lincoln's first day in Washington, see the *New York Tribune*, February 25, 1861.

66. *New York Tribune*, February 26, 1861. The Baltimore press, especially the prosecessionist *Sun,* denied that Lincoln would have faced danger in Baltimore. The authoritative *Philadelphia North American,* however, concluded from the evidence that "certain desperate characters were ready to avail themselves" of his open presence in the city "to execute a fiendish plot against his life." As reported in the *Boston Daily Advertiser,* February 27, 1861.

67. Washburne, "Abraham Lincoln in Illinois, Part II," 455, 458. For an evaluation of the authenticity of Lamon's account, see Cuthbert, ed., *Lincoln and the Baltimore Plot,* xix–xxii. Though Lamon supplied the materials for *The Life of Abraham Lincoln from His Birth to His Inauguration as President* (Boston: James R. Osgood, 1872), Chauncey F. Black wrote the book.

68. *New York Tribune*, February 25, 1861; Daniel M. Barringer to his wife, February 24, 1861, Daniel Moreau Barringer Papers, Southern Historical Collection, University of North Carolina Library, Chapel Hill.

69. Message to Congress in Special Session, July 4, 1861, *CW*, 4: 437.

70. Villard and Villard, eds., *Lincoln on the Eve of '61,* 102–103.

71. William H. Seward to AL, February 24, 1861, John G. Nicolay and John Hay, *Abraham Lincoln: A History,* 10 vols. (New York: Century, 1890), 3: 319–321 (quotes). A list of the changes is found in William H. Seward, Suggested Changes to First Inaugural Address [February 1861], PAL.

72. Orville H. Browning to AL, February 17, 1861, PAL. In addition to Seward and Browning, Carl Schurz and David Davis read a draft of the inaugural address. There is no record that Schurz or Davis recommended changes.

73. *New York Times*, February 27, 1861; *New York Tribune*, February 26, 1861; Baringer, *A House Dividing,* 309–310; entries for February 25 and 26, 1861, Thomas Bragg Diary, Southern Historical Collection, University of North Carolina Library, Chapel Hill.

74. *Recollected Words of Abraham Lincoln,* ed. Don E. Fehrenbacher and Virginia

Fehrenbacher (Stanford, Calif.: Stanford University Press, 1996), 35. The words "dissatisfied fellow countrymen" appeared in Lincoln's inaugural address.

75. *New York Herald,* March 1, 1861; Response to a Serenade, February 28, 1861, *CW,* 4: 247 and 248n.

76. Entries for March 1–3, 1861, *Lincoln Day by Day: A Chronology, 1809–1865,* ed. Earl Schenck Miers (Washington, D.C.: Lincoln Sesquicentennial Commission, 1960), 3: 23–24.

EPILOGUE: INAUGURATION

1. *New York Times,* March 4, 5, 1861; Charles P. Stone, "Washington on the Eve of the War," *Battles and Leaders of the Civil War,* ed. Robert U. Johnson and Clarence C. Buel, 4 vols. (New York: Century, 1887–1888), 1: 24.

2. *New York Times,* March 5, 1861.

3. Ibid.; *Chicago Tribune,* March 5, 1861.

4. First Inaugural Address—Final Text, March 4, 1861, *CW,* 4: 262–263.

5. Ibid., 4: 263–264.

6. Ibid., 4: 264.

7. Ibid., 4: 265.

8. Ibid., 4: 266.

9. Ibid., 4: 267–268.

10. Ibid., 4: 268–270.

11. Ibid., 4: 270–271.

12. Ibid., 4: 271. The last paragraph had been suggested and drafted by Seward; it was "polished into prose akin to poetry by Lincoln." Ronald C. White, *The Eloquent President: A Portrait of Lincoln through His Words* (New York: Random House, 2005), 87. The *New York Times,* March 5, 1861, reported that the closing of the address "upset the watering pot [eyes] of the hearers, and at this point alone did the melodious voice of the President-elect falter" with emotion.

13. *New York Times,* March 5, 1861.

14. David M. Potter, *The Impending Crisis, 1848–1861,* comp. and ed. Don E. Fehrenbacher (New York: Harper and Row, 1976), 568.

15. *Providence Daily Post,* March 8, 1861, as quoted in *Northern Editorials on Secession,* ed. Howard Cecil Perkins, 2 vols. (1942; reprint, Gloucester, Mass.: Peter Smith, 1964), 2: 647.

16. As quoted in Paul Revere Frothingham, *Edward Everett: Orator and Statesman* (Boston: Houghton Mifflin, 1925), 415.

17. John G. Nicolay and John Hay, *Abraham Lincoln: A History,* 10 vols. (New York: Century, 1890), 3: 334; William E. Baringer, *A House Dividing: Lincoln as President Elect* (Springfield: Abraham Lincoln Association, 1945), 334.

BIBLIOGRAPHICAL ESSAY

No effort is made in this essay to provide a comprehensive account of the vast Lincoln literature. Rather, my purpose is to give the reader an idea of the main trends in recent Lincoln studies, particularly for the prepresidential years. Suffice to say, many of the earlier biographies failed the test of historical scholarship and often contributed to the Lincoln legend that had begun with his martyrdom. The late nineteenth-century image of Lincoln's early life was greatly influenced by William H. Herndon's lectures as well as by his biography of his famous law partner, written in collaboration with Jesse W. Weik and with an introduction by Horace White, entitled *Abraham Lincoln: The True Story of a Great Life,* 2 vols. (New York: D. Appleton, 1892). A new edition of this biography has recently been published with an excellent introduction and valuable annotations by editors Douglas L. Wilson and Rodney O. Davis (Urbana and Chicago: Knox College Lincoln Studies Center and the University of Illinois Press, 2006). Herndon sought to portray Lincoln in a realistic way, particularly regarding his personal habits and political ambition, but he also exaggerated or ignored many aspects of the story. A decade before the end of the century, John G. Nicolay and John Hay, Lincoln's secretaries, produced a ten-volume work entitled *Abraham Lincoln: A History* (New York: Century, 1890), which concentrated on the Civil War and, despite its title, often neglected Lincoln himself. Nicolay and Hay's massive study, though generally accurate, was uncritical of Lincoln, as might be expected from friends. Numerous writers referred to the volumes, but the books were largely unread.

Beginning in the 1920s, professional historians entered the field of Lincoln studies, along with a few discerning amateurs, such as Albert J. Beveridge, bringing with them critical standards of scholarship. The period from the 1920s to the 1960s was a golden age of Lincoln scholarship, highlighted by the contributions of James G. Randall, Paul M. Angle, Benjamin P. Thomas, Richard N. Current, Harry V. Jaffa, and a young David Donald. Still, the most popular life of Lincoln during this period was the poet Carl Sandburg's six-volume work, which the historian Charles A. Beard described as "more like a diary or a saga" than a true biography. This set includes *Abraham Lincoln: The Prairie Years,* 2 vols. (New York: Harcourt, Brace, 1926), and *Abraham Lincoln: The War Years,* 4 vols. (New York: Harcourt Brace, 1939). An informative survey and analysis of the early writings on Lincoln to the 1960s can be found in Don E. Fehrenbacher, *The Changing Image of Lincoln in American Historiography* (Oxford: Clarendon Press, 1968).

The disillusionment with the Vietnam War and with the unfulfilled promises of the Civil Rights revolution, beginning in the late 1960s, produced a radical change in the viewpoint of scholars and writers, particularly the young, in interpreting the American past and its greatest hero, Abraham Lincoln. So-called "New Left" scholars, disdainful of America's role in modern history, could hardly contain their scorn for Lincoln, whom they viewed as racist, self-serving, and hypocritical. It is a truism that the changing interpretations of Lincoln have reflected contemporary circumstances and issues more than the realities of the American past. Nowhere was this more evident than in the New Left's condemnation of the Civil War president. African American intellectuals and others often joined in the disparagement of Lincoln's reputation as an antislavery foe and a friend of blacks. With a few exceptions, scholars of the late twentieth century, perhaps partly influenced by the triumph of Lincoln's democratic principles in the Cold War, abandoned or greatly modified this hostile interpretation of Lincoln. However, they still pointed out his less than perfect racial views and policies. It remains to be seen what impact the divisive Iraqi War and the conflict with militant Islamists will have on Lincoln scholarship.

During the past two decades, the history of Lincoln's presidency has attracted outstanding scholars who in well-researched and judicious accounts have demonstrated the complexities of the problems that Lincoln faced during the Civil War. These studies have provided a deeper understanding and a greater appreciation of Lincoln's political leadership in winning the war and ending slavery. Three outstanding examples of this scholarship come quickly to mind: Mark E. Neely, Jr., *The Fate of Liberty: Abraham Lincoln and Civil Liberties* (New York: Oxford University Press, 1991); Phillip Shaw Paludan, *The Presidency of Abraham Lincoln* (Lawrence: University Press of Kansas, 1994); and Allen C. Guelzo, *Lincoln's Emancipation Proclamation: The End of Slavery in America* (New York: Simon and Schuster, 2004). Also during this period, David Herbert Donald's *Lincoln* (New York: Simon and Schuster, 1995), the best single-volume biography of this great American, was published. Donald's thesis, which has been criticized by some scholars, is that Lincoln was a passive leader who reacted to events rather than controlling them. A recent book by Doris Kearns Goodwin, *Team of Rivals: The Political Genius of Abraham Lincoln* (New York: Simon and Schuster, 2005), demonstrates that well-written popular history can also be good scholarship. Goodwin provides fascinating biographical information on Lincoln and his cabinet members and their relationship before and during the Civil War. Her account, however, is at times perhaps too uncritical of Lincoln.

Lincoln's political rise has not received the same thorough treatment as has his presidency. During the past two or three decades, a number of scholars have studied Lincoln's state of mind, philosophy, religion, private life, and sexual orientation. Some studies have been highly controversial and have produced stinging rebuttals. For example, C. A. Tripp in *The Intimate World of Abraham Lincoln* (New York: Free Press, 2005) claims that Lincoln was bisexual. Lincoln biographers have rightly concluded that the Tripp book, which elicited extensive media coverage, has added a new myth to the story of this great American. (See, for example, David Herbert Donald's criticism of Tripp's study in *"We Are Lincoln Men": Abraham Lincoln and His Friends* [New York: Simon and Schuster, 2003], 33–39.) Most of the other recent studies, often employing innovative methods, have provided new insights into Lincoln's private life and views. However, they have achieved mixed results in relating their accounts to political events and developments associated with Lincoln's rise to the presidency.

Some scholars purporting to understand Lincoln from a psychoanalytic perspective have created virtually a new field in Lincoln studies. Influenced by twentieth-century advances in the social sciences, they have sought to explain Lincoln's psychological makeup and inner conflicts by analyzing his early experiences. In the process, they have drawn far-reaching and controversial conclusions about his personality and ambitions. The publication of three books in 1979–1982 can fairly be said to have begun the psychoanalytic approach to understanding Lincoln. Two of the books, George B. Forgie's *Patricide in the House Divided: A Psychological Interpretation of Lincoln and His Age* (New York: W. W. Norton, 1979) and Dwight G. Anderson's *Abraham Lincoln: The Quest for Immortality* (New York: Knopf, 1982), though differing in particulars, argue that Lincoln sought a Napoleonic role in American history and that his ambition was to achieve or even exceed the fame of the Founders. The third book, Charles B. Strozier's *Lincoln's Quest for Union* (New York: Basic Books, 1982), maintains that Lincoln's private experiences and inner struggles shaped his public positions. These psychobiographic accounts were based on limited source materials and a weak historical context. Conventional Lincoln scholars and historians immediately found the Forgie, Anderson, and Strozier efforts to psychoanalyze this American icon both improbable and disturbing. Gabor S. Boritt, however, as editor of *The Historian's Lincoln: Pseudohistory, Psychohistory, and History* (Urbana: University of Illinois Press, 1988), concluded that the studies, though partly "well-argued mythmaking" accounts, shed new light on Lincoln's private self and his motivations.

Though controversial, the works of the early psychobiographers inspired some more historically grounded accounts of Lincoln's private life and mental state. Michael Burlingame, who approached Lincoln as a historian rather than a psychologist, published a well-researched and well-written book aptly entitled *The Inner World of Abraham Lincoln* (Urbana: University of Illinois Press, 1994). Burlingame's book, according to Allen C. Guelzo, writing in *Civil War News,* marked "a turning point in understanding the Lincoln behind the mask of melancholy." Burlingame, however, probably overstated when he described Lincoln's aversion to women, the misery in his marriage that helped to drive him to the presidency, and the "tyranny" of his father that caused him to empathize with the slaves and feel "a special urgency about freeing them" (pp. xv, 325).

Other scholars have followed Burlingame in attempting to explain Lincoln's melancholy, or depression, and its importance in his life. The most intriguing effort along this line is Joshua Wolf Shenk's *Lincoln's Melancholy: How Depression Challenged a President and Fueled His Greatness* (New York: Houghton Mifflin, 2005), which claims that Lincoln's suffering from chronic depression caused him to move away from goals of personal satisfaction and provided him with the desire and the strength to accomplish noble actions. Lincoln scholar William Lee Miller, in *Washington Post Book World* (October 2, 2005), correctly entered an important caveat to Shenk's interpretation and, by implication, to other efforts to overpsychoanalyze Lincoln. Miller pointed out that the fact that a person suffers from depression "does not do all" Shenk claims "unless there is something strong that the suffering prods into action. Lots of people suffer; not all of them become great." Miller suggested that "Lincoln had intellectual and moral self-confidence, deep conscientiousness, a powerful desire to achieve something worthy, a romantic idea of his country and an unusual sympathy for creatures in distress—all independent of his being depressed."

Miller is a part of another important trend in research and writing on Lincoln. These studies focus on Lincoln's moral and intellectual development. In *Lincoln's Virtues: An Ethical Biography* (New York: Knopf, 2002), Miller describes Lincoln's "moral formation" from childhood to his presidency. Lincoln as a politician, according to Miller, practiced the virtues of "moral realism," in contrast to the "radical individualism" of the evangelical Protestant culture in the North (pp. 181, 230). High-minded principles had little meaning to Lincoln unless they could be realistically brought to bear on political affairs. Miller is at his best in describing Lincoln's moral development; its relationship to Lincoln's political success, however, is not as clearly drawn.

Harry V. Jaffa, in *A New Birth of Freedom: Abraham Lincoln and the Coming of the Civil War* (Lanham, Md.: Rowman and Littlefield, 2000) is a wide-ranging examination of Lincoln's political thought. A long-awaited sequel to his *Crisis of the House Divided: An Interpretation of the Issues in the Lincoln-Douglas Debates* (Garden City, N.Y.: Doubleday, 1959), the book portrays Lincoln as America's greatest egalitarian and, in contrast to Stephen A. Douglas and John C. Calhoun, a staunch supporter of the Declaration of Independence's natural rights philosophy. The book is grounded in political philosophy, not history, and is uncritical of Lincoln.

In *Father Abraham: Lincoln's Relentless Struggle to End Slavery* (New York: Oxford University Press, 2006), Richard Striner portrays the sixteenth president as a "fervent idealist" whose "feelings," even in the 1850s, supported not only an early end of slavery but also black civil rights. But unlike the abolitionists, whose side he was on, Lincoln, according to Striner, recognized that "the summoning of power" to accomplish these goals required "strategy as well as ideals" (pp. 1, 2, 47–48). In a somewhat similar vein, Carl F. Wieck, in *Lincoln's Quest for Equality: The Road to Gettysburg* (DeKalb: Northern Illinois University Press, 2002), contends that Lincoln, influenced by the abolitionist Theodore Parker, "had considerably stronger ties to abolitionism than has previously been suggested." Wieck, however, admits that Lincoln "cautiously preserved discreet public distance from avowed abolitionists like Parker" because it "might endanger his political career" (p. 3). The fact that Parker is never mentioned in Lincoln documents leaves Wieck's interpretation weak.

Other recent scholars have sought to explain Lincoln's moral philosophy and even his political success from a religious perspective, a subject long neglected or given short shrift by biographers. Though admitting that as a young man Lincoln was a religious skeptic and that he never outgrew his distrust of church doctrines, Wayne C. Temple, in *Abraham Lincoln: From Skeptic to Prophet* (Mahomet, Ill.: Mayhaven, 1995), concludes that after he joined the antislavery crusade during the mid-1850s he became increasingly drawn to the Bible. Likewise, Allen C. Guelzo, in *Abraham Lincoln: Redeemer President* (Grand Rapids, Mich.: Wm. B. Eerdmans, 1999), deftly describes Lincoln's religion, which was nonsectarian and along Calvinistic predestination lines. Guelzo suggests, however, that Lincoln read the Bible more from a literary standpoint than for religious instruction.

In *Lincoln, Religion, and Romantic Cultural Politics* (DeKalb: Northern Illinois University Press, 2003), Stewart Winger associates what he calls Lincoln's "romantic religion" with his Whig political values, which stressed a positive moral government for America. Mark A. Noll, an authority on the history of American religion, wrote that Winger's study is "one of the best books for showing how Lincoln's religion fits into the broader commitments that motivated his aspirations as an ambitious Whig and his actions as a Republican president." Still, Noll was critical of Winger's interpretation. He contended that "Lincoln was never so simply a 'romantic' as he was definitely a [rational] Whig" ("Review Essay: Stewart Winger, *Lincoln, Religion, and Romantic Cultural Politics,*" *Journal of the Abraham Lincoln Association* 25 [Winter 2004]: 98, 103–104). Joseph R. Fornieri, writing in *Abraham Lincoln's Political Faith* (DeKalb: Northern Illinois University Press, 2003), insisted that religion was foremost in Lincoln's mind and that he "viewed the politics of the Civil War era," including the antislavery cause, "in terms of civil theology" (p. 1). Similarly, in *Lincoln's Sacred Effort: Defining Religion's Role in American Self-Government* (Lanham, Md.: Lexington Books, 2000), Lucas Morel maintains that Lincoln's statesmanship owed a great deal to "his accommodation to the religious sentiments of his countrymen." Lincoln, Morel wrote, thus was able "to direct religious sentiment toward responsible democracy or self-government" for America (p. 1).

With literary grace and original argument, Richard J. Carwardine, in *Lincoln* (London: Pearson Longman, 2003), contends that Lincoln's use of evangelical Protestantism proved a key reason for his political success. Lincoln, according to Carwardine, in his rise to power rather cynically combined appeals to Whig Protestant morality with the Declaration of Independence's natural rights philosophy. I disagree with Carwardine's view. Though Lincoln sometimes used biblical metaphors to make a point (for example, in his House Divided Speech), I have not found that he used the Scriptures to obtain political support. Furthermore, I believe Carwardine is incorrect in viewing Lincoln as "a typical New England Whig in his easy acceptance of religion's role in public affairs" and in concluding that Lincoln and the Republicans primarily owed their success in 1860 to the enthusiastic support of moralistic evangelicals.

Perhaps inspired by Garry Wills's *Lincoln at Gettysburg: The Words That Remade America* (New York: Simon and Schuster, 1992), some scholars have turned their attention to Lincoln's speeches and sought their larger meaning. Ronald C. White, Jr., following his book on Lincoln's second inaugural address (*Lincoln's Greatest Speech: The Second Inaugural* [New York: Simon and Schuster, 2002]), wrote *The Eloquent President: A Portrait of Lincoln through His Words* (New York: Random House, 2005), which tracks the evolution of the president's rhetoric in eleven speeches and documents, beginning with his Farewell Address at Springfield on February 11, 1861. White joins other recent scholars who have described the intensity of Lincoln's religious feelings and concluded that he did not use religious language simply for political effect.

In *Lincoln at Cooper Union: The Speech That Made Abraham Lincoln President* (New York: Simon and Schuster, 2004), Harold Holzer, a prolific scholar in the Lincoln field, tells the story of Lincoln's most famous prewar speech—his Cooper Union address on February 27, 1860. Holzer demonstrates again the importance of this speech in advancing Lincoln's presidential aspirations among influential eastern Republicans. He splendidly narrates the background for the speech, provides a penetrating description of Lincoln's remarks at Cooper Union, and concludes that the address marked the beginning of Lincoln's successful challenge to William H. Seward for the Republican nomination. I question, however, Holzer's contention that there was "nothing conservative about [the speech] by 1860 standards" (pp. 134–144).

Lincoln's use of language and its significance are also the subject of a recent book by Douglas L. Wilson. Entitled *Lincoln's Sword: The Presidency and the Power of Words* (New York: Knopf, 2006), the book emphasizes two aspects of Lincoln as a writer: his habits and practices as a lifelong writer, and the role that writing came to play in his presidency.

No study of Lincoln's early life and circumstances is more illuminating than Wilson's *Honor's Voice: The Transformation of Abraham Lincoln* (New York: Knopf, 1998). In it Wilson describes certain aspects and episodes in young Lincoln's life that occurred during his New Salem and early Springfield years, a period of eleven years. The theme of Wilson's book is Lincoln's successful efforts to improve himself and gain distinction in the community. Lincoln's self-education, his struggle to find a vocation, his pursuit of honor, his religious skepticism, and his less-than-noble treatment of his opponents—and women—are vividly described without resort to the sentimentality of the Lincoln legend. Wilson writes little about political issues and the slavery question; a notable exception is his account of the unsuccessful Lincoln-Stone resolution in the legislative session of 1836–1837 characterizing the institution of slavery as "founded on both injustice and bad policy." Wilson's critical mining of the materials collected by Lincoln's law partner, William H. Herndon, has contributed greatly to the rehabilitation of the latter's reputation as a faithful recorder of Lincoln's early life.

Kenneth J. Winkle, in *The Young Eagle: The Rise of Abraham Lincoln* (Dallas: Taylor, 2001), provides a fresh approach to Lincoln's early life. He focuses on Lincoln's coming of age at a critical time in the transformation of America from a frontier and rural society to an urban, market economy. Winkle probably exaggerates the dramatic socioeconomic change that occurred in central Illinois during the 1840s and 1850s; and in stressing the social environment, Winkle sometimes neglects the broader political scene, especially Lincoln's national emergence in 1858–1860. Still, this historian's detailed, community-based study is an important contribution to our understanding of Lincoln's early life and the obstacles that he had to overcome in his rise to prominence.

Finally, the recent and magnificent work of the Lincoln Legal Papers Project in collecting and making available documents relating to Lincoln as an attorney has renewed interest in his law practice. The project, which is sponsored by the Illinois Historic Preservation Agency and cosponsored by the Abraham Lincoln Association and the University of Illinois at Springfield, has produced a wealth of material on the communities where Lincoln practiced law and the people who lived in them. Mark E. Steiner, a former associate editor of the project, in his *An Honest Calling: The Law Practice of Abraham Lincoln* (DeKalb: Northern Illinois University Press, 2006), has demonstrated the value of studies based on the Lincoln Legal Papers collection. Clearly, as accounts by Steiner and other scholars have revealed, research and writing on Abraham Lincoln continues to produce important scholarship. Students and readers are the beneficiaries of the new information and fresh perspectives that this scholarship brings to our understanding of the man whose place in American history is second to none.

INDEX

The initials AL refer to Abraham Lincoln.